The Evaluation and Measurement of Library Services

The Evaluation and Measurement of Library Services

SECOND EDITION

Foreword by Lisa Hinchliffe

Joseph R. Matthews

LIBRARIES UNLIMITED™

An Imprint of ABC-CLIO, LLC

Santa Barbara, California • Denver, Colorado

Library of Congress Cataloging-in-Publication Data

Names: Matthews, Joseph R., author.
Title: The evaluation and measurement of library services / Joseph R. Matthews.
Description: Second edition / foreword by Lisa Hinchliffe. | Santa Barbara, CA : Libraries Unlimited,
    [2018] | Includes bibliographical references and indexes.
Identifiers: LCCN 2017044826 (print) | LCCN 2017023250 (ebook) | ISBN 9781440855375 (eBook) |
    ISBN 9781440855368 (paperback : acid-free paper)
Subjects: LCSH: Libraries—United States—Evaluation. | Public services (Libraries)—
    United States—Evaluation. | Libraries—Evaluation. | Public services (Libraries)—Evaluation.
Classification: LCC Z678.85 (print) | LCC Z678.85 .M37 2018 (ebook) | DDC 027.473—dc23
LC record available at https://lccn.loc.gov/2017044826

ISBN: 978-1-4408-5536-8
EISBN: 978-1-4408-5537-5

22 21 20 19 18   1   2   3   4   5

This book is also available as an e-book.

Libraries Unlimited
An Imprint of ABC-CLIO, LLC

ABC-CLIO, LLC
130 Cremona Drive, P.O. Box 1911
Santa Barbara, California 93116-1911
www.abc-clio.com

This book is printed on acid-free paper ∞

Manufactured in the United States of America

This book is dedicated to Professor Frederick Wilfred ("Wilf") Lancaster, who taught at the University of Illinois, Urbana, library school for 20 years and was named professor emeritus from 1992–2013. I had the opportunity of meeting and chatting with Wilf several times and always valued him as a mentor, scholar, and writer.

Lancaster's book The Measurement and Evaluation of Library Services *was published in 1977 and, over time, has become recognized as one of the seminal works in the field of library and information science: he received the American Library Association's Ralph Shaw Award for Library Literature in 1978. A second edition of his* Measurement *book came out in 1991. Both editions provide a survey and synthesis of the library evaluation literature.*

The title of this book, The Evaluation and Measurement of Library Services, *is a not-so-discreet acknowledgment of the important contributions Wilf has made to the concept of the evaluation of library services, for which we are all indebted.*

Contents

Part I
Evaluation: Process and Models

Part II
Methodology Concerns

Part III
Evaluation of Library Operations

Part IV
Evaluation of Library Services

Part V
Evaluation of Library Outcomes

Foreword

Over the past decade, libraries of all types have embraced a strategy of evidence-based advocacy to complement metaphorical claims of being the heart of the campus, the people's university, and the like. Gathering, analyzing, using, and communicating data are typical assessment activities in all types of libraries. Demonstrating library value and documenting library impact are integral to what we do and embedded into regular workflows.

Both the Association of College and Research Libraries and the Public Library Association have launched initiatives to support assessment and evaluation work: the *Value of Academic Libraries Initiative* and *Project Outcome*, respectively. The American Association of School Libraries has continued its long tradition of documenting the impact of school libraries and librarians on student success.

Concomitant with the emergence of performance measurement as an expected area of library management and administration has been a focus on user experience, usability, and service design. We have seen a rise in the number of positions responsible for assessment as well as increased attention to marketing and public relations. It is heartening to see commitment to developing services that meet user needs and to assessing their effectiveness in order to demonstrate value and direct continuous improvement.

These evolutions (and sometimes revolutions) in library service development have led to a demand for library workers who have experience and expertise in assessment and measurement. Libraries rely on staff to implement evaluation programs and design processes for continuous improvement, as well as on library leaders with a vision for how data can feed into organizational development and staff training efforts.

The Evaluation and Measurement of Library Services (2nd Edition) is a welcome addition to the toolkit that library and information science educators and practitioners rely upon in designing services and assessing their effectiveness. As library and information science education programs add coursework addressing evaluation and measurement, this book can serve as a course text, providing both theory and practical guidance. Similarly, the book is a useful blend of general guidance and methodological direction for library practitioners. The reader will find answers to the "what" and "why" of evaluation as well as specifics for "how" and "when."

Taken as a whole, the book is a comprehensive guide to library assessment and communicating library value. Pragmatically, this book helps overcome the main barriers to successfully implementing library evaluation and measurement programs, which are lack of knowledge and skills.

The text's wealth of information is an obvious antidote to lack of knowledge. *Part I—Evaluation: Process and Models* offers a succinct overview of developing an evaluation project as well as evaluation models, key terminology, and sage advice on the published literature and collegial connections to ensure one's evaluation project is informed by and builds on existing professional knowledge and best practices. *Part II—Methodology Concerns* continues to develop the reader's knowledge base while also providing skill development through general introductions to qualitative and quantitative tools as well as descriptions of foundational concepts and processes in data analysis.

Part III—Evaluation of Library Operations and *Part IV—Evaluation of Library Services* address the development of skills in the context of specific applications of assessment tools to evaluation and measurement questions. Given that most readers will likely approach the text with a specific assessment project in mind, the organization of these sections by library operations and services provides for easy access to relevant tools and methods as well as discussions of challenges and opportunities specific to those operations and services. These chapters also work as stand-alone introductions to assessing specific operations and services; they can be read in the context of the rest of the text or consulted separately. *Part V—Evaluation of Library Outcomes* furthers the development of knowledge and skills through a framework for understanding how to communicate evaluation and measurement results.

In concluding, let me share that it has been my privilege to learn from Joe Matthews—through his writing and scholarship as well as conference presentations and informal conversations. His passion for libraries and commitment to helping them succeed through evaluation and performance measurement is clear to all who know him. We are fortunate to have his wisdom and experience to guide us!

Lisa Janicke Hinchliffe
University of Illinois at Urbana-Champaign

Acknowledgments

As anyone who has written a book will attest, the final product is the result of the contributions of many talented people. The library profession and I are particularly indebted to the many librarians who take the time to prepare articles about their evaluation and assessment efforts. The many interesting and valuable evaluation and assessment projects often reflect the talents of multiple library staff members who gather, organize, and analyze the data. Just a quick glance at the citations included in this book will provide an overview of the depths and breadth of the evaluation and assessment activities that are going on in libraries today.

Thanks to Teri Roundenbush, head of the Interlibrary Loan department at the California State University San Marco Library. Teri and her staff always manage to find the requested books and articles while remaining cheerful in the face of a formidable workload. I also would like to acknowledge the willingness of every library that shares resources using the interlibrary loan system—your sharing is appreciated.

Finally, thanks much to Barbara Ittner, Senior Acquisitions Editor; to Emma Bailey, Senior Production Coordinator; and to Kathryn Suarez, publisher of Libraries Unlimited, for your positive encouragement. I do appreciate your efforts on my behalf.

Joe Matthews
Carlsbad, CA

Introduction

The evaluation and measurement of library services are critical parts of the management of any library. In the special and public library arena, the term *evaluation* is most often used, whereas in school and academic library environments, the term *assessment* is more often preferred. In my mind, the terms "evaluation" and "assessment" can be used interchangeably. In addition, it is important to recognize that there are significant differences between "evaluation" and "research," as shown in Table I.1. Research most often is aimed at testing theory and determining causality usually employing rigorous research methods while evaluation is more change and action oriented with a focus on practicality and usefulness. Evaluation is intensely local and is focused on "improving."

In concept, an evaluation project would start out with clear and specific objectives that would in turn lead to the selection of the most appropriate measurement tools. However, in many cases an evaluation starts out as a nagging feeling that something should be explored. John Tukey called this latter process exploratory data analysis, a form of detective work.[1] Comparing a variety of performance measures with a group of peer libraries may reveal some anomalies that deserve a closer look. Bob Molyneux has called this exploration of what the data might have to say "noodling around in the numbers."

The individual or team involved with the evaluation determines:

- Whether there has been a change in performance over a selected period of time,
- Whether the change is in the preferred direction, and
- The extent of the change.

Evaluation is a part of the feedback loop on how well the library is performing. In order for evaluation to be particularly meaningful, the process requires objectives as criteria.

Most librarians are content to continue what libraries have traditionally done to provide services to customers. Occasionally a library will introduce a new service, but rarely does a library embrace the concept of using evaluation as a part of its day-to-day activities. Evaluation is most helpful if applied in an ongoing manner to determine how we can improve an existing service or decide whether an existing service should be stopped.

This book is directed at three main audiences. It is intended primarily for library directors and managers in all types of libraries who are interested in learning about what prior evaluations of a library service have revealed. The second audience are librarians who are interested in learning about the variety of evaluation techniques that have been used in the past to evaluate a specific library service. These librarians will then be better able to choose one or more methods that will prove to be most useful in their particular library setting. A third audience are library school students, who, it is hoped, will find the content to be valuable in a number of courses as they prepare for a wonderful career in librarianship.

The purpose of this book is to provide a set of tools that will assist any library in evaluating a particular library service, whether covered in this book or not. The goal is to remove some of the mysteries surrounding the process of evaluation so that many librarians will see the value of performing evaluation/assessment in their libraries. It is possible to overcome the concerns identified by Don Revill many years ago about research in librarianship. These concerns include:

1. You can't do research in librarianship.
2. And if you can:
    a. It shouldn't be called research, and
    b. It can't be generalized to any other library or situation.
3. But if research can be done, no one does so because he or she can't understand the research.
4. And if someone did understand the research, he or she wouldn't accept it.
5. And if someone did, he or she would be deluding himself or herself, because the research wouldn't work.[2]

Table I.1. Differences between Research and Evaluation

	Research	**Evaluation**
Objective	Aimed at testing theory, determining causality, generating new knowledge	Change- and action-oriented, aimed at determining impact, informing decision making
Driven by	Curiosity, hypothesis	Key questions
Design	Prove something	Improve something
Data	High-quality data carefully gathered and analyzed	Often the quality of the data is limited in some manner
Sample size	Usually large populations with carefully selected samples	Much smaller sample sizes—often quite small
Focus	Determining the best approach and increasing or improving the knowledge base "How it works"	Focus on activities, outcomes, impacts on participants, understanding context "How well it works"
Standards	Theory, causality, generalizability, reproducibility, best methodology	Practical, useful, appropriate methodology given constraints of time and budget
Setting	Controlled setting and controls for variables	Changing priorities, resources, timelines, and stakeholders
Costs	Usually expensive	Range from low to moderate
Results	Draw conclusions, publish results, make conference presentations	Report to stakeholders, basis for decision making
Use	Often uncertain results given the desire to advance knowledge	Real opportunity to use results to make changes
Intent	Research can be generalized to other situations, conditions, and times	Evaluation is local

This book is divided into four parts. Part I introduces the concept of evaluation, explores a number of evaluation models that might be used, and discusses a number of issues surrounding the process of evaluation.

Part II is concerned with methodological issues. A number of different tools are discussed so that the librarian will know more about the strengths and limitations of any particular tool or methodology.

Part III presents a number of chapters that are focused on evaluating a specific library service. Each chapter includes a definition of the service, a discussion of possible methods that can be or have been used to evaluate that service, and a summary of the available research pertaining to a particular topic.

Part IV presents an overview of the models with which the value of all the services and functions of a library can be determined. Chapters pertaining to the accomplishments of an individual library, as well as the economic and social impacts of the library, are presented. Frameworks that have been used for a library-wide evaluation can be particularly helpful when communicating with the library's funding stakeholders. This part closes with some suggestions for communicating the value of the library to stakeholders and other key individuals.

This second edition of *The Evaluation and Measurement of Library Services* has been extensively rewritten and nine new chapters in total have been added.

NOTABLES IN THE FIELD

Figure I.1 presents a library Evaluation/Assessment Tree that has three broad branches: methods, use, and value (value has two main categories: outcome perspectives and economic perspectives). The tree identifies a number of individuals who have made notable contributions to the field of library assessment/evaluation over the course of the last few decades.

The methods of evaluative research and evaluation dominated the early days of library evaluation and assessment. This focus is understandable in that the early pioneers were developing theory while trying out various methods they borrowed from the fields of social science and the more practical evaluation tools that are used routinely today.

The use branch began with a focus on how users interacted with information. In particular, those working in this branch hoped to gain a better understanding of how different segments of the population used and interacted with information and library services.

The value branch of the tree has focused on understanding the outcomes or impacts of libraries and their services. This branch has two main limbs: the outcomes perspectives and the economic perspectives. Don't be surprised when you encounter several citations to the work of these luminaries. Our profession owes much to these evaluation and assessment gurus.

Svanhild Aabø is a professor in the Department of Archivistics, Library and Information Science at the Oslo and Akershus University College of Applied Sciences, and focuses on information economics and social capital, especially within the public library arena.

Rachel Applegate is an associate professor in the Department of Library and Information Science at the Indiana University-Purdue University Indianapolis; her research interests include library evaluation and academic library outcomes.

John Carlo Bertot is a professor in the College of Information Studies at the University of Maryland, and his research interests include information policy, public service innovation, and social innovation.

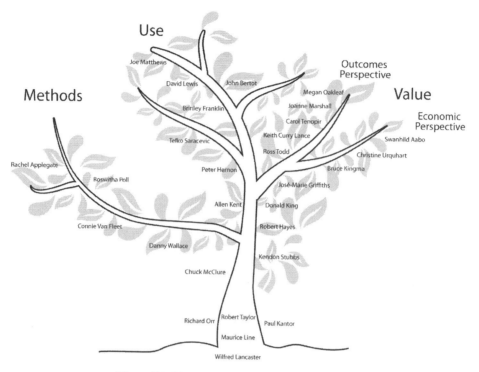

Figure I.1. Library Assessment Evaluation Tree

Brinley Franklin is the library director at the University of Connecticut and helped developed the MINES for Libraries survey.

José-Marie Griffiths is the president of North Dakota State University (formerly vice-president for academic affairs at Bryant University) and earned her doctor of information science degree from University College London. Previously José-Marie was a professor at the School of Information and Library Science at the University of North Carolina, and she has received a number of awards.

Robert Hayes is Professor Emeritus and former dean of the Library School at UCLA.

Peter Hernon, recently retired, was a professor at Simmons College Graduate School of Library and Information Science. Peter is a prolific author and researcher and was the long-time co-editor of the journal *Library & Information Science Research.*

Paul Kantor is Professor Emeritus in the School of Communication and Information at Rutgers University. Paul focused on the rigorous evaluation of information systems for storage and retrieval systems.

Allen Kent, an information scientist, introduced the notion of precision and recall and is best known for his study of the University of Pittsburgh collection.

Donald W. King is a long-time researcher and active member of the American Society for Information Science and Technology; he is an adjunct professor at the School of Information Sciences at the University of Tennessee.

Bruce Kingma is an economist and professor at the School of Information Studies, Syracuse University; his research interests include the economics of information and library management.

Frederick Wilfred Lancaster, or "Wilf," was a professor at the University of Illinois, Urbana, and published broadly in the field of library and information science for more than four decades. He is perhaps best known for his book *The Measurement and Evaluation of Library Services.*

David Lewis is dean of the University Library at the Indiana University-Purdue University Indianapolis campus; he is a prolific author and is active in state and national professional library organizations.

Maurice Line, a UK librarian and prolific author, was the Director General of the British Library Lending Division.

Joanne Gard Marshall is a professor and former dean of the School of Information & Library Science at the University of North Carolina at Chapel Hill who focused on improving research and practice in health library and information services.

Joseph Matthews is a library consultant with extensive experience in working with academic, public, and special libraries to evaluate services and determine the value of libraries. His most recent book is *Adding Value to Libraries, Archives, and Museums.*

Charles "Chuck" McClure is the Francis Eppes Professor of Information Studies and Director, Information Use Management & Policy Institute College of Communication & Information, Florida State University. Chuck has been involved in a number of noteworthy research projects and is a prolific author.

Megan Oakleaf is an Associate Professor in the iSchool at Syracuse University. She is best known for her publication *Value of Academic Libraries Comprehensive Review and Report*, and her research interests include assessment and evidence-based decision making.

Richard Orr introduced the concepts of input, process, outputs, and outcomes measures to the library and information science community. He wrote a classis analysis that explored the concept of "library goodness."

Roswitha Poll was a professor at the University of Munster, Germany; was active in the International Federation of Libraries Association (IFLA); and served as chair of the ISO TC 46 SC 8: Quality—Statistics and Performance Evaluation committee (which is now a standard).

Tefko Saracevic is a Distinguished Professor Emeritus in the School of Communication & Information at Rutgers University and a long-time active researcher and member of the American Society for Information Science and Technology.

Kendon Stubbs had a 41-year career at the University of Virginia Library and is a recognized authority on measuring academic research libraries. Kendon developed the ARL Library Index.

Robert Saxton Taylor was a scholar and information scientist who was Dean of the Syracuse University School of Information Studies, who is best known for his book *Value-Added Processes in Information Systems.*

Carol Tenopir is the Chancellor's Professor, School of Information Sciences, University of Tennessee, Knoxville, and has received numerous research grants. She received the Award of Merit from the American Society for Information Science and Technology.

Ross Todd is an Associate Professor in the School of Communication & Information at Rutgers University and a long-time active researcher in the field of school librarianship.

Christine Urquhart is a Senior Lecturer (retired) in the Department of Information Studies at Aberystwyth University in Wales.

Connie Van Fleet was a professor at the School of Library and Information Studies at the University of Oklahoma; she focused her research in the areas of library evaluation and public library services.

Danny Wallace was a professor and EBSCO Chair of Library Service at the School of Library & Information Studies at the University of Alabama, and was active in the Association for Library and Information Science Education.

NOTES

1. John W. Tukey. *Exploratory Data Analysis.* Reading, MA: Addison-Wesley, 1970.
2. Don Revill. You Can't Do Research in Librarianship. *Library Management News*, 11, February 1980, 10–25.

Part I

Evaluation:
Process and Models

1

Evaluation Issues

*We are continually faced with a series of great opportunities
brilliantly disguised as insoluble problems.*

—John W. Gardner[1]

What distinguishes evaluation is not planning, methodology, or subject matter, but *intent*—
the purpose for which it is done. Unlike research, with its concern about rigorous methodology
and publication, an evaluation employs standard research methods for evaluative purposes. As
Thomas Childers and Nancy Van House have noted:

> Evaluation is the assessment of goodness. It consists of comparing the organ-
> ization's current performance against some standard or set of expectations. Eval-
> uation has two parts: the collection of information . . . about the organization's
> performance; and the comparison of this information to some set of criteria. The
> collection of information is not itself evaluation: a critical component of evalua-
> tion is the exercise of judgment in which criteria are applied to the organization's
> current reality.[2]

Evaluation, especially in public library circles, is usually referred to as *evaluation*, whereas
in academia, evaluation is most often referred to as *assessment*. I will use the terms interchangeably (although I will most often use the term *assessment* when referring to studies done in
academic library settings).[3]

Evaluation is often broadly divided into two types—summative and formative.

Formative evaluation is focused on the collection and analysis of data to strengthen,
improve (sometimes referred to as continuous improvement), or enhance the activity under
analysis. Think of the chef in the kitchen tasting the dish while it is being prepared: this tasting is done (often several times) to make the dish better.

Summative evaluation is concerned with the effect or outcome of a library's program or
service. Think of the customer in a restaurant tasting the dish.

Evaluation can also be characterized from several different perspectives, among them the following:

- Evaluation is concerned with *service-derived questions*—the quality, cost, or effectiveness of a service or program. Typically an evaluation study represents matters of administrative and programmatic interest.
- Evaluation compares "what is" with "what should (could) be." The element of *judgment* against criteria (implicit or explicit) is basic for all evaluations.
- Acknowledging that an evaluation study can take on a life of its own, it is important to remember the service or program is *serving* people—the library's customers.
- The focus of evaluation is *improvement,* so changes that are made should be checked periodically to ensure that positive results continue to occur.
- Only a fraction of evaluation reports are turned into journal articles. In contrast, the underlying aim of most research is *publication* and the dissemination of results.
- Given its focus on the real world, evaluation is often called *action research*, whereas basic research focuses on explanation or prediction.
- An evaluation project may be designed to evaluate *alternatives* such as commercial vendor options.
- *Communicating* the results of an evaluation closes the feedback loop and shows that the library is improving its services.
- An evaluation project may be designed to *enhance* the visibility of library services, describe their impact, and strengthen the library's political position among stakeholders.

For many years the library profession has wrestled with the definition of "goodness." So, how is *goodness* defined for a library? Is it possible to compare the library with an ideal or a set of standards? These are important issues for anyone who is involved with the preparation of an evaluation study.

Evaluation should be an essential tool for any manager. Richard Orr suggested that a manager has four primary responsibilities:[4]

- To define the goals of the organization;
- To obtain the resources needed to reach these goals;
- To identify the programs and services required to achieve those goals, and to optimize the allocation of resources among these programs and services; and
- To see that the resource allocations for a particular activity are used wisely (cost efficiency).

Clearly the latter two responsibilities imply the use of evaluation methods. The third responsibility focuses on evaluating the outcomes of a program or service; this is sometimes called *effectiveness*. The fourth responsibility must of necessity focus on how efficient a library program or service is.

In a similar vein, Peter Drucker, the renowned management guru, would ask five core questions that were at the heart of his philosophy:[5]

1. What is our mission?
2. Who is our customer?
3. What does the customer value?

4.   What are our results?

5.   What is our plan?

José-Marie Griffiths and Don King identified some principles for high-quality evaluation research:[6]

- Evaluation must have a purpose.
- There is no need to evaluate without the potential for some action.
- Evaluation must go beyond description and understand the relationships among operational performance, users, and organizations.
- Evaluation should be ongoing rather than sporadic.
- Ongoing evaluation provides a means for monitoring, diagnosis, and improvement.
- Evaluation can be a tool for communication among staff and users.
- Evaluation should be dynamic, reflecting new knowledge and changes in the environment.

WHO DECIDES

The types of individuals involved in the process of gathering data depends on the focus of the evaluation effort. As shown in Table 1.1, an evaluation can have an internal orientation (library-centric view) or an external perspective (customer-centric view), or be a combination of the two. Each of these perspectives answers a different "how" question.

Table 1.1. Answering the "How" Questions

Library-centric View	Combination View	Customer-centric View
How much?	How reliable?	How well?
How many?	How accurate?	How courteous?
How economical?	How valuable?	How responsive?
How prompt?		How satisfied?

The *library-centric view* has an internal or operations viewpoint. The focus of evaluation efforts is on processes, functions, and services. The things that are measured in this type of evaluation are typically transactions and the performance of the library. In order to provide a comparison, a group of "peer" libraries may be selected. Telltale signs of when the library is not performing well include errors, higher costs than peer libraries, delays, customer complaints, and staff complaints about other staff members or activities (or lack of activity) in another department.

Evaluating the internal operations of a library requires those involved to answer some important questions:

- How do our costs compare to our peers?
- How do our service delivery times compare to our peers?

- Will an alternate resource mix produce better results? Should we consider outsourcing a process?
- Does the library have the needed resources?
- Does the library's staff have the necessary mix of skills?
- What criteria will be used to select "peer" libraries?

The *combination view* requires both the library and the customer to answer service quality questions. Here the expectations of customers are an important part of the assessment process (it is also possible to identify and quantify the gaps in service). The evaluation may examine the differences that exist between customer expectations and the quality of service actually delivered. And the only standard that counts is the customer's!

Notice that this view will not rely on traditional library *output* measures, which include such performance measures as annual circulation and number of reference transactions. Rather, it may require the library to start exploring the use of *outcome* measures to answer the question of "how valuable" the library is. *Outcome* is defined as a change in attitude, behavior, knowledge, skill, status, or condition. Thus, outcome-based evaluation is a systematic way to assess the extent to which a program or a service has achieved its intended results. Among the key questions that might be addressed are the following:

- What are the impacts or consequences for those who utilize a service?
- What are the real results rather than the rhetoric of intent?
- How has this program or service made a difference in the life of the customer?
- What do stakeholders expect this service or program to deliver?
- What outcome measures should be used to measure impacts?

The *customer-centric view* requires some effort to prepare an evaluation that will produce meaningful and valuable results. Customers form expectations based on their experiences in other competitive environments—bookstores, video rental stores, used bookstores, music stores. The customer creates these expectations based on prior visits both to physical and virtual (Web site) stores. Libraries are increasingly turning to customer surveys to determine the extent to which the library is or is not meeting the customer's expectations.

Libraries typically develop a set of collections and services to meet the needs of their customers. Special libraries typically have a specific focus and a restricted set of customers to serve, such as employees of a hospital, medical, legal, business, or technical organization. School libraries serve children and their teachers. Academic libraries, which are a part of a college or university, serve students, faculty, and researchers, who are engaged in teaching, learning, and research. Public libraries usually serve their communities from one or more locations. Any evaluation should start with a clear understanding of the needs of those served by the library.

A more extensive list of "how" questions was developed by Peter Hernon and Ellen Altman (see Table 1.2).[7]

Table 1.2. Components of the "How" Question

Library Control				Library and Customers Decide				Customers Decide		
How much?	How many?	How economical?	How prompt?	How valuable?	How reliable?	How accurate?	How well?	How courteous?	How responsive?	How satisfied?
Magnitude	Magnitude	Resources used	Cycle times	Effort expanded	Dependability	Completeness	Accuracy	Attentive	Anticipatory	Expectations met
Percent of change last year	Change	Units processed	Turnaround time	Cost	Access	Comprehensiveness	Promptness	Welcoming	Helpful	Materials obtained
Percent of overall change			Anticipatory	Benefit obtained	Accuracy	Currency	Courtesy		Empathetic	Personal interaction
Cost							Expertise			Ease of use
										Equipment used
										Environment
										Comfort
										Willingness to return
										Willingness to recommend

Peter Hernon and Ellen Altman. *Assessing Service Quality: Satisfying the Expectation of Library Customers.* Chicago: American Library Association, 1998, 56.

What the library thinks its customer wants
Is not necessarily the same as
What the library thinks it has to offer
Is not necessarily the same as
How the customer experiences a library service
Is not necessarily the same as
What the customer really wants.

AN EVALUATION ACTION PLAN

Preparing an evaluation involves a number of discrete activities, including:

- Identifying the problem
- Determining the scope of the analysis
- Determining whether the answer already exists
- Determining the kind of analysis to do
- Deciding what data will be needed
- Conducting the analysis and preparing a report
- Using the results for service improvement (the feedback loop)

Identifying the Problem

Selecting a topic or area as a candidate for evaluation is, in most cases, fairly straightforward. The library should pay attention to the following:

- **Production bottlenecks.** Are there any backlogs? Bottlenecks may be symptomatic of staffing shortages, poor supervision, cumbersome procedures, or inadequate training. It is important to note that bottlenecks are rarely the fault of staff.
- **Tasks that are performed frequently.** The more frequently a task is performed, the better a candidate it becomes for evaluation. Some obvious candidates are circulation, reference, interlibrary loan, and technical services.
- **Activities that require frequent movement.** The movement may be people, forms, equipment, book trucks, and so forth. Even frequent movement involving short distances can translate into high costs. An evaluation in this area should consider and identify optimum physical arrangements.
- **Declining budgets.** Every library will face this challenge sooner or later. Consider activities or services that consume large portions of the budget. The evaluation will have to identify what alternatives exist for accomplishing the same tasks, along with the associated costs for each alternative.

A brief statement of the evaluation project or a problem statement should be prepared. This statement should not suggest any solutions or attempt to identify the causes of the problem. It should answer the following:

- What is the problem or perceived problem? What is the current performance of the process or activity (if known or can be quantified) that it is proposed to evaluate?
- What are the symptoms pointing to the problem?

- What is problematic or unacceptable about this performance?
- When and where do problems occur?
- What is the impact of the problem from the perspective of library customers?

The following are examples of a problem statement or proposed evaluation:

> Statement A—The acquisitions budget is likely to be reduced. We are unsure of the amount of use our librarians and customers make of our fairly extensive print reference collection. We should determine the extent of and type of actual use, especially in light of our fairly large expenditures for licensing electronic databases. We may be able to reduce our expenditures for reference print materials without compromising the quality of service.

> Statement B—Determine why ILL is taking longer than our customers expect. Currently our turnaround time for borrowing interlibrary loan books is averaging X days for 80 percent of our transactions. Our customers are requesting materials in Y days, based on a recent ILL customer survey. We need to gather data about the time it takes to place requested materials in the hands of our customers. Will we be able to reduce the delivery time?

Determining the Scope of the Analysis

It is important to determine what will and will not be evaluated. Will the evaluation take an internal perspective that focuses on library operations, or will an external focus be included and customers be involved in some way? Perhaps both perspectives might be included in the evaluation.

A number of other important issues have to be addressed as the planning for the evaluation takes place:

- Are the current patterns of use cause for concern? Has demand for a service dropped off? Has demand suddenly peaked?
- Will costs have to be determined? If so, does the budget provide sufficient details to identify all of the cost components for providing the service?
- Should customers of the library be involved? If so, what will be the manner of their participation?
- What evaluation methodology and design will be used? How will the data be collected?
- What is the purpose for doing the evaluation? Is the library attempting to improve its operational efficiencies (an internal focus), or is the study being done to better understand the effectiveness of a library service (an outward focus)?

Determining Whether the Answer Already Exists

Prior to actually starting to collect data, it is important to learn what your colleagues have done in the area. Your might chat with or send an e-mail to a colleague in a similar type of library or someone whom you know has completed a similar evaluation project. Other resources are available, including checking with a professor at a library school or a consultant or posting a query on a listserv. Discovering the experiences of others will help the library avoid some of the pitfalls that others have encountered the hard way—through trial and error.

Preparing a literature review, especially of recently published articles, will help the library to better shape the evaluation study and, ultimately, improve the results of the project. A content analysis has shown that research on evaluation ranges from 15 to 57 percent of the published literature, depending upon the year.[8]

When preparing a literature review, a serious challenge arises, as the literature will often present a confusing and contradictory picture. Thus, it is necessary to assess and prioritize the results of the literature and the studies discussed in various articles and books. It is particularly important to identify whether any systematic review articles have been prepared that summarize the research in a particular subject area. Systematic reviews are typically written by two or more authors, in order to minimize possible bias, using orderly and explicit methods to identify, select, and appraise relevant research.[9] Such an article will summarize a number of prior studies that meet specific criteria for inclusion in the analysis. Once a systematic review article has been prepared in draft form, it is subjected to a rigorous peer review process involving several knowledgeable individuals. One of the byproducts of the systematic review article is that it will identify "best practices."

Systematic reviews are useful for a number of reasons:[10]

- *Large amounts of information are summarized therein,* and the summary produced by the review will mean that less research and reading are required.
- *Explicit methods limit bias* in identifying and including studies in the review.
- *They resolve discrepancies* and may help more clearly define the issues and identify the inconsistencies across studies.
- *To plan for new research,* a systematic review may be produced to identify fruitful methods.
- *They provide teaching or training materials,* as a review provides significant depth of analysis.

Recently the practice of evidence-based evaluation has emerged from within the library community. Building on the tradition and history of evidence-based medicine, evidence-based librarianship provides a method for categorizing or rating the various research and evaluation studies reported in the literature, in order to determine a set of recommendations that is based on sound research rather than feeling and experience. In some ways, this is reflective of the call for developing a "culture of assessment."[11]

One survey of librarians found that reading evidence summaries provided reassuring information or uncovered new information that was helpful at the individual level as well as at the group level (department, library, or organization).[12]

Andrew Booth and Anne Brice, both involved in the development of evidence-based librarianship, suggest that more weight should be given to the findings of research studies that are more rigorous from a methodological point of view.[13] They suggest prioritizing the research in the following manner (from best to worst):

I. **Experimental study using randomized controlled trials.** In clinical medicine, randomized controlled trials are considered the "gold standard" for assessing the effectiveness of a treatment, because the trial can provide the strongest evidence for (or against) the effectiveness of an intervention. Very few randomized controlled trials have been conducted in the library environment.

II. **Experimental study without randomization.** This includes cohort studies and case-control studies. In the medical environment, cohorts are identified prior to the appearance of the disease under investigation. The study groups so defined are observed over a period of time to determine the frequency of disease among them. Again, in the library environment, no cohort studies have been conducted.

The case-control study begins with the identification by researchers of an outcome or effect (e.g., lung cancer, heart disease, or even longevity), and a number of potential causative factors. A group of cases is selected that exhibit the outcome under investigation. A number of subjects (or controls) are then chosen who do not exhibit the outcome or effect under investigation. These controls should match the cases as closely as possible with respect to the nonrisk variables; this allows the proposed nonrisk variables to be ignored in the analysis. The case and control groups are then compared on the proposed causal factors, and statistical analysis is used to estimate the strength of association of each factor with the studied outcome. In the library environment, only a few studies have been conducted that used case-control methodology.

III. **Observational study without a control group.** This includes cross-sectional studies, before-and-after study designs, and case studies. Rather than using large samples and following a rigid protocol to examine a limited number of variables, the case study method involves an in-depth examination of a single instance or event—a case. An observational study provides a systematic way of looking at events, collecting data, analyzing information, and reporting the results. As a result, the researcher may gain a sharpened understanding of why the instance happened as it did, and what might become important to look at more extensively in future research.

IV. **Case reports.** In medicine, a case report is a detailed report of the diagnosis, treatment, and follow-up of an individual patient. Case reports may contain a demographic profile of the patient, but usually they describe an unusual or novel occurrence. The library literature is replete with case reports—or "how I done it good in my library."

This category also includes ideas, editorials, and opinions. This category encourages the discussion of new ideas that are as yet unsupported by any data or research, but may have real value.

The majority of library research employs case studies or case-control studies, including qualitative research reports. Future library research and evaluation studies would be much improved by the use of cohort studies and controlled trials or at least the use of a control group, especially when attempting to measure the outcomes of the use of library resources and services. The increased use of experimental designs would also be beneficial.

The result of the literature review typically is a section in the evaluation report or in an article submitted for publication. It should also be noted that the literature review may reveal "best practices," which will suggest a course of action that does not require further study.

Determining the Kind of Analysis to Do

In general, there are two broad methodologies that can be used to gather information about a library service: quantitative and qualitative. Each method is discussed in some detail in subsequent chapters of this book.

Quantitative methods gather numerical data using a variety of techniques. The resulting data can then be subjected to data analysis, ranging from simple descriptive statistics to more complex statistical analysis.

Library research has been for the most part pragmatically oriented, yet it appears to be so closely tied to professionally acceptable solutions that it seldom contemplates alternatives which might cause pronounced upheaval in the existing order.

—P. Wasserman and M. Bundy[14]

Qualitative methods gather information about a library service that is not numerical in nature. The purpose of a qualitative method is insight. Insight is, roughly, the recognition of connections or patterns. Typical qualitative methods include observations, in-depth interviews, and focus groups. Insight studies can often point to the reasons behind the results of a study that a quantitative study cannot identify. Qualitative methods allow for a much more in-depth exploration of a topic.

The literature review will have identified several methods other libraries have used to conduct an evaluation study. These methods obviously are prime candidates for a library to follow, as it is easier to replicate a study done elsewhere (and compare and contrast the results) than to pioneer a new method.

The specific procedures that will be used in the evaluation project should be decided upon and documented. It may be necessary for some staff members to be trained so that they can assist in the data collection process. The individual or individuals who will be responsible for the various aspects of an evaluation should be specified in the project plan. In addition, the project plan should include a time frame for the completion of the project and any intermediate milestones.

A review of the procedures may indicate the need for some resources to be allocated to the project or for some volunteers to be recruited and trained. It may be necessary to develop a budget for the evaluation project.

Deciding What Data Will Be Needed

The choice of evaluation method will determine, in large part, what data will be needed. Having a clear picture of the evaluation objectives will ensure that unnecessary data are not collected and, even more important, that needed data are actually gathered.

If a survey is being distributed, then the responses will have to be gathered and analyzed. Depending on the complexity of planned data analysis, it may be necessary to have the information in a format that can be imported into a data analysis software package.

One suggestion is to run a prototype of the study, including the collection and analysis of a limited amount of data. This "dry run" will often expose some unanticipated problems that can be resolved before the library incurs the time and costs associated with a much larger data collection effort.

However, it is important to note that

> [p]erfect data are impossible to obtain. Near-perfect data can take so long to obtain that the opportunity will pass you by or the problem will engulf you. Settle for good enough data to get the job done.[15]

If data are to be collected from individuals in an academic setting, then most likely permission will be required from the campus institutional review board, which exists to protect people's privacy and rights. Typically the library will have to follow a specific and detailed process to gain the approval of this board.

Conducting the Analysis and Preparing a Report

After the quantitative data collection process or the qualitative information-gathering process is completed, the resulting information must be analyzed. After all, the purpose of analysis is insight! This is especially important since the library has gone to considerable efforts to prepare for and conduct the evaluation.

The function of the evaluation report is to document the purpose and focus of the evaluation, how the project was conducted, what the quantitative data or qualitative information have to say, and what results and recommendations are being made. The audience for the report may be the library's top management team, the library's funding decision makers, or those involved in a program review, as in the case of an academic library. For any audience, it is important not to use library jargon (if any jargon is used, make sure it is the jargon of the decision makers). Also, as this audience is normally fairly busy, the report should include a one- or two-page executive summary of the evaluation project.

Using the Results for Service Improvement: The Feedback Loop

With the results of the evaluation known, the library will most likely want to make changes in processes or procedures to implement the recommendations of the evaluation study. Communicating with staff during the evaluation about the project and its findings will assist in getting the cooperation and enthusiasm needed to make the changes occur smoothly.

OBSTACLES TO EVALUATION

The commonsense and intuitive approaches to managing a library ignore the reality that today a library—any library—is more complex than ever before and involves many variables that may prevent the library from delivering high-quality services. Without the objective information about a service provided by an evaluation, a library will simply continue to muddle along, believing that all is well.

It is also important to acknowledge that an evaluation might be misused. For example, an evaluation might:

- Have a hidden political agenda (e.g., despite the quality and use of a service, it might be scheduled for termination)
- Only examine those components of a program that generate positive results, without looking at the total program
- Cover up program failures or limited use
- Be used to delay taking action in the short term (it will require time to design the evaluation project, gather and analyze the data, and prepare the report)
- Be sabotaged by staff who refuse to gather data in the prescribed manner, and thus skew the results
- Be suppressed by the management team, who are concerned that an evaluation will show resources are being wasted or misapplied
- Be flawed because those involved in the evaluation project have not received the training to correctly complete the tasks needed for the project

As Peter Hernon and Ellen Altman have observed, "Evaluation, after all, is most productive in an open organization truly interested in planning and self-improvement, and in demonstrating its *worth* and *value*."[16]

One of the continuing challenges with research in any field is the issue of **replication**. In the fields of psychology and medicine, it has been found that only about half of the research being reported can be reliably reproduced. The human brain is quite good at recognizing patterns—even when these patterns do not exist. Thus, the issue of false positives must be considered, especially during the design of a study and while the data analysis is being conducted.

For example, one study found that 65 percent of medical studies were inconsistent when retested, and only 6 percent were completely reproducible.[17] Another study published in *Nature* noted that 47 out of 53 cancer research papers were irreproducible.[18] The National Academies Press has published an interesting and very readable report focused on the issue of reproducibility of scientific results.[19]

The lack of reproducibility is of serious concern in that it leads to distrust of scientific findings among a wide variety of people. Although there are many factors that contribute to the lack of reproducibility, in the end any evaluation effort must carefully document the process used to gather data so that others can assess the degree of confidence they feel with the published results.

ETHICS OF EVALUATION

The Joint Committee on Standards for Educational Evaluation created standards in four areas to help guide evaluators:

- **Utility.** The goal of evaluation is to ensure that the information needs of intended users are met. This may include stakeholder identification; scope and selection of the evaluation; and report clarity, timeliness, and dissemination.
- **Feasibility.** The focus is to ensure that the evaluation will be realistic, follow accepted research methods, and not be too costly.
- **Propriety.** The evaluation should be conducted legally, ethically, and with due regard for the welfare of those involved with the evaluation. This might include rights of human subjects, disclosure of findings, and complete and firm assessment.
- **Accuracy.** The evaluation should reveal accurate information about the program or service being evaluated. Thus, the source of the data, methods for collecting the data, and analysis of the data must be included in the evaluation report.[20]

PHILOSOPHICAL QUESTION

In an interesting article, Hilary Yerbury posits that our understanding of the field of library and information science and its development is guided by a notion of an accepted way of working, and that research is conducted using a "business as usual" model. This "business as usual" model is intricately entwined with the required structure of a journal article and the peer review process. Yerbury argues that our profession is being held back by the "business as usual" model, which is "cramping the development of new knowledge and understanding."[21]

NOTES

1. John Gardner. *On Leadership.* New York: Free Press, 1993, 47.
2. Thomas A. Childers and Nancy A. Van House. *What's Good? Describing Your Public Library's Effectiveness.* Chicago: American Library Association, 1993.
3. See Joseph R. Matthews. *Library Assessment in Higher Education: Second Edition.* Westport, CT: Libraries Unlimited, 2015.

4. Richard H. Orr. Measuring the Goodness of Library Services: A General Framework for Considering Quantitative Measures. *Journal of Documentation*, 29, 1973, 315–32.

5. Peter Drucker. *The Five Most Important Questions You Will Ever Ask About Your Organization.* San Francisco: Jossey-Bass, 2008.

6. José-Marie Griffiths and Donald W. King. *A Manual on the Evaluation of Information Centers and Services.* New York: American Institute of Aeronautics and Astronautics Technical Information Service, 1991.

7. Peter Hernon and Ellen Altman. *Assessing Service Quality: Satisfying the Expectation of Library Customers.* Chicago: American Library Association, 1998, 56.

8. Denise Koufogiannakis and Ellen Crumley. Research in Librarianship: Issues to Consider. *Library Hi Tech*, 24 (3), 2006, 324–40.

9. Sue Phelps and Nicole Campbell. Systematic Reviews in Theory and Practice for Library and Information Studies. *Library and Information Research*, 36 (112), 2012, 6–15.

10. Ann McKibbon. Systematic Reviews and Librarians. *Library Trends*, 55 (1), Summer 2006, 202–15.

11. Amos Lakos. Opinion Piece: The Missing Ingredient—Culture of Assessment in Libraries. *Performance Measurement and Metrics*, August 1999, Sample Issue, 3–7; Amos Lakos and Shelley Phipps. Creating a Culture of Assessment: A Catalyst for Organizational Change. *portal: Libraries and the Academy*, 4 (3), July 2004, 345–61.

12. Lorie Kloda, Denise Koufogiannakis, and Alison Brettle. Assessing the Impact of Evidence Summaries in Library and Information Practice. *Library and Information Research,* 38 (119), 2014, 29–46.

13. Andrew Booth and Anne Brice. *Evidence-Based Practice for Information Professionals: A Handbook.* London: Facet, 2004. A new Internet-based journal called *Evidence Based Library and Information Practice* is available. Visit https://journals.library.ualberta.ca/eblip/index.php/EBLIP/issue /archive for all of the issues.

14. P. Wasserman and M. Bundy. *Reader in Research Methods in Librarianship.* NCR Microcard Editions, 1970, 257.

15. Denise Troll Covey. Using Data to Persuade: State Your Case and Prove It. *Library Administration & Management*, 19 (2), Spring 2005, 84.

16. Peter Hernon and Ellen Altman. *Service Quality in Academic Libraries.* Norwood, NJ: Ablex, 1996, 18.

17. Florian Prinz, Thomas Schlange, and Khusru Asadullah. Believe It or Not: How Much Can We Rely on Published Data on Potential Drug Targets? *Nature Reviews Drug Discovery* 10, 2011, 712.

18. Glenn Begley and Lee Ellis. Drug Development: Raise Standards for Preclinical Cancer Research. *Nature*, 483, 2012, 531–33.

19. National Academies of Sciences, Engineering, and Medicine. *Statistical Challenges in Assessing and Fostering the Reproducibility of Scientific Results: Summary of a Workshop.* Washington, DC: National Academies Press, 2016.

20. Joint Committee on Standards for Educational Evaluation. *The Program Evaluation Standards.* 2nd ed. Thousand Oaks, CA: Sage, 1994.

21. Hilary Yerbury. When Our Data Doesn't Match the Concepts: Reflections on Research Practice. *Australian Academic & Research Libraries*, 47 (1), 2016, 18–29.

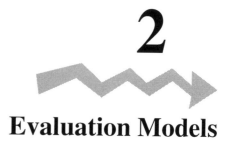

2

Evaluation Models

An original idea. That can't be too hard.
The library must be full of them.

—Stephen Fry

Evaluation is the process of determining the worth, merit, or value of something. It consists of comparing "what is" to "what ought to be." Implicit in the comparison is the need to select one or more measures, often called performance measures, to use as the basis for comparison. Measurement is the precursor to an evaluation done in order to fully understand a system, service, or process. Measurement entails the quantification of a service or process or is a qualitative assessment of a service or process.

An evaluation can be done using one of these four broad levels of analysis:

- **Individual.** An individual library customer's experience could be the basis for an evaluation, but it is difficult to generalize based on a single observation or interaction. Thus, most evaluations are done at a higher level.

- **Service.** A program or service is the focus of a majority of library evaluation projects. In this case, the experience of a group of library customers may be evaluated in order to draw some conclusions.

- **Organizational.** Another option would evaluate all of the library's services. This type of evaluation typically is internally focused. That is, the evaluation would compare one library to a group of peer libraries.

- **Societal.** The final level of analysis examines the impact of the library on the local community (community would mean a city or county for a public library; the degree to which a university has achieved its goals and objectives; the parent organization of a special library).

Having a clear understanding of the level of analysis that a library will be performing is important because it will affect which methodology will be used and the tools that can be used to analyze the resulting data.

EVALUATION MODELS

Evaluation models are used to assist in our understanding of the functions and services provided by a library. Although a number of models have been developed, only a few of the more notable models are presented here. The use of a particular model may be helpful for a specific library depending on the characteristics of the larger organization.

Several models have adopted the use of a matrix in an effort to convey the different types of evaluation studies. Blaise Cronin has suggested a broad and generic evaluation model.[1] He developed the evaluation matrix shown in Figure 2.1 and suggested that a library could focus its evaluation efforts on costs, benefits, and effectiveness, while acknowledging that three different perspectives would influence the type of evaluation that would be prepared. The choice of a particular perspective will influence the expectations of the library's stakeholders. Typically, an evaluation will focus on a single cell within the matrix.

	User	Management	Sponsor
Cost			
Effectiveness			
Benefits			

Figure 2.1. Cronin's Evaluation Matrix. Blaise Cronin. Taking the Measure of Service. *ASLIB Proceedings*, 34 (6/7), 1982, 273–94.

José-Marie Griffiths and Donald King developed a similar evaluation matrix, which suggested that five evaluation perspectives were possible (the library, user, organization of which the library is a part, industry, and society at large) as well as what could be evaluated, as shown in Figure 2.2.[2] This particular model is most often applied in the corporate environment.

	Library	User	Organization	Industry	Society
Entire library					
Functions					
Services/Products					
Activities					
Resources					

Figure 2.2. Griffiths's and King's Evaluation Matrix. Adapted from Figure 14 in José-Marie Griffiths and Donald King. *Special Libraries: Increasing the Information Edge.* Washington, DC: SLA, 1993, p. 45.

Scot Nicholson suggested a slightly simpler evaluation matrix, shown in Figure 2.3.[3] Nicholson employed an internal-focus (the library) or an external-focus (the customer) perspective. Similarly, the evaluation effort could look at the library or its use. Comparing the library's efficiency with its benefits is a way to prepare a cost-benefit analysis. Similarly, examining the quality and effectiveness from the customer's perspective is a way to determine the relevance of the library.

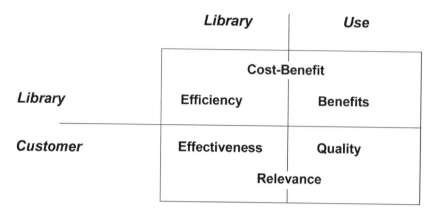

Figure 2.3. Nicholson's Evaluation Matrix. Adapted from Figure 1 in Scot Nicholson. A Conceptual Framework for the Holistic Measurement and Cumulative Evaluation of Library Services. *Journal of Documentation,* 60 (2), 2004, 164–82.

Unfortunately, all of the models presented so far ignore the reality that efforts to measure change must focus on a specific group of individuals (the targets for a program or service) and on evidence that changes in this target population were produced by program activities. One of the early evaluation pioneers was Edward Suchman, who developed a circular six-step model (see Figure 2.4) in order to suggest that evaluation efforts are or should be ongoing activities in an organization.[4] The final step is comparison of results to initial planned goals and objectives.

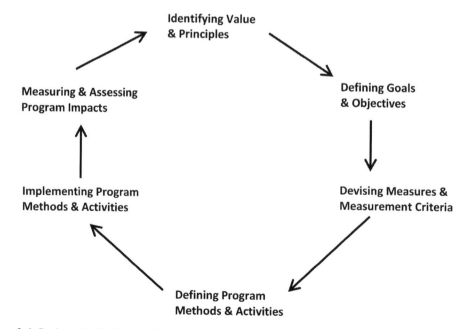

Figure 2.4. Suchman's Evaluative Model. Adapted from figure in Edward Suchman. *Evaluative Research: Principles and Practice in Public Service and Social Action Programs.* New York: Russell Sage, 1967.

Alexander Astin developed a model that has been used for some time in the academic environment (see Figure 2.5).[5] This is a fairly straightforward model that suggests a progression moving from inputs to the environmental setting of the university, to the outcomes generated by the university. Examples of the factors that constitute each component of the model are shown in Figure 2.5.

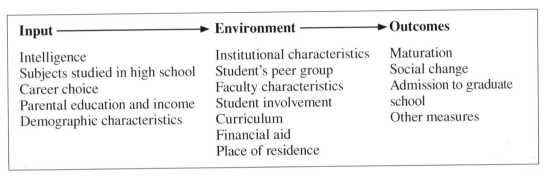

Input →	Environment →	Outcomes
Intelligence	Institutional characteristics	Maturation
Subjects studied in high school	Student's peer group	Social change
Career choice	Faculty characteristics	Admission to graduate
Parental education and income	Student involvement	school
Demographic characteristics	Curriculum	Other measures
	Financial aid	
	Place of residence	

Figure 2.5. Academic (Astin's) Evaluation Model. Alexander Astin. *What Matters in College?* San Francisco: Jossey-Bass, 1993.

One of the oldest, and certainly the most frequently cited, evaluation model in library literature was developed by Richard Orr in 1973. His Input-Process-Output-Outcomes model, shown in Figure 2.6, has value in this context because its structure is clearly applicable in a library setting.[6] Astin's Input-Environment-Outcome model is very similar to Orr's and reflects a process orientation for evaluation. Both models differentiate library efforts (resources and capabilities) from benefits.

Resources — Input measures   Capability — Process measures   Utilization — Output measures   Impact or Effect — Outcomes for the individual community, or organization

Figure 2.6. Orr's Evaluation Model. Richard Orr. Measuring the Goodness of Library Services. *Journal of Documentation*, 29 (3), 1973, 315–52.

According to Orr, when a library is established, it is provided with a set of *resources*. Those resources are organized and directed so that they become transformed and have the *capability* to provide a set of services. These capabilities are then *utilized*. Once used, the information and service that have been provided have the potential to make a positive, beneficial *impact or effect* on the individual and ultimately on the organization or community.

Input measures are the easiest to quantify and gather and have been used by librarians for a long time. Typically, input measures are grouped into five broad categories: budget, staff, collections, facilities, and technology. Input measures are usually counts or a numerical value.

Process measures or *productivity measures* are focused on the activities that transform resources into services offered by the library, and as such are internally directed. Process measures are reflected in an analysis that will quantify the cost or time to perform a specific task or activity. Process measures are ultimately about efficiency and thus answer the question, "Are we doing *things right*?" Usually a library will compare its process measures with a group of peer libraries in order to make an assessment of how efficient the library is.

Output measures are used to indicate the degree to which the library and its services are being utilized. More often than not, output measures are simply counts to indicate volume of activity. Historically, use of output measures has been regarded as a measure of goodness—after all, the library's collection (physical and electronic) and its services were being used, often intensively so! Therefore, the library was doing "good." A multiplicity of measures exist to demonstrate use of services, use of the collection (physical and electronic), use of facilities (gate count, program attendance), visits to the library's Web site, and so forth.

Broadly speaking, *outcomes* indicate the effect of the library's collections, programs, or services in the life of the customer. It is also important to note that outcomes can be planned (sometimes called goals) or unintended, and that the actual outcomes may be less than, equal to, or greater than what was intended. Outcomes occur first in an individual and then in the larger context—the organization or community. Outcomes allow a library to assess its effectiveness and to answer a very important question, "Are we doing the *right things?*"

Assessment of outcomes, sometimes called impact analysis or impact evaluation, is typically done to determine which outcome changes occur as a result of natural forces such as experience or maturation and which occur as a result of the interventions provided by a program or service. In some cases, these positive outcomes from a service or program are called benefits.

An extension of Orr's model answers the "how, who, what, and why" questions, as shown in Figure 2.7.[7]

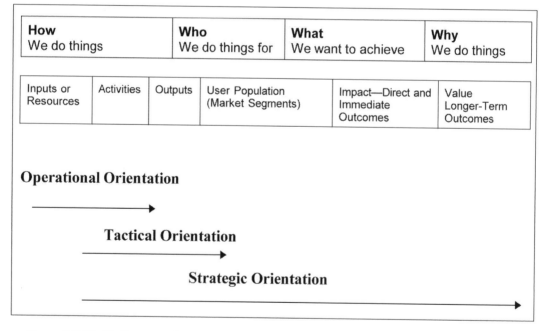

How We do things			**Who** We do things for	**What** We want to achieve	**Why** We do things
Inputs or Resources	Activities	Outputs	User Population (Market Segments)	Impact—Direct and Immediate Outcomes	Value Longer-Term Outcomes

Operational Orientation

Tactical Orientation

Strategic Orientation

Figure 2.7. The Performance Spectrum. Adapted from Jennifer Cram and Valerie Shine. Performance Measurement as Promotion: Demonstrating Benefit to Your Significant Others. Paper presented at the School Library Association of Queensland Biennial Conference, 29 June–1 July 2004, Gold Coast, Queensland.

A focus on operations is reflected in the use of input and process performance measures. A tactical orientation will find a library using process and output measures. A strategic orientation requires the use of output measures to demonstrate use of the library (an implied value) as well as use of outcome measures.

The outcomes that may occur in an individual include changes in

- attitude,
- skill, knowledge, behavior, and
- status or condition.

Rhea Rubin has suggested that focusing on outcomes is beneficial for many reasons, including:[8]

- Assumptions are made explicit.
- It is good for collaboration with users and stakeholders.
- Milestones can be identified as the library selects interim and long-range outcomes.
- It focuses staff and stakeholders on the goals of a program or service.
- Improvements and innovations can result from an examination of outcomes.
- It provides insights into how and why a program or service is being used by some and not by others.
- Outcomes become a vehicle for determining the contributions a library makes to the lives of its customers.

Table 2.1 provides a number of generic outcomes that a library could consider using as part of an evaluation plan to demonstrate the value of the library in the lives of its users.

Peter Hernon and Robert Duggan have noted that an output is institutionally or organizationally based, whereas some outcomes, such as a student's learning outcomes, occur within an individual. Further, there need not be a progression from outputs to outcomes, although this can occur in some cases.[9] Outputs are measurable and are typically compiled, counted, or gathered, whereas outcomes or impacts are often not so easily measured.

Outcomes or impacts may be what was intended or a surprise, positive or negative, short-term or long-term, and significant or trivial. To be considered meaningful, an outcome must be identified as being sensitive to change and intervention.

Combining the Griffiths and King model described earlier with Orr's Input-Process-Output-Outcomes model results in a conceptual framework for library metrics, as shown in Figure 2.8.

Leonor Pinto and Paula Ochoa prepared a meta-evaluation model that highlights the evolution of library performance evaluation models over time, as shown in Table 2.2. Their article suggests that more recently, libraries have been embracing more holistic models of library performance evaluation models.

Peter Brophy has suggested that it might also be useful to consider the magnitude of outcomes, using a levels-of-impact model as shown in Figure 2.9.

Additional problems that may arise when attempting to identify the outcomes or impacts of the library on the lives of its customers include:

- A library service can have a different value and outcome for different user groups.
- Data that might be relevant for demonstrating impact are not available (or are only available with considerable effort) due to considerations of protecting the privacy of individuals.
- Because various methods have been used in different libraries to identify impacts, the results are difficult to compare and synthesize.
- Long-term effects cannot be assessed if the library customer is not available for follow-up tests, surveys, or interviews.

- It is difficult to isolate the contribution of the library from the contributions of others—friends, teachers, family, the Internet, and so forth.
- Rarely is the impact the result of a single encounter with the library's collection or service, and this makes attempting to determine the impact in an individual's life even more challenging.[10]

Table 2.1. Generic Outcomes

Knowledge and Understanding	Knowing about something Learning facts/information Making sense of something Learning how libraries operate Giving specific information—naming things, people, or places Making links and relationships between things Using prior knowledge in new ways
Skills	Knowing how to do something Being able to do new things Intellectual skills—reading, thinking critically and analytically, making judgments Key skills—numbers and statistics, literacy, use of IT, learning how to learn Information management skills—finding, assessing, and using Social skills Communication skills
Attitudes and Values	Feelings Perceptions Opinions about ourselves, e.g., self-esteem Opinions of or attitudes toward other people Increased capacity for tolerance Empathy Increased motivation Attitudes toward the library Positive and negative attitudes in relation to experience
Enjoyment, Inspiration, and Creativity	Having fun Being surprised Innovative thoughts Creativity Exploration and experimentation Being inspired
Activity, Behavior, and Progression	What people do What people intend to do (intention to act) What people have done A change in the way people manage their time Reported or observed actions

Adapted from Jennifer Cram and Valerie Shine, Performance Measurement as Promotion: Demonstrating Benefit to Your Significant Others. Paper presented at the School Library Association of Queensland Biennial Conference, 29 June–1 July 2004, Gold Coast, Queensland, Australia.

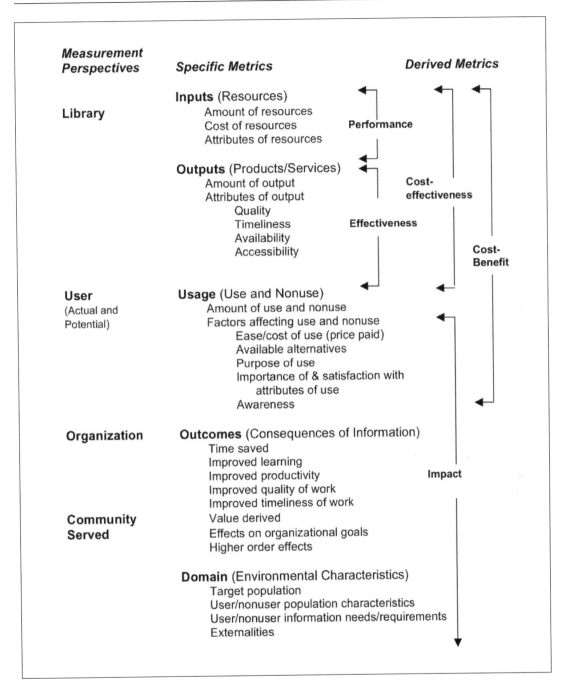

Figure 2.8. Conceptual Framework for Library Metrics. King, Donald W., Boyce, Peter B., Montgomery, Carol Hansen, Tenopir, Carol. "Library Economic Metrics: Examples of the Comparison of Electronic and Print Journal Collections and Collection Services." *Library Trends* 51:3 (2003), p. 379, Fig. 1. © 2003 The Board of Trustees, University of Illinois. Reprinted with permission of Johns Hopkins University Press.

Table 2.2. Portuguese Performance Evaluation Models and Practice Types

| | | TOPIC | |
		Library	**Use**
PERSPECTIVE	**Internal (Library)**	Inputs Results–products Processes Goals Statistics Benchmarking Standards (1998) PLNN* Model of Performance Information Management System LMLN* System for Collecting and Report Performance Information KRCN* Performance Model ISO 9001 certificate (2004)	Results–library use User studies (focus on library use) Bibliometric studies Goals Statistics Benchmarking Standards (1998) PLNN Model of Performance Information Management System LMLN System for Collecting and Report Performance Information KRCN Performance Model
	External (Users and Other Stakeholders)	Needs and expectations of customers KRCN Quality Observation Model LMLN Service Quality Model	Customer satisfaction Service Quality Impact on users Social and economic impact KRCN Quality Observation Model LMLN Service Quality Model ENTITLE-LMNL Impact Assessment Framework
	Holistic	(Total) Quality Management EFQM CAF BSC Integrated models MonitorDoc IU-ME Quality Program LMLN Performance Evaluation Integrated System SIADAP Model Mix-Model CAF-BSC (AHP) Digital Library Integrated Evaluation Model School Libraries Self-Assessment Model	

AHP=Analytic Hierarchy Process
BSC=Balanced Scorecard
CAF=Common Assessment Framework
EFQM=European Foundation for Quality Management
ENTITLE=Europe's New libraries Together In Transversal Learning Environments
IU-ME=Information Unit of the General Secretariat of the Portuguese Ministry of Education
KRCN=Knowledge and Resources Centres Network
LMLN=Lisbon Municipal Libraries Network
PLNN=Public Libraries National Network
SIADAP=Sisterna Integrado de Avaliacao de Desempenho da Administracao Publica (an integrated management and performance evaluation system in public administration in Portugal)

Reprinted from Leonor Pinto and Paula Ochoa. Information Society and Library Evaluation Transitions in Portugal: A Meta-Evaluation Model and Frameworks (1970-2013). *LIBER Quarterly,* 23 (3), 2013, 222. Used with permission.

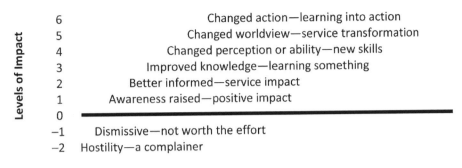

Levels of Impact		
6	Changed action—learning into action
5	Changed worldview—service transformation
4	Changed perception or ability—new skills
3	Improved knowledge—learning something
2	Better informed—service impact
1	Awareness raised—positive impact
0	
−1	Dismissive—not worth the effort
−2	Hostility—a complainer

Kind of Impact

Figure 2.9. Levels of Impact Model. Adapted from Peter Brophy. The Development of a Model for Assessing the Level of Impact of Information and Library Service. *Library & Information Research*, 29 (93), Winter 2005, 43–49.

Since Congress passed the Government Performance and Results Act (GPRA), federal government agencies have been encouraged (read: mandated) to embrace outcome-based evaluation. Outcome-based evaluation (OBE) is a systematic way to assess the extent to which a program or service has achieved its goals. OBE is designed to answer two key questions: (1) How has this program or service made a difference? and (2) How are the lives of the program or service recipients better?

A program or service is developed as a result of assumptions about people's needs. Thus, outcome-based evaluation focuses on the following:

- **Need.** A condition, want, or deficit common to a group of individuals.
- **Solution.** A program or service that will change attitudes, skills, knowledge, behaviors, status, or condition.
- **Desired results.** The change or improvement that is expected.

Outcome-based evaluation is designed to get an organization, such as a library, to answer a crucial question:

We do *what*, for *whom*, for what *outcomes* or *benefits*?

Figure 2.10 presents the same information found in Orr's model (see Figure 2.5) from a slightly different perspective, in order to indicate the relationship between quality and value and the fact that the library (the organization or community) is influenced and constrained by its external environment.

Note that an evaluation of quality occurs between the capability of the library and its staff members and the use of the collection and library services by the library's customers. The perception of the customer is much more important than any objective measure of the quality of the service being delivered. That is, if a library delivers a high-quality service and yet the customers view the service as so-so, then the service is only so-so in the eyes of the most important stakeholders—the customers of the library! The value of library services can only be determined after the service or product is used by the customer and the customer has ascertained its value.

Over the last couple of decades a number of nonprofit organizations have embraced the use of a logic model. A logic model links outcome or impacts (including short-term and long-term) with program or service activities/processes and the underlying assumptions/principles of the program. The logic model starts with impact or effect and moves right to left towards Capability and Resources as shown in Figure 2.11.[11]

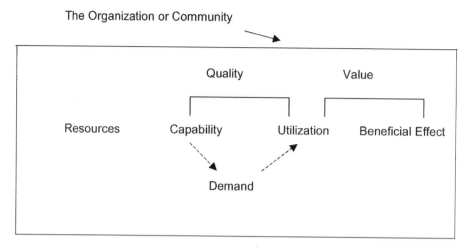

Figure 2.10. Variation on Orr's Evaluation Model

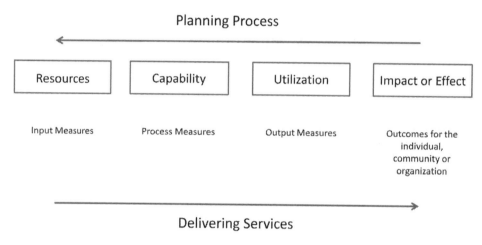

Figure 2.11. The Logic Model

Bill Irwin and Paul St. Pierre have developed a more inclusive model, as seen in Figure 2.12, that demonstrates how an organization can progress through a series of stages, moving from output-based performance metrics to an organizationally aligned outcome-based evaluation system that illustrates the need for operational and cultural transformations if change is going to be lasting.[12]

OTHER NOTABLE MODELS

Donald and James Kirkpatrick developed a model for evaluating training programs that encompassed four levels:[13]

1. Reaction—the feelings and thoughts of participants after the training
2. Learning—a change in knowledge, skills, or attitude (usually involving a test or a demonstration of skills)
3. Behavior—transfer of skills, knowledge, or attitude to the job (evaluation occurs 3 to 6 months after the training)

Dimension		Stage 0	Stage 1	Stage 2	Stage 3	Stage 4
	Purpose	Complacency	Justification	Self-Awareness	Alignment	Actualization
	Motivation	Inertia	Fear & Survival	Toward sense of self-efficacy	Enlightenment	Success, Internalization
	Organizational Impact / Tactical Strategic	Resistance Evaluation is 'busy work'	Tactical: Short-term		Strategic: Long-term	
			Buy-in	Shift from systems, to individual, to patron/staff focus	Habituation	Inculcation
	Organizational Impact Internal / External	Closed system	Internal (staff)	Toward an open system	Broad stakeholder inclusion	Infusion (beware of gaming)
	Inhibitors & Enablers	Lack of education, lack of meaningful results, inertia	Lack of personal involvement. Buy-in not enough	Cautious engagement	Enthusiasm; Coordinating many voices	Unintended consequences (positive or negative)
	Implications	Diminishing budgets, failure	Awakening	Organizational learning	Shared leadership	Assessment is continual, naturally occurring

Figure 2.12. Irwin's and St. Pierre's Framework for Cultural Change and Evaluation.
Bill Irwin and Paul St. Pierre. Creating a Culture of Meaningful Evaluation in Public Libraries: Moving Beyond Quantitative Metrics. *Sage Open,* October–December 2014, 1–14. Used with permission.

4. Results—final results as evidenced by improved productivity, reduced on-the-job injuries, and so forth.

England's National Health Service has developed a Library Quality Assurance Framework that includes criteria in five domains:[14]

Domain 1   Strategic Management

Domain 2   Finance and Service Level Agreements

Domain 3   Human Resources and Staff Management

Domain 4   Infrastructure and Facilities

Domain 5   Library/Knowledge Service Delivery and Development.

In the public library arena, two self-evaluation frameworks have been developed. The first, the *Public Library Quality Improvement Matrix* (PLQIM), developed in Scotland, has seven quality indicators (with six quality levels):[15]

1. **Access to Information**—How well are local and wider information resources made accessible? To what extent are the information needs of the community met?

2. **Personal and Community Participation**—How well does the library contribute to a sense of place and identity? How does library staff support the development of individuals and communities?

3. **Meeting Reader's Needs**—How well does the collection meet the requirements of a broad range of reading interests and abilities? Is a range of reading choices and events provided?

4. **Learners' Experiences**—How do the library environment and staff promote learning? How does the library meet the needs of different market segments?

5. **Ethos and Values**—How does the library demonstrate inclusion and opportunity for all? Are individuals welcomed when they enter the library? How do stakeholders view the library?

6. **Organization and Use of Resources & Space**—How are services marketed? How are facilities evaluated? Are there a sufficient number of trained and motivated staff?

7. **Leadership**—How well is the vision communicated and realized? How are staff supported and empowered? What new innovative services have recently been introduced?

In addition, the State Library of Victoria developed a self-evaluation framework that focuses on five key areas:[16]

Area 1: **Offering access to information, learning, and leisure**
• Adequacy, variety and suitability of resources
• Provisions for access
• Staff expertise of tools and user support

Area 2: **Developing individual skills, competence, and well-being**
• Encouraging lifelong learning
• Presenting 21st-century literacies
• Inspiring a reading culture

Area 3: **Expanding social capital**
• Providing a welcoming civic space
• Reinforcing social connections and embracing all segments of the community
• Acting in partnerships

Area 4: **Showing leadership**
• Embracing innovation at all levels
• Engaging the community
• Building organizational strength through staff

Area 5: **Creating, managing, and enhancing systems and processes**
• Simplifying policies and procedures
• Expending resources wisely
• Focusing on continuous improvement

LIMITATIONS

One of the disappointments of the library profession is that it has been unable to develop a predictive model of library service. That is, the cause-and-effect relationships among inputs, outputs, and outcomes are not understood. Consider, for example, the following facts.

- Two public libraries from different communities are of similar size and socioeconomic characteristics, yet the budgetary support for each library will vary—often significantly. Use of each library will also vary, as evidenced by in-library use of materials and annual circulation numbers, attendance at programs, use of reference services, and so forth.
- Two academic libraries serving a similar size faculty and number of students will have quite different size library buildings, size of collections, and use of library resources.
- Two school libraries, often in the same school district, will have different budgets and support from other teachers and the school principal.
- Two special libraries, for example, in law firms, will have different budgets and number of staff. In one law firm, the library is viewed as helping the firm meet its objective of providing high-quality service to its clients and contributing to the bottom line. In the other firm, the library is viewed as administrative overhead that drags down the bottom line.

SUMMARY

Choosing an evaluation model can assist the library in better understanding the relationships between the resources it is provided and the outputs and outcomes it achieves. In most cases, unless otherwise stated, libraries will implicitly choose Orr's Input-Process-Output-Outcomes model. The reason for this is the relation of the model to the reality experienced by the library. Most libraries are accustomed to reporting inputs and outputs to a variety of agencies. Thus, expanding these measures to include process and outcome measures does not require a big leap.

NOTES

1. Blaise Cronin. Taking the Measure of Service. *ASLIB Proceedings*, 34 (6/7), 1982, 273–94.

2. José-Marie Griffiths and Donald King. *Special Libraries: Increasing the Information Edge.* Washington, DC: SLA, 1993.

3. Scot Nicholson. A Conceptual Framework for the Holistic Measurement and Cumulative Evaluation of Library Services. *Journal of Documentation*, 60 (2), 2004, 164–82.

4. Edward Suchman. *Evaluative Research: Principles and Practice in Public Service and Social Action Programs.* New York: Russell Sage, 1967.

5. Alexander Astin. *What Matters in College?* San Francisco: Jossey-Bass, 1993.

6. Richard Orr. Measuring the Goodness of Library Services. *Journal of Documentation*, 29 (3), 1973, 315–52.

7. Adapted from Jennifer Cram and Valerie Shine. *Performance Measurement as Promotion: Demonstrating Benefit to Your Significant Others.* Paper presented at the School Library Association of Queensland Biennial Conference, 29 June–1 July 2004, Gold Coast, Queensland.

8. Rhea Joyce Rubin. *Demonstrating Results: Using Outcome Measurement in Your Library.* Chicago: American Library Association, 2006.

9. Peter Hernon and Robert E. Duggan. Continued Development of Assorted Measures, in *Outcomes Assessment in Higher Education: Views and Perspectives.* Westport, CT: Libraries Unlimited, 2004, 309–18.

10. Roswitha Poll and Phillip Payne. Impact Measures for Libraries and Information Services. *Library HiTech*, 24 (4), 2006, 547–62.

11. Kellogg Foundation. *Logic Model Development Guide: Using Logic Model to Bring Together Planning, Evaluation, and Action.* Battle Creek, MI: W. K. Kellogg Foundation, 2004.

12. Bill Irwin and Paul St. Pierre. Creating a Culture of Meaningful Evaluation in Public Libraries: Moving Beyond Quantitative Metrics. *Sage Open*, October-December 2014, 1–14.

13. Donald Kirkpatrick and James Kirkpatrick. *Implementing the Four Levels: A Practical Guide for Effective Evaluation of Training Programs*. Oakland, CA: Berrett-Koehler Publishers, 2007.

14. NHS. *NHS Library Quality Assurance Framework (LQAF) England*. Leeds, England: National Health Service, April 2016.

15. Scottish Library & Information Council. *Building on Success: A Public Library Quality Improvement Matrix for Scotland*. Glasgow, Scotland: March 2007.

16. State Library of Victoria. *Being the Best We Can: Key Results for Public Library Service*. Melbourne, Australia: June 2011.

Part II

Methodology Concerns

3

Qualitative Tools

Understanding requires the grasping of explanatory and other coherence-making relationships in a large and comprehensive body of information. One can know many unrelated pieces of information, but understanding is achieved only when informational items are pieced together.

—Jonathan Kvanvig[1]

Qualitative research methods are particularly helpful when attempting to better understand complex relationships among and between variables or to understand the "qualities" of an experience. Qualitative methods have been called "naturalistic research" because it is possible to develop multiple interpretations of reality. Qualitative methods use smaller samples, which means that making generalizations is much more difficult. Qualitative data can include interactions among individuals, groups, and organizations as well as descriptions of phenomena. Qualitative methods are used to define the "why," whereas quantitative tools are typically used to define the "what" and "how many." Table 3.1 provides an overview of the features of qualitative and quantitative research.

Rather than attempting to quantify a library service or activity, qualitative methods seek to document the complexities of what is experienced or observed. The strength of qualitative data is their rich descriptions that facilitate a better understanding of the "why" and "how" of a particular topic or activity by capturing the thoughts, feelings, and behaviors of individuals.

Qualitative analysis techniques were developed in the social sciences, where researchers are unable to control many of the variables relevant to the topic under investigation. Within the field of library and information science, researchers have been using qualitative methods to better understand information seeking and information retrieval, among many other topics. One of the keys to high-quality qualitative research is the use of multiple methods, often called *triangulation*, to improve the reliability of results. For example, one study used three qualitative methods (semi-structured interviews, direct observation, and document analysis) to investigate essential elements of community engagement in public libraries.[2]

Table 3.1. A Comparison of Qualitative and Quantitative Research

Qualitative	Quantitative
The aim is a complete, detailed description that provides depth.	The aim is to classify and count features, and then construct a statistical model in an attempt to explain what is observed.
Typically used during the early phases of a research project.	Typically used during the later phases of a research project.
As few people are involved, a sense of openness is encouraged.	Allows for a broader view involving a greater number of participants.
Researchers rarely know what they are looking for.	Researchers have a clear understanding of what they are looking for.
Design emerges as the study proceeds.	The design is carefully constructed before any data are collected.
The researcher observes and records all data.	The researcher uses tools such as surveys or equipment to gather mostly numerical data.
Data are in the form of words, objects, and pictures.	Data are in the form of numbers and statistics.
The process of gathering data is time consuming and data are more difficult to generalize.	Data gathering is efficient and can test hypotheses.
Researcher is immersed in the subject matter and may have difficulty maintaining objectivity.	Researcher is separated from the subject matter and it is easier to remain objective.

Not surprisingly, the qualitative research field has evolved its own terminology to address important research-related topics, as shown in Table 3.2.

A central concept of qualitative methods is the idea of a "case study," which attempts to provide in-depth understanding about a particular topic, activity, or process. David Silverman provides an overview of qualitative methods that includes exploring meanings rather than behaviors, to craft studies that generate hypotheses rather than test hypotheses.[3] David Bawden focuses on the use of qualitative tools as a better means of gaining an understanding of a topic or subject.[4]

The strength of qualitative methods is that they can provide:

• Greater sensitivity to the needs of and the impact of a library service on the life of a user

• An understanding of how responsive a library service is to a changing environment and various user groups

• Awareness of time and history

Table 3.2. A Comparison of Conventional and Naturalistic Inquiry

Criterion	Conventional Term	Naturalistic Term	Naturalistic Techniques
Truth value	Internal validity	Credibility	Prolonged engagement Persistent observation Triangulation Referential adequacy: use of content-rich materials Peer debriefing Member checks Reflexive journal
Applicability	External validity	Transferability	Thick description Purposive sampling Reflexive journal
Consistency	Reliability	Dependability	Dependability audit Reflexive journal
Neutrality	Objectivity	Confirmability	Confirmability audit Reflexive journal

Adapted from Yvonna S. Lincoln and Egon G. Guba. *Naturalistic Inquiry.*
Newbury Park, CA: Sage Publications, 1985, 79.

- A better understanding of the context of a library program or service
- An opportunity to immerse an observer without preconceptions to better understand what is happening
- Greater flexibility of perspective[5]

In almost all cases, researchers employ multiple qualitative methods rather than simply relying on a single method. These methods can be subdivided into three categories: no contact with an individual, one-to-one interaction, and interaction with a group.

No contact

- Examining documents
- Diaries

One-to-one interaction

- Observation
- Interviewing
- Grounded theory
- Think aloud/think after verbal protocol
- Ethnographic methods
- Netnographic methods
- Phenomenography

Group interaction

- Focus groups
- Delphi method
- Critical incident technique
- Concept mapping

NO CONTACT

Examining Documents

This methodology is rarely used because there are few documents in a library that are not much more susceptible to quantitative analysis. For example, examining the paper copies of the patron registration forms would reveal information about the registered library cardholders. However, because the same information is stored in the library's automated system, quantitative reports can be quickly generated.

Some libraries have found it helpful to analyze the customer complaint forms submitted to the library. This analysis might reveal some patterns of reported problems that should be addressed. It is also possible to analyze the responses to open-ended questions when a survey is completed.

Other documents that can be analyzed are the library's policy manual and the memos that are periodically distributed throughout the organization. Some have studied job announcements in an attempt to understand the changing competency requirements for librarians and other staff members. Others have examined reference interviews (person-to-person or virtual conversations).

In some cases, the analysis of text is called *hermeneutics,* which relates to the development and study of theories of the interpretation and understanding of texts.

Content analysis involves the researcher using analytical constructs or rules to draw inferences about recurring identifiable aspects of text content. The key is making the analytical construct explicit.[6] For example, Danuta Nitecki examined phrases that contained the word stem "librar."[7] Green performed a similar study analyzing the use of the word "information."[8] Karen Davies analyzed the origins and data collection methodologies of research articles published in three information science journals.[9] Lili Luo and Margaret McKinney used content analysis to examine the peer-reviewed articles published in *The Journal of Academic Librarianship* over a 10-year span.[10] These two authors found that information literacy was the most popular topic and that surveys and content analysis were the two most frequently used research methods.

Diaries

Some evaluation studies and research projects have asked respondents to keep a diary of their activities, thoughts, motivations, and emotions throughout the life of the project. For example, Carol Kuhlthau asked a group of high school students to use diaries in an information-seeking study.[11] If a group of respondents faithfully records all that they are experiencing, the result is a deep and rich repository of ideas and thoughts that can be mined to extract nuggets of insight. Participants need some instruction about how much detail to provide, how often they should make an entry, and so forth.

A variation of this approach is to ask a group of respondents to carry a timer that will go off at random intervals during the day. Each time the timer alerts the respondents, they are asked to record what activity they are engaged in at that moment: talking on the telephone, reading, in a meeting, and so forth.

Another variation asks respondents to use an audiotape recorder and to record their comments as they complete a task or activity.

ONE-TO-ONE INTERACTION

Observation

Observation is a method for learning about the activities of a library customer. Although it is possible to observe how a collection is used, this approach has so many problems—e.g., exactly which item is being used—that it is rarely used in evaluation studies.

Activity sampling can provide accurate estimates of time spent on various activities. Having two observers simultaneously recording the activities of customers in the library will improve the consistency and accuracy of the results. One study that employed two observers noted that consistency ranged from 80 to 92 percent.[12]

Another variation of this method is to approach customers while they are in the library and either conduct a brief interview (if they agree) or ask them to complete a questionnaire about their activities.

Another form of observation has been used in unobtrusive evaluations of reference service by using volunteers or paid observers to approach a reference desk seeking assistance. The approach can be made in person or via the telephone. A variation of this approach that some libraries have employed is to use "mystery shoppers" to observe and evaluate a library facility and its services during a visit.[13]

One of the most significant challenges facing those who would be observers in an evaluation study is to decide ahead of time the role they will play. That is, is the observation technique to be used only that of an observer, of an observer and participant (with some interaction with the participant), or of a participant with the individual being observed? Each approach has obvious positive and negative attributes, and the bias of the observer will creep in unless the method is carefully chosen. Note that some librarians may have difficulty in not assisting the participant, even if asked not to do so.

Those involved in an observation study must decide the number of participants, whether the participants will be staff or library customers, the setting or activities that will be observed, and how broad or narrow the focus of the inquiry will be.

Interviewing

An interview offers the opportunity of gaining a better and more in-depth understanding of a situation from the point of view of the library customer. The interview format can vary from formal or structured—an orally administered questionnaire—to semi-structured, from a loose framework for the questions to a completely unstructured discussion. The strength of the interview method is that it allows the questioner to probe and ask clarifying questions in order to gain a better understanding.

Semi-structured and unstructured interviews are more appropriate for use in an exploratory study, where the researcher is attempting to gain some initial understanding of a situation or subject—where it is not known what is not known. This type of interview, which provides great depth on a relatively narrow topic, has been called "river-and-channel" because the questions follow the current of conversation no matter where it leads.[14]

Structured interviews are more reliable because the same questions are asked of a group of people. The questioner has some knowledge of the topic, even though that knowledge is not complete. This interviewing approach has been called "tree-and-branch": the questions are designed to explore each branch of the tree to the same extent.[15]

Although most one-on-one interviews occur face-to-face, it is also possible to conduct one-on-one interviews using the telephone. Typically an interview will start off with some "icebreaker" questions, which allow the respondent to feel safe in answering. As the respondent becomes more comfortable, the interviewer can move to more difficult questions.

The different types of questions that can be asked depend on the type of study. Among these are the following:

- **Experience and behavior questions** probe what a person does or has done, with the intent of eliciting descriptions of behaviors, actions, and activities that are observable.
- **Feeling questions** seek to elicit the emotional responses of people based on their experiences and thoughts. The researcher is looking for adjectives that describe feelings, words such as *happy, frustrated, upset,* and *anxious.*
- **Opinion and value questions** are aimed at understanding the cognitive processes of the respondent. The researcher is seeking information pertaining to goals, desires, values, and intentions.
- **Knowledge questions** are asked to determine the level of knowledge and information the respondent has about a particular topic.
- **Sensory questions** ask about what is seen, heard, touched, tasted, and smelled. For example, "When you walk into the library, what do you see?"
- **Demographic questions** identify the characteristics of the respondent.

A summary of a number of studies that examined the use of e-mail as a means for conducting interviews found the approach to be a viable alternative to face-to-face and telephone interviewing. However, there are problems with this format, as with any methodology.[16]

If the interviews are recorded and then transcribed, hundreds of pages of transcripts can be the result. This may require the use of a software tool to analyze the transcripts to assist in identifying themes, frequently occurring phrases, and so forth.

Tips for conducting a successful interview include the following.

DO'S

- Develop rapport with the participant.
- Divide the interview into major sections.
- Provide transition between major topics.
- Be alert to your own biases and remain neutral.
- Know when to stop probing for more detail.
- Keep the participant focused on the topic.

DON'TS

- Interrupt the participant.
- Attempt to fill every silence.

- Insert your own observations.
- Disagree with the participant.
- Allow the discussion to ramble.

Often the results of one or more interviews and observations will be written up in the form of a case study. The concept of the case study arises from law schools, in which a single case before a court is carefully examined. The use of the case study in law school was popularized by the movie and TV show *The Paper Chase*. Other professional preparation programs, most notably the Harvard Business School and other MBA programs, use the case study approach.

First used in the library arena in 1984 by Fidel, and subsequently by many others, the case study methodology must ameliorate a number of shortcomings:[17]

- Study effect—the very act of studying something may change it (sometimes this is called the "Hawthorne Effect" or the "Observer Effect")
- Participant bias
- Observer bias.

Grounded Theory

Grounded theory was developed as a systematic methodology, and its name underscores the generation of theory from data. When the principles of grounded theory are followed, the researcher will formulate a theory about the phenomena being studied that can be evaluated. In some cases the observer will have prepared a data-coding sheet to assist in gathering data. Others suggest that a coding sheet will prevent the researcher from really understanding what is happening.[18]

Think Aloud/Think After Verbal Protocol

Another kind of interview asks the library customer to perform a prescribed task or activity. The respondent is asked to verbalize what he or she is thinking while doing this activity. This is the think aloud protocol, sometimes called the protocol analysis. Using this methodology requires that the respondents be highly verbal in nature. Caution should be used with this methodology because it will likely affect people's cognitive processes as well as their behavior.[19]

A variation of this is to ask the respondent to describe his or her thoughts after completing the task. Respondents using the think after method will likely "forget" steps they may have taken in the middle of their tasks.

In most cases when this method is used, the respondents are asked for their permission to record their comments with an audio- or videotape recorder. The resulting comments are then transcribed for analysis. Computer software programs are available that can be used to analyze the text.[20] Such software is particularly helpful if the evaluation project is going to involve a fair number of participants, with the resulting transcriptions being quite voluminous and difficult to analyze manually. The amount of data generated using the think aloud or think after method depends on the complexity of the task to be performed and the number of nonproductive "dead ends" encountered by the respondent.

This approach has been applied to studies of library online catalogs and library Web sites. For example, Jennifer Branch used both methods to study the information-seeking processes of adolescents.[21]

Ethnographic Methods

Tools have been developed by cultural anthropologists to better understand people in different cultural settings. Cultural data assume the form of directly observable material items (tools, cultivated fields, houses, statues, clothing), individual behaviors and performances (ceremonies, fights, games, meals), and ideas and arrangements that exist only in people's heads. From the perspective of the culture concept, anthropologists must first treat all these elements as is and must record observations with due attention to the cultural context and the meanings assigned by the culture's members and practitioners. These demands are met through two major research techniques: participant observation and key informant interviewing.

In reality, most information seeking happens outside the library, so using ethnographic techniques allows librarians to unobtrusively "follow the users" to their home, office, or other places in the community (or on campus) in order to gain a clearer picture of how people solve their information-related problems. The more interesting methods include:

- Drawing a picture or a map
- Taking photographs
- Using a map to track activities
- Videotaping environments

Perhaps the best-known ethnographic study in an academic setting was a project conducted for several years at the University of Rochester Libraries. Nancy Foster and Susan Gibbons employed a variety of methods to better understand how undergraduate students used and did not use the library.[22]

A group of Illinois academic libraries participated in an ethnographic research project called the ERIAL Project. Researchers asked students to prepare cognitive maps, a campus mapping diary, photo journals, research journals, interviews, and a space design workshop as part of a process to better understand how students completed research.[23] Diane Mizrachi used ethnographic methods to study undergraduate information and library behaviors at the University of California, Los Angeles, campus.[24]

Michael Khoo, Lily Rozaklis, and Catherine Hall summarized 81 studies in libraries that used ethnographic methods and found that five methods were most frequently used: observation, interviews, fieldwork, focus groups, and cultural probes.[25]

Netnographic Methods

Online communities develop for a variety of reasons, and the interactions of the participants will, over time, create a culture and develop a sense of identity and attachment. *Netnography* is the use of ethnographic methods to study online communities through immersion. Netnographers typically keep observational and reflective field notes and at some point will move from being "lurkers" to introducing themselves to the group and explaining what they are attempting to do—including asking for permission to use specific posts in a discussion list or on other social media sites.

Phenomenography

Phenomenography focuses on learning and the experience of learning in different contexts and can be used to better understand how people conceptualize, perceive, experience, and understand various aspects of phenomena in the world. Christine Yates, Helen Partridge, and Christine Bruce provided an overview of how phenomenography has been applied to better understand information experiences.[26]

GROUP INTERACTION

Focus Groups

A *focus group* is a group interview designed to learn about the beliefs and attitudes people hold and how those beliefs influence behavior. Typically such a discussion starts broadly and then narrows to focus more specifically on the topic being studied: hence the name focus group. The value of a focus group is that the comments of one individual will often trigger really valuable comments from others.

Libraries have used focus groups to address a number of topics, including customer information needs, community analysis, marketing studies, learning more about how a promotion might affect use of a planned or existing library service, value and utility of the library's collections, assessing existing or planned library facilities, and much more.

Focus groups typically have from seven to twelve people as participants. Volunteers are recruited who are representative of a particular group. In some cases, multiple focus group sessions are held with participants from different groups of the population served by the library. Typically, an outside trained moderator is used to facilitate the discussion and keep the comments on track. Thus, depending upon the number of focus group sessions, the costs can mount up quickly.

Focus groups usually run from one to two hours in length and are held in a comfortable room that is free from outside distractions. Refreshments help keep the atmosphere comfortable. The library should work with the moderator to develop a list of topics that will be discussed. It is the moderator's responsibility to ensure that one or two individuals do not monopolize the conversation and to encourage the participation of all attendees. The moderator is there to provide some guidance in order to keep the discussion flowing, but is not to judge or edit the discussion.

In addition to recording the session—with audio- or videotape equipment—the library should have one or two staff members in attendance to take notes and record pertinent comments and observations. The text of the recording is usually transcribed (it may take three to four hours to transcribe one hour of conversation) and is usually subjected to content analysis using a software package. In general, the software will produce a summary of the text and identify recurring themes. Some text-mining software will summarize the text, identify and extract entities, and produce theme "maps" showing the relationships or links among the themes.[27]

Having two or more people review the transcripts of the focus group sessions will assist in producing a summary of what the groups had to "say." This will help reduce any bias that may creep in. Focus groups have been used in libraries to explore a number of topics, including services to youth[28] and the reliability of services.[29]

Delphi Method

The Delphi method is a systematic interactive forecasting method based on the independent contributions of selected experts who answer a series of questionnaires. The name "Delphi"

¯derives from the Oracle of Delphi. The Delphi method recognizes the value of expert opinion, experience, and intuition. The selection of well-informed leading authorities in a particular field is crucial to the success of the Delphi method.

Questions are usually formulated as hypotheses, and experts react to each of these. Each round of questioning is followed with feedback on the preceding round of replies, usually presented anonymously. The experts are thus encouraged to revise their earlier answers in light of the replies of other members of the group. It is believed that during this process the range of the answers will decrease and the group will converge toward "consensus." The following key characteristics of the Delphi method help the participants focus on the issues at hand and separate Delphi from other methodologies:

- Structuring of information flow
- Regular feedback
- Anonymity of the participants

The panel director controls interactions among the participants by processing the information and filtering out irrelevant content. This prevents the negative effects of face-to-face panel discussions and solves the usual problems of group dynamics.

The Delphi method has been used for a number of studies within the library community. For example, Delphi studies have considered the library as place, the future of the academic library, the future of library school instruction, the future of the electronic journal, and the importance of the stakeholder in performance measurement, among others.[30]

Critical Incident Technique

The critical incident technique is a method for analyzing critical incidents—any observable human activity that is sufficiently complete in itself to permit inferences and predictions to be made about the persons performing the act. Typically the critical incident technique is used to gather and analyze data pertaining to the most memorable experience, not necessarily the most recent. John Flanagan and others developed this technique in the 1950s.[31]

The technique is used to evaluate and identify ways to increase effectiveness of service in a variety of fields, including libraries. The critical incident technique has been shown to be a reliable and valid explanatory method as well as useful for gathering information about human behavior in a survey.

The procedures typically used in a critical incident evaluation include the following:

- **General aims.** A brief statement of the focus of evaluation is prepared.
- **Plans and specifications.** If observations are going to be made, the groups and behaviors to be observed are identified and data collection forms are prepared. If a survey is to be used, the survey is designed and pretested.
- **Data collection.** The observer records the data, or the surveys are distributed and then collected.
- **Data analysis.** The data are described and summarized. In some cases, the text of transcripts might be analyzed using a software program, or survey data might be input into a statistical package.
- **Interpretation and reporting.** In addition to presenting the data, the possible limitations to the data collection and analysis should be identified.

Marie Radford applied the critical incident technique in a study of the reference process. Radford analyzed not only the content of the message but also the manner in which the message was delivered—interpersonal skills.[32] Marie Radford also used the critical incident technique as part of a qualitative evaluation of the Connecting Libraries and Schools Project in New York City. In this project, 2,416 fifth- and seventh-grade students shared their perceptions of interactions with urban public librarians and library staff.[33]

Donald King, Carol Tenopir, and colleagues have been using the critical incident method for a number of years to investigate how faculty members, both in the United States and in the United Kingdom, spend their time reading print and e-journals.[34]

Concept Mapping

Concept mapping is any process that represents ideas in pictures or maps. The process provides a structured methodology for organizing ideas of a group or for forming a common framework that can be used for planning and evaluation. It integrates structured group processes such as brainstorming, unstructured idea sorting, and rating tasks with statistical methods to produce maps.[35]

Generally, concept mapping involves six steps:

1. *Preparation*
   - **Focus.** The desired outcomes for the use of concept mapping must be articulated. What is the question(s) that should be addressed?
   - **Who will participate?** The number and types of stakeholders to be involved in the process should be identified. In some cases, the names of specific individuals will be identified.
   - **Scheduling.** The time frame in which group interaction will occur must be identified. The group may meet physically or virtually.
2. *Generating ideas*
   - **Generating statements.** The process might involve brainstorming or another idea-generating process.
   - **Ideas analysis.** The idea statements are sorted and modified into a large set.
3. *Structuring the statements.* This activity might involve several steps, including
   - **Unstructured idea sorting**—asking each individual to sort the ideas into groups and labeling each group.
   - **Sorting by stakeholder groups**—organizing the ideas by the group that generated the ideas.
   - **Ratings**—assigning values to each idea (ratings might be obtained for feasibility, value or importance, and so forth)
4. *Concept mapping analysis.* This step can involve a number of statistical analysis techniques that are used to generate the concept maps. Among the maps that can be produced using a computer software program are a point map, point cluster map, cluster map, point rating map, and cluster-rating map. A sample point cluster map is shown in Figure 3.1.
5. *Interpreting the maps.* Once prepared, the maps are shared with the stakeholders to obtain their understanding, and to develop ownership of the results.

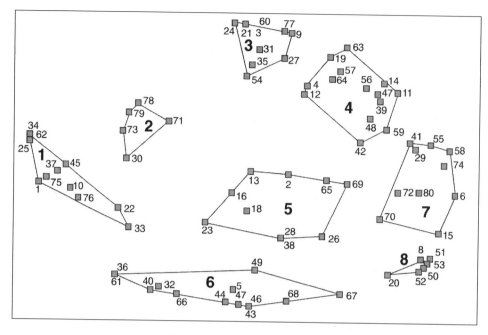

Figure 3.1. Point Cluster Map

6. *Utilization.* For evaluation purposes, the concept maps will identify the types of performance measures that should be used so that the measures are linked to the desired outcomes.

Concept mapping has also been applied in analysis of open-ended responses to survey questions if the number of responses is quite high.

ANALYSIS OF QUALITATIVE DATA

One popular way to approach the analysis of qualitative data is the construction of themes. In some cases, themes are developed as a part of the process of planning the study, whereas in other cases the themes are constructed after the data have been gathered. Coding is an important part of the qualitative data analysis in that it allows the observer to group participant responses and observations into categories based on similar concepts, themes, or ideas.

Some of the challenges associated with qualitative data analysis include:

- *Confidentiality*—the privacy of those who provide data must be protected so there is no possibility of repercussions should their identity become known in some way.
- *Summarizing*—the reality is that a significant amount of data must be condensed in some meaningful manner. It is important to ensure that the results are rooted in the data, that the results not be oversimplified, and that the volume of data not overwhelm the researcher.
- *Expertise*—the analysis of qualitative data requires some training; those collecting the data cannot simply rely on "common sense."
- *Reflexivity*—the researchers should candidly discuss their interactions with the subjects in the field, including what problems were encountered and how those problems were addressed.

PRESENTATION OF FINDINGS

In many cases, the "voice" of those participating in a qualitative study are presented using verbatim quotations. Verbatim quotations can be used for many purposes:

- Presenting quotations as evidence
- Presenting discourse as the matter of inquiry
- Presenting spoken words for explanation
- Using quotations as illustration
- Using quotations to deepen understanding
- Using spoken words to enable voice
- Using quotations to enhance readability of the report

SUMMARY

As noted in this chapter, a number of different qualitative methods might be employed in an evaluation project. A sample of 12 to 20 can generate useful data for thoughtful reflection and analysis. All of these methods consume a fair amount of time and generate a considerable amount of rich data that must be analyzed. This analysis process can, in and of itself, be time consuming. Although the analysis can be done manually, usually a text analysis tool is used to assist in the process. A number of software packages can be downloaded for free or purchased for a modest amount.[36]

The amount of data in raw form, as well as the output from a text analysis software program, can be considerable—hundreds of pages of transcripts from a few hours of interviews.

The usefulness of a qualitative method depends on the researcher thinking carefully about what is being said and done. The goal is to identify the patterns and themes that are present in the data and to develop meaningful categories in an effort to understand what is being evaluated. In some cases, qualitative data analysis is called *content analysis* or *thematic analysis*. The conclusions being drawn must be supported by the data.

The strengths and limitations of qualitative research methods include the following.

Strengths

- Due to the involvement of the researcher, the researcher gains a clearer view of the topic and associated issues
- Qualitative descriptions can play an important role in suggesting possible processes, relationships, causes and effects.
- Qualitative research provides a fair amount of "meat" to chew on and consider when preparing an analysis.

Limitations

- Due to the subjective nature of qualitative data, it is difficult to apply conventional standards of reliability and validity.
- It is almost impossible to replicate events, situations, conditions, and interactions, thus making generalizations problematic.
- The time required for data collection, analysis, and interpretation is significant.
- Viewpoints of both participants and the researcher have to be identified due to issues of bias.

NOTES

1. Jonathan Kvanvig. *The Value of Knowledge and the Pursuit of Understanding*. Cambridge, UK: Cambridge University Press, 2003

2. Hui-Yun Sung, Mark Hepworth, and Gillian Ragsdell. Investigating Essential Elements of Community Engagement in Public Libraries: An Exploratory Qualitative Study. *Journal of Librarianship and Information Science*, 45 (3), 2012, 206–18.

3. David Silverman. *Doing Qualitative Research: A Practical Handbook*. London: Sage, 2000.

4. David Bawden. On the Gaining of Understanding: Synthesis, Themes and Information Analysis. *Library and Information Research*, 36 (112), 2012, 147–62.

5. Carol H. Weiss. *Evaluation: Methods for Studying Programs and Policies*. Upper Saddle River, NJ: Prentice Hall, 1998.

6. Marilyn Domas White and Emily E. Marsh. Content Analysis: A Flexible Methodology. *Library Trends*, 55 (1), Summer 2006, 22–45.

7. Danuta A. Nitecki. Conceptual Models of Libraries Held by Faculty, Administrators and Librarians: An Exploration of Communications in the *Chronicle of Higher Education*. *Journal of Documentation*, 49 (3), 1993, 255–77.

8. R. Green. The Profession's Models of Information: A Cognitive Linguistic Analysis. *Journal of Documentation*, 47, 1991, 130–48.

9. Karen Davies. Content Analysis of Research Articles in Information Systems (LIS) Journals. *Library and Information Research*, 36 (1), 2012, 16–28.

10. Lili Luo and Margaret McKinney. JAL in the Past Decade: A Comprehensive Analysis of Academic Library Research. *The Journal of Academic Librarianship*, 41, 2015, 123–29.

11. Carol Kuhlthau. *Seeking Meaning: A Process Approach to Library and Information Services*. 2nd ed. Norwood, NJ: Ablex, 2004.

12. D. E. Campbell and T. M. Shlecter. Library Design Influences on User Behavior and Satisfaction. *Library Quarterly*, 49 (1), January 1979, 26–41.

13. For example, the Chula Vista (CA) Public Library, the Newport Beach (CA) Public Library, and the Cerritos (CA) Library have used mystery shoppers.

14. Herbert J. Rubin and Irene S. Rubin. *Qualitative Interviewing: The Art of Hearing Data*. Thousand Oaks, CA: Sage, 1995.

15. Rubin and Rubin, *Qualitative Interviewing*.

16. Lokman Meho. E-Mail Interviewing in Qualitative Research: A Methodological Discussion. *Journal of the American Society for Information Science and Technology*, 57 (10), 2006, 1284–95.

17. Lisl Zach. Using a Multiple-Case Studies Design to Investigate the Information-Seeking Behavior of Arts Administrators. *Library Trends*, 55 (1), Summer 2006, 4–21.

18. A. Strauss. *Qualitative Analysis for Social Scientists*. Cambridge, England: Cambridge University Press, 1987; B. Glaser. *Basics of Grounded Theory Analysis*. Mill Valley, CA: Sociology Press, 1992; K. Charmaz. *Constructing Grounded Theory: A Practical Guide Through Qualitative Analysis*. Thousand Oaks, CA: Sage, 2006.

19. Timothy D. Wilson. The Proper Protocol: Validity and Completeness of Verbal Reports. *Psychological Science*, 5, 1994, 249–52.

20. Among the software packages are ATLAS.ti, Code-A-Text, The Ethnograph, Kwalitan, MAXQDA, Qualrus, TAMS Analyzer, and Transana. Some of the software can be downloaded for free.

21. Jennifer L. Branch. Investigating the Information-Seeking Processes of Adolescents: The Value of Using Think Alouds and Think Afters. *Library & Information Science Research*, 22 (4), 2000, 371–92.

22. Nancy Foster and Susan Gibbons. *Studying the Students: The Undergraduate Research Project at the University of Rochester*. Chicago: Association of College and Research Libraries, 2007.

23. Andrew Asher and Susan Miller. *So You Want to Do Anthropology in Your Library?: A Practical Guide to Ethnographic Research in Academic Libraries*. Chicago, IL: ERIAL Project, 2011.

24. Diane Mizrachi. Undergraduates' Academic Information and Library Behaviors: Preliminary Results. *Reference Services Review*, 38 (4), 2010, 571–80.

25. Michael Khoo, Lily Rozaklis, and Catherine Hall. A Survey of the Use of Ethnographic Methods in the Study of Libraries and Library Users. *Library & Information Science Research*, 34, 2012, 82–91.

26. Christine Yates, Helen Partridge, and Christine Bruce. Exploring Information Experiences Through Phenomenography. *Library and Information Research*, 36 (112), 2012, 96–119.

27. Kimberly Neuendorf. *The Content Analysis Guidebook*. Thousand Oaks, CA: Sage, 2001.

28. S. Hughes-Hassell and K. Bishop. Using Focus Group Interviews to Improve Library Services for Youth. *Teacher Librarian*, 32 (1), 2004, 8–12.

29. J. Ho and G. H. Crowley. User Perceptions of the "Reliability" of Library Services at Texas A&M University: A Focus Group Study. *The Journal of Academic Librarianship*, 29 (2), 2003, 82–87.

30. L. Ludwig et al. Library as Place: Results of a Delphi Study. *Journal of the Medical Library Association*, 93 (3), July 2005, 315–26; B. Feret et al. The Future of the Academic Library and the Academic Librarian: A Delphi Study. *IATUL Proceedings*, 15, 2005, 1–23; S. Baruchson-Arbib et al. A View to the Future of the Library and Information Science Profession: A Delphi Study. *Journal of the American Society for Information Science and Technology*, 53 (5), March 2002, 397–408; John B. Harer and Bryan R. Cole. The Importance of the Stakeholder in Performance Measurement: Critical Processes and Performance Measures for Assessing and Improving Academic Library Services and Programs. *College & Research Libraries*, 66, March 2005, 149–70; Yunfei Du. Librarians' Responses to "Reading At Risk": A Delphi Study. *Library & Information Science Research*, 31 (1), January 2009, 46–53; Chaminda Jayasundara. Business Domains for Boosting Customer Satisfaction in Academic Libraries. *The Journal of Academic Librarianship*, 41 (3), May 2015, 350–57.

31. John C. Flanagan. The Critical Incident Technique. *Psychological Bulletin*, 51 (4), July 1954, 327–58.

32. Marie L. Radford. Communication Theory Applied to the Reference Encounter: An Analysis of Critical Incidents. *Library Quarterly*, 66 (2), 1996, 123–37.

33. Marie L. Radford. The Critical Incident Technique and the Qualitative Evaluation of the Connecting Libraries and Schools Project. *Library Trends*, 55 (1), Summer 2006, 46–64.

34. See, for example, Donald W. King, Carol Tenopir, Songphan Choemprayong, and Lei Wu. Scholarly Journal Information Seeking and Reading Patterns of Faculty at Five U.S. Universities. *Learned Publishing*, 22 (2), April 2009, 126–44; Carol Tenopir, Donald W. King, Sheri Edwards, and Lei Wu. Electronic Journals and Changes in Scholarly Article Seeking and Reading Patterns. *Aslib Proceedings: New Information Perspectives*, 61 (1), February 2009, 5–32.

35. Mary Kane and William M. K. Trochim. *Concept Mapping for Planning and Evaluation*. Thousand Oaks, CA: Sage, 2007.

36. Text analysis software uses several different programming languages and runs on different operating systems. Among the many software programs available are AnnoTape; Aquad Five; ATLAS. ti; Automap—Extract, Analyze and Represent Individual Mental Models; C-I-SAID—Code-A-Text Integrated System for the Analysis of Interviews and Dialogues; ESA—Event Structure Analysis; Ethno; The Ethnograph; EZ-TEXT; HyperResearch; KEDS—Kansas Event Data System; Kwalitan; MAX-QDA; QSR NUD*IST—Non-numerical Unstructured Data Indexing Searching and Theorizing; QSR NVivo; Prospero; QDA-Miner; QMA—Qualitative Media Analysis; Qualrus; SuperHyperqual; TABARI—Text Analysis By Augmented Replacement Instructions; and Weft QDA.

Quantitative Tools

You can use all the quantitative data you can get,
but you still have to distrust it
and use your own intelligence and judgment.

—Alvin Toffler

Any evaluation study usually gathers numerical data using one and sometimes several data collection methods; the resulting data are then subjected to analysis. Quantitative research is usually used to estimate or predict a future outcome or to diagnose the existing or current state of a service.

Numerical data can be collected using a variety of methods. Frequently used quantitative methods include:

- Counting
- Measuring
- Surveys
- Conjoint analysis
- Transaction log analysis
- Experiments

COUNTING

Libraries have been counting things for a long time, perhaps as long as they have been in existence. Whether the counts are reflected as input measures or as output measures, the results are a variety of numbers that typically may be found in library directories, the library's annual report, and so forth.

A variety of means may be used to capture the counts: an automated system may record an activity or transaction, a physical counter may be located in a gate, or staff members may make tick marks on a form. Clearly some methods will deliver higher accuracy and consistency than others.

Aside from reporting the counts to various agencies, the library may wish to use the counts to improve control of the various processes found in the library. This latter use of the count information, sometimes called *statistical process control*, is discussed in Chapter 6.

MEASURING

Measurement assists the library in understanding each activity in a process. The goal is to collect and display data that will assist in our understanding of a process. It is critical to verify that each performance measure or metric is actually measuring what it purports to. If the same value for the measure occurs when an identical activity is performed, the measure is said to be "reliable."

Many measurements capture time parameters and requirements. In addition to measuring the time to complete a particular activity, it is also important to measure the waiting time between activities.

SURVEYS

Whenever a survey is used in a library setting, it almost certainly will be a descriptive one. A descriptive survey is used to explain the characteristics of a population of interest, estimate the proportions in a population, make specific predictions, and test for possible relationships in the data.

Surveys are like bikinis. What they reveal is interesting, but what they conceal is essential.
—Kenneth Boulding[1]

The respondents' answers to the questions in the survey may reflect their perceptions, expectations, intentions, and imperfect memories rather than their actual experiences. Thus, great care must be exercised both in developing and administering the survey and also in analyzing the resulting data.

Other types of surveys exist, including the following:[2]

- **Trend study:** Uses almost all the same questions repeatedly over time so as to identify trends and change in patterns.
- **Cohort study:** Collects data from the same population group more than once. The same people may not be surveyed, but all of the people in the group are selected from the same population.
- **Panel study:** Collects data from the same people over time. The trend study and panel study are sometimes referred to as a *longitudinal study*.
- **Parallel samples study:** Covers a specific topic, but data are collected from two or more groups (for example, students and faculty in an academic library setting).
- **Contextual study:** Focuses on a single individual, gathering data from multiple perspectives to better understand a task or problem.
- **Cross-sectional study:** Examines phenomena across a representative sample of the population; must have a large sample size (e.g., Gallup poll).

For a descriptive survey, the first step is to create an instrument or questionnaire. Designing unambiguous and clear questions is difficult. At this point, it is important to try to adhere to the old adage of "not reinventing the wheel." A number of state libraries maintain copies of survey instruments that have been used in one or more libraries; other resources are also available.[3] Not surprisingly, questionnaires have both strengths and weaknesses, as noted in Table 4.1.

A survey is only as good as the wording.
—Carol Tenopir[4]

Table 4.1. Advantages and Disadvantages of Questionnaires

Advantages	Disadvantages
Frank answers are encouraged due to the anonymity of the respondent.	They eliminate personal contact between the respondent and the observer.
They eliminate possible interviewer bias.	Answers cannot be qualified easily.
Quantitative data are easy to collect and analyze.	There is a general resistance to mail questionnaires.
They can be relatively inexpensive to administer.	Nonresponse rates for surveys can be high.

Types of Questions

The kind of information needed from a survey will usually dictate the types of questions to be asked. Among the types of questions are the following:

- **Factual questions:** Used to determine the respondent's age, gender, and so forth. The resulting data are objective in nature.
- **Opinion and attitude questions:** Used to ascertain inclinations, prejudices, ideas, and so forth. The resulting data are subjective in nature.
- **Self-perception questions:** Restricted to the respondents' opinions of themselves.
- **Information questions:** Designed to measure the respondent's knowledge of a topic.
- **Standards of action questions:** Used to determine how the respondent would act in a specific situation.
- **Past or present behavior questions:** Result in subjective information about the respondent's behavior. More accurate data are obtained when asking about present behavior than about past behavior.
- **Projective questions:** Allow respondents to answer indirectly by projecting their attitudes and beliefs onto others (peers, colleagues, and so forth).

Form of Questions

A question may take one of two basic forms: fixed response or structured questions, and open-ended or unstructured questions. This section illustrates types of structured questions.

Checklists

Each item may require a response. For example:

	Yes	**No**
Borrow a book?	1	2
Borrow an audio CD?	1	2
Borrow a video?	1	2

Items may require the selection of a "best" answer. For example:

> What is the primary reason you visit a library? (*Circle one number only.*)
>
> | Borrow materials | 1 |
> |---|---|
> | Use materials in the library | 2 |
> | Make photocopies | 3 |
> | Meet with friends to study | 4 |
> | Use the computers | 5 |

Items may have categories. For example:

> What is the highest grade of school completed? (*Circle one number only.*)
>
> | Grade school | 08 | | | |
> |---|---|---|---|---|
> | High school | 09 | 10 | 11 | 12 |
> | College | 13 | 14 | 15 | 16 |
> | Beyond college | 17 | | | |

There may be grouped responses. For example:

> What is your age group? (*Circle one group only.*)
>
> | 1–12 | 13–18 | 19–39 | 40–59 | 60+ |
> |---|---|---|---|---|

Fill in the Blank

In some cases, more accurate information will be reported if questions ask the respondent to fill in the blank as a way of responding. For example:

> How many miles do you live or work from this library? _____ miles

Scaled Responses

There may be a specific category scale. For example:

How important is each of the following? (*Circle one number on each line.*)				
Item	**Very Important**	**Of Some Importance**	**Of Little Importance**	**Not Important**
More hours	1	2	3	4
More parking	1	2	3	4
Helpful staff	1	2	3	4

There may be a graphic rating scale on which the respondent can mark along a continuum. For example:

Indicate your degree of agreement by marking along the continuum.

The library has a sufficient number of Internet workstations.

Strongly Disagree   Strongly Agree

The library needs to sell coffee and soft drinks.

Strongly Disagree   Strongly Agree

A rank-order scale may be used. For example:

Indicate the relative importance of library services on a scale of 1 to 5, with "1" being the most important and "5" being the least important.

Borrowing books   _____

Borrowing audios and videos   _____

Study facilities   _____

Internet computers   _____

Magazines and newspapers   _____

A differential scale may be used. Sometimes called a Thurston scale, this instrument presents a series of statements with equal distances between them. This type of scale is very difficult to use to design questions that represent values equidistant from one another while avoiding bias on the part of those developing the questions. Use of such a scale is not recommended.

A Likert scale uses questions that represent favorable or unfavorable positions. A Likert scale is also called a summated scale. For example:

Item	Strongly Disagree	Disagree	Agree	Strongly Agree
An acquisitions librarian should consider requests from customers as the top priority for ordering.	SD	D	A	SA

Another way to present a Likert scale is to use numbers rather than letters for the response. For example:

Item	Strongly Disagree	Disagree	Agree	Strongly Agree
An acquisitions librarian should consider requests from customers as the top priority for ordering.	1	2	3	4

A semantic differential scale provides pairs of synonyms and antonyms along with a five- or seven-option rating scale. For example:

For each pair below, circle the number that comes closest to describing service at the reference desk. (*Circle one number on each line.*)

	Extremely	Moderately	Neither	Moderately	Extremely	
Friendly	1	2	3	4	5	Reserved
Active	1	2	3	4	5	Passive
Effective	1	2	3	4	5	Ineffective
Rapid	1	2	3	4	5	Slow

A cumulative scale consists of related statements with which the respondent can agree or disagree. Because the statements are related to one another, the respondent "should" respond to subsequent items in a similar manner.

Self-ratings do have limitations, most resulting primarily from potential bias and the subjectivity of questions included in the survey instrument.

Open-Ended Questions

These unstructured questions allow respondents to make whatever comments they wish and thus are much more difficult to analyze and categorize. Response rates to open-ended questions are typically lower because they require the respondent to take some time to formulate and write answers. Nevertheless, open-ended responses can be categorized, and there are software tools to assist in the process if the amount of text is large. The following are a few examples of such unstructured questions:

What I like best about this library is . . .

When I visit the library I . . .

The library service I use the most is . . .

Question Construction

The development of questions in a survey should be done carefully. This is not the time to become creative, as people have been exposed to many surveys. Usually survey questions proceed from the general to the specific. Demographic information is typically asked last because some respondents are not inclined to reveal personal information. If possible, use questions that have been used in other library surveys. Following are some recommendations about writing questions.

- Use simple language—one- or two-syllable words are better than three- and four-syllable words.
- Questions should be fewer than 20 words in length.
- Be specific and clear about what is being asked.
- Only ask the question if you need to know the answer.
- Don't use library jargon, and if necessary, define a term in the question itself. Questions using such terms as "access tools," "electronic journals," "users," "service problems," and "information skills" are meaningless to respondents.
- Avoid "yes-no" questions.
- Avoid double negatives.
- Don't combine two or more categories; for example, "Did you attend a program and borrow materials while visiting the library?"
- Use wording normally found in surveys. Avoid slang.
- Avoid "gift" questions that most people would agree to.
- If necessary, include information to jog people's memories.
- Avoid shorthand or incomplete sentences.
- Ask respondents about their experiences, not the experiences of others.
- Be sensitive to cultural differences.
- Ask participants to discuss desired outcomes.
- Double-check to ensure that each question is necessary and that the resulting data will be useful in the analysis.

One study asked two groups the same question but used two different words in a single question—"should" and "might." This slight change in the wording of the question evoked very different responses from those taking the survey.[5]

Surveys that are short and focused are more likely to be answered and yield useful information. Write an introduction to the survey that will invite cooperation from the participants. Once the questionnaire has been developed, it should be pretested to discover any ambiguity in the wording of the questions or other problems that may arise. Pretesting should be done with a small sample of the intended participants, not library staff members or others who are handy. Once revised (and in some cases, pretested again), the questionnaire is ready to go. Well, you hope it is ready to go. Pretesting after revision is advisable.

Distributing the Survey

When a survey is distributed can have an effect on the results. For example, in the academic environment, surveys at the start of the semester will likely yield different results than those distributed during the middle or at the end of the semester.

There are five ways to administer the survey questionnaire: through the mail (sometimes called a self-administered survey), using e-mail, on the telephone, in face-to-face interviews, and on the Web.

Mail Survey

The mail survey has been long used by researchers in a variety of fields. It is sent to the desired group of respondents, only a portion of whom will complete the survey and return it. The number of returned questionnaires compared to the total number of surveys distributed is the *response rate*. In general, the higher the response rate, the more generalizable the results—assuming that a representative sample responds to the survey. If the library wants to have a fairly large sample of respondents, it may be necessary to distribute a much larger number of questionnaires. In some cases, it may be necessary to send out a second round of surveys to improve the number of responses.

Research has shown that higher response rates will result if a stamped, self-addressed envelope is sent to the respondent with the questionnaire. Normally a library will ask that the completed questionnaire be returned within 10 to 14 days.

A variation of mailing the survey is to approach someone entering the library and ask if he or she would be willing to complete the survey. Keith Curry Lance and his colleagues used this approach in the Counting on Results project. Interestingly, the respondents had the choice of completing a paper-based survey or using a Palm Pilot to enter their responses to the survey questions.[6]

E-Mail Survey

A questionnaire can be distributed by sending e-mail to potential respondents. The survey instrument can be contained within the body of the e-mail or be provided as an attachment. The respondents can use the e-mail reply feature or return the completed survey using e-mail or regular mail.

The difficulties in using an e-mail survey include the fact that it can only be distributed to those whose e-mail address is known. This may mean that it will be difficult to obtain a random sample of the population. Further, the response rate may be low because the e-mail may be viewed as spam.[7]

Telephone Survey

Telephone surveys are popular and can be an effective method for garnering the required data for a study. However, telephone surveys must be carefully constructed and cannot be too long, as the time required to complete the survey may be too much for respondents, sometimes called "responder burden." The final questions in a survey may not be answered if respondents reach their patience threshold and simply hang up before the survey is completed.

One important advantage of this method is that the responses are normally entered into a computer database, which makes the data analysis relatively simple. However, all across the United States, people are dropping the use of their regular "land-line" telephones in favor of using their cell phones exclusively. This change in telephone technology is making it increasingly difficult to generate a truly representative sample for a survey.

The Face-to-Face Interview

Administering the survey questions in a face-to-face meeting can be useful because it allows the person conducting the interview to follow up and ask clarifying questions. However, it is important to avoid rephrasing the questions, as this will lead to a different response to a seemingly different question and, in turn, lead to difficulties in comparing the responses among all the respondents. Showing emotions, such as surprise or shock, at any of the responses is to be avoided. Developing an answer sheet with codes for anticipated responses will improve the accuracy of the data collection effort. With the respondent's permission, recording open-ended questions will ensure accuracy when notes taken during the interview are later transcribed.

Web-Based Survey

The survey can be administered using the Internet. The respondent is asked to click on a link to complete the survey. The survey can be administered using the library's Web site, or the library can use one of several free Internet sites that provide free online surveys—with some restrictions on the length of the survey.[8]

Because survey fatigue is now a common problem, offering respondents a choice of formats should increase the response rate. All of the responses are stored in a database, which can then be accessed for the data analysis.

An analysis of surveys distributed in three ways showed that the Web-based survey had slightly lower response rates than the paper survey distributed by mail. The importance of carefully designed follow-up procedures to ensure an adequate response rate cannot be overemphasized.[9] A comparison of a Web-based and a paper survey found small differences in the responses of library patrons.[10]

The strengths and limitations of each method of gathering the survey data are shown in Table 4.2.

Types of Sampling

There are two broad types of sampling methods: nonprobability and probability.

Probability Sampling

Probability sampling enhances the prospect that the sample used in a study will be reflective of the entire population and that the resulting data can be used with some assurance that the sample is representative of the total population. Each element in the sample has the same possibility of being included as the other elements in the total population.

Table 4.2. Comparison of Methods of Distributing a Survey

	Mail*	Telephone	In Person	Web-Based
Turnaround time	Slow	Fast	Moderate	Moderate
Cooperation rate	Low	Moderate	Highest	Moderate
Geographic coverage	Excellent	Excellent	Difficult	Excellent
Interviewer bias	None	Moderate	Substantial	None
Interviewer supervision	None required	Excellent	Poor	Excellent
Quality of response	Poor	Better	Best	Better
Questionnaire structure	Simple	Complex	Complex	Complex
Who is in control?	Respondent	Interviewer	Interviewer	Interviewer
Obtrusiveness	Low	High	High	Low
Ability to cope with interruptions	Easy	Difficult	Difficult	Easy
Length of interview	Short	Medium	Long	Long
Cost	Low	Moderate	High	Low

*Snail mail or e-mail

- **Simple random sample.** Using this method means that every individual or item in the population list has an equal chance of being selected for the sample. In theory, after being selected the item should go back into the population list so that the probability of being selected remains constant. However, due to practical considerations, once selected an item is not returned.

     Selecting a sample usually involves use of a random number table, which is used to make selections from the population list—rather than choosing every nth item. A random number chart can be found on the Internet or in a research methods book.
- **Systematic sample.** This method selects every nth element in the population list—starting from a random point in the list—until the desired sample size has been achieved. For practical purposes, an alphabetical list can be considered a random list.
- **Stratified random sample.** This approach requires that the total population be divided into groups, and a random sample is then drawn from each group. One approach when using a stratified random sample is to ensure that the size of the sample for each group is proportional to the total size of the group in relation to the total population. Thus, in an academic environment, undergraduates might account for 70 percent of the population, graduate students make up another 20 percent, and faculty and staff the remaining 10 percent. The sample that is selected should have the same relative percentages for each group. This is the approach that many researchers normally use.

The other alternative, called a disproportionate stratified sample, allows for over-representation of a group to ensure a sample size that is adequate for making comparisons across all groups.

A variation of a stratified random sample is use of a cluster sample when the total population is very large and it would be difficult to create a population list. In this case, the population is divided into clusters (from which a list can be created), from which a random sample is drawn.

Nonprobability Sampling

Nonprobability sampling methods are used when it is not possible to determine the probability of any one unit being included in the sample. However, the primary problem is that statistical inferences cannot be made because the selection probabilities are unknown—the sample is not random. Nevertheless, nonprobability sampling may be appropriate because an evaluation study most likely will not be using sophisticated statistical analysis that requires a probability sample.

- **Accidental sampling.** With this method (sometimes called a convenience, opportunistic, or available sample), no attempt is made to generate a random sample. Rather, whatever is available is used. Thus, a library might choose participants on a first-come, first-asked basis until the desired sample size is reached.

- **Quota sampling.** This method is similar to accidental sampling, but it is used to ensure that different groups within a population are included in the sample, hopefully in the same proportion that they occur in the overall population. A variation of the quota sample is the snowball sample, which asks members of a group for assistance in locating similar members of that group.

- **Purposive sampling.** An evaluation study might be exploring the use of a new service. This method samples other libraries that are already using the service, which might be appropriate to learn about the strengths and weaknesses of the proposed service. Clearly, this method is susceptible to bias.

- **Self-selected sampling.** With this method, an evaluation team might publish a notice asking for volunteers to participate in a study. The data resulting from such an approach will only be reflective of those who participate, for whatever reasons.

- **Incomplete sampling.** An incomplete sample might be the result of a very low response rate or of a sample that was selected with incomplete or inaccurate information about the characteristics of the population. Obviously, any data from such a sample must be used with great care or not be used at all.

- **Extreme case sampling.** In this method, a small sample focuses on cases or situations that are rich in information because they are unusual in some way.

- **Intensity sampling.** This method consists of a small to moderate-sized sample of information-rich cases that are unusual in some way—excellent service provider, low-cost service provider, and so forth.

- **Homogenous sampling.** A small, homogenous sample may be selected and then studied in some depth. Focus group interviews are an example of homogenous sampling.

Determining Sample Size

In a library setting, sampling can be done for just about every activity or physical object. For example, libraries have done evaluation studies involving a sample of different locations, customers, items in the collection, activities or processes, and time.

Determining the size of a sample is a balancing act: while the larger the sample the better, a sample that is too large wastes money and other resources. A sample that is too small (say less than 100) will not be representative of the population. Criteria to determine an appropriate sample size include the following:

The degree of accuracy, sometimes called *precision*, between the sample and the population. The need for more accuracy means a larger sample is needed.

The method of sampling to be used.

The variability of the population. The greater the variability, the higher the sample size.

The type of data analysis that is planned. Some statistical analysis tools require larger sample sizes.

Although it is possible to use a formula to determine the necessary sample size, in most cases those involved with evaluations use a table to determine a random sample size, with precision of .05, as shown in Table 4.3. Note that the sample size requirements are fairly large when the population is small, while the sample size grows quite slowly in proportion as the population increases rapidly.

Table 4.3. Table for Determining Sample Size*

Population Size	Sample Size	Population	Sample Size
100	80	2,000	322
200	132	3,000	341
300	169	4,000	351
400	196	5,000	357
500	217	10,000	370
750	254	20,000	377
1,000	278	50,000	381

*Reflects 95 percent confidence level and a±5 standard deviation.

Survey Nonresponse

Jacquelyn Burkell examined the response rates of surveys published in three major library and information science journals over a six-year period and found that the average response rate was 63 percent. Almost three-fourths of the surveys had a response rate of less than 75 percent—the level generally held to be required for generalizability. Nonresponse always results in a biased sample. The question is whether the bias affects survey results or whether data from nonrespondents would have changed the survey conclusions.[11] Peter Hernon has observed that it is more common for studies to report response rates below 50 percent, perhaps in the 20 to 40 percent range.[12] One study that distributed a request to some 60,000 residents in a community in a utility bill, asking for people to participate in a library online survey, resulted in a survey response rate of 1.1 percent—this ought to give anyone pause for concern and question any of the conclusions and recommendations.[13]

Strategies to improve response rates include pre-notification; personalized cover letters; the use of reminders; incentives with the invitation to participate (including small monetary incentives of $2 to $5 or returned surveys qualifying for the drawing of a prize); and the use of stamped, self-addressed envelopes for the return of mail surveys.

If nonresponse rates remain low despite efforts to boost the number of completed surveys, then care must be exercised to limit survey conclusions appropriately.

Caveats

Problems can arise when using surveys. Assuming a reasonable response rate, the library is not sure that those who did respond to the survey have different characteristics than those who chose not to participate. Obviously they are different in at least one dimension: willingness to complete a survey.

A second problem is that most libraries will ask those who are physically present in the library to participate in a study. This approach to distributing a survey is based on convenience and excludes the views of those who visit the library infrequently or not at all.

Despite the fact that all statistical analyses have a margin of error or a level of confidence, plus or minus "x" percent, managers and decision makers tend to forget the limitations of the data and rely on them as a certainty. The size of the error is affected by four factors:

- Sample size—the larger the sample, the smaller the error
- Sample size relative to population size
- Inherent variability of observations
- Choice of statistical sampling method

Other nonsampling errors may also occur. Sources of these errors include improper questionnaire design, choice of an inadequate sampling method, nonresponses, mistakes in responding to questions, mistakes in clerical processing, and analyst error.

After the sample size and type of sample have been determined, selecting the sample is crucial. Rather than selecting every nth record in a file, for example, it is better to use a random number table (available from various Web sites) to select the sample. This will improve the reliability of the results.

It is important to recognize that bias can be introduced in several different ways when conducting a survey:

1. *Selection bias*—the manner in which potential respondents are identified and approached
2. *Nonresponse bias*—the number of people who decide to complete a survey
3. *Question bias*—the choice of wording (leading questions) can be problematic
4. *Administration bias*—the manner in which the survey is administered may introduce bias
5. *Response bias*—the respondent is not truthful (provides a response that the individual thinks is correct or desirable)
6. *Item bias*—the construction of the survey itself may introduce gender bias, age bias, cultural bias, and other biases

Some of the biggest problems with library research and evaluation projects are unsatisfactory sampling techniques, primitive survey instruments, and studies conducted on too small a scale to permit generalizations.

CONJOINT ANALYSIS

Conjoint analysis, also called multi-attribute compositional models, is a statistical technique that was developed by Paul Green at the Wharton School of the University of Pennsylvania.[14] Today it is used in many of the social sciences and applied sciences, including marketing, product management, and operations research. The objective of conjoint analysis is to determine what combination of attributes is most preferred by respondents. It is used frequently in testing customer acceptance of new product designs and assessing the appeal of advertisements.

Respondents are shown a set of products, prototypes, mock-ups, or pictures. Examples are similar enough that consumers will see them as close substitutes, but they are dissimilar enough that respondents can clearly determine a preference. Each example is composed of a unique combination of product or service features. The data may consist of individual ratings, rank-orders, or preferences among alternative combinations. The two most frequently used variations of this tool are adaptive conjoint analysis and choice-based conjoint analysis.

Any number of algorithms may be used to estimate utility functions. These utility functions indicate the perceived value of the feature and how sensitive consumer perceptions and preferences are to changes in product features.

The advantages of conjoint analysis include that it

- Measures preferences at the individual level and
- Estimates psychological tradeoffs that consumers make when evaluating several attributes together.

The disadvantages include that

- Only a limited set of features can be used, because the number of combinations increases very quickly as more features are added;
- The information-gathering stage is complex; and
- Respondents are unable to articulate attitudes toward new categories.

A research project in Germany, described by Reinhold Decker and Antonia Hermelbracht, used conjoint analysis in a study that reached almost 5,000 respondents to explore new academic library services. Their Web-based survey used a combination of text and pictures to describe each alternative. A total of 118 services or service concepts were analyzed.[15] Another project used conjoint analysis to model public library use and choice behavior.[16]

TRANSACTION LOG ANALYSIS

Most computer systems will keep a log of all transactions: inputs from the user and system outputs. These transaction logs can then be analyzed, although it can be difficult to decide how to separate each of the data elements and to choose the most useful statistics, as most logs squeeze all the data together as a single string of characters. Transaction log analysis, also called log analysis, log file analysis, log tracking, Web logging, or Web log analysis, will most likely require a computer programmer to create a file in a prescribed format that can then be imported into a statistical data analysis software package such as *Microsoft Access* or *SPSS*, two of the more frequently used statistical analysis tools. Lisa Goddard provides an excellent review of the challenges facing those who wish to use transaction log analysis and what information is available from shareware or commercial software analysis tools.[17]

Although it is possible to select a sample of transactions for analysis, typically all transactions that occurred during a particular period of time—a day, a week, a month, a year—are used for the analysis because the computer can make quick work of calculating the data if dealing with thousands of transactions or hundreds of thousands of transactions. Logs can typically be generated by information retrieval systems, library online catalogs, Web sites, intranets, and Web-based database systems.

System designers have used transaction log analysis to examine the actual behavior of users of an online catalog to compare their behavior to that anticipated.[18] In some cases, the analysis has been restricted to periodical title searching in an online catalog.[19] In other cases, the technique has been used to identify the actual content used in five different online health information systems.[20] Karen Markey used this method to examine spelling errors in online catalogs.[21] This method has also been used to examine a wide variety of Web sites.

However, it is important to note that transaction log analysis does have limitations:

- The log represents a snapshot in time.
- Various user characteristics and experience in searching cannot be identified.
- Users' linguistic skills are not revealed.
- Users' understanding of a domain of knowledge cannot be determined.

EXPERIMENTS

Experimental research is most likely the most rigorous of all research methods. If correctly designed, an experiment allows the testing of cause-and-effect relationships. Experimental research is most rigorous when one variable is being tested to determine the presence or absence of an effect or consequence. In the social sciences, a variety of factors are often tested to determine their contribution to a certain event happening. If X, the independent variable, is a necessary condition for Y, the independent variable, to occur, then Y will never occur unless X is present.

However, it is usually impossible to demonstrate that one variable causes another. Thus, cause-and-effect relationships are typically inferred based on an analysis of the available data. As with any methodology, care must be taken when planning and conducting an experiment not to compromise the results. Among the problems to avoid are having too small a sample, selecting a nonrepresentative sample, using poorly designed data collection instruments, not including all of the likely variables, and not using the most appropriate statistical tools.

Experiments have been designed by Pauline Atherton to test the impact of enhancing the bibliographic record with additional table-of-contents and back-of-the-book information;[22] by Karen Drabenstott, who tested search systems with additional Dewey-related information included as part of one test system;[23] by Ray Larson, who used experiments in testing an online catalog system called Cheshire;[24] and by researchers in England, who tested various features of an online catalog called Okapi.[25]

In almost all cases an experimental design is not used to evaluate a library service, because too many variables are outside the control of the researcher.

SUMMARY

This chapter has reviewed the strengths and limitations of a wide variety of quantitative tools that a library is likely to find useful as it plans for and conducts an evaluation of library services. The two broad methodologies available for an evaluation study—qualitative and quantitative—have strengths and limitations, which are summarized in Table 4.4.

Table 4.4. Comparison of Qualitative and Quantitative Methods

	Qualitative	Quantitative
Key Concept	Meaning	Statistical relationships
Design	Flexibility	Structured, predetermined
Data	People's own words, field notes, behavior	Counts, measures, numbers
Data Collection	Less structured	More structured
Sampling	Small, nonrepresentative	Large, random, stratified, representative of the population
Methods	Observations, interviews, review of documents	Survey instruments, data sets
Relationships with Subjects	Personal, emphasis on trust	Short-term, distant, impersonal
Instruments	Researcher, tape recorder, video recorder, camera	Questionnaires, computer
Replication	Difficult	Easier to repeat and thus higher reliability
Data Analysis	Ongoing, evolving, inductive	Deductive, statistical, and objective
Advantages	Flexibility, goal is to gain understanding	Ease of use, high acceptance
Disadvantages	Time, hard to study groups, difficult to distill the data	Controlling other variables, oversimplification

There are several strengths and limitations associated with quantitative research methods.

Strengths
- Control—The sampling method and design of a study influence control, which is essential to provide unambiguous answers to a set of questions.
- Precision—the reliability of the data collection method has a clear impact on the accuracy of the data being collected.
- The ability to explore causality using experiments and statistical techniques.
- Replication—The study design and data collection method must be reliable so that the research may be replicated.

Limitations

- It is almost impossible to control for all variables.
- Some may assume that the facts are "nothing but the facts" and are the same for all people all of the time.
- Quantification and statistical analysis may become the end in itself.
- The researcher is subjectively involved in the choice of research topic and research methods and thus the results may not be truly objective.

NOTES

1. Quoted in Bruce Heterick and Roger C. Schonfeld. The Future Ain't What It Used to Be. *Serials,* 17 (3), November 2004, 226.

2. Gary Golden. *Survey Research Methods.* Chicago: Association of College & Research Libraries, 1982.

3. Sample surveys are available at http://www.webjunction.org/documents/webjunction/Sample _Information_Gathering_Tools.html.

4. Carol Tenopir. What User Studies Tell Us. *Library Journal,* 128 (14), September 1, 2003, 32.

5. Abraham Bookstein. Questionnaire Research in a Library Setting. *The Journal of Academic Librarianship,* 11 (1), March 1985, 24–28.

6. Keith Curry Lance, Marcia J. Rodney, Nicolle O. Steffen, Suzanne Kaller, Rochelle Logan, Kristie M. Koontz, and Dean K. Jue. *Counting on Results: New Tools for Outcome-Based Evaluation of Public Libraries.* Aurora, CO: Bibliographic Center for Research, 2002.

7. Peter Hernon and John R. Whitman. *Delivering Satisfaction and Service Quality: A Customer-Based Approach for Libraries.* Chicago: American Library Association, 2001, 125.

8. Among the many Web-based sites that offer free surveys are Zoomerang.com, FreeOnline Surveys.com, SurveyConsole.com, SurveyMonkey.com, and QuestionPro.com. The data are displayed using some simple charts, and the data analysis tools are fairly limited. The number of respondents to a survey is typically limited (e.g., 100), and it is not possible to download the survey data into a spreadsheet or database for further analysis. A subscription, which generally costs about $20 per month, provides access to a greater range of capabilities.

9. Michele M. Hayslett and Barbara M. Wildemuth. Pixels or Pencils? The Relative Effectiveness of Web-Based Versus Paper Surveys. *Library & Information Science Research,* 26, 2004, 73–93.

10. Gay Helen Perkins and Haiwang Yuan. A Comparison of Web-Based and Paper-and-Pencil Library Satisfaction Survey Results. *College & Research Libraries,* 62 (4), July 2001, 369–77.

11. Jacquelyn Burkell. The Dilemma of Survey Nonresponse. *Library & Information Science Research,* 25, 2003, 239–63.

12. Peter Hernon. Components of the Research Process: Where Do We Need to Focus Attention? *The Journal of Academic Librarianship,* 27 (2), March 2001, 81–89.

13. Susan A Henricks and Genevieve M. Henricks-Lepp. Multiple Constituencies Model in the Identification of Library Effectiveness. *Library Management,* 35 (8/9), 2014, 645–65.

14. Paul Green and V. Srinivasan. Conjoint Analysis in Consumer Research: Issues and Outlook. *Journal of Consumer Research,* 5, September 1978, 103–23; Paul Green, J. Carroll, and S. Goldberg. A General Approach to Product Design Optimization via Conjoint Analysis. *Journal of Marketing,* 43, Summer 1981, 17–35.

15. Reinhold Decker and Antonia Hermelbracht. Planning and Evaluation of New Academic Library Services by Means of Web-Based Conjoint Analysis. *The Journal of Academic Librarianship,* 32 (6), November 2006, 558–72. See also Antonia Hermelbracht and Bettina Koeper. ProSeBiCA: Development of New Library Services by Means of Conjoint Analysis. *Library HiTech,* 24 (4), 2006, 595–603.

16. Akio Sone. An Application of Discrete Choice Analysis to the Modeling of Public Library Use and Choice Behavior. *Library & Information Science Research*, 10, 1988, 35–55.

17. Lisa Goddard. Getting to the Source: A Survey of Quantitative Data Sources Available to the Everyday Librarian: Part 1: Web Server Log Analysis. *Evidence Based Library and Information Practice*, 2 (1), 2007, 48–67.

18. Susan Jones, Mike Gatford, Thien Do, and Stephen Walker. Transaction Logging. *Journal of Documentation*, 53 (1), January 1997, 35–50.

19. Patricia M. Wallace. Periodical Title Searching in Online Catalogs. *Serials Review*, 23 (3), September 1997, 27–35.

20. David Nicholas, Paul Huntington, and Janet Homewood. Assessing Used Content Across Five Digital Health Information Services Using Transaction Log Files. *Journal of Information Science*, 29 (6), 2003, 499–515.

21. Karen M. Drabenstott and Marjorie S. Weller. Handling Spelling Errors in Online Catalog Searches. *Library Resources & Technical Services*, 40 (2), April 1996, 113–32.

22. Pauline Atherton. *Books Are for Use: Final Report of the Subject Access Project to the Council on Library Resources.* Washington, DC: Council on Library Resources, 1978.

23. Karen M. Drabenstott et al. Analysis of a Bibliographic Database Enhanced with a Library Classification [Online Catalog Incorporating DDC Subject Terms]. *Library Resources & Technical Services*, 34, April 1990, 179–98; Karen M. Drabenstott. Searching and Browsing the Dewey Decimal Classification in an Online Catalog. *Cataloging & Classification Quarterly*, 7, Spring 1987, 37–68; Karen M. Drabenstott et al. Findings of the Dewey Decimal Classification On-line Project. *International Cataloguing*, 15, April 1986, 15–19; Karen M. Drabenstott. Class Number Searching in an Experimental Online Catalog. *International Classification*, 13 (3), 1986, 142–50.

24. Ray R. Larson. TREC Interactive with Cheshire II. *Information Processing & Management*, 37 (3), May 2001, 485–505; Ray R. Larson et al. Cheshire II: Designing a Next-Generation Online Catalog. *Journal of the American Society for Information Science*, 47, July 1996, 555–67; Ray R. Larson. Evaluation of Advanced Retrieval Techniques in an Experimental Online Catalog [Probabilistic SMART Retrieval Methods in a Cheshire Catalog]. *Journal of the American Society for Information Science*, 43, January 1992, 34–53; Ray R. Larson. Classification Clustering, Probabilistic Information Retrieval, and the Online Catalog [Experimental Cheshire System Employing SMART Principles]. *The Library Quarterly*, 61, April 1991, 133–73.

25. The Okapi Project produced a plethora of publications. See, for example, Edward M. Keen. The Okapi Projects. *Journal of Documentation*, 53, January 1997, 84–87; Stephen E. Robertson. Overview of the Okapi Projects. *Journal of Documentation*, 53, January 1997, 3–7; Stephen E. Robertson, Stephen Walker, and Micheline Hancock-Beaulieu. Large Test Collection Experiments on an Operational, Interactive System: Okapi at TREC. *Information Processing & Management*, 31, May/June 1995, 345–60; Micheline Hancock-Beaulieu. Query Expansion: Advances in Research in Online Catalogues. *Journal of Information Science*, 18 (2), 1992, 99–103.

5

Analysis of Data

What gets measured, gets managed.

—Peter Drucker[1]

A point of view can be a dangerous luxury when substituted for insight and understanding.

—Marshall McLuhan[2]

For most evaluations, the analysis of data is relatively simple and will not involve the dreaded "S" word—*statistics*. Regardless of the method selected to assist in the analysis of data, it is important to remember:

The purpose of analysis is **insight**!

The analysis of data can be divided into two broad groups:

- **Descriptive methods** for organizing, summarizing, and presenting information; in short, making sense of the data. Using these tools, the librarian can identify trends, perform comparisons, and make better-informed decisions. Descriptive statistics are normally applied to population data rather than sample data.

- **Inferential statistics** allow the librarian to make generalizations using sample data. From the sample it is possible to infer the characteristics of the whole population—if it could be analyzed. Inferential statistics have a probabilistic component because the analysis might be wrong. Thus, if a .05 level is associated with a statistic, this indicates there is a 1 in 20 probability that the analysis is wrong.

It is helpful to understand the meaning of a number of frequently used terms when talking about the analysis of data. Some of these important terms are:

- **Population** is a group of items having at least one shared characteristic. Items may be objects (such as materials found in the library's collection), people, measurements, or observations.

- An **attribute** may be used to define or place limits around a population. For example, a population may be limited to the students attending a specific college.
- A **target population** is the segment of the total population that is the focus of the evaluation study.
- A **variable** is any characteristic of the population that may vary. For example, a collection of books can vary by age, size, author, subject, and so forth.
- A **score** is the value of the variable. For example, the number of years since a book has been published is the score for the variable "age of item."
- **Attribute data** can be described by a word—author, subject headings, place of publication. Attribute data can also be numerical—library card bar code number or driver's license number.
- A variable can be placed into **categories**, in which case the scores of the variables must be mutually exclusive. For example, materials in a library's collection can be placed in material type categories—books, audio, video, microforms, and so forth.

Some data are more meaningful than other data depending on how they have been measured and categorized. There are four different ways of measuring data:

- **Nominal scale measurement** gives a variable meaning by assigning a name or label to the score; it reflects only equality or inequality. For example, a nominal scale might include type of library, type of college or university, book publisher names, and so forth.
- **Ordinal scale measurement** reflects categories that have some associated order, be it hierarchical or some other manner of organizing the data. Thus, the order of the categories is important. For example, the amount of education a person has received is typically reflected in the categories "grade completed"—1 through 8 for elementary school, 9 through 12 for high school, and so forth. Also, ordinal scale measurement does not reflect the distance between categories.
- **Interval scale measurement** is used to rank variables that have equal intervals between values. The purpose of this type of measurement is to compare values, and it is permissible to add and subtract values. A thermometer is an example of an interval scale measurement.
- **Ratio scale measurement** is anchored by true zero. For example, this type of scale can be used to identify the number of children in a family—from zero on up. Absolute zero exists for measuring such units as temperature, weight, time, area, and volume. Using a ratio scale, it is possible to make such statements as "three times as many" or "twice as fast."

In order to be assured that decision makers are using the appropriate data, two additional characteristics of data must be discussed: reliability and validity.

Reliability is concerned with consistency, stability, and predictability of the data. That is, each time a data variable is measured using the same method, the same result should be obtained if the circumstances are identical. For example, one library might treat the renewal of an item as a check-in and then a checkout, whereas another library would only extend the due date and not adjust (increase) the statistical counts. Cronbach's alpha, a statistical analysis test, is often performed to determine the reliability of specific questions.

Data **validity** is concerned with the relationship between the evidence and the argument; that is, determining whether the correct variable is being used appropriately. Validity focuses on the meaning that is being attributed to the data. Consider a library trying to understand customer complaints about the time it takes to get materials reshelved. The library collects data about the length of the time people wait in the queue at the circulation desk. Although these data might be interesting, they are not germane to what is being evaluated: how long it takes to get a recently returned item back on the shelf.

Bias is the enemy of validity. It can be introduced through poor sampling, faulty wording, and sloppy administration of the data collection instrument (survey or interview); inaccurate data recording; and inappropriate interpretation of the results. Pretesting may alert the participants or educate them about the topic under study and thus introduce bias.

DESCRIPTIVE STATISTICS TECHNIQUES

Typically, the analysis of data will begin with a count of the scores for each variable. These *frequency distributions* can be reported in a table and include simple, cumulative, percentage, and grouped distributions. However, it does not take too much data before a table full of numbers becomes fairly meaningless. It is interesting to note that most library monthly management reports use tables to report their statistics. It would be much more helpful to convert some, but not all, of these tabular data into charts or graphs, because they help reveal interesting patterns present in the data.

> *He uses statistics as a drunken man uses lamp-posts . . . for support rather than illumination.*
>
> —Andrew Lang[3]

Converting tables of data into charts or graphs will make the data much more understandable. The widespread availability of spreadsheet programs makes the production of charts and graphs a simple task. The greatest value of any chart or diagram is that it *forces* the observer to notice the unexpected.

Thermometer Chart

Responses to a one-dimensional scale can be shown effectively using a "thermometer" chart. Figure 5.1 shows a typical thermometer chart, displaying the ratings library customers assign to various service attributes.

Histogram

A histogram is a graph composed of a series of rectangles with their base on the horizontal or X-axis. Figure 5.2 shows the copyright dates of books in a hypothetical library.

Frequency Polygon

A frequency polygon is a graph that plots category frequency with the category midpoints. The number of values or observations in a category is assumed to be concentrated at the midpoint. Figure 5.3 presents a sample frequency showing the distribution of a hypothetical library's nonfiction book collection using call number range. Each category midpoint is connected with

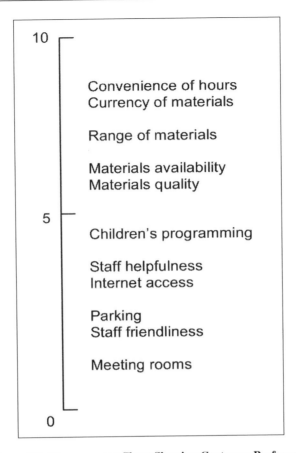

Figure 5.1. Thermometer Chart Showing Customer Preferences

a line to adjacent midpoints. The relative frequency information, when expressed as a percent, must total 100 percent.

A cumulative frequency distribution is constructed by adding the distribution frequencies of successive classes together. Figure 5.4 shows the histogram in Figure 5.2 with a cumulative frequency distribution line added.

Bar Charts

Both horizontal and vertical bar charts effectively compare related items. Because one chart can accommodate many bars, a fair amount of information can be presented and understood by the reader. The bar chart can be organized to reflect numerical order, decreasing values, chronology, and so forth. Bar charts can be arranged in a variety of ways, and the bars can be subdivided, paired, or grouped. Figure 5.5 presents a bar chart that compares circulation with holdings for a public library.

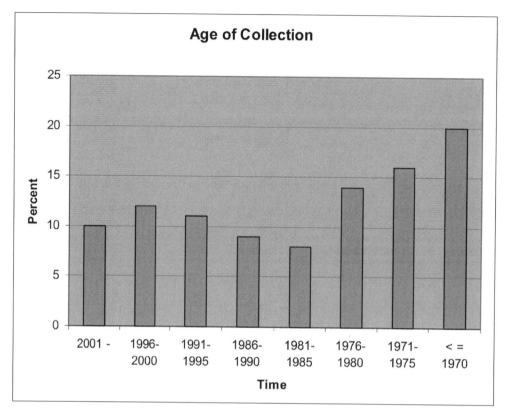

Figure 5.2. Age of Library Book Collection

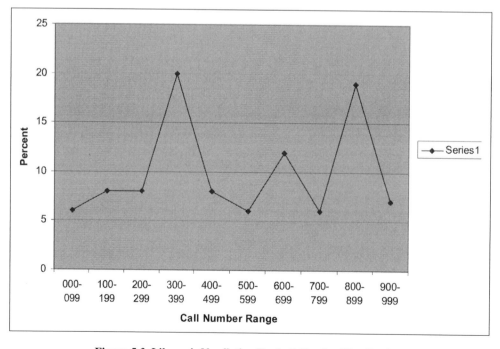

Figure 5.3. Library's Nonfiction Book Collection Distribution

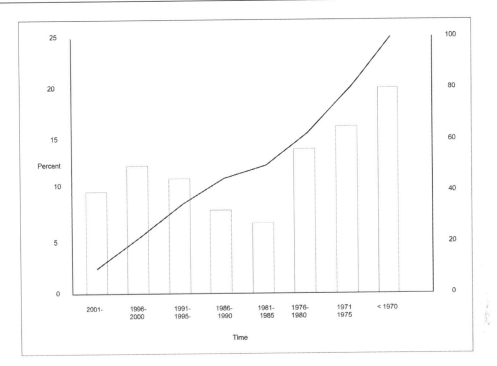

Figure 5.4. Age of Collection with a Cumulative Frequency

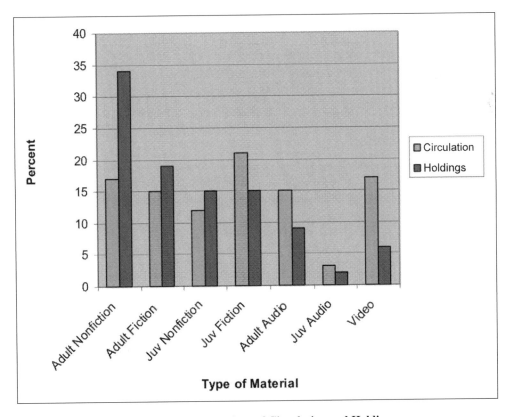

Figure 5.5. A Comparison of Circulation and Holdings

Line Charts

A line chart or line graph is especially effective at showing trends—that is, the rise and fall of a variable. A line chart is particularly useful when comparing this year's performance with that achieved last year, as shown in Figure 5.6. A quick look at this figure indicates that circulation has increased for almost every month compared to the previous year's circulation numbers.

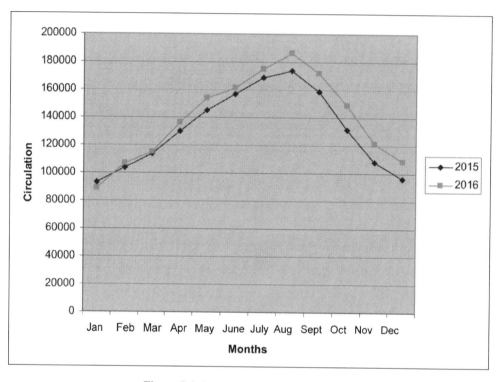

Figure 5.6. Annual Circulation by Month

Pie Charts

A pie chart or circle graph segregates and identifies the components of the whole, such as budgets, portions of the collection, segments of the population who actively use the library's services, and so forth. Each component is identified as a wedge-shaped portion of a circle. A pie chart illustrating the components of a library's budget is shown in Figure 5.7. In general, pie charts should not contain more than five or six segments.

MEASURES OF CENTRAL TENDENCY

The data collected can be organized into tables, frequency distributions, and charts. However, the characteristics of a distribution are important to understand; these include the spread of a distribution, the middle value of the distribution, and the general shape of the distribution. In addition, the measures of central tendency allow the side-by-side comparison of two or more distributions.

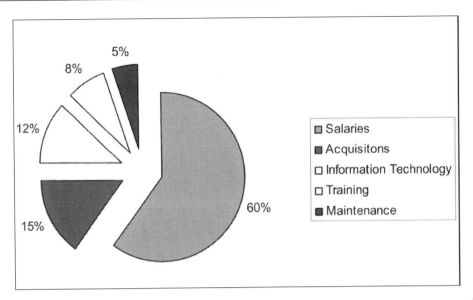

Figure 5.7. Library Budget Components

The Mode

The distribution's center, called the mode, is the data score or data point that occurs *most frequently* in the distribution. Although most distributions will have a single mode, in some cases a distribution will have two modes. The latter situation is described as bimodal.

For example, in the data set [3, 3, 4, 5, 5, 5, 6], the mode is 5, because 5 occurs most frequently. However, it should be noted that a data set might not contain a mode.

The Median

The median divides the distribution in half. Arranging the scores in a distribution from smallest to largest will assist in identifying the midpoint value of the data set. Thus, half the scores of the distribution will be less than the median and the remaining half will be greater than the median value.

For example, in the data set [1, 1, 2, 2, 3, 4, 4, 5, 5], the median is 3—the midpoint score. When the data point contains an even number of scores, the median is the value between the two scores closest to the middle. For example, in the data set [1, 2, 3, 4, 5, 6, 7, 8], the median is the number that lies between the fourth and fifth scores, or 4.5. In this case, the median is rounded because it must be a discrete value: 5.

A box-and-whiskers diagram illustrates the spread of a set of data. It also displays the upper and lower quartile. For example, consider the data set [14, 13, 3, 7, 9, 12, 17, 4, 9, 10, 18, 18]. The upper and lower values are 3 and 18, so the range is 15 and the median (the midpoint) has the value of 11. The upper quartile is the median value for 12, 13, 14, 16, 17, 18, or midway between 14 and 16: 15. The lower quartile is the median value for 3, 4, 7, 9, 9, 10, or midway between 7 and 9: 8.

The box in the box-and-whiskers diagram is composed of the upper and lower quartiles. The whiskers connect the upper and lower quartiles, and the median is also shown in the middle, as illustrated in Figure 5.8.

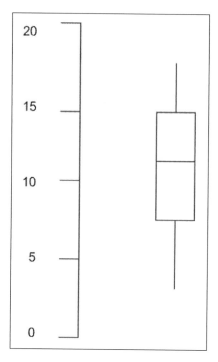

Figure 5.8. Box-and-Whiskers Diagram

The Mean

Adding all the scores in the data set and dividing by the number of scores determines the arithmetical mean or average. For example, in the data set [1, 2, 3, 4, 5, 6, 7, 8], the mean is 4.5. Because the mean is sensitive to extreme values, it may be helpful to calculate two means—one that includes the extreme value(s) and one that does not.

A Distribution's Shape

The distribution of data can be separated into two broad categories: the scores in the data set clustering at the center of the distribution and the scores tending to cluster toward the higher or lower values of the distribution.

A *symmetric distribution* occurs when the median and mean are equal. The most well-known symmetric distribution is the *normal distribution,* also called the Gaussian distribution, illustrated by the bell-shaped distribution shown in Figure 5.9 (more about the bell-shaped curve in the later discussion of inferential statistics). Another variation of a symmetric distribution, called a *unimodal distribution,* is also illustrated in the same figure.

Distributions are said to be *skewed* when the median and mean are not the same. Because the bulk of the scores in the data set are located at either the low or the high end of the distribution, the resulting curve representing the data seems to have a "tail," as shown in Figure 5.10. Note that a great deal of library-related data is skewed and does not reflect a bell-shaped distribution!

When the highest frequency occurs in the first or last category in a data set, it is called a J-distribution, because graphically the curve resembles the letter J (or a reversed letter J), as

Box 5.1. What Is An Average?

Consider the 9,206 public libraries in the United States. They serve populations ranging in size from 19 to 3,912,200, but the vast majority of libraries serve populations that are quite small, as shown in Chart 1.

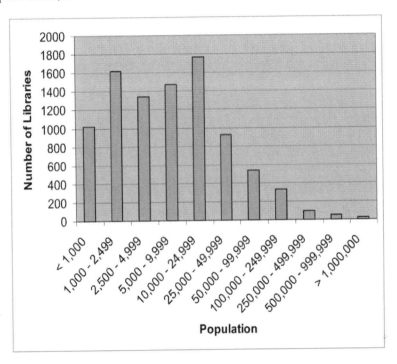

Chart 1. Number of Public Libraries by Population Served

So, what could be considered an average population served for a public library?

The *mean* population served is 30,788.
The *median* population served is 6,598.
The *mode* of the population served is 5,387.

Given the extremely wide range of population size, it is not surprising that the *standard deviation* is also large: 123,165.

shown in Figure 5.11. The J-distribution has been popularized by Chris Anderson, who wrote a book about the "long tail" in which he suggested that there are an infinite number of niche markets that are economically viable due to falling distribution costs of the Internet, and in the aggregate they represent sizeable sales potential.[4]

Vilfredo Pareto, a 19th-century economist, developed the 80/20 rule after examining the distribution of wealth in Italy. This is another example of the J-distribution or J-curve. A Pareto

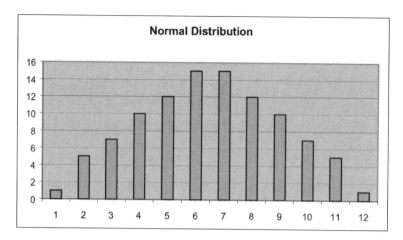

Figure 5.9. Normal Distribution

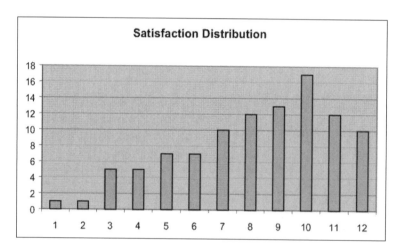

Figure 5.10. Skewed Distribution

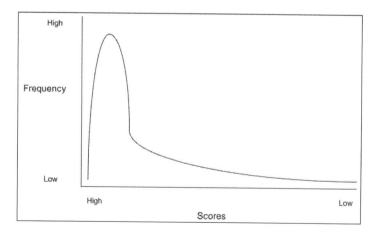

Figure 5.11. High Value Skew Distribution

distribution has been observed in the library environment in a number of different contexts. For example, 80 percent of a library's circulation is typically accounted for by about 20 percent of the library's customers.

MEASURES OF VARIABILITY

To better understand a specific data set, measures of central tendency (mean, median, mode) should be augmented by measures of variability, sometimes called *measures of dispersion*. Such measures will assist in judging the reliability of the central tendency measures.

Range

Range is the difference between the two extreme values in a data set. The greater the range of data, the more spread out or dispersed are the scores. Though helpful, range does not indicate the dispersion of data within the data set. For example, the range in this data set [1, 2, 3, 4, 5, 6, 7, 8, 9, 10] is 9 (10-1), whereas a different data set with the same range could be entirely different [1, 8, 8, 8, 9, 9, 9, 10, 10, 10].

Percentiles

Percentiles divide a large data set that is in rank order (lowest to highest) into 100 equal parts. For anyone who has taken one of the many standardized tests—GRE, SAT, ACT, and so forth—the results provide two numbers to indicate performance. The first is the individual's test score as reflected in the point score (questions answered correctly compared to the total possible points). The second number reflects the individual's test score as compared to all who took the test (percentile). Consider someone who is in the 75th percentile: 25 percent of all test takers scored higher than this individual.

Note that the median is the 50th percentile—the median divides the distribution into two equal data sets. Dividing the distribution into four equal parts will produce *quartiles*.

Standard Deviation

One of the most readily recognized measures of a data set is the standard deviation, which tells how far the typical score is from the mean of the distribution. It is called *standard* because it applies uniformly to all scores in the distribution, and *deviation* refers to the differences in the scores. In other words, standard deviation refers to the spread or dispersion of the data away from the distribution's mean. The Greek character sigma is used to refer to the standard deviation. A large standard deviation means that the data points are far from the mean; a small standard deviation means that they are clustered about the mean.

Calculating the standard deviation can be accomplished in four steps:

1. Determine the mean of the data set.
2. Subtract the mean from each score in the data set and double the resulting value; this is called a squared deviation.
3. Add all the squared deviations together—this is called the sum of the squares—and divide the result by (n - 1), where n = the number of scores in the data set.
4. Calculate the square root of the quotient found in step 3.

To spare you the tedious task of manually calculating the standard deviation, most spreadsheets and statistical software packages will do this for you.

The Russian mathematician P. L. Chebyshev noticed that for any set of data, the formula $1 - (1/k^2)$ would predict the proportion of data that lies within k standard deviations of the mean. For a normal distribution of data, the interval within 1 standard deviation on either side of the mean contains 68 percent of all scores, and within 1.5 standard deviations, 86.6 percent of all scores can be found.

Within the quality movement, the goal for really high quality is often expressed as achieving six sigma: three standard deviations to the left of the mean and three to the right of the mean, or virtually all scores within a data set. To achieve six sigma, a process must not produce more than 3.4 defects per million opportunities.

INFERENTIAL STATISTICS

In some cases, a research project or evaluation study will formulate a hypothesis. A variety of definitions of *hypothesis* exist, but for our purposes a hypothesis can be thought of as the proposition guiding the investigation of a problem. Generally a hypothesis will involve attempting to understand the relationship between two or more variables.

Inferential statistics are used to test hypotheses using tests of statistical significance to determine if observed differences between variables are "real" or merely due to chance. Inferential statistics are usually divided into two groups, parametric and nonparametric. *Parametric statistics* assume a normal population or distribution. *Nonparametric statistics* are regarded as distribution free.

The use of inferential statistics simply does not happen in most evaluation studies. Thus, a detailed description of the various inferential statistical tests and methods is not provided here but can be found elsewhere.[5]

Among some of the better known inferential parametric statistical tests encountered in the literature are Pearson's correlation coefficient, student's *t*-test, analysis of variance (ANOVA), and regression analysis. An example of a nonparametric test is the chi-square test.

- A **correlation** is the extent to which two variables are related, and a *correlation coefficient* is the mathematical expression of the relationship. A correlation coefficient can take on values that range from –1.0 to +1.0; not surprisingly, the plus sign indicates that the relationship is positive and the negative sign that the relationship is negative. When there is no relationship between the two variables, the value of the correlation coefficient is zero. However, it is important to note that the correlation coefficient does not imply cause and effect between the two variables.

  Greater understanding is gained by calculating the *coefficient of determination* by squaring the coefficient correlation, which explains the proportion of the variability of scores in one variable that can be associated with another variable. For example, if the coefficient correlation between college grades and the GRE is .60, then 36 percent (.60 squared) of the variability in GRE scores and college GPA can be explained by achievement. Or, 74 percent of the variability of GPA is unrelated to academic achievement. Note that correlation coefficients of .40 and lower should not be used to explain any relationships!

- The **student's *t*-test** is used to determine whether a relation exists between a two-group nominal or ordinal variable—gender, full-time versus part-time variable—and a second variable measured on an interval or ratio scale. This test evaluates the difference between two groups' mean scores on the ratio or interval variable. For example, the *t*-test could be used to determine whether women had higher grade point averages than men.

- **Analysis of variance (ANOVA)** is a multigroup extension of the *t*-test that compares means. When the grouping variable has more than two categories, the ANOVA test must be used. The ANOVA test will indicate only that no less than one of the possible pairs of the group means is statistically significant—and it will not reveal which one(s).

  Pauline Atherton's *Books Project* created two different databases for searching (one with enhanced bibliographic records and one without enhanced records). Participants then searched one of the systems, and the retrieved records were analyzed for relevance and precision and recall scores were calculated. ANOVA was then used to determine if the differences between the two average recall and two average precision scores were significant. They were![6]

  The word *significant* should only be applied to inferential data, because statistical significance is a measure that the conclusion can be applied to the entire population. Statistical significance between two means depends on four factors: the absolute difference in size, the variance of responses around the mean, the size of the sample, and the level of precision at which the difference is being considered. Given a large enough sample, virtually all differences will be determined statistically significant.

  Statistical significance does not equate to importance. A finding may be true without being important.

- **Regression analysis** models the relationship between one or more response variables (sometimes called dependent variables, explained variables, or predicted variables) and the predictors (also called independent variables, explanatory variables, or control variables). Simple linear regression and multiple linear regressions are related statistical methods for modeling the relationship between two or more random variables using a linear equation. Simple linear regression refers to a regression on two variables, whereas multiple regressions refer to a regression on more than two variables. Linear regression assumes that the best estimate of the response is a linear function of two or more parameters. If the predictors are all quantitative, the multiple regressions method is used.

  Path analysis is a technique that uses linear regression techniques to test the causal relations among variables. A drawing is created based on a theory or a set of hypotheses, and the direct and indirect effects are noted by calculating the path coefficients between each node in the diagram.

- The **chi-square test** of association or goodness-of-fit evaluates whether two variables are related, but this test provides no information about the strength of the relationship. The test indicates whether a relationship is real as opposed to being a chance occurrence.

OCLC *Perceptions of Libraries* Report, 2010

The OCLC *Perceptions of Libraries* report has been widely distributed, discussed, and cited.[7] Yet, as Ray Lyons discusses in his perceptive and interesting blog, *Lib(rary) Performance* blog, the methodology used to conduct the survey and report the data raises a host of issues that have rarely been considered. As Lyons notes about a single survey, regardless of the number of responses, "At best, the findings are well-calculated estimates, at worst they can be really bad guesses . . . some level of uncertainty is always embedded in the information."[8] Some of the issues with any survey, including the OCLC Perceptions report, include:

- **Convenience sample.** Several problems can be found with the way in which the data for this survey was gathered. First, the Americans invited to participate were included in the Harris Interactive Inc.'s Harris Poll Online panel—millions of people that Harris can contact online. What is not disclosed is the number of people included in the Harris Poll Online group (is it 2 million?, 5 million?, 10 million?, more?). Given that the U.S. population is in excess of 310 million, the available pool of potential respondents is not likely to be representative of the total population (although Harris does make statistical adjustments in an attempt to make survey results representative).

  In addition, the *Perceptions* report indicates that 77 percent of the U.S. population has Internet access, whereas 23 percent do not have access. Thus, the roughly 71 million people with no Internet access are excluded from the possibility of participating because the data are collected using an online survey.

  Also, though the total number of American respondents who completed the survey is impressive (1,334 individuals), there is no indication of the number of people who were invited to participate or the number of people who started to complete the survey but dropped out at some point and were thus excluded from the data analysis.

  All of this is briefly acknowledged in page 102 of the report with this disclosure: "The online [American] population may or may not represent the general [American] population." Thus, although the report makes lots of bold statements, the reality is that the conclusions are in many ways simply a guesstimate.

- **Creative interpretation of data.** Never let it be said that OCLC is not selective in how it uses the data from the survey. For example, as Ray Lyons points out, the report states on page 44 that "[m]illions of Americans, across all age groups, indicated that the value of the library has increased during the recent recession (from 16 percent to 36 percent of the different age groups perceived the library as more valuable)." What the report does not mention is that from 64 percent to 84 percent of the age groups did not perceive libraries as more valuable. Thus, each age group has twice as many (or more) reporting no increased value. In his blog, Ray also notes several other ways in which data have been presented is the best possible light.

- **Large percentages**. The OCLC folks really like using large percentages—for example, 1,544 percent growth in e-book sales. Percentages like this are simply overstatements to capture attention; people don't realize that the large percentage is simply the result of the baseline or starting point for the calculation being fairly small (adjust the starting point and the percentage goes down). The report writers like to use sensational adjectives to describe results—"rocketing," "soaring," "exploding," and "exponential."

- **Distortion of data**. The OCLC report has charts that are designed to look attractive but do not accurately reflect the data. For example, a chart on page 12 uses a ribbon rather than a line to reflect the data—and due to the thickness of the ribbon there can be a difference of up to 20 million. Data visualization experts such as Edward Tufte and others call for clarity, not visual appeal, when designing a chart. Tufte calls the lack of clarity "chart junk."[9]

However, despite all of the limitations in conducting and reporting the results of the survey, we can use the report to our benefit if we both acknowledge the uncertainty that is found in the data itself and carefully examine what the data is saying (rather than what the report is stating). This is especially true since people begin to think that the data applies to the total US population when in reality it more than likely only applies to just the survey respondents.

Ray provides a similar critique of the OCLC report in his article on *From Awareness to Funding: A Study of Library Support in America.*[10]

VISUALIZATION

One important way to assist in data analysis is to employ a set of data visualization tools. Data visualization can often reveal interesting patterns in the data—and besides, sometimes the data just look better in a visual format that you can explore with your eyes and brain. Consider the data shown in Figure 5.12, which was created using a tool called Haystacks developed by the Harvard University Library Innovation Lab (http://haystacks.law.harvard.edu/).

Other popular data visualization tools include Chart.js, Tableau, Raw, ZingChart, Timeline, and Visual.ly. Many of these tools can be used for no cost and some are open source.

META-ANALYSIS

Systematic reviews (sometime called meta-analyses) provide transparency about the searching process used to identify studies pertaining to a particular topic, as well as the criteria that were used to assess the quality of each study in order to determine what should be included in or excluded from the review. When you hear the phrase "systematic review," think of the Cochrane Collaboration that provides systematic reviews about health care topics. In the library sector, the journal *Evidence Based Library and Information Practice* provides critiques and summaries of research studies for practitioners. The *Annual Review of Information Science and Technology* (which ceased publication in 2011) provided a traditional literature review generally organized by theme, chronology, or study design.

It is possible to prepare a systematic review of both qualitative and quantitative studies. When a meta-analysis is prepared that examines quantitative studies, it is hoped that the resulting analysis will be more robust and be able to calculate results that have great statistical significance due to the larger sample sizes (data from multiple studies are aggregated).

In two interesting and readable articles, Eric Trahan[11] and Mathew Saxton[12] explore the ways meta-analysis has been used in library and information science. Typically the criteria used to assess the research include quality and accuracy of evidence, credibility (of the author or organization), timeliness and practicality of results, and accessibility.[13] Leonor Gaspar Pinto

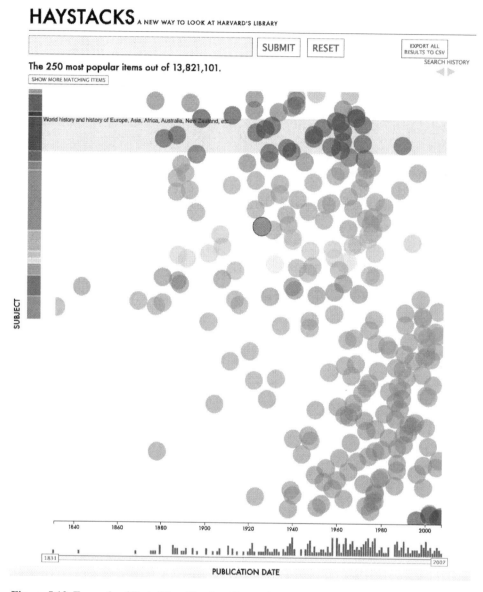

Figure 5.12. Example of Data Visualization. Harvard Haystacks. Reproduced with permission.

and Paula Ochoa have further explored the use of a meta-evaluation model in Portugal.[14] Qing Ke and Ying Cheng thoroughly explore the application of meta-analysis in the field of library and information science and suggest that it is important to carefully distinguish between narrative review, systematic review, meta-synthesis, and meta-analysis.[15]

As a precursor to the preparation of a systematic review or meta-analysis, a scoping study might be prepared. The key aim of a scoping study is to rapidly map the key concepts underpinning a research area. Such a study follows steps similar to those taken in a traditional review.[16]

SUMMARY

This chapter has presented an overview of the variety of methods that can be used to analyze data, ranging from the simple (descriptive) to the more complex statistical analysis techniques. The use of statistics is a means to an end, which is learning what the data have to say so that we can use the results of the data analysis to inform the library leadership team about the *insights* we have gleaned.

NOTES

1. Peter Drucker. *The Effective Executive*. New York: HarperBusiness, 2006, 78.

2. Marshall McLuhan and Quentin Fiore. *The Medium Is the Message*. 9th ed. New York: Ginko Press, 2001, 114.

3. Andrew Lang. Retrieved from http://www.goodreads.com/quotes/93716-he-uses-statistics-as-a-drunken-man-uses-lamp-posts-for.

4. Chris Anderson. *The Long Tail: Why the Future of Business Is Selling Less of More*. New York: Hyperion, 2006.

5. See, for example, Arthur W. Hafner. *Descriptive Statistical Techniques for Librarians*. Chicago: American Library Association, 1998.

6. Pauline Atherton. *Books Are for Use: Final Report of the Subject Access Project to the Council on Library Resources*. Syracuse, NY: School of Information Studies, 1978.

7. Cathy De Rosa et al. *Perceptions of Libraries, 2010: Context and Community. A Report to the OCLC Membership*. Dublin, OH: OCLC Online Computer Library Center, 2010. Also, a search on Google Scholar by the author in January 2014 for "Perceptions of Libraries" returned more than 1,500 citations.

8. Ray Lyons blog Lib(rary) Performance may be found at https://libperformance.com/.

9. Edward Tufte. *The Visual Display of Quantitative Information*. 2nd Ed. New York: Graphics Press, 2001.

10. Ray Lyons. Critiquing Advocacy Research Findings: An Illustration from the OCLC Report, From Awareness to Funding: A Study of Library Support in America. *Public Library Quarterly*, 28 (3), 2009, 212–26.

11. Eric Trahan. Applying Meta-Analysis to Library and Information Science. *Library Quarterly*, 63 (1), January 1993, 73–91.

12. Matthew Saxton. Meta-Analysis in Library and Information Science: Method, History, and Recommendations for Report Research. *Library Trends*, 55 (1), Summer 2006, 158–70.

13. Kristin Olsen and Sheelagh O'Reilly. *Evaluation Methodologies*. Sheffield, UK: IO PARC, June 2011.

14. Leonor Gaspar Pinto and Paula Ochoa. Information Society and Library Evaluation Transitions in Portugal: A Meta-Evaluation Model and Frameworks (1970–2013). *LIBER Quarterly*, 23 (3), 2013, 214–36. See also Leonor Gaspar Pinto. Library Performance Continuum and the Imperative of Meta-Evaluation. *Performance Measurement and Metrics*, 15 (3), 2014, 86–98.

15. Qing Ke and Ying Cheng. Applications of Meta-Analysis to Library and Information Science Research: Content Analysis. *Library & Information Science Research*, 37, 2015, 370–82.

16. Hilary Arksey and Lisa O'Malley. Scoping Studies: Towards a Methodological Framework. *International Journal of Social Research Methodology*, 8 (1), February 2005, 19–32.

Part III

Evaluation of
Library Operations

6

Evaluation of Operations

Continuous improvement teaches that when improving a service delivery chain, reducing non-value-added activities, and streamlining value-added activities, it is a nonstop effort; there is always room for improvement.

—John Huber[1]

Operating a library in an efficient manner and transparently demonstrating the library's efficiency to key stakeholders is important to the continued sustainability of the library. One important tool in managing efficiency is acknowledging that one's view of the world can affect how one perceives potential problems. For example, an organizational perspective reflecting an organizational chart—the vertical view—does not really show how the work is done. A horizontal (or process) perspective provides a different focus on how problems are analyzed, resources are allocated, and so forth. James Harrington has suggested that these different perspectives lead to the comparisons shown in Table 6.1.[2] The process perspective acknowledges that processes are not self-sustaining and thus get better or worse over time; they rarely stay the same. Processes that are not monitored will deteriorate and begin to produce waste.

This chapter provides information about several tools that will assist the library in evaluating its operations. The goal of this chapter is to create a toolbox that will assist the librarian in analyzing a library service. Among these tools are:

- Benchmarking
- Activity-based costing
- Cost-benefit analysis
- Lean tools
- Statistical process control

Table 6.1. View of the World Perspectives

Organizational Focus	Process Focus
Employees are the problem	The process is the problem
Do my job	Help to get things done
Measure individuals	Measure the process
Change the person	Change the process
Can always find a better employee	Can always improve the process
Motivate people	Remove barriers
Control employees	Develop people
Don't trust anyone	We are all in this together
Who made the error?	Reduce variation
Understand my job	Know how my job fits into the total process

H. James Harrington. *Business Process Improvement*. New York: McGraw-Hill, 1991, 5.

BENCHMARKING

One of the challenges for any organization is to recognize and acknowledge that competing organizations are constantly evolving and changing their processes in order to boost their productivity. This is further complicated by the fact that new entrants to the competitive arena are using the Internet to re-engineer processes by placing data and software applications in the cloud, thus introducing new low-cost (and in some cases no-cost) options in the marketplace. One way for a library to "see how it is doing" is to benchmark an activity or process against other similar or "peer" libraries.

Benchmarking may be used to evaluate services against a set of performance standards (to see if the services are improving over time) or against the performance of a set of peer libraries. Benchmarking offers a great deal of flexibility in that it can be used to assess almost any organizational activity. In general, benchmarking requires that key performance measures be identified, measured, analyzed, and compared to provide a basis for possible improvement.

The key to effective benchmarking is the recognition by all that continuous improvement and change management are necessary. Really effective organizations challenge themselves to perform better than they did a month ago and, in a month, to perform better than they are today. The goal is not the benchmarking process itself, but rather to use benchmarking as a tool for improving the library.

Although a library could partner with several other libraries to gather benchmarking data, most libraries use published data to compare their performance to that of its peers. Most public and academic libraries participate in nationwide statistics gathering programs, which can be used for peer comparisons.

Academic Library Statistics

The National Center for Education Statistics (NCES), a part of the U.S. Department of Education, collects expenditures, staffing, and service-related data biennially from some 3,700 degree-granting colleges and universities. The NCES Web site provides a "Compare Academic Libraries" tool that allows one library to compare itself with a set of peer libraries. Data can be downloaded into a spreadsheet for local analysis, charting, and graphing.

NCES is also responsible for another important source of data: the annual Integrated Postsecondary Education Data System (IPEDS) survey that gathers data pertaining to enrollments, program completions, graduation rates, faculty and staffing levels, finances, and student financial aid.

The Association of College and Research Libraries (ACRL) collects statistics through an annual "Academic Library Trends and Statistics" survey that gathers information about expenditures, collections, staffing, technology, and service activities.

Public Library Statistics

The Institute of Museum and Library Services (IMLS) conducts the annual Public Libraries Survey and the State Library Agencies Survey. Data are reported by each public library to the state library and are then aggregated at the national level. Most states prepare an annual report of public library statistics that is published in print format or can be downloaded as a PDF file.

Box 6.1. *ACRLMetrics* and *PLAmetrics*

Both the Association of College and Research Libraries and the Public Library Association make their survey data accessible online through a subscription service known as *ACRLMetrics* and *PLAmetrics*, administered by Counting Opinions (SQUIRE) Ltd.

Since 2000, *ACRLMetrics* has provided access to data supplied by libraries collected by the ACRL and the National Center for Education Statistics. In addition, a subset of data from the Integrated Postsecondary Education Data System is provided to subscribers.

PLAmetrics provides access to the annual Public Library Data Service (PLDS) as well as the data supplied by public libraries to the Institute of Museum and Library Services (IMLS) each year through the state library. The PLDS data are also published each year in an issue of *Public Libraries*.[i]

The book *Managing with Data* provides a roadmap for using these data services so that a library can prepare a series of benchmarking comparisons exploring budgets, staffing levels, expenditures, size of facilities, technology being used, and so forth.[ii] In addition to raw numbers, it is also possible to easily prepare an analysis that uses per capita or per student comparisons that will likely be of more value. A library could also explore the "cost per . . . ," such as the cost per journal article downloaded, acquisitions budget per capita, electronic materials spending per student, workstation use rates, or attendance at programs per capita, among many other options.

i. Ian Reid. The 2015 Public Library Data Service Statistical Report: Characteristics & Trends. *Public Libraries*, 55 (3), 2016, 24–33.
ii. Peter Hernon, Robert Dugan, and Joseph Matthews. *Managing with Data: Using ACRLMetrics and PLAmetrics*. Chicago: American Library Association, 2015.

The criteria used to identify a set of "peer" libraries are important (and should be disclosed for transparency purposes), as different libraries will be included or excluded depending upon the criteria selected. Important questions to consider in the selection process include:

- Should the libraries be from the same state?
- Should the population of the service area be a consideration?
- Should the size of the overall budget be the most important criterion?
- Should library staffing levels be a consideration?
- Should the number of service outlets be included?

Some organizations have already identified a set of peers, so the question may be moot; in some cases, the larger organization may have also identified a set of "aspirational" peers. Two peer comparison charts are shown in Figures 6.1 and 6.2 to illustrate the power of using benchmarking data.

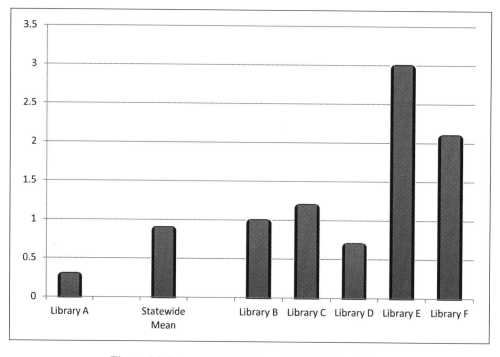

Figure 6.1. Internet Workstations Per 1,000 Population

ACTIVITY-BASED COSTING

The vast majority of libraries, and their parent organizations, use a line-item budget. Using broad categories—personnel, equipment, materials, supplies, utilities, travel, and so forth—every individual and item is accounted for in the budget. Unfortunately, a line-item budget is unable to determine the costs for providing a service.

Originally developed by Robin Cooper and Robert Kaplan, activity-based costing gathers costs into functional cost pools and then allocates them on the basis of activity cost drivers.[3]

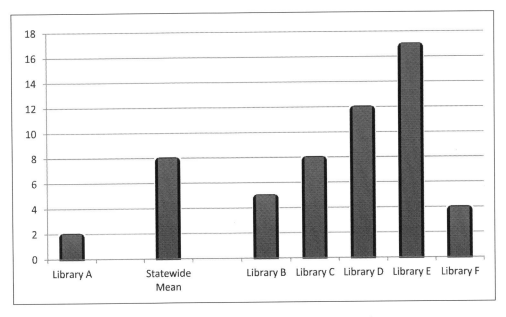

Figure 6.2. E-Books as a Percent of Book Collection

The generators of costs are called *cost drivers*, and variations in a cost driver will cause costs to vary in turn. Activity-based costing (ABC) can be used to identify the costs for almost all activities in a library. The library can control the level of analysis, but allocating all costs to a service that is too broad—for example, public services—will do little to assist in understanding the library's cost structure. As librarians gain awareness of the true costs of providing a service, they can make choices to better utilize limited resources. Snyder and Davenport provide a lucid description of some of the issues involved in activity-based costing.[4]

There is a four-step approach to implementing activity-based costing:

- Identify the key activities and relevant cost drivers.
- Allocate staff time to activities.
- Attribute staff salaries and other costs to activity cost pools.
- Determine a cost per cost driver.

Step 1—Identify Key Activities and Relevant Cost Drivers

Identifying Key Activities

Ascertaining the key activities in the library is a relatively straightforward task. The process may involve engaging in conversations with staff and the library's management team. In some cases, the library may find that preparing a flow chart of a process is helpful, because it may reveal hidden cost categories such as information technology.

The activities within technical services may be broken up into several smaller activities, which will assist in better understanding the cost structure within this broad activity. For example, ordering, receiving materials, handling invoices, cataloging, processing, and so forth can be a useful group of activities to analyze.

Identifying Cost Drivers

Discovering the cost driver for each activity is the next step. It is important to determine the underlying cause-and-effect relationship so that the cost driver selected by the library will control the costs associated with a key activity. Table 6.2 provides some examples of key activities (the cost pool) and their associated cost drivers.

Table 6.2. Cost Pools and Associated Cost Drivers

Cost Pool	Cost Driver
Borrowing an item	Number of checkouts
Returning an item	Number of returns
Renewing an item	Number of renewals
Overdue items	Number of overdue items
Shelving an item	Number of returns
Interlibrary loan requests	Number of items requested
Interlibrary loan supplied	Number of items supplied
Computer maintenance	Computer use
Reference desk	Number of inquiries
Copy cataloging	Number of records available
Original cataloging	Number of items with no records
Physical processing	Number of items added
Programs	Number of programs offered
Public computers	Number of public use computers

Step 2—Allocate Staff Time to Activities

This step will apportion library costs to the activity cost pools. Depending on the size of the library, some staff members will work full-time on a particular task or activity—for example, physical processing of materials. However, most staff members will spend a portion of their time working on two or more activities. Asking staff to estimate the time spent on each activity is one frequently used method, but this approach has the potential for a large margin of error. Another approach is to ask staff to complete a small survey over the course of a week or two in which they track how much time they spend accomplishing each activity. This latter approach will increase the costs of the process slightly but will significantly improve the reliability of the information. In some cases, a library will have a duty roster that indicates time spent on various activities.

Once all of the staff members' hours have been accounted for, the results are tallied by activity, as a percentage of the total hours worked by each staff member. Table 6.3 provides a simplified illustration of the percent of staff time allocated to activities.

Table 6.3. Staff Time Allocated to Activities

Employee	Checkout (%)	Check In (%)	Overdues (%)	Shelving (%)	ILL (%)	Total (%)
A	50	50				100
B	25	25	50			100
C	50	50				100
D	25	25		50		100
E	25	25		50		100
F	25			75		100
G	25	25			50	100

Step 3—Attribute Staff Salaries and Other Costs to Activity Cost Pools

Typically staff salaries will constitute the largest cost category for each cost pool. Salary costs are allocated by multiplying the individual salary costs for each employee by the proportion of time spent on each activity. Usually the actual costs for each employee are used because there are not that many employees. For large libraries, it may be easier to use the average salary for each employee classification than attempt to use each employee's actual salary. Library managers' and administrative staff's time will have to be allocated to each cost pool using a proportional basis to distribute their costs. One method is to apportion the costs based on the percent of employee hours within the cost pool.

In addition, it will be necessary to add in the costs associated with the overhead of fringe benefits: vacation pay, health benefits, sick leave, and so forth. In most cases, a different fringe benefit overhead rate is used for different employee classifications—for example, 27 percent, or 43 percent. Table 6.4 identifies the costs for the activity cost pools. The amounts in the activity columns were then added to arrive at the total cost per activity.

Accounting for Other Indirect and Direct Costs

Other costs found in the library's line-item budget will have to be allocated in a proportional manner to all the activity cost pools. Among these other costs are utilities, maintenance, information technology overhead (maintenance of the servers, software, local area network, Internet connection, and IT staff costs), equipment replacement, insurance, travel, supplies, and so forth. Some libraries have allocated IT costs using the proportion of computers for each activity.

Table 6.4. Allocation of Staff Costs to Activity Cost Pools

Employee	Checkout ($)	Check In ($)	Overdues ($)	Shelving ($)	ILL ($)	Total ($)
A	15,360	15,360				30,720
B	8,740	8,740	17,480			34,960
C	17,120	17,120				34,240
D	6,550	6,550		13,100		26,200
E	6,550	6,550		13,100		26,200
F	6,550			19,650		26,200
G	9,470	9,470			18,940	37,880
Totals	70,340	63,790	17,480	45,850	18,940	216,400

The method for the proportional allocation of the other costs is not particularly important, but the method should be rational and justifiable.

Step 4—Determine Cost Per Cost Driver

Having determined the total cost for each activity, the next step calculates the cost per cost driver. This is accomplished by dividing the total activity cost pool by the cost driver volume, as illustrated in Table 6.5. The result is the cost per activity (the driver), a figure that can be used in a number of ways.

Increased demands for accountability, plus the desire to provide quality services, often in the face of declining or stable budgets, mean the library will have to do more with less. Having a clear understanding of the costs to provide a service will allow the library to make comparisons with a set of peer libraries to ensure that the local library is operating in an efficient manner. The comparison with peer libraries can be done in a formal way, such as participating with a group of libraries in a benchmarking study. Alternatively, the cost information can be used in preparing an internal evaluation report. In addition, knowing the cost of the various activities needed to provide a service is the foundation for greater understanding of existing procedures and processes so that changes can be made.

Activity-based costing has been used in higher education libraries in the United States, England, and Australia.[5] Madeline Daubert provides a thorough review of various methods to analyze library costs, including activity-based costing.[6] The topic of managerial accounting and activity-based costing is thoroughly discussed in a book by Stevenson Smith.[7] A case study in two academic libraries demonstrated the value of using activity-based costs as the foundation tool during a benchmarking project.[8]

Once the library has a clear understanding of the costs associated with providing each service, it should also consider the *opportunity costs*. Key to understanding opportunity costs is the recognition that the use of resources in one way prevents their use in other ways. Thus, the opportunity costs are the benefits lost because the next best alternative was not selected. For example, if a library staff member is involved with providing programming in a library, the library is forfeiting the time of that staff member that could be spent performing other activities.

Table 6.5. Activity Cost Driver Table

Activity	Cost Driver	Total Cost ($)	Driver Volume	Cost per Driver ($)
Borrowing an item	no. of checkouts	70,340	42,789	1.64
Returning an item	no. of returns	63,790	42,600	1.50
Overdue items	no. of overdue items	17,480	4,500	3.88
Shelving an item	no. of returns	45,850	42,600	1.08
ILL requests	no. of items requested	14,205	4,125	3.44
ILL supplied	no. of items supplied	4,735	650	7.28
Reference desk	no. of inquiries	194,620	36,940	5.27
Copy cataloging	no. of records available	60,613	4,100	1.48
Original cataloging	no. of items	32,642	895	36.47
Physical processing	no. of items added	116,350	4,995	23.29
Programs	no. of programs offered	46,200	250	184.80
Public computers	no. of public-use computers	112,420	48	2,633.75

COST-BENEFIT ANALYSIS

A cost-benefit analysis can provide fundamental and (it is hoped) balanced information on which to base a decision concerning the most cost-effective alternative for an expenditure of funds. Cost-benefit analysis has long been used both in private industry and local governments to explore alternatives before making an investment decision. Although identifying the likely costs of a project is fairly straightforward, the most challenging task is to reduce all of the benefits to quantifiable terms: dollars and cents, or, as one critic noted, "dollars and sense." The trick is not to become overwhelmed with the details of the analysis, but to expend a level of effort in preparing the analysis that is proportional to the importance of the decision.

Cost-benefit studies have been prepared by libraries before making investments in automated library systems, RFID-based materials return sorting systems, delivery services, shared storage systems, shared integrated library systems, shared reference services, and so forth.

Five possible methods are available to compare alternatives in the preparation of a cost-benefit analysis.[9] These include:

1. Maximize benefits for a given cost
2. Minimize costs for a given level of benefits
3. Maximize the ratio of benefits over costs
4. Maximize the net present value (present value of benefits minus the present value of costs)
5. Maximize the internal rate of return on the investment.

Notice that the criterion, "Maximize benefits for minimum costs," is a contradiction in terms, although its appeal to politicians is undeniable. A series of examples will best illustrate the viability of a specific method—depending on the circumstances, of course.

First, if your library only has $10,000 (or whatever the number actually happens to be), then the first method is the best choice. Clearly you want to derive as much value as possible for a fixed investment.

Second, if you know the precise level of benefits you wish to achieve (even if additional benefits are available for an additional cost), then the second method of analysis would be appropriate—"minimize costs for a given level of benefits."

Third, in many cases the alternatives being considered vary widely in costs as well as range of benefits that accrue from each option. In this case, the third method, "Maximize the ratio of benefits over costs," would be the best choice. However, this method does not recognize that some alternatives will achieve their benefits at different points in time over the coming few years or that these "benefit streams" often have different starting points. Note that libraries, particularly public libraries, use this method of comparing the ratio of the value of benefits to costs when a return on investment (ROI) calculation is made, in an effort to communicate the value of the library to funding decision makers.

For example, one study found that a manual sorting system for the statewide delivery of library materials was more cost effective than to an RFID-based automated materials handling system (that had higher up-front capital costs).[10]

Fourth, a majority of firms in the private sector utilize the fourth method: "Maximize the net present value" of an investment. The major benefit of the net present value methodology is that it establishes the value of money today, taking into account the time value of money.

The time value of money, often referred to as a *discount rate*, is based on the concept that a dollar today is worth more than a dollar tomorrow. Most organizations use the interest rate that is charged by a bank, or (for local governments) the interest rate to be paid should bonds be issued. The data necessary to calculate the net present value for each alternative are:

- *Discount rate* refers to the interest rate.
- *Present value cost* is the expected annual cost divided by its discount rate (and then summed over all years of the expected project life).
- *Present value benefits* means the value of each year's expected benefits divided by its discount rate (and then summed over all years of the expected project life).
- *Net present value* is the difference between present value benefits and present value costs.

A more objective cost-benefit analysis can be prepared if the following suggestions are heeded:

- If it can't be quantified, the benefit should not be included in the cost-benefit analysis. Rather, a separate section in the report detailing the analysis should identify all of the qualitative aspects of each alternative.
- Quantify the benefits and costs of each alternative in terms of dollar benefits and dollar costs.
- Be conservative in estimating the value of benefits and liberal in estimating costs.
    - Identify and quantify benefits *first*.
    - Review the value of benefits for each alternative with the management team. The management team should accept the benefit valuations before identifying costs.
    - Identify and calculate project costs for each alternative.

If these suggestions are followed, it will help prevent the value of benefits almost always exceeding project costs. It is not too often that you hear someone say "we are experiencing runaway benefits" (rather than "runaway costs").

Among the more noteworthy library cost-benefit studies are these:

- Lori Ayre prepared a report for the Palo Alto (California) Public Library that compared RFID versus barcodes for self-checkout and return sorting systems. The analysis identified the fact that although RFID was more expensive, the benefits were greater and the investment payback period was seven years.[11] Lori also provided an analysis for the Washington County Cooperative Library System (Oregon) in which she suggested changes to the shared integrated library system (ILS) and recommended improvements to the delivery system and implementation of RFID in all of the member libraries.[12]

- Ping Fu and Moira Fitzgerald examined staffing models when they compared existing ILSs with some of the newer next-generation library management systems.[13]

- Ruth Kowal explored possible options for implementing "mediated" interlibrary loan for the Massachusetts Library System.[14]

- Linda Riewe compared open-source ILS systems with proprietary systems and found that libraries choosing open-source systems did so for reasons of affordability.[15]

LEAN TOOLS

Starting in the early 1990s, Michael Hammer and James Champy introduced the notion of reengineering the organization, suggesting that three forces were driving organizations into unfamiliar territory: customers, competition, and change. Customers were becoming empowered because they had access to more information, via the Internet, about alternative product and service providers. In addition, competition was increasing, and change is a constant. Hammer and Champy defined *reengineering* as the fundamental rethinking and radical redesign of processes to achieve dramatic improvements in critical, contemporary measures of performance, such as cost, quality, service, and speed.[16] In the government sector, David Osborne and Ted Gaebler had a similar message.[17] These authors suggested creating teams to accomplish a broad range of activities, empowering the team members to make decisions, and eliminating all activities that were wasteful or did not add value for the customer. Eliminating tasks that duplicate one another or are unnecessary from the customer's perspective can significantly speed the throughput times of a process.

More recently, a new effort, called *lean*, aims to improve the quality of products and services for customers while also reducing costs and improving productivity. Lean is aimed at the elimination of waste by organizing processes that add value for the customer. The four basic lean principles are:

- *Add nothing but value* while eliminating waste.
- *Do it right the first time.* The key to rapid delivery is small batch sizes.
- *People doing the work are adding value.* They should be the center of the resources, information, process design, and decision-making authority.
- *Deliver on demand* means that work isn't done until a downstream process requires it— make only what the next process needs, when it needs it.[18]

Waste comes from a variety of sources, including the following:

- **Overproduction:** Producing more, sooner, or faster than needed by the next process.
- **Inventory:** Any form of batch processing, whether it is electronic or physical.

- **Extra processing steps:** Reentering data, requiring extra copies, producing unused reports, expediting, travel expense reporting.
- **Motion:** Walking to perform an activity, such as picking up reports from a printer, fax machine, or other offices; moving book trucks; picking up supplies to complete a task.
- **Defects:** Data entry errors, errors in invoices, receipt of damaged materials, staff turnover.
- **Waiting:** System downtime, system response times, approval for others, information from vendors, information from others within the department/library, scheduled times to complete activities.
- **Transportation:** Movement of materials and paperwork, including multiple hand-offs, multiple approvals, excessive e-mail attachments.

John Huber, a knowledgeable and experienced consultant who has focused his career on the tools, concepts, and principles of lean, has articulated 11 strategies that will assist libraries in reducing costs and improving customer service.[19] These strategies include:

1. Recognize, benchmark, and measure your service performance compared to for-profit competitors.
2. Transform your change-resistant culture.
3. Understand how delivery service chains drive your library's performance.
4. Align your performance metrics with your delivery service chains.
5. Transform your new book delivery service chain.
6. Transform your customer holds/reserves delivery service chain.
7. Transform your cost-control philosophy to a lean service improvement philosophy by eliminating waste.
8. Transform your overall library service performance metrics.
9. Transform your digital research delivery service chain.
10. Transform your delivery service chain from a "Push" to a "Pull" philosophy.
11. The design of a physical space can transform how customers interact with collections, equipment, and services.

Huber carefully explains the lean concepts that are used in each strategy and provides detailed step-by-step instructions to accomplish service delivery improvements in all areas of a library.

NISO has also created a set of "Recommended Practices" for library physical delivery of materials.[20]

Jeremy Nelson, in a very readable book called *Becoming a Lean Library*, thoughtfully explores the concepts of lean in a library setting.[21]

STATISTICAL PROCESS CONTROL

In addition to its role as a means of communicating a variety of statistics about the library, a line chart is an important tool when a library is attempting to understand and improve any process using a method called *statistical process control*. The basic tool of this method is a plot of the data using a line chart. For example, Figure 6.3 shows the amount of time (in number of days) it takes to fill an interlibrary loan request (the average number of days to fill the requests completed each day). Clearly there is variability in the process: the average is 15.5 days.

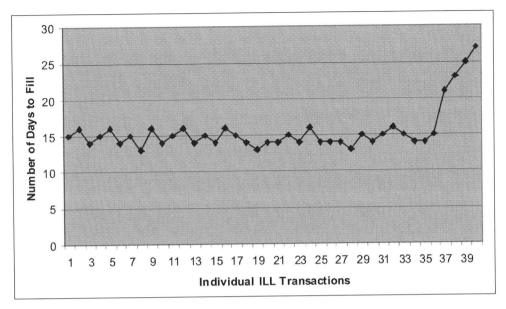

Figure 6.3. ILL Request Fill Rate

An important factor in understanding the statistical process control methodology is the recognition that every process will have variability. The issue is whether the process is under control, and the variability is within normal limits; or whether the process is out of control. To determine the normal limits of variability, take the following steps:

Step 1. Calculate the moving ranges between each value (determine the difference in successive daily values) and create a moving ranges graph (see Figure 6.4). In this example, the moving range average is 1.4 days.

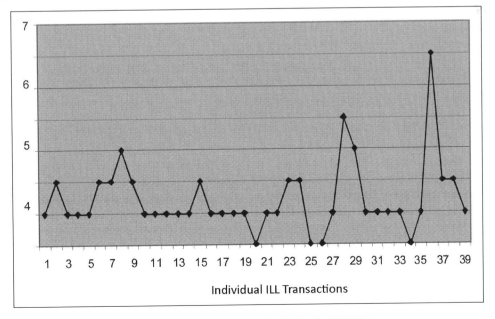

Figure 6.4. Moving Ranges Graph for the ILL Data

Step 2. Calculate the upper natural process limit by multiplying the average moving range by 2.66 (1.4 days x 2.66=3.7 days) and add the result to the average processing time of 15.5 days. The result is 19.2 days.

Step 3. Calculate the lower natural process limit by multiplying the average moving range by 2.66 (1.4 days x 2.66=3.7 days) and subtract the result from the average processing time of 15.5 days (see Figure 6.5). The result is 11.8 days.

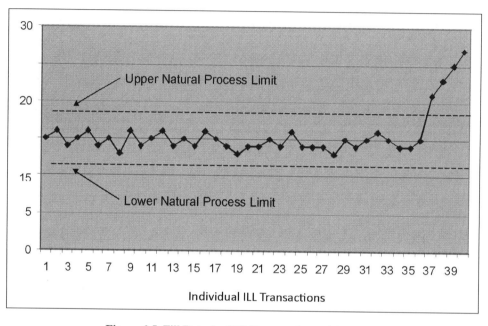

Figure 6.5. Fill Rate for ILL Transactions with Limits

Step 4. Add the upper natural process limit and the lower natural process limit to the line chart. Thus, the existing ILL processes that are being used to fill requests for journal articles will operate in a range from 11.8 to 19.2 days.

The process is neutral as to whether or not the library likes the upper and lower limits. The procedures and activities that compose the existing process will determine the results—sometimes this is called the "Voice of the Process." When a request is filled in a time period that exceeds the upper limit, that is a signal that something is not operating correctly.

Converting the raw data into a chart with its associated upper and lower limits helps the library better understand the data and begin to ask interesting and important questions. A library wishing to gain a deeper understanding of statistical process control techniques should consult one of the many books published in this area.

The existing performance of a process may or may not be acceptable. The library should initiate a dialogue with its customers to better understand their expectations, using focus groups, analysis of complaints, and so forth. The customer's expectations have been referred to as the "Voice of the Customer."[22]

SUMMARY

This chapter has provided an overview of several tools that can be employed to improve library operations by measuring, benchmarking, and reporting operational data. Among the techniques discussed were activity-based costing, cost-benefit analysis, lean tools, and statistical process control.

NOTES

1. John Huber. *Lean Library Management: Eleven Strategies for Reducing Costs and Improving Customer Service*. New York: Neal-Schulman, 2011, 169.

2. H. James Harrington. *Business Process Improvement*. New York: McGraw-Hill, 1991, 5.

3. Robin Cooper and Robert S. Kaplan. Measure Costs Right: Make the Right Decisions. *Harvard Business Review*, 66 (5), September/October 1988, 96–103.

4. Herbert Snyder and Elisabeth Davenport. What Does It Really Cost? Allocating Indirect Costs. *The Bottom Line*, 10 (4), 1997, 158–64.

5. L. Tatikonda and R. Tatikonda. Activity-Based Costing for Higher Education Institutions. *Management Accounting Quarterly*, Winter 2001, 16–27; James R. Montgomery and Julie K. Snyder. Costing a Library: A Generic Approach. *Research in Higher Education*, 30, 1989, 48–54; Jennifer Ellis-Newman. Activity-Based Costing in User Services of an Academic Library. *Library Trends,* 51 (3), Winter 2003, 333–48; Jennifer Ellis-Newman and P. Robinson. The Cost of Library Services: Activity-Based Costing in an Australian Academic Library. *The Journal of Academic Librarianship*, 24, 1998, 373–79; Michael Heaney. Easy as ABC? Activity-Based Costing in Oxford University Library Services. *The Bottom Line*, 17 (3), 2004, 93–97.

6. Madeline J. Daubert. *Analyzing Library Costs for Decision-Making and Cost Recovery*. Washington, DC: Special Libraries Association, 1997.

7. G. Stevenson Smith. *Managerial Accounting for Libraries & Other Not-for-Profit Organizations*. Chicago: American Library Association, 2002.

8. Lorena Siguenza-Guzman, Andres Auquilla, Alexandra Van den Abbeele, and Dirk Cattrysse. Using Time-Driven Activity-Based Costing to Identify Best Practices in Academic Libraries. *The Journal of Academic Librarianship,* 42, 2016, 232–46.

9. John King and Edward Schrems. Cost-Benefit Analysis of Information Systems Development and Operation. *Computing Surveys*, 10 (1), March 1978, 22–34.

10. Lori Ayre, Greg Pronevitz, and Catherine Utt. Label-Less Library Logistics: Implementing Labor-Saving Practices in Massachusetts' High Volume Resource Sharing System. *Collaborative Librarianship*, 3 (3), 2011, 163–73.

11. Lori Ayre. *Analysis, Evaluation and Recommendations for Materials Handling System and RFID at Palo Alto City Library: Final Report*. Petaluma, CA: The Galecia Group, May 2009.

12. Lori Ayre. *Washington County Cooperative Library Services: Library Materials Handling and Collection Management Study*. Petaluma, CA: The Galecia Group, April 2010.

13. Ping Fu and Moira Fitzgerald. A Comparative Analysis of the Effect of the Integrated Library System on Staffing Models in Academic Libraries. *Information Technology and Libraries*, September 2013, 47–58.

14. Ruth Kowal. *Massachusetts Library System (MLS) Mediated Interlibrary Loan Service Models: Review and Evaluation*. Boston: Strategic Assessment and Planning Services, May 2012.

15. Linda Riewe. *Survey of Open Source Integrated Library Systems* (Paper 3481). San Jose, CA: San Jose State University MLS Thesis, 2008.

16. Michael Hammer and James Champy. *Reengineering the Corporation: A Manifesto for Business Revolution*. New York: HarperBusiness, 1993.

17. David Osborne and Ted Gaebler. *Reinventing Government: How the Entrepreneurial Spirit Is Transforming the Public Sector.* New York: Addison-Wesley, 1992.

18. Mary Poppendieck. *Principles of Lean Thinking.* Available at http://sel.unsl.edu.ar/ApuntesMaes /Anteriores/MetodologiasAgiles/LeanThinking.pdf.

19. John Huber. *Lean Library Management: Eleven Strategies for Reducing Costs and Improving Customer Service.* New York: Neal-Schulman, 2011.

20. Gregory Pronevitz and Valerie Horton. Creating NISO's Library Physical Delivery Recommended Practices. *Collaborative Librarianship,* 4 (2), 2012, 67–75.

21. Jeremy Nelson. *Becoming a Lean Library: Lessons from the World of Technology Startups.* London: Chandos Publishing, 2016.

22. Donald J. Wheeler. *Understanding Variation: The Key to Managing Chaos.* Knoxville, TN: SPC Press, 2000.

7

Evaluation of Technical Services

To achieve the results they need, technical service departments need breakthrough, double-digit improvements in cost, time and effectiveness.
—Karen Calhoun[1]

SERVICE DEFINITION

The activities that comprise technical services are important because they support the services that the library's customers interact with. Selecting, cataloging, and processing the physical and electronic materials that are added to the library's collection are all activities that add value. However, because technical services are providing service to other areas within the library and not directly to the customer, the focus of performance measurement and evaluation activities is, in almost all cases, necessarily internal.

EVALUATION QUESTIONS

Among the questions technical services evaluations have addressed, shown in Figure 7.1, are the following:

- How much time does it take to complete a task?
- How much does it cost to perform this task?
- How much will workflow analysis improve productivity of technical services?
- How efficient are our operations compared to a set of peer libraries?
- How can we compare in-library processing to using an outsourced vendor?
- What is the quality of work completed in technical services?
- Are enhanced bibliographic records something that will benefit the user?

	Qualitative	Quantitative
Library Perspective	Suggestion box Interviews Focus groups	Gathering statistics Survey of public services staff Survey of technical services staff Benchmarking Workflow analysis Quality assessment
Customer Perspective		Customer surveys

Figure 7.1. Technical Services Evaluation Methods

INTRODUCTION

There is no doubt about it: the elephant in the technical services room is OCLC, as evidenced by the fact that OCLC's WorldCat now holds more than 376 million bibliographic records (as of October 2016), with some 2.4+ billion holdings linked to the bibliographic records. As shown in Figure 7.2, the growth of the OCLC WorldCat bibliographic database started slowly, but as more libraries joined, the faster the database grew to become the behemoth it is today.

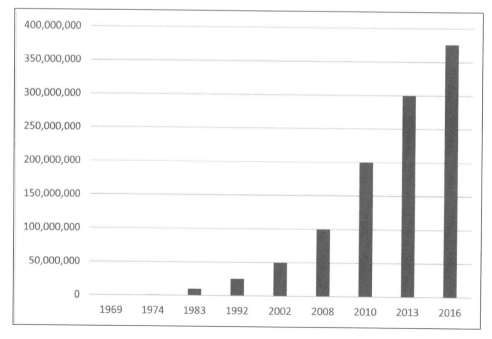

Figure 7.2. Growth of the OCLC WorldCat Bibliographic Database Over Time. Data courtesy of OCLC.

Ruth Fischer and Rick Lugg conducted an important study of the North American MARC Records Marketplace, prepared at the behest of the Library of Congress in 2009.[2] The study found:

1. Library of Congress cataloging continues to be widely valued
2. The Library of Congress subsidizes portions of the market
3. LC records are significantly underpriced
4. Cataloging backlogs continue to grow in many areas and market segments
5. There is adequate cataloging capacity in North America to meet the collective need
6. Cooperative cataloging has not realized its full potential
7. The market for cataloging records is conflicted
8. The market provides insufficient incentives to stimulate additional original cataloging
9. 80 percent of libraries edit records for English-language monographs in their local catalog
10. 78 percent of libraries are unaware of any restrictions on MARC record use or redistribution restrictions.

Among the alternatives for obtaining bibliographic records from sources other than OCLC are:

- Online access, including SkyRiver
- Other libraries, using Z39.50
- Internet resources
- Vendors that supply physical and electronic resources
- Outsourcing cataloging vendors

Any discussion of alternatives must, of necessity, explore a variety of perspectives or topics in order to better understand the strengths and limitations of each alternative. In this case, the factors that determine the ultimate utility of each alternative include:

- **Breadth of the Database**—size and diversity of the bibliographic database. The larger the database and the more diverse the database in terms of language and type of formats, the more likely a library will find a record it needs and it will not have to create an original cataloging record
- **Quality of the Database**—quality is determined by the amount of records that do not adhere to certain prescribed standards and the number of duplicate records. Library catalogs *typically* contain very good metadata because they are created and maintained using content standards, classification, and authority control to describe and collocate related materials. However, not every record is necessarily of acceptable quality in any database—even in the case of OCLC.
- **Ease of Use of the Database**—the user interface for searching, viewing, selecting, and then using a bibliographic record controls the ease of use. The ease of use will have a significant impact on the overall productivity for performing a specific activity (assuming the library has worked to optimize its workflows and processes to accomplish an activity). Ease of use is further complicated by the fact that users often are attempting to complete two different tasks: known item searching, and browsing to find something of interest. For users, ease of use and convenience trump quality of information.
- **Costs of Use of the Database**—the database provider determines the cost associated with downloading one or more records.

The activities of library technical services can be grouped into three broad supply chain models:

- The library assumes responsibility for all selection, cataloging, and processing of materials in-house, often with very customized processing requirements.
- The library fully outsources acquisition and supply of shelf-ready library materials.
- The library purchases its materials using a combination of the first two options.

EVALUATION METHODS

A variety of qualitative and quantitative methods have been used to evaluate technical services, as shown in Table 7.1. A survey of academic libraries found that three-fourths had done some form of evaluation of cataloging, whereas a little more than two-thirds had evaluated acquisitions.[3] Despite the importance of technical services, there is a lack of literature reporting evaluation efforts, and the literature that can be found often lacks detail that would be important should others wish to replicate a study.

Table 7.1. Examples of Cataloging Monograph Productivity

	Simple Copy Cataloging	Original Cataloging	Complex Original Cataloging
Professional catalogers	2 per hour	1 per hour	1 per hour
	3–4 per hour	0.5 per hour	2 per hour
	5 per hour	2 per hour	3–5 per hour
	225 per month	3 per hour	100 per month
		6 per day	120 per month
		90 per month	200 per month
Paraprofessionals	1–2 per hour	1 per hour	0.5 per hour
	2–3 per hour	1 per 1.3 hours	1–5 per hour
	3–10 per hour	7 per hour	5 per hour
	300–350 per month	6 per day	100 per month
	225–1,000 per month	100 per month	200 per month

Claire-Lise Benaud et al. Cataloging Production Standards in Academic Libraries. *Technical Services Quarterly,* 16 (3), 1999, 43–67.

PRIOR EVALUATIONS AND RESEARCH

Gathering Statistics

Libraries record counts of activities such as titles and volumes ordered, cataloged, and processed that are reported to a variety of agencies. These same data can be used for comparative purposes to a set of peer libraries.

Time

We all attempt to prioritize and allocate a specific amount of time to various activities. One of the components of efficiency is the time it takes to order, receive, catalog, and process an item until it finally reaches the shelf. Time can also be broken into two components: the time to accomplish a particular task or activity and the time spent waiting between process activities.

One simple method of tracking time is for each staff member to record the start and end times of the task being performed on a slip of paper placed in each item. The slips or forms might be divided into two columns: tasks and time. Assigning a unique ID number to each slip or form will ensure that all forms are returned and analyzed. In some cases, the slips are pre-printed with a broad range of activities. These slips are used for a period of time sufficient so that a minimum of at least 500 slips can be collected. The information is then tallied. Dividing the total time by the number of items handled for each task will reveal the average time required to complete an activity or task for a single item.

Another approach is to use a alarm unit that is carried by each staff member. When the alarm goes off at random intervals, the staff member records the activity he or she is engaged in. If the alarm is used for a two- to three-week period, the resulting data will allow the library to prepare a chart of the time spent on each activity by each staff member.

Tasks that are repetitive in nature are ideal candidates for establishing performance standards. The standard is a specific, measurable statement of what is required for a job to be performed within a specified amount of time.

One study found that the time it took a firm order to move from being received to being placed on the shelf averaged 45 days—the range was from 1 to 170 days. The firm orders required cataloging to be accomplished by the library. *PromptCat* orders come with cataloging records, and the elapsed time averaged 38 days—with a range of 10 to 58 days.[4] A time-activity study found that 83 percent of monographs were cataloged in less than 15 minutes. Further, the time from date cataloged to the date placed on the shelf was 1 to 5 days for 56 percent of the monographs.[5]

A survey of 25 academic libraries (tracking both professional and paraprofessional time) found that overall cataloging efficiency ranged from 5,056 volumes cataloged per FTE to a low of 866 volumes cataloged per FTE.[6]

Costs

Those managing technical services are obviously concerned about total costs as well as the unit costs of performing each activity. A cost analysis can be done for a variety of reasons:

- It is useful as a management tool for controlling technical service activities.
- It is helpful in taking a progressive and proactive approach to management.

- It is useful for comparing costs with a set of peer libraries.
- It can be used to demonstrate transparent cost efficiency to funding decision makers.

As shown in Chapter 6, it is not too difficult to calculate the costs for a specific activity using activity-based costing (ABC). However, caution must be used when attempting to compare the costs of one library with those of another because the cost figures were most likely not calculated in the same manner (for example, the cost of benefits may be included, or they may be ignored). The use of a time-based activity-based costing model in an European university library led to improvements in the acquisitions area.[7]

One interesting measure is the TSCORE—Technical Services Cost Ratio—which is calculated by dividing the total salaries for technical services by the amount spent on purchasing materials in the same period.[8] For example, if a library spends $350,000 annually to purchase materials and pays $190,000 in salaries to those who work in technical services, then the library's TSCORE would be 190/350 or $.54. In this case, the library is spending an additional 54 cents on technical services for every dollar it spends to acquire materials for its collection.

In a survey of 10 university libraries, TSCOREs ranged from a low of 45 cents to a high of $1.00, and the TSCORE varied directly with the size of the library: larger libraries have higher TSCOREs. Interestingly, a group of 12 large public libraries had an inverse relationship between the TSCORE and the size of the book budget: the larger the book budget, the smaller the technical services costs.[9]

The costs of technical services should be related to the tasks that are performed and the time it takes to perform each task. Difficulties arise when attempting to replicate research about the costs and efficiencies of technical services (and in particular, copy cataloging) because the majority of studies are based on locally produced (and undefined) data and they typically focus on the productivity of individuals rather than the productivity of the system in place.

The Iowa State University library conducted a series of time and cost studies from 1994 to 2001. During the period of the studies, cataloging costs per title declined consistently due to the collaborative efforts of catalogers and improved workflow procedures.[10] One interesting finding was that although automation had reduced costs and improved productivity, the library had for the most part only automated processes and activities that existed in the manual environment, and had not been taking advantage of technology to transform the processes within technical services. Although the library has made some changes to improve productivity, it has recognized that further change will require staff members to leave their present "comfort zones."[11] The bottom line demonstrated that acquiring a monograph is now comparatively expensive relative to the costs of cataloging.[12] In addition to tracking costs for monographs, the Iowa State team also identified the time and costs to perform a number of tasks associated with the processing of serials.[13]

A thorough time and cost analysis was prepared at the University of Oregon library, which found that upgrading an OCLC record cost $9.23 per title and that original cataloging cost $24.92 per title.[14] John Buschman and William Chickering of Rider University reviewed the available research and concluded that a rough benchmark of copy cataloging output ranges from 1.4 to 1.7 volumes/records per hour.[15]

Taking a much broader perspective, Lawrence et al. estimated the life cycle costs of collections. Their analysis demonstrated that the purchase price of library materials is a small fraction of the life cycle ownership costs of maintaining library collections. The researchers found that the expected cost of owning a monograph was more than seven times the original purchase price, consuming 95 percent of library life cycle expenditures.[16]

Many libraries have used an analysis to compare the costs of vendors. Paul Orkiszewski compared the costs of using Amazon.com with the library's existing vendor and found that the existing vendor offered better discounts to the library. Amazon.com compared favorably in terms of selection, availability, and fulfillment and ranked considerably better in terms of speed.[17]

Dana Miller and Teressa Keenan suggest that when preparing a activity-based costing project, it is best to:[18]

- Use a simple, straightforward data collection instrument.
- Recognize that clear instructions are necessary.
- Know that communication and transparency are essential.
- Include everyone in the department.
- Understand that time management studies have a variety of potential uses.
- Time your data collection carefully.
- Consider the limitations.
- Consider combining with other data.

Surveys

A library can conduct surveys of its technical services staff and its public services staff, as well as its customers, and ask them to rate and comment on a wide range of issues pertaining to technical services.

Technical Services and Public Services Staff Survey

Some libraries have conducted surveys of technical services staff as a means of soliciting participation in making productivity improvements within the department. Public services staff are less frequently involved in an assessment of technical services operations.

Customer Survey

One little-used method to assess technical services is to directly involve library customers in the evaluation process. The Wagga Wagga City Library in New South Wales, Australia, distributed a contingent valuation survey (more about this kind of survey in a later chapter of this book) to 336 randomly selected homes in the city. Respondents were asked to provide a value for library services as well as an estimated value for technical services. The analysis suggested that the benefit-cost ratio for technical services was 2.4:1.[19]

Workflow Analysis

The whole field of improving operational efficiencies of any organization most often is referred to as "lean." Any activity that does not add value (in the eyes of the customer) is either waste or is considered as incidental. Waste is the archenemy of lean. Waste may be the result of:

- Transportation—moving things from location to location unnecessarily (shorten the distances)
- Processing—doing something that has no value from the customer's perspective

- Waiting—staging material (waiting for a full book truck)
- Motion—unnecessary handling, touching of materials
- Defects—needing to fix or redo something
- Inventory—having too much or not the right inventory

A team of library staff members can do remarkable work if they are unleashed and are actively involved in making changes.

A workflow analysis creates a diagram of how materials move about in the technical services area. Create a diagram of the technical services area that is to scale and then use the information from the time-tracking forms (used in the time analysis discussed earlier in this chapter). A good workflow will minimize the number of individuals who have to touch the materials as they move from receiving, to cataloging, to processing, and out the door. Another useful tool is to create a value stream map. Myung Sung explains the use of flow charts and other techniques to significantly improve the productivity of technical services and, as a result, eliminate a substantial backlog of materials.[20]

The Kent State University library, working with its book vendor, reengineered its workflow by asking computers to perform the easy, repetitive, and dull work. The results were a significant decrease in the cost of cataloging and a reduction in the time it takes to get materials on the shelf.[21]

Staff members at the University of Chicago library used several lean methods and were able to reduce the number of days till a book was reshelved once it had been returned from 4 to 2 days, primarily by reducing the batch size (eliminating wait time for full book trucks).[22]

Tip! Buy John Huber's *Lean Library Management* book. This is an excellent resource that provides easy-to-follow, step-by-step instructions.[23]

Efficiency

Efficiency measures divide the time or cost information for an activity by the volume of activity to create a time/activity or cost/activity ratio. Efficiency measures help the library determine whether it is doing things right. For example, if the library is spending $58,000 for original cataloging for a total of 1,460 titles over the course of the year, then the cost per title is $39.73. Similarly, if the library spends a total of 3,200 hours to complete all of the cataloging, then the time per title to complete original cataloging is 2.2 hours.

Due to the increasing pressures on the budgets of most libraries, there is an almost unrelenting need to ensure that the library is operating in a cost-efficient manner. Nevertheless, most technical service departments continue to operate using a host of nonessential and time-honored wasteful practices.

Penn State University libraries used re-engineering principles to reorganize the cataloging processes for monographs, with good results.[24] The University of Southern Mississippi libraries merged their acquisitions and cataloging units and found that by revising the workflows within the new unit, the ordering lag time was decreased to 60 days.[25] Workflows can be streamlined by combining processes performed at one workstation and reducing the number of staff who handle materials.

One sign that cataloging is a challenge for many libraries is the fact that

> [v]ast cataloging backlogs in many libraries provide even more convincing evidence that the cost of cataloging is too high. In many cases, though not all, backlogs exist because cataloging departments still seek to provide a level of service that is not supported by the institution. Backlogs can be eliminated by changing either the process or the product.[26]

A suggestion in 1999 that the profession should develop production expectations is still waiting for the standards to be developed, and the data about productivity expectations that do exist are quite variable and dated.[27] Smith suggested that a cataloger should be expected to catalog 250 to 400 titles a month and that original cataloging should take between 30 and 60 minutes per item, depending on its complexity.[28] Clearly, the creation of cataloging production standards must encompass both quantity and quality measures.

One analysis of semi-automatic metadata generation tools concludes that each tool addresses only part of the issue of metadata generation (providing solutions to one or a few metadata elements) rather than the full complement of metadata elements.[29]

OUTSOURCING

Not surprisingly, outsourcing can engender considerable emotion. Ellen Duranceau suggested that

> [t]he question of whether and when to pay a vendor to do the work of professional in-house catalogers strikes to the very heart of our identity as librarians, calling into question our assumptions about our ultimate purpose, our place in the scholarly information chain, and how we can best serve our institutions.[31]

> *There is nothing more wasteful than doing efficiently that which is not necessary.*
> —Sir Royce[30]

James Rush expresses a contrary point of view: "I have long been fascinated by the fact that libraries spend so much of their scare resources on cataloging with so little resultant benefit."[32]

Outsourcing involves the purchasing, from an outside source, of goods and services that a library previously provided for itself. Outsourcing is done to reduce costs or improve the speed of the service. Some libraries have contracted out some, but not all, technical services functions to vendors in the private sector, including collection development (approval plans and blanket orders), cataloging and authority control, materials processing, bindery services, and serials subscription service.

Prior to signing a contract for an outsourced service, the library should prepare a cost analysis for that particular activity. A number of cost studies have compared in-library versus outsourced cataloging services (see Table 7.2).

Table 7.2. In-House Versus Outsourced Cataloging Costs

Library	In-House Costs	Outsourced Costs
City University of New York[i]	$7.50	$3.25
Michigan State University[ii]	6.22	3.99
University of Alabama[iii]	3.44	9.80

i. Douglas Duchin. Outsourcing: Newman Library, Baruch College CCNY. *The Bottom Line*, 11 (3), 1998, 111–15.
ii. Mary M. Rider and Marsha Hamilton. PromptCat Issues for Acquisitions: Quality Review, Cost Analysis and Workflow Implications. *Library Acquisitions: Practice and Theory*, 20 (1), 1996, 9–21.
iii. Debra W. Hill. To Outsource or Not: University of Alabama Libraries Engage in Pilot Project with OCLC's TechPro. *Cataloging & Classification Quarterly*, 26 (1), 63–73.

Wright State University outsourced all of its technical services, including cataloging activities, and saved the library about $253,000 per year.[33] Some libraries have outsourced the cataloging of materials that are difficult to complete—for example, cataloging foreign-language, legal, and medical materials. In some cases, outsourcing is used because it may be difficult to fill a cataloging position with a required set of skills. Original cataloging was outsourced at the central Oregon Community College library, with turnaround time, error rates, and costs all declining.[34]

The acquisition of shelf-ready material—cataloging, bar codes, spine labels, covers, and the like—is another popular form of outsourcing. The University of Vermont found in-house processing costs of $6 to $7 per volume, whereas shelf-ready outsourcing cost $3 to $4 per volume.[35] Other libraries, including Adelphi University,[36] the University of Arizona,[37] and the Fort Worth Public Library,[38] found similar cost savings. The Brigham Young University libraries conducted a time-task cost study and found that shelf-ready books were 6 percent less expensive, took 47 percent less processing time, and arrived on the shelves 33 days faster than books processed in-house.[39]

Outsourcing the selection and processing for shelf-ready, opening-day collections for branch libraries has been employed by a number of public libraries.

Another variation of outsourcing is having a consortium of libraries centralize all technical services activities. Stumpf analyzed the feasibility of centralized cataloging and processing for a group of public libraries and determined that the concept would save the individual libraries money while improving throughput times.[40]

The topic of outsourcing is well summarized by James Sweetland,[41] and useful annotated bibliographies have been prepared by Marylou Colver[42] and Benaud and Bordeianu.[43] Using a matrix to determine which services might be outsourced is a helpful technique suggested by David Ball.[44] One survey of academic librarians found that only half felt that outsourcing provided the desired result.[45]

Among the questions that might be asked when considering outsourcing are the following:

- Does the service "define" the library?
- Are the costs for providing the service high?
- Is the turnaround time to provide a service greater than customer expectations?
- Has performance been declining of late?

Any outsourcing agreement should ensure that all terms and standards are clearly defined. Regardless of the scope or specific service being outsourced, it is important to create an agreement that clearly identifies what is to be delivered (and for what price), as well as what performance measures will be used to verify the quality and timeliness of services.

To improve the efficiency of technical services, the department should adopt a mantra:

- Simplify it!
- Eliminate it!
- Automate it!

QUALITY

The presence of a typographical error in a bibliographic record can negatively affect the ability of an individual to find needed information. This reality leads to my favorite definition of a library catalog: a place where bibliographic records get lost alphabetically.

Typographical and other kinds of errors can occur in almost any part of the record itself. Errors in the primary fields—author, title, subject headings—are going to present more problems during searching, especially if the error occurs in the first word or two, than errors occurring in other parts of the record.[46]

Jeffery Beall brought the importance of errors to the attention of librarians when he suggested the use of the "Dirty Database Test," which entailed performing keyword searches for 10 misspelled words and counting the number of records that were retrieved.[47] Terry Ballard systematically examined the database of Adelphi University and corrected more than 800 errors in a database that contained some 117,000 words. Most of the errors were found in the title proper, and in 40 percent of the cases, the error occurred in the first three words.[48]

Another study analyzed the typographical errors found in a library's catalog and noted that the frequently misspelled words tend to have eight or more letters and at least three syllables. In addition, common words are more likely to have typos than esoteric technical terms.[49] Valid subject headings entered as a search request by users of the online catalog contained a spelling error in 6 percent of the requests. The 6 percent does not include spelling errors that failed to match the controlled vocabulary and keyword terms in the catalog.[50]

Another study that examined the filing problems with initial articles in bibliographic records found that the number of errors was quite high.[51] Another study found that in almost all cases, a record contained a spelling error.[52] Although the quality of the OCLC bibliographic database is quite good, the organization has an ongoing program to improve quality and reduce the number of misspellings.[53]

Sylvia Gardner classified spelling and typographical errors into four groups: errors of letter omission, errors of letter insertion, errors of letter substitution, and errors of letter transposition.[54] Gentner et al. developed a more precise definition of errors.[55]

A library can perform an audit to determine the quality of its catalog. A sample of cataloging records is compared to the physical items and all errors are noted. Similarly, a sample of physical items can be selected and then compared to their bibliographic records. Using this method, one library found that about one-third of its catalog records contained at least one error.[56]

ENHANCED RECORDS

Adding additional content to a bibliographic record will improve the end user's chances for success in searching because the number of words that can be used to retrieve a record has been increased. Pauline Atherton first articulated the concept of enhanced records in 1978. The additional content might come from the table of contents, an abstract, a book jacket summary, entries from an index, or the preface.[57] The notion of adding content to improve search results caused much discussion at the time, but seems slightly amusing now given the popularity of indexing every word in millions of books as is the case with the *Google Books Project.*

Several studies showed an increase in circulation for titles to which additional content had been added.[58] For example, Peis and Fernandez-Molina found that precision and recall will improve simultaneously when the user is searching enhanced records compared to nonenhanced bibliographic records, as shown in Figure 7.3.[59]

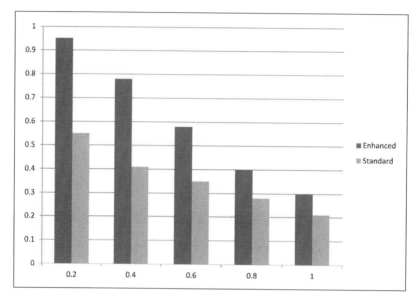

Figure 7.3. Utility of Enhanced MARC Records. Adapted from E. Peis and J. C. Fernandez-Molina. Enrichment of Bibliographic Records of Online Catalogs Through OCR and SGML Technology. *Information Technology and Libraries,* 17 (3), March 1998, 161–72.

SUMMARY

A review of the research pertaining to technical services suggests that:

- Time and cost of technical services activities are quite variable. A library should periodically identify its performance and compare itself with a set of peer libraries.
- Workflow analysis and work simplification can assist a library in reducing the activities it performs that do not add value from the customer's perspective.
- Cataloging productivity is quite variable and seems to reflect management's expectations and the local culture of the library.
- Outsourcing, although controversial, can be selectively used to improve the time to get new materials on the shelf and may reduce costs.
- Options for obtaining bibliographic and authority control records should be explored.
- A library should consider eliminating its technical services and moving these activities to a consortium.

One of the realities facing every library is that the value being added by staff members performing repetitive activities, such as in technical services departments, is being diminished as staff costs grow while the use of the collection remains stagnant or is declining. Libraries are also facing a number of other realities that should be causing libraries to serious consider the use of consortia. Among these factors are:

- A higher proportion of academic library collections are being stored offsite in shared regional facilities (or in some cases, in on-site automated storage and retrieval systems).
- Shared technology infrastructure reduces costs, improves services in many cases, and offers staff the opportunity for better training.
- Shared workloads will help keep transaction costs low through the use of standardization.
- Unique skills and expertise can be better shared than attempting to recruit and retain staff locally.

Ruth Fischer, Rick Lugg, and Kent Boese[60] suggest that a number of business principles have specific relevance for any library technical services. These principles include:

- Know your library's current cost structures
- Control the "expert mentality"
- Adhere to standards
- Maximize use of available resources
- Design and produce an economically viable product
- Adjust capacity to meet demand
- Automate and/or outsource
- Establish production goals and measure performance
- Control quality via sampling
- Be strategic

NOTES

1. Karen Calhoun. Technology, Productivity and Change in Library Technical Services. *Library Collections, Acquisitions & Technical Services*, 27 (3), Autumn 2003, 283.

2. Ruth Fischer and Rick Lugg. *Study of the North American MARC Records Marketplace*. Washington, DC: Library of Congress, October 2009.

3. Stephanie Wright and Lynda S. White. *SPEC Kit 303 Library Assessment*. Washington, DC: Association of Research Libraries, 2007.

4. Patricia Dragon and Lisa Sheets Barricella. Assessment of Technical Services Workflow in an Academic Library: A Time-and-Path Study. *Technical Services Quarterly*, 23 (4), 2006, 1–16.

5. Terry Hurlbert and Linda L. Dujmic. Factors Affecting Cataloging Time: An In-House Survey. *Technical Services Quarterly*, 22 (2), 2004, 1–14.

6. Cheryl McCain and Jay Shorten. Cataloging Efficiency and Effectiveness. *Library Resources & Technical Services*, 46 (1), 2002, 23–31.

7. Kristof Stouthuysen et al. Time-Driven Activity-Based Costing for a Library Acquisition Process: A Case Study in a Belgian University. *Library Collections, Acquisitions, & Technical Services*, 34 (2), 2010, 83–91. See also Kate-Riin Kont. How Much Does It Cost to Catalog a Document? A Case Study in Estonian University Libraries. *Cataloging & Classification Quarterly*, 53, 2015, 825–50.

8. H. W. Tuttle. TSCORE: The Technical Service Cost Ratio. *Southeastern Librarian*, 19, 1969, 15–25.

9. H. M. Welch. Technical Service Costs, Statistics, and Standards. *Library Resources & Technical Services*, 11, 1967, 436–42.

10. Dilys E. Morris, Collin B. Hobert, Lori Osmus, and Gregory Wool. Cataloging Staff Costs Revisited. *Library Resources & Technical Services*, 44 (2), April 2000, 70–83.

11. David C. Fowler and Janet Arcand. Monographs Acquisitions Time and Cost Studies: The Next Generation. *Library Resources & Technical Services*, 47 (3), July 2003, 109–24.

12. Dilys E. Morris, Pamela Rebarcak, and Gordon Rowley. Monograph Acquisitions: Staffing Costs and the Impact of Automation. *Library Resources & Technical Services*, 40 (4), 1996, 301–18; Dilys E. Morris, Collin B. Hobert, Lori Osmus, and Gregory Wool. Cataloging Staff Costs Revisited. *Library Resources & Technical Services*, 44 (2), 2000, 70–83.

13. David C. Fowler and Janet Arcand. A Serials Acquisitions Cost Study: Presenting a Case for Standard Serials Acquisitions Data Elements. *Library Resources & Technical Services*, 49 (2), April 2005, 107–22.

14. Nancy Slight-Gibney. How Far Have We Come? Benchmarking Time and Costs for Monograph Purchasing. *Library Collections, Acquisitions, & Technical Services*, 23 (1), 1999, 47–59; Nancy Slight-Gibney. Defining Priorities and Energizing Technical Services: The University of Oregon Self-Study. *Library Acquisitions: Practice and Theory*, 22 (1), 1998, 91–95.

15. John Buschman and William F. Chickering. A Rough Measure of Copy Cataloging Productivity in the Academic Library. *Library Philosophy and Practice*, 2007, Paper 139.

16. Stephen R. Lawrence, Lynn Silipigni Connaway, and Keith H. Brigham. Life Cycle Costs of Library Collections: Creation of Effective Performance and Cost Metrics for Library Resources. *College & Research Libraries*, 62, November 2001, 541–53.

17. Paul Orkiszewski. Notes on Operations: A Comparative Study of Amazon.com as a Library Book and Media Vendor. *Library Resources & Technical Services*, 49 (3), July 2005, 204–9.

18. Dana Miller and Teressa Keenan. The Time Management Study as a Tool for New Technical Services Managers. *Library Leadership & Management*, 30 (1), 2015. https://journals.tdl.org/llm/index.php/llm/article/view/7124/6354.

19. Philip Hider. How Much Are Technical Services Worth? Using the Contingent Valuation Method to Estimate the Added Value of Collection Management and Access. *Library Resources & Technical Services,* 52 (4), 2008, 254–62.

20. Myung Gi Sung. Increasing Technical Services Efficiency to Eliminate Cataloging Backlogs. *Public Libraries*, 43 (6), November/December 2004, 52–43.

21. Margaret Beecher Maurer and Michele L. Hurst. Library-Vendor Collaboration for Re-Engineering Workflow: The Kent State Experience. *Library Collections, Acquisitions, & Technical Services*, 27, 2003, 155–64.

22. Nancy J. Kress. Lean Thinking in Libraries: A Case Study on Improving Shelving Turnaround. *Journal of Access Services*, 5 (1–2), 2008, 159–72.

23. John Huber. *Lean Library Management: Eleven Strategies for Reducing Costs and Improving Customer Service.* New York: Neal-Schuman, 2011.

24. Robert B. Freeborn and Rebecca L. Mugridge. The Reorganization of Monographic Cataloging Processes at Penn State University Libraries. *Library Collections, Acquisitions, & Technical Services*, 26, 2002, 35–45.

25. Ann Branton and Tracy Englert. Mandate for Change: Merging Acquisitions and Cataloging Functions into a Single Workflow. *Library Collections, Acquisitions, & Technical Services*, 26, 2002, 345–54.

26. Ruth Fischer, Rick Lugg, and Kent C. Boese. Cataloging: How to Take a Business Approach. *The Bottom Line*, 17 (2), 2004, 50.

27. Claire-Lise Benaud, Sever Bordeianu, and Mary Ellen Hanson. Cataloging Production Standards in Academic Libraries. *Technical Services Quarterly*, 16 (3), 1999, 43–67.

28. P. M. Smith. Cataloging Production Standards in Academic Libraries. *Technical Services Quarterly*, 6 (1), 1988, 3–14.

29. Jung-Ran Park and Andrew Brenza. Evaluation of Semi-Automatic Metadata Generation Tools: A Survey of the Current State of the Art. *Information Technology and Libraries*, September 2015, 22–42.

30. Quoted in Dorsey J. Talley. *Total Quality Management: Performance and Cost Measurement—the Strategy for Economic Survival*. Milwaukee, WI: ASQC Quality Press, 1991, 31.

31. Ellen Duranceau. Vendors and Librarians Speak on Outsourcing, Cataloging, and Acquisitions. *Serials Review*, 20 (3), Fall 1994, 69–83.

32. James E. Rush. A Case for Eliminating Cataloging in the Individual Library, in *The Changing Face of Technical Services*. Dublin, OH: OCLC, 1994, 1.

33. Arnold Hirshon. Letter to the Editor. *The Journal of Academic Librarianship*, 22 (5), 1996, 392.

34. Carol G. Henderson. Freelance Cataloging: Outsourcing Original Cataloging at Central Oregon Community College Library, in K. A. Wilson and Marylou Colver (Eds.). *Outsourcing Library Technical Services Operations: Practices in Academic, Public, and Special Libraries*. Chicago: American Library Association, 1997, 38–45.

35. A. J. Joy and R. Lugg. The Books Are Shelf-Ready, Are You? *Library Acquisitions: Practice and Theory*, 22 (1), 1998, 71–89.

36. B. Horenstein. Outsourcing Copy Cataloging at Adelphi University Libraries. *Cataloging & Classification Quarterly*, 28 (4), 1999, 105–16.

37. T. H. Marshall and J. W. Tellman. Processing Foreign Language Books Without Catalog Librarians at the University of Arizona Library. *Against the Grain*, 12 (3), 2000, 28–29.

38. C. A. Dixon and F. G. Bordonaro. From Selection to Shelf: Outsourcing Book Selection, Copy Cataloging, and Physical Processing at Forth Worth Public Library, in K. A. Wilson and Marylou Colver (Eds.). *Outsourcing Library Technical Services Operations: Practices in Academic, Public, and Special Libraries*. Chicago: American Library Association, 1997, 124–43.

39. Rebecca Schroeder and Jared L. Howland. Shelf-Ready: A Cost-Benefit Analysis. *Library Collections, Acquisitions, & Technical Services*, 35 (4), 2011, 129–34.

40. Frances F. Stumpf. Centralized Cataloging and Processing for Public Library Consortia. *The Bottom Line*, 16 (3), 2003, 93–99.

41. James H. Sweetland. Outsourcing Library Technical Services—What We Think We Know, and Don't Know. *The Bottom Line*, 14 (3), 2001, 164–75.

42. Marylou Colver. Selected Annotated Bibliography, in K. A. Wilson and Marylou Colver (Eds.). *Outsourcing Library Technical Services Operations: Practices in Academic, Public, and Special Libraries*. Chicago: American Library Association, 1997, 193–220.

43. Claire L. Benaud and Sever M. Bordeianu. Outsourcing in Academic Libraries: A Selective Bibliography. *Reference Services Review*, 27 (1), 1999, 78–89.

44. David Ball. A Weighted Decision Matrix for Outsourcing Library Services. *The Bottom Line*, 16 (1), 2003, 25–30.

45. Laurie Lopatin. Review of the Literature: Technical Services Redesign and Reorganization, in *Innovative Redesign and Reorganization of Library Technical Services: Paths for the Future and Case Studies*. Westport, CT: Libraries Unlimited, 2004, 9.

46. Terry Ballard. Spelling and Typographical Errors in Library Databases. *Computers in Libraries*, 12 (6), June 1992, 14–19.

47. Jeffery Beall. The Dirty Database Test. *American Libraries*, 22, March 1991, 97.

48. Terry Ballard. Spelling and Typographical Errors in Library Databases. *Computers in Libraries*, 12 (6), June 1992, 14–19, 15.

49. Terry Ballard and Arthur Lifshin. Prediction of OPAC Spelling Errors Through a Keyword Inventory. *Information Technology and Libraries*, 11, June 1992, 139–45.

50. Karen M. Drabenstott and Marjorie S. Weller. Handling Spelling Errors in Online Catalog Searches. *Library Resources & Technical Services*, 40 (2), April 1996, 113–32.

51. Ralph Nielsen and Jan M. Pyle. Lost Articles: Filing Problems with Initial Articles in Databases. *Library Resources & Technical Services*, 39 (3), 1995, 291–92.

52. Joseph J. Pollock and Antonio Zamora. Collection and Characterization of Spelling Errors in Scientific and Scholarly Text. *Journal of the American Society for Information Science*, 34 (1), 1983, 51–58.

53. Edward T. O'Neill and Diane Vizine-Goetz. The Impact of Spelling Errors on Databases and Indexes, in *Proceedings of the 1989 National Online Meeting, 9–11 May 1989, New York*. Medford, NJ: Learned Information, 1990, 313–20; Edward T. O'Neill and Diane Vizine-Goetz. Quality Control in Online Databases. *Annual Review of Information Science and Technology*, 23, 1988, 125–56.

54. Sylvia A. Gardner. Spelling Errors in Online Databases: What the Technical Communicator Should Know. *Technical Communications*, 39, 1992, 50–53.

55. D. R. Gentner, J. T. Grudin, S. Larochelle, D. A. Norman, and D. E. Rumelhart. A Glossary of Terms Including a Classification of Typing Errors, in William E. Cooper (Ed.). *Cognitive Aspects of Skilled Typewriting*. New York: Springer-Verlag, 1983, 39–43; *Typographical Errors in Library Databases*. 2009, February 20. Available at http://www.terryballard.org/typos/typoscomplete.html.

56. Ann Chapman and Owen Massey. A Catalogue Quality Audit Tool. *Library and Information Research News*, 26 (82), Spring 2002, 26–37.

57. Pauline Atherton. *Books Are for Use: Final Report of the Subject Access Project to the Council on Library Resources*. Washington, DC: Council on Library Resources, 1978.

58. Ruth C. Morris. Online Table of Contents for Books: Effect on Usage. *Bulletin of the Medical Library Association*, 89, 2001, 29–36.

59. E. Peis and J. C. Fernandez-Molina. Enrichment of Bibliographic Records of Online Catalogs Through OCR and SGML Technology. *Information Technology and Libraries*, 17 (3), March 1998, 161–72.

60. Ruth Fischer, Rick Lugg, and Kent Boese. Cataloging: How to Take a Business Approach. *The Bottom Line*, 17 (2), 2004, 50–54.

8

Evaluation of Interlibrary Loan

We live in a radically different information world from the one that gave rise to ILL. Rather than resisting that reality, we should embrace it, rejoicing in the ways it allows us to serve our patrons better.

—Rick Anderson[1]

SERVICE DEFINITION

Libraries are unable to build a collection that will meet 100 percent of the needs of their customers (due to both financial and space constraints). The sharing of resources, called *interlibrary loan* (ILL), assists libraries in bridging the gap of unmet needs. Typically, journal articles are obtained from other libraries or a document delivery supplier, whereas books are normally borrowed from another library. The majority of journal articles are provided to the user as a PDF file. Academic libraries, in general, have seen a significant growth in interlibrary loan borrowing over the last 10 years.

The disruptive impact of the Internet (in its ability to reduce transaction costs) is also being felt in traditional services such as interlibrary loan. Academic libraries are increasingly being asked to support the entire information chain in the research process, and almost all of the links in this chain are operating at the network level.[2] Libraries are struggling to manage open-access materials as part of their collection management responsibilities.

EVALUATION QUESTIONS

The evaluation of interlibrary loan and document delivery is done for a variety of purposes:

- Assist requesting libraries in deciding among alternative supply sources;
- Garner the customer's perspective;
- Assess the impact of user-initiated ILL requests;

- Identify areas of weakness in order to make improvements;
- Explore document delivery in lieu of ILL;
- Track performance over time to demonstrate improved levels of service, reduced costs, and so forth.[3]

EVALUATION METHODS

A variety of measures can be used to evaluate document delivery and interlibrary loan, as shown in Table 8.1.

Table 8.1. Methods for Evaluating Interlibrary Loan

	Qualitative	Quantitative
Library Perspective		Statistics (counts) Speed (turnaround time) Fill rate Costs Requested items owned by the library Concentration and scatter of requested materials
Customer Perspective	Interviews Focus groups	User surveys

Among the other factors that have been evaluated include tracking the number of requests received, growth over time of the ILL service, document quality, safety of materials, and partner satisfaction. One fruitful evaluation approach is to use a communication framework, as suggested by Peter Lor:[4]

- Who—requesting customers and libraries
- Requests what—requested materials
- Through which channel—procedures, channels, and transmission media
- From whom—supplying library or vendor
- With what effect—outcomes of requests

PRIOR EVALUATIONS AND RESEARCH

Thorough reviews of the interlibrary loan literature have been provided by Thomas Waldhart's 1985 article[5] and Joan Stein's 2001 article[6], as well as the ongoing set of reviews authored by Mike McGrath in the journal *Interlending and Document Supply*.[7] Rather than organizing the prior research around methods that have been used, this material is presented by examining the variables that have been studied.

Speed (Turnaround Time)

The speed of the ILL service is known by many names: delivery time, turnaround time, turnaround, and delivery speed. Typically *turnaround* is defined as the time elapsed between submission of the request and the item being received by the library.

The *ISO 11620 Information and Documentation: Library Performance Indicators* standard includes measurement of speed of interlibrary lending.[8] This standard requires the library to construct a log and collect the dates of

- receiving the request from the user,
- initiating the search for materials,
- deciding on and initiating the interlibrary borrowing procedure,
- ordering the document from an external source,
- receiving the document from an external source, and
- notifying the user.

Typically, a commercial document delivery firm provides faster but more expensive service. Turnaround times reported in the literature are shown in Table 8.2.

Table 8.2. ILL Turnaround Times

Author	Data From	Turnaround Time
Thomas Nisonger[i]	75 studies	7 to 38 days using ILL 1 to 23 days using a document delivery service
Mary Jackson[ii]	97 ARL libraries	16-day average
Sue Burkholder[iii]	Oregon Document Delivery Service	1 to 2 days for 95 percent of requests
Victoria Nozero & Jason Vaughn[iv]	University of Nevada, Las Vegas	1 to 2 days

i. Thomas E. Nisonger. Accessing Information: The Evaluation Research. *Collection Management*, 26 (1), 2001, 1–23.

ii. Mary E. Jackson. Loan Stars: ILL Comes of Age. *Library Journal*, 123 (2), February 1, 1998, 44–47.

iii. Sue A. Burkholder. By Our Own Bootstraps: Making Document Delivery Work in Oregon. *Computers in Libraries*, 12, December 1992, 19–24.

iv. Victoria A. Nozero and Jason Vaughan. Utilization of Process Improvement to Manage Change in an Academic Library. *The Journal of Academic Librarianship*, 26 (6), November 2000, 416–21.

Reported average turnaround times can often mask a great deal of variability. From the customer's perspective, consistency of speed may be more important than a service that is sometimes "fast." Several studies have found that delivery speed (turnaround time) is not correlated with customer satisfaction, and that interactions with service staff have a greater impact.[9]

Among the variables that affect the results of the various studies are:

- The definition used for *turnaround time*;
- How time is measured—calendar days or work days;
- How the request is transmitted—electronically via an ILL management system, via e-mail, or via U.S. mail;
- Whether the library is participating in a small group of libraries that provide "fast" service to one another; and
- Whether the requests are verified.

Figure 8.1 illustrates that the clock calculations to start and stop turnaround time can vary—often significantly. The majority of interlibrary loan studies start the clock when the request is transmitted to the first library (not when the request is received from the user) and stop the clock when the material is received by the library (not in the hands of the customer). Starting the clock when the patron submits the request and stopping it when the patron receives the item is known as "satisfaction time."

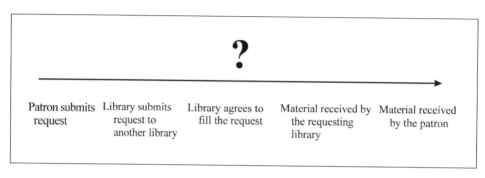

Figure 8.1. When Does the Turnaround "Clock" Start and Stop?

A survey of faculty found that 75 percent of the faculty did not want to wait longer than one to two weeks for document delivery.[10]

The Colorado State University Libraries have developed RapidILL, a system that includes the holdings for each participating library. The resource-sharing database allows a library to exclude items that are oversized or rare, as well as missing issues from print journal title runs, thus routing requests to libraries for materials they are willing to loan (and have the material on the shelf). Libraries using RapidILL have lower costs and improved turnaround times.[11]

Clearly, the ready availability of electronic journals and other online materials is having an impact on interlibrary loan. An interlibrary loan article sharing data from the 26 largest libraries in Illinois shows a 26 percent drop in overall article requests over a three-year period.[12]

Fill Rate

The fill rate, success rate, or satisfaction rate is the proportion of requested items that were received by the library, within a defined period of time, compared to the total number of requests. The majority of studies report a fill rate that exceeds 80 percent for the borrowing library.

Factors that influence the results of a fill rate analysis include:

- whether the analysis includes all designated suppliers or only the first designated supplier (the customer is only concerned with getting the material and not the number of suppliers approached);
- the type of item requested (books, journal articles, media, other types of materials);
- whether potential or actual fill rates are being calculated;
- the point in the process at which the fill rate is being measured;
- the location of the measurement activity—requesting or supplying library; and
- whether the calculation is based on the number of requests or the number of attempts.

One interesting study calculated four different fill rates (using different alternative methods). This revealed that the manner in which data are collected is critical:[13]

- **Monthly statistical returns.** Suppliers had an overall fill rate of 74 percent for all requests. Requesters had a final fill rate of 80 percent, counting the final successful attempt.
- **Transaction tracking—longitudinal.** This approach yielded a 92 percent final fill rate, taking all attempts into account, over a long period of time.
- **Transaction recording—cross-section.** This method provides a snapshot view of the request status at one point in time and thus yields a lower fill rate of 78 percent.
- **A questionnaire to determine customer perceptions of fill rates.** Results varied depending on the time interval between the request and when the material was received by the customer.

An analysis of interlibrary loan data over a three-year period for a consortium of large academic libraries (Committee on Institutional Cooperation) found that 19 percent of borrowing requests were unfilled.[14] Table 8.3 identifies the reasons why libraries are unable to fill requests. Reasons for the "owned but not available" category include items in circulation, not found on the shelf, and so forth.

Table 8.3. Reasons for Unfilled ILL Requests

Study*	Year	Volume Not Owned	Loan Prohibited	Owned But Not Available
Seaman	1992	60%	44%	38%
Guyonneau	1993		29% b	41% b
		53% j		27% j
Medina & Thornton	1996	39%		38%

b=books
j=journal articles
   *Scott Seaman. An Examination of Unfilled OCLC Lending and Photocopy Requests. *Information Technology and Libraries*, 11 (3), 1992, 229–35; Christine H. Guyonneau. Performance Measurements for ILL: An Examination. *Journal of Interlibrary Loan, Document Delivery & Information Supply*, 3 (3), 1993, 101–26; and Sue Medina and Linda Thornton. Cannot Supply: An Examination of ILL Requests Which Could Not Be Filled by Members of the Network of Alabama Libraries. *Journal of Interlibrary Loan, Document Delivery & Information Supply*, 6 (4), 1996, 11–33.

Costs

Although the majority of studies examine costs at the individual library level, some cost studies have been prepared at the state level and at the network or consortium level. Most libraries will track the cost per filled request, and the mean costs can be quite variable—from about $1 to slightly more than $18 per filled request.[15] The costs for materials filled by a commercial supplier are also variable—from a little more than $8 to slightly more than $33 per request. A summary of the costs and delivery speed for a number of studies is shown in Table 8.4.

Please note that a great deal of caution should be exercised when attempting to compare costs from one library to another. Unless a group of libraries is participating in a cost analysis that carefully defines all cost components and provides a consistent process for capturing, reporting, and analyzing the data, the comparisons are not very meaningful.

Table 8.4. Summary of Interlibrary Loan Findings

Study*	Year	Cost of Borrow Request ($)	Cost of Lending Request ($)	Borrow + Lending Cost ($)	Average Turnaround Time (Days)	Borrowing Fill Rate
Roche	1993	18.62	10.93	29.55		
Stolt	1995	14.72			10.5	82%
Levene —U of AR —IA State U	1996	2.11 1.46			15.4 8.4	
Naylor	1997	8.51	4.68			86%
Jackson —research —college	1998			27.83 19.33	15.6 10.8	85% 91%
Jackson —mediated ILL —RAPID	2004	17.50 5.41			7.6 3.4	

*Marilyn M. Roche. *ALG/RLG Interlibrary Loan Cost Study: A Joint Effort by the Association of Research Libraries and the Research Libraries Group.* Washington, DC: Association of Research Libraries, 1993; Wilbur A. Stolt, Pat L. Weaver-Meyers, and Molly Murphy. Interlibrary Loan and Customer Satisfaction: How Important Is Delivery Speed?, in Richard Amrhein (Ed.). *Continuity and Transformation; The Promise of Confluence: Proceedings of the Seventh National Conference of the Association of College and Research Libraries, Pittsburgh, Pennsylvania, March 29–April 1 1995.* Chicago: Association of College and Research Libraries, 1995; Lee-Allison Levene and Wayne A. Pedersen. Patron Satisfaction at Any Cost? A Case Study of Interlibrary Loan in Two U.S. Research Libraries. *Journal of Library Administration*, 23 (1–2), 1996, 55–71; Ted Naylor. The Cost of Interlibrary Loan Services in a Medium-Sized Academic Library. *Journal of Interlibrary Loan, Document Delivery & Information Supply*, 8, 1997, 51–61; Mary E. Jackson. *Measuring the Performance of Interlibrary Loan Operations.* Washington, DC: Association of Research Libraries, 1998; Mary E. Jackson. *Assessing ILL/DD Services: New Cost-Effective Alternatives.* Washington, DC: Association of Research Libraries, 2004.

Among the variables that will influence the calculations of cost figures are the following:

- What components are included in the cost calculation[16]
- Staff—can account for 75 percent or more of interlibrary loan operations in a library
- Networking/communications
- Delivery method
- Photocopying/scanning
- Supplies
- Software and computer equipment
- Rental and maintenance

- Direct borrowing costs
- Indirect borrowing costs.
- The pay rates for different personnel classifications
- Whether indirect costs (benefits) and copyright cost are included
- The year the study was conducted

Interlibrary resource sharing costs more than $30 per transaction, one-third of which is borne by the lending institution.[17]

Access versus Ownership

Historically libraries focused on building their just-in-case collections by purchasing and providing access to a variety of material types, but the bulk of materials purchased were books. More recently, libraries have been focusing less on building collections and more on providing access to content by licensing e-resources. The literature suggests that there are two approaches in preparing an analysis of the issue of access versus ownership:

- Comparing actual expenses for purchasing material to the hypothetical cost of providing access; and
- Comparing the costs of providing access (interlibrary loan/document delivery) to the hypothetical costs of purchase.

As shown in Table 8.5, the majority of studies suggest that access is considerably less expensive than ownership. In 1995, Eleanor Gossen and Suzanne Irving at the SUNY Albany campus found that the cost of providing access to all periodical subscriptions (based on observed usage) would have been $2,900,456, while the actual subscription costs were $1,273,531.[18] Gossen and Irving suggest that access is cost-effective for any serial title used five times or fewer during the year. Rather than using a rule of thumb, Bruce Kingma has suggested using graphs or a mathematical model to determine the access "break-even point"—when access is more cost effective than ownership.[19]

One study found no impact on the number of ILL requests after a significant journal cancellation project.[20]

Requested Items Owned by the Library

Requests made directly by users of an interlibrary loan system, often called an unmediated service, are frequently for materials already owned by the library. The percent of requests owned by the library varies greatly—from 15 percent to as much as 76 percent, according to several studies. There may be a number of reasons for this:

- The library's catalog is not consulted prior to making an interlibrary loan request.
- The library's catalog may not clearly reveal what holdings are owned by the library.
- The customer may prefer document delivery rather than retrieving the article from the library.
- The desired item may not be on the shelf—that is, it may be missing or checked out.

An average of 25 percent of ILL borrowing requests were canceled due to local availability—the range was from 8 to 33 percent—in a study conducted by a consortium of large academic libraries.[21]

Table 8.5. Cost of Ownership vs. Access

Focus of Study	Cost of Ownership ($)	Cost of Access ($)	Author*	Location of Study
Journals accessed 5 times or more	220,000	4,034	Anthes	Wichita State University library
Journals requested 10 times or more	28,229	5,629	Kleiner & Hamaker	Louisiana State University library
Electrical engineering journal articles requested	89,544	6,264	Ferguson & Kehoe	Columbia University
Physics journal articles requested	33,628	1,872	Ferguson & Kehoe	Columbia University
Biology periodical articles requested	343,926	28,674	Ferguson & Kehoe	Columbia University
Journal articles requested	62,800	8,700	Fuseler	Colorado State University Libraries
Providing access to 1,060 articles from 480 canceled journals	207,000	12,278	Currie	Louisiana State University library
Access to articles from canceled journals	53,344	7,123	Wilson & Alexander	Texas A&M University library

*Mary Anthes. An Experiment in Unmediated Document Delivery: EbscoDOC at Wichita State University. *Library Collections, Acquisitions & Technical Services*, 23, Spring 1999, 1–13; Jane P. Kleiner and Charles A. Hamaker. Libraries 2000: Transforming Libraries Using Document Delivery, Needs Assessment and Networked Resources. *College & Research Libraries,* 58, July 1997, 355–74; Anthony W. Ferguson and Kathleen Kehoe. Access vs. Ownership: What Is Most Cost Effective in the Sciences. *Journal of Library Administration*, 19 (2), 1993, 89–99; Elizabeth A. Fuseler. Providing Access to Journals—Just in Time or Just in Case? *College & Research Libraries News*, 55, March 1994, 130–32, 148; Debra L. Currie. Serials Redesign: Using Electronic Document Delivery to Reshape Access to Agricultural Journal Literature. *Journal of Agricultural & Food Information*, 3 (2), 1995, 13–22; Mary Dabney Wilson and Whitney Alexander. Automated Interlibrary Loan/Document Delivery Data Applications for Serials Collection Development. *Serials Review*, 25 (4), 1999, 11–19.

An analysis at the University of Colorado at Boulder compared interlibrary loan requests to the number of titles owned in 25 subject areas and found that for every request, the library owned from 9 to 144 titles.[22]

One study compared the time to recall an item in circulation to the time to retrieve the same item using interlibrary loan from anther library and found that recalled items were returned to the library in an average of 6.3 days, while interlibrary loan took an average of 7.3 days. The materials then sat on the hold shelf for the patron for another 3.2 days for recalled items and 4.5 days for ILL materials.[23]

Concentration and Scatter in Requested Materials

The customers of any library will find a majority of what they need in the library's physical and electronic collections. In addition, it stands to reason that the majority of interlibrary loan requests will be for materials that are infrequently used. These infrequently used or "scattered" resources are similar to what Chris Anderson describes as the "long tail."[24]

The "long tail" was described much earlier and is known as Bradford's Law, which demonstrates that a subject area's journals can be divided into zones: a small number of highly used titles and a large number of infrequently used titles.

Analysis of interlibrary lending data from 1956 led to Urquhart's Law, which states that interlibrary loan demand for a periodical is, as a rule, highly skewed, with less than 10 percent of the journal collection accounting for about 80 percent of the loans, and the number of loans of given journals was highly correlated with the number of UK libraries holding these journals. Urquhart further suggested that the use of a single serial can be modeled by a Poisson distribution.[25] Table 8.6 provides summary information about other studies that have examined the distribution of ILL requested materials.

Table 8.6. Distribution of Requested Materials

Study	Percent of Titles Requested Multiple Times	Percent of Titles Requested Once
Lacroix[i]	Less than 10% requested 10+ times	76%
Prabha and Marsh[ii]	16% of 120 titles requested 5+ times	48%
Gossen and Kaczor[iii]	6 titles requested 5+ times	80%

i. Eve-Marie Lacroix. Interlibrary Loan in U.S. Health Sciences Libraries: Journal Article Use. *Bulletin of the Medical Library Association*, 82, October 1994, 363–68.
ii. Chandra Prabha and Elizabeth C. Marsh. Commercial Document Suppliers: How Many of the ILL/DD Periodical Article Requests Can They Fulfill? *Library Trends*, 45, Winter 1997, 551–68.
iii. Eleanor A. Gossen and Sue Kaczor. Variation in Interlibrary Loan Use by University of Albany Science Departments. *Library Resources & Technical Services*, 41, January 1997, 17–28.

Impact of a Discovery Service

Penn State University libraries conducted an analysis four years after the implementation of a discovery service (in this case, Summon) to better understand the possible impact of the new system on interlibrary loan. The analysis showed that there was a 22 percent reduction in interlibrary loan borrowing (especially among undergraduate students). The number of ILL requests that were cancelled due to local ownership dropped significantly.[26]

In general, most libraries using the WorldCat Local Discovery Service experienced an increase in interlibrary loan borrowing following implementation (see studies at the University of Washington,[27] University of Maryland and Ohio State University, and Washington State University.[28]) Other studies offer a contrary perspective in that requests for journal articles have declined while requests for books have increased,[29] and others report that ILL remains flat.[30]

Other Topics

Clearly, it is possible to conduct any number of studies pertaining to interlibrary loan and document delivery. Among the topics might be characteristics of the users of this service, characteristics of the requested materials, and reasons for not being able to fulfill a request.

An analysis of ILL transaction data over a two-year period at the University of Tennessee at Chattanooga revealed that using a centered moving average with seasonal variation would accurately forecast the demand for ILL services (which would be helpful in scheduling staff).[31]

An evaluation of unfilled interlibrary lending requests at the University of Indianapolis identified a number of reasons for the unavailability of the requested items. Problems within the library included poor working habits of the staff, cataloging errors, and loss of materials.[32]

PATRON-DRIVEN ACQUISITIONS

Patron-driven acquisitions (PDAs)—not to be confused with "public displays of affection"—respond to patron requests by purchasing (e-books or print books) on demand. PDA moves the library to a just-in-time delivery model by involving the library's customers in the process of building a collection. A number of observers have suggested that the just-in-case collection-building model is no longer sustainable.

But what has been the impact of PDA (sometimes called demand-driven acquisitions) on interlibrary loan? Several articles have suggested that PDA is a success in terms of cost-effectiveness and appropriateness of selections, based on studies at Purdue University libraries,[33] California State University, Fullerton,[34] and Stetson University library (59 percent of the purchased e-books were used more than once).[35]

The University of Nebraska at Lincoln library found that its PDA program was a cost-effective way to acquire materials suitable for its collection, but that the materials also met the needs of several patrons. In addition, PDA materials circulate at higher rates and experience elevated amounts of repeat circulation.[36]

However, the Brigham Young University Libraries compared the costs of monograph ILL with the costs of monograph accession, including staffing overhead costs for both. The analysis revealed that the costs of an ILL purchase-on-demand was $58.83 per title and that four uses of the title makes purchasing the title more cost-effective.[37]

CUSTOMER PERSPECTIVE

User Surveys

Libraries frequently conduct one-time or periodic surveys of interlibrary loan users using a Likert scale to determine levels of customer satisfaction. Usually the results are reported as the percent of satisfied customers.

The ARL ILL/DD Performance Measures Study surveyed a random sample of users from each participating library and found high levels of satisfaction for timeliness, quality and completeness of materials, and staff helpfulness.[38]

Françoise Hébert used a SERVQUAL type of survey instrument and found that public library users of ILL ranked reliability as the most important dimension, followed by responsiveness. Again, staff interactions had a greater impact on overall customer satisfaction ratings than did turnaround times.[39] For more about SERVQUAL and customer satisfaction, see Chapter 18.

In addition to doing a survey, some libraries have used a focus group to learn more about the perceptions of interlibrary loan users and their needs. Focus groups of ILL customers have been used at Emory University[40] and Carnegie Mellon University.[41]

One study of academic library users examined ILL customer satisfaction and found that the highest priority should be on obtaining material, regardless of speed and cost.[42] An analysis of comments from another customer satisfaction survey of ILL services found that users value the service when staff interactions are experienced positively.[43]

One study compared ILL services at three different libraries using a patron survey and found, not surprisingly, that their users valued the services, especially the convenience and speed of delivery.[44]

Mark Kinnucan used the conjoint analysis approach in a series of interviews with faculty and graduate students and found that the price of the document was the most important consideration ($3 or less) and that turnaround time had only a modest effect.[45]

A service at the Texas A&M University Libraries called deliverEdocs provides desktop delivery of any article, even those on the Texas A&M library shelves. A customer survey revealed that 43 percent felt they should receive the article within two days and 32 percent within three days for materials owned locally. Further, 41 percent felt that interlibrary loan materials should be available within four to seven days, and 32 percent felt that two weeks was acceptable.[46]

INTERLIBRARY LOAN OPTIONS

Some libraries have been experimenting in order to determine the effectiveness of some ILL alternatives, including print-on-demand, pay per view, Circ-to-Circ systems and document delivery.

Print-on-demand (POD) is being used by some libraries to print older books, especially those no longer covered by copyright, in lieu of absorbing the costs of storing and requesting the specific item from storage. Some libraries ask that the POD item not be returned to the library.[47] William Dougherty suggested that it costs about $10 to print a book on demand using an Expresso Book Machine, whereas most ILL studies suggest that the cost to borrow an item from another library runs about $30.[48]

Pay per view (PPV), sometimes called article-level acquisitions, may be an affordable option for journals to which a library does not subscribe. Some libraries use both a library-mediated approach (staff access and retrieve articles for a patron) and an unmediated approach (patrons have direct access to all of a publisher's journals). The University of Tennessee Health Science Center used PPV (a volume discount made this option viable) and was able to provide access to some 700 journal titles in a revenue-neutral manner (by cancelling subscriptions).[49] In general, libraries employing PPV report fiscal savings and high levels of customer satisfaction. Nevertheless, the PPV approach is not likely to replace ILL in the short-term future.[50]

Circ-to-Circ systems provide a shared catalog among all of the consortia member libraries. Patrons place a "hold" on a specific item located in another library and the item is delivered in a timely manner using a delivery service. One study found that the cost of a Circ-to-Circ system borrowed item was $3.85, whereas traditional ILL borrowing cost $12.11 per item—a savings of $8.26 per request.[51]

An analysis of the existing ILL service provided to the Massachusetts Library System member libraries revealed that the use of OCLC ILL system plus all other associated costs meant that each per-member library request transaction totaled slightly more than $20. The use of a shared "discovery service" that allowed patrons to search and make their own requests would significantly lower the per-request cost.[52]

Document delivery is another option that some libraries use to provide access either to specific journal titles or to a subject area that receives relative few ILL requests. Document delivery also ensures copyright compliance (this also frees up library staff from needing to do copyright compliance for these requests).[53] In addition to the traditional document delivery suppliers, new players are entering the marketplace with new business models (consider Deep Dyve, which allows one-time viewing of an article for a reasonable price). One library found that using a single service, in this case ReadCube, was more cost-effective than licensing "big deals."[54]

BEST PRACTICES

Lee Hilyar, in an interesting article, suggests best practices for operating and managing interlibrary loan services in libraries.[55] The Greater Western Library Alliance (GWLA) created an Interlibrary Loan Best Practices Task Force, which developed an noteworthy framework:

Conceptual Best Practices—includes the goals, standards, benchmarks, and philosophical framework within which interlibrary loan operates.

Structural Best Practices—includes the staff, equipment, technology, and organizational structures necessary to support ILL.

Procedural Best Practices—the daily routines, activities, and procedures for handling the ILL workload.

GWLA noted a 77 percent improvement in the delivery of journal articles within 24 hours, along with a 16 percent improvement of the delivery of books within 4 days.[56] GWLA member libraries use the RapidILL system.

An ILL unit can cut its greenhouse emissions in half by reusing packaging materials. In addition, padded mailers are easier on the environment than cardboard boxes and nylon bags are better than plastic bins.[57]

The ALA RUSA "Rethinking Resource Sharing Initiative" has developed the STAR Checklist to provide staff with an opportunity to reflect and review on their resource sharing/interlibrary loan policies, procedures, and services (the checklist is available at http://rethinkingresourcesharing.org/star-checklist-2/). The value of the checklist is that it provides the impetus for conversations about ways to improve services in each library.

SUMMARY

After reviewing the research pertaining to interlibrary loan and document delivery, it is possible to reach the following conclusions:

- The ILL/DD fill rates are about the same for libraries and commercial firms.
- Commercial document delivery is more expensive but typically faster than interlibrary loan.
- Access to licensed e-resources is the dominant method for a majority of libraries.
- The ILL demand for books is declining.

- A significant proportion of requests are for materials owned by the library.
- Libraries can make improvements in workflow procedures to improve turnaround times.
- User satisfaction is not related to speed of delivery.
- Any library using a patron unmediated interlibrary loan service will need to modify its workflow procedures to check whether the requested item is owned by the library, in order to keep costs down.

It is also important to recognize that ILL is a part of a larger delivery system (from the perspective of the customer) and thus it is suggested that libraries should evaluation ILL activities within a broader context. Specifically,

- Customers are looking to be able to discover, request, and track the progress of a desired item
- The objective is to get the desired item into the hands of the customer within the expected time frame (the shorter the time frame, the more expensive the process will be)
- The system should reduce the need for physical delivery when possible (finds the closest available copy or offers a digital surrogate)
- The system selects the "least expensive" copy in terms of transportation costs (by exploring a number of options automatically—scan on demand, print on demand, delivery of an electronic copy, purchase on demand, and interlibrary loan)

NOTES

1. Rick Anderson. To Share or Not to Share? Peer to Peer Review. *Library Journal*, October 25, 2012.

2. Lorcan Dempsey, Constance Malpas, and Brian Lavoie. Collection Directions: The Evolution of Library Collections and Collecting. *portal: Libraries and the Academy*, 14 (3), 2014, 393–423.

3. Maurice Line. Performance Measurement Within Interlending and Document Supply Systems, in *Interlending and Document Supply: Proceedings of the Second International Conference*. Boston: IFLA Office for International Lending, 1992, 5–13.

4. Peter Lor. The Analysis of ILL Systems: A Taxonomy of Variables. *Journal of Interlibrary Loan, Document Delivery & Information Supply*, 1 (1), 1990, 43–66.

5. Thomas J. Waldhart. Performance Evaluation of ILL in the United States: A Review of the Research. *Library & Information Science Research*, 7 (4), 1985, 313–31.

6. Joan Stein. Measuring the Performance of ILL and Document Supply: 1986 to 1998. *Performance Measurement and Metrics*, 2 (2001), 11–72.

7. Mike McGrath. Interlending and Document Supply: A Review of the Recent Literature: No. 91. *Interlending and Document Supply*, 44 (1), 2016, 1–6; Mike McGrath. Interlending and Document Supply: A Review of the Recent Literature: No. 90. *Interlending and Document Supply*, 43 (3), 2015, 160–66; Mike McGrath. Interlending and Document Supply: A Review of the Recent Literature: No. 89. *Interlending and Document Supply*, 43 (2), 2015, 62–67; Mike McGrath. Interlending and Document Supply: A Review of the Recent Literature: No. 88. *Interlending and Document Supply*, 43 (1), 2015, 53–58; Mike McGrath. Interlending and Document Supply: A Review of the Recent Literature: No. 87. *Interlending & Document Supply*, 42 (4), 2014, 199–204.

8. ISO. *ISO 11620 Information and Documentation: Library Performance Indicators*. Geneva: International Organization for Standardization, 1998.

9. Wilbur Stolt, Pat Weaver-Meyers, and Molly Murphy. Interlibrary Loan and Customer Satisfaction: How Important Is Delivery Speed, in *Continuity and Transformation: The Promise of Confluence: Proceedings of the Seventh National Conference of the Association of College and Research*

Libraries. Chicago: Association of College and Research Libraries, 1995, 365–71; Lee-Allison Levene and Wayne Pedersen. Patron Satisfaction at Any Cost? A Case Study of Interlibrary Loan in Two U.S. Research Libraries. *Journal of Library Administration,* 23 (1–2), 1996, 55–71; Pat L. Weaver-Meyers and Wilbur A. Stolt. Delivery Speed, Timeliness and Satisfaction: Patrons' Perceptions About ILL Service. *Journal of Library Administration,* 23 (1–2), 1996, 23–42; Sheila Walters. User Behavior in a Non-Mediated Document Delivery Environment: The Direct Doc Pilot Project at Arizona State. *Computers in Libraries,* 15, October 1995, 22–24, 26.

10. Elizabeth P. Roberts. ILL/Document Delivery as an Alternative to Local Ownership of Seldom-Used Scientific Journals. *The Journal of Academic Librarianship,* 18, March 1992, 32, 34.

11. Jane Smith. The RAPIDly Changing World of Interlibrary Loan. *Technical Services Quarterly,* 23 (4), 2006, 17–25.

12. Lynn Wiley and Tina E. Chrzastowski. The Impact of Electronic Journals on Interlibrary Lending: A Longitudinal Study of Statewide Interlibrary Loan Article Sharing in Illinois. *Library Collections, Acquisitions, & Technical Services,* 29, 2005, 364–81.

13. Peter Lor. Measuring the Outcomes of Southern African Interlending Requests: A Comparison of Measurement Approaches. *South African Journal of Library and Information Science,* 57 (4), 1989, 362–71.

14. Anne K. Beaubien, Jennifer Kuehn, Barbara Smolow, and Suzanne M. Ward. Challenges Facing High-Volume Interlibrary Loan Operations: Baseline Data and Trends in the CIC Consortium. *College & Research Libraries,* 67 (1), January 2006, 64–84.

15. Thomas E. Nisonger. Accessing Information: The Evaluation Research. *Collection Management,* 26 (1), 2001, 1–23.

16. Anthony W. Ferguson and Kathleen Kehoe. Access vs. Ownership: What Is Most Cost Effective in the Sciences. *Journal of Library Administration,* 19 (2), 1993, 89–99.

17. Marilyn M. Roche. *ARL/RLG Interlibrary Loan Cost Study.* Washington, DC: Association of Research Libraries, 1993.

18. Eleanor A. Gossen and Suzanne Irving. Ownership Versus Access and Low-Use Periodical Titles. *Library Resources & Technical Services,* 39, January 1995, 43–52.

19. Bruce R. Kingma. Economic Issues in Document Delivery: Access Versus Ownership and Library Consortia. *Serials Librarian,* 34 (1–2), 1998, 203–11; Bruce R. Kingma. Interlibrary Loan and Resource Sharing: The Economics of the SUNY Express Consortium. *Library Trends,* 45, Winter 1997, 518–30; Bruce R. Kingma and Suzanne Irving. The Economics of Access Versus Ownership: The Costs and Benefits of Access to Scholarly Articles via Interlibrary Loan and Journal Subscriptions. *Journal of Interlibrary Loan, Document Delivery & Information Supply,* 6 (3), 1996, 1–79.

20. Kristin Calvert, Rachel Fleming, and Katherine Hill. Impact of Journal Cancellations on Interlibrary Loan Demand. *Serials Review,* 39 (3), 2013, 184–87.

21. Anne K. Beaubien, Jennifer Kuehn, Barbara Smolow, and Suzanne M. Ward. Challenges Facing High-Volume Interlibrary Loan Operations: Baseline Data and Trends in the CIC Consortium. *College & Research Libraries,* 67 (1), January 2006, 64–84.

22. Jennifer E. Knievel, Heather Wicht, and Lynn Silipigni Connaway. Use of Circulation Statistics and Interlibrary Loan Data in Collection Management. *College & Research Libraries,* 67 (1), January 2006, 35–49.

23. David J. Gregory and Wayne A. Pedersen. Book Availability Revisited: Turnaround Time for Recalls Versus Interlibrary Loans. *College & Research Libraries,* 64, July 2003, 283–99.

24. Chris Anderson. The Long Tail. *Wired,* 12 (10), October 2004; Chris Anderson. *The Long Tail: Why the Future of Business Is Selling Less of More.* New York: Hyperion, 2006.

25. Stephen J. Bensman. Urquhart's Law: Probability and the Management of Scientific and Technical Journal Collections. Part 1. The Law's Initial Formulation and Statistical Bases. *Science & Technology Libraries,* 26 (1), 2005, 11–68; Part 2. Probability in the Development of a Central Document Delivery Collection. *Science & Technology Libraries,* 26 (2), 2005, 5–31; Part 3. The Law's Final Formulation and Implications for Library Systems. *Science & Technology Libraries,* 26 (2), 2005, 33–69.

26. Linda R. Musser and Barbara M. Coopey. Impact of a Discovery System on Interlibrary Loan. *College & Research Libraries,* September 2016, 643–53.

27. Thomas Deardoff and Heidi Nance. WorldCat Local Implementation: The Impact on Interlibrary Loan. *Interlending & Document Supply*, 3 (7), 2009, 177–80.

28. Zinthia Brice-Rosales. OCLC WorldCat: Interactivity and Mobility Create a Winning Circulation, in Discovering What Works: Librarians Compare Discovery Interfaces. *Library Journal Reviews*, December 7, 2011.

29. Kristin Calvert. Maximizing Academic Library Collections: Measuring Changes in Use Patterns Owing to EBSCO Discovery Service. *College & Research Libraries*, 76 (1), January 2015, 81–99.

30. Jody Fagan and Meris Mandernach. Discovery by the Numbers: An Examination of the Impact of a Discovery Tool Through Usage Statistics. *Proceedings of the Charleston Library Conference, 2011.* Charleston, SC: Purdue University Press.

31. Mohammad Ahmadi, Parthasarati Dileepan, and Sarla Murgai. Predicting Demand of Inter-Library Loan Requests. *The Bottom Line*, 26 (3), 2013, 116–28.

32. Christine H. Guyonneau. Performance Measurements for ILL: An Evaluation. *Journal of Interlibrary Loan & Information Supply*, 3 (3), 1993, 101–26.

33. Kristine Anderson, Robert S. Freeman, Jean-Pierre V. M. Hérubel, Lawrence J. Mykytiuk, Judith M. Nixon, and Suzanne M. Ward. Buy, Don't Borrow: Bibliographers' Analysis of Academic Library Collection Development Through Interlibrary Loan Requests. *Collection Management*, 27 (3/4), 2002, 1–11.

34. William Breitbach and Joy E. Lambert. Patron-Driven Ebook Acquisition. *Computers in Libraries*, 31 (6), 2011, 17–20.

35. Debbi Dinkins. Individual Title Requests in PDA Collections. *College & Research Libraries News*, 73 (5), May 2012, 249–55.

36. David C. Tyler, Yang Xu, Joyce C. Melvin, Marylou Epp, and Anita M. Kreps. Just How Right Are the Customers? An Analysis of the Relative Performance of Patron-Initiated Interlibrary Loan Monograph Purchases. *Collection Management,* 35 (3–4), 2010, 162–79.

37. Gerrit van Dyk. Interlibrary Loan Purchase-on-Demand: A Misleading Literature. *Library Collections, Acquisitions, & Technical Services*, 35 (2–3), 2011, 83–89.

38. Mary Jackson, *Measuring the Performance of Interlibrary Loan Operations in North American Research and College Libraries.* Washington, DC: Association of Research Libraries, 1998.

39. Françoise Hébert. An Unobtrusive Investigation of ILL in Large Public Libraries in Canada. *Library & Information Science Research*, 16, 1994, 3–21; Françoise Hébert. Service Quality: ILL in the Public Library, in J. Watkins (Ed.). *Interlending and Document Supply: Proceedings of the Fourth International Conference. Papers from the Conference Held in Calgary, June 1995.* Boston: IFLA, 1996, 111–17.

40. Molidori Group, Inc. *Emory University General Libraries ILL User Survey: Executive Summary.* Atlanta: Emory University General Libraries, 1997.

41. Joan Stein. ILL User Focus Groups: Final Report, Carnegie Mellon University Libraries. Unpublished report. Contact Joan at joan@andrew.cmu.edu.

42. Anna H. Perrault and Marjo Arseneau. User Satisfaction and Interlibrary Loan Service: A Study at Louisiana State University. *RQ*, 35, Fall 1995, 90–100.

43. Yem S. Fong. The Value of Interlibrary Loan: An Analysis of Customer Satisfaction Survey Comments. *Journal of Library Administration*, 23 (1/2), 1996, 43–54.

44. Micquel Little and Lars Leon. Assessing the Value of ILL to Our Users: A Comparative Study of Three US Libraries. *Interlending & Document Supply*, 43 (1), 2015, 34–40.

45. Mark Kinnucan. Demand for Document Delivery and ILL in Academic Settings. *Library & Information Science Research*, 15, 1993, 355–74; Mark Kinnucan. Modeling User's Preferences for Document Delivery. *OCLC Systems and Services*, 10, 1994, 93–98.

46. Zheng Ye (Lan) Yang. Customer Satisfaction with Interlibrary Loan Service—Deliver Edocs: A Case Study. *Journal of Interlibrary Loan, Document Delivery & Information Supply*, 14 (4), 2004, 79–94.

47. Suzanne Wilson-Higgins. Could Print-on-Demand Actually Be the "New Interlibrary Loan"? *Interlending & Document Supply*, 39 (10), 2011, 5–8.

48. William Dougherty. Print on Demand: What Librarians Should Know. *The Journal of Academic Librarianship*, 35 (2), 2009, 184–86.

49. R. Fought. Breaking Inertia: Increasing Access to Journals During a Period of Declining Budgets: A Case Study. *Journal of the Medical Library Association*, 102 (3), 2014, 192–96.

50. Heather Brown. Pay-per-View in Interlibrary Loan: A Case Study. *Journal of the Medical Library Association*, 100 (2), April 2012, 98–103; Patrick Carr and Marie Collins. Acquiring Articles Through Unmediated, User-Initiated Pay-per-View Transactions: An Assessment of Current Practices. *Serials Review*, 35 (4), December 2009, 272–77; L. Schell, K. Ginanni, and B. Heet. Playing the Field: Pay-per-View E-Journals and E-Books. *Serials Librarian*, 58 (1–4), January 2010, 87–96; C. Chamberlain and B. MacAlpine. Pay-per-View Article Access: A Viable Replacement for Subscriptions? *Serials,* 21 (1), March 2008, 30–34; Mindy King, Aaron Nichols, and Michael Hanson. Pay-per-View Article Delivery at the University of Wisconsin–Stevens Point. *Serials Librarian*, 60 (1–4), January 2011, 223–28.

51. Lars Leon and N. Kress. Looking at Resource Sharing Costs. *Interlending & Document Supply,* 40 (2), 2012, 81–87.

52. Ruth Kowal. *Massachusetts Library System (MLS) Mediated Interlibrary Loan Service Models: Review and Evaluation.* Marlborough, MA, May 2012. Available at http://www.masslibsystem.org /wp-content/uploads/MLS-Final-5-5-121.pdf.

53. CLS UC Article Delivery Service Exploration Task Force. *Article Delivery Services: Environmental Scan of Content, Services, and Business Models for US Libraries.* Berkeley, CA: CLS UC Article Delivery Service Exploration Task Force, University of California, May 5, 2014.

54. Mark England and Phill Jones. (2013). Diversification of Access Pathways and the Role of Demand Driven Acquisition—A Case Study at the University of Utah. Presentation at NASIG Conference, Buffalo, NY, June 6, 2013.

55. Lee Andre Hilyer. Interlibrary Loan and Document Delivery: Best Practices for Operating and Managing Interlibrary Loan Services in All Libraries. *Journal of Interlibrary Loan, Document Delivery & Electronic Reserve*, 16 (1/2), 2006, 1–147.

56. Carol Kochan and Lars Leon. Revisiting Interlibrary Loan Best Practices: Still Viable? *Interlending & Document Supply*, 41 (4), 2013, 113–19.

57. Dennis Massie. *Greening Interlibrary Loan Practices.* Dublin, OK: OCLC Research, 2010.

9

Evaluation of Automated Systems

To err is human, but to really foul things up requires a computer.

—Phillip Howard[1]

SERVICE DEFINITION

Libraries of all types and sizes have embraced information technology (IT) to such a great degree that any effort to evaluate automated systems seems almost a waste of time. However, information technology is so pervasive that many aspects deserve to be put under the microscope so that the impacts of IT can be better understood.

EVALUATION QUESTIONS

Historically, the evaluation of automated systems was focused on the suitability of a particular system being implemented in a library (with specific needs). The evaluation of systems has meant that the various systems exist alongside one another (often this is referred to as silos). Of late, there is increasing interest in library management systems that integrate several silo systems into one comprehensive system. In addition, there is increasing interest in determining how information technology provides value to the end user of the various automated systems. Thus, some of the questions that might be considered are:

- What are the risks and rewards of moving to a cloud-based library solution?
- What silo system can be integrated into a new library management system and what financial benefits can be achieved?
- How does the use of information technology in a library setting provide value to the library customer?
- What are the risks and benefits of sharing information technology with a group of libraries?

EVALUATION METHODS

Rather than iterating the various methods that might be used to evaluate automated systems, the chapter is organized around themes that will likely arise in the coming years.

PRIOR EVALUATIONS AND RESEARCH

Among the important issues or topics in evaluation of information technology are:

- Should my library move to the next-generation library management system?
- Should we continue to house and maintain information technology servers (in or near the library), or should we move to cloud-based solutions?
- Should the library choose an open-source solution, or continue to use a vendor-provided solution?
- Should we join (or create) a consortium sharing a library management system?
- What is the best way to evaluate a new discovery system?
- How do we evaluate the library's Web site?
- How important is increased bandwidth in the library to our customers?

Next-Generation Library Management Systems

Libraries have been adopting and using integrated library systems (ILSs) for more than 30 years. However, although the ILS is clearly in the sunset of its usefulness, the next-generation automated system, most often referred to as a library service platform (LSP)—or a library management system, in Europe—is not being implemented as an ILS replacement by libraries at an increasing rate.

Before exploring LSP solutions, it is important to understand one very important term: **multi-tenant software**. Multi-tenant software is an architecture in which a single instance of the software application serves multiple customers. Each customer of the software is called a tenant, and while each tenant has some ability to customize the software in terms of how it looks and acts, the underlying application software cannot be customized. The primary advantage of multi-tenant software is that the vendor needs to make only a single update to the software. Multi-tenant applications can support massive large-scale services such as gmail, Facebook, and Amazon.

The advantages of multi-tenant software from a vendor's perspective should be obvious (significantly reduced costs). The library should also benefit with reduced prices (compared to the same system running in an SaaS—software as a service—mode). More importantly, software updates can be quickly and transparently installed to address security issues, fix bugs, or introduce new features.

Due to the increasing performance of computer system, issues such as system reliability, response times, expandability, ease of use, adherence to standards, and so forth are no longer of primary concern to the library. However, traditional issues such as functionality, support for data standards such as RDA and BIBFRAME, security, and multi-tenant architecture continue to drive the next-generation LSP system selection process.

An LSP differs from the traditional integrated library system in that it:[2]

- Consolidates the management of print and electronic resources
- Provides for extensive metadata management by supporting MARC, XML standards, Dublin Core, RDA, and BIBFRAME
- Replaces several existing products that complement an ILS
- Supports multiple procurement workflows for licensed, purchased, and open-access materials
- Operates using a Web-based interface (Web browser)
- Relies on a services-oriented software architecture
- Exposes application programming interfaces (APIs) for extensibility and interoperability
- Provides for advanced collection analysis and assessment
- Utilizes several knowledge bases for print and electronic resources

Table 9.1 provides an overview comparison of ILS systems compared to LSPs.

Table 9.1. Comparison of ILSs versus LSPs

Category	Integrated Library System (ILS)	Integrated Library System plus additional systems	Library Services Platform (LSP)
Resources managed	Physical	Print, electronic	Electronic, print
Procurement models	Purchase	Purchase, license	License, purchase
Technology	Server-based	Server-based	Multi-tenant
Hosting option	Local installation, vendor hosting	Local installation, vendor hosting	SaaS only
Interoperability	Proprietary APIs, batch transfer	Batch transfer, RESTful APIs	APIs (mostly RESTful)
Knowledge bases	None	None	E-holdings, bibliographic
Patron interface	Browser-based	Browser-based	Browser-based
Staff interface	Graphical desktop (Windows, Mac OS, Java Swing)	Browser-based	Browser-based
Products	SirsiDynix Symphony, Millennium, Polaris	Sierra, SirsiDynix BLUEcloud, Polaris, Apollo	Alma, ProQuest Intota, Sierra, Worldshare Management Services

Among the LSP offerings are systems from EBSCO Discover Service (EDS), Ex Libris (Alma), Innovative Interfaces (Sierra), OCLC (Worldshare Management System or WMS) and SirsiDynix (Blue Sky).

Tip! Important LSP-Related Resources

American Libraries[3] has an annual article about the automation marketplace, as does *Library Journal*.[4] In addition, check out Marshall Breeding's Website, Library Technology Guides, for all things related to automation (www.librarytechnology.org/).

If you are interested in LSP specifications, visit Ken Chad's Web site (UK).[5]

Carl Grant wrote an interesting article, "The Future of Library Systems," in *Information Standards Quarterly*.[6]

Merits of Cloud-Based Solutions

Before exploring cloud-based solutions, it is important to understand some terminology and definitions.

- **SaaS**—Software as a service is an option provided by a vendor in which the vendor assumes responsibility for maintaining the system (performing backups, installing new software, and so forth) rather than the library using a locally installed server. A vendor must make a software update for each customer individually. This service generally frees up a staff person or two. Vendors have been offering this service for a number of years.
- **Cloud computing**—A generally accepted definition of cloud computing is a system that supports[7]
    - **C**—Computing resources
    - **L**—Location independent
    - **O**—Online access
    - **U**—Utility
    - **D**—on-Demand availability

Vendors describe their use of cloud computing in many different ways and thus care should be exercised when using the term "cloud computing." Cloud-based services are delivered over the Internet.

The primary benefit of a cloud-based ILS or LSP is that the library is freed up from the responsibility for the care and maintenance of one or more servers, handling software updates, ensuring that data backups are performed nightly, and so forth. Many libraries have found using an SaaS- or cloud-based library system to be beneficial. The risk is that the system might be slow (this depends in large part on the bandwidth connectivity to and from the library).

Note that some libraries may have restrictions as to where the servers and data can be located for a cloud-based solution.

Open-Source Options

Open-source software (OSS) library systems have been in the marketplace for some time. In order to qualify as open-source software, the source code and technical documentation should be available to be downloaded under a GNU general public license, and the software should be installed and operating in a number of libraries. Not surprisingly, the primary benefit of choosing an open-source solution is economic: libraries need not pay an up-front fee to a vendor to license its software products. Also, in many cases, the support costs are lower with an open-source product than with a commercial product (for the same size library).

The two primary OSS ILS systems are Evergreen (built to scale to very large systems) and Koha (installed in many small and medium-size libraries). As most libraries cannot afford to recruit and retain competent software programmers, several commercial firms offer support for the library open-source software systems (ByWater Solutions, Equinox, and LibLime). Vendors typically charge for data conversion services, hosting a server (SaaS), training, and support. A library (or group of libraries) can ask a vendor to develop software for a fee and have the resulting source code made available for others to use at no cost. Vandana Singh conducted a survey of libraries using open-source ILS systems and found that because there are many channels of technical support, librarians are generally pleased with their ILS systems.[8] Another analysis concluded that there were no significant differences between open-source and proprietary ILS systems in the marketplace.[9]

It should be noted that several versions of the source code for Koha are available (depending on the vendor providing support, as no single repository is being used for Koha worldwide). Edmund Balnaves has suggested that any evaluation of open-source options should consider the developer and support community, the source code characteristics, and the information schema.[10]

The Georgia Public Library System created Evergreen in 2006; Koha was created in New Zealand in 1999. There are now more than 2,500 libraries worldwide that use either Koha or Evergreen solutions.[11] Bob Molyneux explores the past, present, and future of Evergreen in a thoughtful article.[12] Another study explored staff use of the Evergreen system at nine public libraries over the course of a year and found that the primary benefits included the ability to see the availability of materials at other libraries, as well as the ability to place reserves on materials at other libraries.[13]

The Kuali Open Library Environment project, an attempt to develop an open-source library system for large academic libraries that has spent more than $5 million, announced in June 2016 that it was suspending the project.

Merits of a Consortium

Library consortia exist for two possible reasons: to provide a set of services that are lower in cost than an individual library can provide, and to provide services collectively that a single library is unable to perform by itself.

George Machovec has suggested that the most common programmatic areas served by consortia include shared purchasing and sharing technology. Specifically, George identifies the "buying club," shared integrated library systems, shared discovery and delivery systems, shared digital repositories, and shared print archiving.[14] The consortium might be limited to a specific type of library or to libraries in a region. More recently, some consortia have formed that encompass libraries from several states; an example is the Orbis Cascade Alliance, a nonprofit consortium of 39 colleges and universities in Oregon, Washington, and Idaho that offers a range of services including a shared automated system (Ex Libris Alma). Other large consortia include OhioLINK (serving 121 academic libraries), the Illinois Digital Academic Library (with 150 academic institutions as members), Northern Ireland (100 public libraries sharing a SirsiDynix Symphony system), Illinois Heartland Library System (427 libraries sharing a Polaris system), public libraries of the State of South Australia, and the BIBSYS consortium in Norway (105 members sharing Alma), among many others.

The services most frequently provided by consortia include: resource sharing/ILL/document delivery—45 percent; shared automated system—41 percent; cooperative purchasing—38 percent; and electronic resource content licensing—33 percent.[15] In challenging times of budget restrictions or little-or-no annual increases, consortia of all types (but especially statewide consortia) must clearly understand and communicate their value proposition.[16]

A survey of library directors found that societal and economic benefits are at the heart of a decision to join (or leave) a consortium.

> [W]hen given the opportunity to expand access by sharing collections with other college and university libraries, academic library directors should take a broader user perspective that includes their surrounding communities and region. . . . There is also the potential for fostering regional economic development when presented the opportunity to share a larger, more academically-focused collection.[17]

One Colorado consortium prepared a cost-benefit analysis to demonstrate the value of collaborative purchasing (one campus library receives $8.15 of benefits for every dollar it spends), and found positive results.[18]

Two well-known consultants, Rick Lugg and Ruth Fischer, suggest that consortia will play an increasingly important role in the future for five reasons:[19]

1. Shared workloads will keep transaction costs low
2. A higher percentage of collections will be stored offsite in shared regional facilities
3. Tangible collections require proximity to the items being managed
4. Shared technology infrastructure reduces costs and improves service and training
5. Scare expertise and staff capacity can be better distributed regionally

Discovery System Tradeoffs

A discovery system or discovery service (sometimes called a Web-scale discovery service or a resource discovery service) provides a set of tools and user interface that gives patrons the ability to search (and browse) library collections, including electronic resources. A discovery service replaces the library's online public access catalog (OPAC). A library's OPAC typically only provides access to what has been cataloged and is accessible in the library's ILS database: books, media, and some portion of special collections.

The library's ILS database is provided to a discovery service provider and is housed on a remote server (located in the cloud). The discovery service provider also maintains a database of electronic resources that the library subscribes to. The user of the discovery service is able to enter a search in a single search box (similar to a Google search) and retrieve journal articles, physical resources owned by the library, and other electronic resources. In addition to the single search box, discovery products typically also provide relevancy-ranked results, faceted navigation, recommendations, and enriched records. Undergraduate students are seen as the primary users and beneficiaries of a discovery service.

Doug Way has suggested that it is possible to group discovery service literature into five categories:[20]

1. Comparison of products with each other and with Google Scholar
2. Reports on a discovery service implementation at a particular library
3. The impact a discovery service has on other library systems and resources
4. The usability and design of the discovery service
5. The perceptions of students and librarians regarding the discovery service

A literature review focusing on the evaluation and assessment of Web-scale discovery services explored the criteria for choosing a particular discovery service and usability studies.[21] Joseph Deodato has recommended that a discovery service selection process should be inclusive, goal-oriented, data-driven, user-centered, and transparent.[22]

One study asked a group of individuals to perform typical search tasks; the quality (*quality* defined as a resource from a scholarly source) of search results was judged and the results indicated that the EBSCO Discovery Service produced the "highest quality" results, compared to Summon and Google Scholar.[23] Yet another study comparing various discovery service products found no significance differences between products.[24] A study using actual user searches compared Summon, EDS, and Google Scholar and found no significance differences for known-item searches, although Google Scholar did better for topical searches. Helen Timpson and Gemma Sansom found that Google Scholar was the least successful resource in terms of precision when compared to Summon and two publishers' discovery platforms (Emerald and Sage). The authors concluded that although subject-specific databases are more effective than search engines, the complexities involved with accessing the invisible Web are hindering their use.[25]

Using a combination of an online survey and a series of focus groups, another study found general overall satisfaction with the ease of use and the utility of the resource revealed when a discovery service is used.[26]

Marshall Breeding provides a thorough review of the various discovery service options in the marketplace in an issue of *Library Technology Reports*.[27] In a systematic review of 80 articles pertaining to discovery services, Jenny Bossaller and Heather Moulaison Sandy suggest that the move to improve user experiences when confronting the library's online catalog has meant a move to embrace the single search box so that patrons can find the different kinds of materials housed in various places in the library.[28] The reality imposed by a single search box was revealed when one study analyzed more than 1 million search transactions and found that:[29]

- Almost one-fourth of search requests were for resources outside the library
- A small number of popular search queries account for a disproportionate share of the total queries (such queries may reveal latent demand for resources)

Kristin Calvert found that after implementing a discovery service, use of e-resources experienced strong growth, while use of the physical collection declined sharply.[30] Linda Musser and Barbara Coopey report that four years after implementing a discovery service (Summon), interlibrary loan requests dropped 27 percent; requests by undergraduates dropped even more (57 percent), suggesting that a user of a discovery service finds more of value licensed or housed in the library.[31] The perception of increased usage of library resources following the implementation of a discovery service are borne out by usage data.[32]

Nevertheless, a team of librarians at Auburn University, after demonstrations of several discovery services that involved actual reference questions, concluded that the "resources and staff required to implement a discovery system were unacceptably high when measured against perceived benefits to users." The team further concluded that the discovery services were deficient in two areas: controlled vocabularies and ontologies necessary for deeper and smarter connections to other resources and supportive structures for development of information literacy skills.[33]

Carl Grant has argued that the next step after implementing a discovery service is the development of knowledge creation platforms.[34] Despite the large number of discovery service products installed (mostly in academic libraries), the reality is that "discovery mostly happens elsewhere," as was so famously articulated by Lorcan Dempsey, vice-president of OCLC.[35]

Roger Schonfeld has noted that scholars in the academic environment gain access to relevant content using a variety of approaches:[36]

- Google and Google Scholar are the starting point for many individuals
- The platforms of major content providers (ScienceDirect, Emerald Insight, Taylor and Francis Online, and SagePub) experience high volumes of traffic that has not been redirected from a library Web site
- Various third-party discovery services such as ResearchGate and Academia.Edu are growing in importance
- Library-provided discovery services account for a minor share of search-driven discovery

Evaluating Web Sites

Despite the very discouraging statistic that only 1 percent of people start an information search at a library Web site, evaluating and improving upon a library's Web site is an important activity.[37] Jakob Nielsen, a long-time usability guru, has suggested that the most important aspect of any Web site is usability, that is, how easy user interfaces are to use. Nielsen further suggests that usability has five components: learnability, efficiency, memorability, errors, and satisfaction. One study from Finland applied Nielsen's heuristics as a way to evaluate Web sites, and obtained good results.[38] When considering the usability of any Web site, it is also important to remember Mooers' Law: an information retrieval system will tend not to be used whenever it is more painful and troublesome for a customer to have information than for him not to have it.

An analysis of public library Web sites suggests that it is important to understand how the availability (or lack thereof) of content influences the decision to use (and return) to a library Web site. One study found that libraries focused more on providing guidance on library services rather than helping children find resources that are germane to assisting with their school projects and learning in general.[39] A comparable study conducted to evaluate young adult (YA) public library Web pages had similar results.[40]

Not only must libraries provide access to a wealth of information on their Web site to folks using a desktop computer and Web browser, libraries must also ensure that the Web site is accessible to those individuals with disabilities, as well as to the myriad of individuals who are constantly using their handheld mobile phones, tablets, and laptop computers. An analysis of the top 50 ranked university libraries showed that 80 percent provide mobile library Web site services and only 34 percent provided a library app.[41]

An analysis of the 127 Urban Library Council member libraries revealed that almost 75 percent did not provide users with the option to change font size at the request of the user. Slightly more than half of the Web sites did not allow the user to convert a Web page to versions readable by screen readers and/or braille display (a Safari browser is required). Almost every Web site has problems related to contrast (the combination of colors between the text or image and the background). Pages with low contrast are difficult to read for individuals with vision or color blindness problems.[42]

Many libraries face the reality that they need to completely redo their Web site. The team at the Queens College Libraries illustrated that following best practices will result in the development of a high-quality and functional Web site.[43] A team at the Olivet Nazarene University library thoughtfully explained the steps they followed in developing a new library Web site.[44] Other useful discussions of the issues surrounding a Web site redesign are provided by Sandra Shropshire,[45] and Kyle Felker and Su Chung.[46]

Best practices in Web design include:

- Keep information consistent through the use of a taxonomy
- Let the functionality of the Web site drive the resulting form (the site should be device neutral)
- Adopt the latest standards, including W3C standards of Extensible Hypertext Markup Language (XHTML) and Cascading Style Sheets (CSS) and Unicode for text
- Employ frequently used programming languages—JavaScript (client-side) and PHP (server side)

Increasing Bandwidth

The broadband bandwidth connecting a library to the Internet can be best though of as a pipe: the larger the pipe, the faster the information moves to and from the Internet. Networks that utilize coaxial cable typically have data transmission speeds in the 1 to 100 Mbps (megabits per second; 1 million bits per second), whereas networks that use fiber-optic cables typically have speeds that range from 1 to more than 100 Gbps (gigabits per second; 1,000 Mbps). Many communities across the United States are working to install fiber-optic networks; an area that has done this is sometimes referred to as a "Gig City." Google Fiber is installing fiber-optic networks in selected cities across the United States; Kansas City is one example.

A library can ask its Internet service provider (ISP) to provide a report of the current use of the available bandwidth. If the report shows that there are periods of the day where there is 70 to 75 percent or more use of the available bandwidth, then users are experiencing periods when their Internet connection slows down measurably. As more and more varied content is being moved across the Internet every day (downloading files, streaming video and audio files, viewing Web sites, and so forth), the library will need to ensure that its Internet connection has sufficient bandwidth. Some of the development challenges for developing a Web site that is compatible with mobile devices are discussed by Lih-Juan Chan and Lin Wei-Hsiang Hung.[47]

Also, as more and more people bring their electronic handheld devices with them to the library, there is increasing demand for high-speed WiFi access. Of course, the WiFi network connects to the Internet so that people can view their desired content: e-mails, Web pages, Facebook, Snapchat, and so much more. Thus, a WiFi puts increasing pressure on the bandwidth required for the library's Internet connection.

One study examined how the prevalence of information technology in the daily lives of high school students has influenced their perception and use of libraries. The analysis found that the teenagers view libraries as largely outdated institutions with little relevance to their technology-focused daily information practices.[48]

SUMMARY

A library should periodically assess all of its various automated system and information technology infrastructure to ensure that the technology is assisting the library in meeting its needs. The library may wish to compare its installed systems with those of a set of peer libraries to determine if the level of investment in technology is providing adequate benefits for library staff members and, more importantly, for library customers.

Given little differences in the performance among and between various discovery service products, a library's decision to select a specific product is more likely to be based on other considerations such as price, the user interface, customer service, and/or technical issues.

Remember that technology is a tool and a means to the end of providing services that add real value in the life of the library's customer.

NOTES

1. Phillip Howard. Quoted in *The Times*, February 25, 1987.

2. Marshall Breeding. Library Service Platforms: A Maturing Genre of Products. *Library Technology Reports*, May/June 2015, 1–38.

3. Marshall Breeding. Library Systems Report 2016: Power Plays. *American Libraries,* May 2016.

4. Matt Enis. All Systems Go | Library Systems Landscape 2016. *Library Journal*, April 6, 2016.

5. Ken Chad. *Specification for a Unified (Next Generation) Library Resource Management System*, version 2. Ken Chad Consulting, August 2012. Available at https://libtechrfp.wikispaces.com/Unified+library+resource+management+specification.

6. Carl Grant. The Future of Library Systems: Library Services Platforms. *Information Standards Quarterly*, 24 (4), Fall 2012, 4–15.

7. Mayank Yuvaraj. Cloud Computing Applications in Indian Central University Libraries: A Study of Librarians' Use. *Library Philosophy and Practice*, 2013. Retrieved from http://digitalcommons.unl.edu/cgi/viewcontent.cgi?article=2397&context=libphilprac

8. Vandana Singh. Expectations Versus Experiences: Librarians Using Open Source Integrated Library Systems. *The Electronic Library*, 32 (5), 2014, 688–709.

9. Joseph Pruett and Namjoo Choi. A Comparison Between Select Open Source and Proprietary Integrated Library Systems. *Library Hi Tech*, 31 (3), 2013, 435–54.

10. Edmund Balnaves. Open Source Library Management Systems: A Multidimensional Evaluation. *Australian Academic & Research Libraries*, 39 (1), 2008, 1–13.

11. Matt Enis. Open Source Options | Library Systems Landscape. *Library Journal*, April 10, 2014. Retrieved from http://lj.libraryjournal.com/2014/04/technology/open-source-options-library-systems-landscape/#_

12. Robert E. Molyneux and Mike Rylander. The State of Evergreen: Evergreen at Three. *Library Review*, 59 (9), 2010, 667–76.

13. Barbara Albee and Hsin-liang Chen. Public Library Staff's Perceived Value and Satisfaction of an Open Source Library System. *The Electronic Library*, 32 (3), 2014, 390–402.

14. George Machovec. Library Networking and Consortia. *Journal of Library Administration,* 53, 2013, 199–208.

15. OCLC. *U.S. Library Consortia: A Snapshot of Priorities & Perspectives.* Dublin, OH: OCLC, 2013.

16. Faye A. Chadwell, Donald Campbell, and Delpha Campbell. Assessing the Value of Academic Library Consortia. *Journal of Library Administration*, 51 (7/8), 2011, 645–61.

17. Dennis Krieb. *Academic Library Directors' Perceptions of Joining a Large Library Consortium Sharing an Integrated Library System: A Descriptive Survey.* 2011. Educational Administration:

Theses, Dissertations, and Student Research. Paper 54. Available at http://digitalcommons.unl.edu /cehsedaddiss/54

18. Denise Pan and Yem Fong. Return on Investment for Collaborative Collection Development: A Cost-Benefit Evaluation of Consortia Purchasing. *Collaborative Librarianship*, 2 (4), 2010, 183–92.

19. Rick Lugg and Ruth Fischer. Future Tense—The Library on the Ground: 5 Reasons Why Consortia Matter More than Ever. *Against the Grain*, February 2010, 84–85.

20. Doug Way. The Impact of Web-Scale Discovery on the Use of a Library Collection. *Serials Review*, 36 (4), 2010, 214–20.

21. Nadine Ellero. An Unexpected Discovery: One Library's Experience With Web-Scale Discovery Service (WSDS) Evaluation and Assessment. *Journal of Library Administration*, 53 (5/6), 2013, 323–43.

22. Joseph Deodato. Evaluating Web-Scale Discovery: A Step-by-Step Guide. *Information Technology and Libraries*, 34 (2), June 2015, 19–75.

23. Andrew Asher, Lynda Duke, and Suzanne Wilson. Paths of Discovery: Comparing the Search Effectiveness of EBSCO Discovery Service, Summon, Google Scholar, and Conventional Library Resources. *College & Research Libraries*, 75 (5), 2013, 464–88.

24. Jonathan Rochkind. A Comparison of Article Search APIs Via Blinded Experiment and Developer Review. *Code4Lib Journal*, 19, 2013, 1–15.

25. Helen Timpson and Gemma Sansom. A Student Perspective on e-Resource Discovery: Has the Google Factor Changed Publisher Platform Searching Forever? *The Serials Librarian*, 61, 2011, 253–66.

26. Courtney Lundgrigan, Kevin Manuel, and May Yan. "Pretty Rad": Explorations in User Satisfaction with a Discovery Layer at Ryerson University. *College & Research Libraries,* 77 (1), January 2016, 43–62.

27. Marshall Breeding. Library Resource Discovery Products: Library Perspectives, and Vendor Positions. *Library Technology Reports*, January 2014, 1–45.

28. Jenny Bossaller and Heather Moulaison Sandy. Documenting the Conversation: A System Review of Library Discover Layers. *College & Research Libraries*, 78 (6), September 1, 2017 (forthcoming).

29. Cory Lown, Tito Sierra, and Josh Boyer. How Users Search the Library from a Single Search Box. *College & Research Libraries,* 75 (5), May 2013, 227–41.

30. Kristin Calvert. Maximizing Academic Library Collections: Measuring Changes in Use Patterns Owing to EBSCO Discovery Service. *College & Research Libraries,* 77 (1), January 2015, 81–99.

31. Linda Musser and Barbara Coopey. Impact of a Discovery Service on Interlibrary Loan. *College & Research Libraries*, 77 (6), September 2016, 643–53.

32. Valerie Spezi, Claire Creaser, Ann O'Brien, and Angelea Conyers. *Impact of Library Discovery Technologies: A Report for UKSG*. Loughborough, England: Loughborough University, November 2013.

33. Nadine Ellero. An Unexpected Discovery: One Library's Experience with Web-Scale Discovery Service (WSDS) Evaluation and Assessment. *Journal of Library Administration*, 53, 2013, 323–43.

34. Carl Grant. Knowledge Creation Platforms: The Next-Step After Web-Scale Discovery. *027.7* [title of the journal], 2, 2013, 67–73.

35. Lorcan Dempsey. Thirteen Ways of Looking at Libraries, Discovery, and the Catalog: Scale, Workflow, Attention. *Educause Review*, December 10, 2012. Available at http://www.educause.edu/ero /article/thirteen-ways-looking-libraries-discovery-and-catalog-scale-workflow-attention

36. Roger Schonfeld. *Does Discovery Still Happen in the Library? Roles and Strategies for a Shifting Reality*. New York: Ithaka S+R, 2014.

37. Cathy De Rosa et al. *Perceptions of Libraries and Information Resources*. Dublin, OH: OCLC, 2005, 1–17.

38. Marjo-Riitta Aitta, Saana Kaleva, and Terttu Kortelainen. Heuristic evaluation applied to library web services. *New Library World*, 109 (1/2), 2008, 25–45.

39. Midori Kanazawa, Yukiko Maruyama, and Akihiro Motoki. An Analysis of Children's Web Pages in Public Library Web Sites in Japan. *Public Library Quarterly*, 30, 2011, 270–85.

40. Midori Kanazawa. An Evaluation of Young Adult Web Pages in Public Library Websites in Japan. *Public Library Quarterly*, 33 (4), 2014, 279–95.

41. Paula Torres-Pérez, Eva Méndez-Rodríguez, and Enrique Orduna-Malea. Mobile Web Adoption in Top Ranked University Libraries: A Preliminary Study. *The Journal of Academic Librarianship*, 42 (4), June 2016, 329–39.

42. Stephanie L. Maatta Smith. Web Accessibility Assessment of Urban Public Library Websites. *Public Library Quarterly*, 33 (3), 2014, 187–204.

43. James T. Mellone and David J. Williams. Applying Best Practices in Web Site Redesign: The Queens College Libraries Experience. *OCLC Systems & Services: International Digital Library Perspectives*, 26 (3), 2010, 177–97.

44. Ann Johnston, Pamela Greenlee, Matthew Marcukaitis, and Ian Lopshire. Building a New Academic Library Web Site. *Library Hi Tech News*, 32 (8), 2015, 1–15.

45. Sandra Shropshire. Beyond the Design and Evaluation of Library Web Sites: An Analysis and Four Case Studies. *The Journal of Academic Librarianship*, 29 (2), March 2003, 95–101.

46. Kyle Felker and Su Kim Chung. "If at first you don't succeed . . .": Web Site Redesign at the UNLV Libraries. *Library Hi Tech*, 23 (1), 2005, 50–65.

47. Lih-Juan Chan and Lin Wei-Hsiang Hung. Usability and Evaluation of a Library Mobile Web Site. *The Electronic Library*, 34 (4), 2016, 636–50.

48. Denise Agosto, Rachel Magee, Michael Dickard, and Andrea Forte. Teens, Technology and Libraries: An Uncertain Relationship. *The Library Quarterly*, 86 (3), July 2016, 248–69.

10

Evaluation of Automated Materials Handling Systems

Not everything that can be counted counts, and not everything that counts can be counted.

—William Bruce Cameron[1]

SERVICE DEFINITION

Evaluating the possible service delivery improvements while recognizing that the installation of a self-service checkout system or of a return and sorting system (usually involving the use of RFID tags) will lead to the preparation of a cost-benefit analysis that will assist the library in making an investment decision. Self-service is an evolving part of the landscape for both academic and public libraries as it drives and enables further change.

Among the types of automated materials handling (AMH) systems that may be installed in a library setting are:

- Customer self-service checkout equipment
- Return and sorting systems
- Large-scale sorting systems
- Material dispensing machine (books, CDs, DVDs)
- Automatic storage and retrieval systems (AS/RSs).

EVALUATION QUESTIONS

Among the questions that may arise when considering the use of a materials handling system are:

- What are the initial and ongoing costs to install a system?
- What is the reliability of such systems?

- What are the anticipated impacts of staff when a system is installed?
- What are the risks for selecting a specific system?

Of course, many other questions may also arise, depending on the nature and size of the library.

EVALUATION METHODS

Both qualitative and quantitative methods can be used to assess the implications of using a materials handling system. Studies that examine the qualitative aspects of a materials handling system typically focus on improved customer service, freeing up staff to focus on activities that add more value, and improved staff morale. Studies that use quantitative approaches typically prepare a cost-benefit analysis that focuses on reduced risk of repetitive motion injuries, more efficient operations, delivering materials to customers in a more timely manner, and so forth.

PRIOR EVALUATIONS AND RESEARCH

Rather than focusing on the methods used to evaluate the different types of systems, this chapter uses the types of systems as the means of organization.

RFID

Radio frequency identification (RFID) uses an electromagnetic field to track tags attached to objects (similar to a barcode). Radio waves from a RFID reader activate the tag or transponder which then "transmits" stored information. Typically a RFID reader can read several RFID-tagged items simultaneously. RFID tags are used in many industries; a tag can be implanted into pets, livestock, products, and containers.

Libraries that wish to utilize automated materials handling systems must apply a unique RFID tag to each item in the library's collection—thus eliminating the need for barcodes. Depending on the volume purchased, RFID tags will range in cost from 25 to 75 cents per tag. Tags are normally installed inside a book or case and typically only contain a unique identification number. Each RFID ID number must be linked to the item record in the library's integrated library system (ILS) system. For the more technically inclined reader, Douglas Blansita,[2] as well as Shien-Chiang Yu,[3] provides a thorough overview of RFID strengths and its limitations. The document *RFID in U.S. Libraries,* detailing a recommended practice of the National Information Standards Organization (NISO), created the opportunity for cooperation between various RFID-based systems and the assorted ILS systems in the marketplace.[4]

The outcomes typically associated with RFID in libraries include:[5]

- Productivity improvements
- Improved record keeping and inventory control
- Occupational health and safety (reduced repetitive motion syndrome injuries)
- Security
- Improved collection management
- Better customer service (reduce waiting in queues)
- More staff time for transformational interactions
- Increased customer privacy

- Freeing-up of expensive library space
- Image

RFID tags interact with equipment that is linked to a library's integrated library system. These self-service units are using the Standard Interchange Protocol or SIP2 (or the more recent SIP3) developed by 3M, which is now a NISO standard (X39.100). More recently, the Library Communications Framework (LCF) was developed in the United Kingdom to perform many RFID-enabled transactions (including those performed by SIP).[6] And to further muddy the waters, the NISO Circulation Interchange Protocol (NCIP) allows ILS systems to communicate for resource-sharing purposes.[7]

Customer Self-Service Checkout Units

One of the major drivers of the installation of customer self-checkout systems in libraries (and in retail establishments) is the desire to improve customer service and improve the security of materials, while reducing staffing costs. Provided that sufficient self-service checkout units are installed, a reduction in the lines at the circulation area will most likely result.

Although a library can purchase self-service checkout units that continue to use barcodes, most libraries install RFID tags in all items in the collection before installing self-service checkout machines. The costs and benefits associated with self-service checkout units are shown in Table 10.1.

Table 10.1. Costs and Benefits of Self-Service Checkout Units

Type	Cost	Benefit	Value of Benefit
Purchase self-service checkout units	$15,000 to $20,000	Reduced staff costs	$ To be calculated
Maintenance of self-service checkout units	15% of purchase price annually	Improved equipment reliability	$ To be calculated
Software interface to ILS system	$7,000 to $10,000	Reduced theft and missing items	$ To be calculated
RFID tags	$2,000 per 1,000 tags	Reduction in staff time off due to injuries	$ To be calculated
Staff time to add tag to an item and link to the ILS system (1 item per minute)	Varies by library; estimated at $25 per hour	Able to handle increased workload without adding staff	$ To be calculated
Totals	$ To be calculated		$ To be calculated

One study of self-service checkout units found that customer service improved as a result:[8]

- Being more responsive
- Providing consistent and reliable service
- Providing accurate and timely information

- Shifting staff to services that add value in the life of the customer
- Learning more about the customer
- Being flexible and delivering service the way the customer prefers it

Libraries that use kiosks (and eliminate circulation desks) seem to have a higher proportion of circulation checkouts being completed without staff assistance. The important message to staff and library customer is that self-service offers the opportunity for more customer-staff interaction. One study found that the payback period of implementing an RFID system, ignoring the staff cost savings, ranged from three to five years.[9]

Lori Ayre has suggested a set of best practices for self-service checkouts:[10]

1. Implement RFID self-check.
2. Involve staff in implementation planning.
3. Implement self-service holds pickup.
4. Choose self-service checkout units with an appealing design and intuitive use.
5. Get enough self-check units (1 unit per 125,000 circulations).
6. Locate self-check units adjacent to the exit.
7. Use supportive signage at self-check machines.
8. Allow for the payment of fines and fees at the self-check unit.
9. Eliminate the "circulation desk."
10. Communicate to staff and customers the reasons for the move to use self-service units (give staff more opportunities to engage with staff).
11. Train staff to assist patrons at the self-service checkout units.

Return and Sorting Systems

Some libraries have installed systems that sort materials when the customer returns them to the library. Items are placed on a conveyor belt, the system reads the RFID tag and sends a message to the ILS system to check in the item, and the item is then sorted into one of several sorting bins. These return sorting systems, often called automated materials handling (AMH) systems, bring a range of benefits to the library, including:

- Items are immediately checked in and security is reapplied
- Returned items will be returned to the shelves quicker, resulting in increased use of a library's collection
- Items are sorted into several categories, thus reducing the amount of handling by staff members
- Items in the hold queue are identified and sorted into a separate bin

The number of bins to be installed is typically based on size and budget constraints. Increasing the number of sorting bins allows for an increased number of sorting categories, which improves staff productivity.

A library can also install a real-time, book-drop check in of materials returned.

Materials Dispensing Machines

A materials dispensing machine or vending machine offers the opportunity to lend books, CDs, and DVDs to library patrons in areas not served by the library—rapid transit stations, shopping malls, and so forth—or the dispensing machine may be located in the library itself.

The Richmond Public Library (British Columbia, Canada) has used a dispensing machine to loan DVDs (more than 10,000 transactions per month) since 2005. The primary benefit of this approach is the increased safety and security for an expensive collection.[11] A free-standing material dispensing machine was employed by the Contra Costa County (California) Library when it introduced its "Library-a-Go-Go" service located at a rapid transit BART station. The machine holds up to 400 paperback books, and patrons use their library card to borrow and return books. At any given time, about one-fourth of the collection is checked out. The cost of a vending machine is about $100,000.[12]

Large-Scale Sorting System

The King County Library System (KCLS) in Washington and the New York Public Library (NYPL) operate large-scale mechanized sorting systems located in a distribution center. The KCLS system processes more than 14 million RFID-tagged items annually, whereas the NYPL BookOps system handles about 8 million on its 238-foot-long conveyor. The two library systems hold an annual "sorting smackdown" (Battle of the Book Sorters) to see who can sort more books in one hour.[13]

Installing the $3 million system in the NYPL BookOps saved about 45,000 person-hours a year. Other libraries with large-scale sorting systems include the Seattle Public Library and the Minneapolis Public Library.

Lori Ayre prepared a cost-benefit study for the King County Library System that demonstrated significant cost savings when a materials handling system was used in four areas: the "cost" of unavailable items due to backlogs in processing, the costs of front-line staff time spent on requests related to materials handling, the cost of backroom staff assigned to materials handling processing, and the costs to customers.[14]

Automatic Storage and Retrieval System

For some libraries, an automated storage and retrieval system (AS/RS) provides a cost-effective alternative to either (an on-site or off-site) depository or compact shelving. An AS/RS is a computer-controlled system for placing and retrieving objects from storage locations. A library AS/RS places books and other materials in bins (typically sorted by size of materials) that are retrieved by a robotic crane. The system, linked to the library's online catalog, can typically retrieve an item from storage within 10 minutes.

The benefits of an AS/RS include accurate tracking of inventory, near-elimination of pilferage, reduction of mis-shelving of items, reduced space requirements to store the materials, and reduced annual operating costs to provide access to traditional open stacks in a library. More than 30 libraries worldwide are using AS/RS systems.

The CSU Northridge Oviatt Library installed an AS/RS system in 1991 for a cost of $2 million and annual maintenance costs of about $35,000; the anticipated benefits from the system were estimated at more than $250,000 annually.[15] The life expectancy of an AS/RS system is about 20 years. The CSU Northridge AS/RS sits in an 8,000-square-foot, 40-foot-high room that contains 13,260 bins providing access to more than 850,000 volumes. In 2012, the system underwent a major renovation of hardware, and the system currently handles more than 15,000 retrievals annually.[16]

Some of the libraries using AS/RS include the University of Nevada, Las Vegas; Eastern Michigan University; University of Nevada, Reno; Santa Clara University Library; University of British Columbia; University of Chicago; Cornell University; Sonoma State University; Utah State University; and the University of Louisville.[17]

Patricia Bravender and Valeria Long provide a readable discussion of the process the Grand Valley State University library followed to discard a sizable number of items from an AS/RS system.[18] The Eastern Michigan University Library recommends that a marketing program be put into place stressing the benefits of an AS/RS.[19]

The major benefit of an AS/RS is a dramatic reduction in the storage space required to house library materials. This in turn frees up space to be used for other purposes.

SUMMARY

The biggest challenge for any library considering a materials handling solution is the high up-front costs for such systems. An AS/RS can easily cost more than a million dollars, depending on the number of storage bins and robotic cranes (used to place and retrieve the bins).

Libraries that use one or more of the materials handling system options discussed here achieve a number of benefits and, in general, customers experience few problems when using one of these systems.

NOTES

1. William Bruce Cameron. *Informal Sociology: A Casual Introduction to Sociological Thinking.* New York: Random House, 1963, 159.

2. Douglas Blansita. RFI Terminology and Technology: Preparing to Evaluate RFID for Your Library. *Journal of Electronic Resources in Medical Libraries*, 7 (4), 2010, 344–54.

3. Shien-Chiang Yu. RFID Implementation and Benefits in Libraries. *The Electronic Library*, 25 (1), 2007, 54–64.

4. NISO. *RFID in U.S. Libraries* (NISO RP-6-2012). Baltimore, MD: National Information Standards Organization, 2012.

5. Alan Butters. RFID in Australian Academic Libraries: Exploring the Barriers to Implementation. *Australian Academic & Research Libraries*, 39 (3), September 2008, 198–206.

6. BIC. *Library Interoperability Standards—Library Data Communication Framework for Terminal Applications (LCF).* Version 1.0. London: Book Industry Communication, 10 January 2014.

7. NISO. *NISO Circulation Interchange Protocol* (Z39.83). Baltimore, MD: National Information Standards Organization, 2012.

8. *Customer Service Excellence in the Self-Service Public Library.* Melbourne, Victoria, Australia: State Library of Victoria, 2009.

9. Joel Tiu and Shawn Bahk. *A Cost Benefit Analysis of Radio Frequency Identification (RFID) Implementation at the Naval Postgraduate School's Dudley Knox Library.* Monterey, CA: Naval Postgraduate School, December 2006.

10. Lori Ayre. Best Practices for Self-Service Check-Out. The Galecia Group blog, April 25, 2016. Available at http://galecia.com/blogs/lori-ayre/best-practices-self-service-check-out.

11. Mark Ellis. Dispensing with the DVD Circulation Dilemma. *Computers in Libraries*, February 4, 2008, 11–13, 48.

12. Michele Hampshire and Cathy E. Sanford. Library-a-Go-Go: Bringing the Library to the People. *New Library World*, 110 (11/12), 2009, 541–49.

13. Emily Rueb. Libraries in New York and Seattle Area Staging a Battle of the Sorters. *New York Times*, November 6, 2015.

14. Lori Ayre. *Cost Comparison of Automated versus Manual Materials Handling Operations at King County Library System*. Petaluma, CA: The Galecia Group, January 2006. http://galecia.com/sites/default/files/blog_files/Report%20on%20AMH%20and%20Non%20AMH%20Cost%20Comparison_FINAL.pdf.

15. Norma Creaghe and Douglas Davis. Hard Copy in Transition: An Automated Storage and Retrieval Facility for Low-Use Library Materials. *College & Research Libraries*, September 1986, 495–99.

16. Helen Heinrich and Eric Willis. Automated Storage and Retrieval System: A Time-Tested Innovation. *IFLA Conference*, 22 June 2012, 1–11. See also Helen Heinrich and Eric Willis. Automated Storage and Retrieval System: A Time-Tested Innovation. *Library Management*, 35 (6/7), 444–53.

17. Claudene Sproles and Randy Kuehn. Managing Items in an Automated Storage and Retrieval System (AS/RS). Journal of Access Services, 11 (4), 2014, 219–28.

18. Patricia Bravender and Valeria Long. Weeding an Outdated Collection in an Automated Retrieval System. *Collection Management*, 36 (4), 2011, 237–45.

19. Linda Shirato, Sarah Cogan, and Sandra Yee. The Impact of an Automated Storage and Retrieval System on Public Services. *Reference Services Review*, 29 (3), 253–61.

Part IV

Evaluation of Library Services

11

Library Users and Nonusers

Libraries are really about transforming people through access to information.

—Andromeda Yelton[1]

The mission of librarians is to improve society through facilitating knowledge creation in their communities.

—David Lankes

SERVICE DEFINITION

Having a clear understanding of actual and potential customers in a community or academic environment can assist the library in better understanding its customer needs. Information about various segments of a population is usually assembled when the library is involved in a planning process.[2]

EVALUATION QUESTIONS

Identifying who uses and does not use the library is necessary in order to respond to the following types of evaluation questions:

- What are the characteristics of the frequent library user; the occasional library user; and those who do not use the library at all?
- What services are used by different segments of the community?
- What other options are available to segment library users other than demographics?
- What stops nonusers from using the library (physically or virtually)?
- To what degree does the geographic location of the library influence use of the library?
- What services might attract more people to use the library?

EVALUATION METHODS

A number of evaluation methods have been used to better understand library users and nonusers. Each of the methods reveals different information about the various segments of a population. These methods include

- Desk work analysis
- Focus groups
- Surveys of library users and of the community

PRIOR EVALUATIONS AND RESEARCH

Five different methods can be used to segment a population:

- Demographics
- Lifestyles
- Geography
- Volume of use
- Benefits or purpose

This segmentation process can involve a population of citizens living in a city or county, persons connected with a college or university, or employees of a government agency or company. The real value occurs when two or more segmentation techniques are applied simultaneously, reflecting the truism that the whole is greater than the sum of its parts. Combining demographics and geographic information or combining demographics with lifestyle information can reveal a great deal about a community.

Organizations use market segmentation to gain insight into their customers and to become customer-centric organizations. Public and academic libraries that have used market segmentation have found they achieve growth in the number of customers served and higher utilization rates of their collections; in addition the information gained assists in the strategic planning process.

Demographics

Historically, census information has been used by public libraries to put together a profile of their community. This allows the library to segment citizens according to age, education, sex, ethnicity, marital status, family income, number of children, and so forth. For example, age-related information assists a library in identifying the possible need for preschool programs or large-print materials for seniors.

In almost all cases, census information is analyzed at the city or county level, although it is possible to present the information at the census tract or census block level (about 1,000 people in a block).

A combination of demographic factors is often more important than a single characteristic. Characteristics of the public library user that have been discussed and analyzed in a number of user studies include:

- **Education.** The more education an individual has, the more likely he or she is to use the public library.[3] While it is true that income, occupation, and education are all inter-correlated, regression analysis demonstrates that everything disappears except education.

- **Age.** There is evidence suggesting that those who use the library the most are young adults, and that use of the library declines with age. According to a 2016 Pew survey, individuals who visited in the library in the last year were:[4]

18–29	54%
30–49	47%
50–64	38%
65+	36%

  One survey found that only 8 percent of public libraries offer specific programs for older adults.[5]

- **Number of small children.** Adults with small children are more likely to have a library card and to visit the library on a fairly regular basis (the greater the number of children, the more frequently the library is used) than those without children—61 percent compared to 35 percent.[6]

- **Family income.** Individuals with higher incomes will use the local library more frequently (use is greater among middle-income levels than among the rich). It may be that low use of the library by the poor is related to poor reading skills. In 2002, one-quarter of library user households earned from $25,000 to $49,999, whereas more than one-third earned $50,000 or more.[7] With increased income comes discretionary time for reading and information-seeking activities.

  One study, using a "library activity" index composed of circulation, in-library use of materials, number of reference transactions, and annual program attendance, found that higher incomes tended to be associated with higher library usage rates per capita.[8] Another study of public libraries across the United States found that libraries in lower-income or rural neighborhoods were relatively less funded and offered fewer information resources.[9]

- **Sex.** Women are more likely to use the library than men, although taking employment status into consideration and holding education constant, the dominant use by women disappears.[10]

- **Marital status.** Single individuals use the library more than married people.

- **Ethnicity.** Depending on the ethnic population within a community, use of the library will generally reflect the relative proportions of the population—see Figure 11.1.[11]

  One study found that patrons of color use the library for educational support and information gathering more than do their Caucasian counterparts.[12] Racial and ethnic minority groups are growing at a much faster pace than the general U.S. population. Thus, a public library should periodically review the demographic shifts that are occurring within its geographic and service area boundaries in order to better respond to changing demands for services.

Lifestyles

Market researchers have categorized consumers according to their lifestyles. The lifestyles approach combines demographic information with how people spend their time and money. Although income influences a choice of lifestyle, it is influenced only slightly by education.[13]

One study analyzed more than 8 million circulation transactions in 10 different communities and found that circulation patterns were similar across the communities.[14] Despite community characteristics or lifestyles, fiction and audiovisual materials accounted for about

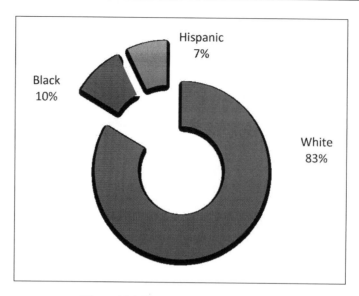

Figure 11.1. Ethnicity of Library Users

two-thirds of all circulations. An analysis of circulation patterns among 21 branches of the Indianapolis-Marion County (Indiana) Public Library found that people borrowed similar types of materials regardless of the characteristics of the populations served by each branch.[15]

A 2016 study examined the patron registration and circulation transaction data for 10 large public library systems across the United States using lifestyle data to complement the analysis. The study focused on "core customers" who are the top 20 percent of the most active (most frequent) borrowers of library materials. Overall, the study found that core customer characteristics and behaviors are not homogenous nationally. Rather, core customers are unique and complex, distributed in distinctive patterns that reflect the local communities of each library. In short, the business of public libraries is hyperlocal.[16] Figure 11.2 shows the distribution of lifestyle segments for the Anythink Libraries in Colorado.

Geography

Geographic information system (GIS) software allows individuals to create a map of a community using information containing addresses in a map-based form. Library systems with branches especially benefit because it is possible to assign each census tract to a service area adjacent to each branch location. This allows the decision makers the opportunity to visually see the information in graphic map format. Many local government agencies use GIS for planning the location of facilities: police and fire stations, police patrol areas, and much more.

America's shifting demographics require that public libraries shift their tactics to better respond to the needs of a changing population.[17] The resulting maps can be helpful at the time of budget hearings, for exploring alternative branch site locations, and for reporting to the library's stakeholders.

The importance of branch library location cannot be overemphasized. People *choose* to spend time and resources traveling from home or a workplace to visit the library. The average library customer will not travel more than two to three miles to visit a library. The old real estate maxim holds true: location, location, location.[18] One study found that the national average

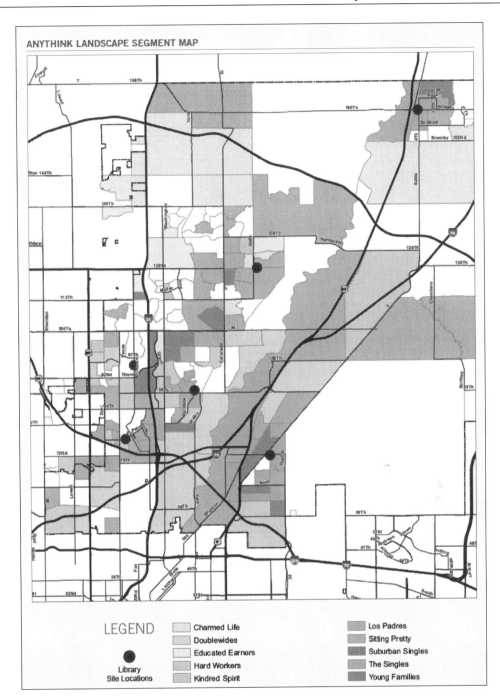

Figure 11.2. Anythink Libraries Lifestyles Segment Map. From Marc Futterman and Danielle Patrick Milam. Core Customer Intelligence: Public Library Reach, Relevance and Resilience. March 2016, 37. Available at http://civictechnologies.com/core-customer-intelligence

population-weighted distance to the nearest public library is 2.1 miles (however, the data also reveal significant regional variations in terms of accessibility).[19]

One study mapped demographic and library use data and found that branch libraries serving primarily minority populations had higher in-library use, higher reference transactions, and greater program attendance, while at the same time having lower circulation figures.[20] This is significant because most public library systems will use circulation as the sole indicator of a branch library's performance. Another study used GIS mapping software to better understand market segments and deliver more relevant customer services.[21]

Yet another study found that children's programming is immune to competition, whereas job-related and informational uses of the library are reduced if the community has a local book store.[22]

Several studies used multivariate analysis (multiple regression analysis) in modeling public library use and postulated that a resident's library use is a function of his or her socioeconomic and locational characteristics.[23] Demographic variables alone do not accurately predict library use, but topographical features, hours of operation, size of the building, and unique population characteristics will affect library use.[24]

Volume of Use

Use is a word that frequently appears in library and information science literature and, in fact, as Rachael Fleming-May notes, "has multiple facets of meaning that are deployed in diverse contexts."[25] Fleming-May created a typology of library use with four broad categories: use of the library as an abstraction, use of the library as an implement or tool, use of the library as a transaction, and use of the library as a complex process.

It is possible to segment the population by use, which results in the classic split of users and nonusers. The more optimistic prefer to call nonusers "potential users." With today's automated systems, it is possible to obtain a set of reports that will sort the registered borrowers into several groups:

- Customers are "card-carrying individuals" who use the library. They can be subdivided into three groups:
    - *Frequent users* are those who use the library on a monthly or more frequent basis.
    - *Moderate users* are those will use the library at least quarterly.
    - *Infrequent users* are those who will use the library at least once a year.
- "Lost or lapsed customers" are people who have a library card but have not used the library for more than a year. So, although they "found" the library once, they are now "lost." Depending on how often library user records are purged from an automated system, as much as 30 to 40 percent of registered library users will fall into the lost category.
- Nonusers are people within a community who may or may not be aware of the location of the library and the range of services it offers. Note that nonusers can be divided into two groups: those who can be enticed into the library and those who will never, under any circumstances, use the library.

    Identifying the number of nonusers is a straightforward calculation. Subtracting the number of registered library borrowers from the total population of the jurisdiction will provide the number of nonusers. Note that the total number of registered borrowers may exceed the total population of a jurisdiction due to nonresidents becoming registered library cardholders.

A study that applied a discrete choice analysis in a public library setting found that lost users and nonusers alike did not use the library primarily due to distance, inconvenience of hours, and their preference to purchase their own materials. In a similar vein, it found that adding to the collection would entice lost customers to return, while adding more locations and hours would attract nonusers to the library.[26]

Perhaps the biggest failure of the majority of library user studies is that researchers have "looked at the user in the life of the library rather than the library in the life of the user."[27]

Benefit Segmentation

Another relatively new segmentation technique is to identify the benefits people receive from a physical or virtual visit to the library. A study at the Dover Public Library identified eight task-related reasons for a visit to the library—see Figure 11.3:[28]

- **Experience seekers** look to the library as a venue for entertainment or social connection.
- **Explorers** are individuals who are curious and love to learn but do not have a content or subject agenda prior to the visit.
- **Problem solvers** have a specific question or problem they want to solve.
- **Facilitators** are users who are there to support someone else in their use of the library—their children or a friend.
- **Patrons** are individuals with a strong sense of belonging to the library. They belong to the "Friends" group and will often volunteer at the library.
- **Scholars** are those with a deep interest in and a history of research work in one topic area, such as genealogy or religion.
- **Spiritual pilgrims** will focus on the library as a place of reflection or rejuvenation.
- **Hobbyists** are individuals looking to further their interest in a particular area.

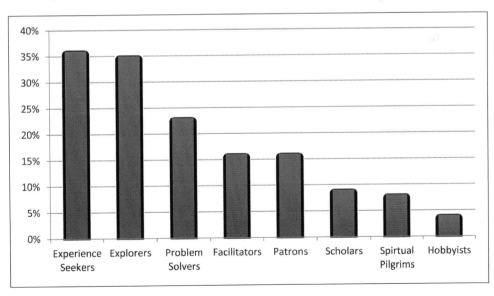

Figure 11.3. Task-Related Reasons for Library Use. Adapted from Institute for Learning Innovation. *Dover, DE Library User Identity—Motivation Pilot Study.* Dover: Delaware Division of Libraries, December 2005.

The benefit segmentation approach raises an important question: "How could a library organize its services to better meet the needs of each benefit segment to complete a task? In Singapore, an analysis suggested:[29]

- **Career-minded people** hold strong beliefs about education and family and turn to the library first for their reading.

- **Active information seekers** possess a moderate education, have an entrepreneurial spirit, and place greater importance on social status and material well-being.

- **Self-suppliers** prefer to purchase their own books, are better educated, and hold managerial or executive positions.

- **Group readers** have an avid appetite for reading and are heavy library users.

- **Narrowly focused learners** are students who read to fulfill a course requirement.

- **Low motivators** have little interest in reading.

- **Facilitators** are females with lower education levels who highly value the importance of the library for their children.

As shown in Figure 11.4, identification of the reasons for possible use of the library leads to insights about reading habits and visits to the library.

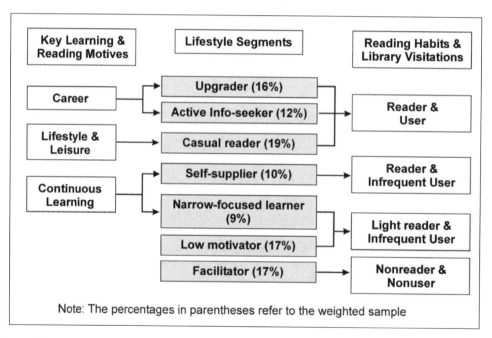

Figure 11.4. Summary Findings of the Seven Segments. Kau Ah Keng, Kwon Jung, and Jochen Wirtz. Segmentation of Library Visitors in Singapore: Learning and Reading Related Lifestyles. *Library Management,* 24 (1/2), 2003, 20–33.

Joan Durrance and Karen Fisher interviewed users of specific library services to determine the outcomes of the library service in the life of the customer.[30]

USERS

The analysis of library users helps develop a profile of various market segments and how they use the library. An individual chooses to visit the library—physically or virtually—when the benefits of using the library are greater than going to the next-best alternative. The individual compares the value of the service minus the price and waiting costs at each alternative, choosing the source with the highest net value.[31]

Surveys range from those designed to improve services in a specific library to those designed to lead to broad conclusions and support for theory. In addition to the quantitative data that result from surveys, libraries have also used interviews (one-on-one and focus groups) and observation to understand how people use the library. The characteristics most frequently examined in user studies are sex, age, education, family income, marital status, and the number of small children living at home.

Carol Kronus prepared an analysis which suggested that education, urban residence, and family life cycle factors predicted rate of library use.[32]

George D'Elia developed a model that included such items as individual characteristics, patron awareness of library services, perceived accessibility, and ease of library use.[33] He concluded that users of the public library perceived the library as more accessible than did nonusers, and that frequency and intensity of use were related to awareness of the range of available library services. Ronald Powell found no link between personality type and use of the library.[34]

A Pew Research survey conducted in late 2015 found that 44 percent of adults have visited a public library in the past year, and that 31 percent used a public library website.[35] A nationwide Australian survey of library nonusers and users of the state libraries and public libraries found that only 30 percent of the population had used the library in the past year.[36] A Province of Ontario (Canada) survey of child and youth services revealed that although circulation of children's materials accounted for 24 percent of overall circulation, the children's materials acquisitions budgets made up only 17 percent of total acquisitions budgets.[37]

One interesting study in a public library setting asked customers to complete a time diary to estimate the time spent using library facilities and circulated materials for a month. Patrons used the facilities, services, and collections for an estimated 182,000 hours (90 percent of use occurred outside the library through the use of borrowed materials—reading, listening, and watching).[38]

Brenda Dervin suggests using an alternative set of categories that describe a person at a particular moment in time and space rather than across time and space.[39]

A survey of faculty members in a sample of California colleges found a broad spectrum of user types, ranging from the nonuser, to the inexperienced novice, to the highly proficient. Faculty used digital resources to integrate primary materials into their teaching, to include materials that would otherwise be unavailable, and to improve student learning.[40]

The Principle of Least Effort

The principle of least effort states that most people, even academic scholars and scientists, will choose easily available information sources, even if they are of low quality. Further, people tend to be satisfied with whatever can be found easily, in preference to tracking down high-quality sources that would require a greater expenditure of effort.

The principle of least effort, sometimes called the "principle of information seeking parsimony," is also known as Zipf's Law of Least Effort.[41] The reality is that people tend to choose perceived ease of access over quality of content. In short, people will choose free, convenient, and good enough over quality information (that may require some effort to obtain) every time. And people will "satisfice"—a word coined by Herb Simon to indicate that individuals will set modest goals and then stop searching when these goals are reached.

Evidence for the validity of this principle is substantial and covers many decades of study. In his investigation of information-seeking behavior, Victor Rosenberg found that the guiding principle for the design of any information system should be the system's ease of use rather than the amount or quality of information provided.[42] Peter Gerstberger and Thomas Allen arrived at a similar conclusion and noted that there was a direct relationship between the perceived accessibility of an information channel and several objective measures of use.[43]

John Salasin and Toby Cedar found that an information source was chosen based on the perceived ease of use rather than other criteria.[44] Herbert Poole noted that 43 out of 51 studies that focused on the information behavior of scientists demonstrate the principle of least effort.[45] Similar results were observed in a study which reported that social scientists tended to rely on footnote chasing and forgo use of indexes to the literature.[46]

William Paisley noted that the level of frustration in using libraries is high for most people, and that people "are conditioned to feeling that the library is a place . . . [they] almost have to drag something out of."[47] Thomas Mann challenged the library profession, observing that it was time to stop blaming library users for being "lazy":

> Ironically, disregarding the Principle of Least Effort is itself a result of the same principle at work: it is easier for many library managers and information scientists to concentrate on "hard" problems of technology than to do the difficult library research on "soft" human behavior.[48]

Even OCLC's *Perceptions* survey found that 84 percent start their search for information using a search engine, and only 1 percent visit a library Web site. On a list of sources of information identified as "trusted," the library was last.[49]

The implications of this principle are serious indeed and have been ignored by the library profession for far too long! It is time to focus on usability of the library's physical and virtual collections. Hoping that library users will recognize that the library contains quality resources and start using the library in increasing numbers is simply delusional thinking.

OCLC released a very interesting and readable report, *The Library in the Life of the User: Engaging with People Where They Live and Learn*, in which they asked (and answered) several important questions:[50]

- Is it possible to identify how people find information as well as how and why they get information; and with that knowledge as a foundation, could librarians provide systems and services that meet people's needs where they are (being in the flow of the user without acting as a barrier)?

- Given the reduction in resources being provided to libraries, is it still possible to innovate and deliver services that are of value to the user?

- Should libraries focus on their existing users (and ignore their nonusers) by providing personalized boutique services?

NONUSERS

Some people, for a variety of reasons, will never obtain a public library card. Part of the planning process should be to recognize what proportion of the population "might" be interested in public library services and then determine how the library can best meet the needs of "prospective users."

Public libraries do very little to encourage people who have not used the library in more than a year to return. A library could use a brief mail survey, a focus group, or other means to identify the reasons for failing to return to the library. A survey of former library users who had not used the library in more than a year revealed that the typical "once but no-longer a user" was an employed (one-third were retired), well-educated Caucasian over the age of 50.[51] In short, the typical "lost customer" was an "empty nester" who either was too busy or would rather buy books than visit the local public library. Another more comprehensive survey of non-users in a community found other reasons for nonuse; see Figure 11.5.[52]

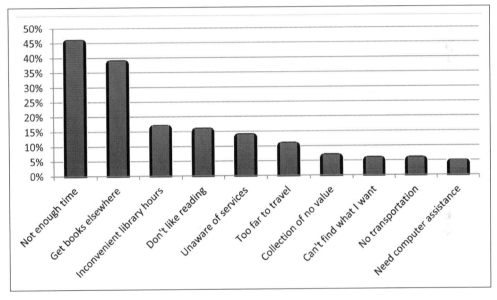

Figure 11.5. Reasons for Nonuse of a Public Library. Louise Flowers. Non-Users of the Upper Goulburn Library Service. *The Australian Library Journal,* 44, May 1995, 67–85.

The Glasgow Public Libraries conducted an online survey of nonusers (more than 1,000 respondents) and found that 90 percent of nonusers had been users in the past and that today the group of nonusers could be split into two equal groups: the affluent and the financial distressed.[53]

Almost all undergraduate students procrastinate about academic activities such as studying for an examination or writing a term paper,[54] and almost two-thirds of graduate students procrastinate due to fear of failure and task averseness.[55] One study found that task averseness was related to barriers with library staff, affective barriers, comfort with the library, and knowledge of the library.[56] These findings are similar to those in other studies pertaining to procrastination.[57]

SUMMARY

This chapter has presented information about a variety of tools that can be used to learn more about the characteristics of library users and nonusers. Having a clear understanding of the actual and potential users of a library is critical to any planning for and evaluation of library services.

NOTES

1. Andromeda Yelton. Across Divided Networks blog, October 15, 2015. Available at https://andromedayelton.com/2015/

2. Jennifer Rowley. Focusing on Customers. *Library Review*, 46 (2), 1997, 81–89; Ana Reyes Pacios Lozano. A Customer Orientation Checklist: A Model. *Library Review*, 49 (4), 2000, 173–78; Jennifer Rowley. Managing Branding and Corporate Image for Library and Information Services. *Library Review*, 46 (4), 1997, 244–50; Jennifer Rowley and Jillian Dawes. Customer Loyalty—A Relevant Concept for Libraries? *Library Management*, 20 (6), 1999, 345–51.

3. This summary of the user characteristics is based on a review of the work of Berelson, Kronus, and D'Elia in Ronald R. Powell. *The Relationship of Library User Studies to Performance Measures: A Review of the Literature* (Occasional Paper Number 181). Champaign: University of Illinois, Graduate School of Library and Information Science, 1988.

4. Lee Rainie. *Libraries and Learning*. Pew Research Center, April 2016, Available at http://www.pewinternet.org/2016/04/07/libraries-and-learning/

5. Renee Bennett-Kapusniak. Older Adults and the Public Library: The Impact of the Boomer Generation. *Public Library Quarterly*, 32, 2013, 204–22.

6. Mary Jo Lynch. Using Public Libraries: What Makes a Difference? *American Libraries*, 28 (10), November 1997, 64–65.

7. KRC Research & Consulting. @ *Your Library: Attitudes Toward Public Libraries Survey*. June 2002. Available at http://www.ala.org/research/sites/ala.org.research/files/content/librarystats/attitudes towardpubliclibrariessurvey.pdf

8. Mary Kopczynski and Michael Lombardo. Comparative Performance Measurement: Insights and Lessons Learned from a Consortium Effort. *Public Administration Review*, 59 (2), March/April 1999, 124–34.

9. Sei-Ching Joanna Sin. Neighborhood Disparities in Access to Information Resources: Measuring and Mapping U.S. Public Libraries' Funding and Service Landscapes. *Library & Information Science Research*, 33, 2011, 41–53.

10. Carol I. Kronus. Patterns of Adult Library Use: A Regression and Path Analysis. *Adult Education*, 23, 1973, 115–31.

11. Mary Jo Lynch. Using Public Libraries: What Makes a Difference? *American Libraries*, 28 (10), November 1997, 64–65.

12. George D'Elia and Eleanor J. Rodger. Public Library Roles and Patron Use: Why Patrons Use the Library. *Public Libraries*, 33 (3), 1994, 135–44.

13. Michael J. Weiss. *The Clustering of America*. New York: Harper, 1988; Michael J. Weiss. Clustered America: The Communities We Serve. *Public Libraries*, 28 (3), June 1989, 161–65.

14. Hazel M. Davis and Ellen Altman. The Relationship Between Community Lifestyles and Circulation Patterns in Public Libraries. *Public Libraries*, 36 (1), January/February 1997, 40–45.

15. John R. Ottensmann, Raymond E. Gnat, and Michael E. Gleeson. Similarities in Circulation Patterns Among Public Library Branches Serving Diverse Populations. *Library Quarterly*, 65, January 1995, 89–118.

16. Marc Futterman and Danielle Milam. *Core Customer Intelligence: Public Library Reach, Relevance and Resilience*. March 2016. Available at http://civictechnologies.com/core-customer-intelligence

17. Christie Koontz and Dean Jue. Unlock Your Demographics. *Library Journal*, 129 (4), March 1, 2004, 32–33.

18. Christie M. Koontz. Public Library Site Evaluation and Location: Past and Present Market-Based Modeling Tools for the Future. *Library & Information Science Research*, 14 (4), 1992, 379–409; Christie M. Koontz. *Library Facility Siting and Location Handbook*. Westport, CT: Greenwood, 1991.

19. Francis Donnelly. Regional Variations in Average Distance to Public Libraries in the United States. *Library & Information Science Research*, 37, 2015, 280–89.

20. Christie M. Koontz. Technology—Pied Piper or Playground Bully, or Creating Meaningful Measures Using Emerging Technologies: Separating the Reality from the Myths. *Proceedings of the 4th Northumbria International Conference on Performance Measurement & Libraries & Information Services*. New Castle, England: University of Northumbria, 2001.

21. Marc Futterman and Judy Michaelson. Data Rules: How Mapping Technology Drives Better Customer Service. *Public Library Quarterly*, 31, (2), 2012, 141–52.

22. Jeffrey A. Hemmeter. Household Use of Public Libraries and Large Bookstores. *Library & Information Science Research*, 28, 2006, 595–616.

23. George D'Elia. The Development and Testing of a Conceptual Model of Public Library Use Behavior. *Library Quarterly*, 50, 1980, 410–30; Janet M. Lange. *Public Library Users, Nonusers and Type of Library Use*. Doctoral dissertation, Claremont Graduate University, California, 1984.

24. Christie M. Koontz. Public Library Site Evaluation and Location: Past and Present Market-Based Modeling Tools for the Future. *Library & Information Science Research*, 14 (4), 1992, 379–409.

25. Rachel Fleming-May. What Is Library Use? Facets of Concept and a Typology of Its Application in the Literature of Library and Information Science. *Library Quarterly*, 81 (3), 2011, 297–320.

26. Akio Sone. An Application of Discrete Choice Analysis to the Modeling of Public Library Use and Choice Behavior. *Library & Information Science Research*, 10, 1988, 35–55.

27. Douglas Zweizig. *Predicting Amount of Library Use: An Empirical Study of the Role of the Public Library in the Life of the Adult Public*. Doctoral dissertation, Syracuse University, New York, 1973, 76.

28. Adapted from Figure 2 in Institute for Learning Innovation. *Dover, DE Library User Identity—Motivation Pilot Study*. Dover: Delaware Division of Libraries, December 2005.

29. Kau Ah Keng, Kwon Jung, and Jochen Wirtz. Segmentation of Library Visitors in Singapore: Learning and Reading Related Lifestyles. *Library Management*, 24 (1/2), 2003, 20–33.

30. Joan C. Durrance and Karen E. Fisher. *How Libraries and Librarians Help: A Guide to Identifying User-Centered Outcomes*. Chicago: American Library Association, 2005.

31. Nancy A. Van House. A Time Allocation Theory of Public Library Use. *Library & Information Science Research*, 5, 1983, 356–84; Nancy A. Van House. *Public Library User Fees: The Use and Finance of Public Libraries*. Westport, CT: Greenwood Press, 1983.

32. Carol I. Kronus. Patterns of Adult Library Use: A Regression and Path Analysis. *Adult Education*, 23, 1973, 115–31.

33. George D'Elia. The Development and Testing of a Conceptual Model of Public Library User Behavior. *Library Quarterly*, 50, 1980, 410–30.

34. Ronald R. Powell. Library Use and Personality: The Relationship Locus of Control and Frequency of Use. *Library & Information Science Research*, 6, 1984, 179–90.

35. Lee Rainie. Libraries and Learning. Pew Research Center, April 2016, Available at http://www.pewinternet.org/2016/04/07/libraries-and-learning/

36. Colin Mercer and Tony Bennett. *Navigating the Economy of Knowledge: A National Survey of Users and Non-Users of State and Public Libraries*. Brisbane, Australia: Institute for Cultural Policy Studies Griffith University, 1995.

37. Ontario Library Association. *Children's Services Benchmark and Statistical Report 2016*. Toronto: Ontario Library Association, 2016.

38. John Shepherd, Kaitlyn Vardy, and Allan Wilson. Quantifying Patron Time-Use of a Public Library. *Library Management*, 36 (6/7), 2015, 448–61.

39. Brenda Dervin. Users as Research Inventions: How Research Categories Perpetuate Inequities. *Journal of Communication*, 39 (3), Summer 1989, 216–32.

40. Diane Harley, Jonathan Henke and Shannon Lawrence. *Use and Users of Digital Resources: A Focus on Undergraduate Education in the Humanities and Social Sciences.* Berkeley, CA: Center for the Studies in Higher Education, April 2006. Available at http://www.cshe.berkeley.edu/sites/default /files/shared/research/digitalresourcestudy/report/digitalresourcestudy_final_report_goal1.pdf.

41. George K. Zipf. *Human Behavior and the Principle of Least Effort.* Cambridge, MA: Addison-Wesley, 1949.

42. Victor Rosenberg. Factors Affecting the Preference of Industrial Personnel for Information Gathering Methods. *Information Storage and Retrieval*, 3 (3), July 1967, 119–27.

43. Peter G. Gerstberger and Thomas J. Allen. Criteria Used by Research and Development Engineers in the Selection of an Information Source. *Journal of Applied Psychology*, 52 (4), August 1968, 272–79; see also Thomas J. Allen and Peter G. Gerstberger. *Criteria for Selection of an Information Source.* Cambridge, MA: MIT Press, 1967.

44. John Salasin and Toby Cedar. Person-to-Person Communication in an Applied-Research Service Delivery Setting. *Journal of the American Society for Information Science*, 36 (2), March 1985, 103–15.

45. Herbert Poole. *Theories of the Middle Range.* Norwood, NJ: Ablex, 1985.

46. L. Uytterschaut. Literature Searching Methods in Social Science Research: A Pilot Inquiry. *American Behavioral Scientist*, 9 (9), May 1966, 14–26.

47. William J. Paisley. Information Needs and Uses. *Annual Review of Information Science and Technology*, 3, 1968, 18.

48. Thomas Mann. *Library Research Models: A Guide to Classification, Cataloging, and Computers.* Oxford, UK: Oxford University Press, 1993, 98.

49. Cathy De Rosa, Joanne Cantrell, Diane Cellentani, Janet Hawk, Lillie Jenkins, and Alane Wilson. *Perceptions of Libraries and Information Resources.* Dublin, OH: OCLC, 2006. See also Cathy De Rosa, Joanne Cantrell, Janet Hawk, and Alane Wilson. *College Students' Perceptions of Libraries and Information Resources.* Dublin, OH: OCLC, 2006.

50. Lynn Silipigni Connaway. *The Library in the Life of the User: Engaging with People Where They Live and Learn.* Dublin, OH: OCLC, 2015.

51. Kathy L. Harris. Who Are They? In Search of the Elusive Non-User. *Colorado Libraries*, 27 (4), Winter 2001, 16–18.

52. Louise Flowers. Non-Users of the Upper Goulburn Library Service. *The Australian Library Journal*, 44, May 1995, 67–85.

53. Glasgow Libraries. *Almost a Faded Feeling? Online Non-User Survey Report.* Glasgow, Scotland: Glasgow Libraries, April 2015.

54. Albert Ellis and William J. Knaus. *Overcoming Procrastination.* New York: Institute for Rational Living, 1977.

55. Mary B. Hill. A Survey of College Faculty and Student Procrastination. *College Student Journal*, 12 (2), Fall 1978, 256–62.

56. Mary B. Hill. A Survey of College Faculty and Student Procrastination. *College Student Journal*, 12 (2), Fall 1978, 256–62.

57. Laura J. Solomon and Esther D. Rothblum. Academic Procrastination: Frequency and Cognitive-Behavioral Correlates. *Journal of Counseling Psychology*, 31, October 1984, 503–9; Joseph R. Ferrari, Johnson L. Judith, and William G. McCowan. *Procrastination and Task Avoidance: Theory, Research, and Treatment.* New York: Plenum, 1995.

12

Evaluation of the Physical Collection

One problem with collecting everything to get the "good" is that we are not sure of the impact of every "bad" volume on a "good" collection.
—Elizabeth Futas and David Vidor[1]

SERVICE DEFINITION

Historically, the physical collection has been the raison d'être of almost every library. Perhaps due to the decades spent building and maintaining a library's physical collection, a plethora of literature exists about the evaluation of a library's collection.

EVALUATION QUESTIONS

The evaluation of a library's collections has been focused on a number of topics, including:

- Gaining a better understanding of the nature, depth, and utility of the collection
- Assessing the collection development policy and methods, or sources for acquiring resources
- Assessing the capacity of the collection to support research or the curriculum
- Developing tools for collection planning and pruning (weeding)
- Identifying possible gaps in library holdings
- Assessing the collection's ability to meet demand
- Providing a rational basis for the allocation of the acquisitions budget
- Defending the materials acquisitions budget
- Understanding the annual costs for maintaining books on shelves
- Considering moving a portion of the collection to storage of some kind

Perhaps the central evaluation question is: What constitutes a *good* collection? Although size has been used as an indirect measure for decades in many libraries, what counts most is having the right resource at the right time to meet the needs of the user.

171

Libraries are in a period of transition: as we move from the traditional "book-centered" paradigm (what some call the library as warehouse) to a "learning-centered" paradigm, the amount of space occupied by the shelving and the collection it stores is being questioned. A rethinking of library collections is long overdue, and in academic libraries declining circulation and use of reference services provides additional evidence of this.

As we will see later in this chapter when overlap studies are discussed, a sizable amount of a library's collection (think monographs) is widely held and available elsewhere. In addition, given the speed with which the Google Books project is digitizing collections (more than 30 million books at last count), many people, especially students and faculty members, now have access to digital copies via the Hathi Trust Digital Library. Thus the importance of the evaluation of the physical collection for every type of library.

PRIOR EVALUATIONS AND RESEARCH

The wide variety of both qualitative and quantitative methods that have been used to evaluate library physical collections is shown in Figure 12.1.

	Qualitative	Quantitative
Library Perspective	Expert opinion Checking lists Conspectus	Size Analyzing use Comparison with peers using bibliographic records Overlap studies Citation studies Interlibrary loan analysis Loss rate analysis
Customer Perspective		User surveys Shelf availability studies Document delivery In-library use studies Formula approach Curriculum analysis Analysis of ILL stats Weeding Value

Figure 12.1. Collection Evaluation

Qualitative Methods

It is safe to say that quantitative data are not necessarily more objective than qualitative information, but when assessing a collection the qualitative approach is subjective in nature. Although qualitative methods can be made less subjective through the use of appropriate tools, criteria, guidelines, and procedures, in the end the method relies on subjective judgment. The qualitative approach may make it more difficult to defend results to the library's funding decision makers.

Expert Opinion

Shelf scanning or examining the materials on the shelves is an effective way to assess a collection, particularly smaller and more specialized collections. Such an approach obviously requires a knowledgeable and skilled professional who is a subject specialist. The expert performing the shelf scan typically produces a written report of the findings.

There are obvious problems with this approach. A subject specialist is not necessarily an expert in the literature in that subject area, or may not be familiar with the needs of the library's customers. Attempting to use experts in a larger collection will require numerous evaluators, and the cost may mount quickly.

Core lists that are considered essential for teaching and research can be created by a faculty survey. One study compared the results of a faculty survey with data based on citation analysis and circulation transactions and found the core lists of journals almost identical.[2] Another study found that the "subjective" judgments made by librarians to cancel specific journal subscriptions were almost identical to faculty recommendations.[3]

Checking Lists

Depending on the type of library, an individual or team can check its holdings against a published list or series of bibliographies. The list or bibliographies must be well chosen (check the complete list or a sample of the list); then they must complete the comparison and prepare a report. Checking lists is one of the oldest forms of collection assessment. Typically list checking is combined with another form of collection assessment. Criticisms of this method include that the lists have a short life expectancy, and they do not identify the reality that comparable books owned by the library are not on the lists.

Several techniques are available that can be adapted to serve the needs of most libraries:

- A check of a list of **monographic titles** that has been published for a particular type of library. A variation of this approach is to compare the local library's holdings against those of several peer libraries.
- A check of a list of **journal titles** deemed appropriate for a particular type of library.
- Creation of a list from the **citations** in selected journals.
- Creation of a list and selection of a sample of citations from the first list to create a second list. A sample of citations from the second list is used as a third list. This successive generation of lists is called **"tiered" list checking**. Each list is used to check the availability of holdings in the library.
- A check of **bibliographies** or citation lists from works of significance to local users or programs.
- Checks of lists of most-used, **most-cited titles**—from reading lists, subject reading lists, or departmental bibliographies.

Dennis Ridley and Joseph Weber completed a list-checking study combined with an analysis of in-library study of customer browsing of the collection.[4] List checking in conjunction with citation analysis was used in another study to evaluate Northwestern University's economics collection.[5] Russell Dennison used the tiered checklist approach to assess a library's collection.[6]

White's *Brief Tests of Collection Strength* compares short lists of items to library holdings (brief tests) and includes the conspectus levels as a part of the evaluation effort.[7] White's approach has been tested and judged to be efficacious by McMinn and others.[8]

Conspectus

The development of the conspectus, popular in the 1980s and 1990s, allowed an academic library to assess the depth or comprehensiveness of its collection. The assessment (using a 1–5 rating, with 5 reflecting the greatest depth and indicating a first-rate research collection) typically used a variety of tools to assist in the process, but in the end the rating was subjective.[9] It was hoped that the conspectus would help facilitate cooperative collection development and work as a planning tool to upgrade portions of a library's collection. There is a growing skepticism that measures of collection size or depth are adequate measures of the collection's quality or its benefit to the university community.

A variation of the conspectus approach was developed by Howard White and is based on comparing short lists—what White calls brief tests—to a library's holdings. White's brief tests method is based on the premise that comparing a library's collection to another library does not reveal whether the library has the right mix of items for the subject area or the correct mix of levels for the curriculum.[10] David Lesniaski has suggested a simplification of the brief tests method.[11]

Quantitative Methods

The attractiveness of the quantitative approach is grounded in the reality that the method provides numbers that are rather comforting: "compared to our peers, this library has 10 percent more holdings" or "our users find 70 percent of what they are looking for, while other libraries have availability rates that are lower." Despite the attractiveness of this approach, quantitative methods must be used judiciously, as a statistic can be misinterpreted or lead to unsound conclusions.

Size

The absolute size of a collection is one characteristic that can be used for evaluation. In fact, counts of a library's materials are probably one of the oldest measures for assessing and comparing libraries. For decades the size of a library's collection was compared to a standard. Standards existed for school, public, junior college, college, and special libraries. The use of standards generally fell out of favor during the 1980s, although some states still use standards for public libraries. One of the principal problems of standards is that decision makers often regard a "minimum" standard as a "maximum," thus inhibiting the growth of a given library.

Creating large "just-in-case" collections made sense in a print-only environment. If the collection contains what students and faculty are looking for, then it will be used (at least that was the hope!). Most academic libraries responded to the expressed needs of faculty and used the positive feelings engendered by faculty to get more money to build ever-larger collections. This approach, of course, led to judging quality by size (as in the case of the Association of

Research Libraries [ARL] rankings), and libraries, in good times and bad, were held captive to this standard. The end result, as Allan Pratt and Ellen Altman have wryly noted, is that the library will "live by the numbers, and die by the numbers."[12] Johann Van Reenen demonstrated that it is unrealistic to expect any particular library to move up more than five points in the ARL rankings, due to budgetary and other resource constraints.[13]

In addition to raw counts, there are numerous permutations of measures that reflect size: number of volumes per capita, volumes per full-time equivalent (FTE) student, counts of sub-divisions of the collection (by type of material and call number range), growth of the collection, and so forth.

Analyzing Use

Preparing an analysis of use of the library's collection is another frequently employed method to assess the adequacy of the collection. The analysis will reveal collection areas that receive little or no use as well as areas that are intensively used. A. K. Jain[14] and George Bonn[15] developed the theory of use relative to holdings. Bonn suggested creating a "use factor" by divid-ing the circulation percentage of a given subject by the holdings percentage of the same sub-ject. Large use factors (e.g., 2.1) represent portions of the collection that are intensively used, and perhaps the acquisitions budget should be expanded in this area. Conversely, small use factors (e.g., 0.3) represent portions of the collection that are not used very much, and perhaps fewer of the acquisitions dollars should be spent in this area. A use factor of 1.0 indicates a balance between holdings and use. Paul Metz called the "use factor" a proportional use statistic.[16]

Terry Mills expanded this concept and suggested that Bonn's use factor should be multi-plied by 100 to create the "percentage of expected use." If the expected use of a subject area is 100 percent, which sounds logical, then subject areas that are above 100 percent are overused, while those below 100 percent are underused.[17]

Rather than relying on subjective demarcation lines, Ken Dowlin and Lynn Magrath rec-ommended using the standard deviation as a more objective way to define overuse and under-use.[18] William Aguilar suggested preparing a "ratio of interlibrary loan borrowings to holdings" to complement a "holdings/use" analysis.[19]

Getting the availability of use information by title or copy is relatively simple given the reporting capabilities of today's automated library systems. One helpful analysis is to compare percent holdings (by type of material and call number range) with percent circulation using the categories shown in Figure 12.2A. This analysis has been called the "circulation/holdings ratio," the "circulation/inventory ratio," "stock turnover ratio," "inventory use ratio," and "inten-sity of circulation."

Plotting the current percent of the acquisitions budget for the same "circulation/holdings" ratio categories will highlight areas of the budget that may have to be adjusted. Similar charts can be prepared for the nonfiction collection (no more than 20 categories should be included in the analysis)—see Figure 12.2B; percent circulation to percent acquisitions budget—see Figure 12.2C, and many other variations.

An analysis of fiction and nonfiction bestseller titles in 10 public libraries found that although the ratio of holds to copies averaged about 2.7:1, fiction titles had about twice the num-ber of copies as nonfiction titles.[20]

Some types of libraries, such as those in academic institutions, will have relatively few duplicate titles, whereas in a public library, especially with a large number of branches, the

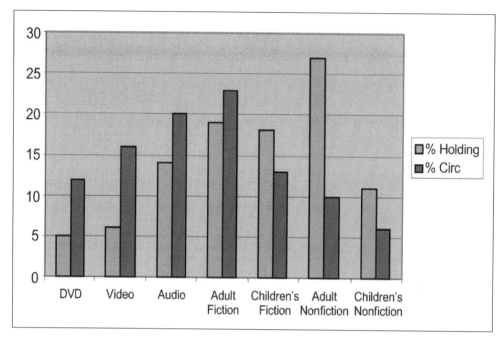

Figure 12.2A. Percent Holding Compared to Percent of Circulation

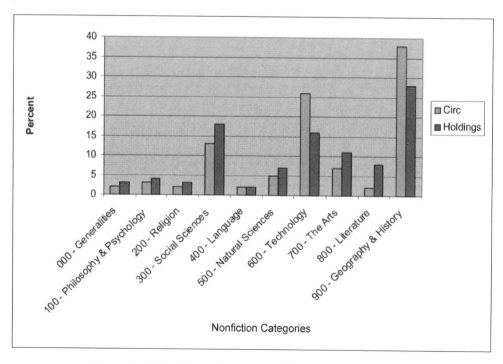

Figure 12.2B. Holdings Compared to Circulation for Nonfiction

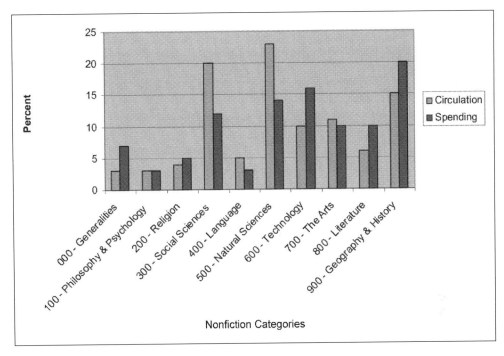

Figure 12.2C. Circulation and Spending for Nonfiction

number of volumes can be quite high compared to the number of unique titles. A majority of public libraries will routinely prepare a report indicating the number of holds to the number of copies of a title, so that additional copies of the title can be ordered if the hold/holdings ratio exceeds a defined threshold.

An analysis of circulating children's books found that:

- Best-seller lists infrequently contain award-winning books
- Best-seller lists contain many series books, such as the *Harry Potter* series or the *Series of Unfortunate Events* books
- Bestsellers rather than prize-winning books are found on the shelves
- Prize-winning books rarely stimulate children to read more[21]

Dennis Carrigan suggests using data from a library's automated circulation system to determine the proportional use by subject classification of a library's collection to reveal both under-selection and over-selection.[22] First introduced by George Bonn, the concept has been used at Virginia Tech libraries, among others.[23] A library would also need to prepare an analysis of interlibrary loan and document delivery data for a complete picture of the value of the collection development decisions that are being made on behalf of the library.

The 80/20 Rule. Richard Trueswell introduced the 80/20 rule, sometimes called the Power Law distribution, by showing that a small proportion of the print collection (about 20 percent) would account for 80 percent (or more) of circulation.[24] Trueswell also noted that the 80/20 rule was not a hard-and-fast rule and that sometimes the data might reflect a 75/25 rule; the important point is to note that a small proportion of active users account for a large percent of the total circulation. The University of Tennessee, Knoxville, library prepared an analysis that confirmed the applicability of the 80/20 rule for the entire collection, but found that the rule did not apply to various sections of the Library of Congress classification system (80 percent of the circulation within a class would require from 6 to 40 percent of the holdings).[25]

Not surprisingly, the 80/20 rule prompted some discussion in the profession. Seymour Sargent reported on a study done at the University of Wisconsin-Oshkosh library. Owing in part to the relatively young age of the library's collection, a shelf time of only 7½ years could account for 99 percent of circulation, and only 12 percent of the sample had never circulated.[26] In addition, Trueswell used data reflecting historical usage, whereas other authors, such as Eldredge[27] and Blecic et al.,[28] have analyzed monographs acquired over the course of a specific time period that may bias the results. Nisonger summarized a set of studies that analyzed the 80/20 rule and found that most studies were in fact in the general ballpark of 80/20. Jacob Nash has written a thoughtful review of Trueswell's original article and its contribution to collection evaluation and management.[29]

The 80/20 rule, sometimes known as the Pareto effect, was developed by Italian economist Vilfredo Pareto in 1906. In a similar vein, Joseph Juran recognized the same universal principle—which he called the "vital few and trivial many"—when he identified 20 percent of the defects causing 80 percent of the problems.

Consider a portion of the collection. The more heavily used it is, the more likely it is that any particular item will not be on the shelf when looked for by a customer. This intensive use and its impact on the customer are called "shelf bias." An example will help illustrate this phenomenon. During the day, one customer after another retrieves items from the shelf in a specific area of the collection and finds fewer choices. As the day wears on, the selection of available items becomes less and less interesting as shelf bias increases. The end result is that the shelves will contain items that nobody wants.[30]

Regardless of where oversized items were shelved, these materials experienced significantly less circulation than the rest of the collection.[31]

Paul Kantor and Wonsik Shim analyzed ARL circulation data and formulated the "Square Root Law": circulation is proportional to the square root of the product of reader population (number of FTE students) and the fractional power of the collection size.[32]

The University of Pittsburgh Study (sometimes called the Kent Study or the Pitt Study). Allen Kent and his colleagues conducted a very important study when they examined the 36,892 books cataloged in 1969 and found that 40 percent (actually 39.8 percent) had never circulated six years later (and suggested that the uncirculated items would never be used). The team also examined in-library use of materials and concluded that circulation data can be utilized with a high degree of confidence to measure total book use. An examination of print journal use found that usage was generally low, and what journals were used were primarily current ones. The study also calculated cost per use for books and journals.[33] Not surprisingly, the study generated a fair amount of controversy.[34] Kent and his co-authors responded to the criticism, noting that the team's analysis was conservative.[35]

The data collected by Kent and his colleagues suggest that after a book is added to the collection, there is only a 50 percent chance that it will ever be used. After the first two years in the library, the chance that it will ever be used drops to 25 percent; if it is not used after the first six years, the probability that it will ever be used drops to 4 percent.

Larry Hardesty replicated and validated the Pittsburgh Study at DePauw University in Indiana, noted that 30 percent of the books accounted for 80 percent of the circulation, roughly confirming Trueswell's 80/20 Rule.[36]

The Pittsburgh Study was replicated a second time by Hardesty at Eckerd College in Florida and found that approximately one-third of the books did not circulate even once. A high correlation was found between in-library use of materials and borrowed materials.[37] Thus, it would seem that regardless of the size of the academic library, building a "just-in-case" collection will result in a large proportion of the materials never being used!

Robert Hayes analyzed the data from the Pittsburgh Study and asserted that circulation data do not adequately represent the total use of a research collection. He suggested that if circulation data were the only criterion to relegate material to remote storage, up to 25 percent of in-library use would be adversely affected.[38]

Also, in a classic study conducted at the University of Chicago, Herbert Fussler and Julian Simon found that past use is a good predictor of present use and, thus, present use is likely a good predictor of future use.[39]

Using data collected over long periods of time (a semester or a full year) will even out any variations in use that may occur during a semester. Illustrating this point is a study that examined one year of circulation data for the 6.6 million titles held by the OhioLINK academic libraries. It was found that circulation rates varied widely by language, subject, age of material, and institution. The analysis revealed that the proportion of items from the collective collection that are not used, are used only once, or are used more than once stays relatively constant from year to year; however, individual titles will move between the three groups in a somewhat random process. Interestingly, *80 percent* of the circulation among all of Ohio's academic institutions is driven by *6 percent* of the collection.[40]

Nevertheless, a number of studies in ARL libraries and medium-sized academic libraries belie the claim that a 45 percent circulation rate in 20 years is typical—66 percent of 1.3 million books purchased by the CARLI libraries circulated within five years[41]; the University of Denver found that 58 percent of imprints were borrowed at least once within 5 years of being acquired[42]; 62.5 percent of books purchased by Kent State over a two-year period had circulated after three years[43]; and the Lingnam University Library in Hong Kong found that 67 percent of books had circulated at least once within 6 years of being added to the collection.[44]

Exemplifying the need to determine use patterns in a specific library, two studies reflecting monograph use at an academic health sciences library are of interest. Jonathan Eldridge at the University of New Mexico School of Medicine found that most monographs (84 percent) had circulated at least once in the four years following acquisition.[45] The second study found that 81 percent had circulated once during the first three years of shelf life—39 percent occurred in the first year, 32 percent in the second year, and 29 percent in the third year.[46] Both studies observed that a low monograph-to-user ratio might account for their atypical use pattern.

Taking into account the size of a library's collection and the type of library, it would be fair to say that a good ballpark estimate is that about 40 percent of a libraries physical collection will go unused. The very diversity of all of the studies makes these findings fairly consistent and quite compelling. So, the obvious question that should arise in the mind of the reader is: "What do the circulation data in my library reveal about our collection?"

One academic library removed fines and reduced fees and found that there was no significant effect on return rates and circulation numbers.[47]

In-Library Use

Documenting the in-library use of the collection is typically accomplished by recording items (manually or using an automated scanner) found on the desks before returning these items to the shelves. This method will underreport actual use because the library's customers will return items to the shelves, even when asked not to do so. Two reshelving studies using the sweep method found that it yielded results that underreported actual use from 20 to 40 percent.[48] In addition, this method will not identify use that is relatively short because the customer did not carry the item to a desk.

An alternative approach is to use direct observation to gain an estimate of total in-library use of the book or serial collection. During randomly assigned blocks of time, users are observed to see how many items are used and returned to the shelf and how many are left on the tables. Adding reshelved items to the items left on the tables provides a more accurate indication of in-library use.[49] Another study calculated the browsing ratio: volumes used in the library plus volumes checked out.[50]

One college used journal use, subscription prices, and academic department enrollment to calculate cost per use and use per department in an effort to determine low-usage journals that could be moved to storage.[51]

Studies have suggested that there tends to be a stable *ratio* of total circulation to total in-library use of a library's collection, although the ratios noted in some studies have varied significantly (from less than 1:1 to more than 10 in-library uses to 1 borrowed item). Anthony Hindle and Michael Buckland found that books that circulate little get relatively little in-library use, and the more heavily borrowed books also have a higher in-library use.[52] They also noted that 40 percent of the collection had no recorded circulation, yet accounted for nearly 20 percent of the in-library use.

Determining the ratio in a particular library is important to get a better understanding of the total use of a library's collection. Joan Stockard et al., who found a wide range of ratios when they examined in-library use in three libraries, underscored this point in a study.[53]

Harris[54] found that in-library collection use was as much as 20 times the use reflected in materials left on tables; Lawrence and Oja suggested that in-library use of books was six times greater than circulation data in two University of California libraries.[55] The Seton Hall University Library found that 30 percent of "possible" circulation transactions were for materials that were used in-house (and not borrowed).[56]

This suggests that circulation statistics do not represent the totality of the use of the physical collection.

Patron-Driven Acquisitions

Patron-driven acquisition (PDA) programs have been called by many titles: collaborative collection development, demand-driven acquisitions, just-in-time acquisitions, patron-driven acquisitions, patron-initiated acquisitions, patron-initiated collection development, purchase on demand, and user-driven acquisitions (and there are no doubt more titles for this type of program). Rather than a library purchasing materials on behalf of the customer (a just-in-case approach), PDA enables the customer to trigger the purchase of materials (either physical or digital) by clicking on a catalog link. PDA is a "just-in-time" approach to collection building.

Among the reasons a library may adopt such a program include:[57]

- *Cost-effectiveness*—Only materials that the customer actually wants are purchased. In addition to reducing expenses for collection development, PDA may provide more rapid turnaround time and reduce ILL staff workload.

- *Increased usage*—The desired item is purchased at the point of need as expressed by the customer's request; the content will be read at least once. And research suggests that if an item is used once, it will most likely be used several more times.
- *Collection development*—Customer-driven acquisitions, in their various forms, help create a balanced (and used) collection by filling in gaps in the collection, encourage patron collaboration in collection development, and improve overall customer satisfaction.

Libraries might create criteria to make a purchase decision; for example, set a maximum cost, only books, English language, published within the last X years, speed of acquiring the desired title, and so forth.

The Purdue University Libraries initiated a program of purchasing rather than borrowing books requested through ILL (a kind of indirect patron-driven acquisition program). After 10 years of operation, an analysis of this *Books on Demand* program suggests the books were appropriate additions to the collection. The study also found that books acquired through this program had much higher circulation rates than books acquired through the normal acquisitions process (a mean of 4.1 compared to a mean of 2.4)[58] However, the librarians involved in the study argue against the idea that collection development should be left *completely* up to users. A similar program in a small college compared book requests from undergraduates that were purchased in lieu of ILL borrowing. Items acquired through this popular program were circulated more frequently and cost $39.70 on average (costs of items acquired using the normal acquisitions process were not provided).[59]

The Texas A&M University Libraries "Suggest a Purchase" program has met with very high levels of satisfaction among both students and faculty members. Of the more than 13,000 requests:[60]

- 75 percent were added to the collection
- 15 percent were already owned by the library
- 6 percent were not yet published
- 3 percent were for journal titles
- 78 percent of the added titles were borrowed within the first 3 years

The Brigham Young University (BYU) Libraries employ five PDA programs: suggest a book online, faculty expedited orders, ILL requests, e-books, and multiple holds triggers. An analysis of the effectiveness of these PDA programs measured use, cost, and cost-per-use and found that the PDA models were more cost-effective in acquiring library resources than the traditional just-in-case models.[61] An earlier analysis by BYU determined that only 50 percent of its acquisitions had been used within 10 years of being purchased.[62]

A group of librarians created the *Getting It System Toolkit* (GIST) that automated selected library processes to support better and more informed decisions about the borrow-or-purchase decision.[63] For more about this helpful open-source toolkit, visit http://www.gistlibrary.org/. Another study found that librarians and patrons often choose the same titles of the same level of usefulness and sophistication.[64]

Still, it should be noted that PDA programs have both intended and unintended consequences, as noted by Robert Kieft and Lizanne Payne:

> Demand-driven acquisition of print and electronic text initially served local library interests by reducing the number of volumes purchased. Such programs, however,

soon fostered print-on-demand services through consortial or state-based production facilities, the establishment of regional acquisition programs for print monographs that did not find a demand-driven market, and the intensification of programs for consortial licensing of e-books.[65]

Patron-driven acquisition of e-books is discussed in another chapter.

Comparing Holdings

Given the ready availability of machine-readable bibliographic records, it is possible to prepare an analysis that compares the holdings in a specific library with the holdings of a peer group of libraries.

OCLC provides a service called *WorldShare Collection Evaluation* that allows a library to compare its collection with a group of peer libraries (up to 50). Comparisons can be made for specific subject areas or for the entire collection. The analysis will cover size, age, growth, title, and uniqueness.[36] One of the reports is a list of titles held by the other libraries that are not owned by the "target" library. This list of titles does not, however, indicate whether these titles have ever been circulated or used in the library. The service can assist libraries when they are deselecting (identify titles that are unique in your collection), adding content (what titles are widely held), and undergoing accreditation (what titles other libraries with similar programs hold).

One study of eight public libraries, using the *WorldShare Collection Evaluation* service, found that 80 percent of the collection was represented by 20 percent of the subject categories.[66] Another study by an academic library revealed that its collection was older than those of comparable libraries and that e-books provided access to resources that were more intensively used than had been realized.[67] A study of the Seton Hall University Libraries collection found that only 22 percent of the collection circulated over a 5-year period (circulation was higher in areas with more current collections).[68]

Overlap Studies

An overlap study will determine how materials are distributed among a number of libraries. Overlap studies are intended to provide information on the amount of overlap or duplication among collections while also revealing materials that are *not* duplicated. An overlap study is useful in planning cooperative or distributed programs among libraries.

Sampling methods that may be used to prepare an overlap analysis include:

• Comparing specific subject areas to determine which material is held in common
• Sampling from external lists such as a national bibliography or a subject bibliography
• Selecting random samples from each library and checking them against the other libraries involved (each sample should be proportional to the size of the collection)
• Comparing recent acquisitions

In addition, it is possible to compare the total holdings of one library with one or more other libraries using machine-readable bibliographic records; in effect, this is a 100% sample. Constance Malpas from OCLC examined the Hathi Trust Digital Library database and found that 24 percent of the digital holdings were also held in print by more than 100 libraries.[69]

One type of overlap study will determine the overlap of titles held by two or more libraries as well as identifying the distribution of unique titles. A study of overlap among the University of California libraries found that 75 percent of Berkeley's holdings were unique among the northern UC libraries, and 45 percent of UCLA's titles were unique among the southern UC libraries. Also, 53 percent of the Berkeley and UCLA holdings were duplicated in another UC library.[70]

During the late 1970s, 82 percent of all titles added in the University of Wisconsin system libraries were held by just one library, and only 18 percent were held by two libraries.[71] The SULAN libraries in Indiana found that 45 percent of titles were unique, and that another 26 percent were held by two libraries.[72] A higher rate of 52 percent was noted by Thomas Nisonger when he examined the holdings of 17 Texas libraries.[73] An even higher rate of original titles was found by William Potter when he examined the holdings of 21 academic libraries in Illinois.[74]

An analysis of the OhioLINK consortium's holdings was made to determine the amount of duplication of recently published materials as well as the number of copies available for patron-initiated borrowing.[75] It was found that there is a high level of duplication (70 percent of purchased copies were not being used), and that over time the level of duplication increases.

A study in two hospital health science libraries found an overlap that ranged from 20 to 26 percent for monographs and 45 to 58 percent for serial titles.[76] Although it is now slightly dated, William Potter prepared an excellent review of collection overlap studies.[77]

William McGrath prepared a table showing the overlap between 60 libraries, similar to a table showing distances between cities in a road atlas. McGrath's table is an example of a multidimensional scaling technique. An analysis showed a clustering by type of library and that regional location did not seem to affect overlap.[78]

Citation Studies

Bibliometrics, the term introduced by Alan Pritchard in 1969,[79] uses statistical data to analyze patterns pertaining to the use of documents and scholarly communication. The main branch of bibliometrics is citation studies—an analysis of references in and citations to documents such as books and articles. Among the uses of citation studies are:

- Identifying the core journals for a discipline, which will allow the library to satisfy the majority of demand while minimizing the number of subscriptions
- Analyzing a discipline's structure in terms of language, age, and place of publication
- Identifying the most productive authors, departments, universities, and nations
- Identifying the growth, obsolescence, and scattering of a discipline
- Identifying little-cited journals as candidates for cancellation
- Determining whether serial/monograph expenditure ratios are appropriate
- Checking textbook citations against a library's holdings
- Evaluating university faculty's research productivity

The value of a citation analysis is that citations are treated seriously by scholars and are used to look for additional materials related to a topic. Citation analysis is most frequently done in the academic environment, although it has been used in some special libraries. Citation analysis is attractive as a focus for study because the citations are readily available and unobtrusive. Co-citation is the frequency with which two documents are cited together.

The *Journal Citation Reports* provides four types of citation data for thousands of scientific journals:

- *Total Citations* details the aggregate number of citations received by all issues of a journal during the year.
- *Impact Factor* provides the ratio of citations received to articles published by the journal. These citation data are available for a specific institution for a fee through *Local Journal Utilization Reports,* a product offered by the Institute for Scientific Information (ISI).
- *Cited Half-Life* designates the median age of the articles cited from a specific journal.
- *Immediacy Index* reveals how quickly a journal's articles are cited.

Francis Narin concluded that bibliometric measures correlate highly with more subjective and survey-based measures of productivity, eminence, and quality of research.[80]

> *The impact factor may be a pox upon the land because of the abuse of that number.*
> —Robert Austin[81]

A number of studies that have examined journal impact factors have produced decidedly mixed results. For example:

- Global journal impact factors do not correlate with use of print journals in individual libraries.[82]
- Journals grouped by subject, scope, and language show a positive correlation between journal impact factor and use of print journals.[83]
- One study found no relationship between citation-based measures and holding counts.[84]
- One study concluded that citation-based measures could be used without correcting for journal self-citation. Self-citations do exert a major effect on the rankings for a small number of journals.[85]
- Other studies have yielded inconclusive results.[86]

Blecic found correlations between local citation and publication data and in-library use as measured by print journal reshelving data, circulation, and citation by faculty.[87] Joanna Duy and Liwen Vaughn found that local citation data are a valid reflection of total journal usage.[88] Robin Devin and Martha Kellogg, after reviewing a number of citation studies, developed a table that recommends a percent of the acquisitions budget that should be spent on serials, subdivided by subject.[89]

As disenchantment with impact factors has grown, some new tools have emerged to help evaluate scientists and their research. Among these are the following:

- **The Faculty of 1,000,** which uses 2,000 scientists to rate each paper they read each month from some 800 journals. This approach will identify important articles published in journals with high- or low-impact factors.
- **The h-index,** developed by physics professor Jorgu Hirsh, identifies the highest number of papers each researcher has published that receive the same number of citations.[90] One study calculated the h-index for U.S. library and information science school faculty members (Nicholas Belkin had the highest score of 20), and found that there was a strong correlation between an individual's h-index and the total number of citations an individual received.[91]
- **The Number Needed to Read (NNR)** is an index of how many papers in a journal have to be read to find one of adequate clinical quality and relevance.[92]

- **Relative Citation Ratio (RCR)** is a new article-level quality metric that measures the relative citation strength of an article. The RCR normalizes articles to their field, to their year of publication, and to an average score of 1.0.[93]

Bibliometric Laws. Six basic bibliometric "laws" are often mentioned in the citation analysis literature:

- **Bradford's Law,** sometimes called the "law of scattering," is based on the distribution of publications in a discipline or of articles in a set of journals. The "law" states that there is a high degree of concentration of related papers in a relatively small number of "core" journals. Stated another way, a small percentage of journals accounts for a large percentage of what articles are published, and an even smaller percentage accounts for what is cited. Beyond the small nucleus of "core" journals, Bradford identified "zones" of less-productive journals, each zone providing reduced yield as an increasing number of marginally productive journals are added.

   The number of the groups of journals to produce nearly equal numbers of articles is roughly in proportion to 1: n: n^2 . . . , where n is called the Bradford multiplier.[94] When Bradford scattering data are plotted as a log-normal graph, the central portion becomes a straight line. There are usually deviations from this straight line for both core journals and the most peripheral journals. The latter deviation is now referred to as "Groos droop."[95]

- **Garfield's Law of Concentration** states that all disciplines combined produce a multidisciplinary literature core for all of science that consists of 500 to 1,000 journals.

- **Lotka's Law** is based on the number of authors publishing in a discipline or other defined field. The number of authors publishing a certain number of articles is a fixed ratio to the number of authors publishing a single article. As the number of articles published increases, authors producing the same number of publications become less frequent. There are one-quarter as many authors publishing two articles within a specified time period as there are single-publication authors, one-ninth as many publishing three articles, one-sixteenth as many publishing four articles, and so on. Though the law itself covers many disciplines, the actual ratios involved are very discipline-specific.

- **Zipf's Law** is based on word-frequency rankings in a defined set of documents. The frequency of any word is roughly inversely proportional to its rank in the frequency table. The most frequent word will occur approximately twice as often as the second most frequent word, which occurs twice as often as the fourth most frequent word, and so on. In other words, people are more likely to select and use familiar rather than unfamiliar words.

- **Half-Life Law.** The half-life of a literature is the time during which one-half of the currently active literature was published.[96] The half-life of a subject area can be determined and is sometimes used as a descriptive measure of a particular subject; for example, the physics literature might have a half-life of 9.4 years. Charles Bourne demonstrated that although there are differences, they are not dramatic differences in various subject areas.[97] Depending on the method used, either 400 or 580 items are needed to estimate the half-life within a 10 percent margin of error.[98]

- **Price Index**. De Solla Price analyzed a large number of citations and found that in any given year, 35 percent of all existing papers are not cited at all, 49 percent are cited once, and the remaining 16 percent are cited an average of 3.2 times.[99] He further noted that only 1 percent of all papers are cited six or more times a year. The "Price Index" is the proportion of references to papers published in the last five years compared to the total volume of papers in a discipline (the value can range from 0 to 100 percent). Price also noted that recent papers tended to be cited more often than the amount of recent literature might suggest and called this difference the "immediacy factor." He suggested that the immediacy factor might vary among disciplines, as some relied more on older literature than others.

Stern conducted a study of the characteristics of the literature of literary scholarship and found that monographic literature was heavily cited. Primary sources and older materials were heavily used; about 50 percent of the citations were 20 years old or older.[100] A citation analysis study of eight humanity fields found that monographs remain the dominant format of cited sources, and that French- and German-language materials are the most frequently cited foreign-language items.[101] An examination of citations from six biological journals found that authors included more citations for articles published in 1998 than in 1968. And while there is a clear bias toward citing the recent literature, that bias seems to be no greater now than it was in 1968, before the advent of computer databases.[102]

Undergraduate use of an academic library's collection will not be reflected in citation studies. Rose Mary Magrill and Gloriana St. Clair prepared a citation analysis of undergraduate papers at four academic institutions. They found that science students used twice as many references in their papers as humanities or social sciences students. Further, a clear majority (66 percent) of the citations used by the science undergraduates were to journal articles, whereas two-thirds of the citations used by the humanities undergraduates were to books.[103]

Hoffmann and Doucette, in a review of 34 cited reference analysis studies or citation studies, found that most studies do not provide sufficient detail for their study to be replicated.[104]

Analyzing the references contained in faculty publications or in doctoral dissertations is problematic. Several studies have shown that the principle of least effort has a significant impact on the information-seeking behavior of faculty and students: the more accessible an information source; the more likely it will be used.[105]

Soper has suggested that accessibility influences citation behavior—the more accessible a source, the more likely it will be cited.[106] Liu has suggested that a "normative theory of citing" exists—the more an electronic journal article is read, the more it is cited.[107] Supporting evidence for this theory was found on the Web-based NASA Astrophysics Data System.[108]

Lois Kuyper-Rushing examined music dissertation citations from across the United States and concluded that analysis of a single institution would likely result in a skewed list of journals; she raised the issue of whether an analysis of doctoral dissertation citations as a basis for collection decision is justified.[109] A more recent study by Penny Beile and her colleagues also found that analysis of a single institution can result in a skewed list of core journals.[110]

Johanna Tuñón and Bruce Brydges developed a rubric for assessing the quality of citations that included currency, type of document, and other document-specific criteria. They also developed a second rubric for the subjective assessment of citations based on five criteria: number and variety of documents cited, depth of understanding through the inclusion of theoretical and background documents, scholarliness, currency, and relevance of the resources. These authors found that most students failed to include retrieval statements, and thus the use of bibliometric information about students' use of electronic resources will be murky.[111]

An analysis of citations obtained from several sources found that the University of Illinois library owned some 77 percent of items cited in monographs, 87 percent cited in periodicals, and 91 percent cited in dissertations. The study concluded that:

- Monographs used as sources of citations are best suited to assess the strength of a collection in terms of foreign-language materials, general monographs, and older materials

- Periodicals used as sources of citations are best suited to assess the strength of a collection in relation to recently published materials, its own periodical coverage, and its comprehensiveness in terms of "other" types of materials
- Dissertations used as sources of citations are best suited to assess the strength of a collection in relation to its holdings of conference proceedings, dissertations, and reports[112]

Yet several cautions must be noted:

- Core journals can change rapidly due to editorial changes, a new title, or changes in emphasis in a field.
- Citation studies are useful to predict use of research and scholarly materials and not for other purposes.
- Citation analysis resources are readily available for the sciences and social sciences but less so for other subject areas.
- It is necessary to ensure that the citations used for analysis come from more than one institution, to prevent bias.[113]
- It is easy to focus on the mathematical distributions without seeking the meaning behind the numbers.
- Citation analysis should be just one of several factors in the decision-making process.

Loss Rate Analysis

The library may want to identify the amount of material that is no longer in its collection due to theft. Typically a loss rate analysis is prepared when a library is considering installing a theft detection system, but it also has value in identifying materials the library may wish to replace in its collection. Losses may be items that have been checked out to a customer but never returned, as well as materials that are "borrowed" from the library but not checked out—often the latter is called theft.

A library may generate a report from its automated library system identifying the titles of materials that have been borrowed but not returned in more than three to six months. This list can be used to identify titles that the library will order again to ensure that they are found in its collection. The total number of items that have not been returned after 12 months compared to total circulation will yield a percent loss rate.

Other libraries have selected a sample of titles from their shelf lists and then checked to see whether the items are on the shelf or have been borrowed by a customer. It is then possible to calculate a percent loss rate: number of items not "found" compared to the total number of items checked in the sample. One survey of a nonrepresentative sample of 74 libraries found that libraries "share consistent theft patterns."[114]

A library should also ensure that the theft or nonreturn of materials is addressed as part of its collection development policies, especially if theft is a persistent problem.

User Surveys

Some libraries have asked their customers to rate the library's collection in terms of how well it meets their needs and to suggest or identify areas that are weak. In some cases, additional demographic information is obtained so that the results can be compared among different groups—young vs. old, student vs. faculty, and so forth. It should be noted that the focus of this type of survey is on the library's collection, and it is not a general customer satisfaction survey.

A number of studies have demonstrated that users of academic libraries select materials on the basis of subject matter and topicality.[115] Other studies have found that the most desirable sources were those that were accessible and easy to understand.[116] A study that examined undergraduate student selection criteria showed that the content, table of contents, and book organization were the most important factors.[117]

If a user survey is used, it should be complemented with other methods to evaluate the library's collection. Daniel Gore asked a group of students to keep a diary of their book searches over an academic semester. A total of 422 items were sought, and the library owned 90 percent of them. Of the items owned, 88 percent were found on the shelf—an availability rate of 88 percent.[118]

The Availability Study

An availability study examines the reasons customers are unable to find the items they are looking for when they visit the library. An availability study has also been called a "shelf availability study," a "frustration study," or a "failure study." Such studies have been conducted chiefly at academic libraries. The reasons an item might not be available range from being it checked out, missing, or misplaced on the shelf, to the customer searching incorrectly or the item not being owned by the library. In general, these studies reveal that a library customer has only about a 60 percent chance of getting the item, as shown in Figure 12.3.[119]

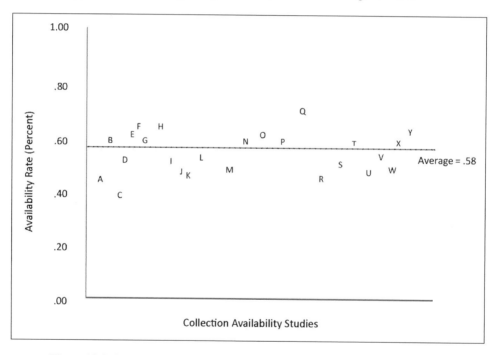

Figure 12.3. Summary of Collection Availability Studies in Academic Libraries

Other, library-centric, collection assessment methods include:

- Obtaining a sample from the shelf list. The bias inherent in this approach can be overcome with some creative analysis.[120]
- Using citations selected by experts in a subject field.
- Using indexes, abstracts, or general bibliographies.

Involving the customers is a method that asks them to record on a form what they are looking for and whether the desired item was found. The forms are distributed as the customer enters the library. Alternatively, a staff member could interview customers as they begin their search among the shelves. Staff then analyzes the completed forms to determine the cause of failure, if any. A sample data collection form is shown in Figure 12.4.

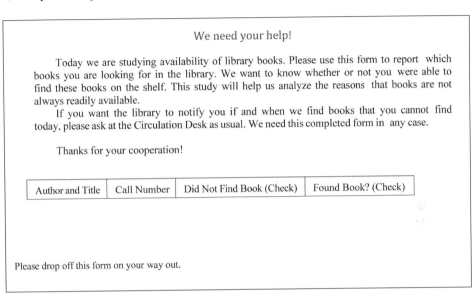

Figure 12.4. Sample Book Availability Study Data Collection Form

The availability study examines the success experienced by the customer when looking for a known item. This approach can be easily adapted for use in any type of library. One study noted that its customers found about 81 percent of the journal articles they were seeking.[121]

The sample sizes of the availability studies summarized in this section ranged from slightly more than 200 to more than 2,300, with an average of 802. Clearly the library management team will have more confidence in the results of an analysis with a larger sample size, but this must be balanced with the costs associated with the data collection effort.

Paul Kantor developed a branching technique to illustrate the relationship among the various categories (see Figure 12.5). Available items were seen as flowing through a pipeline, some being sidetracked along branches for various reasons and thus becoming unavailable. Those items emerging at the end of the pipe were available for use by the customer.[122]

Reasons an item might not be available include the following:

- **Collection Failure:** The library does not own the desired item about 10 percent of the time. An analysis of customer requests to purchase titles for the collection, as well as of interlibrary loan requests, will assist in reducing customer frustrations.
- **In Circulation:** The desired item has been checked out to another customer or is on the hold shelf waiting to be checked out for about 15 to 20 percent of the items.
- **Library Error:** The item should be on the shelf but it is waiting to be shelved (yet to be sorted, on a sorting shelf or a book truck), is missing, is reported lost, or is shelved incorrectly about 13 percent of the time.
- **Catalog Error:** The customer cannot find the item in the catalog about 7 percent of the time. Among the factors that might be examined are the complexity of the user interface with the

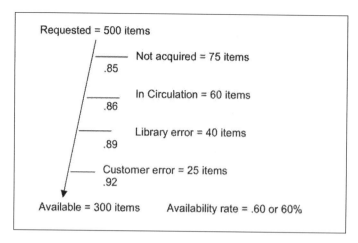

Figure 12.5. Kantor's Branching Diagram

library's online catalog, the clarity of information (information overload) displaced as the result of a search, the number of misspellings in the catalog, and so forth.

- **Customer Error:** The customer brings an incorrect citation, wrote down the call number incorrectly, or can't locate the item on the shelf about 10 percent of the time.

The Kantor branching diagram approach has been used in a number of academic libraries,[123] a specialized academic library,[124] a public library,[125] and a study of the availability of periodicals.[126] Haseeb Rashid suggested that a broader perspective that captured information about more categories of failure or disappointment would assist a library management team in understanding how they could make improvements. Rashid proposed 13 categories that should be tracked:[127]

- Quality of information brought to the library by the patron
- Whether the title is owned by the library
- If the item is not owned by the library, whether the item meets the collection development policies of the library
- Whether the call number is recorded correctly
- Whether the item is located in a special collection/location identified in the library catalog
- Whether the item is located in a special collection/location *not* identified in the library catalog
- Whether the item has been properly shelved but not located by the patron
- Whether the item has been mis-shelved
- Whether the item is in use in the library
- Whether the item has been checked out
- Whether the item is in a pre-shelving area
- Whether the item is missing or reported lost
- Other factors

Anne Ciliberti et al. expanded on the Kantor branching diagram by slightly revising the model for known-item searching and developing a parallel model for subject searching, shown in Figure 12.6.[128] She and her colleagues further elaborated the model by identifying the hurdles encountered in journal title searches.[129] This study revealed a number of problems that customers encountered that were unsuspected by library staff, including the need for better inventory control, better signage, and removing abbreviations from the catalog.

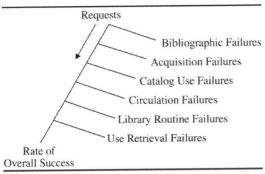

Known-Item Searches

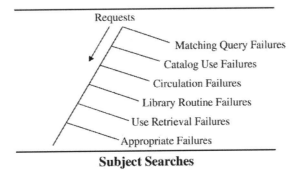

Subject Searches

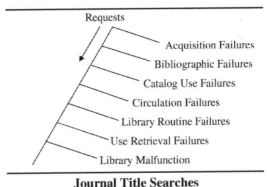

Journal Title Searches

Figure 12.6. Ciliberti Branching Diagrams. Anne C. Ciliberti, Mary Casserly, Judy Hegg, and Eugene Mitchell. Material Availability: A Study of Academic Library Performance. *College & Research Libraries*, 48, November 1987, 513–27; Anne Ciliberti, Marie L. Radford, Gary P. Radford, and Terry Ballard. Empty Handed? A Material Availability Study and Transaction Log Analysis Verification. *The Journal of Academic Librarianship*, 59, July 1998, 282–89.

Another study, by Eugene Mitchell et al., successfully applied the Kantor branching diagram to subject searches and found the approach to be helpful in identifying needed improvements for the library's procedures.[130] Three primary factors affect availability of a particular item: the item's popularity (best-seller list, recommendation by a professor, and so forth), the number of copies available for loan, and the length of the loan period.[131]

An alternative to the availability study is for the library to conduct a snapshot inventory. Topsy Smalley suggests sampling 3 percent of the library's circulating collection to determine the percent of the sample that is unavailable (neither on the shelf nor checked out).[132]

Thomas Nisonger prepared a thorough review of more than 50 studies and found availability rates for known-item searches by actual library users of about 61 percent, which was almost identical to an earlier review that Nisonger had prepared.[133]

Neal Kaske has suggested that as "just-in-case" collections are losing their utility, so too the availability study may no longer be useful. The traditional availability studies ignore the "just-in-time" efforts made by a library to meet a specific demand from a customer (purchasing the item with 24- to 48-hour delivery, recalling an item, interlibrary loan, document delivery, and so forth), as well as the increasing availability of print materials in electronic formats. Kaske suggests the need for a new measure that focuses on the time the customer waits for the desired item.[134]

Document Delivery Tests

A document delivery test creates a pool of citations from a broad range of recently published literature. The degree of accessibility is then determined for each title in the pool of citations. It is assumed that the citation pool will represent the information needs of real users.

Richard Orr and his colleagues in biomedical libraries conducted a major document delivery test. The research team created a citation pool of 300 citations and assigned a speed code as an indication of the degree of accessibility; possibilities ranged from immediate shelf availability to loan using an interlibrary loan service.[135] The speed of delivery used a scale of 1–5:

1. Document available in less than 10 minutes
2. Document available in more than 10 minutes but less than 2 hours
3. Document available in more than 2 hours but less than 24 hours
4. Document available in more than 24 hours but less than 7 days
5. Document not available in less than 7 days

The team also developed a Document Delivery Capability Index, with a maximal value of 100 only if all the sample documents were found "on the shelf" and available in less than 10 minutes. The Capability Index ranged from a low of 47 to a high of 88 in the sample of participating libraries.

A study team created three citation pools to test the availability of recently published books, current periodical literature, and other titles known to be in the libraries' collections. The goal was to determine the probability that an item was owned and, if owned, the probability that it was available for use—called the "Probability of Availability." Using a pool of 500 citations, Ernest DeProspo and his colleagues checked the catalogs of 20 participating libraries to determine if something was owned and then checked the shelf to determine its availability. The Probability of Availability was then calculated for each library.[136]

Curriculum Analysis

Another method involves assigning Library of Congress classification numbers to each course offering, sometimes called *course analysis*. The numbers of holdings for the corresponding classification numbers are counted in order to identify the resources available to support individual courses of instruction.[137] William McGrath used this approach at the University of Southwestern Louisiana and felt that it was a superior method to identify the scholarly interests in the campus departments.[138] McGrath's approach was replicated at the University of Nebraska at Omaha by Barbara Golden, who also added the number of enrolled students for each class to the analysis.[139] Similar analyses were prepared by Jenks and Burr.[140]

Richard Dougherty and Laura Bloomquist used course analysis to compare collections at branch libraries on a large academic campus.[141] Others have used course analysis to improve acquisitions, prepare a collection development policy, and evaluate the collection.[142] Gwen Lochstet added faculty research activity to the course analysis approach and demonstrated its value for three departments at the University of South Carolina.[143]

Course analysis allows the library to identify potential gaps in the collection. In addition, faculty will gain an understanding of the collection and how it supports the curriculum—and librarians will find their knowledge of the library's collection much improved. The disadvantage with this approach is that it is extremely time-consuming.

Interlibrary Loan Analysis

Another method of measuring collection adequacy against customer demand is to analyze a fairly large sample of interlibrary loan (ILL) requests. The ILL requests are sorted by subject or program, publication date, language of publication, and format. Such an analysis can reveal whether there is unmet demand based on weaknesses in the library's collection.

Albert Henderson developed a library Collection Failure Quotient (CFQ), which is the ratio of interlibrary borrowing to collection size.[144] Using data from 36 academic libraries, Henderson noted that the average CFQ score had doubled between 1974 and 1992. Henderson also prepared a similar analysis for 80 university libraries and calculated their CFQ scores between 1974 and 1998; the results indicate that all scores doubled or tripled during the 25-year time frame of the analysis.

A graph that shows the number and subject distributions of recent book acquisitions and of books borrowed using interlibrary loan can be an indication of current collection strength and balance, particularly for small to medium-sized libraries.[145] Jennifer Knievel and her colleagues suggest constructing a table of subject classifications and comparing the percent of holdings, the percent of circulation, and the ratio of holdings to interlibrary loan requests, to provide greater clarity when making collection management decisions.[146] Another study examined ILL requests and noted that they were indicators of subject needs, of recent publication, favorably reviewed, and easy to obtain, which led to the recommendation to buy rather than borrow most ILL requests.[147]

A longitudinal study prepared by Lynn Wiley and Tina Chrzastowski examined the number of ILL article requests among the 26 largest libraries in Illinois. Forty-four percent of the requests were filled in-state, and items from the sciences were requested by a two-to-one ratio over items from the social sciences and humanities. The results showed a significant decline (26 percent reduction) as the result of these same libraries offering greater access to electronic journals; use of the full-text database increased about 10 percent per year.[148]

Bruce Kingma analyzed the tradeoffs associated with use of ILL versus journal subscription costs and found that economic savings can be achieved from an increased use of ILL as long as the number of article requests for a specific journal is below a prescribed threshold.[149]

Right-Sizing the Collection

Another form of collection evaluation occurs when weeding items from the collection. The need for weeding is based on the reality that most items now being borrowed were previously borrowed in the fairly recent past (thus the use of the last circulation date as a weeding criterion as suggested by Slote),[150] and very few items that are now borrowed have sat on the shelves for a long period of time.

Rick Lugg and Ruth Fischer provide eight reasons why substantial weeding programs in academic libraries should be considered:[151]

1. Increasing access to digital content
2. Improved tools and infrastructure for resource sharing
3. It is possible to quickly reacquire an item previously discarded
4. Use of print materials has been steadily declining
5. Collection size is no longer a leading indicator of value
6. Increased access to data from several sources to make decisions
7. Space for physical collections is quite expensive (and reoccurs each year)
8. The status quo is no longer sustainable

In addition to the withdrawal of items from the collection, increasingly libraries are attempting to "free up" space from the shelving of collections for other uses. A library also has the option of "right-sizing" or deselecting materials other than through weeding by moving them to storage or participating in a shared print management program. Rick Lugg has suggested that this can be accomplished by:[152]

- Reducing the number of low-use surplus copies
- Minimizing the number of low-use copies held in open stacks
- Ensuring that withdrawn content is archived in both print and digital form
- Co-ordinating regionally (and nationally) to ensure that sufficient copies are retained
- Ensuring that deselected content remains accessible to users (should the need ever arise)

Lugg further argues that a library can use a multiplicity of factors to make decisions about weeding, storage, and shared print programs, including examining circulation, reserve borrowing, holdings in other libraries regionally and nationally, publication date, and Hathi Trust holdings (in-copyright and in the public domain).

Cynthia Snyder suggests that multiple criteria should be used when considering a title for deselection:[153]

- Book was added before X date
- Book has not been circulated or used in-house since Y date
- Title is owned by more than 100 other libraries
- Book is not in a specific list (e.g., *Resources for College Libraries*)
- Book is not about Z topic
- Multiple copies exist

Colin Taylor developed his 15/5 rule as a way to identify items that are candidates for storage (on or off campus). He suggested that all volumes of a title that were published in the last 15 years and that had not been borrowed during the last 5 years should be moved to storage.[154] Also, many libraries continue to expand their e-book collections partially as a way to discard a print book. Walton suggests that it is important for libraries to adopt a hybrid model of providing access to both print and digital formats, as students prefer print books for many reasons.[155]

Lorcan Dempsey, Constance Malpas, and Brian Lavoie argue persuasively that, given recent trends in scholarly communications:[156]

1. Libraries are becoming embedded in networks of cooperation, collaboration, and consolidation that require the reassessment of collections.

2. Customers are increasingly operating in a network environment that is rich in available resources (reducing the value and centrality of the local collection).

Shared Storage Facilities

About 20 percent of the 70 or so storage facilities are shared by two or more libraries.[157] And while there can be challenges in the administration of such services, shared storage facilities offer libraries the prospect of lowering costs while still preserving one or two copies of older, less-frequently used materials. Yet, ironically, the cost of weeding collections deposited from several libraries into one facility may be greater than the cost of storage.[158]

One survey of library directors suggested that trust, good communication policies, leadership, and use of appropriate technology are what is needed to make a shared repository work well.[159] Clearly, larger academic libraries are embracing the need to move from simply warehousing little-used print materials to collaborating in the creation of shared print facilities. This allows participating libraries to draw down their print collections in a responsible manner while still ensuring access.

Preservation

An evaluation or assessment may be made from the perspective of the condition of the library's collection. The assessment is designed to identify that portion of the collection that may have to be repaired in order to preserve it. The evaluation collects data regarding the condition, age, paper pH, type of binding, date of last circulation, and so forth using a statistical sampling technique.[160]

Value

The vast majority of libraries assign a replacement value for the library's collection for insurance purposes. There is, however, a much more important value that is difficult to conceptualize and quantify. That is, what are the consequences of use of the library's collection in the lives of its customers?

A few public libraries have attempted to identify the value of the benefits of using the library's collection using a cost-benefit analysis. Special libraries are in a fairly unique position in that they can ask their clients, usually employees of the organization, to identify and quantify the benefits that arise from use of the library—time savings, cost savings, generating new revenues, and so forth.

Recently, several academic libraries have calculated the value of their collections and services by focusing on the time savings (and thus also identifying the cost savings) that result from library services, as a part of the *LibValue Project*. This project was funded by the Institute of Museum and Library Services (IMLS), and its principal investigator was Carol Tenopir.[161]

Life Cycle Costs

Although purchase and processing costs of library materials are fairly easily identified, total life cycle costs of a library's collection are rarely considered. Using annual data reported by the Association of Research Libraries, costs are allocated to collections based on the size of the collection and its relative space. The analysis revealed that the life cycle costs of collections are many multiples of their purchase costs—seven times for monographs. And the life cycle costs of monograph collections overwhelm the costs of other collections, accounting for as much as 95 percent of all costs.

Paul Courant and Buzzy Nielsen estimated that holding books in open stacks costs $4.26 per volume per year and only 86 cents per volume per year in high-density storage.[162] The conclusion is inescapable: low use and the high annual costs for providing access to print monographs sitting on shelves is a premise that is no longer sustainable. Library customers need the space for other purposes.

COLLECTION DEVELOPMENT

Though the evaluation of collections might be viewed as an acceptable proxy for the evaluation of collection development, the reality is that over-selection and under-selection are not identified when the collection is evaluated. Under-selection results when materials that should have been acquired are not; over-selection results when materials are acquired but never used. Under-selection can be mitigated through the use of interlibrary loan and document delivery services.

The consequences of over-selection are serious, even ignoring the costs to purchase, process, and shelve the item for many years to come. More importantly, the opportunity cost of the item—the value to the library's customers of what was *not* acquired due to the item that was selected—must be acknowledged. Moving little-used and never-used materials to a storage facility may lower the costs slightly, but ongoing costs to continue to store the materials and provide access are also significant.

SUMMARY

This chapter has presented a wide variety of methods that can be used to assess a library's physical collection. Among the more notable conclusions that can drawn from this discussion are the following:

- A small proportion of the collection receives the greatest proportion of use.
- Although the 80/20 rule is valid for many libraries, some libraries will have a slightly different ratio of circulation to holdings due to their age and size.
- Circulation is not an accurate measure of total use, and the ratio of in-library use to circulation varies greatly.
- Some research libraries have significant in-library use of low-circulation items.
- Evaluating collection development is different than evaluating the collection, although similar tools are used for the analysis.

An analysis of faculty publishing suggests that an author needs between 40 and 50 publications to produce a single article. One organization found that it needed access to 90,000 publications to produce nearly 2,000 original articles in a single year. Nearly a quarter of all references were to articles less than 4 years old, and another quarter of the cited references were to materials 16 years or older. Thus, faculty need access to current publications as well as continuing access to publications for decades.[163]

As resources available to libraries decline, it is critical that collections and services be continually and systematically reviewed, with the goal of keeping them aligned with the mission of the organization and the needs of the customers. To present a balanced view of any evaluation, it is suggested that two or more methods be used. Each evaluation methodology has strengths and weaknesses, which must be considered when making plans to assess a specific library's collection. The goals and objectives of the evaluation will usually determine what methodology should be used.

For any type of library, consideration should be given to constructing and completing outcome studies that identify the benefits and impacts of the library's resources and its services on the lives of its customers.

David Lewis has argued persuasively that academic libraries are living in rapidly changing times and has issued a call to action:

> If academic libraries are to be successful, they will need to: deconstruct legacy print collections; move from item-by-item book selection to purchase-on-demand and subscriptions; manage the transition to open access journals; focus on curating unique items; and develop new mechanisms for funding national infrastructure.[164]

NOTES

1. Elizabeth Futas and David L. Vidor. What Constitutes a "Good" Collection? *Library Journal*, 112, April 15, 1987, 45–47, at 45.

2. Diane Schmidt, Elizabeth B. Davis, and Ruby Jahr. Biology Journal Use at an Academic Library: A Comparison of Use Studies. *Serials Review*, 20 (2), 1994, 45–64.

3. Robert N. Broadus. The Measurement of Periodical Use. *Serials Review*, 11 (2), 1985, 30–35.

4. Dennis R. Ridley and Joseph E. Weber. Toward Assessing In-House Use of Print Resources in an Undergraduate Academic Library: An Inter-Institutional Study. *Library Collections, Acquisitions, & Technical Services*, 24, 2000, 89–103.

5. Harriet Lightman and Sabina Manilov. A Simple Method for Evaluating a Journal Collection: A Case Study of Northwestern University's Economics Collection. *The Journal of Academic Librarianship*, 26 (3), May 2000, 183–90.

6. Russell F. Dennison. Quality Assessment of Collection Development Through Tiered Checklists: Can You Prove You Are a Good Collection Developer? *Collection Building*, 19 (1), 2000, 24–26.

7. Howard White. *Brief Tests of Collection Strength: A Methodology for All Types of Libraries*. Westport, CT: Greenwood Press, 1995.

8. Stephen McMinn. Evaluation of Motor Vehicles, Aeronautics, Astronautics Collections Using White's Power Method of Collection Analysis. *Collection Management*, 36 (1), 2010, 29–52. See also Jay Bernstein. From the Ubiquitous to the Nonexistent: A Demographic Study of OCLC WorldCat. *Library Resources & Technical Services*, 50, 2006, 79–90.

9. Nancy E. Gwinn and Paul H. Mosher. Coordinating Collection Development: The RLG Conspectus. *College & Research Libraries*, 44, March 1983, 128–40.

10. Howard White. *Brief Tests of Collection Strength: A Methodology for All Types of Libraries*. Westport, CT: Greenwood Press, 1995.

11. David Lesniaski. Evaluating Collections: A Discussion and Extension of Brief Tests of Collection Strength. *College & Undergraduate Libraries*, 11 (1), 2004, 11–24.

12. Allen D. Pratt and Ellen Altman. Live by the Numbers, Die by the Numbers. *Library Journal*, 122, April 15, 1997, 48–49.

13. Johann Van Reenen. Library Budgets and Academic Library Rankings in Times of Transition. *The Bottom Line*, 14 (4), 2001, 213–18.

14. A. K. Jain. Sampling and Data Collection Methods for a Book-Use Study. *Library Quarterly*, 39, July 1969, 245–52.

15. George S. Bonn. Evaluation of the Collection. *Library Trends*, 22, January 1974, 265–304.

16. Paul Metz. *The Landscape of Literatures: Use of Subject Collections in a University Library.* Chicago: American Library Association, 1983.

17. Terry R. Mills. *The University of Illinois Film Center Collection Use Study* (CAS Paper). Urbana: University of Illinois-Urbana, 1981.

18. Ken Dowlin and Lynn Magrath. Beyond the Numbers: A Decision Support System, in *Proceedings of the 1982 Clinic on Library Applications of Data Processing.* Urbana: University of Illinois, Graduate School of Library and Information Science, 1983, 27–58.

19. William Aguilar. The Application of Relative Use and Interlibrary Demand in Collection Development. *Collection Management*, 8 (1), Spring 1986, 15–24.

20. Michelle Gordon, Allison Haack, Rebecca Vernon, Tiffany Saulter, and Debora Shaw. Multiple Copies of Bestsellers in Public Libraries: How Much Is Enough? *Public Library Quarterly*, 33, 2014, 145–54.

21. Joanne Ujiie and Stephen Krashen. Are Prize-Winning Books Popular Among Children? An Analysis of Public Library Circulation. *Knowledge Quest*, 34 (3), January/February 2006, 33–35.

22. Dennis P. Carrigan. Collection Development—Evaluation. *The Journal of Academic Librarianship*, 22 (4), July 1996, 273–78.

23. George S. Bonn. Evaluation of the Collection. *Library Trends*, 29, January 1974, 272–73.

24. Richard W. Trueswell. Some Behavioral Patterns of Library Users: The 80/20 Rule. *Wilson Library Bulletin*, 43, January 1969, 458–61.

25. William A. Britten. A Use Statistic for Collection Management: The 80/20 Rule Revisited. *Library Acquisitions: Practice & Theory*, 14, 1990, 183–89.

26. Seymour H. Sargent. The Uses and Limitations of Trueswell. *College & Research Libraries*, 40, September 1979, 416–23.

27. Jonathan Eldredge. The Vital Few Meet the Trivial Many: Unexpected Use Patterns in a Monographs Collection. *Bulletin of the Medical Library Association*, 86(4), 1998, 496–503.

28. Deborah Blecic, Stephen Wiberley, Joan Fiscella, Sara Bahnmaier-Blaszczak, and Rebecca Lowery. Deal or No Deal? Evaluating Big Deals and Their Journals. *College & Research Libraries*, 74(2), 2013, 178–94.

29. Jacob Nash. Richard Trueswell's Contribution to Collection Evaluation and Management: A Review. *Evidence Based Library and Information Practice*, 11 (3), 2016, 118–24.

30. Michael K. Buckland. An Operations Research Study of a Variable Loan and Duplication Policy at the University of Lancaster. *Library Quarterly*, 42, 1972, 97–106.

31. D. Yvonne Jones. Oversized and Underused: Size Matters in Academic Libraries. *College & Research Libraries*, 67 (7), July 2006, 325–33.

32. Paul B. Kantor and Wonsik Shim. Library Circulation as Interaction Between Readers and Collections: The Square Root Law. *Proceedings of the American Society for Information Science*, 35, 1998, 260–66.

33. Allen Kent, Jacob Cohen, K. Leon Montgomery, James G. Williams, Stephen Bulick, Roger R. Flynn, William N. Sabor, and Una Mansfield. *Use of Library Materials: The University of Pittsburgh Study.* New York: Marcel Dekker, 1979.

34. Jasper G. Schad. Missing the Brass Ring in the Iron City. *The Journal of Academic Librarianship*, 5, May 1979, 60–63; Melvin J. Voight. Circulation Studies Cannot Reflect Research Use. *The Journal of Academic Librarianship*, 5, May 1979, 66; Leslie Peat. The Use of Research Libraries: A Comment About the Pittsburgh Study & Its Critics. *The Journal of Academic Librarianship*, 7, September 1981, 229–31.

35. Allen Kent. A Rebuttal. *The Journal of Academic Librarianship*, 5, May 1979, 69–70; Allen Kent et al. A Commentary on "Report on the Study of Library Use at Pitt by Professor Allen Kent et al." The Senate Library Committee, University of Pittsburgh, July 1969. *Library Acquisitions: Practice & Theory*, 4 (1), 1980, 87–99.

36. Larry Hardesty. Use of Library Materials at a Small Liberal Arts College. *Library Research*, 3, Fall 1981, 261–82.

37. Larry Hardesty. Use of Library Materials at a Small Liberal Arts College: A Replication. *Collection Management*, 10 (3/4), 1988, 61–80.

38. Robert M. Hayes. The Distribution of Use of Library Materials: Analysis of Data from the University of Pittsburgh. *Library Research*, 3, Fall 1981, 215–60.

39. Herbert H. Fussler and Julian L. Simon. *Patterns in the Use of Books in Large Research Libraries*. Chicago: University of Chicago Press, 1969.

40. Edward O'Neill and Julia A. Gammon. Consortial Book Circulation Patterns: The OCLC-OhioLINK Study. *College & Research Libraries*, 75 (6), 2014, 791–807. See also Julia Gammon and Edward T. O'Neill. *OhioLINK OCLC Collection and Circulation Analysis Project 2011*. Dublin, OH: OCLC, 2011.

41. Lynn Wiley, Tina Chrzastowski, and Stephanie Baker. A Domestic Monograph Collection Assessment in Illinois Academic Libraries: What Are We Buying and How Is It Used? *Interlending & Document Supply*, 39 (4), 2011, 167–75.

42. Michael Levine-Clark. "Developing a Multiformat Demand-Driven Acquisition Model. *Collection Management*, 35 (3–4), 2010, 201–7.

43. Kay Downey, Yin Zhang, Cristobal Urbano, and Tom Klinger. A Comparative Study of Print Book and DDA Ebook Acquisition and Use. *Technical Services Quarterly*, 31 (2), 2014, 139–60.

44. Sheila Cheung, Terry Chung, and Frederick Nesta. Monograph Circulation Over a 15-Year Period in a Liberal Arts University. *Library Management*, 32 (6/7), 2011, 419–34.

45. Jonathan D. Eldridge. The Vital Few Meet the Trivial Many: Unexpected Use Patterns in a Monographs Collection. *Bulletin of the Medical Library Association*, 86 (4), October 1998, 496–503.

46. Deborah D. Blecic. Monograph Use at an Academic Health Science Library: The First Three Years of Shelf Life. *Bulletin of the Medical Library Association*, 88 (2), 2000, 145–51.

47. Kathleen Reed, Jean Blackburn, and Daniel Sifton. Putting a Sacred Cow Out to Pasture: Assessing the Removal of Fines and Reduction of Barriers at a Small Academic Library. *The Journal of Academic Librarianship*, 40, 2014, 275–80.

48. Colin R. Taylor. A Practical Solution to Weeding University Library Periodicals Collections. *Collection Management*, 1 (3/4), 1977, 27–45.

49. C. Wenger and J. Childress. Journal Evaluation in a Large Research Library. *Journal of the American Society for Information Science*, 28 (5), September 1977, 293–99.

50. Joseph E. Weber and Dennis R. Ridley. Assessment and Decision Making: Two User-Oriented Studies. *Library Review*, 46 (3), 1997, 202–9.

51. Steve Black. Journal Collection Analysis at a Liberal Arts College. *Library Resources & Technical Services*, 41 (4), 1997, 283–94.

52. Anthony Hindle and Michael K. Buckland. In-Library Book Usage in Relation to Circulation. *Collection Management*, 2 (4), Winter 1978, 265–77.

53. Joan Stockard, Mary Ann Griffin, and Clementine Coblyn. Document Exposure Counts in Three Academic Libraries: Circulation and In-Library Use, in *Quantitative Measurement and Dynamic Library Service*. Phoenix, AZ: Oryx Press, 1978, 136–47.

54. C. A. Harris. A Comparison of Issues and In-Library Use of Books. *ASLIB Proceedings*, 29, 1977, 118–26.

55. Gary S. Lawrence and A. R. Oja. *The Use of General Collections at the University of California*. Sacramento: California State Department of Education, 1980. ERIC ED 191 490.

56. Lisa M. Rose-Wiles and John P. Irwin. An Old Horse Revived? In-House Use of Print Books at Seton Hall University. *The Journal of Academic Librarianship*, 42, 2016, 207–14.

57. Lisa Shen, Erin Cassidy, Eric Elmore, Glenda Griffin, Tyler Manolovitz, Michelle Martinez, and Linda Turney. Headfirst into Patron-Driven Acquisition Pool: A Comparison of Librarians Selection Versus Patron Purchases. *Journal of Electronic Resources Librarianship*, 23, 2011, 203–18.

58. Kristine J. Anderson, Robert S. Freeman, Jean-Pierre V. M. Hérubel, Lawrence J. Mykytiuk, Judith M. Nixon, and Suzanne M. Ward. Liberal Arts Books on Demand: A Decade of Patron-Driven Collection Development, Part 1, *Collection Management*, 35 (3–4), 2010, 125–41. See also Marianne Stowell Bracke. Science and Technology Books on Demand: A Decade of Patron-Driven Collection Development, Part 2. *Collection Management*, 35 (3–4), 2010, 142–50; Judith M. Nixon & E. Stewart Saunders. A Study of Circulation Statistics of Books on Demand: A Decade of Patron-Driven Collection Development, Part 3. *Collection Management*, 35 (3–4), 2010, 151–61.

59. Jeffery Waller. Undergrads as Selectors: Assessing Patron-Driven Acquisition at a Liberal Arts College. *Journal of Interlibrary Loan, Document Delivery, & Electronic Reserve*, 23 (3), 2013, 127–48.

60. Leslie J. Reynolds, Carmelita Pickett, Wyoma vanDuinkerken, Jane Smith, Jeanne Harrell, and Sandra Tucker. User-Driven Acquisitions: Allowing Patron Requests to Drive Collection Development in an Academic Library. *Collection Management*, 35 (3–4), 2010, 244–54.

61. Jared Howland, Rebecca Schroeder, and Thomas Wright. Brigham Young University's Patron-Driven Acquisitions: Does It Stand the Test of Time?, in Karl Bridges (Ed.). *Customer-Based Collection Development: An Overview.* Chicago: American Library Association, 2013, 174–89.

62. Rebecca Schroeder. When Patrons Call the Shots: Patron-Driven Acquisition at Brigham Young University. *Collection Building*, 31 (1), 2012, 11–14.

63. Tim Bowersox, Cyril Oberlander, Kate Pitcher, and Mark Sullivan. *Building Responsive Library Collections with the Getting It System Toolkit.* Geneseo, NY: IDS Project Press, 2014.

64. Lisa Shen et al. Head First into the Patron-Driven Acquisition Pool: A Comparison of Librarian Selections Versus Patron Purchases. *Journal of Electronic Resources Librarianship,* 23 (3), 2011, 203–18.

65. Robert Kieft and Lizanne Payne. Collective Collection, Collective Action. *Collection Management*, 37, 2012, 137–52, at 141.

66. Matthew Kelly. An Evidence Based Methodology to Facilitate Public Library Nonfiction Collection Development. *Evidence Based Library and Information Practice*, 10 (4), 2015, 40–61.

67. Elizabeth Henry, Rachel Longstaff, and Doris Van Kampen. Collection Analysis Outcomes in an Academic Library. *Collection Building*, 27 (3), 2008, 113–17.

68. Lisa Rose-Wiles. Are Print Books Dead? An Investigation of Book Circulation at a Mid-Sized Academic Library. *Technical Services Quarterly*, 30 (2), 2013, 129–52.

69. Constance Malpas. *Cloud-Sourcing Research Collections: Managing Print in the Mass-Digitized Library Environment.* Dublin, OH: OCLC Research, 2011.

70. W. S. Cooper, D. D. Thompson, and K. R. Weeks. The Duplication of Monograph Holdings in the University of California System. *Library Quarterly*, 45, 1975, 253–74.

71. B. Moore, I. J. Miller, and D. L. Tolliver. Title Overlap: A Study of Duplication in the University of Wisconsin System Libraries. *College & Research Libraries*, 43, 1982, 14–22.

72. Ruth H. Miller and Martha W. Niemeier. A Study of Collection Overlap in the Southwest Indiana Cluster of SULAN. *Indiana Libraries*, 9 (2), 1990, 45–54.

73. Thomas Nisonger. Editing the RLG Conspectus to Analyze the OCLC Archival Tapes for Seventeen Texas Libraries. *Library Resources & Technical Services*, 29, October/December 1985, 309–27.

74. William Gray Potter. Collection Overlap in the LCS Network in Illinois. *Library Quarterly*, 56 (2), 1986, 119–41.

75. Rob Kairis. Consortium Level Collection Development: A Duplication Study of the OhioLINK Central Catalog. *Library Collections, Acquisitions, & Technical Services*, 27, 2003, 317–26.

76. Sue Stroyan. Collection Overlap in Hospital Health Sciences Libraries: A Case Study. *Bulletin of the Medical Library Association*, 73 (4), October 1985, 358–64.

77. William G. Potter. Studies of Collection Overlap: A Literature Review. *Library Research*, 4, Spring 1982, 309–21.

78. William E. McGrath. Multidimensional Map of Library Similarities. *Proceedings of the American Society for Information Science*, 18, 1980, 298–300.

79. Alan Pritchard. Statistical Bibliography or Bibliometrics? *Journal of Documentation*, 25, December 1969, 48–49.

80. Francis Narin. *Evaluative Bibliometrics: The Use of Publication and Citation Analysis in the Evaluation of Scientific Activity*. Cherry Hill, NJ: Computer Horizons, 1976.

81. Robert H. Austin, as quoted in Richard Monastersky. The Number That's Devouring Science. *The Chronicle of Higher Education*, October 14, 2005, 12.

82. P. Scales. Citation Analysis as Indicators of the Use of Serials: A Comparison of Ranked Title Lists Produced by Citation Counting and from Use Data. *Journal of Documentation*, 32, 1976, 17–25; E. Pan. Journal Citation as a Predictor of Journal Usage in Libraries. *Collection Management*, 2, 1978, 29–38.

83. T. Stankus and B. Rice. Handle with Care: Use and Citation Data for Science Journal Management. *Collection Management*, 4, 1982, 95–110; M. Tsay. The Relationship Between Journal Use in a Medical Library and Citation Use. *Bulletin of the Medical Library Association*, 86, 1998, 31–39.

84. Danny P. Wallace and Bert R. Boyce. Holdings as a Measure of Journal Value. *Library & Information Science Research,* 11, 1989, 59–71.

85. Thomas E. Nisonger. Use of the *Journal Citation Reports* for Serials Management in Research Libraries: An Investigation of the Effect of Self-Citation on Journal Rankings in Library and Information Science and Genetics. *College & Research Libraries*, 61 (3), May 2000, 263–75.

86. B. Rice. Selection and Evaluation of Chemistry Periodicals. *Science & Technology Libraries*, 4, 1983, 43–59; Diane Schmidt et al., Biology Journal Use at an Academic Library: A Comparison of Use Studies, *Serials Review* 20 (2), 45–64; J. Wulff and N. Nixon. Quality Makers and Use of Electronic Journals in an Academic Health Sciences Library. *Journal of the Medical Library Association*, 92, 2004, 315–22.

87. D. Blecic. Measurements of Journal Use: An Analysis of the Correlations Between Three Methods. *Bulletin of the Medical Library Association*, 87 (1), 1999, 20–25.

88. Joanna Duy and Liwen Vaughn. Can Electronic Journal Usage Data Replace Citation Data as a Measure of Journal Use? An Empirical Examination. *The Journal of Academic Librarianship*, 32 (5), September 2006, 512–17.

89. Robin B. Devin and Martha Kellogg. The Serial/Monograph Ratio in Research Libraries: Budgeting in Light of Citation Studies. *College & Research Libraries*, 51, January 1990, 46–54.

90. Richard Monastersky. Impact Factors Run into Competition. *The Chronicle of Higher Education,* October 14, 2005, 17.

91. Blaise Cronin and Lokman Meho. Using the h-index to Rank Influential Information Scientists. *Journal of the American Society for Information Science and Technology*, 57 (9), 2006, 1275–78. See also Charles Oppenheim. Using the h-index to Rank Influential British Researchers in Information Science and Librarianship. *Journal of the American Society for Information Science and Technology*, 58 (2), 2007, 297–301.

92. Ben Toth. The Number Needed to Read—A New Measure of Journal Value. *Health Information and Libraries Journal*, 22, 2005, 81–82.

93. B. Ian Hutchins, Xin Yuan, James Anderson, and George Santangelo. Relative Citation Ratio (RCR): A New Metric That Uses Citation Rates to Measure Influence at the Article Level. *PLOS Biology*, September 6, 2016. doi:10.1371/journal.pbio.1002541; Lutz Bornmann and Robin Haunschild. Relative Citation Ratio (RCR): An Empirical Attempt to Study a New Field-Normalized Bibliometric Indicator. *Journal of the Association for Information Science and Technology,* 68 (4), April 2017, 1064–67.

94. Note that Bradford multipliers may vary from zone to zone based on an analysis by I. K. R. Rao. An Analysis of Bradford Multipliers and a Model to Explain the Law of Scattering. *Scientometrics*, 41 (1/2), 1998, 93–100.

95. O. V. Groos. Bradford's Law and the Keenan-Atherton Data. *American Documentation*, 18, 1967, 46.

96. R. E. Burton and R. W. Kebler. The "Half-Life" of Some Scientific and Technical Literature. *American Documentation*, 11 (1), January 1960, 18–22.

97. Charles P. Bourne. Some User Requirements Stated Quantitatively in Terms of the 90 Percent Library, in Allen Kent and Orrin E. Taulbee (Eds.). *Electronic Information Handling*. Washington, DC: Spartan Books, 1965, 93–110.

98. B. C. Brookes. The Growth, Vitality and Obsolescence of Scientific Periodical Literature. *Journal of Documentation*, 26 (4), 1970, 283–94; B. C. Brookes. Obsolescence of Special Library Periodicals: Sampling Errors and Utility Curves. *Journal of the American Society for Information Science*, 21 (5), 1970, 320–29.

99. D. J. De Solla Price. Networks of Scientific Papers. *Science*, 149, 1965, 510–15.

100. M. Stern. Characteristics of the Literature of Literary Scholarship. *College & Research Libraries*, 44, 1983, 199–209.

101. Jennifer E. Knievel and Charlene Kellsey. Citation Analysis for Collection Development: A Comparative Study of Eight Humanities Fields. *Library Quarterly*, 75 (2), 2005, 142–68.

102. Jan A. Pechenik, J. Michael Reed, and Melissa Russ. Should Auld Acquaintance Be Forgot: Possible Influence of Computer Databases on Citation Patterns in the Biological Literature. *BioScience*, 51 (7), July 2001, 583–88.

103. Rose Mary Magrill and Gloriana St. Clair. Undergraduate Term Paper Citation Patterns by Disciplines and Level of Course. *Collection Management*, 12 (3/4), 1990, 25–56.

104. Kristin Hoffmann and Lise Doucette. A Review of Citation Analysis Methodologies for Collection Management. *College & Research Libraries*, 73 (4), 2012, 321–35.

105. T. J. Allen and P. G. Gerstberger. Criteria for Selection of an Information Source. *Journal of Applied Psychology*, 52, 1968, 272–79; Victor Rosenberg. The Application of Psychometric Techniques to Determine the Attitudes of Individuals Toward Information Seeking. *Information Storage and Retrieval*, 3, 1967, 119–27.

106. M. E. Soper. The Relationship Between Personal Collections and the Selection of Cited Reference. *Library Quarterly*, 46, 1976, 397–415.

107. M. Liu. Progress in Documentation—The Complexities of Citation Practice: A Review of Citation Studies. *Journal of Documentation*, 49, 1993, 17–25.

108. H. D. White and K. W. McCain. Bibliometrics. *Annual Review of Information Science and Technology*, 24, 1989, 119–86.

109. Lois Kuyper-Rushing. Identifying Uniform Core Journal Titles for Music Libraries: A Dissertation Citation Study. *College & Research Libraries*, 60, 1999, 153–63.

110. Penny M. Beile, David N. Boote, and Elizabeth K. Killingsworth. A Microscope or a Mirror?: A Question of Study Validity Regarding the Use of Dissertation Citation Analysis for Evaluating Research Collections. *The Journal of Academic Librarianship*, 30 (5), September 2004, 347–53.

111. Johanna Tuñón and Bruce Brydges. Improving the Quality of University Libraries Through Citation Mining and Analysis Using Two New Dissertation Bibliometric Assessment Tools. Presentation at the 71st IFLA General Conference, 14–18 August 2005, Oslo, Norway.

112. Silas Marques De Oliveira. *Collection Evaluation Through Citation Checking: A Comparison of Three Sources*. Doctoral dissertation. University of Illinois at Urbana-Champaign, 1991.

113. Penny M. Beile, David N. Boote, and Elizabeth K. Killingsworth. A Microscope or a Mirror?: A Question of Study Validity Regarding the Use of Dissertation Citation Analysis for Evaluating Research Collections. *The Journal of Academic Librarianship*, 30 (5), September 2004, 347–53.

114. Shelley Mosley, Anna Caggiano, and John Charles. The "Self-Weeding" Collection. *Library Journal*, 119, October 15, 1996, 38.

115. Michelle Twait. Undergraduate Students' Source Selection Criteria: A Qualitative Study. *The Journal of Academic Librarianship*, 31 (6), 1995, 567–73; Yunjie (Calvin) Xu and Zhiwei Chen. Relevance Judgment: What Do Users Consider Beyond Topicality? *Journal of the American Society for Information Science and Technology*, 67 (7), 2006, 961–73.

116. Carol L. Barry. User-Defined Relevance Criteria: An Exploratory Study. *Journal of the American Society for Information Science*, 45 (3), 1994, 149–59; Vicki Tolar Burton and Scott A. Chadwick.

Investigating the Practices of Student Researchers: Patterns of Use and Criteria for Use of Internet and Library Sources. *Computers and Composition*, 17 (3), 2000, 309–28.

117. Thomas Stieve and David Schoen. Undergraduate Students' Book Selection: A Study of Factors in the Decision-Making Process. *The Journal of Academic Librarianship,* 32 (6), November 2006, 599–608.

118. Daniel Gore. The Mischief in Measurement. *Library Journal*, May 1, 1978, 933–37.

119. A=Anne C. Ciliberti, Mary F. Casserly, Judith L. Hegg, and Eugene S. Mitchell. Material Availability: A Study of Academic Library Performance. *College & Research Libraries*, 48, November 1987, 513–27;

B=Terry Ellen Ferl and Margaret G. Robinson. Book Availability at the University of California, Santa Cruz. *College & Research Libraries*, 47, September 1986, 501–8;

C, D, E, F, G=Katherine A. Frohmberg, Paul B. Kantor, and William A. Moffett. Increases in Book Availability in a Large College Library. *Proceedings of the 43rd ASIS Annual Meeting.* Washington, DC: ASIS, 1980, 292–94;

H, I=Paul B. Kantor. The Library as an Information Utility in the University Context: Evaluation and Measurement of Services. *Journal of the American Society of Information Science*, 27, 1976, 100–12;

J, K=Paul B. Kantor. Availability Analysis. *Journal of the American Society of Information Science,* 27, 1976, 311–19;

L=Stuart J. Kolner and Eric C. Welch. The Book Availability Study as an Objective Measure of Performance in a Health Sciences Library. *Bulletin of the Medical Library Association*, 73 (2), April 1985, 121–31;

M=John Mansbridge. *Evaluating Resource Sharing Library Networks.* Doctoral dissertation. Case Western University, Cleveland, OH, 1984;

N=Elliot S. Palais. Availability Analysis Report, Arizona State. *User Surveys and Evaluation of Library Services.* Bethesda, MD: ERIC, 1981, 73–82. ED 214 541;

O, P, Q=Neil A. Radford. Failure in the Library—A Case Study. *Library Quarterly*, 53 (3), 1983, 328–39;

R, S=Tefko Saracevic, William M. Shaw, and Paul B. Kantor. Causes and Dynamics of User Frustration in an Academic Library. *College & Research Libraries*, 38, 1977, 7–18;

T=James L. Schofield and D. H. Waters. Evaluation of an Academic Library's Stock Effectiveness. *Journal of Librarianship*, 7, 1975, 207–27;

U, V=William M. Shaw. Longitudinal Studies of Book Availability, in Neal Kaske and William Jones (Eds.). *Library Effectiveness: A State of the Art.* Chicago: American Library Association/LAMA, 1980, 337–49;

W=Rita Smith and Warner Grande. AL Report, Undergraduate Library Availability Study 1975–1977, University of Tennessee. *User Surveys and Evaluation of Library Services.* Bethesda, MD: ERIC, 1981, 83–90. ED 214 541;

X=Jo Bell Whitlach and Karen Kieffer. Service at San Jose State University: Survey of Document Availability. *Journal of Academic Librarianship*, 4, 1978, 197–99;

Y = Yvonne Wulff. Book Availability in the University of Minnesota Bio-Medical Library. *Bulletin of the Medical Library Association*, 66, 1978, 349–50.

120. Paul B. Kantor. Demand-Adjusted Shelf Availability Parameters. *The Journal of Academic Librarianship*, 7 (2), 1981, 78–82.

121. Julia Shaw-Kokot and Claire de la Varre. Using a Journal Availability Study to Improve Access. *Bulletin of the Medical Library Association*, 89 (1), January 2001, 21–28.

122. Paul B. Kantor. The Library as an Information Utility in the University Context: Evaluation and Measurement of Services. *Journal of the American Society of Information Science*, 27, 1976, 100–12; Paul B. Kantor. Availability Analysis. *Journal of the American Society of Information Science,* 27, 1976, 311–19. See also Paul B. Kantor. *Objective Performance Measures for Academic and Research Libraries.* Washington, DC: Association of Research Libraries, 1984.

123. K. A. Frohmberg and W. A. Moffett. *Research on the Impact of a Computerized Circulation System on the Performance of a Large College Library: Part One—The Main Library.* Oberlin, OH:

Oberlin College Library, 1981; Thomas R. Kochtanek. *User Satisfaction in the Hugh Stevens College Library.* Columbia, MO: University of Missouri, September 1979. ED 190 164; E. S. Palais. *Availability Analysis Report.* SPEC Kit 71. Washington, DC: Association of Research Libraries, 1981; G. K. Rinkel and P. McCandless. Application of a Methodology Analyzing User Frustration. *College & Research Libraries*, 44, 1983, 29–37.

124. Yvonne Wulff. Book Availability in the University of Minnesota Bio-Medical Library. *Bulletin of the Medical Library Association*, 66, 1978, 349–50; Haseeb F. Rashid. Book Availability as a Performance Measure of a Library: An Analysis of the Effectiveness of a Health Sciences Library. *Journal of the American Society for Information Science*, 41 (7), 1990, 501–7.

125. J. B. Wood, J. J. Bremer, and S. A. Saraidaridis. Measurement of Service at a Public Library. *Public Library Quarterly*, 2, 1980, 49–57.

126. M. E. Murfin. The Myth of Accessibility: Frustration and Failure in Retrieving Periodicals. *The Journal of Academic Librarianship*, 6, 1980, 16–19.

127. Haseeb F. Rashid. Book Availability as a Performance Measure of a Library: An Analysis of the Effectiveness of a Health Sciences Library. *Journal of the American Society for Information Science*, 41 (7), 1990, 501–7.

128. Anne C. Ciliberti, Mary Casserly, Judy Hegg, and Eugene Mitchell. Material Availability: A Study of Academic Library Performance. *College & Research Libraries*, 48, November 1987, 513–27.

129. Anne Ciliberti, Marie L. Radford, Gary P. Radford, and Terry Ballard. Empty Handed? A Material Availability Study and Transaction Log Analysis Verification. *The Journal of Academic Librarianship*, 59, July 1998, 282–89.

130. Eugene S. Mitchell, Marie L. Radford, and Judith L. Hegg. Book Availability: Academic Library Assessment. *College & Research Libraries*, 55, January 1994, 47–55.

131. Michael K. Buckland. *Book Availability and the Library User.* New York: Pergamon, 1975.

132. Topsy N. Smalley. Assessing Collection Availability: A Snapshot Inventory. *Community & Junior College Libraries*, 5 (2), 1988, 69–75.

133. Thomas E. Nisonger. A Review and Analysis of Library Availability Studies. *Library Resources & Technical Services*, 51 (1), January 2007, 30–49.

134. Neal K. Kaske. Materials Availability Model and the Internet. *The Journal of Academic Librarianship*, 20, November 1994, 317–18.

135. Richard H. Orr, Vern M. Pings, Irwin H. Pizer, and Edwin E. Olsen. Development of Methodological Tools for Planning and Managing Library Services: I. Project Goals and Approach. *Bulletin of the Medical Library Association*, 56 (3), July 1968, 235–40; Richard H. Orr, Vern M. Pings, Irwin Pizer, Edwin E. Olsen, and Carol C. Spencer. Development of Methodological Tools for Planning and Managing Library Services: II. Measuring a Library's Capability for Providing Documents. *Bulletin of the Medical Library Association*, 56 (3), July 1968, 241–67; Richard H. Orr, Vern M. Pings, Edwin E. Olsen, and Irwin H. Pizer. Development of Methodological Tools for Planning and Managing Library Services: III. Standardized Inventories of Library Services. *Bulletin of the Medical Library Association*, 56 (3), July 1968, 380–403; Richard H. Orr. Development of Methodological Tools for Planning and Managing Library Services: IV. Bibliography of Studies Selected for Methods and Data Useful to Biomedical Libraries. *Bulletin of the Medical Library Association*, 58 (3), July 1970, 350–70.

136. Ernest R. DeProspo, Ellen Altman, and Kenneth E. Beasley. *Performance Measures for Public Libraries.* Chicago: American Library Association, 1979.

137. William E. McGrath. Significance of Book Use According to a Classified Profile of Academic Departments. *College & Research Libraries*, 33, 1972, 212–19; William E. McGrath. Measuring Classified Circulation According to Curriculum. *College & Research Libraries*, 29, 1968, 347–50.

138. William McGrath and Norma Durand. Classifying Courses in the University Catalog. *College & Research Libraries*, 30, November 1969, 553–59.

139. Barbara Golden. A Method for Quantitatively Evaluating a University Library Collection. *Library Resources & Technical Services*, 18 (3), Summer 1974, 268–74.

140. G. M. Jenks. Circulation and Its Relationship to the Book Collection and Academic Departments. *College & Research Libraries*, 37, 1976, 145–52. See also Robert L. Burr. Evaluating Library Collections: A Case Study. *The Journal of Academic Librarianship*, 5, 1979, 256–61.

141. Richard M. Dougherty and Laura L. Bloomquist. *Improving Access to Library Resources: The Influence of Organization of Library Collection and of User Attitudes Toward Innovative Services.* Metuchen, NJ: Scarecrow Press, 1974.

142. John H. Whaley Jr. An Approach to Collection Analysis. *Library Resources & Technical Services*, 25, July/September 1981, 330–38; Elliot Palais. Use of Course Analysis in Compiling a Collection Development Policy Statement for a University Library. *The Journal of Academic Librarianship*, 13, March 1987, 8–13; Michael R. Gabriel. Online Collection Evaluation, Course by Course. *Collection Building*, 8 (2), 1989, 20–24.

143. Gwen S. Lochstet. Course and Research Analysis Using a Coded Classification System. *The Journal of Academic Librarianship*, 23, September 1997, 380–89.

144. Albert Henderson. The Library Collection Failure Quotient: The Ratio of Interlibrary Borrowing to Collection Size. *The Journal of Academic Librarianship*, 26 (3), May 2000, 159–70.

145. Gary D. Byrd, D. A. Thomas, and Katherine E. Hughes. Collection Development Using Interlibrary Loan Borrowing and Acquisitions Statistics. *Bulletin of the Medical Library Association*, 70 (1), January 1982, 1–9.

146. Jennifer Knievel, Heather Wicht, and Lynn Silipigni Connaway. Use of Circulation Statistics and Interlibrary Loan Data in Collection Management. *College & Research Libraries*, 67 (1), January 2006, 35–49.

147. Margie Ruppe. Tying Collection Development's Loose Ends with Interlibrary Loan. *Collection Building*, 25 (3), 2006, 72–77.

148. Lynn Wiley and Tina E. Chrzastowski. The Impact of Electronic Journals on Interlibrary Lending: A Longitudinal Study of Statewide Interlibrary Loan Article Sharing in Illinois. *Library Collections, Acquisitions, & Technical Services*, 29, 2005, 364–81.

149. Bruce R. Kingma. The Economics of Access Versus Ownership. *Journal of Library Administration*, 26 (1–2), 1999, 145–57.

150. Stanley J. Slote. *Weeding Library Collections: Library Weeding Methods.* Westport, CT: Libraries Unlimited, 1997.

151. Rick Lugg and Ruth Fischer. Future Tense—The Disapproval Plan: Rules-Based Weeding & Storage Decisions. *Against the Grain*, 20 (6), 2008, Article 32.

152. Rick Lugg. Data-Driven Deselection for Monographs: A Rules-Based Approach to Weeding, Storage, and Shared Print Decisions. *Insights*, 25 (2), July 2012, 1–7.

153. Cynthia Ehret Snyder. Data-Driven Deselection: Multiple Point Data Using a Decision Support Tool in an Academic Library. *Collection Management*, 39, 2014, 17–31.

154. Colin R. Taylor. A Practical Solution to Weeding University Library Periodicals Collections. *Collection Management*, 1 (3/4), 1977, 27–45, at 38.

155. Edward Walton. Why Undergraduate Students Choose to Use E-Books. *Journal of Librarianship and Information Science*, 46 (4), 2014, 263–70.

156. Lorcan Dempsey, Constance Malpas, and Brian Lavoie. Collection Directions: Some Reflections on the Future of Library Collections and Collecting. *portal: Libraries and the Academy*, 14 (3), July 2014, 393–423.

157. Lizanne Payne. *Library Storage Facilities and the Future of Print Collections in North America.* Dublin, OH: OCLC, 2007.

158. Paul Gherman. The North Atlantic Storage Trust: Maximizing Space, Preserving Collections. *portal: Libraries and the Academy*, 7 (3), 2014, 273–75.

159. Cathy Maskell, Jennifer Soutter, and Kristina Oldenburg. Collaborative Print Repositories: A Case Study of Library Directors' Views. *The Journal of Academic Librarianship*, 36 (3), 2010, 242–49.

160. Brian J. Baird. *Library Collection Assessment Through Statistical Sampling.* Toronto: Scarecrow Press, 2004.

161. The LibValue Project Website may be accessed at http://libvalue.cci.utk.edu/. The project's reports, presentations, and published articles are available on the Web site. Most notable of these are Donald W. King and Carol Tenopir. Linking Information Seeking Patterns with Purpose, Use, Value, and Return on Investment of Academic Library Journals. *Evidence Based Library and Information Practice*, 8 (2), 2013, 153-62; Donald W. King. *Methods to Assess the Use, Value, Cost and ROI of All Academic Library Services*. Knoxville, TN: University of Tennessee, 2015; Bruce Kingma. LibValue: Values, Outcomes, and Return on Investment on Academic Libraries, Phase III: ROI of the Syracuse University Library. *College & Research Libraries*, 76, January 2015, 63–80.

162. Paul Courant and Matthew "Buzzy" Nielsen. On the Cost of Keeping a Book, in *The Idea of Order: Transforming Research Collections for 21st Century Scholarship*. Washington, DC: Council on Library and Information Resources, June 2010, 81-105. See also Stephen R. Lawrence, Lynn Silipigni Connaway, and Keith H. Brigham. Life Cycle Costs of Library Collections: Creation of Effective Performance and Cost Metrics for Library Resources. *College & Research Libraries*, 62 (6), November 2001, 541–53.

163. Christopher Belter and Neal Kaske. Using Bibliometrics to Demonstrate the Value of Library Journal Collections. *College & Research Libraries*, 77 (4), July 2016, 410–22.

164. David Lewis. From Stacks to the Web: The Transformation of Academic Library Collecting. *College & Research Libraries*, March 2013, 159–76.

13

Evaluation of Electronic Resources

Libraries store the energy that fuels the imagination. They open up windows to the world and inspire us to explore and achieve, and contribute to improving our quality of life.

—Sidney Sheldon

SERVICE DEFINITION

Libraries of all types and sizes are facing unrelenting pressure to provide access to an increasing number of electronic journals and other digital resources: e-books, streaming audio, and video files. The appeal for users is that they have desktop access to the electronic resources 24/7 without requiring a trip to the library. Libraries can provide access to electronic journals and to indexing and abstracting databases, as well as to other electronic content. Clearly, digital collections save the library space, but moving toward an increasing amount of digital resources will likely require new skill sets.

EVALUATION QUESTIONS

Libraries are in a period of transition as they move from traditional physical collections to a largely digital environment—some have called this a "hybrid" library. Having a clear understanding of who uses electronic resources and why they are being used can be helpful to libraries as they adjust their service delivery strategies to better meet the needs of their customers. Among the important questions that have been evaluated are the following:

- Do users of electronic resources differ from users of the library's physical collection?
- Do some users focus on electronic resources exclusively?
- Do others use the library's physical and digital collections?
- Where is the greatest demand for electronic resources coming from?
- Other than convenience, why do people use electronic resources?

- Do users of electronic resources focus their use on a small number of resources, or do they explore a wider range of resources?
- What problems do people encounter when using a variety of electronic resources, each with its own unique user interface?
- What problems do libraries face when attempting to interpret access and download statistics?
- How can libraries provide access to the staggering amount of journal articles published each year while at the same time allocating their budgets in a prudent manner?

Among the types of measures used to assess electronic resources are the following:

- **Transaction-based measures** include counts of search sessions, types of searches performed, number of records retrieved, and so forth.
- The transaction log file can also be examined to calculate **time-based measures** such as length of search sessions, system peak periods, time spent browsing versus downloading files, and so forth.
- **Cost-based measures** analyze the cost of providing the resources; determine the cost of providing the required hardware, software, networking, training, and site licensing; and so forth.
- **Use-based measures** examine the number of unique users, the number of times users return each month, number of items viewed online, number of articles downloaded, user satisfaction, and so forth.

EVALUATION METHODS

Libraries can learn more about users and the uses of electronic resources through a variety of means, as shown in Table 13.1.

Table 13.1. Electronic Resources Evaluation Methods

Qualitative	Quantitative
Interviews	Surveys
Focus groups	Transaction log analysis
Observation	Download statistical analysis
Keeping a journal	Cost analysis
Paper prototypes and scenarios	Cost-benefit analysis
Card-sorting tests	

Jill Grogg and Rachel Fleming-May illustrate the complexity of attempting to evaluate electronic resources and in particular, urge caution with the lack of definitions and consistent "usage" of terminology such as *use, use study, users, session,* and *download*.[1]

PRIOR EVALUATIONS AND RESEARCH

In 2006, about 2.5 million articles were published each year across all disciplines and languages in the roughly 25,000 peer-reviewed journals and refereed conference proceedings.[2] According to the 2015 STM report, the number of scholarly peer-review English-language journals in 2014 totaled 28,100 (the total increases to 34,585 if non-English journals are included), while the number of journal articles remains fairly static at 2.5 million per year.[3]

The result is that a great deal of this publishing effort is losing some portion of its potential research impact (usage and citations) because the article is not discoverable by various search engines (such as Google), a library's catalog, or even the publisher's discovery platform, for any number of reasons.[4] In addition, there has been a consolidation within the scientific publishing industry: the top five dominant publishers account for more than 50 percent of all papers published in 2013.[5]

Carol Tenopir prepared an excellent summary of user studies that have focused on electronic resources.[6] Tenopir divided these studies into two categories. Tier 1 included major studies involving hundreds or thousands of subjects that employed a variety of evaluation methods and resulted in many publications. The Tier 2 category summarized the smaller, individual research studies.

Users

Obviously, no single "user" is going to represent all users of electronic resources. In the academic environment, users of electronic resources are typically categorized into four primary groups—undergraduate students, graduate students, faculty, and researchers—and each group's use of electronic resources varies considerably. Public libraries will usually sort users into four groups as well: students, families, businesspeople, and senior citizens. Special libraries may separate users into two or three groups, but often users are analyzed in a single group.

The user of electronic journals will vary with subject discipline and the status of the individual:

- Faculty who use e-journals for research vary from a low of 61 percent (law) to a high of 83 percent (biological sciences).
- Faculty who use electronic journals for teaching range from a low of 28 percent (law) to a high of 56 percent (biological sciences).
- Student use also varies, from a low of 35 percent (law) to a high of 62 percent (biological sciences).[7] Of all survey respondents, 75 percent prefer online access to journal articles. Also, most respondents use online sources to find articles contained in e-journals.
- Visits to the physical library by faculty and graduate students have declined, whereas visits to the virtual library have been increasing.[8]
- Graduate, postdoctoral students and faculty make disproportionately more use, whereas undergraduates' use is low compared to their population size.[9]

Motivations for use. Among the factors affecting choice of print or online journal articles, the time spent to acquire articles may have the strongest correlation to preference of format. Described by Barry Schwartz as a "satisficing" behavior, people may take what is available rather than seeking the best available due to time pressures, efficiency, ease of access, and around-the-clock availability of electronic resources from anywhere.[10] Several studies have shown that accessibility is associated with the amount of database use.[11]

Different motivations or information needs will affect information seeking and use. A study of students and faculty at the University of West England found that the greatest predictor of use of electronic resources was whether or not the individual was engaged in research.[12] Another study found that level of instruction is not correlated to amount of database use.[13] Yet another study determined that there was no relationship between instruction in the use of electronic resources and increased use of those resources.[14]

For faculty, about half of the articles they read are identified by browsing recently published journals issues, as a byproduct of keeping up with the literature and conducting background research. About a fourth of all readings are selected as the result of online searching of abstracting and indexing databases, Web search engines, and online journal collections, or of receiving a current awareness message. Other articles are identified as the result of a citation in another publication or from another colleague.[15] One analysis suggests that electronic resources are likely to be used most heavily in fields in which directed searching is the dominant search method and less in fields in which browsing and chaining are the preferred search methods.[16]

A study at the Vanderbilt University Medical Center biomedical library found that students, residents, and fellows preferred electronic journals due to convenient access; faculty preferred print journals (print journals have higher quality text and figures).[17]

Faculty and students vary in their preferences for using print or online formats of journals. Most students preferred the convenience of online journal articles, whereas faculty members were more inclined to seek the best articles regardless of format.[18] In a comparison of the use of journals by faculty and students, Kathleen Joswick and Jeanne Stierman found that students preferred to use more generalized journals, whereas faculty often used highly specialized journals.[19] At the University of Maryland, faculty members were more likely to use electronic journals than print journals on a weekly or daily basis.[20] Faculty members who publish more frequently are more aware of and are more likely to submit articles to electronic journals.[21] Junior faculty members tend to use electronic resources more than senior faculty.[22]

The finding that high school students and undergraduates prefer to search the Internet for school-related tasks has clearly and consistently been shown in a number of studies: see, for example, OCLC,[23] the Pew studies,[24] and Leah Graham.[25]

A Web-based survey has been developed that measures both in-library and remote usage of networked electronic resources. The instrument, called MINES for Libraries—Measuring the Impact of Networked Electronic Services—asks survey respondents to indicate the purpose of their searching. The survey discovered that remote users of electronic resources exceed in-library use by a four-to-one or larger margin. Not surprisingly, those conducting sponsored research use the electronic resources from their offices rather than visiting the library. In addition, in-library and on-campus use of the electronic resources greatly exceeds off-campus usage. Faculty, staff, and researchers did most of the usage for sponsored research.[26] Grant-funded research accounts for almost one-third of networked electronic services activity, and this searching was done from on campus but not from within the library.[27]

Use

Time spent reading. Scientists spend well over 100 hours per year of their time reading journal articles.

During the 1990s, scientists averaged 120 readings of scholarly journal articles per year; surveys in the 2000s indicate that the average has risen to 130. University scientists read more—they average 188 readings per year—and three-fourths of the readings are for research purposes. Forty percent of the readings are for teaching purposes. It is interesting to note that, on average, scientists whose work is recognized through achievement awards read more than non-award winners.[28] Medical scientists read much more than others, and engineers read the least. Although medical faculty read more articles than others, they prefer to have the information digested in a way that saves them time.[29]

The majority of readings came from articles published in the previous year. Typically, for articles older than two years, the scientists reading the articles reported that they were *re-reading* them.[30] An analysis of the impact of online journals on the citation patterns of medical faculty over a 10-year period found that the number of journals cited per year increased and that the researchers were not more likely to cite online journals or less likely to cite journals only available in print.[31]

All of this reading is done to improve the quality of teaching and research and to save time and money. The information is sought for a number of reasons, including:

- Primary research
- Current awareness or continuing education
- Communications-related purposes (making presentations, writing, consulting), and background research

Analytics

Collecting data. Gathering a variety of data pertaining to the downloading and use of electronic resources is a continuing challenge. Should libraries rely on data that they collect, or should they focus on vendor-provided data? Project COUNTER (Counting Online Usage of Networked Electronic Resources) was developed to ensure that the data were defined, collected, and reported in the same way to each library. COUNTER is an international initiative to improve the reliability of online usage statistics from vendors. Project COUNTER has published a Code of Practice that specifies the content, format, delivery mechanisms, definitions, and rules for a set of core usage reports.

So far, there are three COUNTER Codes of Practice:

1. **Code of Practice for e-Resources** (Release 4 was issued in 2014)
2. **Code of Practice for Articles** provides a standard for recording and reporting of usage at the individual journal article level
3. **Code of Practice for Usage Factors** based on COUNTER standards

Publishers, aggregators, and other vendors can go through an auditing process to become COUNTER-compliant. Once certified, they are listed on the Project COUNTER Web site (www .projectcounter.org/code_practice.html).

As libraries were gaining experience in using COUNTER reports, it became apparent that attempting to correlate and consolidate the COUNTER reports from various vendors was a time-consuming and frustrating experience. This frustration led to the development by NISO of SUSHI (Standardized Usage Statistics Harvesting Institute). The library's client service (initiated by a library management platform, an electronic resources management system [ERMS], or other library system) connects to the vendor's SUSHI server service, identifies itself to the vendor, and then downloads the appropriate COUNTER report to the library. Typically the library sets up its client service so that the entire process is automatically repeated monthly for each vendor that the library does business with that is capable of providing COUNTER-compliant reports.

The importance of library gateways to electronic journals cannot be overemphasized. The biggest generators of *ScienceDirect* traffic are library gateways, followed by PubMed. In August 2005 *ScienceDirect* received more than 4 million referrals from PubMed. Forty-three percent of full-text usage of *ScienceDirect* was for articles less than a year old, nearly 20 percent from articles one to two years old, and 27 percent for articles more than three years old.[33]

> *One thing is clear. Users use what's available. And increasingly available means immediately.*
>
> —Carol Diedrichs[32]

Google Scholar plays an important role in university students and faculty members discovery of e-resources. One study suggests that half of all engineering master's students use *Google Scholar* as a means of identifying journal articles that might be of value.[34] The students acknowledge "satisficing" as they operate at the network level to find information that will meet their needs.

Increasingly, libraries will be using data from a number of sources so that they can better understand the connections between usage and purchasing/licensing decisions. In the long term, it is hoped that libraries will be able to share such data in order to maximize the return on investment that libraries make in providing access to e-resources.

Social media. More and more people are using social media platforms such as Facebook on a daily basis, and individuals often recommend journal articles they are reading that they find interesting and post this information, as they believe some of their friends might find the article of value—yet another example of people operating at the network level.

What the data say. At Ohio State University, 69 percent of survey respondents use electronic resources weekly, yet half of all undergraduates never use any electronic resources or are not aware of the availability of such resources.[35] OhioLINK mounts more than 8,000 journals on its own automated library system, providing to its users a single user interface to access electronic journals regardless of the source (publisher or aggregator) and allowing OhioLINK to track actual usage of this resource. The number of journal articles that have been downloaded has increased dramatically, to 12,000,000 in July 2014, as shown in Figure 13.1. The licensing of the electronic journals by the OhioLINK consortium has meant that each library saves money and still is able to provide its students and faculty access to a much larger array of journals than they would have on their own.[36] Forty percent of the journal titles account for 85 percent of the article downloads, and 1 percent of the journal titles account for about 10 percent of the downloads. Slightly more than half (58 percent) of the articles downloaded were from journals not held in print at the downloading user's library.[37]

However, a large geographic consortium may not always be the best model. Philip Davis analyzed the use of 200 titles in the sciences and social sciences among the member libraries of the NorthEast Research Libraries Consortium and found that larger institutions used a wider range of journal titles, whereas smaller institutions only used about 30 percent of the electronic resources.[38] Davis suggested that consortia based on size and type of library may be more cost-effective.

A large percentage of use is concentrated in a small proportion of the journal titles—another manifestation of the 80/20 rule, which seems to hold true for electronic journals, as noted by several studies that examined transaction logs.[39] James Stemper and Janice Jaguszewski

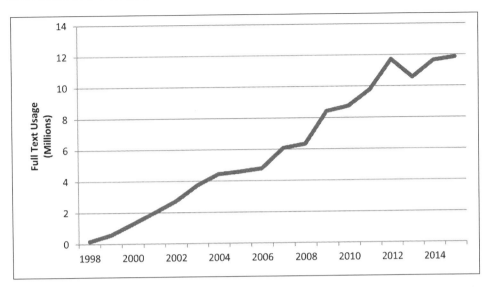

Figure 13.1. OhioLINK Electronic Journal Articles Downloaded Annually. Electronic journal center e-journal packages, 1998-2015. Data provided by OhioLINK. Used with permission.

suggest that the rule is closer to 70/30 in the online environment, in a project that compared vendor and local data.[40]

During a six-month period at the University of Southern California Medical Library, 28,000 full-text articles were viewed online, while only 1,800 uses were made of the corresponding print volumes.[41] Another study demonstrates that although size of institution influences overall usage data, institutions with large graduate and professional schools show more usage. In addition, selecting the most appropriate e-resource collections to match the needs of your campus users is key to usage.[42]

Having access to the wealth of data provided by COUNTER reports provides an opportunity for creativity. Several libraries have created a list of all titles by source (publisher or aggregator) which can then be sorted to identify the journal titles that are accessible in more than one source (this was valuable when the library needed to reduce the number of subscriptions).

Loyola Marymount University Libraries in Los Angeles tracked every interaction with library users over the course of a year. They then used a social network analysis tool to discover that while a group of e-resources was normally recommended in response to a specific query, half of the available e-resources were not mentioned once by staff members during the year.[43]

Print or view online. Most individuals report that they print selected articles from online sources for later reading and for their own archives, and they do not like the HTML format for printing.[44] Slightly more than three-fourths of the scholars begin their searching at a multijournal Web site with links to full text, such as PubMed, ScienceDirect, Medline, or EBSCOHost, rather than at a specific journal Web site.

Cost Analysis

Electronic resources have come to represent an increasing proportion of library acquisitions budgets. For example, some of the ARL libraries may spend $10 million or more on e-resources annually. Traditionally, the providers of e-resources sell bundled online subscriptions to their entire list of journals (the "Big Deal") for prices lower than the sum of their á la carte prices. However, the prices paid by each institution for the "Big Deal" are generally restricted by the licensing agreement and vary by size and type of institution (tiered pricing).

A 2014 study examined 360 licensing agreements between universities and publishers for bundled subscriptions and used cost per citation as a measure of cost-effectiveness. The article demonstrates the quite variable pricing for the same bundle of journals across a range of universities. The study concluded that even with discounts resulting from bundled purchases, prices to large PhD-granting universities by major commercial publishers are much higher than those charged by nonprofit publishers. The study also demonstrates that some library staff members responsible for negotiating are much more effective than their counterparts in other universities.[45]

A majority of libraries create a cost-per-use or cost-per-download report (normally a spreadsheet) in order to determine whether the current mix of electronic resources is appropriate for the needs of library customers. However, as Belinda Nicolson-Guest and Debby Macdonald note:

> The "Reality" is that the spreadsheet has more footnotes than a thesis and in most cases still requires a certain amount of discussion (to explain the footnotes).[46]

The authors detail all of the challenges that arise when attempting to create an "apples-to-apples" comparison of download statistics from various suppliers. The short answer is that the resulting analysis represents a best effort but the confidence levels for the results are very limited.

Libraries can also prepare a title-level analysis that compares the cost per use of a print subscription with a cost per download for online access to the same journal title. This type of analysis can be rewarding in identifying usage patterns and identifying print journal title subscriptions that might be eliminated, as noted by Anthony McMullen.[47]

Determining what print subscriptions to cancel will require the library to analyze use of both the print and electronic collections. How should download statistics that are provided by vendors be used? Parker Ladwig and Andrew Sommese suggest adjusting use statistics using a journal's ISI *Journal Citation Reports* half-life. These authors contend that total use will be undercounted, but that the undercounting will be proportional across disciplines. Their approach allows a library to calculate an adjusted cost per use that can be used to assist in making cancellation decisions.[48]

Denise Pan and Yem Fong prepared a consortium-level return-on-investment (ROI) analysis (using both qualitative and quantitative methods) that demonstrated the value of collaborative purchasing to university stakeholders.[49]

Open-Access Journals

Open access (OA) refers to all forms of published materials including peer-reviewed and nonpeer-reviewed academic journal articles, presentations, conference papers, book chapters, and books that are free of all restrictions on access and free of certain copyright and license restrictions.

Authors can provide open access to their work in several ways. First, an author can have an article published and then self-archive it in a repository (institutional or a central repository such as PubMed). Some publishers may require the author to wait for a period of time after publication in a journal before the article can be placed in the repository (this approach is known as "green" open access).

Second, an author can choose to make an article immediately available ("gold" open access) by choosing an open-access journal that has no restrictions or choosing a hybrid open-access journal. In the latter case, the author (or the author's institution or the research funder) will pay a fee (an article processing charge) to ensure that the article is immediately available to all.

Creating an institutional repository is a first (but insufficient) step in providing access to the breadth of materials being produced by faculty members, as the self-archiving rate is only about 20 percent.[50] A number of institutions worldwide and research funders have adopted OA self-archiving mandates, with the result that deposit rates grow substantially and in many cases begin to approach 100%.[51]

For the casual Internet user or nonaffiliated researcher, about 35 percent of the peer-reviewed literature is accessible (given variations in different disciplines).[52]

One important study found that OA articles are cited significantly more often than articles in the same journal and year that were not OA. This has been called the "OA advantage" and its effects are real, independent, and casual (although related to quality: the top 20 percent of articles receive about 80 percent of all citations).[53]

An analysis of 1.3 million journal articles placed each article into one of two categories: open access or not open access. The findings suggested that open-access articles received more citations than those in the nonopen-access group, although questions were raised about the averaging of averages.[54] Within the field of computer science, the more highly cited articles, and more recent articles, are more likely to be online.[55] Presenting an opposing point of view, a study that used a randomized controlled trial found that there was no evidence of a citation advantage for open-access articles in the first year after publication.[56]

The challenge, however, is that author characteristics (prior citation history, reputation, total publication count, funding organizations, disciplines, etc.) confound any analysis that attempts to better understand the relationship between open access and citations. Iain Craig and colleagues explore a number of methodological issues in an interesting article for those wishing to explore the topic in greater detail.[57]

One interesting study focused on the quality of epidemiological studies in OA and non-OA journals and found the same methodological quality and quality of reporting in both types of journals.[58]

Customer Satisfaction

Users of electronic journals typically search journal tables of contents, briefly scan the full text of the article, and then request a PDF version of the article for printing or archiving. Younger scholars report that they are frequent e-journal users; older scholars tend to be troubled by the user interface at multijournal Web sites and thus use e-journals less frequently.[59] Focus groups noted that many of the databases licensed by the academic library are too complex to use, and there is not enough time or frequency of use to learn how to use them well.[60]

Ziming Liu surveyed graduate students and found that 84 percent use electronic resources all or most of the time.[61] College and university students report that they are frustrated with their campus libraries and would like the library to:[62]

- Become more customer focused
- Make it easier to use and access library information
- Offer interactive maps, study guides, and resource guides
- Provide links to quality Web sites and other library catalogs
- Make it easier to access electronic resources remotely

The Urban Libraries Council sponsored a large-scale telephone survey in early 2000 and found a difference in service ratings for the library and the Internet:[63]

Greater service ratings for the library	*Greater service ratings for the Internet*
Ease of use	Ease of getting there
Low cost	Time to get there
Availability of paper copy	Hours of access
Accuracy of information	Range of resources
Helpfulness of librarians	Expect to find what is sought
Privacy	Able to act immediately
Currency of information	Enjoyment of browsing
Able to work alone	Fun

Accuracy

Online journal articles in full-text databases are not always fully equivalent to print. Nancy Sprague and Mary Beth Chambers found that 45 percent of full-text articles were not as current as the print journal, 17 percent of major articles were missing, and many graphics were omitted in the databases.[64] It is unclear why more research is not directed at the issue of accuracy and comprehensiveness of the available electronic resources.

Impact on Print Journals

The availability and use of electronic journals can have a significant impact on the use of the library's print journal collection. A comparison of a matched set of biomedical journals available in print and online demonstrated that users overwhelmingly selected journals in the online format.[65] Others noting a reduction in the use of print journals include Vaughan (a 47 percent drop from 1999 to 2002),[66] Obst (30 percent decrease over a two-year period),[67] Black (34% decrease from 1996 to 2003),[68] and Sennyey et al. (a 41 percent decrease from 1998 to 2000).[69] Chandra Prabha analyzed ARL data from 2002 to 2006 and noted a sevenfold increase in subscriptions to electronic-only journals and a reduction in subscriptions to print-only journals of more than 50 percent, while subscriptions to both print and electronic journals remained about the same.[70]

Providing a contrary view, Tammy Siebenberg et al. found that online availability definitely increased the total use of print journals. From the user's perspective, quality and pertinence are still the dominant factors in journal selection.[71]

Impact on the Library

As demand for electronic resources has grown, there has been unrelenting pressure to spend more money on such resources, as evidenced by the increased percentage of the acquisitions budget spent on them.

Health science libraries have also noted a decline in the number of photocopies made, interlibrary loan requests, and physical attendance in the library as the result of providing access to a broad set of electronic resources.[72]

A study at the University of Pittsburgh found that *if* the library's journal collection—physical and electronic—*were not available*, faculty would spend an additional 250,000 hours and some $2.1 million to use alternative sources to locate the desired articles.[73]

Providing access to electronic resources requires that a library reorganize its workflows and procedures. It will also have to hire or train staff with a new set of skills to negotiate the licenses for the electronic resources. David Lewis noted, during a presentation at the 2006 Living the Future Conference, that unless current collection practices are changed, libraries cannot change except on the margins. He suggests that academic libraries need to "follow the user" and revise their collection development strategies by significantly reducing the number of books and print journal subscriptions and supporting open access by claiming responsibility for the institutional repository.[74]

Value of E-Resources

Don King and his colleagues used a contingent valuation methodology, which asks survey respondents how much time and money they would spend to obtain the information they currently receive from the library's journal collection if the library collection were unavailable. Further analysis suggested that the total value of the library's journal collection to the university is $13.48 million, less the $3.43 million costs for creating and maintaining the collection, for a net value of $11.61 million. In other words, if there were no university library journal collection—print and electronic—it would cost the university 4.38 times the cost of the current library collection in faculty time and other expenditures for the same amount of research and information gathering to be carried out.

Another way to determine the value of e-resources is the value associated with the reclamation of stack space devoted to books, reference collections, government documents, and so forth.[75]

SUMMARY

A review of the available research about the availability and use of electronic resources suggests the following:

- Customers prefer online access to electronic resources that are licensed by the library.
- Libraries are spending an increasing percentage of their acquisitions budget on electronic resources.
- A library should calculate a cost per use of a journal or a package of journals as part of an ongoing assessment process.
- Use of some electronic resources is quite high.
- Vendors need to improve the statistics that they provide to comply with the COUNTER standards.
- The purchase of back files should be considered, as their cost is typically fairly moderate.
- Libraries will need to be more creative in communicating the availability of electronic resources to their current and prospective customers.
- The increasing use of electronic resources means that a library must adjust its expenditures on print journals and will likely need to restructure staff positions to cope with licensing and access issues.

A majority of the research studies identified in this chapter typically only used basic descriptive statistics to analyze the data, with the result that it is difficult to generalize the results with any level of confidence. Given that the majority of studies were case-study or survey-based, it is understandable that there were few replication studies (which are needed).

The skill set for librarians responsible for e-resources will have to change as we continue to move to a world of network connections. Specifically, this skill set may look like:

> To increase operational efficiencies, library workflows will have to be more intelligent and data-aware, using demand-side usage data to trigger acquisitions, collection balancing between institutions, triage for digitization, consolidation in shared print environments, transfer or withdrawal decisions, and so on.[76]

FUTURE RESEARCH

A number of libraries, especially larger academic libraries, are involved in digitizing special collections and other unique materials. In a parallel vein, Google is involved in a mass digitization project that will ultimately scan more than 100 million books. Clearly, having such a massive amount of content available online is going to have serious implications and consequences for all types of libraries, which will need to be studied. Among the issues that will likely be investigated and evaluated in the near future are the following:

- Should some portion of materials now housed in a library be moved to storage facilities?
- How does the availability of electronic resources affect a faculty member's ability to teach?
- Do the increasing amounts of electronic resources that are downloaded (saved or printed) increase the research productivity of users?
- Do graduate students who use electronic resources have better academic success?
- How can a library communicate the value of high-quality electronic resources to users in a way that will affect their learning behaviors?
- In short, what are the impacts of the ready availability of electronic resources?

NOTES

1. Jill Grogg and Rachel Fleming-May. The Concept of Electronic Resource Usage and Libraries. *Library Technology Report*, 46 (6), August/September 2010, 1–34.

2. Andrew Odlyzko. The Economic Costs of Toll Access, in Neil Jacobs, (Ed.), *Open Access: Key Strategic, Technical and Economic Aspects*. Oxford, England: Chandos Publishing, 2006, 63–77.

3. Mark Ware and Michael Wabe. *The STM Report: An Overview of Scientific and Scholarly Journal Publishing*. 9th ed. The Hague, The Netherlands: International Association of Scientific, Technical and Medical Publishers, 2015.

4. Steve Hitchcock. The Effect of Open Access and Downloads ('Hits') on Citation Impact: A Bibliography of Studies. 2013. Available at http://opcit.eprints.org/oacitation-biblio.html

5. Vincent Larivière, Stefanie Haustein, and Philippe Mongeon. The Oligopoly of Academic Publishers in the Digital Era. *PLoS One*, 10 (6), June 10, 2015, e0127502.

6. Carol Tenopir. *Use and Users of Electronic Library Resources: An Overview and Analysis of Recent Research Studies*. Washington, DC: Council on Library and Information Resources, August 2003.

7. Amy Friedlander. *Dimensions and Use of the Scholarly Information Environment: Introduction to a Data Set*. Washington, DC: Council on Library and Information Resources, 2002. See also Leigh Watson Healy, Lynn Dagar, and Katherine Medaglia Wilkie. *Customer Report for the Digital Library Federation/Council on Library and Information Resources*. Burlingame, CA: Outsell, 2002.

8. Steve Hiller. How Different Are They? A Comparison by Academic Area of Library Use, Priorities and Information Needs at the University of Washington. *Issues in Science and Technology Librarianship*, 33, Winter 2002, n.p.

9. Tschera Harkness Connell, Sally A. Rogers, and Carol Pitts Diedrichs. OhioLINK Electronic Journal Use at Ohio State University. *portal: Libraries and the Academy*, 5 (3), 2005, 371–90.

10. Barry Schwartz. The Tyranny of Choice. *Scientific American*, 290, April 2004, 70–75.

11. Yumin Jiang, Jeanne A. Baker, and Lynda S. Kresge. Toward Better Access to Full-Text Aggregator Collections. *Serials Librarian*, 39, 2000, 291–97; Jie Tian, Sharon Wiles-Young, and Elizabeth Parang. The Convergence of User Needs, Collection Building and the Electronic Publishing Marketplace. *Serials Librarian*, 38, 2000, 333–39.

12. Dianne Nelson. The Uptake of Electronic Journals by Academics in the UK, Their Attitudes Towards Them and Their Potential Impact on Scholarly Communication. *Information Services & Use*, 21 (3/4), 2001, 205–14.

13. Carol Tenopir and Eleanor J. Read. Patterns of Database Use in Academic Libraries. *College & Research Libraries*, 61, 2000, 234–46.

14. Debbie Malone and Carol Videon. Assessing Undergraduate Use of Electronic Resources: A Quantitative Analysis of Works Cited. *Research Strategies*, 15 (3), 1997, 151–58.

15. Donald W. King, Carol Tenopir, Carol Hansen Montgomery, and Sarah E. Aerni. Patterns of Journal Use by Faculty at Three Diverse Universities. *D-Lib Magazine*, 9 (10), October 2003, n.p.

16. Sanna Talja and Hanni Maula. Reasons for the Use and Non-Use of Electronic Journals and Databases: A Domain Analytic Study in Four Scholarly Disciplines. *Journal of Documentation*, 59 (6), 2003, 673–91.

17. Nila A. Sathe, Jenifer L. Grady, and Nunzia B. Guise. Print Versus Electronic Journals: A Preliminary Investigation into the Effect of Journal Format on Research Processes. *Journal of the Medical Library Association*, 90 (2), April 2002, 235–43.

18. Juris Dilevko and Lisa Gottlieb. Print Sources in an Electronic Age: A Vital Part of the Research Process for Undergraduate Students. *The Journal of Academic Librarianship*, 28 (6), November 2002, 381–92.

19. Kathleen E. Joswick and Jeanne Koekkock Stierman. Perceptions vs. Use: Comparing Faculty Evaluations of Journal Titles with Student Usage. *The Journal of Academic Librarianship*, 21 (6), November 1995, 454–58.

20. Irma F. Dillon and Karla L. Hahn. Are Researchers Ready for the Electronic-Only Journal Collection? Results of a Survey at the University of Maryland. *portal: Libraries and the Academy*, 2 (3), 2002, 375–90.

21. Susan E. Hahn, Cheri Speier, Jonathan Palmer, and Daniel Wren. Advantages and Disadvantages of Electronic Journals: Business School Faculty Views. *Journal of Business and Finance Librarianship*, 5 (1), 1999, 19–31.

22. Erin T. Smith. Changes in Faculty Reading Behaviors: The Impact of Electronic Journals on the University of Georgia. *The Journal of Academic Librarianship*, 29 (3), 2003, 162–68.

23. Cathy De Rosa, Joanne Cantrell, Janet Hawk, and Alane Wilson. *College Students' Perceptions of Libraries and Information Resources.* Dublin, OH: OCLC, 2006.

24. Steve Jones. *The Internet Goes to College.* New York: Pew Internet & American Life Project, 2002; Douglas Levin and Sousan Arafeh. *The Digital Disconnect: The Widening Gap Between Internet-Savvy Students and Their Schools.* New York: Pew Internet & American Life Project, 2002.

25. Leah Graham. Of Course It's True; I Saw It on the Internet!: Critical Thinking in the Internet Era. *Communications of the ACM*, 46 (5), 2003, 71–75.

26. Brinley Franklin and Terry Plum. Networked Electronic Services Usage Patterns at Four Academic Health Sciences Libraries. *Performance Measurement and Metrics*, 3 (3), 2002, 123–33. See also Brinley Franklin and Terry Plum. Successful Web Survey Methodologies for Measuring the Impact of Networked Electronic Services (MINES for libraries). *IFLA Journal*, 32 (1), 2006, 28–40.

27. Brinley Franklin and Terry Plum. Library Usage Patterns in the Electronic Information Environment. *Information Research,* 9 (4), July 2004. Available at http://www.informationr.net/ir/9-4/paper187.html

28. Carol Tenopir and Donald W. King. The Use and Value of Scientific Journals: Past, Present and Future. *Serials*, 14 (2), July 2001, 113–20.

29. Carol Tenopir, Donald W. King, and Amy Bush. Medical Faculty's Use of Print and Electronic Journals: Changes over Time and in Comparison with Scientists. *Journal of the Medical Library Association*, 92 (2), April 2004, 233–41.

30. Carol Tenopir, Donald W. King, P. Boyce, M. Grayson, and K. L. Paulson. Relying on Electronic Journals: Reading Patterns of Astronomers. *Journal of the American Society for Information Science and Technology*, 56 (8), April 2005, 786–802.

31. Sandra L. De Groote, Mary Schultz, and Marceline Doranski. Online Journals' Impact on the Citation Patterns of Medical Faculty. *Journal of the Medical Library Association*, 93 (2), April 2005, 223–28.

32. Carol Pitts Diedrichs. E-Journals: The OhioLINK Experience. *Library Collections, Acquisitions, & Technical Services*. 25 (2), 2001, 191–210, 208.

33. Alex Lankester. What We Know about ScienceDirect User Behavior. *Library Connect*, 4 (1), 2006, 10–11.

34. Paula Johnson and Jennifer Simonsen. Do Engineering Master's Students Know What They Don't Know? Exploring Abstracting and Indexing Service Use and Non-Use. *Library Review*, 64 (1/2), 2015, 36–57.

35. Tschera Harkness Connell, Sally A. Rogers, and Carol Pitts Diedrichs. OhioLINK Electronic Journal Use at Ohio State University. *portal: Libraries and the Academy*, 5 (3), 2005, 371–90.

36. Carol Pitts Diedrichs. E-Journals: The OhioLINK Experience. *Library Collections, Acquisitions, & Technical Services*. 25 (2), 2001, 191–210.

37. Thomas J. Sanville. A Method Out of the Madness: OhioLINK's Collaborative Response to the Serials Crisis Three Years Later: A Progress Report. *Serials Librarian*, 40 (1/2), 2001, 129–55; Anita Cook and Thomas Dowling. Linking from Index to Primary Source: The OhioLINK Model. *The Journal of Academic Librarianship*, 29 (5), September 2003, 320–26.

38. Philip M. Davis. Patterns in Electronic Journal Usage: Challenging the Composition of Geographic Consortia. *College & Research Libraries*, 63 (6), 2002, 484–97.

39. M. P. Day. Electronic Journal Usage and Policy at UMIST. *Information Services & Use*, 21 (3/4), 2001, 135–37; Philip M. Davis. Patterns in Electronic Journal Usage: Challenging the Composition of Geographic Consortia. *College & Research Libraries*, 63 (6), 2002, 484–97; Hans Roes. Promotion of Electronic Journals to Users by Libraries—A Case Study of Tilburg University Library. Presented at the UK Serials Group Promotion and Management of Electronic Journals in London, 28 October 1999.

40. James A. Stemper and Janice M. Jaguszewski. Usage Statistics for Electronic Journals: An Analysis of Local and Vendor Counts. *Collection Management*, 28 (4), 2003, 3–22.

41. David H. Morse and William A. Clintworth. Comparing Patterns of Print and Electronic Journal Use in an Academic Health Science Library. *Issues in Science and Technology Librarianship*, 28, Fall 2000. doi:10.5062/F42B8W0Z

42. Barbara Gauger and Carolyn Kacena. JSTOR Usage Data and What It Can Tell Us about Ourselves: Is There Predictability Based on Historical Use by Libraries of Similar Size? *OCLC Systems & Services: International Digital Library Perspectives*, 22 (1), 43—55.

43. Marie Kennedy and David Kennedy. The "Use" of an Electronic Resource from a Social Network Analysis Perspective. *Library and Information Research*, 38 (118), 2014, 17–34.

44. Institute for the Future. *E-Journal Usage and Scholarly Practice*. 2002. Available at http://ejust.stanford.edu/findings/full_0801.pdf. See also Institute for the Future. *Final Synthesis Report of the E-Journal User Study*. 2002. Available at https://web.stanford.edu/dept/SUL/library/ejust/SR-786.ejustfinal.pdf

45. Theodore Bergstrom, Paul Courant, Preston McAfee, and Michael Williams. Evaluating Big Deal Journal Bundles. *PNAS*, 111 (26), July 1, 2014, 9425–30.

46. Belinda Nicolson-Guest and Debby Macdonald. Are We Comparing Bananas and Gorillas? Interpreting Usage Statistics for Cost Benefit and Reporting: A Presentation to the Council of Australian University Librarians. Available at http://www.caul.edu.au/content/upload/files/stats/online2013 nicholson-guest-statistics.pdf

47. Anthony McMullen. Comparison of Usage Data of a Print Journal Title Versus Electronic Counterpart. *The Bottom Line*, 27 (4), 2014, 126–28.

48. Parker Ladwig and Andrew J. Sommese. Using Cited Half-Life to Adjust Download Statistics. *College & Research Libraries*, 66, November 2005, 527–42.

49. Denise Pan and Yem Fong. Return on Investment for Collaborative Collective Development: A Cost-Benefit Evaluation of Consortia Purchasing. *Collaborative Librarianship*, 2 (4), 2010, 183–92.

50. Bo-Christer Björk, Patrik Welling, Mikael Laakso, Peter Majlender, Turid Hedlund, and Guðni Guðnason. Open Access to the Scientific Journal Literature: Situation 2009. *PLoS One*, June 23, 2010. Available at http://journals.plos.org/plosone/article?id=10.1371/journal.pone.0011273

51. Arthur Sale. The Acquisition of Open Access Research Articles. *First Monday*, October 2011. Available at http://firstmonday.org/ojs/index.php/fm/article/view/1409

52. Bruce White. Total Availability of Journal Articles to Internet Users. *Library Review*, 63 (4/5), 2014, 295–304.

53. Yassine Gargouri, Chawki Hajjem, Vincent Larivière, Yves Gingras, Les Carr, Tim Brody, and Stevan Harnad. Self-Selected or Mandated, Open Access Increases Citation Impact for Higher Quality Research. *PLoS One*, October 18, 2010. Available at http://journals.plos.org/plosone/article?id=10.1371/journal.pone.0013636

54. Chawki Hajjem, Stevan Harnad, and Yves Gingras. Ten-Year Cross-Disciplinary Comparison of the Growth of Open Access and How It Increases Research Citation Impact. *Bulletin of the IEEE Computer Society Technical Committee on Data Engineering*, 28, 2005, 39–47.

55. Steve Lawrence. Free Online Availability Substantially Increases a Paper's Impact. *Nature*, 411, 31 May 2011, 521.

56. Philip Davis, Bruce Lewenstein, Danile Simon, James Booth, and Mathew Connolly. Open Access Publishing, Article Downloads, and Citation: Randomized Controlled Trial. *BMJ*, 2008, a568.

57. Iain D. Craig, Andrew M. Plume, Marie E. McVeigh, James Pringle, and Mayur Amin. Do Open Access Articles Have Greater Citation Impact? A Critical Review of the Literature. *Journal of Informetrics*, 1 (3), July 2007, 239–48.

58. Roberta Pastorino, Sonja Milovanovic, Jovana Stojanovic, Ljupcho Efremov, Rosarita Amore, and Stefania Boccia. Quality Assessment of Studies Published in Open Access and Subscription Journals: Results of a Systematic Evaluation. *PLoS One*, May 11, 2106.

59. Institute for the Future. *E-Journal Usage And Scholarly Practice: An Ethnographic Perspective on the Role and Impact Of E-Journal Usage Among Users Of Biomedical Literature*. Palo Alto, CA: Stanford University, Institute for the Future, 2001.

60. Steve Hiller. Evaluating Bibliographic Database Use: Beyond the Numbers. *Against the Grain*, 15 (6), December 2003–January 2004, 26–30.

61. Ziming Liu. Print vs. Electronic Resources: A Study of User Perceptions, Preferences, and Use. *Information Processing & Management*, 42, 2006, 583–92.

62. Steve Jones. *The Internet Goes to College*. New York: Pew Internet & American Life Project, 2002; Douglas Levin and Sousan Arafeh. *The Digital Disconnect: The Widening Gap Between Internet-Savvy Students and Their Schools*. New York: Pew Internet & American Life Project, 2002. See also OCLC. *How Academic Librarians Can Influence Students' Web-Based Information Choices* (OCLC White Paper on the Information Habits of College Students). Dublin, OH: OCLC, June 2002.

63. George D'Elia, Corinne Jorgensen, Joseph Woelfel, and Eleanor Jo Rodger. The Impact of the Internet on Public Library Use: An Analysis of the Current Consumer Market for Library and Internet Services. *Journal of the American Society for Information Science and Technology*, 53 (10), 2002, 802–20.

64. Nancy Sprague and Mary Beth Chambers. Full Text Databases and the Journal Cancellation Process: A Case Study. *Serials Review*, 26 (3), October 2000, 19–31.

65. David H. Morse and William A. Clintworth. Comparing Patterns of Print and Electronic Journal Use in an Academic Health Science Library. *Issues in Science and Technology Librarianship*, 28, Fall 2000.

66. K. T. L. Vaughan. Changing Patterns of Print Journals in the Digital Age: Impacts of Electronic Equivalents on Print Chemistry Journal Use. *Journal of the American Society for Information Science and Technology*, 54 (12), October 2003, 1149–52.

67. Oliver Obst. Patterns and Costs of Printed and Online Journal Usage. *Health Information and Libraries Journal*, 20, 2003, 22–32.

68. Steve Black. Impact of Full Text on Print Journal Use at a Liberal Arts College. *Library Resources & Technical Services*, 49 (1), 2005, 19–26.

69. Pongracz Sennyey, Gillian D. Ellern, and Nancy Newsome. Collection Development and a Long-Term Periodical Use Study: Methodology and Implications. *Serials Review*, 28 (1), Spring 2002, 38–44.

70. Chandra Prabha. Shifting from Print to Electronic Journals in ARL University Libraries. *Serials Review*, 33 (1), 2007, 4–13.

71. Tammy Siebenberg, Betty Galbraith, and Eileen E. Brady. Print Versus Electronic Journal Use in Three Sci/Tech Disciplines: What's Going on Here? *College & Research Libraries*, 65 (5), September 2004, 427–38.

72. Suzetta Burrows. A Review of Electronic Journal Acquisitions, Management, and Use in Health Science Libraries. *Journal of the Medical Library Association*, 94 (1), January 2006, 67–74.

73. Donald W. King, Sarah Aerni, Fern Brody, Matt Hebison, and Amy Knapp. *The Use and Outcomes of University Library Print and Electronic Collections.* Pittsburgh: University of Pittsburgh, Sara Fine Institute for Interpersonal Behavior and Technology, April 2004; Donald W. King, Sarah Aerni, Fern Brody, Matt Hebison, and Paul Kohberger. *Comparative Cost of the University of Pittsburgh Electronic and Print Library Collections.* Pittsburgh: University of Pittsburgh, Sara Fine Institute for Interpersonal Behavior and Technology, May 2004. See also Roger C. Schonfeld, Donald W. King, Ann Okerson, and Eileen Gifford Fenton. Library Periodicals Expenses: Comparison of Non-Subscription Costs of Print and Electronic Formats on a Life-Cycle Basis. *D-Lib Magazine*, 10 (1), January 2004; Donald W. King, Carol Tenopir, Carol Hansen Montgomery, and Sarah E. Aerni. Patterns of Journal Use by Faculty at Three Diverse Universities. *D-Lib Magazine*, 9 (10), October 2003.

74. David W. Lewis. Reflections on the Future of Library Collections. Presentation made at the *Living the Future 6 Conference,* 6 April 2006, Tucson, Arizona.

75. Kay Downey. Thoughts on Collection Development of eResources, in Douglas King (Ed.), *How Can Libraries Determine the Value in Collecting, Managing, Preserving, and/or Cataloging E-Resources? Journal of Electronic Resources Librarianship*, 21 (2), 2009, 131–40. See also Kay Downey, Why Did We Buy That? New Customers and Changing Directions in Collection Development. *Collection Management*, 38 (2), April 2013, 90–103.

76. Lorcan Dempsey, Constance Malpas, and Brian Lavoie. Collection Directions: Some Reflection on the Future of Library Collections and Collecting. *portal: Libraries and the Academy,* 14 (3), 2014, 420.

14

Evaluation of E-Books

I want to be able to seamlessly go back and forth between reading with my eyes and reading with my ears (Audible audiobook).

—Joshua Kim[1]

SERVICE DEFINITION

E-books are becoming increasingly popular among library users, and thus almost every library needs to ensure that the e-books available to its users are meeting their needs. To add to the complexity of the picture, in addition to the e-books available (in some cases) from traditional publishers, there is the blizzard of self-published e-books from a variety of sources.

EVALUATION QUESTIONS

Among the many questions that have been raised as libraries provide increasing access to e-books are:

- Should e-books be provided from more than one vendor?
- How many e-books is "enough" at any point in time?
- Should we use a vendor's platform, or should the library host its own e-book platform?
- Should e-books be purchased or licensed?
- Should bibliographic records be a part of the library's catalog (or discovery system)?
- Should the library provide a kiosk so patrons can browse available e-books?
- Is it possible to loan the same e-book to two different people at the same time?
- How problematic are proprietary file formats?
- What are the best practices in terms of licensing restrictions?

EVALUATION METHODS

Libraries have relied on use statistics (primarily, number of downloads), analysis of proxy server transaction data, and customer satisfaction surveys to evaluate e-books in a library.

PRIOR EVALUATIONS AND RESEARCH

According to a variety of sources, as many as 95 percent of American public libraries offer access to an e-book collection, often times in excess of 10,000 titles. Note: The issues and concerns surrounding the decision by some vendors not to license e-books to public libraries, or the fact that some vendors place restrictions on the number of times an e-book can be borrowed before it must be relicensed, are not addressed in this chapter. Though these are important concerns, no research has been (or will ever likely be) conducted, as these are marketing and pricing decisions made by the publishers. In addition, the impact that such services as Kindle Unlimited and Oyster.com, which provide unlimited e-book reading for a flat monthly fee, will have on public libraries has yet to be assessed.

William Walters has provided a overview of the challenges associated with e-books in a library setting.[2] Sottong defined eight criteria that can be used for the evaluation of e-book technology: quality, durability, initial cost, continuing cost, ease of use, features, standardized, and have extra features. Sottong used the criteria in 2001 and concluded that e-books failed on six of the eight criteria.[3] In 2016, it is safe to say, using the same criteria, that e-books would score 100 percent, as evidenced by the number of and popularity of e-book readers and the significant number of e-books downloaded each year.

Jeff Staiger prepared a thoughtful and thoroughly readable literature review of e-book studies covering the years 2006 to 2011.[4]

Comparing Availability of Print versus E-Books

Although academic libraries may be interested in moving more of their acquisitions budget to e-books, several studies have shown that only a small proportion of published academic materials are available as e-books.[5]

A study at the Jawaharlal Nehru University Library in New Delhi compared the availability of print titles versus the e-book format and found that an average of 57.5 percent of titles were available in e-book format (availability varied depending upon subject area from a low of 39.5 percent to a high of 70 percent). The study also noted that the purchase price of print books was cheaper than e-books (ignoring the continuing costs to store and provide access to library physical collections).[6]

Comparing Use of Print versus E-Books

Analyzing only titles that were available in both formats, a study at the University of Pittsburgh found a definite preference for e-books.[7] A comparison of electronic and print formats at the University of Louisiana State University found a weak correlation between use of a print book and use of the e-book.[8]

A comparison of 7,490 print book titles and the same titles available as electronic books (e-books) at Duke University found that e-books received 11 percent more use than their print counterparts.[9] Another study at a large academic library found that almost all of the 20,000-plus demand-driven acquisition e-books were used the first year, and 90 percent had two to nine uses. Also, 62.5 percent of the print books were used within the first three years of being purchased. Interestingly, the cost per use for print and e-books was about the same. However, it was found that demand-driven acquisition of e-books leads to more overall active use.[10]

Students like e-books for several reasons:[11]

- **Convenience:** Content is available immediately in digital format (PDF format is preferred—especially without any use or access restrictions).
- **Cost savings:** They reduce the number of books that must be purchased for classes.
- **Currency:** Recent content is valued.
- **Efficiency:** Users can browse or search and then print just those portions of interest. Students find reading online too disjointed.
- **An alternative copy:** They are available when the print version is checked out or no print version is available.

Subject Area of Use

Several studies have focused on how e-book usage varies across scholarly disciplines, and have concluded that the highest usage rates are found in computers, technology, business, and the sciences, while the lowest usage occurs in the arts and humanities.[12]

A study of NetLibrary e-book use found that titles in economics, business, and computer science were most heavily used.[13] An analysis of Questia, a commercial online library service that provides access to e-books, found that literature was the most popular subject for research, followed by sociology and history, at the University of Rochester.[14]

The California State University campuses evaluated their shared e-book collection by analyzing use statistics and a customer satisfaction survey.[15] A similar analysis was prepared at Oakland University; that study also determined in what subject areas e-books were more heavily used.[16] An analysis of use and nonuse among both print and electronic collections at Seton Hall University found that among science books, very similar rates were observed among the two formats.[17]

Steven Knowlton used a technique called Percent of Expected Use (PEU) to compare print and e-book collections at the University of Memphis libraries. Percent of Expected Use, first advocated by Bonn,[18] compares the ratio of use to holdings in a specific subject area(s). Knowlton found that there was a strong overall preference for print (except in a few subject areas where patrons strongly preferred e-books).[19] An analysis of ProQuest's *Electronic Book Library* at the University of Massachusetts Amherst Library compared a set of books available in both print and e-book formats. Although more use of print books was found, 40 percent of the e-book users did not borrow any print books—indicating that the availability of e-books created new users.[20]

Nisa Bakkalbasi and Melissa Goertzen at the Columbia University Libraries used a combination of search terms captured by Google Analytics and COUNTER e-book usage data and found that e-books are used primarily to read chapters or articles for study purposes.[21]

As the librarians at Louisiana State University remind us, it is important to weed e-book collections so outdated content is removed and the digital e-book collection is kept fresh and relevant.[22]

One analysis tracked the number of days a patron would need to wait in order to borrow popular e-books in three large public libraries and found that the wait time exceeded 21 days—while attempting to maintain a 6:1 holds-to-copy ratio of popular e-book titles. Recommended changes included shortening the lending period for e-books to 14 days, limiting the number of e-books that can be borrowed at one time, and limiting the e-book hold requests.[23]

Customer Surveys

A survey of faculty members, students, incoming students, and alumni at the University of Denver (more than 2,000 respondents) found no correlation between the awareness of e-books collections within disciplines and e-book usage rates. Further, the analysis reveal that awareness ranged from 49 to 69 percent across disciplines. Interestingly, most users "use rather than read" e-books and more than half of the users are only reading a chapter or an article within the book.[24]

A similar survey conducted at the University of Illinois found that more than 75 percent of e-book use was for research purposes and half used e-books for study purposes.[25]

Consortia Purchases

Consortia will, in many cases, license e-books for their members. The specific characteristics of each vendor agreement will, of necessity, reflect the needs of consortium members. Recognizing that e-books and print formats are not in an either-or competition, the Triangle Research Libraries Network (TRLN) worked with Oxford University Press to create a financially sustainable model whereby the libraries would systematically increase e-book acquisitions while at the same time reducing print intake over time and keeping net costs constant. The parties involved with this creative project found that they needed to remain flexible as issues such as licensing, pricing, and providing access were being addressed.[26]

Wen-ying Lu and Mary Beth Chambers[27] explored the changes required for the shared purchasing and cataloging of patron-driven acquisition of e-books among five geographically separate University of Colorado campuses. The authors' suggested best practices include:

- Establish a standard for vendor-supplied metadata
- Create positive relationships with various vendor personnel
- Provide a means for assessing the collection and monitoring the budget
- Revise and streamline local workflow procedures

SUMMARY

From the perspective of the user, electronic resources are so attractive and heavily used because:

- They provide access to information quickly
- They provide access to a wide range of information
- Desktop access to information is easy—it saves time and energy—and can be done anytime and anywhere; and downloading and printing of articles is now fairly routine
- Patron-driven acquisition of e-books should now be a standard operating procedure for a majority of academic libraries (rather than being a pilot program)[28]
- E-books offer the typical academic library several benefits including:
  - Users prefer e-books for quick consultation of sections and print books for reading the entire book
  - Low cost for the acquisition of content

- Low cost per use
- Require less space for the physical storage of a title
- Require less staff time to lend
- User can access e-book content 24/7
- Enables higher usage per book compared to a print book

NOTES

1. Joshua Kim. On Choosing Technologies that We Know Will Diminish Quality. *Inside Higher Ed*, August 23, 2016.

2. William Walters. E-Books in Academic Libraries: Challenges for Acquisition and Collection Management. *portal: Libraries and the Academy*, 13 (2), 2013, 187–211.

3. S. Sottong. E-Book Technology: Waiting for the "False Pretender." *Information Technology and Libraries*, 20 (2), 2001, 72–80.

4. Jeff Staiger. How E-Books Are Used: A Literature Review of the E-Book Studies Conducted from 2006 to 2011. *Reference & User Services Quarterly*, 51(4), 2012, 355–65.

5. Sarah Pomerantz. The Availability of E-Books: Examples of Nursing and Business. *Collection Building*, 29 (1), 2010, 11–14; William H. Walters. E-Books in Academic Libraries: Challenges for Acquisition and Collection Management. *portal: Libraries and the Academy*, 13 (2), 2013, 187–211; Suresh Jindal and Ankur Pant. Availability of E-books in Science: Case Study of University of Delhi. *The Electronic Library*, 31 (3), 2013, 313–28.

6. K. Nageswara Rao, Manorama Tripathi, and Sunil Kumar. Cost of Print and Digital Books: A Comparative Study. *The Journal of Academic Librarianship*, 42, 2016, 445–52.

7. Lynn Silipigni Connaway, Kaia Densch, and Susan Gibbons. The Integration and Usage of Electronic Books (eBooks) in the Digital Library, in Carol Nixon (Ed.). *Computers in Libraries 2002: Collected Presentations*. Medford, NJ: Information Today, 2002, 18–25.

8. Marilyn Christianson and Marsha Aucoin. Electronic or Print Books: Which Are Used? *Library Collections, Acquisitions, & Technical Services*, 29, 2005, 74–79.

9. Justin Littman and Lynn Silipigni Connaway. A Circulation Analysis of Print Books and E-Books in an Academic Research Library. *Library Resources & Technical Services*, 48 (4), 2004, 256–26.

10. Kay Downey, Yin Zhang, Cristobo Urbano, and Tom Klinger. A Comparative Study of Print Book and DDA E-Book Acquisition and Use. *Technical Services Quarterly*, 31 (2), 2014, 139–60.

11. Peter Hernon, Rosita Hopper, Michael R. Leach, Laura L. Saunders, and Jane Zhang. E-book Use by Students: Undergraduates in Economics, Literature and Nursing. *The Journal of Academic Librarianship*, 33 (1), January 2007, 3–13.

12. Timothy Bailey. Electronic Book Usage at a Master's Level 1 University: A Longitudinal Study. *The Journal of Academic Librarianship*, 32(1), 2006, 52–59; Marilyn Christianson. Patterns of Use of Electronic Books. *Library Collections, Acquisitions, & Technical Services*, 29(4), 2005, 351–63; Jeff Staiger. How E-Books Are Used: A Literature Review of the E-Book Studies Conducted from 2006 to 2011. *Reference & User Services Quarterly*, 51(4), 2012, 355–65.

13. Carol Ann Hughes and Nancy L. Buckman. Use of Electronic Monographs in the Humanities and Social Sciences. *Library Hi Tech*, 19 (4), 2001, 368–75.

14. *netLibrary eBook Usage at the University of Rochester Libraries*. 2001, September 27. Available at http://www.lib.rochester.edu/main/ebooks/studies/analysis.pdf

15. Marc Langston. The California State University E-Book Pilot Project: Implications for Cooperative Collection Development. *Library Collections, Acquisitions, & Technical Services*, 27 (1), 2003, 19–32.

16. Robert Slater. E-Books or Print Books, 'Big Deals' or Local Selections—What Gets More Use? *Library Collections, Acquisitions, & Technical Services*, 33, 2009, 31–41.

17. Lisa Rose-Wiles. Are Print Books Dead? An Investigation of Book Circulation at a Mid-Sized Academic Library. *Technical Services Quarterly*, 30, 2013, 129–52.

18. George Bonn. Evaluation of the Collection. *Library Trends*, 22, 1974, 273.

19. Steven Knowlton. A Two-Step Model for Assessing Relative Interest in E-Books Compared to Print. *College & Research Libraries,* 77 (1), January 2016, 20–33.

20. Rachel Lewellen, Steven Bischoff, and Terry Plum. EBL Ebook Use Compared to the Use of Equivalent Print Books and Other Eresources: A University of Massachusetts Amherst—MINES for Libraries Case Study. *Performance Measurement and Metrics*, 17 (2), 2016, 150–64.

21. Nisa Bakkalbasi and Melissa Goertzen. Scholarly E-Book Use across Disciplines: Content Analysis of Usage Reports and Search Terms, in Ann Fiddler (Ed.). *Reinventing Libraries: Reinventing Assessment Innovative Practices and Ideas That Challenge the Status Quo—Proceedings of the CUNY Library Assessment Conference*, 2014. Available at http://academicworks.cuny.edu/ols_proceedings _lac/4/.

22. Mike Waugh, Michelle Donlin, and Stephanie Braunstein. Next-Generation Collection Management: A Case Study of Quality Control and Weeding E-Books in an Academic Library. *Collection Management*, 40 (1), 2015, 17–26.

23. Laura Ridenour and Wooseob Jeong. Are We There Yet? Calculating Wait Time for Popular Digital Titles. *Public Library Quarterly*, 35 (2), 2016, 136–51.

24. Michael Levine-Clark. Electronic Books and the Humanities: A Survey at the University of Denver. *Collection Building,* 26(1), 2007, 7–14.

25. Wendy Shelburne. E-Book Usage in an Academic Library: User Attitudes and Behaviors. *Library Collections, Acquisitions, & Technical Services*, 33, 2009, 59–72.

26. Luke Swindler. New Consortial Model for E-Books Acquisitions. *College & Research Libraries*, May 2016, 269–85.

27. Wen-ying Lu and Mary Beth Chambers. PDA Consortium Style: The CU MyiLibrary Cataloging Experience. *Library Resources & Technical Services,* 57 (3), 2013.

28. Graham Stone and Briony Heyhow-Pullar. The Customer Is Always Right? Assessing the Value of Patron-Driven Acquisition at the University of Huddersfield. *Insights*, 28 (1), March 2015, 22–31.

15

Evaluation of Reference Services

We need big servers and the geeks to take care of them. What are we going to cut to be able to hire a geek? We are going to cut reference staff. Reference is dead.

—Eli Neiburger[1]

I actually relish the idea that the present, passive reference model is dead, and that something more agile, flexible and proactive will replace it.

—Colin the Librarian[2]

SERVICE DEFINITION

It is generally acknowledged that the beginning of reference service occurred back in the 1870s when Samuel Green suggested that reference had four functions: answering patron queries, instructing patrons how to use the library, assisting patrons to select resources, and promoting the library within the community.[3]

A library customer may approach a staff member at a number of service locations, be it a circulation desk, information counter, reference desk, or customer service—as well as via the telephone or the Internet (e-mail, instant messaging, or a virtual "Ask a librarian" service). Ignoring the quickly dispatched directional queries and the need to provide technical assistance with computers, printers, and so forth, the focus of this chapter is the evaluation of reference services. As shown in Figure 15.1, the provision of reference service involves a customer, a librarian, the interaction between the two, and access to a set of resources that can be used to answer the question.

The customer interacts with the librarian to resolve an information need using a variety of methods: face-to-face in the library, over a telephone, via e-mail, in a 24/7 chat-based electronic tool, via instant messaging, Skype, and so forth. The customer's knowledge about his or her information need may be complete and accurate or quite limited and ill-defined. More important is the customer's ability to accurately communicate and interact with the reference librarian to fulfill the information need.

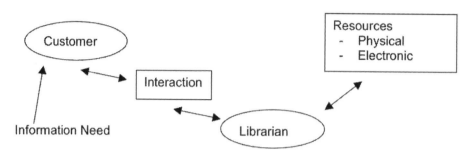

Figure 15.1. Components of Reference Service

The librarian's ability to provide an accurate answer and a total experience that the customer will consider professional and satisfactory depends on a number of factors:

- The experience and training of the librarian
- The librarian's familiarity with the library's collection
- The librarian's knowledge of and available electronic resources
- The number of people waiting for service
- The "reference interview" communication skills
- The attitude of the librarian and his or her commitment to providing quality and friendly service
- The communication skills of the user to describe the information need
- Implementation of reference policies, reflected in management policies and reward and recognition practices

EVALUATION QUESTIONS

Libraries have examined a variety of issues surrounding reference service, including the following questions:

- Is use of reference services declining or increasing?
- Is an answer to a question provided?
- Is the answer provided accurate?
- How long does a customer wait for reference service?
- Is the customer satisfied with the answer provided?
- Is the customer satisfied with the complete reference experience?
- What interpersonal and other skills are important?
- What categories are used to record each reference transaction?
- What proportion of the physical reference collection is being used?
- What reference electronic resources are being used? Are other electronic resources needed?
- What is the cost to the library to answer each question?
- How does the cost to the library vary if service is provided in person, over the telephone, via e-mail, via fax, or via an electronic system?
- What is the value of providing reference to a library's customers?

EVALUATION METHODS

In general, there are a number of means for evaluating reference services. The more frequently used methods include surveys, focus groups, interviews, and observation. Figure 15.2 shows a broader classification of these methods.

	Qualitative	Quantitative
Library Perspective	Descriptive Analysis Observation	Obtrusive Methods
Customer Perspective	WOREP Survey	Unobtrusive Methods Conjoint Analysis Cost-Benefit Analysis

Figure 15.2. Reference Services Evaluation Methods

PRIOR EVALUATIONS AND RESEARCH

Ellen Altman and William Katz reviewed the literature on the evaluation of reference services, and both authors suggested that there is no standard for measuring the efficiency and effectiveness of reference services.[4] More recently, Jean McLaughlin noted that there is no generally accepted set of standard approaches, study methodologies, and reporting formats for analysis and comparison.[5]

Libraries as a Source of Information

Some would suggest that libraries are either losing or have lost their quest to be the primary information provider for their service populations. Google has become the "go to" source for information. The recent evidence is fairly compelling. The use of reference services in large academic and public libraries has been declining in recent years. A 2005 OCLC survey found that people turn first to the Internet to get answers to their questions. Libraries are rarely, if ever, thought of as a potential source of information. Some 65 percent of survey respondents do not seek assistance, either while online or visiting the library.[6] However, of those who do seek assistance, more than three-fourths prefer to interact directly with a librarian. The survey respondents also indicated that search engines deliver better quality and quantity of information than librarian-assisted searching—and at greater speed. In addition, a study found that answers to ready reference questions on the Internet are very likely to be accurate, especially if the site is in the top five retrieved by Google. Many of the commonly proposed indicators of accuracy—for example, no advertising being present—were in fact not related to accuracy.[7]

A survey of ARL libraries found that the number of reference transactions had declined 77 percent from 1999 to 2015. In addition, library customers now use a variety of methods to communicate with reference librarians: telephone, e-mail, chat reference, and reference question Web forms.[8]

Yet this is not a recent phenomenon, as Ching-chih Chen and Peter Hernon discovered more than 35 years ago when they surveyed 2,400 New England residents to learn about their information needs. The library ranked ninth, behind such sources as own experience; friends and acquaintances; newspapers or books; someone in a store or business; co-workers; professors, doctors, or lawyers; government officials; and television.[9]

Historically, libraries have gathered counts of reference transactions to demonstrate the value of the service to funding decision makers (use equals value) and to better align staffing and service hours. Traditionally libraries have recorded each reference transaction as "directional," "ready reference," or "search/instructional." However, reference staff are inconsistent about how they class and record data, regardless of the categories used. One study found as much as 45 percent variation in how staff recorded service transactions.[10]

The READ Scale

The READ Scale (Reference Effort Assessment Data) is a six-point scale for recording qualitative data by recording effort, knowledge, skills, and teaching used by staff during a reference transaction. The READ Scale, which was developed in 2007, includes:

1. Least of amount of effort—typically directional inquiries and rudimentary machine assistance—less than 5 minutes.

2. Nominal amount of effort—general library or policy information, minor machine assistance.

3. Requires some effort and time; use of resource materials is usually necessary. Basic instruction on use of a resource or machine.

4. Requires the consultation of multiple resources—reference knowledge and skills needed.

5. More substantial time and effort spent assisting with finding information and research. More in-depth "back and forth" discussion of an information need.

6. Requires the most time and effort—in-depth meetings and instruction.

Testing in 14 academic libraries with some 24 service points found that more than half of all transactions were directional (Level 1), 27 percent were Level 2, 15 percent were Level 3, 6 percent were Level 4, and only 1 percent were Level 5.[11]

Librarian Skills

The library profession has developed two guidelines for recommended behavior of reference service providers: *Facets of Quality for Digital References Services* and the RUSA *Guidelines for Behavioral Performance of Reference and Information Service Providers*. Reference staff members will adopt such behaviors through training and feedback about their actual performance.

> *With all of the demands that we have in trying to remain relevant, what is the value of having a highly skilled subject specialist sitting at a desk?*
>
> —Steven Bell[12]

A study by George Hawley suggested that libraries need to view reference as a service that incorporates a broader perspective, and admit that they do a poor job of referring customers to other libraries or sources to satisfy the information need of the customer.[13]

Several studies have shown that a library customer does not know who is a professional librarian and who is a paraprofessional.[14] Actual behaviors have a strong impact on the perceived performance of service providers.[15] Nonverbal communication also plays an important role in the user's perception of the librarian's approachability. One study found that eye contact signaled to the user that the reference librarian was approachable.[16]

The interpersonal skills so necessary in a face-to-face reference transaction are also necessary, though modified, in a virtual reference situation.[17] Periodically reviewing the virtual reference session transcripts offers an opportunity for improvement and feedback. The transcripts can be useful in a training setting.[18]

Historically, the evaluation of reference has had a system-centric view of the world. However, thanks to the efforts of Brenda Dervin's sense-making communication theory,[19] Carol Kuhlthau's diagnosis-intervention orientation model,[20] and Diane Nahl-Jakobovits's self-witnessing behavior model,[21] the user-centered perspective has been gaining strength. User-centered is a way of defining, measuring, and explaining the behavior of library users. Diane Nahl has prepared a thorough review of the research in this area.[22]

Descriptive Analysis

Most studies examining the quality of reference services are, by design, internally focused, and consider such topics as the reference interval, service times, queuing times, librarian–customer interactions, and so forth. A majority of libraries collect output measures, which are gathered at the reference desk: number of customers served (often divided into blocks of time), time spent with each customer, and so forth. These statistics can be helpful in scheduling staff at the service desk, and the reporting of these measures in some manner is usually mandated. However, collecting these statistics is *not* a form of evaluation, because they cannot be used to assess quality or understand why people use reference services.

Other studies of reference have categorized those who use the service (age, occupation, academic class standing, and so forth), degree of satisfaction with the service, visibility of the service, willingness of people to approach the service desk, types of questions asked (and answered), sources used, and so forth. The majority of the early studies focused on actual reference transactions as the unit of study. It is interesting to note that approximately 25 percent of reference transactions in public libraries are reported to be for someone else.[23] And those who came to the library on behalf of someone else rated library services higher than those who came seeking answers for their own questions.[24]

Assessing the customer's satisfaction with the reference interaction can provide valuable information, but it is only an indirect measure of reference service. Satisfaction has been defined as "the emotional reaction to a specific transaction or service encounter."[25] Customer satisfaction is basically a comparison between the expectations of the customer and his or her experience receiving the service. One study found evidence that customers appear to distinguish between their satisfaction with the service provided and satisfaction with the information that they obtain.[26]

Given the easy availability of options, it is not surprising that customers have high expectations for the skills of library staff and the overall quality of service they will receive. A study by Vicki Coleman et al. examined the quality of library services at three libraries and found that customers rated the libraries below or just barely above their minimum expectations.[27] In an earlier study, people sitting in an academic library were asked if they would approach a librarian for help if they had an information need. Of those with an information need, 42 percent indicated they would not ask for assistance because they were dissatisfied with service they had previously received.[28]

Jo Bell Whitlatch has suggested that because customers separately evaluate different aspects of service, a variety of performance measures, such as success in locating the desired information, should be analyzed.[29] She found that although customer and librarian ratings for service outcomes were almost always identical, substantial differences arose concerning the sufficiency of information provided and the usefulness of the information provided.

Obtrusive Methods

An obtrusive method is a technique to evaluate the use of a particular service during which the observer and user of the service directly interact. In the case of evaluating reference services, the observer, customer, and librarian would talk with one another about what they are doing and thinking. The observer could ask clarifying questions. In addition, a survey can be distributed to the customer or the librarian, or both.

A Library Survey

Some libraries have developed local surveys to determine the quality of reference services. It seems that satisfaction surveys can determine whether the service was quick and whether the librarian was courteous and professional, but are not able to assist in judging the accuracy of the provided information.

In a study that involved five academic libraries in northern California, Jo Bell Whitlatch asked both users and librarians to complete a questionnaire regarding the reference transaction. The study found that requests for specific factual information are a small proportion of reference service: 12 percent.[30] Yet the librarians judged factual questions to be more difficult because responding to these queries involves the use of less familiar, less frequently used sources. Carolyn Jardine found that the reference librarian's attitude, behavior, interest, and enthusiasm influence customers' perceptions of the librarian and the service they receive.[31] Another study found that college students valued the availability of high-quality, quick, and personalized reference assistance using chat and instant messages.[32]

The WOREP Survey

One well-grounded tool is the Wisconsin-Ohio Reference Evaluation Program (WOREP), which asks the library customer to complete a short checklist about his or her query; the librarian fills out a corresponding form. The WOREP instrument—called the Reference Transaction Assessment Instrument—has been subjected to a rigorous set of reliability measures and validity tests.[33] A transaction is scored as successful only when the customer reports finding exactly what was wanted, marks being fully satisfied, and does not check any of the nine listed reasons for dissatisfaction. A library using WOREP can compare itself with similar types of libraries (for example, public libraries) as well as libraries of similar size. The survey is easy to administer and inexpensive to use, and the return rate is typically quite high.[34]

Wichita State University Library used the WOREP survey, and staff were surprised to learn that the two highest user groups were freshmen and graduate students, contrary to the staff's impression that upper-level undergraduates were the biggest users.[35] An analysis of 7,013 reference transactions in 74 general reference departments in academic libraries around the United States found a mean success rate of 57 percent and also found that quality varies by size of library: small 30 percent, medium 46 percent, and large only 28 percent.[36] Quality reference service was defined as providing an accurate answer (in the opinion of the customer) and having the customer rate the experience as satisfactory. Not surprisingly, having insufficient time for most customers and their questions usually had a negative effect on success in all sizes of libraries. June Parker reported similar results in a study of a government documents department.[37]

The use of WOREP allows a library to discover its strengths and weaknesses and to compare itself to a set of peer libraries that have also completed the WOREP survey. The strength of the WOREP methodology is that it uses actual queries brought to the library by the customer or asked via the telephone, rather than using "test questions." The WOREP survey can be used repeatedly to track improvements resulting from staff training.[38]

Although large libraries, with their larger funding, collections, electronic resources, and trained staff, are able to provide a breadth and depth of reference services that simply cannot be duplicated in a smaller library, the large libraries may have too many resources and may provide a lower quality of service than their medium-sized peers.

Quick and Easy Reference Evaluation

Jonathan Miller developed a "Quick and Easy Reference Evaluation" survey with only four questions that are asked of both the customer and the staff member:

1. The user gets the information he or she needs.
2. The user learns something about how to find information.
3. The user learns something about how to evaluate information.
4. The user is satisfied with the interaction.

The survey confirmed the library's LibQUAL results—public-service staff members receive high marks for quality service.[39]

Unobtrusive Testing

When the unobtrusive testing method is used, library staff members are unaware that they are being tested as they attempt to respond to a query. "Proxies" playing the role of customers pose questions with predetermined answers. The questions may be specifically created for the study or derived from actual reference interactions. After the interaction the proxy completes a checklist to report answers, sources used, attitudes, and so forth.

The quality of reference service can be defined as the accuracy of the information being provided in response to fact-type questions. In 1971, Terence Crowley and Thomas Childers initiated a tradition of unobtrusive observation testing of reference services when they published the results of their dissertations.[40] This type of study uses the correct answer rate—the proportion of correct answers to the total number of answers received (expressed as a percentage)—as a measure of reference performance.

Peter Hernon and Charles McClure explored the results of a number of studies, and they noted that numerous studies found a consistent and low reference success rate. This led Hernon and McClure to suggest

> the "55 percent rule": Anyone asking an information question in a library has about a 55 percent chance of receiving the correct answer![41]

Among the more notable unobtrusive studies was one conducted by McClure and Hernon in which they examined the quality of reference service in government depository libraries; they found that correct responses ranged from 6 to 82 percent.[42] A similar study, performed by Juris Dilevko and Elizabeth Dolan in Canadian government depository libraries, found that accuracy ranged from 15 to 79 percent.[43] This latter study used four categories to code or score each question: complete answer, partially complete answer, referral, and no or incorrect answer.

In general, despite the many reference accuracy studies done, there are inconsistent operational definitions of "accuracy" and outcome variables included in the analysis. Other problems with most of these studies include simplistic statistical analysis, a lack of random sampling, informational queries being only a part of the services offered at the reference desk, limited reliability of the study design, and so forth.[44]

Thomas Childers, reflecting on his participation in launching a series of research projects that have evaluated reference service, noted:

> The bad news about investigating queries with short, factual, unambiguous answers is that, in the minds of many—especially those interested in evaluating performance—it has assumed unrealistic proportions and come to stand for the whole of the reference function, yet there is no empirical foundation for it, no literature that links performance of one kind of reference service with performance on another kind of service.[45]

The inaccuracy of information provided by reference services has the potential for serious negative consequences, depending on how the information will be used. Paul Burton provided a summary of the numerous studies in this area and suggests that other professionals do not get it wrong 45 percent of the time. Burton recommends that librarians do more research into the contribution of information to work that users do and the environment in which their information needs arise.[46]

Kenneth Crews provides a valuable overview of most of the accuracy studies and suggests the need for further research.[47] In a comprehensive assessment and critique of the various reference accuracy studies, Matthew Saxton and John Richardson assert that there are a number of methodological difficulties, including the following:

- "Fact type" queries account for many and perhaps a majority of all queries received at the reference desk. "Open-ended" questions typically require more interaction and negotiation to arrive at a satisfactory answer from the customer's perspective.
- There are difficulties in determining categories for types of questions.
- Definitions of independent and outcome variables are inconsistent from one study to another.
- Bias arises from self-selected samples and low sample sizes.
- Simplistic statistical techniques are used.
- Reporting of findings is inconsistent, and there is a general lack of attention to theory.[48]

A meta-analysis by Saxton and Richardson of more than 9,000 reference queries found that more than 90 percent of the answers were judged to be completely accurate or partially accurate, or the user was referred to another agency. The problem with this rosy assessment is that the authors are grouping together accurate and partially accurate categories, when in reality the answer is either accurate or it is not accurate.

More recently, Andrew Hubbertz has expressed three fundamental concerns about unobtrusive testing that raise serious questions about this type of research:[49]

- All libraries in such tests must be administered the same test—in other words, be asked the same questions. This will allow the identification of varying results to a single variable—library performance. Wondering about the wide variation in accuracy results, Hubbertz states that the difficulty of the questions or the skill, experience, training, and tenacity of the librarian could account for the differences, since the same questions were not administered at all locations.

- Such tests are principally useful for measuring relative performance rather than assessing the overall quality of service. The test questions do not represent the universe of questions that an individual library receives. That is, different libraries receive different mixes of reference queries, and the questions actually have to be representative of the entire mix the library receives in order to assess the overall quality of service of that library.

- Usually, possible questions are pretested, and those that score higher than 75 percent or lower than 25 percent are rejected. In reality, the range of accuracy scores varies from about 35 percent to 80 percent—about what one should expect given the design of the tests.[50] Hubbertz reanalyzed the two government depository studies and sorted the questions into "easy" and "hard" categories based on accuracy success; not surprisingly, the "easy" questions had higher accuracy success.

- This type of test should be used for the evaluation of reference collections and assessing the various modes of delivering service—in-person, 24/7 virtual reference, telephone, e-mail, chat, and so forth. Accuracy information about the comparative performance of each mode would be helpful to almost every library.

Joan Durrance examined the setting of the reference interview and found that customers were "willing to return" to a staff member who had made them feel more comfortable, was friendly, and appeared interested in their information need.[51] In an earlier study, Helen Gothberg found that customers of reference service were more satisfied when they encountered librarians who expressed warmth, empathy, and genuineness.[52] Roma Harris and Gillian Mitchell concluded from their study that the demeanor of the librarian during the reference interview might be as important as retrieving the correct information in terms of customer satisfaction.[53] Continuing education and reference training seem to have little or no effect on accuracy.[54]

Patricia Dewdney and Catherine Ross found a positive correlation between the helpfulness of the answer and the friendliness of the staff member and overall satisfaction.[55] Dissatisfaction resulted from the absence of good listening skills and poor interpersonal skills. Similar results were noted in studies conducted by Janine Schmidt[56]; Lynda Baker and Judith Field[57]; Virginia Massey-Burzio[58]; Danny Wallace[59]; and JoAnn Jacoby and Nancy O'Brien.[60]

One study found that only 12 percent of reference librarians concluded a reference transaction with the question, "Does this answer your question?" When that question was asked, correct answers were provided 76 percent of the time; if it was not asked, the accuracy rate dropped to 52 percent.[61]

Providing reference services via chat, instant messaging, or use an electronic reference product affords the opportunity for testing but does raise different methodological issues. Marilyn White et al. performed a pilot study to understand and address the methodological concerns.[62] One of the byproducts is a transcript of the session, which can later be analyzed or used for teaching or mentoring. One useful tool is Hirko and Ross's *Virtual Reference Training*.[63]

A library might provide a chat-based service using one of the more popular instant messaging programs available from several Internet services (e.g., AOL, Yahoo). Effective marketing efforts have used e-mails, listserv advertisements, and professional networking.[64] Despite the efforts of some libraries to promote chat-based reference services and high levels of user satisfaction with the service, use of chat services has declined or never gained much momentum.[65]

Observation

A librarian can observe peers as they interact with customers at the reference desk. Acting as a coach or mentor, the librarian can offer specific suggestions for improving the way those peers interact with customers. In addition, the mentor might provide some coaching in the use of electronic resources or sources in the library that might be consulted. Users are aided to the extent that the answers to their questions help them accomplish something.

In the virtual environment, analysis of chat reference transcripts is another form of observation. NCknows is a collaborative, statewide, chat-based reference service in North Carolina. An analysis of the chat reference transcripts found that the quality of the chat-based reference service is high.

- NCknows librarians are more engaged with users but are no more skilled in research or use of information sources
- Although public librarians provide superior service, academic librarians provide superior referrals.[66]

A study of student shelvers in an academic setting found that they received directional and item location questions.[67]

Two other methods that have been used to better understand reference service, but have not been used widely, nevertheless provide an interesting perspective: conjoint analysis and cost-benefit analysis.

Conjoint Analysis

A few studies used a technique developed by market researchers to develop a model of users' preferences for a particular product or service when all the attributes are considered together. This technique, called conjoint analysis, allows all levels of each attribute to be compared to all levels of the other attributes. Attributes might be the speed of service, friendliness of the staff member, quality of the answer, and so forth. Applied within the context of academic reference services, several studies found that college students prefer a definite (rather than an uncertain) answer for which they only had to wait a brief period of time, and desire that the answer be provided in a timely manner—no real surprise here.[68]

Cost-Benefit Analysis

One survey used the contingent valuation method to estimate the economic value that patrons attach to reference desk service at the Virginia Commonwealth University. Students were willing to pay $5.59 per semester to maintain current reference hours, whereas instructional faculty were only willing to pay about $22 per semester.[69]

The quality and costs of providing reference services are becoming much more visible. A study at Cornell University indicated that *Google Answers*, an e-Bay-like marketplace for people with questions and others who are prepared to answer these questions, was half the cost of comparable reference services at Cornell.[70] In addition, 94 percent of the students who used Google Answers indicated that they would use the service again. (Google Answers is no longer available.)

Reference Resources

One study noted that reference librarians use electronic resources six times more than print sources to respond to customer queries.[71] The top five sources used to respond to reference questions were electronic databases (24 percent), other librarians (24 percent), the library catalog (15 percent), an internal Web page (12 percent), and reference books (9 percent). It is interesting to note that during the two semesters that the data were gathered, only 173 of the library's 9,587 reference collection titles were used—that is, less than 2 percent of the library's print reference collection. And for 75 percent of the questions, the librarians only referred to a single source for an answer. The switch by students to the direct use of Internet-based resources (search engines) and avoiding the need to visit—in any way—the library has even been noticed by the popular press.[72]

For a significant number of years, libraries have been building and maintaining print reference collections. As reference librarians increasingly turn to electronic resources to respond to customer queries, an important question should be addressed: Is the print reference collection too large? Starting in 2000, libraries have been shifting a significant portion of their reference collection budget to electronic resources—27 percent or more in some libraries.[73] Librarians at the University of Georgia library report that they cancelled all their print indexes in favor of Web-based versions and now meet most of their undergraduates' needs without a print collection.[74]

A number of options exist for measuring the use of a print reference collection. Among them are the following:

- **Touch techniques:** A substance is placed on the print item that is affected in some way if the item is moved. The substance can be infrared dust, beads on the top of the book, or unexposed photographic paper. This method does not rely on the user for assistance in any way.

- **Tally slip:** A slip of paper is placed in each volume or on the spine of the item, and the user is asked to mark the slip of paper each time he or she opens a volume. Because this method depends on the cooperation of the user, results are problematic.

- **Interviews:** Interviewers approach each user of the reference collection during a sampling period and ask him or her to respond to a few questions. Not all individuals will be willing to participate, and the user's memory of what resources he or she has used will vary considerably.

- **Questionnaires:** Fussler and Simon placed a short questionnaire in a sample of volumes. When a volume was opened, the individual was asked to answer four questions: why the item was removed from the shelf; where and for what purpose the item would be used; and how valuable the item was to the user.[75]

- **Reshelving techniques (the "dot" method):** The specific volume is recorded in some manner as it is reshelved. Some libraries have scanned the bar code and stored the information in a spreadsheet. Others have placed dots on the item for later counting. Different colored dots can be used to identify use by librarians. This method is problematic because patrons can use an item at the shelf and then reshelve it—even if there are signs requesting that items not be reshelved.[76] Others have printed a shelf list of reference materials and then manually recorded usage.

Eugene Engeldinger examined the use of the print reference collection at the University of Wisconsin-Eau Claire over a five-year period (using the dot method) and found that 35 percent of the collection was unused and 16 percent of the reference items had only been used once.[77] Mary Biggs and Victor Biggs reported that their survey of 471 libraries found that very few libraries (less than 10 percent) actually conducted use studies of their reference collections. As a result, the authors called into question the need for a library to maintain such large print reference collections.[78] A more recent survey of 550 college and university libraries found that few libraries weed their reference collections on a regular basis. The dominant reason was lack of staff time.[79]

In a study conducted at Stetson University, library staff collected reference materials from desks, tables, and shelves and recorded bibliographic information into a database over a four-month period. During the study period there were 9,755 titles and 25,626 volumes in the reference collection. The study found that only 8.5 percent of the total volumes in the print reference collection were used even once.[80]

SUMMARY

Despite the relatively consistent research findings suggesting that reference librarians are correct only about 55 percent of the time, the methodological problems inherent in the studies of the unobtrusive testing of reference accuracy call into question a very large body of research. In sum, this research is murky, contradictory, and generally leads to misinformation—for both practicing reference librarians and their customers.

Obtrusive testing using the WOREP survey provides a foundation that is built on solid ground and includes the perspectives of both customer and librarian regarding a "real" reference transaction.

Other conclusions that can be drawn from the research include the following:

- The print reference collection should be evaluated for use and then extensively weeded (or eliminated entirely).
- The budget should be adjusted to provide more funding for electronic resources.
- Training for reference staff may be needed so that they are more knowledgeable about electronic resources.
- Using several methods to evaluate reference services will provide a more complete picture of the range of services offered and their value.

NOTES

1. Michael Kelley. Geeks Are the Future: A Program in Ann Arbor, MI Argues for a Resource Shift Toward IT. *Library Journal*, April 26, 2011.

2. *The Cult of Eli Neiburger*. Colin the Librarian blog, April 26, 2011. Available at http://colinthelibrarian-blog-blog.tumblr.com/post/4971100328/the-cult-of-eli-neiburger

3. Samuel S. Green. Personal Relations Between Librarians and Readers. *Library Journal*, October 1, 1876.

4. Ellen Altman. Assessment of Reference, in Gail A. Schlacter (Ed.). *The Service Imperative for Libraries: Essays in Honor of Margaret E. Monroe*. Littleton, CO: Libraries Unlimited, 1982; William A. Katz and Ruth Fraley. *Evaluation of Reference Services*. Haworth Press, 1984.

5. Jean McLaughlin. Reference Transaction Assessment: Survey of a Multiple Perspectives Approach, 2001 to 2010. *Reference Services Review*, 39 (4), 2011, 536–50.

6. Cathy De Rose, Joanne Cantrell, Diane Cellentani, Janet Hawk, Lillie Jenkins, and Alane Wilson. *Perceptions of Libraries and Information Resources*. Dublin, OH: OCLC, 2005, 2–14.

7. Martin Fricke and Don Fallis. Indicators of Accuracy for Answers to Ready Reference Questions on the Internet. *Journal of the American Society for Information Science and Technology*, 55 (3), 2004, 238–45.

8. Eric Novotny. *Reference Service Statistics & Assessment* (SPEC Kit 268). Washington, DC: Association of Research Libraries, September 2002.

9. Ching-chih Chen and Peter Hernon. Library Effectiveness in Meeting Consumer's Information Needs, in *Library Effectiveness: A State of the Art: Preconference on Library Effectiveness*. Chicago: American Library Association, 1980, 50–62.

10. Martin Kesselman and Sarah Barbara Watstein. The Measurement of Reference and Information Services. *The Journal of Academic Librarianship*, 13, March 1987, 24–30.

11. Belia Karr Gerlich and Lynn Berard. Testing the Validity of the READ Scale (Reference Effort Assessment Data): Qualitative Statistics for Academic Reference Services. *College & Research Libraries*, March 2010, 116–37.

12. Steven Bell, quoted in Scott Carlson. Are Reference Desks Dying Out? Librarians Struggle to Redefine—and in Some Cases Eliminate—the Venerable Institution. *The Reference Librarian*, 48 (2), 2007, 25–30.

13. George S. Hawley, *Referral Process in Libraries: Characterization and an Exploration of Related Factors*. Metuchen, NJ: Scarecrow, 1987.

14. Patricia Dewdney and Catherine S. Ross. Flying a Light Aircraft: Reference Service Evaluation from a User's Perspective. *RQ*, 34, 1994, 217–30.

15. *Facets of Quality for Digital References Services*. Chicago: American Library Association, June 2003; MOUSS Management of Reference Committee. *Guidelines for Behavioral Performance of Reference and Information Service Providers*. Chicago: American Library Association, June 2004.

16. Marie L. Radford. Approach or Avoidance? The Role of Nonverbal Communication in the Academic Library User's Role to Initiate a Reference Encounter. *Library Trends*, 46 (4), March 1998, 699–713.

17. Marie L. Radford. Encountering Virtual Users: A Qualitative Investigation of Interpersonal Communication in Chat Reference. *Journal of the American Society for Information Science and Technology*, 57 (8), 2006, 1046–59.

18. Buff Hirko and Mary Bucher Ross. *Virtual Reference Training: The Complete Guide to Providing Anytime, Anywhere Answers*. Chicago: American Library Association, 2004.

19. Brenda Dervin. Useful Theory for Librarianship: Communication, Not Information. *Drexel Library Quarterly*, 13, 1977, 16–32.

20. Carol Collier Kuhlthau. *Seeking Meaning: A Process Approach to Library and Information Services*. 2nd ed. Westport, CT: Libraries Unlimited, 2004.

21. Diane Nahl-Jakobovits. Problem Solving, Creative Librarianship, and Search Behavior. *College & Research Libraries*, 49 (5), 1988, 400–8.

22. Diane Nahl. The User-Centered Revolution: 1970–1995, in Allen Kent and James G. Williams (Eds.). *Encyclopedia of Microcomputers*, vol. 19. New York: Marcel Dekker, 1988, 143–99.

23. Melissa Gross and Matthew L. Saxton. Who Wants to Know? Imposed Queries in the Public Library. *Public Libraries*, 40 (3), May/June 2001, 170–76.

24. Melissa Gross and Matthew L. Saxton. Integrating the Imposed Query into the Evaluation of Reference Service: A Dichotomous Analysis of User Ratings. *Library & Information Science Research*, 24, 2002, 251–63.

25. K. Elliott. A Comparison of Alternative Measures of Service Quality. *Journal of Customer Service in Marketing and Management*, 1 (1), 1995, 35.

26. Marjorie E. Murfin and Gary Gugelchuk. Development and Testing of a Reference Transaction Assessment Instrument. *College & Research Libraries*, 48, July 1987, 321–22.

27. Vicki Coleman, Yi (Daniel) Xiao, Linda Blair, and Bill Chollett. Toward a TQM Paradigm: Using SERVQUAL to Measure Library Service Quality. *College & Research Libraries*, 58, 1997, 237–51.

28. Mary Jane Swope and Jeffrey Katzer. Silent Majority: Why Don't They Ask Questions. *RQ*, 12, 1972, 161–66.

29. Jo Bell Whitlatch. *The Role of the Academic Reference Librarian*. Westport, CT: Greenwood, 1990.

30. Jo Bell Whitlatch. Unobtrusive Studies and the Quality of Academic Library Reference Services. *College & Research Libraries*, 50 (2), March 1989, 181–94.

31. Carolyn W. Jardine. Maybe the 55 Percent Rule Doesn't Tell the Whole Story: A User-Satisfaction Survey. *College & Research Libraries*, 56, November 1995, 477–85.

32. Margie Ruppel and Amy Vecchione. It's Research Made Easier! SMS and Chat Reference Perceptions. *Reference Services Review*, 40 (3), 2012, 423–48.

33. Marjorie E. Murfin and Gary Gugelchuk. Development and Testing of a Reference Transaction Assessment Instrument. *College & Research Libraries*, 48, July 1987, 321–22.

34. Amy Paster, Kathy Fescemyer, Nancy Henry, Janet Hughes, and Helen Smith. Assessing Reference: Using the Wisconsin-Ohio Evaluation Program in an Academic Science Library. *Issues in Science and Technology Librarianship*, Spring 2006. doi:10.5062/F4D50JX8

35. Janet Dagenais Brown. Using Quality Concepts to Improve Reference Services. *College & Research Libraries*, 55 (3), May 1994, 211–19.

36. John C. Stalker and Marjorie E. Murfin. Quality Reference Service: A Preliminary Case Study. *The Journal of Academic Librarianship*, 22 (6), November 1996, 423–29.

37. June D. Parker. Evaluating Documents Reference Service and the Implications for Improvement. *Journal of Government Information*, 23 (1), January/February 1995, 49–70.

38. Carolyn J. Radcliff and Barbara F. Schloman. Using the Wisconsin-Ohio Reference Evaluation Program, in Danny P. Wallace and Connie Van Fleet (Eds.). *Library Evaluation: A Casebook and Can-Do Guide*. Englewood, CO: Libraries Unlimited, 2001, 134-47; see also Eric Novotny and Emily Rimland. Using the Wisconsin-Ohio Reference Evaluation Program (WOREP) to Improve Training and Reference Services. *The Journal of Academic Librarianship*, 31 (3), May 2007, 382–92.

39. Jonathan Miller. Quick and Easy Reference Evaluation: Gathering Users' and Providers' Perspectives. *Reference & User Services Quarterly*, 47 (3), 2007, 218–22.

40. Terence Crowley and Thomas Childers. *Information Service in Public Libraries: Two Studies*. Metuchen, NJ: Scarecrow Press, 1971.

41. Peter Hernon and Charles R. McClure. *Unobtrusive Testing and Library Reference Services*. Norwood, NJ: Ablex, 1984. See also Peter Hernon and Charles R. McClure. Unobtrusive Reference Testing: The 55% Rule. *Library Journal*, 111, April 15, 1986, 37–41.

42. Charles R. McClure and Peter Hernon. *Improving the Quality of Reference Service for Government Publications*. Chicago: American Library Association, 1983.

43. Juris Dilevko and Elizabeth Dolan. *Government Documents Reference Service in Canada: Implications for Electronic Access*. Ottawa: Public Works and Government Services Canada, 1999. See also Juris Dilevko. *Unobtrusive Evaluation of Reference Service and Individual Responsibility: The Canadian Experience*. Westport, CT: Ablex, 2000.

44. Matthew L. Saxton. Reference Service Evaluation and Meta-Analysis: Findings and Methodological Issues. *Library Quarterly*, 67 (3), July 1997, 267–89.

45. Terence Crowley and Thomas Childers. The Effectiveness of Information Service in Medium Size Public Libraries, in *Information Service in Public Libraries: Two Studies*. Metuchen, NJ: Scarecrow Press, 1971, 16–21.

46. Paul F. Burton. Accuracy of Information Provision: The Need for Client-Centered Service. *Journal of Librarianship*, 22 (4), October 1990, 210–15.

47. Kenneth D. Crews. The Accuracy of Reference Service: Variables for Research and Implementation. *Library & Information Science Research*, 10, 1988, 331–55.

48. Matthew L. Saxton and John V. Richardson Jr. *Understanding Reference Transactions: Transforming an Art into a Science*. San Diego: Academic Press, 2002.

49. Andrew Hubbertz. The Design and Interpretation of Unobtrusive Evaluations. *Reference & User Services Quarterly*, 44 (4), Summer 2005, 327–35.

50. Terence Crowley. Half-Right Reference: Is It True? *RQ*, 25 (1), Fall 1985, 59–68.

51. Joan C. Durrance. Reference Success: Does the 55 Percent Rule Tell the Whole Story? *Library Journal*, 114 (7), April 15, 1989, 31–36.

52. Helen M. Gothberg. Immediacy: A Study of Communication Effect on the Reference Process. *The Journal of Academic Librarianship*, 2, July 1976, 126–29.

53. Roma M. Harris and B. Gillian Michell. The Social Context of Reference Work: Assessing the Effects of Gender and Communication Skills on Observers' Judgment of Competence. *Library & Information Science Research*, 8, January–March 1986, 94–99.

54. Ronald R. Powell. An Investigation of the Relationship Between Quantifiable Reference Service Variables and Reference Performance in Public Libraries. *Library Quarterly*, 48, 1978, 1–19.

55. Patricia Dewdney and Catherine Sheldrick Ross. Flying a Light Aircraft: Reference Service Evaluation from a User's Perspective. *RQ*, 34, Winter 1994, 217–30.

56. Janine Schmidt. Evaluation of Reference Services in College Libraries in New South Wales, Australia, in Neal K. Kaske and William Jones (Eds.). *Library Effectiveness: A State of the Art*. Chicago: American Library Association, 1980, 68–84.

57. Lynda M. Baker and Judith J. Field. Reference Success: What Has Changed Over the Past Ten Years? *Public Libraries*, 39, January/February 2000, 23–30.

58. Virginia Massey-Burzio. From the Other Side of the Reference Desk: A Focus Group Study. *The Journal of Academic Librarianship*, 24, 1998, 217–30.

59. Danny Wallace. *An Index of Quality of Illinois Public Library Service, 1983* (Illinois Library Statistical Report No. 14). Springfield: Illinois State Library, 1984.

60. JoAnn Jacoby and Nancy O'Brien. Assessing the Impact of Reference Services Provided to Undergraduate Students. *College & Research Libraries*, 66, July 2005, 324–40.

61. Ralph Gers and Lillie J. Seward. Improving Reference Performance: Results of a Statewide Survey. *Library Journal*, 110, 1985, 32–35.

62. Marilyn Domas White, Eileen G. Abels, and Neal Kaske. Evaluation of Chat Reference Service Quality. *D-Lib Magazine*, 9 (2), February 2003.

63. Buff Hirko and Mary Bucher Ross, *Virtual Reference Training: The Complete Guide to Providing Anytime, Anywhere Answers*. Chicago: ALA Editions, 2004.

64. Deborah Lynn Harrington and Xiaodong Li. Spinning an Academic Web Community: Measuring Marketing Effectiveness. *The Journal of Academic Librarianship*, 27 (3), May 2001, 199–207.

65. Steve Coffman and Linda Arret. To Chat or Not to Chat: Taking Another Look at Digital Reference, Part 1. *Searcher*, 12 (7), July/August 2004, 38–46; Steve Coffman and Linda Arret. To Chat or Not to Chat: Taking Another Look at Digital Reference, Part 2. *Searcher*, 12 (8), September 2004, 49–56. See also Joel Cummings, Lara Cummings, and Linda Frederiksen. User Preferences in Reference Services: Virtual Reference and Academic Libraries. *portal: Libraries and the Academy*, 7 (1), 2007, 81–96.

66. Jeffrey Pomerantz, Lili Luo, and Charles McClure. Peer Review of Chat Reference Transcripts: Approaches and Strategies. *Library & Information Science Research*, 28, 2006, 24–48.

67. Luke Vilelle and Christopher Peters. Don't Shelve the Questions: Defining Good Customer Service for Shelvers. *Reference & User Services Quarterly*, 48 (1), 2008, 60–67.

68. Gregory A. Crawford. A Conjoint Analysis of Reference Services in Academic Libraries. *College & Research Libraries*, 55, May 1994, 257–67; Michael Halperin and Maureen Stardon. Measuring Students' Preferences for Reference Service: A Conjoint Analysis. *Library Quarterly*, 50, 1980, 208–24; Kenneth D. Ramsing and John R. Wish. What Do Library Users Want? A Conjoint Measurement Technique May Yield the Answer. *Information Processing and Management*, 18, 1982, 237–42.

69. David W. Harless and Frank R. Allen. Using the Contingent Valuation Method to Measure Patron Benefits of Reference Desk Service in an Academic Library. *College & Research Libraries*, 60 (1), January 1999, 56–69.

70. Anne R. Kennedy, Nancy Y. McGovern, Ida T. Martinez, and Lance J. Heidig. Google, Meet eBay: What Academic Librarians Can Learn from Alternative Information Providers. *D-Lib Magazine*, 9 (6), June 2003.

71. Jane T. Bradford, Barbara Costello, and Robert Lenholt. Reference Service in the Digital Age: An Analysis of Sources Used to Answer Reference Questions. *The Journal of Academic Librarianship*, 31 (3), May 2005, 263–72.

72. Patrick Boyle. What? Use a Book for Doing Research? College Students Forsake Library Shelves for Computers. *Washington Post*, August 24, 2000, M07.

73. Brian Kenney and Eric Bryant. Reference Budgets: A Slow Revolution. *Library Journal*, 128 (19), November 15, 2003, 8–9, 12; Mirela Roncevic. The E-Ref Invasion—Reference 2006. *Library Journal*, 130 (19), November 15, 2005, 8–13.

74. Mirela Roncevic. The E-Ref Invasion—Reference 2006. *Library Journal*, 130 (19), November 15, 2005, 8–13.

75. Herman H. Fussler and Julian L. Simon. *Patterns in the Use of Books in Large Research Libraries*. Chicago: University of Chicago Press, 1969.

76. Mary Biggs. Discovering How Information Seekers Seek: Methods of Measuring Reference Collection Use, in S. J. Pierce (Ed.). *Weeding and Maintenance of Reference Collections*. New York: Haworth Press, 1990, 103–14.

77. Eugene A. Engeldinger. "Use" as a Criterion for the Weeding of Reference Collections: A Review and Case Study, in Sydney J. Pierce (Ed.). *Weeding and Maintenance of Reference Collections*. New York: Haworth, 1990, 119–28.

78. Mary Biggs and Victor Biggs. Reference Collection Development in Academic Libraries: Report of a Survey. *RQ*, 27, Fall 1987, 66–79.

79. Eugene A. Engeldinger. Weeding of Academic Library Reference Collections: A Survey of Current Practice. *RQ*, 25 (3), Spring 1986, 366–71.

80. Jane T. Bradford. What's Coming off the Shelves? A Reference Use Study Analyzing Print Reference Sources Used in a University Library. *The Journal of Academic Librarianship*, 31 (6), November 2005, 546–58.

16

Evaluation of Information Literacy

Carefully targeted, thoroughly prepared, well-presented, properly evaluated user education will be expensive indeed. We might remember S. R. Ranganathan's Fourth Law of Library Science: Save the Time of the Reader. This is more important than the Principle of Cost Effectiveness: Save the Time of the Librarian.

—Tom Eadie[1]

SERVICE DEFINITION

For a considerable period of time, libraries (generally academic libraries) have been offering and providing bibliographic instruction, sometimes called library research instruction, under one guise or another. It is interesting to note that, historically, little effort has been expended by libraries to reduce the complexity that leads to the need for bibliographic instruction.

EVALUATION QUESTIONS

Among the bibliographic instruction and information literacy evaluation questions that might be raised are:

- Do different types of instructional modes make a difference in acquiring skills?
- How improved are library skills as the result of instruction?
- Are students satisfied with the instruction?
- What are the most effective means of delivering information literacy instruction?
- Are information literacy skills retained and used in later years?
- Do students who receive instruction use the library more often?
- Does academic performance (student learning outcomes) improve as the result of instruction?
- How is the learning environment affected by information literacy instruction?
- What are the costs to deliver information literacy instruction?

EVALUATION METHODS

There is abundant literature pertaining to the evaluation of bibliographic instruction and library instruction programs; however, the bulk of the research is generally focused on methods to improve the instruction program rather than on an assessment of the impact of the program in the lives of the recipients.

The methods used to evaluate bibliographic instruction and library instruction programs include

- Skill surveys
- Satisfaction surveys
- Identification of use of the library
- Identification of improved academic performance

PRIOR EVALUATIONS AND RESEARCH

Bibliographic instruction assessment efforts seem to fall into four categories: opinion surveys, knowledge testing, observing actual library use, and student persistence.[2] These categories are used to structure this chapter.

Opinion Surveys

The evaluation of bibliographic instruction, according to Richard Werking, was not meaningful.[3] Typically the evaluations focused on user satisfaction rather than the development of learning competencies and other outcomes.[4] Aside from having difficulty identifying the benefits of instruction, the surveys and skill tests often lacked validity and reliability.[5] The primary drawbacks of opinion surveys are that the questions often reflected the biases of the instrument's developers and that the data generated did not measure the effectiveness of the instruction. In addition, the self-reported data often lead to validity problems.

One study, which tracked results over a six-year period, found little relationship between students' demographics, previous library instruction, or prior use of library resources and how they evaluated library instruction.[6] Studies that focus on measuring changes in student attitudes do not in any way measure any changes in student learning.

Knowledge Testing

One study used an advanced statistical methodology (multiple regression techniques) to evaluate the retention of library skills over time and their impact on students who took a library skills course. Although the students who actively used the learned skills after the course had the best skills retention (no surprise there), the study found no significant relationship between library skills retention and SAT scores or eventual grade point averages.[7] Another study found no significant correlation between a library information competency class and the students' GPAs.[8]

Self-assessment imposes serious methodological problems. For example, 90 percent of students rated their library skills as adequate, but in a test of competences, only 53 percent proved "minimally competent."[9]

Use of a pretest and posttest methodology offers the potential for more accurate understanding of knowledge transfer, but methodology problems can persist. If the same instrument is used for both tests, reported gains are suspect because students will likely remember questions and naturally improve their scores. Also, if students are tested immediately after receiving instruction, short-term gains are not likely to be sustained. One study using this approach with a sample of 404 students found no difference between pre- and posttest results.[10] Another study, with a larger sample of 1,197 students, found that the library class measurably improved the participants' library skills.[11]

In addition, focusing on a prescribed set of skills does not equate to assessing the impact of instruction on actual use and behavior in a library.

Several studies assessed the quality of term papers prepared by students who had completed a library orientation course, comparing their papers to those of students who did not take the class, and found that the course completers had written better papers and had higher course completion rates.[12] Similar findings were also noted in earlier studies.[13]

Providing a contrary point of view, another analysis found that a library instruction program made little difference in the types of materials students cited in their research papers.[14] In addition, focusing on the style of the citations, the total number of citations, and variety of citations is a library-centric view of the world. It is much more important to determine the degree to which the instruction helped the students write better papers and achieve better grades, among other possible outcomes. A methodological problem associated with term paper analysis is that other variables, such as assistance from a reference librarian or friend, may interfere with the results.

Two studies determined that library use instruction is more highly correlated with skill possession than either inherent intellectual ability or academic diligence.[15]

Donald Barclay suggested that the dearth of quality evaluations of library instructional classes was the result of limited institutional support, time constraints, and the difficulty of developing an effective evaluation process.[16] Barclay's solution was to

"set [our] sights lower and do the best evaluation [we] can with what [we] have."[17]

One study found that online instruction was effective,[18] another suggested that traditional classroom instruction was more effective,[19] and a third study found that neither approach was effective.[20]

One of the fundamental problems is that many instruments developed to measure the effectiveness of library research instruction lack important psychometric properties such as validity and reliability.[21]

Rather than traditional classroom instruction, interactive multimedia Web sites can provide instruction about specific library skills. An evaluation of the LUMENS Project found that users' topic knowledge increased after viewing the interactive materials—based on a pretest and posttest assessment of skills. However, planning the content and mastering the interactive technology requires that librarians be able to work in a multimedia learning environment with few distractions.[22]

These knowledge testing studies are summarized in Table 16.1.

Actual Library Use

At Earlham College, bibliographic instruction was integrated into about 37 percent of course offerings. It was found that the average graduate used the library in 54 percent of courses. Unfortunately, no analysis was made to compare college graduates to dropouts and their use (or nonuse) of the library.[23]

Table 16.1. Summary of Library Instruction Program Studies

Supportive	No Support
Opinion Surveys	
Wong et al. (2006). Positive feelings about instruction [395]	Werking (1980). What bibliographic instruction has been done is not meaningful
	Eadie (1982). Validity and reliability problems with locally developed instruments
	Landrum & Muench (1994). Surveys often reflect the biases of librarians who develop the instruments
	Moore-Jansen (1997). No link between instruction and library use and opinions [403]
	Stamatopols & Mackoy (1998). Student self-assessment of skills increased
Knowledge Testing	
Corlett (1974). Library orientation class was linked to improved GPA scores [81]	Hardesty et al. (1982). No correlation between library skills retention and SAT or GPA scores [162]
	Moore et al. (2002). Library skills class is not linked to GPA scores
	Ware et al. (1986). Self-assessment of skills not linked to reality
	Colborn & Cordell (1998). Pre- and posttest method reveals no improvement in library skills [404]
Breivik (1977). Library orientation course resulted in better term papers	Emmons & Martin (2002). Library use instruction made little difference in type of materials selected for a term paper [250]
King & Ory (1981); Dykeman & King (1983); Kohl & Wilson (1986). Library skills class linked to better term papers	Malone & Videon (1997). Instruction does not lead to increased use of electronic sources in term papers [291]
Selegean et al. (1983). Bibliographic instruction resulted in higher GPA scores [512]	Eyman & Nunley (1977). Library skills course does not lead to improved bibliographic skills

(*continued*)

Table 16.1. Summary of Library Instruction Program Studies (*continued*)

Supportive	No Support
Carter (2002). Bibliographic instruction class resulted in increased use of the library	
Wang (2006). Library instruction course resulted in more scholarly citations and better grades [120 papers, 836 citations]	
Germain et al. (2000). Online instruction resulted in better skills than classroom instruction [284]	Holman (2000). No difference between online and classroom instruction [56 & 27]

[#] = sample size

Gabrielle Wong, Diana Chan, and Sam Chu. Assessing the Enduring Impact of Library Instruction Programs. *The Journal of Academic Librarianship*, 32 (4), July 2006, 384–95; Richard Werking. Evaluating Bibliographic Instruction: A Review and Critique. *Library Trends*, 29, Summer 1980, 153–72; Tom Eadie. Beyond Immodesty: Questioning the Benefits of BI. *RQ*, 21, 1982, 331–33; Eric Landrum and Diana Muench. Assessing Student Library Skills and Knowledge: The Library Research Strategies Questionnaire. *Psychological Reports*, 75, 1994, 1617–24; Cathy Moore-Jansen. What Difference Does It Make? One Study of Student Background and the Evaluation of Library Instruction. *Research Strategies*, 15 (1), 1997, 26–38; Anthony Stamatopols and Robert Mackay. Effects of library instruction on university students' satisfaction with the library: A longitudinal study. *College & Research Libraries*, 59(4), 1998, 323–34; Donna Corlett. Library Skills, Study Habits and Attitudes, and Sex as Related to Academic Achievement. *Educational and Psychological Measurement*, 34 (4), 1974, 967–69; Larry Hardesty, Nicholas P. Lovrich Jr., and James Mannon. Evaluating Library-Use Instruction. *College & Research Libraries*, 43, January 1982, 38–46; Deborah Moore, Steve Brewster, Cynthia Dorroh, and Michael Moreau. Information Competency Instruction in a Two-Year College: One Size Does Not Fit All. *Reference Services Review*, 30, November 2002, 300–6; Susan A. Ware, J. Deena, and A. Morganti. Competency-Based Approach to Assessing Workbook Effectiveness. *Research Strategies*, 4 (9), Winter 1986, 4–10; Nancy W. Colborn and Rossane M. Cordell. Moving from Subjective to Objective Assessments of Your Instruction Program. *Reference Services Review*, 26, Fall/Winter 1998, 125–37; Patricia S. Breivik. Brooklyn College: A Test Case, in *Open Admissions and the Academic Library*. Chicago: American Library Association, 1977, 137–152; Mark Emmons and Wanda Martin. Engaging Conversation: Evaluating the Contribution of Library Instruction to the Quality of Student Research. *College & Research Libraries*, 63 (6), November 2002, 545–60; David N. King and John C. Ory. Effects of Library Instruction on Student Research: A Case Study. *College & Research Libraries*, 42 (1), January 1981, 31–41; Amy Dykeman and Barbara King. Term Paper Analysis: A Proposal for Evaluating Bibliographic Instruction. *Research Strategies*, 1, December 1983, 14–21; David F. Kohl and Lizabeth A. Wilson. Effectiveness of Course Integrated Bibliographic Instruction in Improving Course Work. *RQ*, 26, December 1986, 203–11; Debbie Malone and Carol Videon. Assessing Undergraduate Use of Electronic Resources: A Quantitative Analysis of Works Cited. *Research Strategies*, 15 (3), 1997, 151–58; John C. Selegean, Martha Lou Thomas, and Marie Louise Richman. Long-Range Effectiveness of Library Use Instruction. *College & Research Libraries*, 44 (6), November 1983, 476–80; David Eyman and Alven Nunley. *Effectiveness of Library Science 101 in Teaching Bibliographic Skills*. May 1977. ERIC Document ED150 962; Elizabeth Carter. "Doing the Best You Can with What You Have": Lessons Learned from Outcomes Assessment. *The Journal of Academic Librarianship*, 28 (1), January–March 2002, 36–41; Rui Wang. The Lasting Impact of a Library Credit Course. *portal: Libraries and the Academy*, 6 (1), January 2006, 79–92; Carol Germain, Trudi E. Jacobson, and Sue A. Kaczor. A Comparison of the Effectiveness of Presentation Formats for Instruction: Teaching First-Year Students. *College & Research Libraries*, 61 (1), January 2000, 65–72; Lucy Holman. A Comparison of Computer-Assisted Instruction and Classroom Bibliographic Instruction. *Reference & User Services Quarterly*, 40 (1), 2000, 53–60.

Student Retention Rates

Interestingly, several studies have noted a positive correlation between a freshman orientation course and student persistence and strengthened academic performance. One analysis found that students who participated in the orientation class had higher sophomore return rates and graduation rates despite the fact that many were less prepared academically than their non-participant counterparts.[24] Another study found that the participants reported increased use of university resources such as the library and writing services, their grades were higher, and their overall retention rate was higher than their counterparts.[25] Freshman orientation courses are cost-effective given that they generate revenue due to increased student retention and thus offset the costs of the orientation class.[26]

Despite the studies noted here, the vast majority of libraries did little or no evaluation, because

> Bibliographic instruction seems to be perceived by many librarians simply as a self-evident social good, not needing an extensive rationale or empirical evidence to substantiate its effectiveness or even to support the need for it. Much of the literature of bibliographic instruction resembles a dialectic with the antithesis missing.[27]

In summarizing the plethora of articles reporting studies about library bibliographic instruction, a decidedly mixed picture emerges:

- The vast majority of new students who enter the college environment each year do not avail themselves of the opportunity to attend a library skills or bibliographic instruction class.
- A majority of collegiate courses do not have a bibliographic instruction component that is integrated into the course content.
- A fair amount of the research focuses on opinion surveys and pre- and posttest knowledge and library skill improvements, which do not evaluate how these skills impact student learning.
- The majority of instruments used to assess bibliographic instruction lack important properties such as validity and reliability.
- Improvement in basic library skills is the means and not the end, yet it is the latter that is the focus of most bibliographic instruction evaluation efforts.
- Few studies reported a link between bibliographic instruction and increased use of the library resources and services.
- Even fewer studies have focused on the link between bibliographic instruction and doing better academically (however this might be measured).

EVALUATION OF INFORMATION LITERACY PROGRAMS

Before the various studies of information literacy are reviewed, the topic of critical thinking is considered. Critical thinking is closely related to information literacy and can be defined as the ability to "interpret, evaluate, and make informed decisions about the adequacy of arguments, data, and conclusions."[28]

Starting late in the 1980s, Patricia Breivik and others presented the idea of information literacy, suggesting that it was an essential skill in lifelong learning.[29] These individuals believed that integration of information literacy into the curriculum serves a major goal for the future success of academic libraries. Shirley Behrens provided a conceptual analysis and historical overview of information literacy.[30]

Academic librarians have turned to the concept of information literacy as a way to designate the importance of understanding how information is organized, how to find appropriate information resources, and how to assess information that is encountered during the search process. Unfortunately, "there is a temptation for students to settle for information that meets the 'three Fs' requirement: first, fastest, and full text."[31]

The *Information Literacy Competency Standards for Higher Education*, developed by the Association of College & Research Libraries (ACRL), state:

> Information literacy forms the basis for lifelong learning. It is common to all disciplines, to all learning environments, and to all levels of education. It enables learners to master content and extend their investigations, become more self-directed, and assume greater control over their own learning. An information literate individual is able to:
>
> - Determine the extent of information needed
> - Access the needed information effectively and efficiently
> - Evaluate information and its sources critically
> - Incorporate selected information into one's knowledge base
> - Use information effectively to accomplish a specific purpose
> - Understand the economic, legal, and social issues surrounding the use of information, and access and use information ethically and legally.[32]

Teaching information literacy skills is generally viewed as affecting student outcomes, because these skills support such educational outcomes as critical thinking, problem solving, and lifelong learning. Unfortunately, this view is an assumption that has yet to be proven in a series of studies that can be replicated.

Methods of information literacy instruction include:

- Instruction at the reference desk
- Course-integrated instruction
- For-credit classes
- Tutorials

A systematic review to assess which library instruction methods are most effective for improving the information literacy skills of undergraduate students found that:

- Computer-assisted instruction is as effective as traditional instruction
- Traditional instruction is better than no instruction
- Self-directed, independent learning is more effective than no instruction[33]

Susan Taylor studied three colleges with well-regarded information literacy programs and noted the factors that were common to all:

- There was leadership by the librarians.
- There was faculty interest and support.
- The curriculum required library use.
- The library's collection development involved faculty.[34]

Stephanie Margolin and Wendy Hayden at Hunter College created a Research Toolkit that is designed to meet student and faculty "where they are" by focusing not on the mechanics of information literacy but on the more critical experience of inquiry-based research.[35] The research questions include:

- What is my research question?
- How do I find sources?
- How do I read this stuff?
- How do I use sources in my paper?

The majority of the *information literacy literature* focuses on three topics: opinion/satisfaction surveys, testing of skills of the participants of the information literacy courses, and actual information-seeking behavior. The Information Literacy Test was administered to 3,000 college students from 44 institutions and found that only 13 percent were deemed information literate.[36] Only 49 percent could identify faux Web sites using evaluation criteria of objectivity, authority, and timeliness, and no more than 35 percent knew how to narrow an overly broad search.

Opinion Surveys

Often this literature suggests that improvements should be made to teaching methods and modes of delivery of the information literacy content. For example, one study found that students of color, students satisfied with campus library facilities, and students engaged in interactions with faculty self-reported greatest satisfaction with their information literacy skills.[37]

Skills Testing

One study used testing to gauge gains in information literacy as well as obtaining the perspectives of librarians involved in instruction, but did not use an independent means to verify improved student grades.[38] Two studies found that the differences between those who had attended library information literacy education sessions and those who had not were not that great.[39] Another problem that arises is that "library jargon" is often used in the instruction program, and—as one study noted—students could only correctly define an average of 9 out of 15 terms. The least understood terms included *Boolean logic, controlled vocabulary, truncation,* and *precision.*[40]

Students at the University of California, Berkeley, believe they know more about accessing information and conducting library research than they are able to demonstrate when put to the test.[41] A different study found that students had difficulties defining a problem, determining where to go for quality information, developing an effective search strategy, finding material in the library, and developing insights.[42]

Another study found that students who participated in an information literacy class had improved confidence levels in using the library yet failed to improve their pre- to posttest performance on content questions.[43] Between 35 and 81 percent of the test participants received poor or failing scores. Similar disappointing findings were found in a study at Johns Hopkins University[44] and Indiana University, South Bend.[45]

Challenges arise when a library attempts to use a pre- and posttest method of assessment. Locally developed questions are often not subjected to rigorous analysis to screen out use of jargon or the answer being indicated in another item. If the pretest scores are high, there is very little room to differentiate the impact of the training from incidental changes, including test/retest effects.[46]

The King's College (Pennsylvania) library has spent several years developing a 25-item Information Literacy Assessment instrument, with five questions for each of the five ACRL *Information Literacy Competency Standards*. The library decided to use a relatively brief but rigorous instrument with good reliability.[47] Rather than the traditional librarian-centered instructional class, students are asked to complete 10- to 15-minute pre-class exercises, which are reviewed by the librarian prior to the class meeting. During the class students are asked to demonstrate the concepts so that they learn from each other to make the experience more learning centered.

Project SAILS (Standardized Assessment of Information Literacy Skills) is a Web-based, multiple-choice knowledge test targeting a variety of information literacy skills.[48] A number of academic libraries have administered the test. Participants are presented with 45 randomly generated multiple-choice or multiple-response questions from a test bank of 130 questions. One study found that information literacy skills are complex, that students have difficult gaining these skills on their own, and that participation in an online information literacy class resulted in higher scores than one-shot instruction.[49]

It is also possible to use an evaluation rubric to assess the information literacy skills of individuals. Megan Oakleaf found that multiple raters can use rubrics to produce consistent scoring of information literacy artifacts of student learning. However, different groups of raters arrived at varying levels of agreement.[50]

Observed Behavior

One study found that while students' learning is influenced by their previous experiences, they will engage with information literacy programs only to the extent that they perceive professors and instructors require them to do so.[51] Other studies have raised serious questions about students' abilities to seek and use information.[52]

An analysis of college students found that they are not being exposed to library and information literacy environments, and those students greatly overestimated their skill levels. Few faculty members participate in information literacy skills modeling for students, with the result that students are not familiar with basic library research skills.[53]

Nancy Seamans used a qualitative approach and found that students do not see libraries and library personnel as part of their information-support network. Further, students appear to be generally uncritical in using and evaluating resources.[54] A systematic review of the literature, prepared by Alison Brettle, observed that there is limited evidence to show that training improves skills, insufficient evidence to determine the most effective methods of training, and limited evidence to show whether training leading to increased knowledge of health care actually improves patient health care.[55]

Clearly, the readily availability of a wide range of Internet-based resources (some of dubious quality and value) is having an impact on all types of libraries. The well-publicized decline in ARL reference statistics is one handy indicator. One study of student searching behavior shows that commercial Internet search engines dominate students' information-seeking strategies. Some 45 percent of students use Google as their primary access method when attempting to locate information, while only 10 percent rely on the university library online catalog.[56] A companion survey, sponsored by the Pew Trust, found that 55 percent of college students completely agree that Google provides worthwhile information, compared with only 31 percent for library databases. Internet-based search engines are the first choice for research for 80 percent of the respondents; the online library is the first choice of only 6 percent, and the respondents see little difference between Internet resources and library-provided electronic databases.[57]

The OCLC survey indicates that search engines are used most often to begin information searches (89 percent), whereas a library Web site is selected by just 2 percent of college students.[58] The survey also found that college students favor libraries as a place to study, for free Internet access, and for materials, while they favor bookstores for coffee shops, current materials, and meeting their friends.

An analysis of more than 300,000 student respondents to the College Student Experiences Questionnaire over a 19-year period found that library experiences do not seem to directly contribute to gains in information literacy, to what students gain overall from college, or to student satisfaction.[59]

A summary of the studies related to information literacy is in Table 16.2.

Table 16.2. Summary of Information Literacy Studies

Supportive	No Support
Smalley (2004). High school students with good information literacy skills received better grades than students who attended high schools without librarians [506]	Whitmire (1998). Libraries with large numbers of bibliographic instruction students report that few undergraduates used the library [18,157]
Skills Testing	
Julien & Boon (2004). Claimed gains in information literacy but no testing [28]	Brewer (1999). Information literacy program had no impact on students' searching skills
	Rabine & Cardwell (2000). Few differences between those who attended an information literacy class and those who did not [414]
	Maughan (2001). Students' perceptions of their skills is greater than reality [185]
	Hepworth (1999). Students not retaining information literacy skills
	Dunnington & Strong (2006). Student confidence levels improved but actual skills did not [635]
	Coupe (1993). Student skill levels did not improve
	Schuck (1992). Instruction course produced no improvements

(continued)

Table 16.2. Summary of Information Literacy Studies (*continued*)

Supportive	No Support
Observed Behavior	
	Hartmann (2001). Participation in information literacy is driven by professor requirements [focus groups]
	Turnbull et al. (2003). Students reluctant to seek and use information
	Kuh & Gonyea (2003). Library experiences do not lead to gains in information literacy [300,000]

Topsy N. Smalley. College Success: High School Librarians Make the Difference. *The Journal of Academic Librarianship*, 30 (3), May 2004, 193–98; Ethelene Whitmire. Development of Critical Thinking Skills: An Analysis of Academic Library Experiences and Other Measures. *College & Research Libraries*, 59 (3), May 1998, 1–8; Heidi Julien and Stuart Boon. Assessing Instructional Outcomes in Canadian Academic Libraries. *Library & Information Science Research*, 26, 2004, 121–39; Chris Brewer. *Integrating Information Literacy into the Health Sciences Curriculum: Longitudinal Study of an Information Literacy Program for the University of Wollongong*. Paper presented at the 4th National Information Literacy Conference, Adelaide, South Australia, December 1999; Julie Rabine and Catherine Cardwell. Start Making Sense: Practical Approaches to Outcomes Assessment for Libraries. *Research Strategies*, 17 (4), 2000, 319–35; Patricia Davitt Maughan. Assessing Information Literacy among Undergraduates: A Discussion of the Literature and the University of California-Berkeley Assessment Experience. *College & Research Libraries*, 62 (1), January 2001, 71–85; Mark Hepworth. *A Study of Undergraduate Information Literacy and Skills: The Inclusion of Information Literacy and Skills in the Undergraduate Curriculum*. Paper presented at the 65th IFLA Council and General Conference, Bangkok, Thailand, August 20–28, 1999; Angela Dunnington and Mary Lou Strong. *What's Assessment Got to Do with It?! Exploring Student Learning Outcomes*. Presentation given at the ALA Annual Conference, New Orleans, Louisiana, June 24, 2006; Jill Coupe. Undergraduate Library Skills: Two Surveys at Johns Hopkins University. *Research Strategies*, 11, Fall 1993, 188–201; Brian R. Schuck. Assessing a Library Instruction Program. *Research Strategies*, 10, Fall 1992, 152–60; Elizabeth Hartmann. Understandings of Information Literacy: The Perceptions of First-Year Undergraduate Students at the University of Ballarat. *Australian Academic & Research Libraries*, 32 (2), 2001, 110–22; Deborah Turnbull, Denise Frost, and Nicola Foxlee. *Infoseek, InfoFind! Information Literacy and Integrated Service Delivery for Researchers and Postgraduates*. Paper presented at the Information Online 2003 Conference, Sydney, New South Wales, January 2003; George D. Kuh and Robert M. Gonyea. The Role of the Academic Library in Promoting Student Engagement in Learning. *College & Research Libraries*, 64 (7), July 2003, 256–82.

James Marcum has asked whether "information" is the appropriate literacy. He suggested that other literacies deserved some consideration and were perhaps better suited for a student's long-term success in the job marketplace. Among the possible literacies vying for supremacy are visual literacy, technological literacy, computer-mediated communication literacy, computational literacy, and knowledge media literacy.[60] Perhaps literacy is not the appropriate focus, and academic libraries should instead be concentrating on competencies, fluency, or expertise.

Allan Martin has suggested the term "e-literacy" to describe the combination of computer literacy and information literacy encompassing:

- Awareness of IT and the information environment
- Confidence in using generic IT and information tools

- Evaluation of information-handling operations and products
- Reflection of one's own e-literacy development
- Adaptability and willingness to meet e-literacy challenges[61]

INFORMATION LITERACY STANDARDS

Stephen Foster and Lisa O'Connor raise real concerns about the value and utility of the ACRL *Information Literacy Competency Standards for Higher Education* by suggesting that information literacy is but a "means of professional legitimization."[62] In addition, O'Connor argues that the standards place too much emphasis on workplace preparedness and the relationship between education and upward mobility. Eamon Tewell provides a thoughtful and thorough review of the information literacy literature.[63]

Sue Samson used writing portfolios and research bibliographies (16 students in each group) to assess information literacy learning using a rubric based on ACRL standards. The results provided benchmark data for first-year and capstone students.[64]

FACULTY–LIBRARIAN RELATIONSHIPS

The perception of librarians by academic faculty members will clearly have a major impact on the success of information literacy efforts. Some librarians have observed that faculty members are either apathetic about or obstructive toward their efforts to initiate joint instructional activities. Several studies suggest that librarians are valued for the support services they provide but are not perceived to be academic equals, as evidenced by the lack of scholarly published literature.[65] And while librarians are concerned about their relationships with faculty, faculty members do not seem to be too concerned about theirs with librarians.[66]

The most thorough analysis to date remains Hardesty's 1991 study, which developed the *Library Educational Attitudes Scale* to measure faculty members' attitudes toward the role of the library in undergraduate education.[67] Other studies soon followed, including Cannon,[68] Thomas,[69] and Leckie and Fullerton.[70] The studies suggested that arts and humanities faculty were more likely to invite a librarian to instruct their classes than were their science counterparts. In addition, there is little support among faculty for instructional methods requiring a high degree of library–faculty cooperation, such as team teaching, credit courses, or jointly developed assignments.

Librarians at Oregon State University found that a surprising number of faculty and students did not know about the several one-credit, discipline-specific library research courses, and that a for-credit course was the least preferred method for receiving information literacy instruction.[71] More recently, Claire McGuinness found that faculty believe that students gradually become information literate through class assignments and individual initiative as part of a "law of exposure." The findings lead to the assumption made by faculty that students will develop information literacy skills even though the faculty makes no attempt to design assignments with this outcome in mind.[72]

All of this suggests that librarians need to reconsider their opinions about what students should be taught and how librarians contribute to the student learning process. Implicit in this reconsideration is the need to focus library efforts on the outcomes of information literacy rather than on ways to improve the process of imparting skills or assessing the satisfaction levels of students who complete an information literacy course.

SUMMARY

In summarizing the often conflicting and narrowly directed information literacy literature, a fairly clear picture comes into focus:

- Most of the literature assessing students' information literacy skills focuses on evaluating students in particular courses, assignments, disciplines, or instructional mode.

- Two rigorous systematic reviews by Koufogiannakis and Wiebe as well as Zhang et al. found no difference between computer-aided instruction and traditional teaching methods.[73]

- A majority of the literature has centered on the testing of discrete skills or competencies to improve the delivery of information literacy content. Such a perspective focuses on the instructor, instruction method, or instruction materials and is too narrowly focused.

- Little research has addressed the value of improved information literacy skills and success in the academic environment.

- Faculty members will of necessity have to be involved in the assessment of information literacy outcomes.

- No research has been done to determine the extent to which good information literacy skills assist in lifelong learning and greater success in student careers after graduation—a "big picture" perspective.

- Some information literacy advocates are beginning to call for the use of multiple, mixed research methods and tying information literacy outcomes to institutional learning outcomes.

The challenges facing those interested in attempting to evaluate the impact of information literacy instruction are significant, given that many variables exist within a population of students that will likely affect information literacy learning outcomes.

NOTES

1. Tom Eadie. Immodest Proposals: User Instruction for Students Does Not Work. *Library Journal*, 115 (17), October 15, 1990, 44.

2. John C. Selegean, Martha Lou Thomas, and Marie Louise Richman. Long-Range Effectiveness of Library Use Instruction. *College & Research Libraries*, 44 (6), November 1983, 476–80.

3. Richard Werking. Evaluating Bibliographic Instruction: A Review and Critique. *Library Trends*, 29, Summer 1980, 153–72.

4. Tom Eadie. Beyond Immodesty: Questioning the Benefits of BI. *RQ*, 21, 1982, 331–33.

5. Eric Landrum and Diana Muench. Assessing Student Library Skills and Knowledge: The Library Research Strategies Questionnaire. *Psychological Reports*, 75, 1994, 1617–24.

6. Cathy Moore-Jansen. What Difference Does It Make? One Study of Student Background and the Evaluation of Library Instruction. *Research Strategies*, 15 (1), 1997, 26–38.

7. Larry Hardesty, Nicholas P. Lovrich Jr., and James Mannon. Evaluating Library-Use Instruction. *College & Research Libraries*, 43, January 1982, 38–46.

8. Deborah Moore, Steve Brewster, Cynthia Dorroh, and Michael Moreau. Information Competency Instruction in a Two-Year College: One Size Does Not Fit All. *Reference Services Review*, 30, November 2002, 300–6.

9. Susan A. Ware, J. Deena, and A. Morganti. Competency-Based Approach to Assessing Workbook Effectiveness. *Research Strategies*, 4 (9), Winter 1986, 4–10.

10. Nancy W. Colborn and Rossane M. Cordell. Moving from Subjective to Objective Assessments of Your Instruction Program. *Reference Services Review*, 26, Fall/Winter 1998, 125–37.

11. John S. Riddle and Karen A. Hartman. But Are They Learning Anything? Designing an Assessment of First Year Library Instruction. *College & Undergraduate Libraries*, 7, 2000, 66.

12. Patricia S. Breivik. Brooklyn College: A Test Case, in *Open Admissions and the Academic Library*. Chicago: American Library Association, 1977, 89-103. See also Rui Wang. The Lasting Impact of a Library Credit Course. *portal: Libraries and the Academy*, 6 (1), January 2006, 79–92; Elizabeth Carter. "Doing the Best You Can with What You Have": Lessons Learned from Outcomes Assessment. *The Journal of Academic Librarianship*, 28 (1), January–March 2002, 36–41.

13. Amy Dykeman and Barbara King. Term Paper Analysis: A Proposal for Evaluating Bibliographic Instruction. *Research Strategies*, 1, December 1983, 14–21; David F. Kohl and Lizabeth A. Wilson. Effectiveness of Course Integrated Bibliographic Instruction in Improving Course Work. *RQ*, 26, December 1986, 203–11; David N. King and John C. Ory. Effects of Library Instruction on Student Research: A Case Study. *College & Research Libraries*, 42 (1), January 1981, 31–41.

14. Mark Emmons and Wanda Martin. Engaging Conversation: Evaluating the Contribution of Library Instruction to the Quality of Student Research. *College & Research Libraries*, 63 (6), November 2002, 545–60. See also David Eyman and Alven Nunley. *Effectiveness of Library Science 101 in Teaching Bibliographic Skills*. May 1977. ERIC Document ED150 962.

15. John C. Selegean, Martha Lou Thomas, and Marie Louise Richman. Long-Range Effectiveness of Library Use Instruction. *College & Research Libraries*, 44 (6), November 1983, 476–80. See also Larry Hardesty, Nicholas P. Lovrich Jr., and James Mannon. Library-Use Instruction: Assessment of Long-Term Effects. *College & Research Libraries*, 43, 1982, 38–46.

16. Donald Barclay. Evaluating Library Instruction: Doing the Best You Can with What You Have. *RQ*, 33, Winter 1993, 194–99.

17. Donald Barclay. Evaluating Library Instruction: Doing the Best You Can with What You Have. *RQ*, 33, Winter 1993, 194–99, 196.

18. Carol Germain, Trudi E. Jacobson, and Sue A. Kaczor. A Comparison of the Effectiveness of Presentation Formats for Instruction: Teaching First-Year Students. *College & Research Libraries*, 61 (1), January 2000, 65–72.

19. Lorrie A. Knight. The Role of Assessment in Library User Education. *Reference Services Review*, 30 (1), 2002, 15–24.

20. Lucy Holman. A Comparison of Computer-Assisted Instruction and Classroom Bibliographic Instruction. *Reference & User Services Quarterly*, 40 (1), 2000, 53–60.

21. E. Eric Landrum and Diana M. Muench. Assessing Students' Library Skills and Knowledge: The Library Research Strategies Questionnaire. *Psychological Reports*, 75, 1994, 1619–28.

22. Karen Markey, Annie Armstrong, Sandy De Groote, Michael Fosmire, Laura Fuderer, Kelly Garrett, Helen Georgas, Linda Sharp, Cheri Smith, Michael Spaly, and Joni E. Warner. Testing the Effectiveness of Interactive Multimedia for Library-User Education. *portal: Libraries and the Academy*, 5 (4), 2005, 527–44.

23. Sara J. Penhale, Nancy Taylor, and Thomas G. Kirk. A Method of Measuring the Reach of a Bibliographic Instruction Program. *Association of College & Research Libraries*. Available at http://www.ala.org/acrl/publications/whitepapers/nashville/penhaletaylor

24. M. Shanley and C. Witten. University 101 Freshman Seminar Course: A Longitudinal Study of Persistence, Retention, and Graduation Rates. *NASPA Journal*, 27, 1990, 344–52.

25. C. Wilkie and S. Kuckuck. A Longitudinal Study of the Effects of a Freshman Seminar. *Journal of the Freshman Year Experience*, 1, 1989, 7–16.

26. K. Ketkar and S. D. Bennett. Strategies for Evaluating a Freshman Studies Program. *Journal of the Freshman Year Experience*, 1, 1989, 33–44.

27. J. Benton. Bibliographic Instruction: A Radical Assessment, in C. Oberman-Soroka (Ed.). *Proceedings from the Second Southeastern Conference on Approaches to Bibliographic Instruction, 22–23 March 1979*. Charleston, SC: College of Charleston, 1980, 53–68.

28. Earnest T. Pascarella and Patrick T. Terenzini. *How College Affects Students: Findings and Insights from Twenty Years of Research.* San Francisco: Jossey-Bass, 1991, 118.

29. Patricia S. Breivik and Gordon Gee. *Information Literacy: Revolution in the Library.* New York: American Council on Education/Macmillan, 1989; Patricia S. Breivik. *Student Learning in the Information Age.* Phoenix: American Council on Education/Oryx, 1998.

30. Shirley J. Behrens. A Conceptual Analysis and Historical Overview of Information Literacy. *College & Research Libraries,* July 1994, 309–22.

31. Laurie A. MacWhinnie. The Information Commons: The Academic Library of the Future. *portal: Libraries and the Academy,* 3 (2), 2003, 241-57, at 247.

32. Available at http://www.ala.org/acrl/sites/ala.org.acrl/files/content/standards/standards.pdf

33. Denise Koufogiannakis and Natasha Wiebe. Effective Methods for Teaching Information Literacy Skills to Undergraduate Students: A Systematic Review and Meta-Analysis. *Evidence Based Library and Information Practice,* 1 (3), 2006, 3–22.

34. Susan D. K. Taylor. *An Examination of Course-Integrated Library Instruction Programs at Three Small Private Liberal Arts Colleges.* Manhattan: Kansas State University, 1991.

35. Stephanie Margolin and Wendy Hayden. Beyond Mechanics: Reframing the Pedagogy and Development of Information Literacy Teaching Tools. *The Journal of Academic Librarianship,* 41, 2015, 602–12.

36. Andrea L. Foster. Students Fall Short on 'Information Literacy,' Educational Testing Service's Study Finds. *Chronicle of Higher Education,* 53 (10), October 2006, A36.

37. Ethelene Whitmire. Factors Influencing Undergraduates' Self-Reported Satisfaction with Their Information Literacy Skills. *portal: Libraries and the Academy,* 1 (4), 2001, 409–20.

38. Heidi Julien and Stuart Boon. Assessing Instructional Outcomes in Canadian Academic Libraries. *Library & Information Science Research,* 26, 2004, 121–39.

39. Chris Brewer. *Integrating Information Literacy into the Health Sciences Curriculum: Longitudinal Study of an Information Literacy Program for the University of Wollongong.* Paper presented at the 4th National Information Literacy Conference, Adelaide, South Australia, December 1999. See also Julie Rabine and Catherine Cardwell. Start Making Sense: Practical Approaches to Outcomes Assessment for Libraries. *Research Strategies,* 17 (4), 2000, 319–35.

40. Norman B. Hutcherson. Library Jargon: Student Recognition of Terms and Concepts Commonly Used by Librarians in the Classroom. *College & Research Libraries,* 65 (4), July 2004, 349–54.

41. Patricia Davitt Maughan. Assessing Information Literacy among Undergraduates: A Discussion of the Literature and the University of California-Berkeley Assessment Experience. *College & Research Libraries,* 62 (1), January 2001, 71–85.

42. Mark Hepworth. *A Study of Undergraduate Information Literacy and Skills: The Inclusion of Information Literacy and Skills in the Undergraduate Curriculum.* Paper presented at the 65th IFLA Council and General Conference, Bangkok, Thailand, August 20–28, 1999.

43. Angela Dunnington and Mary Lou Strong. *What's Assessment Got to Do with It?! Exploring Student Learning Outcomes.* Presentation given at the ALA Annual Conference, New Orleans, Louisiana, June 24, 2006.

44. Jill Coupe. Undergraduate Library Skills: Two Surveys at Johns Hopkins University. *Research Strategies,* 11, Fall 1993, 188–201.

45. Brian R. Schuck. Assessing a Library Instruction Program. *Research Strategies,* 10, Fall 1992, 152–60.

46. Joan R. Kaplowitz and Janice Contini. Computer Assisted Instruction: Is It an Option for Bibliographic Instruction in Large Undergraduate Survey Classes? *College & Research Libraries,* 59 (1), 1998, 19–27.

47. Terrence Mech. Developing an Information Literacy Assessment Instrument, in Peter Hernon, Robert E. Dugan, and Candy Schwartz (Eds.). *Revisiting Outcomes Assessment in Higher Education.* Westport, CT: Libraries Unlimited, 2006, 327–50.

48. See the Project SAILS Web site at www.projectsails.org.

49. Yvonne Mery, Jill Newby, and Ke Peng. Why One-Shot Information Literacy Sessions Are Not the Future of Instruction: A Case for Online Credit Courses. *College & Research Libraries*, July 2012, 366–77.

50. Megan J. Oakleaf. *Assessing Information Literacy Skills: A Rubric Approach.* Doctoral dissertation. University of North Carolina at Chapel Hill, 2006.

51. Elizabeth Hartmann. Understandings of Information Literacy: The Perceptions of First-Year Undergraduate Students at the University of Ballarat. *Australian Academic & Research Libraries*, 32 (2), 2001, 110–22.

52. Deborah Turnbull, Denise Frost, and Nicola Foxlee. *Infoseek, InfoFind! Information Literacy and Integrated Service Delivery for Researchers and Postgraduates.* Paper presented at the Information Online 2003 Conference, Sydney, New South Wales, January 2003; Margaret C. Wallace, Allison Shorten, and Patrick Crookes. Teaching Information Literacy Skills: An Evaluation. *Nurse Education Today*, 20, 2000, 485–89.

53. Teresa Y. Neely. *Aspects of Information Literacy: A Sociological and Psychological Study.* Doctoral dissertation, University of Pittsburgh, 2000.

54. Nancy H. Seamans. Student Perceptions of Information Literacy: Insights for Librarians. *Reference Services Review*, 30 (2), 2002, 112–23.

55. Alison Brettle. Information Skills Training: A Systematic Review of the Literature. *Health Information and Libraries Journal*, 20 (Supplement 1), June 2003, 3–9.

56. Jillian R. Griffiths and Peter Brophy. Student Searching Behavior and the Web: Use of Academic Resources and Google. *Library Trends*, 53 (4), Spring 2005, 539–54.

57. Steve Jones. The Internet Goes to College: How Students Are Living in the Future with Today's Technology. *Pew Internet and American Life Project,* September 15, 2002. Available at http://www.pewinternet.org/files/old-media/Files/Reports/2002/PIP_College_Report.pdf.pdf

58. Cathy De Rosa, Joanne Cantrell, Janet Hawk, and Alane Wilson. *College Students' Perceptions of Libraries and Information Resources.* Dublin, OH: OCLC, 2006.

59. George D. Kuh and Robert M. Gonyea. The Role of the Academic Library in Promoting Student Engagement in Learning. *College & Research Libraries*, 64 (7), July 2003, 256–82.

60. James W. Marcum. Rethinking Information Literacy. *Library Quarterly*, 72 (1), January 2002, 1–26.

61. Allan Martin. Towards e-Literacy, in Allan Martin and Hannelore Rader (Eds.). *Information and IT Literacy: Enabling Learning in the 21st Century.* London: Facet, 2003, 18.

62. Stephen Foster. Information Literacy: Some Misgivings. *American Libraries*, 24 (4), 1993, 344–46; Lisa O'Connor. Information Literacy as Professional Legitimization: The Quest for a New Jurisdiction. *Library Review*, 58 (7), 2009, 493–508.

63. Eamon Tewell. A Decade of Critical Information Literacy. *Communications in Information Literacy*, 9 (1), 2015, 24–43.

64. Sue Samson. Information Literacy Learning Outcomes and Student Success. *The Journal of Academic Librarianship*, 36 (3), May 2010, 202–10.

65. See, for example, Margaret K. Cook. Rank, Status and Contribution of Academic Librarians as Perceived by the Teaching Faculty at Southern Illinois University, Carbondale. *College & Research Libraries*, 42, May 1981, 214–22; Robert T. Ivey. Teaching Faculty Perceptions of Academic Librarians at Memphis State University. *College & Research Libraries*, 55, January 1994, 69–82; LeeAnn Withnell. Faculty Opinions of Academic Library Service Policies. *Journal of Interlibrary Loan, Document Delivery & Information Supply*, 4, 1994, 23–79; Gaby Divay, Ada M. Ducas, and Nicole Michaud-Oystryk. Faculty Perceptions of Librarians at the University of Manitoba. *College & Research Libraries*, 48, January 1987, 27–35; Larry R. Oberg, Mary Kay Schleiter, and Michael Van Houten. Faculty Perceptions of Librarians at Albion College: Status, Role, Contribution and Contacts. *College & Research Libraries*, 50, March 1989, 215–30.

66. Lars Christensen, Mindy Stombler, and Lyn Thaxton. A Report on Librarian-Faculty Relations from a Sociological Perspective. *The Journal of Academic Librarianship*, 30, March 2004, 116–21.

67. Larry Hardesty. *Faculty and the Library: The Undergraduate Experience.* Norwood, NJ: Ablex, 1991.

68. Anita Cannon. Faculty Survey on Library Research Instruction. *RQ*, 33, Summer 1994, 524–41.

69. Joy Thomas. Faculty Attitudes and Habits Concerning Library Instruction: How Much Has Changed Since 1982? *Research Strategies*, 12, Fall 1994, 209–23.

70. Gloria J. Leckie and Anne Fullerton. Information Literacy in Science and Engineering Undergraduate Education: Faculty Attitudes and Pedagogical Practices. *College & Research Libraries*, 60, January 1999, 9–29.

71. Jeanne R. Davidson. Faculty and Student Attitudes Toward Credit Courses for Library Skills. *College & Research Libraries*, 62 (2), March 2001, 155–63.

72. Claire McGuinness. What Faculty Think—Exploring the Barriers to Information Literacy Development in Undergraduate Education. *The Journal of Academic Librarianship*, 32 (6), November 2006, 573–82.

73. Denise Koufogiannakis and Natasha Wiebe. Effective Methods for Teaching Information Literacy Skills to Undergraduate Students: A Systematic Review and Meta-Analysis. *Evidence-Based Library and Information Practice*, 1 (3), 2006, 3–43. See also Li Zhang, Erin Watson, and Laura Banfield. The Efficacy of Computer-Assisted Instruction Versus Face-to-Face Instruction in Academic Libraries: A Systematic Review. *The Journal of Academic Librarianship,* 33 (4), 2007, 478–84.

17

Evaluation of Summer Reading Programs

When school is in session, the faucet of resources is on and all children gain equally. When school is out, the resource faucet is off and low-income children do not have access to learning resources.

—Alexander, Entwisle, and Olson[1]

SERVICE DEFINITION

Summer reading programs seek to attract large numbers of children to the library during the summer, a time when reading skills often decline—sometimes called "summer loss," "summer learning loss," or "summer reading setback." One consistent finding of a number of research studies is that summer reading setback—presumably the result of a lack of adequate reading practice—is a very real phenomenon: it impacts children living in poverty the most, and its effects are cumulative.

EVALUATION QUESTIONS

Evaluation of summer reading programs (SRPs) have been designed to accomplish several objectives, including:

- Identify the number of children and teens (and, in some cases, adults) who participate during the "summer"—recognizing that some libraries offer a reading programs several times during the year
- Identify the number of books read during the course of the program
- Identify the total number of minutes read over the "summer"
- Determine the impact of the SRP on the library's circulation of materials
- Identify the time spent reading with a parent/caregiver
- Ask if the child's attitude toward reading became more positive

- Ask if children spent more time voluntarily reading
- Ask if children's reading skills improved over the course of the summer

EVALUATION METHODS

A library's summer reading program can be evaluated using both qualitative and quantitative methods, as shown in Figure 17.1. Note that a majority of research methods used to date are quantitative.

	Qualitative	Quantitative
Library Perspective		Input measures Output measures
Customer Perspective	Journal Surveys	Meta-Analysis Pre- & Post-test Statistical analysis Surveys Experimental

Figure 17.1. Summer Reading Program Evaluation Methods

Summer reading programs have been a staple for many, if not most, public libraries for many decades. Probably 95 percent or more of the public libraries in America offer some form of a summer reading program. The popularity of such programs attests to the continuing value of encouraging reading among primary and secondary grade children in communities across the nation.

One of the common assumptions about summer reading programs is that they are valuable in many ways for the children participating. Reading practice improves word recognition, assists in building vocabulary, improves fluency and comprehension,[2] is a powerful source of world knowledge,[3] and is a way to develop understandings of complex written language syntax and story/text grammars.[4] However, most children do very little reading out of school, and only a small number of children read for extended periods of time.[5]

NATIONAL READING STUDIES

Seven national studies have investigated reading: some of these studies are longitudinal in nature, and others provide a snapshot in time. These studies indicate as follows:

- **Kids & Family Reading Report**—Half of children ages 6 through 17 are reading a book for fun, and although 86 percent of parents say reading for fun is important or extremely important, only 46 percent of kids say the same. There are several predictors that indicate whether children ages 6–17 will be frequent readers: being more likely to rate themselves as "really enjoying reading," a strong belief that reading for fun is important, and having parents who are frequent readers.[6]
- **National Assessment of Educational Progress**—Average reading scores in 2015 for fourth-grade students were not significantly different in comparison to 2013; eighth-grade students scored lower than 2013.[7]

- **Learning at Home**—Nearly half (44 percent) of the screen media that 2- to 10-year-olds use is considered educational by their parents; educational media use occurs most frequently among very young children; children spend far more time with educational TV than they do with educational content on other platforms; and many children have access to and are using electronic reading devices.[8]

- **Parenting in the Age of Digital Technology**—Although new media technologies have become widespread, a majority of parents do not think they have made parenting any easier; parents do not report having many family conflicts or concerns about their children's media use; and parents still turn to family and friends for parenting advice far more often than to new media sources like websites, blogs, and social networks.[9]

- **Zero to Eight**—Children's access to mobile media devices is dramatically higher than it was two years ago; the average amount of time children spend using mobile devices has tripled; and television still dominates children's media time, but new ways of watching now make up a large portion of viewing.[10]

- **Generation M²**—Over the past five years, young people have increased the amount of time they spend consuming media by 1 hour and 17 minutes daily, from 6:21 to 7:38—almost the amount of time most adults spend at work each day, except that young people use media seven days a week instead of five; and an explosion in mobile and online media has fueled the increase in media use among young people.[11]

> *Literally hundreds of correlational studies find*
> *that the best readers read the most*
> *and that poor readers read the least.*
> *These correlational studies suggest that*
> *the more children read, the better their*
> *fluency, vocabulary, and comprehension.*
>   —The National Reading Panel[12]

PRIOR EVALUATION AND RESEARCH

There are four possible approaches for attempting to ameliorate the summer reading slide. These include:

- **Summer camps or day camps**—Expensive and low participation among low socioeconomic status (SES) families. When tutoring, instruction, and reading time are a part of each day, reading skills improve.

- **Books in the home**—Providing books to children to read over the summer may or may not improve reading test scores. When children and their parents get together with others in the program on a weekly basis, reading skills improve, often significantly.

- **After-school programs** (including during the summer)—These types of programs are expensive to provide; however, programs that combine homework assistance and tutoring for reading can be effective provided there is an intentional focus on learning.

- **Library summer reading programs**—More than 90 percent of public libraries offer a summer reading program; about two-thirds offer a separate program for teens. About two-thirds of the libraries prepare a written evaluation report of these programs; a third track reading time; only 3 percent partner with nearby schools.[13]

Although there is a plethora of research about each of these approaches, for obvious reasons only the research about library summer reading programs will be reviewed here.

Qualitative Methods

Two qualitative methods have been used to assess the effectiveness of summer reading programs: journaling and the use of surveys.

Journaling

One study asked 155 fifth-grade students to track a wide range of out-of-school activities using a journal. Data are reported that range from 8 to 26 weeks. Reading books is the best predictor of several measures of reading achievement. However, on most days most children did little or no reading.[14] A child in the 90th percentile in amount of book reading spends nearly five times as many minutes reading per day as the child in the 50th percentile, and more than 200 times as many minutes per day as the child in the 10th percentile. In 2007, Sharon McKool found that most fifth-grade students do very little voluntary reading outside of school: an average of 17 minutes a day reading voluntarily. She also noted that the more television students watch and the more organized activities students take part in, the less voluntary reading they do.[15]

Surveys

A qualitative survey can be used to ask children (parents and teachers could also be included in a survey) about their perceptions of why they read, the benefits of reading, and their perceptions about their skill levels.

A survey by Goldhor and McCrossan of fourth-graders in 35 elementary schools in Evansville, Indiana, showed that participation in a summer reading program was one factor in the retention and improvement of reading skills, but noted two other important factors:

- The bias in allowing children to select program participation. That is, from a research perspective it would be better to assign a child to the experimental group (library summer reading program) or to a control group (no library summer reading program).
- The need to identify the amount and character of reading done by each child.[16]

Quantitative Methods

The value of the quantitative approach to the evaluation of summer reading programs is that it provides a fairly clear picture of the effectiveness of the program. Within the quantitative perspective, a variety of methods can be used that range from the fairly simple to the more complex (using statistical tools, for example). And, as we will see, careful use of these tools must be used to ensure that no bias exists in reporting the results of any one study.

Input Measures

A library may identify the necessary resources, staff time, materials, equipment or performer rental, printing, marketing, and other costs associated with the library's summer reading program. This is typically done for budgeting purposes and/or to share with potential grant funders.

Output Measures

Almost every library that provides a summer reading program collects and reports associated output measures. Among the more frequently captured SRP output measures are:

- Individuals registered for the SRP (children, teens, adults)
- SRP participants as a percentage of school-age children and teens
- Number of individuals attending program events
- Number of individuals completing the SRP (children, teens, adults)
- Number of books the participants read
- Number of children who read a minimum of X books during the program
- Number of checkouts while the SRP was in operation compared to the prior year
- Number of pages read (children, teens, adults)
- Amount of time spent reading alone (children, teens, adults)
- Amount of time spent reading with a parent or caregiver (children, teens, adults)
- Whether the child spends more time reading with a parent or caregiver
- Number of new library cards issued to families of SRP participants
- Number of SRP-related programs
- Total attendance at SRP-related programs (children, teens, adults)

Some libraries also calculate the cost per SRP activity as well as the cost per participant.

Surveys

A survey by Donna Celano and Susan Neuman of Pennsylvania public libraries found that summer reading programs are thriving and attracting large numbers of children and families each year.[17] This study found that:

- Three-fourths of the libraries noted that circulation increases from 6% to 10% during the summer, with the assumption that most of this increase can be attributed to the summer reading program
- The majority of SRP children visit the library weekly
- A third of the libraries report that the SRP attracts more than 200 children
- Children who attend summer library programs read on a higher level than those who do not attend, including those children who attend summer camp programs
- Library events related to a SRP (crafts, songs, drama, storytelling, and puppetry) extend the reading experience
- Summer library programs encourage parents to be involved in their children's reading
- Summer reading programs encourage children to spend more time with books

However, public libraries located in lower SES communities offer inferior collections and services to children in poverty.

A survey of 53 southern California public libraries pertaining to summer reading programs is noteworthy in that it involved a total of 1,637 parent survey responses, more than 2,500 students, and 58 third-grade teachers who provided information on 932 students.[18] An analysis of the data suggests that:

- Children participating in the summer reading program spend more time looking at text and reading than their counterparts
- 11 percent of the parents reported that they spend more time reading with or to their children (15 hours or more per week)
- The amount of reading is substantial: 36 percent of the children read 1–20 books; 17 percent read 21–30; 27 percent read 31–50; and 21 percent read 51 or more books
- Participants are much more enthusiastic about reading
- Teachers reported that 31 percent of the participants had maintained or improved their reading skills compared to 5percent of nonparticipants

The Public Library Association has received a grant from the Gates Foundation to develop outcome measures. Project Outcome has developed a series of brief surveys that individuals attending a library program can complete online. An outcomes-based survey for summer reading programs is available and libraries can use this service for free (visit ProjectOutcome.Org for more information).

Pre- and Posttests

The use of pre- and posttests, typically standardized reading tests, provides a fairly reliable way to assess any program's success, and this method has been used by several studies, For example, Barbara Heyns studied nearly 3,000 sixth- and seventh-grade Atlanta school children over a two-year period. She demonstrates that the single summer activity that is most strongly and consistently related to summer learning is reading. Heyns found that the public library is the primary public institution contributing to the intellectual growth of children during the summer. Among the findings of her research:

- The number of books read during the summer is consistently related to academic gains.
- Children in every income group who read six or more books over the summer gained more in reading achievement than children who did not.
- The use of the public library during the summer is more predictive of vocabulary gains than attending summer school.
- Distance is a deterrent to children using the library, especially for black and less economically advantaged children; those living closer to a public library used it more regularly.
- Girls read more books and their reading seems less dependent on library use than that of boys.[19]

Similar results have been found in several studies that used large-scale surveys conducted in Canada,[20] England,[21] and New Zealand.

More recently, IMLS funded a project, generally referred to as The Dominican Study, that attempted to answer the question, "Do public library summer reading programs close the achievement gap?"[22] The study involved a partnership between a public library and nearby elementary schools. The criteria used to select the 11 sites to participate in the study included:

- 50 percent of more of the students in the school had to qualify for free and reduced-price meals
- 85 percent of the school students would be able to take a reading proficiency test in English

- The public library summer reading program had to be a minimum of six weeks of programming over the summer
- The school and the public library would sign a partnership agreement

Because the study involved school-age children, parents needed to sign a consent form (only 367 were received) so the children could be tested. Although the authors of the Dominican Study asserted that public library summer reading programs do close the achievement gap, there is unfortunately no data to support their claim. As shown in Figure 17.2, reading skills improved from Spring to Fall 2008 for *both* summer reading program participants and nonparticipants.

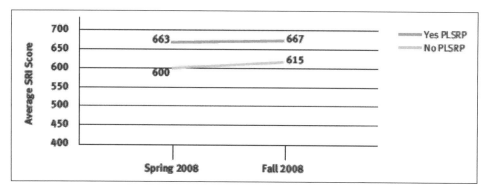

Figure 17.2. Reading Achievement Test Scores Report by Summer Reading Program Attendance. Susan Roman, Deborah Carran, and Carole Fiore. *The Dominican Study: Public Library Reading Programs Close the Reading Gap.* River Forest, IL: Dominican University, Graduate School of Library & Information Science, June 2010.

In a strong critique of the Dominican Study, Ray Lyons argued that there were two primary problems with the study:[23]

- **Nonequivalent groups**—There was no attempt to make the two groups (SRP participants and nonparticipants) as equivalent as possible in terms of socioeconomic status characteristics. The two groups were initially separated by more than 60 points in the reading achievement test scores in Spring 2008 and by 50 points in Fall 2008, so it is impossible to assess the potential contributions of the summer reading programs.
- **Attrition in research subjects**—The initial group of 800 possible participants was reduced to 367 (signed parental consent forms), and this number was further reduced to 149 based on the number of students who completed the reading achievement test in Fall 2008. The final 149 respondents simply constitute too small a sample size to provide any confidence in the results of the study.

Fortunately, there is a model of a good evaluation study that others can emulate. The public libraries and a number of school districts in the Kansas City area partnered with the Kansas City Area Education Research Consortium to prepare an evaluation of summer reading programs.[24] This evaluation used a fairly sophisticated (yet doable) approach to the study:

- Data for 7,224 students with pretest and posttest scores were provided by four school districts
- The public libraries provided the identity of 1,122 students who participated in the summer reading program
- The reading achievement test scores (a different test was used in each of the four school districts) was converted to Lexile-equivalent categories

- A group of equivalent nonparticipants was created to use as a control group
- Students were matched as closely as possible on pretest score; gender, race, and ethnicity; free and reduced-price lunch status; and summer school attendance

The Kansas City study found that:

- **All Participating Students:** Program participants' reading scores increased more from Spring 2013 to Fall 2013 compared to students in the matched comparison group.
- **Male Participants:** Male participants experienced more growth in reading skills than their matched comparison group.
- **Female Participants:** Although an increase was observed in Lexile scores as well as percentile ranking for females in summer programs, the results revealed a nonsignificant statistical trend in the predicted direction.
- **Students with Free and Reduced-Price Lunch Status:** The participating group showed greater increases in their reading assessment scores when compared to students in the matched comparison group.
- **White Students:** The results revealed a nonsignificant trend (there was no significant increase among participating white students), meaning that the observed impact may have happened by chance.
- **Non-White Students:** Students of color who participated in summer reading programs experienced positive growth in reading skills from Spring 2013 to Fall 2013.

Statistical Analysis

A number of studies have used statistical analysis (typically correlation analysis) to explore the potential impact of socioeconomic status characteristics on children's abilities to read. It is interesting to note that no statistical analysis studies have been prepared in the public library environment.

For example, one study found that within the same socioeconomic strata, on average white children have higher achievement test scores than African American children.[25]

Meta-Analysis

A meta-analysis looks at a number of prior studies (that have all used the same statistical measure) in an attempt to aggregate information leading to better statistical results. In effect, the data from all prior studies are pooled in order to conduct research about prior research.

Harris Cooper and his colleagues[26] summarized 13 empirical studies on about 40,000 subjects that focus on "summer learning loss," which show that students who do not engage in educational activities during the summer typically score lower on tests at the end of summer than they did at the beginning. The focus of the studies Harris and his team analyzed is summer programs organized by schools, not libraries, to combat the fact that vacations typically result in an annual achievement gap between rich and poor students of about three months. The principal conclusions that can be drawn from this meta-analysis are:

- Summer school programs that focus on lessening or removing learning deficiencies have a positive impact on the knowledge and skills of participants.
- Summer school programs focusing on the acceleration of learning or on other multiple goals also have a positive impact on participants roughly equal to remedial programs.

- Summer school programs have more positive effects on the achievement of middle-class students than on that of students from disadvantaged backgrounds.
- Remedial summer programs have larger positive effects when the program is run for a small number of schools or classes or in a small community.
- Summer programs that provide small-group or individual instruction produce the largest impact on student outcomes.
- Summer programs that require some form of parental involvement produce larger effects than programs without this component.
- Remedial summer programs may have a larger effect on math achievement than on reading.
- The achievement advantage gained by students who attend summer school may diminish over time.
- Remedial summer school programs have positive effects for students at all grade levels, although the effects may be more pronounced for students in early primary grades and secondary school than in middle grades.
- Summer programs that undergo careful scrutiny for treatment fidelity, including monitoring to ensure that instruction is being delivered as prescribed, monitoring of attendance, and removal from the evaluation of students with many absences, may produce larger effects than unmonitored programs.

Jerome D'Agostino and Judith Murphy prepared a meta-analysis of 36 studies (from a sample of 109 studies) of *Reading Readiness*, an intensive tutorial intervention designed to develop the literacy skills of low-performing first-grade students.[27] Problems confronting those who have prepared evaluations of the Reading Readiness program include the different experience and training of teachers, the amount of instructional time, the number of students instructed per period of time, and the need to construct an equivalent comparison group. In general, the Reading Readiness program results in "graduating" students achieving or surpassing regular student achievements based on pre/post differences using standardized achievement tests.

Other important meta-analyses of summer reading have been prepared by Lauer et al.[28] (a review of studies published between 1986 and 2003), McCombs et al.,[29] and Kim and Quinn[30] (who reviewed studies published from 1998 up to 2011). More recently, NPC Research prepared a meta-analysis for the Collaborative Summer Library Program, which came to three conclusions pertaining to the state of the research:[31]

1. There is clear and consistent evidence that *school-based summer and other out-of-school-time reading programs* can be effective in preventing summer learning loss and improving reading achievement.

2. There is clear and consistent evidence that *home-based summer and other out-of-school-time reading programs* can be effective in preventing summer learning loss and improving reading achievement.

3. The evidence base for the effectiveness of *public library summer and other out-of-school-time reading programs* has yet to be developed. Although a logical argument exists for public libraries playing a key role in children's literacy, especially in terms of access to books and encouragement of voluntary and pleasure reading, rigorous empirical research has yet to be conducted on this topic.

SUGGESTED BEST PRACTICES

Specific library summer reading program best practices include:

- Calculate the number of SRP participants as a percentage of school-age children. A library can quickly obtain information about the number of children in its community using census data. Every public library should be making this calculation as a part of its program goal-setting process.

- Set participation goals that are aggressive—certainly above 15 percent.

- Develop a better understanding of the reasons why children drop out of the SRP; this would allow a library to design a program that is more compelling and keep the attention (and participation) of children over the course of the summer.

- Focus outreach and marketing efforts on children who likely suffer summer reading loss. A public library might need to develop a marketing plan that identified various market segments—children with different characteristics (those who are not readers, the aliterates), readers who are currently nonusers of the library (potential customers, infrequent customers, or frequent customers)—and the associated marketing approaches that would be effective for each market segment.

- Expand outreach efforts by more innovative and effective marketing. For example, the Torrance (California) Public Library placed stickers on the elementary school report cards going home to parents. The stickers exclaimed: "Vacation reading equals better grades. Take your child to the public library for summer reading." As a result of the stickers, the number of children registering for the SRP jumped more than 25 percent.[32]

- Consider an outreach strategy that takes the SRP to children without requiring children to physically visit the library. The public library should be reaching out to latchkey programs, day care centers, the YMCA, the Boys and Girls Clubs, summer camp programs, summer recreation programs, and local home schoolers. This approach also suggests setting some specific targets for each market segment rather than relying on total registration numbers.

- Explore the possibility of developing partnerships with the local schools to involve teachers in assessment of the library's SRP. Linking the results of standardized reading tests with participation in the public library's SRP can potentially lead to more funding.

- Develop an online version of the SRP that would appeal to yet another segment of the community currently not being served by the library. Online SRPs have been successful in many public libraries.

- Track outcomes; consider participating in PLA's Project Outcome to identify summer reading program outcomes in your library.

SUMMARY

This chapter presented a variety of methods that can be used to evaluate a library's summer reading program. Among the more notable conclusions that can be drawn from the various research studies pertaining to summer reading programs are the following:

- Students who do not engage in educational activities during the summer typically score lower on tests at the end of summer than they did at the beginning.

- Summer school programs that focus on lessening or removing learning deficiencies have a positive impact on the knowledge and skills of participants.

- Summer school programs focusing on the acceleration of learning or on other multiple goals also have a positive impact on participants roughly equal to that of remedial programs.

- Summer school programs have more positive effects on the achievement of middle-class students than on students from disadvantaged backgrounds.

- Remedial summer programs have larger positive effects when the program is run for a small number of schools or classes or in a small community.

- Summer programs that provide small-group or individual instruction produce the largest impact on student outcomes.

- Summer programs that require some form of parental involvement produce larger, positive effects than programs without this component.

- The achievement advantage gained by students who attend summer school may diminish over time.

- Remedial summer school programs have positive effects for students at all grade levels, although the effects may be more pronounced for students in early primary grades and secondary school than those in middle grades.

- On most days, the majority of children did little or no reading. A child in the 90th percentile in amount of book reading spends nearly five times as many minutes reading per day as the child in the 50th percentile and more than 200 times as many minutes per day as the child in the 10th percentile.

- Summer reading setback is one of the important factors contributing to the reading achievement gap between rich and poor children.

- There is little difference in reading gains between children from high- and low-income families during the school year. Rather, the differences are the result of what happens during the summer.

- Children from high-income families make superior progress in reading over the summer, and over time the summer advantage can account for the social class differences in reading achievement. This is a result of the fact that children from high-income families tend to read more over the summer.

- Children from lower-income families have more restricted access to books (both in school and out of school) than do their more advantaged peers.

- The more children read, the better their fluency, vocabulary, and comprehension.

NOTES

1. Karl Alexander, Doris Entwisle, and Linda Olson. Schools, Achievement, and Inequality: A Seasonal Perspective. *Educational Evaluation and Policy*, Summer 2001, 171–91.

2. William Naggy, Richard Anderson, and Patricia Herman. Learning Word Meanings from Context During Normal Reading. *American Educational Research Journal*, 14, Summer 1987, 237–70.

3. Keith Stanovich. Does Reading Make You Smarter? Literacy and the Development of Verbal Intelligence, in H. Reese (Ed.). *Advances in Child Development and Behavior*, vol. 24. New York: Academic Press, 1993, 133–80.

4. Carol Chomsky. Stages in Language Development and Reading Exposure. *Harvard Educational Review*, 42, Spring 1972, 1–33.

5. Richard Anderson, Paul Wilson, and Linda Fielding. Growth in Reading and How Children Spend Their Time Outside of School. *Reading Research Quarterly*, 23, 1988, 285–303.

6. *Kids & Family Reading Report*. 5th ed. New York: Scholastic, 2015.

7. The National Assessment of Educational Progress survey results are available at http://nces.ed .gov/nationsreportcard/

8. Victoria Rideout. *Learning at Home: Families' Educational Media Use in America*. New York: The Joan Ganz Cooney Center, January 2014.

9. Ellen Wartella, Vicky Rideout, Alexis Lauricella, and Sabrina Connell. *Parenting in the Age of Digital Technology*. Evanston, IL: Center on Media and Human Development, School of Communication, Northwestern University, June 2013.

10. Common Sense Media. *Zero to Eight: Children's Media Use in America 2013*. Washington, DC: Common Sense Media, Fall 2013.

11. *Generation M²: Media in the Lives of 8- to 18-Year-Olds*. Menlo Park, CA: A Kaiser Family Foundation Study, January 2010.

12. National Reading Panel. *Teaching Children to Read: An Evidence-Based Assessment of the Scientific Literature on Reading and Its Implications for Reading Instruction*. Washington, DC: Government Printing Office, 2000, 15.

13. Joseph Matthews. Evaluating Summer Reading Programs: Suggested Improvements. *Public Libraries*, 49 (4), July/August 2010, 34–39.

14. Richard Anderson, Paul Wilson, and Linda Fielding. Growth in Reading and How Children Spend Their Time Outside of School. *Reading Research Quarterly*, 23, 1988, 285–303.

15. Sharon McKool. Factors That Influence the Decision to Read: An Investigation of Fifth Grade Students' Out-of-School Reading Habits. *Reading Improvement,* 44, 2007, 111–31.

16. Herbert Goldhor and John McCrossan. An Exploratory Study of the Effects of a Public Library Summer Reading Club on Reading Skills. *Library Quarterly,* 36 (1), 1966, 14–24.

17. Donna Celano and Susan Neuman. *The Role of Public Libraries in Children's Literacy Development: An Evaluation Report*. Harrisburg, PA: Pennsylvania Library Association, 2001.

18. Evaluation and Training Institute. *Evaluation of the Public Library Summer Reading Program: Books and Beyond . . . Take Me to Your Reader!* Los Angeles: Evaluation and Training Institute, 2001.

19. Barbara Heynes. *Summer Learning and the Effects of Schooling*. New York: Academic Press, 1978.

20. Adele Fasick, Andre Gagnon, Lynne Howarth, and Ken Setterington. *Opening Doors to Children: Reading, Media, and Public Library Use by Children in Six Canadian Cities*. Regina: Regina Public Library, Canada, 2005.

21. Product Perceptions, Ltd. *Inspiring Children: The Impact of Summer Reading Challenge: The Reading Maze National Participant Survey*. London: Product Perceptions, Ltd., 2003.

22. Susan Roman, Deborah Carran, and Carole Fiore. *The Dominican Study: Public Library Reading Programs Close the Reading Gap*. Forest River, IL: Dominican University, Graduate School of Library & Information Science, June 2010.

23. Ray Lyons. Overstating Summer Reading Impact: The Dominican Study. *Public Library Quarterly*, 30 (1), 2011, 54–61.

24. Leigh Ann Taylor Knight, Hajar Aghababa, Jiaxi Quan, and Pat Oslund. *An Evaluation of Kansas City Reading Programs for Turn the Page Kansas City*. Lawrence, KS: Kansas City Area Education Research Consortium, February 2014.

25. Douglas Downey, Beckett Broh, and Paul von Hippel. Are Schools the Great Equalizer? Cognitive Inequality During the Summer Months and the School Year. *American Sociological Review,* 69, October 2004, 613–35.

26. Harris Cooper, Barbara Nye, and Kelly Charlton. The Effects of Summer Vacation on Achievement Test Scores: A Narrative and Meta-Analytic Review. *Review of Education Research*, 66 (3), Fall 1996, 227–68.

27. Jerome D'Agostino and Judith Murphy. A Meta-Analysis of Reading Recovery in United States Schools. *Educational Evaluation and Policy Analysis,* 26, 2004, 23–38.

28. Patricia Lauer, Motoko Akiba, Stephanie B. Wilkerson, Helen S. Apthorp, David Snow, and Mya L. Martin-Glenn. Out-of-School-Time Programs: A Meta-Analysis of Effects for At-Risk Students. *Review of Educational Research*, 76 (2). 2006, 275–313.

29. Jennifer S. McCombs, Catherine H. Augustine, Heather L. Schwartz, Susan J. Bodilly, Brian Mcinnis, Dahlia S. Lichter, and Amanda B. Cross. *Making Summer Count: How Summer Programs Can Boost Children's Learning* (Monograph Report 1120). Santa Monica, CA: RAND Corporation, 2011. See also Catherine H. Augustine, Jennifer Sloan McCombs, John F. Pane, Heather L. Schwartz, Jonathan Schweig, Andrew McEachin, and Kyle Siler-Evans. *Learning from Summer: Effects of Voluntary Summer Learning Programs on Low-Income Urban Youth.* Santa Monica, CA: RAND Corporation, 2016.

30. James S. Kim and David M. Quinn. The Effects of Summer Reading on Low-Income Children's Literacy Achievement from Kindergarten to Grade 8: A Meta-Analysis of Classroom and Home Interventions. *Review of Educational Research,* 83 (3), 2013, 386–431.

31. NPC Research. *CLSP Summer Reading White Paper.* Mason City, IA: Collaborative Summer Reading Program, July 2015.

32. Walter Minkel. Making A Splash With Summer Reading: Seven Ways Public Libraries Can Team Up With Schools. *School Library Journal*, 49, 2003, 54–56.

18

Evaluation of Customer Service

Many librarians maintain that only they, the professionals, have the expertise to assess the quality of library service . . . . Such opinions about service, in fact, are irrelevant. The only thing that matters is the customers' opinions, because without users there is no need for libraries except as warehouses.

—Ellen Altman and Peter Hernon[1]

SERVICE DEFINITION

Over the course of the last decade or so, surveys have been developed that focus on customer satisfaction. And while it is possible to assess the degree of satisfaction for a specific library service, the focus of this chapter is on the "big picture": determining satisfaction with the library and all of its systems and services. It is important to remember that people *choose to use* libraries, be they physical or virtual.

Phillip Kotler and Alan Andreasen assert that nonprofit organizations that focus on themselves rather than their customers will display specific characteristics, including seeing their services as inherently desirable, blaming customer ignorance when their services are not being used, relegating research about customers to a minor role, tending to define marketing as promotion, and assuming that there is no competition.[2]

When it comes to customer satisfaction, the perception of the customer—right or wrong, informed or uninformed—is the only "reality" that counts. A tendency exists for any library to become defensive about its ratings by asserting that "we really do a better job than the numbers reflect" or "the users just aren't aware of"; these attitudes simply mask the reality that the library could be making improvements. There may be many reasons for lower-than-expected ratings: not delivering the desired services, need for staff training, lack of quality in services, or not communicating the library's value to customers and decision stakeholders.

More than 50 percent of public and academic libraries had no way of quantifiably tracking organizational success and used informal customer feedback as their primary metric of success.[3]

Terry Vavra has suggested that an organization create a chart that identifies what motivates people to use a particular service and determine the associated customer requirements for each use motive.[4] This, in turn, will lead to identifying corresponding performance measures that matter, as shown in Table 18.1.

Table 18.1. The Structure of Customer Requirements

Use Motives	Customer Requirement	Performance Measures
Currency of resources	Library has what I want	Purchase requests/ILL requests
		Turnover rate of collection
		Complaints
Availability of resources	Items available to borrow	Availability survey
		Complaints
Read best sellers	Wait time	Wait time (no. of days)
		Complaints
Proximity of library to home/office	Convenience	Average travel time
		Average travel distance
Ease of navigation in library	Can find my own way	No. of directional questions
		Complaints
Hours of operation	Convenience	Complaints
Cleanliness of library	Comfort and security	Cleanliness index
Courteous staff	Friendly	Customer satisfaction survey
Helpful staff	Help when I need it	Customer satisfaction survey

Adapted from Figure 3.1 in Terry G. Vavra. Improving Your Measurement of Customer Satisfaction: A Guide to Creating, Conducting, Analyzing, and Reporting Customer Satisfaction Measurement Programs. *American Society for Quality,* 1997, 44–60.

EVALUATION QUESTIONS

A number of customer service–related questions have been the focus of evaluation efforts, including:

- How should a library define quality?
- Is customer satisfaction important to a library?
- Should increasing customer satisfaction be important to a library?

- While we are doing "good," what can we do better?
- How can a library improve its customer satisfaction rating?
- What are the tradeoffs of LibSat versus LibQUAL+?
- Is it possible to distinguish between information product and information service satisfaction?

EVALUATION METHODS

The methods that have been used to evaluate customer service can be divided into qualitative and quantitative (see Table 18.2).

Table 18.2. Customer Service Evaluation Methods

Qualitative	Quantitative
Focus groups	Locally developed surveys
Mystery shoppers	Standardized surveys
Complaints	Defining service characteristics

PRIOR EVALUATIONS AND RESEARCH

Service Quality

Service quality has garnered significant attention in the professional management and library literature over the last two decades. It is an antecedent of customer satisfaction that higher-quality service levels will lead to increased customer satisfaction. Yet it is possible to visit the library and receive a quality service and still be unsatisfied, for a variety of reasons. Some writers have confused service quality with or likened it to satisfaction.

Richard Orr, an early proponent of identifying quality of library services, suggests a distinction between quality and value. Orr indicates that *quality* should reflect how good the service is, in comparison to *value*, which should reflect how much good it does.[5]

Service quality has been defined from four primary perspectives:

- **Excellence** is usually externally defined and is used by many organizations. Organizations slowly create the brand of "excellence" over time. However, attributes of excellence may change over time. Excellence is achieving or reaching for the highest standard and never being satisfied with second best.
- **Value** stresses the benefits that will be received by the recipient, whereas quality is the perception of meeting or exceeding expectations. Quality and value are thus different concepts. The focus is on internal efficiency and external effectiveness.
- **Conformance to specifications** requires a detailed specification of requirements, some or most of which the customer may not be aware of. Although this approach facilitates precise measurement, it is an internally focused view of the world. For example, Joseph Juran— one of the pioneers in quality control—separated quality into two components: quality of design and quality of conformance to design specifications. Most customers will not care about service specifications—only the results of the specifications.

- **Meeting and/or exceeding expectations** crosses the boundaries of most service industries, although it should be noted that expectations, although subjective, are customer-centric, and are neither static nor predictable.[6] Customer expectations will change as the result of experiences with other service providers. The majority of research pertaining to service quality and customer satisfaction focuses on this expectations dimension. Service quality can be defined as reducing the gap between the services provided (real or perceived) and customer expectations.

Service quality actually has two components: **what** is provided to the customer (deliverables), and **how** the service is delivered (interactions). Deliverables describe what is provided to the customer. Interactions describe the characteristics of staff and equipment that impact how customers experience the service process. A large amount of the library literature has focused on the "what" to the exclusion of the "how."

Customer satisfaction has been defined as "the emotional reaction to a specific transaction or service encounter."[7] Satisfaction has two components. The first is *service encounter satisfaction*, which is the degree of satisfaction or dissatisfaction experienced by the individual in a specific service transaction. Jan Carlson, former president of SAS Airlines, coined the phrase "moments of truth" to describe any point in time during which a customer comes into contact with an organization.[8] Examples of "moments of truth" in a library might include contact at an information desk, contact at a circulation desk, reading a sign, asking for assistance from a staff member, attempting to locate an item in the collection, and use of the library's Web site.

The second component is *overall service satisfaction*, or the level of client satisfaction or dissatisfaction based on multiple transactions or experiences.[9] Thus, the overall service satisfaction is built up over time and is the result of numerous transactions of varying quality. Others have suggested that *customer satisfaction* refers to a specific transaction, whereas *service quality* is the collective judgment based on all of the previous encounters.

It is possible to conceive of the relationship between satisfaction and performance from two perspectives:

- Library performance is equated with customer satisfaction.
- A series of variables other than performance alone contribute to user satisfaction.

It is possible to distinguish between material and emotional satisfaction, according to Rachel Applegate, and there are three possible models to describe the satisfaction formation process:

- **Material Satisfaction Model.** System performance determines material satisfaction, yet the results from several studies suggest mixed or weak support between performance measurement variables and user satisfaction.[10]
- **Emotional Satisfaction Model—Simple Path.** Emotional satisfaction is caused by material satisfaction in this model. Yet several studies have found weak relationships between emotional satisfaction and performance—almost as if users were reluctant to criticize the library. Applegate called this a "false positive."[11]
- **Emotional Satisfaction Model—Multiple Path.** In this model three variables are analyzed—product settings, product performance, and disconfirmation. Disconfirmation refers to the difference between an individual's expectations of performance and the actual perception of performance. Applegate found in her OPAC retrieval experiment that disconfirmation plays an important role in explaining the formation of satisfaction.[12]

These findings are complemented by a study that separated the measurement of user satisfaction by both information product and information system/service, which were typically measured as one concept in prior studies.[13] Customer satisfaction can also be manifested at the micro level and macro level, as noted by Rowena Cullen.[14] Fei Yu found that it is much easier to achieve specific service use loyalty for repeat users than to achieve general library use loyalty for occasional users.[15]

A simplified model of the interactions among and between client expectations, perceptions, satisfaction, assessment of service quality, and the resulting overall customer satisfaction is shown in Figure 18.1. The various quality-related survey instruments are assessing the perceived quality rather than attempting to determine an objective measure of quality.

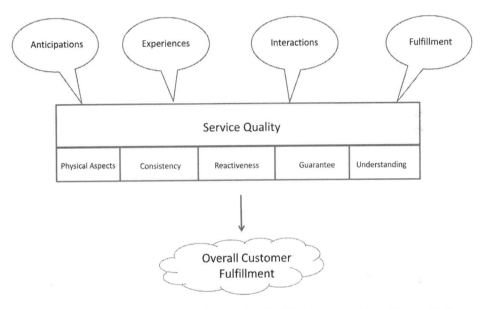

Figure 18.1. Client Satisfaction and Service Quality Model. Adapted from Rowena Cullen. Perspectives on User Satisfaction Surveys. *Library Trends,* 49 (4), Spring 2001, 662–86.

Linking customer satisfaction and service quality in the assessment of the value of libraries is problematic for some. For example, John Budd suggests that such a strategy results in emphasizing the exchange value of libraries and their services to the detriment of relying on use as a value of libraries. In short, Budd argues that it is effective to focus on customer satisfaction as a way for libraries to increase their share of the budget.[16]

SATISFACTION

Satisfaction is a sense of contentment that results from an actual experience in relation to an expected experience. Satisfaction surveys ask the clients to compare the quality and utility of library services they experience with their expectations. If applied in an appropriate manner, a customer satisfaction survey allows the library to learn what matters to customers and apply that information to improve service delivery. Customer satisfaction, by its very nature, is inward and backward looking (a lagging indicator of performance).[17] In order to improve customer satisfaction, the gaps that exist between a customer's expectations and the service actually provided should be reduced over time.

Too often, customer satisfaction is approached as a report card rather than as a source of information about services where improvement and further analysis and thinking are required. George D'Elia and Sandra Walsh suggested that user satisfaction surveys are useful for evaluating the performance of a library but should not be used to compare presumed levels of performance for libraries serving different communities.[18] Illustrating the challenges that will arise from such an effort, Sebastian Mundt reports that a joint user satisfaction survey conducted by 15 German university libraries found the results led to identifying "best practice" activities and revealed structural strengths and weaknesses among the libraries. The libraries decided to keep the results anonymous to avoid the public branding of "winners and losers."[19]

A customer's experience with a library service(s) is dictated by a simple formula:[20]

$$\text{Customer satisfaction} = \text{Performance minus Expectations}$$

Customers are pleased when the perception of performance meets or exceeds their expectations (see Figure 18.2). Libraries must pay attention to both performance and customer expectations. Expectations range on a continuum or hierarchy from worst possible, to low, to minimally acceptable, to high, to ideal.[21] Should a library deliver a service that is below what is expected by the customer, the only result is dissatisfaction. Excitement or delight will only produce very satisfied customers, as the level of service provided is totally unexpected.

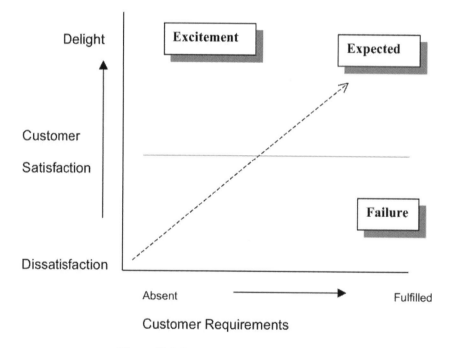

Figure 18.2. Levels of Customer Satisfaction

As noted by Peter Hernon and John Whitman, expectations can be divided into three groups:

- **Core expectations:** Elements of service assumed to be common to all people (courtesy, respect, dignity, and so forth)
- **Learned expectations:** Developed from experience and a widening exposure to the world
- **Anticipated expectations:** An aspect or element of service that is not currently offered[22]

Methods for Determining Satisfaction

It is possible to use either qualitative methods or quantitative techniques to determine the levels of customer satisfaction.

Focus Groups

One popular qualitative method is to use several focus groups, each group representing a different customer segment, and ask them to discuss the library, its services, and the participants' use of the library and their levels of satisfaction.

Mystery Shoppers

The use of a mystery shopper offers the opportunity to discover a new dimension for the assessment of quality and perceived value of services provided by the library. The strength of the mystery shopper approach lies in learning how staff attitudes, attributes, and behaviors influence overall customer satisfaction. The concept of mystery shoppers asks an individual to act as a customer and then to evaluate and report on the total customer experience—from first impressions through to the use of specific resources and services. Of particular note, the consistency, reliability, and accuracy of promised services as well as the responsiveness of staff can be assessed.[23] The "shopper's" experience is documented by completing a survey after each visit.[24] A library can design its own shopping experience questionnaire, and the cost to use a commercial shopping firm is usually modest. Some academic libraries have hired and trained students to act as mystery shoppers.

The University of Wollongong library used mystery shoppers to capture more detailed, qualitative information about its services outside the somewhat artificial focus group setting.[25]

Complaints

Customer complaints are simply a fact of life for any organization. Research conducted by a customer service consulting firm found that the average organization will not hear from 96 percent of unhappy customers (for every complaint, 26 people will not complain). Most importantly, though, 13 percent of those having a problem will relate their experience to 20 or more people.[26]

The important point regarding complaints is what the library does about them. There seem to be two approaches to the "problem" of complaints:

- Complaints indicate a "failure" and are something to be avoided. The emphasis is on taking care of the problem and placating customers. Often the same problems and complaints recur because the library does nothing to correct the underlying root cause. This approach is reflective of an inward-looking, library-centric view of the world.

- Complaints are "welcomed" and the library uses the complaint as an opportunity to learn something from the customer's perspective and to examine the policies and training that led to the problem. This approach is reflective of an outward-looking, customer-centric view of the world. The library keeps a log of all complaints, which are sorted into categories. Although staff may be trained to provide an immediate solution to resolve the customer complaint, the log of complaints is periodically analyzed in an attempt to take corrective actions so that customers do not repeatedly encounter the same problem.

Locally Developed Surveys

Satisfaction surveys can be created and conducted by library staff. A survey can focus on general satisfaction, which is an evaluation of the library as a whole, or on satisfaction with one or more specific library services. The focus of this chapter is on the former; satisfaction with specific library services is addressed in other chapters of this book. A number of library user surveys are available via the Internet.[27]

There are difficulties associated with a satisfaction survey. The challenges are usually technical, such as ensuring that an appropriate sample size is obtained, that the sample is random, and that the questions are appropriately worded. In addition, the numerical values assigned to customer satisfaction ratings are largely misunderstood, misused, and misapplied. The assumed, though incorrect, linear and interval properties of satisfaction ratings can cause serious misunderstandings. And numerical averages, or means, are not a reliable way to summarize or track periodic performance.[28]

However, the chief underlying difficulty connected with any survey is making sure that the right questions are being asked.

A false sense of security. In any survey, the distribution of satisfaction ratings is presumed to be a reflection of "true" satisfaction. Yet, in most library customer satisfaction surveys the distribution of responses is abnormally skewed: that is, the majority of the survey respondents report high levels of satisfaction (see Figures 18.3 and 18.4.[29] When reflecting on the results of a satisfaction survey, libraries must recognize that they are considered a "good thing"—much like apple pie and motherhood.[30] Companies have learned that only when customers rate their buying experience as either completely or extremely satisfied can they count on customers' repeat purchasing behavior.[31] Perhaps frequent library users are those who rate their library experience as "completely or extremely satisfied."

D'Elia and Walsh questioned the value of user satisfaction because the user's expectations of a service are conditioned by what he or she has been used to receiving.[32] In addition, one of the problems with satisfaction surveys is that an individual's expectations may change. An individual may be pleased with a particular product or service (and would rate such a product or service quite high in a satisfaction survey) until he or she discovers an alternative product or service that provides vastly improved levels of satisfaction. Suddenly that person's satisfaction with the old product or service is quite low.[33]

Disconfirmation theory is a popular model for predicting customer satisfaction or dissatisfaction. This model suggests that customers have some standard in their minds to guide their activities—purchase of a product or use of a service. One study found that it is the disconfirmation of user needs and expectations, not user needs or expectations alone, which determines library user satisfaction. This suggests that satisfaction with the information product may be more important for overall satisfaction than is satisfaction with the system or service.[34]

Avoidance of self-absorption. The typical customer satisfaction survey asks, "How are we doing?" To the extent that this perspective fosters an attitude that the library is doing well, it may mean that the library is missing an opportunity to better understand the real needs of its users. As we have seen, the broad customer satisfaction survey responses will typically be very high for the library. But what about the user's satisfaction with particular services and products offered by the library? This requires a probing and inquisitive nature and the ability to move beyond the good feelings that arise when the library is rated highly.

Missed opportunities. Asking users how *they* are doing, perhaps in a series of focus groups, will reveal the motivations and frustrations that they experience in using the library. Perhaps

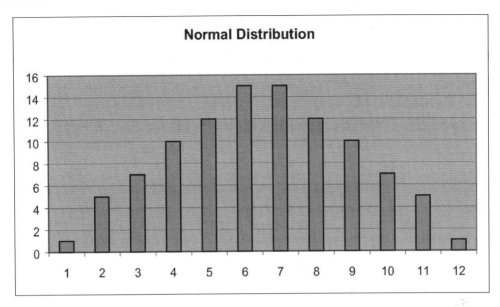

Figure 18.3. Normal Distribution

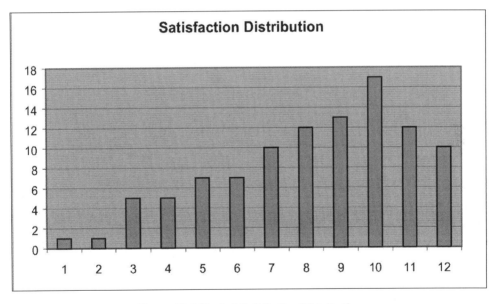

Figure 18.4. Typical Satisfaction Distribution

there are real barriers to access and service that can be eliminated about which the library is unaware or that it never considered from the perspective of the user.

One survey of library users noted that satisfaction levels were quite high (96 percent) when people succeeded in finding what they wanted but dropped almost by half when they failed to find what they wanted.[35] George D'Elia, attempting to ascertain the determinants of user satisfaction in a library setting, found that there were none. He examined user demographics, the various uses of the library by the user, and the user's evaluation of the characteristics of the library used.[36] Although satisfaction is important as a perceived value of library service, it does not demonstrate how the individual or the community has benefited from the services provided by the library.

Failure to understand expectations. Most often customer satisfaction surveys focus on customer *perceptions* of service delivery; they rarely afford the customer a chance to articulate *expectations* of service delivery. Because customers compare their expectations with their experiences, having a good understanding of expectations is important to better serving the needs of library users.

Another problem with satisfaction surveys is that they often fail to probe beneath the surface of responses provided, and in fact respondents may be reluctant to criticize libraries generally. However, one study found that people were willing to suggest or agree with specific criticisms or complaints.

Providing a level of service that users rate as satisfactory may not be enough. In fact, different satisfaction levels may reflect different issues and therefore require different corrective actions. Several research studies have demonstrated that only completely satisfied customers will be loyal.[37]

Perspective. In some cases it is possible to improve the quality, timeliness, and utility of an information service and see a corresponding increase in customer satisfaction surveys over time. Yet, even in the face of objective measures that demonstrate improvements in service levels, satisfaction surveys (a subjective measure) might report the same or only slight increases in customer satisfaction levels. This may be the case because input, process, and output measures typically are collected and reported as administrative performance measures, whereas customers' evaluations are likely to be based on outcomes that are meaningful to them.[38]

Methodology problems. Satisfaction data collected using different means (in-person or telephone surveys versus self-administered survey forms) are not comparable. In some cases, oral data-gathering techniques may increase satisfaction ratings by 10 to 12 percent compared to data gathered using self-administered surveys.[39] Further, how a question is asked appears to affect the level of satisfaction. A positive form of the question ("How satisfied are you?") seems to lead to greater reported levels of satisfaction than a negative form ("Did you experience a problem that led to your being dissatisfied?").

Survey scores don't link to actual performance. Links between the actual performance of a library, as measured by subjective or objective measures, and customer satisfaction survey results have not been established.

Survey fatigue. A great many people are simply turned off by customer satisfaction surveys—too many questions and too many surveys. Their response? Trash them.

How to take corrective action. Once the results of a survey are in, the library management team and the employees of the library simply have no idea how to make improvements so that the library's customer satisfaction scores will go up.

An analysis of customer experiences in using public and academic libraries found that both overall satisfaction and willingness to return to the library were significantly related to the librarian's behavior (smiling and displaying welcoming body language) and the quality of the reference answer.[40] Joan Durrance, who found a strong relationship between overall satisfaction and the friendliness of library staff, noted further support for this finding.[41]

A survey at Valdosta State University library found that students' comments were much more valuable than the objective questions and gave specific insight into each area of customer service.[42]

Single Survey Question

Can a single survey question serve as a predictor of actual customer behavior? In the business world, customer loyalty results in individuals who tend to buy more over time or devote a larger share of their wallets to a company they feel good about. Also, loyal customers talk up a company to their friends, family, and colleagues.

The Net Promoter Score (NPS) is an index, ranging from -100 to 100, that measures the willingness of a customer to recommend an organization's products or services to others. Many consider the NPS a proxy for gauging overall customer satisfaction and customer loyalty. Frederick Reichheld and Bain & Company developed the Net Promoter Score.[43]

A customer is asked one single question:

> One a scale of 0 to 10, how likely are you to recommend this organization's product or service to a friend or colleague?

Respondents can be placed into three categories: detractors, passives, and promoters:

- Detractors, who responded with a score of 6 or less, are not thrilled with the product or service.
- Passives, who gave a score of 7 or 8, are lukewarm about the product or service (neither happy nor dissatisfied).
- Promoters, who responded with a 9 or 10, are enthusiastic about the product or service and are likely to "share their happiness" with others.

The Net Promoter Score is determined by subtracting the percent of customers who are detractors from the percent who are promoters:

$$NPS = \% \ \odot - \% \ \otimes$$

Critics of the NPS suggest that the likelihood-to-recommend question is not a better predictor of growth and customer loyalty,[44] is less accurate than a composite index of satisfaction questions,[45] and has low predictive validity.[46]

Within the library environment, a number of public libraries have used the Net Promoter Score with some success, including the Williamson County Public Library and others.[47]

The Enterprise Rent-a-Car asks its customers a single question when they return a rented car:

> How likely is it that you will recommend Enterprise to a friend or colleague?

The results are tallied for each branch, each day, to develop an Enterprise Service Quality index (ESQi). Employees earn bonuses based on their ESQi ratings. The company found a strong relationship between branches with high ESQi ratings and sustained growth for the branch.[48]

Priority Setting

Asking users about the relevance of existing and possible library services is another form of client satisfaction survey that can have direct and positive impact. The users will benefit because the library will better appreciate what services have the greatest clear-cut impact in the users' personal or professional lives. The library, in turn, can benefit from such a survey in that it will both identify what services are most important and also understand how users rate the library's current performance for each specific service offering.

Using a priority and performance evaluation or PAPE survey, the user is asked to indicate the priority the library should give to each service, as well as how well it is currently doing, using a Likert scale (see Figure 18.5).[49] In addition to asking users to participate in a PAPE survey, asking the library's funding decision makers and library staff to complete the questionnaire also will allow the library to compare and contrast the responses from these three important groups. Any differences that emerge between the groups will require further attention and consideration. One PAPE study found that while there was general congruence between library staff and their customers, there was a tendency for library staff members to underestimate the importance of performing the promised service dependably and accurately.[50]

In your opinion, what priority should the library give each of the following?

	Low Priority <			Very High Priority			Don't Know >	
Availability & accessibility of library staff	1	2	3	4	5	6	7	D
Availability of reference services	1	2	3	4	5	6	7	D
Checking out books	1	2	3	4	5	6	7	D
Able to browse magazines & newspapers	1	2	3	4	5	6	7	D
Interlibrary loan service	1	2	3	4	5	6	7	D
Access to online databases	1	2	3	4	5	6	7	D

And so forth . . .

In your opinion, how well does the library perform in each of the following areas?

	Low Priority <			Very High Priority			Don't Know >	
Availability of reference services	1	2	3	4	5	6	7	D
Checking out books	1	2	3	4	5	6	7	D
Availability & accessibility of library staff	1	2	3	4	5	6	7	D
Access to online databases	1	2	3	4	5	6	7	D
Interlibrary loan service	1	2	3	4	5	6	7	D
Able to browse magazines & newspapers	1	2	3	4	5	6	7	D

And so forth . . .

Figure 18.5. Sample PAPE Questionnaire. Marianne Broadbent and Hans Lofgren. Information Delivery: Identifying Priorities, Performance and Value, in *OPAC and Beyond*. Hilton on the Park, Melbourne, Australia, Victorian Association for Library Automation 6th Biennial Conference and Exhibition, 11–13 November 1991, 185–215; Marianne Broadbent. Demonstrating Information Service Value to Your Organization. *Proceedings of the IOLIM Conference*, 16, 1992, 65–83; Marianne Broadbent and Hans Lofgren. *Priorities, Performance and Benefits: An Exploratory Study of Library and Information Units*. Melbourne, Australia: CIRCIT Ltd. and ACLIS, 1991.

A sample of the results from a PAPE survey is shown in Figure 18.6. In all, 21 library services have been prioritized and evaluated (identified using the letters of the alphabet). Notice that for the first 14 services, the priority assigned by the library's clients exceeded the library's ability to deliver the expected level of service (with three exceptions). And for the services with lower priorities, actual performance exceeded expectations in only two cases. Still, some adjustment of the service levels for these two highly rated services might be advisable.

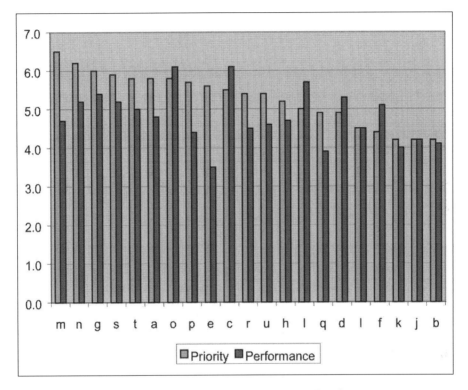

Figure 18.6. Priority and Performance Results

A somewhat similar presentation approach is called a quadrant analysis (see Figure 18.7). Plotting the scores of priority and performance will allow the library to see what services should be focused on in order to make improvements that will have the greatest impact on the library's customers.[51]

Libraries that have used PAPE have found it to be a useful tool that can be administered annually to capture any shifts of the priorities of their users, as well as to track improvements in the services provided.

Budget Allocation

A method of studying user preferences that has been infrequently used in a library setting is to ask a sample of users to allocate hypothetical library budgets over a range of services. The user is given a supplemental budget of $200,000 over the existing budget; a supplemental budget of $100,000 over the existing budget; and a budget with no new funds, forcing the user to make adjustments to the mix of services without increasing the budget. Note that a library will need to adjust the supplemental budget amounts to reflect its own situation. That is, if a library has a budget of $5 million, then the supplemental budget amounts would be higher.

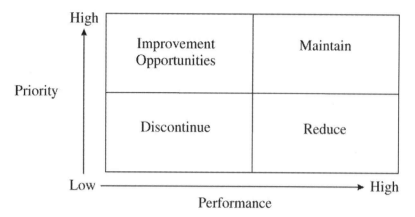

Figure 18.7. Quadrant Analysis Illustration

Jeffrey Raffel and Robert Shishko found that the rank order of services selected varied little at each budget level. Users were principally interested in improving availability of materials and lowering the cost of making photocopies.[52] Slightly different results were obtained when the responses were sorted by type of user.

Combining Cost Per Use and Users' Satisfaction

Aristeidis Meletiou has suggested combining user satisfaction, usage, and cost per use data in an instrument called a Multi-criteria Satisfaction Analysis (MUSA). The end result is a rank order of library services from the customer's perspective which acknowledges that some services are quite expensive to provide.[53]

Standardized Survey

One popular service quality assessment tool developed in the retail industry, called SERVQUAL (Service Quality), has been adapted for libraries.[54] In the SERVQUAL model, quality is defined as "perceived quality" rather than "objective quality" and compares the expectations of customers and performance using five attributes:

- **Tangibles.** Physical appearance of the library, library staff members, equipment, and communication materials (signage, handouts, and so forth).
- **Reliability.** Is the service reliable and consistent? This is the *most* important factor among the five attributes being evaluated by the client.
- **Responsiveness.** How timely is the service? Are staff members willing to provide assistance?
- **Assurance.** Do staff convey competence and confidence? Are they knowledgeable, professional, and courteous?
- **Empathy.** Are staff members cheerful? Do they provide individualized attention to clients?

A shorter, competing survey instrument, called SERVPERF (Service Performance), was developed to better address the issue of predicting overall variance.[55]

The SERVQUAL instrument is based on the Gap Model of Services, developed by a team of marketing researchers.[56] Customer satisfaction constitutes the gap or difference between the service a customer expects to receive and the service received. It is possible to use the data gathered by SERVQUAL to identify five different gaps, as shown in Figure 18.8.[57]

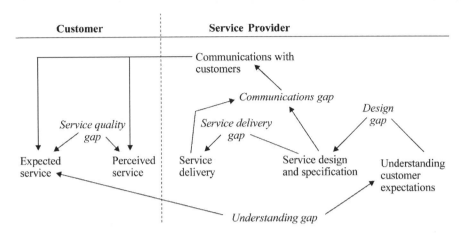

Figure 18.8. Service Quality Gaps. Adapted from Mik Wisniewski and Mike Donnelly. Measuring Service Quality in the Public Sector: The Potential for SERVQUAL. *Total Quality Management,* 7 (4), 1996, 357–65.

The *service quality gap* arises from the difference between the perceived service and the expected service. Other gaps will likely be contributing to the service quality gap.

The *understanding gap* comes about due to the differences between customer service expectations and management's understanding of customer expectations. Such a gap may arise due to a less-than-clear understanding of customer needs or poor communication within the library.

The *design gap* falls between management's understanding of customer expectations and the design and specifications of service quality. The management team provides the training to the library's employees about what constitutes acceptable levels of service. The *delivery gap* will arise due to the gap between the specification of service quality and the actual quality of service delivered.

Finally, the *communications gap* is that between what is actually delivered and what has been promised in terms of external communications, comparison by the customer of experiences with other similar services, and so forth.

There have been several criticisms of the SERVQUAL approach, including fundamental measurement problems, the belief that use of perceptions is better than use of this particular scale, shortcomings in how the scale was developed, the presence of both positive and negative wording of questions, and problems using the scale across organizations.[58] Michael Roszkowski et al. provide a detailed summary of the criticisms leveled at SERVQUAL.[59] These problems arise, in part, because the data are collected after a service encounter, and questions about service expectations may be based on memory or be biased by the services actually received.

Hébert used a version of the SERVQUAL instrument to examine the quality of interlibrary loan services and suggested that there are two service dimensions: technical quality (an objective measure of *what* customers receive) and functional quality (a subjective measure of *how* customers receive a service). Hébert found a mismatch between library measures of interlibrary loan performance (fill rate and turnaround time) and customer perceptions of quality.[60]

Versions of SERVQUAL have been used successfully in a number of library settings.[61] A survey of three academic libraries in the Erie, Pennsylvania, area and an analysis of the data using regression models showed that three factors—assurance, resources, and tangibles (physical condition of the library)—explained about 64 percent of satisfaction. Also, staff responsiveness to customer requests had no effect on user satisfaction. A detailed analysis of the assumptions used to create SERVQUAL has suggested that libraries can enhance the utility of the SERVQUAL survey by:[62]

1. Using separate surveys for different customer segments
2. Using a purposely selected sample rather than attempting to use a random sample
3. Using qualitative methods concurrently with the SERVQUAL survey, focusing particular on unsuccessful or unpleasant library experiences

LibQUAL+

One adaptation of SERVQUAL, which has been named LibQUAL+, includes 22 survey questions providing information about three dimensions: affect of service, information control, and library as place.[63] An additional eight questions deal with general satisfaction and information literacy; there are up to five local library questions, and some demographic questions, and there is an open-ended box for comments from the respondents. Some libraries have found that as many as one-third of all respondents will provide an open-ended comment.

When using LibQUAL+, data can be collected from different groups—undergraduates, postgraduates, academic staff, and library staff. The survey asks the respondent to identify *minimum* levels of service, the *desired* levels of service, and the *actual* level of service. An analysis of the differences and similarities in the ratings between the groups can be revealing and helpful in assessing the quality of library services.

Guidry noted that some LibQUAL+ respondents have difficulty discerning the differences among the three service levels—minimum, desired, and perceived—upon which the gap model is based.[64] Further, Roszkowski et al. analyzed one library's LibQUAL+ data and found that the "perceived ratings" correlated more highly with global measures of library performance than did the "superiority gap" scores (desired minus perceived scores).[65]

An analysis of LibQUAL+ survey responses from several UK university libraries found that undergraduates had lower response rates yet were more likely to use library resources—specifically to obtain texts and readings needed for course assignments. Postgraduates were more likely to use electronic resources, and they were interested in the library's book and journal collections.[66] Further, the analysis of the survey data revealed that samples of less than 400 were used (a sample of 400 would typically be considered the minimum acceptable to provide reasonably accurate results). An analysis at another library found that the "library as place" dimension was an important determinant of perceived service quality and pointed out that cultural biases and experiences will also influence customer satisfaction ratings.[67]

LibQUAL+ does have its critics.[68]

- **Conceptual problems.** The LibQUAL+ instrument is conceptually different from the frameworks suggested by the original service quality research of Parasuraman, Berry, and Zeithaml. Also, the definitions of the tested constructs, expectations, and needs are confusing.

- **Sample problems.** For many campuses, the response rate has been less than 5 percent. Given this low rate, is it possible to use the resulting data with confidence? The LibQUAL+ staff suggests a 10 percent response rate as reasonable, assuming the sample represents the demographic pattern of the total population.
- **Data analysis problems.** Determinants of service quality perception cannot use descriptive statistics.

In another critique of LibQUAL+, William Edgar asks eight questions raising issues that should be seriously considered:[69]

1. How do libraries operate to serve their users?
2. What is the value provided to library users?
3. Are library users able to be self-reliant?
4. Are library users who are satisfied with library service delivery likely to be those who are well served by the service's underlying essence?
5. Are academic library users also its customers?
6. Are library users the only constituency with legitimate claims to library effectiveness?
7. On what basis should obligations of an academic library be distributed?
8. How do users' perceptions of service delivery relate to their perceptions of the service's underlying "essence," its reality?

A further analysis of customer satisfaction suggests that libraries should focus on their resources (the collection and providing access to electronic resources) and staff demeanor or attitude.[70] In Australia, a number of libraries have used a survey developed by the Rodski Research Group that is similar to LibQUAL+.[71]

Customer Satisfaction Domains. University libraries in Sri Lanka developed a service quality survey that includes seven domains—affect of service, building environment, collection and access, furniture and facilities, technology, service delivery and Web services—that ultimately contribute to overall customer satisfaction.[72]

LibSat

An alternative to the LibQUAL+ survey, for both academic and public libraries, is the Lib-Sat survey provided by Counting Opinions. The LibSat survey is available 24/7 for library customers to record their views about the quality of services they receive, so that library staff members can respond in a timely manner to urgent problems that may arise.

LibSat is a continuous, Web-based customer satisfaction survey that is used by a number of public and academic libraries. LibSat, a subscription service provided by Counting Opinions, provides a number of standard reports and allows a customer library to drill into the data to ensure that problems that have been reported by a customer are immediately dealt with.

Local Library Surveys

A library might develop its own version of a customer satisfaction survey. One research project in Japan started first with a series of interviews to determine what services customers valued and then explored, through the use of a survey, how different segments of customers responded to each of these services. The results identified four different customer groups and found that each group valued library services differently.[73]

Walking in the Shoes of the Customer

In addition to conducting surveys of customer satisfaction and quality assessment, a library might perform a "walk-through audit" to assess the total customer experience.[74] Such an audit comprises a number of questions to be answered by a team of library managers that take the managers through the customer's experience stage by stage. The results of the audit can highlight areas in which the library can change or improve the "experience" of going to the library.

DEFINING SERVICE CHARACTERISTICS

The Kano Model. One of the challenges facing any service provider, such as a library, is gaining an understanding of what service characteristics are expected as a matter of course and what characteristics will delight the customer. Dr. Noriaki Kano, a Japanese quality expert, developed the "Kano model" to assist in this process. Kano's model predicts the degree of customer satisfaction, which is dependent on the degree of fulfillment of customer requirements, and recognizes that customers have different types of customer expectations.

The Kano model relates three factors to their degree of implementation (see Figure 18.9). The three factors are basic or expected (must be) factors, normal or fundamental (more is better) factors, and delighter or latent (excitement) factors.

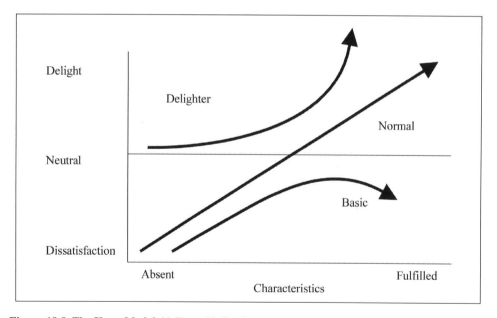

Figure 18.9. The Kano Model. N. Kano, N. Seraku, et al. "Must-Be Quality and Attractive Quality." *The Best on Quality,* 7, 1996, 165.

Basic requirements are those that are so obvious to customers that they do not state them overtly. They are normally so obviously essential to the customer that stating these requirements seems a bit silly. For example, you would expect to hear a dial tone when you pick up a telephone. If you don't, then you are unhappy. Failing to provide basic requirements will result in customer complaints.

Normal requirements are those that a customer is cognizant of and can readily articulate. When these needs are met, customers are satisfied, and when they are not met, dissatisfaction arises. If more than "standard" customer requirements are delivered, then additional perceived benefits are generated.

Delighter requirements or exciting requirements are needs that some or all customers may not be aware of. Thus, these are often referred to as latent requirements. These are out-of-the-ordinary service or product features or characteristics. If a provider understands such a need and fulfills it, the customer is delighted and will have a "wow" reaction. If these needs are not met, there is no customer response because customers are unaware of the need.

A library can analyze an existing or planned service by involving users to discover the types of customer requirements. This is done by using a two-sided question. The same question is asked of a number of users in positive and negative forms. For example:

- How do you feel if our service has feature X?
- How do you feel if our service does not have feature X?
- The respondent is presented with four choices for these two questions:
- I like it.
- It is normally that way [feature is expected].
- I don't care.
- I don't like it.

Features or requirements that have high counts represent one of the three types of customer requirements (see Table 18.3). It should be remembered that over time, some service characteristics would move from delightful to normal and from normal to basic.

Table 18.3. Kano Model Response Table

	Negative Question Answers			
Positive Question	**Like**	**Normal**	**Don't Care**	**Don't Like**
Like		Delightful	Delightful	Normal
Normal				Basic
Don't Care				Basic
Don't Like				

A library can use this methodology to systematically examine all of the characteristics and features of a service in order to discover what characteristics are particularly important to the user. Using a systems analysis approach to break a service down into its component steps and processes can identify these service characteristics. Observing users as they interact with the service can complement this analysis. Questions that should be addressed include the following:[75]

- What do users (customers) find frustrating or confusing about the service?
- Does the user experience any anxiety using the service?
- Are there any time-consuming tasks or wasted time in using the service?

- What things does the user do that are "wrong"?
- What is causing a customer to use the service once and not return?
- Do users experience any other irritants when they use the service?

IMPLEMENTING QUALITY

If a library wants to make improvements in the quality of services that it offers to its customers, then staff will need training and encouragement to embrace change. Improving quality will, almost by definition if not necessity, require changing the way in which the library completes its activities and delivers service.

One project investigated the use of a marketing audit which reviewed the library's mission, vision, goals, and operating environment, combined with an analysis of community demographics and a SWOT (Strengths, Weaknesses, Opportunities, and Threats) analysis. This resulted in a set of recommendations as how to reach various segments of the community with the message that the library had the appropriate set of services to meet the needs of each sement.[76]

It should not be surprising that a library that is attempting to embrace service quality will meet resistance on some level. Peter Hernon et al. articulate 16 reasons why resistance will likely be encountered.[77] Frankie Wilson and Stephen Town suggest that a library will move through several evolutionary stages or levels as it seeks to embrace a culture of continuous improvement. These authors have developed a Quality Maturity Model with five levels so that libraries can recognize these evolutionary stages in their own facilities.[78]

One interesting suggestion is to combine user satisfaction, usage measures, and the costs associated with providing a service. This combination of measures can assist library decision makers in choosing the most appropriate mix of service and improvements according to user needs and the allocated budget.[79]

SUMMARY

This chapter has presented a number of methods that can be used to assess customer satisfaction. Among the more notable conclusions that can drawn from the discussion in this chapter are the following:

- Customer satisfaction surveys are the most popular and frequently used method of assessment.
- Use of two or more methods provides a more complete picture of customer satisfaction.
- User satisfaction is typically contingent upon the context of other variables being considered.
- One of the biggest challenges facing a majority of studies about customer satisfaction is sample selection; specifically, obtaining a representative sample.
- Librarians can make small adjustments in services to increase customer satisfaction.
- Adjusting a service may not lead to improved customer satisfaction ratings.
- Deciding on what expectation to meet has important service delivery implications.
- Focusing on customers requires staff to be trained and to accept that service quality is a worthy goal.
- How the library will assess progress toward the achievement of customer satisfaction goals is an important concern.

Some of the practical suggestions made by a number of librarians to improve customer service and customer satisfaction are:

- **Learn more about your customers**—use surveys and focus groups on a regular basis
- **Create a customer service pledge**—to inform your customers of what they can expect in terms of quality customer service
- **Encourage staff/customer interaction**—have staff move about the library rather than staying behind a service desk
- **Promote community involvement**—Active involvement in organizations outside the library will assist staff in better understanding community needs
- **Re-evaluate customer needs and current services**—explore whether a revised service or introducing a new service will provide more value in the life of your customers

---

Sample Customer Service Pledge

- We will provide courteous, prompt, and accurate service to every customer.
- We will carefully listen and respond to your needs.
- We will provide resources to meet your research needs.
- We will offer opportunities for instruction about our resources and services.
- We will provide an environment conducive to study and research.
- We will not give you the runaround. We will provide the assistance you need, or we will put you in contact with someone who can.

Wright State University Library[80]

- Respecting our customers, partners and peers
- Engaging in direct and prompt communications
- Always smiling and saying thank you.

Guelph Public Library

- We will provide courteous, prompt and accurate service to you.
- We will listen carefully to your needs.
- We will provide the assistance you need or will put you in touch with someone who can.
- We will provide you with information and resources that are based on current and verifiable sources. The information will be clearly communicated and given in a timely manner.
- We will provide an environment that supports our services.
- We will ensure that service to you is our top priority.

Cleveland Heights-University Heights Libraries

NOTES

1. Ellen Altman and Peter Hernon. Service Quality and Customer Satisfaction Do Matter. *American Libraries*, August 1998, 53–54.

2. Phillip Kotler and Alan Andreasen. *Strategic Marketing for Nonprofit Organizations*. Englewood Cliffs, NJ: Prentice-Hall, 1991.

3. Stratton Lloyd. Building Library Success Using the Balanced Scorecard. *Library Quarterly*, 76 (3), July 2006, 352–61.

4. Terry G. Vavra. Improving Your Measurement of Customer Satisfaction: A Guide to Creating, Conducting, Analyzing, and Reporting Customer Satisfaction Measurement Programs. *American Society for Quality,* 1997, 44–60.

5. Richard Orr. Measuring the Goodness of Library Services. *Journal of Documentation*, 29 (3), 1973, 315–52.

6. Carol A. Reeves and David A. Bednar. Defining Quality: Alternatives and Implications. *Academy of Management Review*, 19 (3), 1994, 419–45; Peter Hernon and Danuta A. Nitecki. Service Quality: A Concept Not Fully Explored. *Library Trends*, 49 (4), Spring 2001, 687–708.

7. K. Elliott. A Comparison of Alternative Measures of Service Quality. *Journal of Customer Service in Marketing and Management*, 1 (1), 1995, 35.

8. Jan Carlson. *Moments of Truth*. Cambridge, MA: Balinger, 1987.

9. Peter Hernon and Ellen Altman. *Assessing Service Quality: Satisfying the Expectations of Library Customers.* Chicago: American Library Association, 1998. See also Peter Hernon and Ellen Altman. *Service Quality in Academic Libraries.* Norwood, NJ: Ablex, 1996.

10. Carol H. Fenichel. Intermediary Searchers' Satisfaction with the Results of Their Searches, in A. Benefeld and E. Kazlauskas (Eds.). *Proceedings of the 43rd ASIS Annual Meeting.* New York: Knowledge Industry for ASIS, 1980, 58–63. See also S. E. Hilchey and J. M. Hurych. User Satisfaction or User Acceptance? Statistical Evaluation of an Online Reference Service. *RQ, 24*(4), 1985, 452–59; R. Tagliacozzo. Estimating the Satisfaction of Information Users, *Bulletin of the Medical Library Association*, 65, 1977, 243–49.

11. Rachel Applegate. Models of User Satisfaction: Understanding False Positive, *RQ*, 32(4), 1993, 525–39.

12. Rachel Applegate. User Satisfaction with Information Services: A Test of the Disconfirmation-Satisfaction Model with a Library OPAC. Doctoral dissertation. University of Wisconsin-Madison, 1995.

13. Xi Shi. An Examination of Information User Satisfaction Formation Process. Dissertation Abstracts International. 2000 (UMI No. 3010763); Xi Shi. Satisfaction Formation Processes in Library Users: Understanding Multisource Effects. *The Journal of Academic Librarianship*, 30(2), 2003, 121–31.

14. Rowena Cullen. Perspectives on User Satisfaction Surveys. *Library Trends*, 49 (4), 2001, 662–87.

15. Fei Yu. Users' Emotional and Material Satisfaction at the Micro/Macro Levels in an Academic Library. Doctoral dissertation. University of Pittsburgh, 2006.

16. John M. Budd. A Critique of Customer and Commodity. *College & Research Libraries*, 58, July 1997, 309–20.

17. Jennifer Cram. *Six Impossible Things Before Breakfast: A Multidimensional Approach to Measuring the Value of Libraries.* Keynote address to the 3rd Northumbria International Conference on Performance Measurement in Libraries and Information Services, 27–31 August 1999.

18. George D'Elia and Sandra Walsh. User Satisfaction with Library Service—A Measure of Public Library Performance? *Library Quarterly*, 53 (2), April 1983, 109–33.

19. Sebastian Mundt. Benchmarking Users Satisfaction in Academic Libraries—A Case Study. *Library and Information Research*, 27 (87), Winter 2003, 29–37.

20. Richard L. Lynch and Kelvin F. Cross. *Measure Up! Yardsticks for Continuous Improvement.* London: Basil Blackwell, 1991.

21. Roland T. Rust, Anthony J. Zahorik, and Timothy L. Keiningham. *Return on Quality: Measuring the Financial Impact of Your Company's Quest for Quality.* New York: McGraw-Hill, 1994.

22. Peter Hernon and John R. Whitman. *Delivering Satisfaction and Service Quality.* Chicago: American Library Association, 2001.

23. G. Deane. Bridging the Value Gap: Getting Past Professional Values to Customer Value in the Public Library. *Public Libraries*, 42 (5), 2003, 315–19.

24. Philip Calvert. It's a Mystery: Mystery Shopping in New Zealand's Public Libraries. *Library Review*, 54 (1), 2005, 24–35.

25. Marjie Jantti. Assessing the Service Needs and Expectations of Customers—No Longer a Mystery. Paper presented at the Library Assessment Conference, Charlottesville, Virginia, September 25–27, 2006.

26. Robert G. Sines and Eric A. Duckworth. Customer Service in Higher Education. *Journal of Marketing for Higher Education*, 5, 1994, 1–15.

27. See, for example, the Colorado Library Research Service Web site at https://www.lrs.org/library-user-surveys-on-the-web/.

28. Timothy Keiningham and Terry Vavra. *The Customer Delight Principle: Exceeding Customers' Expectations for Bottom-Line Success*. New York: McGraw-Hill, 2001.

29. Douglas Badenoch, Christine Reid, Paul Burton, Forbes Gibb, and Charles Oppenheim. The Value of Information, in Mary Feeney and Maureen Grieves (Eds.). *The Value and Impact of Information*. London: Bowker Saur, 1994, 9–78.

30. Ruth Applegate. Models of User Satisfaction: Understanding False Positives. *RQ*, 32 (4), 1993, 525–39.

31. Thomas O. Jones and W. Earl Sasser Jr. Why Satisfied Customers Defect. *Harvard Business Review*, 73, November–December 1995, 88–99.

32. George D'Elia and Sandra Walsh. User Satisfaction with Library Service—Measure of Public Library Performance? *Library Quarterly*, 53 (2), 1983, 109–33.

33. John Guaspari. The Hidden Costs of Customer Satisfaction. *Quality Digest*, February 1998, 45–49.

34. Xi Shi, Patricia J. Holahan, and M. Peter Jurkat. Satisfaction Formation Processes in Library Users: Understanding Multisource Effects. *The Journal of Academic Librarianship*, 30 (2), March 2004, 122–31.

35. Barry Totterdell and Jean Bird. *The Effective Library: Report of the Hillingdon Project on Public Library Effectiveness*. London: The Library Association, 1976.

36. George D'Elia. User Satisfaction as a Measure of Public Library Performance, in *Library Effectiveness: A State of the Art. Papers from a 1980 ALA Preconference, June 27 & 28, 1980, New York, NY*. Chicago: American Library Association, 1980, 64–69.

37. Thomas O. Jones and W. Earl Sasser Jr. Why Satisfied Customers Defect. *Harvard Business Review*, 73, November-December 1995, 88–99.

38. Janet M. Kelly and David Swindell. A Multiple-Indicator Approach to Municipal Service Evaluation: Correlating Performance Measurement and Citizen Satisfaction Across Jurisdictions. *Public Administration Review*, 62 (5), September/October 2002, 610–21.

39. Robert A. Peterson and William R. Wilson. Measuring Customer Satisfaction: Fact and Artifact. *Journal of the Academy of Marketing Science*, 20 (1), Winter 1992, 61–71.

40. Patricia Dewdney and Catherine S. Ross. Flying a Light Aircraft: Reference Service Evaluation from a User's Viewpoint. *RQ*, 34, Winter 1994, 217–30.

41. Joan C. Durrance. Reference Success: Does the 55 Percent Rule Tell the Whole Story? *Library Journal*, 114, April 15, 1989, 31–36.

42. Deborah S. Davis and Alan M. Bernstein. From Survey to Service: Using Patron Input to Improve Customer Satisfaction. *Technical Services Quarterly*, 14 (3), 1997, 47–62.

43. Frederick F. Reichheld. The One Number You Need to Grow. *Harvard Business Review*, 81 (12), December 2003, 46–57. See also Frederick F. Reichheld. *The Ultimate Question: Driving Good Profits and True Growth*. Boston: Harvard Business School Press, 2006; Frederick Reichheld and Rob Markey. *The Ultimate Question 2.0: How Net Promoter Companies Thrive in a Customer-Driven World*. Boston: Harvard Business Review Press, 2011.

44. Jenny van Doorn, Peter S. H. Leeflang, and Marleen Tijs. Satisfaction as a Predictor of Future Performance: A Replication. *International Journal of Research in Marketing*, 30 (3), September 2013, 314–18.

45. Birgit Leisen Pollack and Aliosha Alexandrov. Nomological Validity of the Net Promoter Index Question. *Journal of Services Marketing*, 27 (2), 2013, 118–29.

46. Bob Hayes. The True Test of Loyalty. *Quality Progress*, 41 (6), June 2008, 20–26.

47. Joseph R. Matthews. Customer Satisfaction: A New Perspective. *Public Libraries*, 47 (6), November/December 2008, 52-55. See also Nashville Area Chamber of Commerce Research Center. *Economic Impact and Contribution Analysis: Williamson County Public Library*. Nashville, TN: The Research Center, January 2017.

48. Frederick F. Reichheld. The One Number You Need to Grow. *Harvard Business Review*, 81 (12), December 2003, 46–57.

49. Marianne Broadbent and Hans Lofgren. Information Delivery: Identifying Priorities, Performance and Value, in *OPAC and Beyond*. Hilton on the Park, Melbourne, Australia, Victorian Association for Library Automation 6th Biennial Conference and Exhibition, 11–13 November 1991, 185–215; Marianne Broadbent. Demonstrating Information Service Value to Your Organization. *Proceedings of the IOLIM Conference*, 16, 1992, 65–83; Marianne Broadbent and Hans Lofgren. *Priorities, Performance and Benefits: An Exploratory Study of Library and Information Units*. Melbourne, Australia: CIRCIT Ltd. and ACLIS, 1991.

50. Susan Edwards and Mairead Browne. Quality in Information Services: Do Users and Librarians Differ in Their Expectations? *Library & Information Science Research*, 17 (2), 1995, 163–82.

51. Danuta A. Nitecki. Quality Assessment Measures in Libraries. *Advances in Librarianship*, 25, 2001, 133–62.

52. Jeffrey A. Raffel and Robert Shishko. *Systematic Analysis of University Libraries*. Cambridge, MA: MIT Press, 1969.

53. Aristeidis Meletiou. The Evaluation of Library Services Methods: Cost per Use and Users' Satisfaction. *International Journal of Decision Support System Technology*, 2 (2), April-June 2010, 10–23.

54. A. Parasuraman, Valarie A. Zeithaml, and Leonard L. Berry. SERVQUAL: A Multiple-Item Scale for Measuring Consumer Perceptions of Service Quality. *Journal of Retailing*, 64, 1988, 12–37; Valarie A. Zeithaml, A. Parasuraman, and Leonard L. Berry, *Delivering Quality Service: Balancing Customer Perceptions and Expectations*. New York: Free Press, 1990; A. Parasuraman, Valarie A. Zeithaml, and Leonard L. Berry. Reassessment of Expectations as a Comparison Standard in Measuring Service Quality: Implications for Further Research. *Journal of Marketing*, 58 (1), January 1994, 111–24.

55. Joseph J. Cronin and Steven A. Taylor. SERVPERF versus SERVQUAL: Reconciling Performance-Based and Perceptions Minus Expectations of Service Quality. *Journal of Marketing*, 58 (1), January 1994, 125–31.

56. A. Parasuraman, Leonard Berry, and Valarie A. Zeithaml. A Conceptual Model of Service Quality and Its Implications for Future Research. *Journal of Marketing*, 49 (4), 1985, 41–50.

57. Mik Wisniewski and Mike Donnelly. Measuring Service Quality in the Public Sector: The Potential for SERVQUAL. *Total Quality Management*, 7 (4), 1996, 357–65.

58. See, for example, Tom J. Brown, Gilbert A. Churchill Jr., and J. Paul Peter. Improving the Measurement of Service Quality. *Journal of Retailing*, 66 (1), Spring 1993, 127–39; J. Joseph Cronin Jr. and Stephen A. Taylor. Measuring Service Quality: A Re-examination and Extension. *Journal of Marketing*, 56 (3), July 1992, 55–68; James M. Carman. Consumer Perceptions of Service Quality: An Assessment of SERVQUAL Dimensions. *Journal of Retailing*, 66 (1), Spring 1990, 33–55; Emin Babakus and Gregory W. Boller. An Empirical Assessment of the SERVQUAL Scale. *Journal of Business Research*, 24 (3), Winter 1994, 253–68; Syed Saad Andaleeb and Amiya K. Basu. Technical Complexity and Consumer Knowledge as Moderators of Service Quality Evaluation in the Automobile Industry. *Journal of Retailing*, 70 (4), Winter 1994, 367–81.

59. Michael J. Roszkowski, John S. Baky, and David B. Jones. So Which Score on the LibQUAL+Tells Me if Library Users Are Satisfied? *Library & Information Science Research*, 27, 2005, 424–39.

60. Françoise Hébert. Service Quality: An Unobtrusive Investigation of Interlibrary Loan in Large Public Libraries in Canada. *Library & Information Science Research*, 16, 1994, 3–21.

61. Syed S. Andaleeb and Patience L. Simmonds. Explaining User Satisfaction with Academic Libraries. *College & Research Libraries,* 59, March 1998, 156–67; Yoshinori Satoh, Haruki Nagata, Paivi Kytomaki, and Sarah Gerrard. *Performance Measurement and Metrics,* 6 (3), 2005, 183–93; Vicki Coleman, Yi (Daniel) Xiao, Linda Bair, and Bill Chollett. Toward a TQM Paradigm: Using SERVQUAL to Measure Library Service Quality. *College & Research Libraries,* 58, May 1997, 237–51; Susan Edwards and Mairead Browne. Quality in Information Services: Do Users and Librarians Differ in Their Expectations? *Library & Information Science Research,* 17, Spring 1995, 163–82.

62. Liangzhi Yu, Qiulan Hong, Song Gu, and Yazun Wang. An Epistemological Critique of Gap Theory Based Library Assessment: The Case of SERVQUAL. *Journal of Documentation,* 64 (4), 2008, 511–51.

63. Yvonna S. Lincoln. Insights into Library Services and Users from Qualitative Research. *Library & Information Science Research,* 24 (1), 2002, 3–16.

64. Julie Anna Guidry. LibQUAL+™ Spring 2001 Comments: A Qualitative Analysis Using Atlas. ti. *Performance Measurement and Metrics,* 3 (2), 2002, 100–107.

65. Michael J. Roszkowski, John S. Baky, and David B. Jones. So Which Score on the LibQUAL+ Tells Me if Library Users Are Satisfied? *Library & Information Science Research,* 27, 2005, 424–39.

66. Claire Creaser. One Size Does Not Fit All: User Surveys in Academic Libraries. *Performance Measurement and Metrics,* 7 (3), 2006, 153–62.

67. Riadh Ladhari and Miguel Morales. Perceived Service Quality, Perceived Value and Recommendation. *Library Management,* 29 (4/5), 2008, 352–66.

68. Xi Shi and Sarah Levy. A Theory-Guided Approach to Library Services Assessment. *College & Research Libraries,* 66 (3), May 2005, 266–77.

69. William B. Edgar. Questioning LibQUAL+: Expanding Its Assessment of Academic Library Effectiveness. *portal: Libraries and the Academy,* 6 (4), 2006, 445–65.

70. Syed S. Andaleeb and Patience L. Simmonds. Explaining User Satisfaction with Academic Libraries. *College & Research Libraries,* 59, March 1998, 156–67.

71. Nicole Clark and Grace Saw. Reading Rodski: User Surveys Revisited. Paper presented at The 25th IATUL Annual Conference, Krakow, Poland, 2004.

72. Chaminda Jayasundara. Business Domains for Boosting Customer Satisfaction in Academic Libraries. *The Journal of Academic Librarianship,* 41, 2015, 350–57.

73. Haruki Nagata and Lisa Klopfer. Public Library Assessment in Customer Perspective. *Library Management,* 32 (4/5), 2011, 336–45.

74. Jennifer Rowley. Customer Experience of Libraries. *Library Review,* 43 (6), 1994, 7–17.

75. Kurt R. Hofmeister, Christi Walters, and John Gongos. Discovering Customer Wow's. *ASQC 50th Annual Quality Conference Proceedings,* May 13–15 1996. Milwaukee, WI: ASQC, 1996, 759–70.

76. Abigail Leigh Phillips. Systematic Marketing Facilitates Optimal Customer Service: The Marketing Audit of a Rural Public Library System. *Public Library Quarterly,* 33 (3), 2014, 219–35.

77. Peter Hernon, Danuta A. Nitecki, and Ellen Altman. Service Quality and Customer Satisfaction: An Assessment and Future Directions. *The Journal of Academic Librarianship,* 25 (1), January 1999, 9–17.

78. Frankie Wilson and J. Stephen Town. Benchmarking and Library Quality Maturity. *Performance Measurement and Metrics,* 7 (2), 2006, 75–82.

79. Aristeidis Meletiou. The Evaluation of Library Service Methods: Cost per Use and Users' Satisfaction. *International Journal of Decision Support System Technology,* 2 (2), April-June 2010, 10–23.

80. Susan Wehmeyer, Dorothy Auchter, and Arnold Hirshon. Saying What We Will Do, and Doing What We Say: Implementing a Customer Service Plan. *The Journal of Academic Librarianship,* 22 (3), 1996, 173.

19

Evaluation of Social Media

Information technology has become a participatory medium, giving rise to an environment that is constantly being changed and reshaped by the participation itself.

—Douglas Thomas and John Seely Brown[1]

SERVICE DEFINITION

Social media offers a great opportunity for libraries to communicate, interact, and engage with their community. Social media offers the opportunity to expand the definition of "community" beyond simply those who live in a specific city or county (or campus in the case of a academic library) to those interested in the "community" served by the library. This interest might be from those who used to live in a community (or graduated from an academic institution) or from those interested in a library's historical or special collections from around the world or in a particular librarian who is sharing his or her passion with other like-minded individuals around the world. Some libraries use social media to engage users about their favorite author or book series, show off their collections, show what it takes to put together an exhibit or program, and show off their "cool" technologies, as well as highlighting their history.

As has always been the case, a library is a place where ideas, experiences, and opinions can be safely exchanged. And while there will be a continuing role for the professional librarian, the evolution of communication technologies and social media sites offers very real opportunities for everyone to contribute from their own personal perspective.

The obvious challenge is how to measure the value and impact of a library's social media activities; this must obviously go beyond the number of followers or the number of likes.

EVALUATION QUESTIONS

Given that a library can establish a presence on a variety of social media sites, such as Facebook, Twitter, Instagram, Tumblr, Pinterest, YouTube, Flickr, LinkedIn, and Snapchat among others, several questions then arise:

- What is the value of all this posting and interacting for the library?
- What is the value of all this posting and interacting for the customer?
- What performance measures are going to identify value?
- How does the library demonstrate that it is building an engaged online community or network?
- What social media sites do different market segments—teens, young adults, adult women, seniors, and so forth—use most frequently?
- What social media sites should the library be using regularly?

EVALUATION METHODS

Both qualitative and quantitative measures can be employed to assist in the evaluation of social media for a library, as seen in Table 19.1. It is also possible to consider that a user takes direct action when visiting a Web site while, at the same time, leaving footprints and cookie crumbs that can be traced to a specific Web site, as shown in Figure 19.1.

Table 19.1. Social Media Evaluation Methods

	Qualitative	**Quantitative**
Library Perspective	Focus groups Analysis of comments Variety of content posted "Voice" of the posts	Counts of engagement—number of likes and comments Number of click-throughs on links Number of real-time conversations Number of links coming back to the library
Customer Perspective		User surveys

PRIOR EVALUATIONS AND RESEARCH

Keith Quesenberry has categorized social media into nine broad groups:[2]

1. Social Networks—Facebook, LinkedIn, Google+, and . . .
2. Blogs and Forums—Wordpress, Blogger, Tumblr, and . . .
3. Microblogging—Twitter, Pinterest, Vine, Clammr, and . . .
4. Media Sharing—YouTube, Instagram, Snapchat, Flickr, Slideshare, Vimeo, and . . .
5. Geo-location—Foursquare, Swarm, Google My business, Facebook Check-Ins, Nextdoor, and . . .

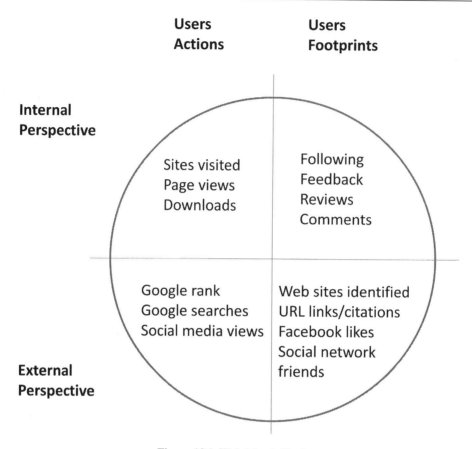

Figure 19.1. Web Metric Tools

6. Ratings and Reviews—Yelp, TripAdvisor, Angie's List, Citisearch, and . . .
7. Social Bookmarking—Reddit, Digg, Buzzfeed, NowThis, and . . .
8. Social Knowledge—Wikipedia, Yahoo! Answers, Quora, Ask.fm, and . . .
9. Podcasts—iTunes, SoundCloud, Stitcher, iHeartRadio, Audible, and . . .

Some libraries have developed goals for social media participation and include such evaluation measures as:

- Visibility of the library in social media searches
- Size and growth of the library's social media community
- Number of comments and likes by community members

Counts

One analysis that evaluated the 125 ARL member library Web sites found that although reference and social networking tools are found in slightly more than half of the Web sites, somewhat fewer are to be found on the home page.[3]

One study examined the frequency with which Twitter was being used in a sample of academic libraries, and found that only 34 percent had an account in 2012—almost certainly this percentage has increased since the time of this study.[4]

Katie Anderson found a growing library presence on Tumblr, a social media site, that is being used by libraries of all types. The University of Iowa Special Collections and University Archives is an excellent example of a Tumblr blog.

Analysis of Comments

A survey of undergraduate and graduate students found that Facebook users had lower GPAs compared to nonusers, and they also spend fewer hours studying than their counterparts[5]; another study found no link between the use of Facebook and academic performance.[6] A further study found that use of social media positively affected collaborative learning among peers and faculty members.[7] An interesting study suggests that academic performance may determine college students' Facebook use, rather than the reverse.[8]

An analysis of 20 U.S. academic library Facebook pages found that 82 percent of users "liked" the library; that 91 percent provided no comments; and that library staff members or employers of the college made most of the posted comments.[9]

Diane Henjyoji[10] used qualitative and quantitative methods to examine the use of social media by four public libraries and found that each library used one tool much more effectively than other social media tools. As a result, she concluded that the libraries were not being strategic in how they approach social media.

A summary of the available literature about the use of Facebook by libraries suggests that it is still being used primarily for promotion and marketing purposes, rather than as a tool to engage more actively with library customers "where they are."[11]

Surveys

Given the potential significant benefits of library engagement in the social media milieu, many if not most libraries have only dipped their toes in the social media pond. Emily Neo and Philip Calvert found in a survey that the adoption of Facebook provides benefits as a marketing and promotional tool, in that it gives the library a better public image. Libraries choosing not to use Facebook were concerned about limited staff resources and poor customer response so far.[12]

A survey of undergraduates and librarians found that the two groups use similar social media platforms for information seeking, as shown in Table 19.2, yet students continue to use superficial clues when evaluating information and its source.[13]

Table 19.2. Social Media Sites Used for Information Seeking

Rank	Students	Librarians
1	Wikis	Wikis
2	Social Q&A sites	Media-sharing services
3	Media-sharing services	Blogs
4	Internet forums	Internet forums
5	Blogs	Microblogs

Kyung-Sun Kima and Sei-Ching Joanna Sin. Use and Evaluation of Information from Social Media in the Academic Context: Analysis of Gap Between Students and Librarians. *The Journal of Academic Librarianship*, 42, 2016, 74–82.

An analysis of a worldwide survey of libraries and archives found that the evaluation of their social media activities was tentative at best; most institutions lack policies and strategies for the preservation and sustainability of their social media activities.[14]

Automated Tools

The challenge for any organization is to confront the reality that a plethora of data exists in the social media world and either try to handle this ocean of data manually or to implement an automated social media analysis tool. Interestingly, a number of free social media monitoring tools are available: Addict-o-matic, Boardreader, HyperAlerts, Klout, Netvibes, Twazzup, and WhosTalkin, among others. One study developed a set of criteria that can be used to evaluate the many commercial social media monitoring products in the marketplace.[15]

Metrics

Avinash Kaushik has suggested that what is important about social media is what happens after you post/tweet/participate/engage. Did you cause people to take action? Did you provoke a response? Are people joining in the conversation? To that end, Kaushik recommends four metrics:[16]

1. **Conversation rate**—the number of conversations per post (its comments on Facebook and LinkedIn; its replies on Twitter).
2. **Amplification rate**—The number of reshares or retweets per post.
3. **Applause rate**—Likes, retweets, and so forth.
4. **Economic value**—cost savings, revenue growth (obviously this is for the for-profit sector). For libraries and other nonprofits, it might be growth of the community engaged with the library.

Kevin Lee suggests the use of Share Score in his Social blog that uses a simple formula:[17]

$$\frac{(\text{Clicks} / \text{Average Clicks})}{3} + \frac{(\text{Shares} / \text{Average Shares})}{3} + \frac{(\text{Replies} / \text{Average Replies})}{3}$$

The value of Share Score is that it is quite easy to customize by adjusting the multiplier (1/3) to something else to reflect what is important for your library.

Darlene Fichter encourages libraries to move beyond counting and work to assess the nature of the sentiment being expressed in social media. Darlene suggests analyzing the length of time a user spends on the library Web site, and asking whether the user rates a page or the contents on it; does the user leave a comment, add a tag, bookmark it, like it, or share with someone else?[18]

Social Network Analysis

It is also possible to use social network analysis software to look at the number and nature of connections between the library and other individuals in a social network environment.[19] To date, such an analysis has not been done in a library setting.

Return on Investment

Nuria Romero suggests that it is possible to calculate a return on investment (ROI) as a tool for demonstrating the value of social media for a library. A comparison can be made of an individual's behavior (amount of borrowing, attendance at programs, and so forth) prior to following a library on social media and after doing so. The use of social media in lieu of traditional marketing avenues, advertising, flyers, and so forth can be compared to low costs of social media.[20]

SUMMARY

The evaluation of social media is most effective when clear goals have been established for the reasons why and how the library will become involved with social media. These social media goals have to be aligned with the goals and objectives of the library itself. It seems clear that any metrics selected by a library should be able to measure four perspectives: exposure, engagement, influence, and results. It is always important to remember, even when considering social media, that we measure to improve.

> *The more we interact with these information spaces,*
> *the more the environment changes,*
> *and the very act of finding information reshapes*
> *not only the context that gives that*
> *information meaning, but also the meaning itself.*
> —Douglas Thomas and John Seely Brown[21]

One study found several challenges that libraries face when they attempt to use social media:[22]

1. Best practices have not been established as to suggested frequency and type of content to post for different types of social media
2. Libraries have a real challenge in establishing a two-way communication channel with their users
3. Opportunities to encourage informal learning are being missed

Gauntner Witte has suggested that a shift is occurring from using social media as a "voice of the institution" to the "voice of the librarian" within the institution.[23]

Some of the important planning and evaluation considerations that should be addressed when deciding how to implement social media in your library and what media to utilize have been summarized in Table 19.3. Each library should revise these suggestions so the resulting plan best meets its specific needs.

David Lee King, someone who is quite knowledgeable about and experienced in using social media, has some great tips for libraries:[24]

- Start with good high-quality content.
- Use the social media channels your users/patrons/students/customers use—be it Facebook, Twitter, Instagram, Snapchat, YouTube, and so forth.
- Get all staff members, especially your creative and energetic staff, to make (find) content. Be helpful, be engaged, and use your sense of humor.
- Tell people where you are in social media—in your newsletter, bookmarks, sign near the exit to the library. Remind folks to Friend your library at the start of programs, meetings, and so forth.
- Measure your success and consider using a dashboard to track your library's level of engagement with its community.

Table 19.3. Social Media Evaluation Plan

Objectives	Measures	Method	Initiatives
Internal			
Create policies & guidelines	Guidelines & policies shared with staff	Hand document to each staff member	
Create interesting content on a regular schedule	Track amount of content posted per platform per month per staff member	Check social media sites	
Increase staff skills & abilities	Provide training classes for each social media site	Training plan	Develop new training programs
		Training records	
Provide tools & technology to interact with social media sites	Number of staff with social media accounts	IT records	
Create a social media culture with multiple voices	Track staff time spent using social media sites	Develop a social media plan	
	Number of social media projects	Update job descriptions	
External			
Promote the brand of the library	Number who receive the library e-newsletter	Web analytics	
Communicate awareness of programs & services	Number of followers of library social media sites	Percent of library patrons who follow library on social media	
Engage with the community	Frequency of interactions	Social media platform	Ongoing evaluation of the reach and effectiveness of the library's social media activities
	Number of forwards	Analytic tools	
Increase interaction	Number of conversations per social media site	Content sentiment analysis	

(continued)

Table 19.3. Social Media Evaluation Plan (*continued*)

Objectives	Measures	Method	Initiatives
Distribute content	Content views on social media sites	Social media platform	
		Analytic tools	
Generate discussion, debate about the (special) collections	Number of comments, replies	Social media platform	
	Frequency of interactions	Analytic tools	
Reach a wider audience	Number of new users outside the community	Social media platform	
		Analytic tools	

When considering the use and evaluation of social media, it is important to keep several things in mind:

- Social media should be integrated with all that your library does so that it simply reflects what you do in the physical library and in the library's virtual arena. The Internet, due to its worldwide reach, is a powerful tool if only libraries will embrace the use of the technology as a means of furthering their mission and vision. Social media is really an extension of what libraries do elsewhere.

- Social media is all about people connecting with other people; it's not about the technology or specific platform used to do so. People interacting with other people use social media platforms as a means of connecting more frequently, more powerfully, and more meaningfully with other like-minded people—wherever they happen to be.

- Social media tools are always changing, but the library brand changes slowly. Change is the only constant when it comes to the digital world; what was hot several years ago is no longer even on the radar. Thus, libraries must be nimble when it comes to choosing social media tools to use and recognize that what is going to be "hot" in a year or two probably does not even exist today.

NOTES

1. Douglas Thomas and John Seely Brown. *A New Culture of Learning—Cultivating the Imagination for a World of Constant Change.* New York: CreateSpace, 2011, 46.

2. Keith Quesenberry. *Social Media Strategy: Marketing and Advertising in the Consumer Revolution.* New York: Rowman & Littlefield, 2015.

3. Leila June Rod-Welch. Incorporation and Visibility of Reference and Social Networking Tools on ARL Member Libraries' Websites. *Reference Services Review*, 40 (1), 2012, 138–71.

4. Darcy Del Bosque, Sam Leif, and Susie Skarl. Libraries Atwitter: Trends in Academic Library Tweeting. *Reference Services Review*, 40 (2), 2012, 199–213.

5. Paul Kirschner and Aryn Karpinski. Facebook and Academic Performance. *Computers in Human Behavior*, 26, 2010, 1237–45.

6. Josh Pasek, Eian More, and Eszter Hargittai. Facebook and Academic Performance: Reconciling Media Sensation with Data. *First Monday*, 15 (5), 2009.

7. Waleed Mugahed Al-Rahmi, Mohd Shahizan Othma, and Mahdi Alhaji Musa. The Improvement of Students' Academic Performance by Using Social Media through Collaborative Learning in Malaysian Higher Education. *Asian Social Science*, 10 (8), 2014, 210–21.

8. Minas Michikyan, Kaveri Subrahmanyam, and Jessica Dennis. Facebook Use and Academic Performance among College Students: A Mixed-Methods Study with a Multi-Ethnic Sample. *Computers in Human Behavior*, 45, 2015, 265–72.

9. Michalis Gerolimos. Academic Libraries on Facebook: An Analysis of Users' Comments. *D-Lib Magazine*, 17 (11/12), November/December 2011.

10. Diane Henjyoji. How "Social" Are New Zealand Public Libraries?: An Evaluation of the Use of Social Media for Relationship Marketing. Thesis submitted to the School of Information Management, Victoria University of Wellington, New Zealand, November 2011.

11. Evgenia Vassilakaki and Emmanouel Garoufallou. The Impact of Facebook on Libraries and Librarians: A Review of the Literature. *Program: Electronic Library and Information Systems*, 48 (3), 2014, 226–45.

12. Emily Neo and Philip Calvert. Facebook and the Diffusion of Innovation in New Zealand Public Libraries. *Journal of Librarianship and Information Science*, 44 (4), 2012, 227–37.

13. Kyung-Sun Kima and Sei-Ching Joanna Sin. Use and Evaluation of Information from Social Media in the Academic Context: Analysis of Gap Between Students and Librarians. *The Journal of Academic Librarianship*, 42, 2016, 74–82.

14. Chern Li Liew, Vanessa King, and Gillian Oliver. Social Media in Archives and Libraries: A Snapshot of Planning, Evaluation, and Preservation Decisions. *Preservation, Digital Technology & Culture*, 44 (1), 2015, 3–11.

15. Ioannis Stavrakantonakis, Andrea-Elena Gagiu, Harriet Kasper, Ioan Toma, and Andreas Thalhammer. An Approach for Evaluation of Social Media Monitoring Tools. In *Proceedings of the Common Value Management Workshop CVM*, co-located with the 9th Extended Semantic Web Conference ESWC2012, Heraklion, Crete, May 28, 2012.

16. Avinash Kaushik. Best Social Media Metrics: Conversation, Amplification, Applause, Economic Value. *Occam's Razor* (blog), October 10, 2011. Available at http://www.kaushik.net/avinash/best-social-media-metrics-conversation-amplification-applause-economic-value/

17. Kevin Lee. 5 Unique Ways to Measure and Evaluate a Social Media Campaign. *Buffer Social* (blog), September 18, 2014. Available at https://blog.bufferapp.com/how-to-evaluate-and-optimize-social-media-content

18. Darlene Fichter. How To—Measure the Results of Your Activity on Social Media Sites. *Marketing Newsletter*, 23 (2), March/April 2009.

19. Kimberly Fredericks and Joanne Carman. *Using Social Network Analysis in Evaluation* (Report to the Robert Wood Johnson Foundation). Princeton, NJ: Robert Wood Johnson Foundation, 2013.

20. Nuria Romero. ROI: Measuring the Social Media Return on Investment in a Library. *The Bottom Line*, 24 (2), 2011, 145–51.

21. Douglas Thomas and John Seely Brown. *A New Culture of Learning—Cultivating the Imagination for a World of Constant Change*. New York: CreateSpace, 2011, 123.

22. Iris Xie and Jennifer Stevenson. Social Media Application in Digital Libraries. *Online Information Review*, 38 (4), 2014, 502–23.

23. Gauntner Witte. Content Generation and Social Network Interaction within Academic Library Facebook Pages. *Journal of Electronic Resources Librarianship*, 26 (2), 2014, 89–100.

24. David Lee King. *Face2Face: Using Facebook, Twitter, and Other Social Media Tools to Create Great Customer Connections*. Medford, NJ: Information Today, 2012.

20

Evaluation of Physical Space

Library after library has sacrificed reader accommodations to the imper-
atives of shelving. The crowding out of readers by reading material is one
of the most common and disturbing ironies in library space planning.

—Scott Bennett[1]

SERVICE DEFINITION

The physical structure of an organization plays a central role in how people interact with one another and determines, in large part, how productive people are as they work and learn. Our ability to work together and learn are deeply influenced by social environments, which are influenced by the physical spaces and boundaries provided by buildings. Clearly, face-to-face communication is heavily influenced by physical proximity, although this is lessening as we increasingly spend more time online and use face-to-face communication tools such as Skype.

The intent of this chapter is to review the available research about the space provided by library buildings.

EVALUATION QUESTIONS

As libraries transition from the totally physically to providing a preponderance of digital services, libraries are being asked to redefine the purpose and uses of their physical spaces. Among the issues and topics that can be examined when evaluating the physical space are:

- What proportion of available space should be devoted to a collection?
- When renovating a library, what activities and functions should the library support?
- How much space should be devoted to individual, small group, and larger group activities and interactions?
- What kinds of furnishings and furniture encourage or discourage group study?

- How much space should be devoted to desktop technology versus providing information technology infrastructure support (allowing people to bring their own devices to the library and having them work using the library's WiFi network)?
- Should space be adjustable by the library's customers?
- How does space affect the ability of a customer to complete a task or activity?

EVALUATION METHODS

A number of qualitative and quantitative methods can be used to evaluate the space in a physical setting, as shown in Table 20.1. Quantitative data provide numerical counts of where students are and what they may be doing at various times of the day. Qualitative data provide the user's perspectives, opinions, and feelings about the spaces within the library building. Compared to other areas of evaluation, there is a dearth of empirical research on the actual use of public libraries as meeting places.

Table 20.1. Space Evaluation Methods

	Qualitative	Quantitative
Library Perspective	Interviews Focus groups Design charrette	Gate counts Floor counts Activity-based costing
Customer Perspective	Ethnographic tools - Keeping a journal - Mapping	Surveys

PRIOR EVALUATIONS AND RESEARCH

Scott Bennett has developed a model of library space using three paradigms as the organizing framework, reflecting the past, present, and future of library design.[2] The paradigms include:

1. *User-centered paradigm*—Library buildings were designed with the needs of a few scholars accessing a relatively small number of printed documents.
2. *Book-centered paradigm*—The explosion of the volume of printed materials led to multi-story library buildings with extensive shelving or stacks.
3. *Learning-centered paradigm*—Library customers use digital materials as they engage in solo and group learning in ways that are social and immersive in nature. Library buildings must support intentional learning where individuals want to take responsibility for learning, especially within a group setting.

The movement to the third paradigm is largely the result of advances in technology that is freeing library spaces from housing collections. In addition, as libraries move to repurpose space, librarians and architects are seeking inspiration from a variety of sources: Apple stores, restaurants, markets, specialist stores, airport lounges, community gathering places, Starbucks, museums, theaters, and other libraries.

Danuta Nitecki[3] identifies the various factors affecting an evaluation of space with relation to the evolving purpose of the library: accumulator, service provider, and collaborative partner in learning and knowledge creation.

Given that users are choosing to come to the library, it is possible to group the activities users engage in into two broad categories: traditional (studying, reading, writing, looking for resources) and social (eating, socializing, utilizing nonlibrary support services).[4] Rudolf Moos and Paul Sommers talk about the importance of congruence and suggest that distance, various amenities, and spatial arrangements have an effect on human behavior.[5]

Within the realm of academic libraries, the repurposed space was often given the name "Information Commons"—a response to user needs for access to technology, group work, social interaction, and knowledge creation. For many libraries, the Information Commons has further evolved into the "Learning Commons" or "Research Commons," where the focus is on the creation of knowledge and self-directed learning.[6] Elizabeth Heitsch and Robert Holley argue that the commons model is being limited by implementation issues such as poor organization, lack of cohesive leadership, and reliance on the mythical "patron" when planning for services.[7]

Helen Shenton reviews various developments, focusing primarily on alternative storage options that are affecting decisions about what materials should be kept on shelves for browsing by customers and what materials should be moved to storage, especially climate-controlled environments.[8]

Interviews

Some libraries have used interviews (both scripted and unscripted) to learn more about how individuals use the physical library. Librarians at the University of New South Wales Library interviewed students and faculty members a year or so after a major refurbishment of the library. The results demonstrated that the library is highly valued, both as a place to interact with a group of people as well as a place to study alone.[9] The students particularly appreciate the flexible and adaptive nature of the learning spaces. The study used student interviews after a renovation project and found that students appreciated the welcoming, flexible spaces with plentiful technology.

In Finland, a combination of interviews and observation was used to develop profiles of people who work in public libraries (not staff members). It was found that people are using libraries as "transitory workspaces" and visit the library at least a couple of hours per week.[10]

Interviews with local government politicians in several cities revealed that the desire to build public library buildings was based on a combination of providing access to resources for everyone and portraying a city as oriented toward knowledge and culture.[11]

Svanhild Aabø, Ragnar Audunson, and Andreas Vårheim used a combination of interviews and observation when they studied visitors in three public libraries in three communities with markedly different demographics (the gentrified community, the multicultural community, and the middle-class community). They found that patrons move between high and low intensive activities within the library (from visit to visit or during the same visit) as they work to complete various tasks.[12] In addition, the study found that many individuals use the library as a place related to education or work, whereas for those in transitory life situations, the library is a place that helps structure everyday life as the workplace does for those who are employed.[13] An analysis of the survey data revealed the library as having six different categories of place:

1. Viewed as a "public square"
2. As a public sphere/space

3. Meeting and interacting with people of different backgrounds
4. Joint activities with friends and colleagues
5. Virtual meetings
6. Location for larger "community" meetings

Visitors to the downtown Seattle Public Library were interviewed; their responses revealed that the building was regarded as serving as a social and meeting place.[14] Another study used interviews to explore public libraries and social capital. The results suggest that frequent library users were more apt to engage in civic activities and that social benefits gained from library use spill over into the community.[15]

Focus Groups

In a focus group, a small group of people is asked about their opinions, beliefs, perceptions, and attitudes about a product or service. A moderator asks the group to discuss a specific and focused set of questions. Focus groups have been used effectively by a number of libraries as they plan new library buildings or remodel existing facilities.

Helen Cartwright used focus groups to gather data for a study that compared bookstores with public libraries. Helen suggested that public libraries were losing young people and middle-income people to the bookstore for a variety of reasons that could be overcome with a refreshing of library buildings and marketing.[16]

Design Charrette

In architectural circles, a *charrette* refers to a collaborative session in which an architect, librarians, and a group of users (sometimes senior stakeholders also participate) work together to create a solution to a design problem. This collaborative design or co-design process offers an important planning approach that has been successfully used by many libraries. Mary Somerville and Lydia Collins[17] provide two case studies that illustrate the power of collaborative design.

Ethnographic Tools

Ethnographic studies rely on directly interaction with users in order to better understand their lives or by observation of their behaviors in and out of the library. Such studies employ tools such as photo surveys, keeping a journal, using a map to track where the users visit within the library or on campus, and observations.

The University of Rochester, in a detailed two-year study, used a variety of ethnographic methods to better understand how the library intersects with students' complicated and busy lives. The focus of all this activity was on the "learner and their needs."[18]

One study gathered data over five months at The Edge—a "bookless" space at the State Library of Queensland in Brisbane, Australia, that is dedicated to coworking, peer collaboration, social learning, and creativity using digital tools. Despite the fact that the physical space was designed with collaboration and open sharing in mind, most users worked as individuals or in pre-organized groups rather than spontaneously interacting with strangers.[19]

Wesleyan University librarians used several ethnographic tools, which proved quite valuable, to assist them in developing a plan for a new study space during a library renovation.[20] Also, Joanna Bryant found that a single individual collecting ethnographic data could yield really useful information.[21]

Librarians at the Illinois State University unleashed a group of students to research the library using ethnographic methods, with very positive results.[22] Librarians at the Brigham Young University used a similar approach with equally positive results.[23]

Gate Counts

Gate counts have been used by libraries to assist in making staffing decisions: what are the busy and slow periods in terms of people actually in the building? These data can be displayed in charts and sorted by time of day and day of week. One interesting study examined more than 100 renovation projects and found that the increase in social spaces (e.g., cafes) did not result in an increase in the gate count.[24] However, for 80 percent of these renovation projects, gate counts went up on average about 37 percent. Factors that led to the greatest increases were the number of data ports, percent of seats with wired network access, and the quality of instruction lab.[25] Visualization tools can also be used to gain a deeper understanding of what the building access data have to say.[26]

Floor Counts

Libraries can observe their customers to determine their numbers, location, and activities they are engaged in. In some cases a library will prepare a form and ask selected staff members at predetermined time intervals to walk around, observe, and gather data unobtrusively. For example, librarians at Rollins College used a combination of preparing an observation chart (and map) so the observers could record the location and activities of each individual in the library at prescribed time periods. This was complemented with several "Design Brainstorm Sessions."[27]

Rachel Applegate observed students in a large academic library and found that gathering data over the course of the semester was important, as there was significant variation in use.[28] Some libraries plot the data to the floor map of the library and color-code the resulting data: blue and green for low-use areas and yellow, orange, and red for high-use areas.

More recently, a staff member can use an app to gather this same data. The resulting data can be used when a library is planning a remodel or repurposing of some of its space. For example, staff at the North Carolina State University Libraries has developed Suma—an open-source, tablet, and Web-based assessment toolkit for collecting observational data about the usage of services and physical spaces (for more information, visit http://go.ncsu.edu/Suma). The app gathers the data and Web-based analysis tools are provided to explore the data.

Several libraries have used photographs of interior space as a means of gathering and then analyzing both the number of people present at a particular time as well as identifying what each individual is doing. A photo study was conducted at the University of Dayton[29] and Georgetown University.[30] Photos are taken at the same spot several times a day over the course of several weeks. The Florida International University Library conducted a seating study using a variety of methods: counting the number of occupied seats at various times of the day and week, asking students to complete a short survey, and collecting observational data (photos of each area within the library). The results revealed higher library use than expected and the data assisted a space redesign project.[31]

Another useful way to gather observation data is to use a video and then to record the movement of individuals within the library from the time they enter until they leave. In some cases, the video camera is set up to gather data for a week or two, and in other cases, a library may use a video from security cameras.

Several libraries have hired the well-known retail-store consulting firm Envirosell to study library services and service attitudes. Among these libraries are the San Jose Public Library, the Hayward Public Library,[32] the Los Angeles County Public Library,[33] and the Metropolitan Library System (located near Chicago). These studies typically measure visitor interactions at touch points within the library, and explore the dynamics of visitor behavior using a combination of interviews, surveys, observation, and video tracking methods. A sample of the resulting map tracking where people move about within a library is shown in Figure 20.1.

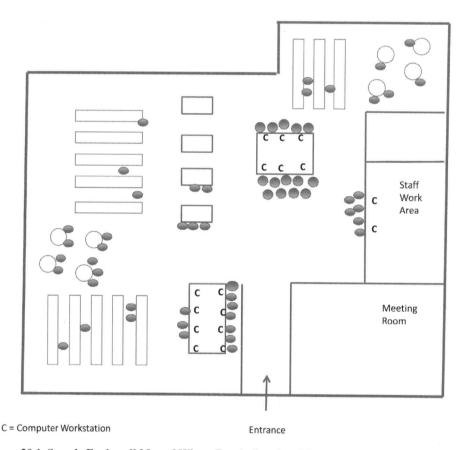

C = Computer Workstation   Entrance

Figure 20.1. Sample Envirosell Map of Where People Stop in a Library. Adapted from Envirosell, *Final Report for the Metropolitan Library System*, April 29, 2008, p. 65.

Four libraries (both public and academic) in the Chicago area were involved with an Envirosell study that analyzed 750 hours of video and interviewed almost 250 people. The study found that 95 percent visited the library monthly and more than half once a week; a majority came to the library alone. Slightly more than half of the visitors spent less than 10 minutes in the library, two-thirds did not know what they wanted before they arrived, and audiovisual materials accounted for a third of items that were borrowed.

Other findings included that a third of the visitors sought assistance at a service desk (two-thirds did not), two-thirds came to the library to read or for conversations, 70 percent of patrons borrowed materials, and age definitely influences behavior (younger visitors used a computer and seldom visited the collection, whereas older patrons visited the collection and seldom used a computer). Also, more than 60 percent received assistance during their visit (compared to 13 percent from prior library studies and 15 percent in retail establishments) and only 12 percent of visitors read library signage.[34]

Among the consistent findings of the Envirosell studies across all of the libraries are the following:

- More than half (60 percent) of customers visit weekly or more frequently.
- The time spent in the library varied by library; the range ran from under 10 minutes to more than 20 minutes.
- The book collection is only of interest to a third of patrons (use increases with age).
- About a third of the customers browse materials (split between books and audiovisuals).
- Only a third of the customers had a specific item in mind.
- More than two-thirds of customers borrow materials.
- Use of computers is more frequent among younger (under age 30) customers.
- About half of the customers interact with staff.
- Signage is invisible to most visitors; only about 10 percent view signs.
- Signage on desk surfaces is typically ignored.
- Lounge areas located near computers and periodicals work well.
- Locating audiovisual materials near the checkout area will increase use.
- Most people (70 percent) don't know what titles they want when they enter.
- More than 90 percent ignore the library catalog.
- Stacks signage is read by about half of the visitors (is this signage the most user friendly?).
- Finding items on the shelf is a problem and generates a need for assistance.
- About a third of patrons wait in line (but not too long—an average of 30 seconds).

Envirosell recommendations included:

- Create a hierarchy of signage.
    - Level 1—Section identification (visible from the main path through the library)
    - Level 2—Theme signage should be visible from outside the section in order to attract patrons
    - Level 3—Call number identification
    - Level 4—Shelf talk; use to direct readers to related titles
- Libraries are too cluttered. Signs should use odd shapes and sizes and create a sense of movement.
- Bring images into the space to create a more visually stimulating environment.
- Offer more ways to pair patrons with materials.
- Expand the audiovisual section.
- Change displays frequently.

Using geographic information system (GIS) software, it is possible to produce a set of maps to display usage data in a map format in order to better convey what the data have to say. This visualization of the data will likely improve the stakeholders' understanding of the ways in which people are using the library.[35]

Observation

Observational studies can be an effective way to gain a better understanding of people's behaviors. One study compared bookstores and libraries and found that more socializing was occurring in the library (e.g., participants at programs and strangers interacting in the stacks).[36] In addition, the library had more varied users in terms of culture, ethnicity, and social standing than did the bookstore.

The University of Huddersfield Library in the United Kingdom conducted a study that employed multiple methods, including observation, to determine the impact of learning spaces on learning behavior and staff and user interactions. Among the results were specific findings that led to the training of student assistants who assisted other students on the floor where help was needed (this initiative led to a significant reduction in the number of IT-related problems).[37]

Researchers used content analysis of the 22 narrated video tours of young adult (YA) public library spaces and found:[38]

- The need for physical comfort is important, as reflected in appealing furniture, attractive lighting, and comfortable furnishings.
- Teens focus on the activities that take place in a given space and appreciate space that can be used for multiple purposes.
- Promoting teen space ownership is important because a variety of activities are typically pursued in a YA space.
- Involving teens in an ongoing discussion of the adequacy of a space is important, as needs (and technology) are constantly changing.

Surveys

A customer survey about space within the library can vary in length and thus collect either a modest amount or a significant amount of data. For example, the librarians at Lehman College, City University of New York, were confronted with the challenge to prepare a plan for the redesign and renovation of the library in a three-month time frame. The librarians used a very brief written survey containing three questions (1 and 2—strongest positive and negative feelings about the library; 3—where the student was at the time of the survey and why he or she was there) distributed to students over a two-week period. The responses were summarized and two categories (replace or improve and add or expand) formed the foundation for the renovation proposal.[39]

Another study illustrated the important of obtaining the views of several different groups of users and then triangulating the responses. Two surveys gathered data on students' perceptions of place and of occupancy rates in the same library. The results identified two contrasting models of place: the traditional model of individual study having immediate access to a collection, and the emerging technology-focused group study model.[40]

Exploring the use of information technology in an academic library, Susan Thompson used both student surveys and observations and found that despite the increasing dependence on handheld electronic devices, students clearly preferred to use desktop computers in the library. In addition, the students who used the computers were more likely to use other library services and physical collections.[41] A study at Andrews University Library used a variety of methods to learn more about how students use space in the library and in other locations on campus. The results suggested that students, regardless of gender and program level, prefer individual student spaces over group study and social spaces.[42]

One study found that students often "mark" their territory with a variety of objects, including backpacks, books, jackets, and laptops, and that this territory is generally respected by others.[43] Howard Silver examined usage of the Bryant University Krupp Library, which has almost 75 percent of public seating allocated to collaborative spaces, and found that 41 percent of nonclassroom study happens in the library.[44] Another study found that students prefer spaces that provide good lighting, comfort, the choice of "quiet" areas, and pleasing aesthetics.[45]

Another study compared "informal learning spaces" on campus and found that although the library's "informal group learning spaces" were preferred by a majority of respondents, there was also demand for silent or quiet spaces for study.[46]

Svanhild Aabø, Ragnar Audunson, and Andreas Vårheim conducted a survey of users of public libraries and found six categories of place:[47]

1. Library as a "square"
2. Meeting diverse people
3. As a public sphere
4. Place for joint activities
5. Metameeting place
6. Place for virtual meetings

A study of a rural public library used multiple methods (surveys, interviews of patrons and staff, and observations) to gather data to determine how newly constructed library facilities were being used by community members. The findings suggest that the libraries serve their communities as informational places, facilitate the generation of social capital, and act as familiarized locales rather than as a "third place."[48]

Christopher Stewart prepared an overview and analysis of new U.S. academic library construction from 2000 to 2014 and found that a majority of the new buildings serve as the main library for the institution (new construction has declined dramatically since 2008), and the majority of new buildings serve undergraduates at public institutions.[49]

Traci Lesneski explores the opportunities, challenges, and implications of reusing "big box" retail stores for library facilities. Lesneski concludes that renovating big box stores is an affordable alternative to building new facilities and that size of the big box store relates to the target library building size for many communities.[50]

SUMMARY

As noted many years ago by Stanley Slote, every library consists of two separate collections: the collection that is used, and the collection that is *not* used. Rick Lugg and Ruth Fischer have noted the historical imperative of shelving encroaching on the user in the academic library:[51]

> More than 40% of the material filling these encroaching shelves [has] never been used, and is unlikely to ever be used. Not only are library users being crowded out by reading material, they are being crowded out by *unwanted* reading material!

By weeding or moving a portion of their collections to storage, libraries have the opportunity to free up a very valuable and expensive resource and repurpose this space for activities and services that will provide real value to the customer.

In addition, Gabriela Sonntag has asserted that it is time to eliminate the reference desk and that the services provided at that location have been largely replaced by course-integrated instruction and research assistance "on-demand."[52] Despite the use of newer information technologies and the emergence of a newer user-centered library-design paradigm, the spatial organizations of most libraries are designed with library materials, the librarian, and library operations in mind far more often than user needs.[53]

When libraries are renovating an existing space or planning for a new facility, it is critical that spaces and services should be:

- **Adaptive**—Both physical and digital spaces must be flexible and adaptive in order to provide space, technology, furnishings, and services that are capable of easy reconfiguration (especially if a group of users wants to make a change on the fly). Students often move chairs, tables, and other furnishings in order to make space "work" for them.

- **Engaging**—Space must be designed to encourage and facilitate social interaction among the users, and between users and library staff members. Libraries should allow food and drink, provide soft furniture, and a high proportion of four- to six-person tables.

- **Transparent**—The activities within the library should be visible and accessible so that all will be encouraged to participate and build a sense of community.

- **Productive**—Increasingly, libraries are "right-sizing" collections in order to provide more space for quiet work, group activities, and socializing, as well as presentations and performances. Space will be provided for interactive learning spaces, multimedia rooms (creating and editing content), sharing, collaborating, and interacting with technology.

- **Responsive**—As technology changes and advances, libraries will be confronted with the need to quickly adapt and adjust. Tools routinely being used today will become passé and users of the library will adopt new tools, often quickly. Libraries must be responsive in order to remain relevant.

- **Sustainable**—Libraries are increasingly being asked to identify their carbon footprint and to build buildings that are "greener," and also to model green and cooperative behaviors in their day-to-day activities.

- **Innovative**—Libraries must strive to provide space and services that go beyond the traditional and provide inspiration and delight. It is also important to recognize that not every experiment will be a success and that we must celebrate (and learn from) failures.

David Lankes argues persuasively that "[t]he mission of librarians is to improve society through facilitating knowledge creation in their communities."[54] If this is the case, libraries must ensure that the spaces they provide within their buildings will encourage the collaboration and engagement of others that Lankes envisions.

NOTES

1. Scott Bennett. *Libraries Designed for Learning.* Washington, DC: Council on Library and Information Resources, 2003.

2. Scott Bennett. Libraries and Learning: A History of Paradigm Change. *portal: Libraries and the Academy,* 9 (2), 2009, 181–97.

3. Danuta Nitecki. Space Assessment as a Venue for Defining the Academic Library. *Library Quarterly*, 81 (1), 2011, 27–59.

4. Sam Demas. From the Ashes of Alexandria: What's Happening in the College Library? in *The Library as Place: Rethinking Roles, Rethinking Space*. Washington DC: Council on Library and Information Resources, 2005, 25–40.

5. Rudolf Moos and Paul Sommers. The Architectural Environment: Physical Space and Building Design, in Rudolf Moos (Ed.). *The Human Context: Environmental Determinants of Behavior*. Malabar, FL: Robert E. Krieger, 1986, 108–40.

6. Robert Seal. Library Spaces in the 21st Century: Meeting the Challenges of User Needs for Information, Technology, and Expertise. *Library Management*, 2015, 36 (8/9), 558–59.

7. Elizabeth Heitsch and Robert Holley. The Information and Learning Commons: Some Reflections. *New Review of Academic Librarianship*, 17, 2011, 64–77.

8. Helen Shenton. Strategic Developments in Collection Storage of Libraries and Archives—Architectural, Technical, Political. *LIBER Quarterly*, 15 (3–4), 2005.

9. Kylie Baylin. Changes in Academic Library Space: A Case Study at the University of New South Wales. *Australian Academic & Research Libraries*, 42 (4), December 2011, 342–59.

10. Mina Di Marino and Kimmo Lapintie. Libraries as Transitory Workspaces and Spatial Incubators. *Library & Information Science Research*, 37, 2015, 118–29.

11. Sunniva Evjen. The Image of an Institution: Politicians and the Urban Library Project. *Library & Information Science Research*, 37, 2015, 28–35.

12. Svanhild Aabø, Ragnar Audunson, and Andreas Vårheim. How Do Public Libraries Function as Meeting Places? *Library & Information Science Research*, 32, 2010, 16–26.

13. Svanhild Aabø and Ragnar Audunson. Use of Library Space and the Library as Place. *Library & Information Science Research*, 34, 2012, 138–49.

14. Karen Fisher, Matthew Saxton, Phillip Edwards, and Jens-Erik Mai. Seattle Public Library as Place: Reconceptualizing Space, Community, and Information at the Central Library. In John Buschman and Gloria Leckie (Eds.), *The Library as Place: History, Community, and Culture*. Westport, CT: Libraries Unlimited, 2007, 135–60.

15. Catherine Johnson and Matthew Griffis. A Place Where Everybody Knows Your Name? Investigating Relationship Between Public Libraries and Social Capital. *Canadian Journal of Information and Library Science*, 33(3/4), 2009, 159–91.

16. Helen Cartwright. Change in Store? An Investigation into the Impact of the Book Superstore Environment on Use, Perceptions and Expectations of the Public Library as a Space, Place and Experience. *Library and Information Research*, 28 (88), Spring 2004, 13–26.

17. Mary Somerville and Lydia Collins. Collaborative Design: A Learner-Centered Library Planning Approach. *The Electronic Library*, 26 (6), 2008, 803–20.

18. Nancy Fried Foster and Susan Gibbons. Library Design and Ethnography, in Nancy Fried Foster and Susan Gibbons (Eds.). *Studying Students: The Undergraduate Research Project at the University of Rochester*. Chicago: Association of College and Research Libraries, 2007, 20–29.

19. Mark Bilandzic and Marcus Foth. Libraries as Coworking Spaces: Understanding User Motivations and Perceived Barriers to Social Learning. *Library Hi Tech*, 31 (2), 2013, 254–73.

20. Kendall Hobbs and Diane Klare. User Driven Design: Using Ethnographic Techniques to Plan Student Study Space. *Technical Services Quarterly*, 27 (4), 2010, 347–63.

21. Joanna Bryant. What Are Students Doing in Our Library? Ethnography as a Method of Exploring Library User Behavior. *Library and Information Research*, 33 (103), 2009, 3–9.

22. Gina Hunter and Dane Ward. Students Research the Library Using Student-Led Ethnographic Research to Examine the Changing Role of Campus Libraries. *College & Research Libraries News*, May 2011, 264–68.

23. Allyson Washburn and Sheila C Bibb. Students Studying Students: An Assessment of Using Undergraduate Student Researchers in an Ethnographic Study of Library Use. *Library and Information Research*, 35 (109), 2011, 55–66.

24. Jeffrey T. Gayton. Academic Libraries: "Social" or "Communal?" The Nature and Future of Academic Libraries. *The Journal of Academic Librarianship*, 34 (1), January 2008, 60–66.

25. Harold B. Shill and Shawn Tonner. Does the Building Still Matter? Usage Patterns in New, Expanded, and Renovated Libraries, 1995-2002. *College & Research Libraries*, 65 (2), March 2004, 123–50.

26. Gary Brewerton and Jason Cooper. Visualising Building Access Data. *Ariadne*, 73, July 2015. Available at http://www.ariadne.ac.uk/issue73/brewerton-cooper

27. Susan Montgomery. Quantitative vs. Qualitative—Do Different Research Methods Give Us Consistent Information about Our Users and Their Library Space Needs? *Library and Information Research*, 35 (111), 2011, 73–86. See also Susan Montgomery. Library Space Assessment: User Learning Behaviors in the Library. *The Journal of Academic Librarianship*, 40, 2014, 70–75.

28. Rachel Applegate. The Library Is for Studying: Student Preferences for Study Space. *The Journal of Academic Librarianship*, 35, (4), July 2009, 341–46.

29. Kathleen M. Webb, Molly A. Schaller, and Sawyer A. Hunley. Measuring Library Space Use and Preferences: Charting a Path Toward Increased Engagement. *portal: Libraries and the Academy*, 8 (4), October 2008, 407–22.

30. Maura Seale. *Beer Cans in the Stacks? Using a Photo Study to Reveal How Library Spaces Are Used*. Presentation at the ACRL Conference, April 10–13, 2013, Indianapolis, IN.

31. Gricel Dominguez. Beyond Gate Counts: Seating Studies and Observations to Assess Library Space Usage. *New Library World*, 117 (5/6), 2016, 321–28.

32. Envirosell. *San Jose Public Libraries and Hayward Public Libraries: Final Report*. New York: Envirosell, February 16, 2007.

33. Envirosell. *Envirosell Presents County of Los Angeles Public Library Study*. New York: Envirosell, February 16, 2007.

34. Envirosell. *Best Practices for the Customer-Focused Library: A Report Prepared for the Metropolitan Library System*. New York: Envirosell, 2008. See also *Envirosell Presents—Why We Borrow: Borrowing Retail Strategies for Library Success*. New York: Envirosell, April 29, 2008.

35. Lauren Mandel. Visualizing the Library as Place. *Performance Measurement and Metrics*, 17 (2), 2016, 165–74.

36. Lynne McKechnie, George Goodall, and Margaret Kipp. Covered Beverages Now Allowed: Public Libraries and Book Superstores. *Canadian Journal of Information & Library Sciences*, 28(3), 2004, 39–51.

37. Bryon Ramsey. Evaluating the Impact of Library Space. *Reference Services Review*, 39 (3), 2011, 451–64.

38. Denise E. Agosto, Jonathan Pacheco Bell, Anthony Bernier, and Meghann Kuhlmann. This Is Our Library, and It's a Pretty Cool Place: A User-Centered Study of Public Library YA Spaces. *Public Library Quarterly*, 34 (1), 2015, 23–43.

39. Jennifer Poggiali and Madeline Cohen. A Low-Hassle, Low-Cost Method to Survey Student Attitudes about Library Space. *Library Leadership & Management*, 28 (3), 2014, 1–7.

40. Michael Khoo, Lilly Rozaklis, Catherine Hall, and Diana Kusunoki. "A Really Nice Spot": Evaluating Place, Space, and Technology in Academic Libraries. *College & Research Libraries*, 77 (1), January 2016, 51–70.

41. Susan Thompson. Student Use of Library Computers: Are Desktop Computers Still Relevant in Today's Libraries? *Information Technology and Libraries*, December 2012, 20–33.

42. Silas M. Oliveira. Space Preference at James White Library: What Students Really Want. *The Journal of Academic Librarianship*, 42, 2016, 355–67.

43. Virginia Young. *Can We Encourage Learning by Shaping Environment? Patterns of Seating Behavior in Undergraduates*. Presentation at the Association of College and Research Libraries Conference, Charlotte, NC, 2003.

44. Howard Silver. *Use of Collaborative Spaces in an Academic Library*. Doctoral dissertation. Simmons College, 2007.

45. Kathleen M. Webb, Molly Schaller, and Sawyer Hunley. Measuring Library Space Use and Preferences: Charting a Path Toward Increased Engagement. *portal: Libraries and the Academy*, 8 (4), 2008, 407–22.

46. Matthew Cunningham and Graham Walton. Informal Learning Spaces (ILS) in University Libraries and Their Campuses: A Loughborough University Case Study. *New Library World*, 117 (1/2), 2016, 49–62.

47. Svanhild Aabø, Ragnar Audunson, and Andreas Vårheim. How Do Public Libraries Function as Meeting Places? *Library & Information Science Research*, 32, 2010, 16–26.

48. Linda Most. The Rural Public Library as Place: A Theoretical Analysis. *Advances in Library Administration and Organization*, 30, 2011, 51–149.

49. Christopher Stewart. *Building with Purpose: A Quantitative Overview and Analysis of New U.S. Academic Library Construction, 2000-2014* (ACRL Occasional Report). Chicago: Association of College & Research Libraries, 2015.

50. Traci Lesneski. Big Box Libraries: Beyond Restocking the Shelves with Books. *New Library World*, 112 (9/10), 2011, 395–405.

51. Rick Lugg and Ruth Fischer. Future Tense—Doing What's Obvious: Library Space and the Fat Smoker. *Against the Grain*, 21 (1), 2009, Article 47.

52. Gabriela Sonntag and Felicia Palsson. No Longer the Sacred Cow—No Longer a Desk: Transforming Reference Service to Meet 21st Century User Needs. *Library Philosophy and Practice*, 111, 2007, 1–16.

53. Matthew Griffiths. Bricks, Mortar, and Control: A Multicase Examination of the Public Library as Organizational Space. *Advances in Library Administration and Organization*, 32, 2014, 1–106.

54. David R. Lankes. *The Atlas of New Librarianship*. Cambridge, MA: The MIT Press, 2011, 15.

21

Evaluation of the User Experience

Relying only on our assumptions and instincts is a very dangerous thing to do.

—Andy Priestner[1]

SERVICE DEFINITION

User experiences are the feelings that result when someone is using a product or service or is interacting with others in a physical space. *User experience,* often abbreviated as UX, is the result of many factors or potential places of interaction, usually referred to as *touchpoints,* which have an overall impact when using a product or service. Note that the product or service may be in the physical or digital world.

It is also important to note that a user experience is intentional and that a library and its collections and services (both in the physical and digital arenas) have numerous touchpoints that will engender positive, negative, or indifference feelings.

EVALUATION QUESTIONS

There is no shortage of possible user experience evaluation questions that might be explored. Some of the most pertinent include:

- Is the library's Web site due for a significant upgrade in order to improve the user experience?
- What are the first impressions when driving to, parking, and entering the library?
- Are the library brand and logo recognized in the community?
- Is it possible to find a specific collection (e.g., audio books) or service within the library by using signage and other clues, without asking for directions?

- Does the library space meet a user's needs for individual study or group interactions and collaboration?
- What frustrations does a user experience when attending a library program?

Obviously, there are many, many more questions that could be added to this list.

EVALUATION METHODS

Both qualitative and quantitative research methods have been used to identify the present experience and improve on the user experience, as shown in Table 21.1.

Table 21.1. Comparison of Qualitative and Quantitative Methods

	Qualitative	Quantitative
Library Perspective	Observation	Usability testing Floor counts
Customer Perspective	Interviews Focus groups Journey mapping Secret shopper	User surveys Ethnographic methods

PRIOR EVALUATIONS AND RESEARCH

Aaron Schmidt and Amanda Etches, in their wonderful UX book *Useful, Usable, Desirable,* suggest that there are eight important user experience design principles:[2]

1. **You are not your user**—the most important perspective is how our actual users will likely interact with library spaces and services. The more we can learn about our users, the better.

2. **The user is not broken**—If something is so complicated in a library that staff think or say "We just need to teach them how to . . . ," then from the user experience perspective, the library has it wrong. The service or signage or . . . is broken, not the user.

3. **A good user experience requires research**—Learning more about library users' lives, hopes, and preferences can help transform problem (from the user's perspective) services into services that deliver real value.

4. **Building a good user experience requires empathy**—Empathy is all about understanding someone else's experience and is partially gained by "walking in the shoes of the user."

5. **A good user experience must be easy before it can be interesting**—Focusing on functionality (making something easy to do, whether it is a digital or physical experience) must be accomplished before focusing on the "sizzle."

6. **Good user experience is universal**—Ensuring that a design works as well for those people with disabilities as for those without disabilities is an important (and often neglected) principle.

7. **Good user experience design is intentional**—Over the course of time, a majority of libraries will see their physical space evolve as furniture and furnishing are added/removed/moved. Unfortunately, what once worked well will not work so well as changes are made. Ask yourself, "What would work best for our users?"

8. **Good user experience is holistic**—A good user experience consists of ensuring that in addition to really good customer service, everything else in the building (or on the Web site) works so that individuals feel that they can accomplish their goals (whatever those may be) when they visit the library.

The better designed libraries are those that are easy to use, intuitive, convenient, and allow users to complete their desired tasks (in a self-service mode if that is what they prefer) or to receive high-quality customer service when they interact with staff members.

There is no shortage of tools and methods that can be employed to evaluate and improve a user experience at your library. Some of the more frequently used methods are identified and discussed in this chapter; however, Courtney Greene McDonald has identified some 30 strategies (techniques) that can be used for transforming library services.[3]

Observation

One of the easiest methods of gaining an understanding of the challenges a user faces when attempting to use a collection, space, or service is simply to observe a group of individuals over a period of time and make detailed notes. Note specifically issues of signage, observing body language that might convey frustrations, the need to seek out staff to answer a question or obtain directions, and so forth. It might be necessary to check with staff to learn about the question or need; this will make your observations even more meaningful.

The University of South Florida library employed direct observation to identify areas of low use, and then used the information gained—with great success—to remodel several areas that were not along natural pathways into well-designed, desirable areas that students will want to visit.[4]

Interviews and Focus Groups

A focus group involves an open, in-depth discussion of 6 to 10 participants led by a trained moderator to explore a predefined topic. Typically the discussion is taped and then transcribed for further analysis. Krueger has suggested that it is possible to categorize a discussion using seven attributes: words; context; internal consistency; frequency and extensiveness of comments; specificity of comments; intensity of comments; and big ideas.[5]

A focus group study at the University of Tartu, Estonia, focused on the quality of online library services. The researchers found that although aspects such as speed, reliability, and user-friendliness were important, criteria such as dialogue and participation were equally important, revealing that two-way communication is, at times, crucial.[6]

Secret Shopper

Secret shopping, sometimes called mystery shopping, is an unobtrusive evaluation method used to assess a variety of services, most often customer service interactions. Libraries have used students, librarians from other libraries, and volunteers from the public, as well as hiring experienced shoppers from a commercial "shopping" firm. One real advantage of the shopper approach is that the library can construct a script that directs the shopper as what specifically is to be "shopped." Candice Benjes-Small and Elizabeth Kocevar-Weidinger suggest that there are six secrets to successful shopping, the most important of which is to communicate frequently with staff as to the purpose and timing of the "shop."[7]

Secret shopping has been used by a number of libraries to evaluate various aspects of public services, including Central Missouri State University library (shop the reference service area),[8] Villanova University library (shop a co-located service desk),[9] Florida International University library (shop student employee training),[10] Illinois Wesleyan University library (shop the user experience received from student employees),[11] and the University of North Carolina at Greensboro libraries (shop the customer service experience).[12]

Public libraries have also employed the secret shopper method for assessing services, including several New Zealand public libraries (shop customer service),[13] several public libraries in Michigan[14] and all of the branches of the Arapahoe Library District in Colorado[15] (shop the user experience), Monroe County Public Library in Indiana (shop the reference experience),[16] and all branches of the Stanislaus County, California, Free Library (shop the total user experience).[17]

Journey Mapping

One really valuable method of evaluating library services and access is *journey mapping*, often called *service blueprinting*. This technique identifies each and every touchpoint as a user completes a specific task in the physical library or on the Web site. The end result is a visual representation of a library transaction, from the point the user initiates the process until its final resolution.

Developed by Lynn Shostack in 1984, the components of a service blueprint include:[18]

- **Customer actions**—The chronological steps a customer takes (before, during, and after) the service delivery process
- **On-stage actions**—Face-to-face interactions between staff and customers
- **Backstage actions**—The supporting activities of employees the customer does not see
- **Support processes**—All of the actions and activities that may or may not be visible to the customer that must be performed in order to deliver a service
- **Physical evidence**—All of the touchpoints a customer interacts with while visiting the library (may include signage, wayfinding, displays, shelving of collections, program attendance, and so forth).

After documenting the process using a service blueprint (or journey map), the "fail points" are identified. A fail point is a process or interaction that is time-consuming, inconsistent, or of low quality.

Several scenarios can be developed and a journey map can be produced for each scenario, as shown in Figure 21.1.

Bulu Maharana and Krushna Chandra Panda discuss the use of service blueprinting in the context of an academic library setting.[19] Judith Andrews and Eleanor Eade used journey mapping to track students as they engaged in a variety of tasks, and then identified service improvements and the likely staffing implications if the improvements were made.[20] Sue Sampson, Kim Granath, and Adrienne Alger used journey mapping to consider physical spaces, service points, policies and customer service, signage and wayfinding, online presence, and the overall experience of using the library from the customer's perspective.[21]

	Entice →	Enter →	Engage →	Exit →	Extend
Thinking	I need to ... I want to ... How can I ... Let's meet ... Let's see what ...	Where can I find ... How can I ... I want to ... I'm looking for ...	I need to ... How can I ... I want to ... I'm looking for ... Need more ...	I accomplished ... Good to have met ... Great I finished ...	I need to follow up ... Add to my "To do's" ... Schedule meetings ...
Activities	Search for ... Interact with ... Find ... Locate ... Discuss with ...	Reading signs ... Asking for ... Finding ... Using ... Attending ...	Just found ... Met ... Interact with ... Used ... Discuss ...	I learned ... I networked ... I found a new perspective ...	Write ... Print ... Email ... Read ... Analyze ...
Feeling	Curious Anxious Determined ...	Curious Anxious Determined Frustrated ...	Focused Exciting Curious Productive ...	Happy Satisfied Productive Tired ...	Satisfied Motivated Engaged ...

Figure 21.1. A Journey Map for a Visit to the Library

Steven Bell has long articulated the value of thoughtful and intentional service, and specifically the value of journey mapping, in his blog (Designing Better Libraries), his writings,[22] and his presentations.[23]

Cassi Pretlow and Karen Sobel also found journey mapping to be quite valuable in identifying areas of the user experience.[24] Librarians at the University of Montana developed scenarios for six areas—physical space; service points; policies and customer service; signage and wayfinding; online presence; and using the library—so they could then use the journey mapping method. After gathering the data and producing a journey map for each scenario, the librarians discovered that many of the stress points or points of failure could be improved with minor adjustments and quick action.[25]

A variation in the journey mapping method is to "walk a mile in the user's shoes." One or more staff members follow the process a user would follow to complete a task and map the results using a journey map, as was done by several librarians at Reed College in Oregon.[26] One of the potential pitfalls with this approach is that staff may not "see" things the same way users will, due to their familiarity with the library and the location of various collections and service points.

Floor Counts

As Linn has noted, seating sweeps provide an excellent, low-cost method of gathering data about user behaviors and identifying areas of need while avoiding the bias of subjective self-reporting.[27] Seating sweeps is just one tool among many that can be used to help answer the question: "What uses do individuals actually make of public space in libraries?" The results can identify areas of high and low use (and how those vary at different points during the day), usage patterns by time of day, and user behaviors.[28]

A study at the Florida International University library used seating sweeps to record the number of individuals seated at several points in time over the course of the data collection period, as well as noting what they were doing. The results of this study, along with a student survey, spurred the addition of more flexible seating, whiteboards, increased electrical power connections, and more seating for collaborative activities.[29]

Envirosell, the retail consulting firm, has conducted several studies in public and academic libraries. The firm installs cameras and tracks the movement of each individual as that person enters, moves about, and then leaves the library. The results of several hundred hours of video are plotted on a floor plan map of the library to show concentration points or "hot spots." In addition, a significant number of people are interviewed as they are leaving the library. The typical report demonstrates that a majority of people do not come to the library with a specific title in mind; more than one-third of materials that are borrowed are audiovisual materials; with the exception of moms with young children, most people arrive at the library alone; and users typically spend about 10 minutes at the library. Other interesting findings include the fact that most signage is not seen by the customer, and given that a majority of people are interested in browsing the collection, libraries should be moving to merchandising of the collections.[30]

Usability Testing

Librarians at the Edith Cowan University Library used a small group of students to test the library's use of a single search box which was introduced as a part of the Web-scale discovery service being implemented in the library (Summon). The results revealed the students' overwhelming preference for a single search box; users found both the materials in the library as well as the journal articles accessible via the library to be of real value.[31]

A usability study at the New York City College of Technology was quite helpful in improving the library Web site and in particular in creating a more user-centric home page.[32] In addition to using usability testing, the authors recommended using a small group of experts who would evaluate a library's Web site using Jakob Nielsen's 10 heuristics.[33] Interesting, the same techniques can be used to assess and improve on an app provided by a library[34] or to ensure that the library's Web site is accessible using a handheld mobile device.[35]

Fagan et al. employed usability testing to measure time, accuracy, and completion rates for nine tasks and found that users had difficult following directions (did not see and read them), skipped tasks, took time-outs to perform other tasks, and did not really focus while they attempted to complete each task.[36] Another popular usability study method is asking users to "think aloud" while recording their activities and words, as was done at the University of Houston Libraries when they were testing their new discovery system.[37]

One study used a survey to ask users about their experiences and frustrations in their interactions with a digital library using a Web browser on a desktop computer, compared to the same resource using a smartphone. The results suggest that users had more challenges using their smartphones when navigating the digital library and concluded that every digital library's Web site must be optimized for handheld devices.[38]

The roles and responsibilities of a team should be openly discussed so that everyone has a clear sense of the goals and objectives of the team and how each member can make a positive contribution.[39] In an effort to improve systems in libraries, Suzanne Chapman and her colleagues have suggested focusing on the development of systems using user experiences principles from the get-go, analyzing available quantitative data, making the evaluation of the user interface a process of continuous improvement, and working more closely with vendors because librarians are actually representing their many users.[40] Highlighting the importance of iterative usability testing, Jeffrey Gallant and Laura Wright showed how even a small library could collect really useful qualitative data that will improve a library's Web site.[41]

Hierarchical Task Analysis

Hierarchical task analysis uses knowledgeable experts to analyze a user interface (and/or system) from a task-oriented perspective: what job is the user attempting to complete? The experts were asked to perform three tasks: 1) find an article, 2) find a book, and 3) find an e-book. Jakob Nielsen's "Goal Composition" heuristics were used as a framework to assess the user experience of using a discovery service.[42] Whereas usability tests are very effective for evaluating specific features of a user interface by observing users as they interact with a system, hierarchical task analysis leads to more systematized results and is good at identifying gaps that may exist between mental models and system design. One study conducted at the Purdue University library found that it was difficult to identify journal titles and revealed that there was no way to limit search results to view e-books only.[43]

Web Analytics

Web analytics collect, measure, analyze, and report Internet data for the purposes of understanding Web site usage. Although a number of commercial Web analytic tools are available, perhaps the most widely known and used tool is *Google Analytics*. Among other data, *Google Analytics* reports such data as Number of Visits, Number of Unique Visitors, Number of Pageviews, Number of Pages Visited/Visit, Average Time of Visit Duration, Number of New Visits, and Bounce Rate. It is important to recognize that the data must be carefully examined and looked at with the needs of the library clearly in mind. For example, a public library might be more concerned about tracking the individuals who live nearby or visit specific pages when a specific program or event is being promoted.

Although *Google Analytics* is free and is easy to install and use, in reality it comes with real costs attached. Google gathers data from installation of the analytical tool on a regular basis, and thus the privacy of the library's patrons is indirectly compromised.

In addition, there are external sites that provide metrics about all Web traffic, so that it is possible to gather ranking information regarding a specific Web site. Among the more popular external ranking services are Alexa, Compete, and Quantcast.

Transaction Log Analysis

It is also possible to analyze the log of a Web server in order to learn more about who comes to visit the site, what pages they visit, how long they stay, where they leave from, and so forth. A number of commercial products are available to provide this level of analysis.

User Surveys

Students at Loughborough University and York University in England participated in a brief survey to better understand how they were using the space and services in the library on each campus. The results suggest that there is a need to provide a range of study spaces to cater to a range of needs, as well as to provide the resources and services that are an essential component of the student study experience.[44]

One study at the University of Oklahoma used three perspectives to examine the library's Web site: 1) the user's perspective, 2) the Web site design perspective, and 3) the library service quality perspective. The findings revealed that different customer segments engaged with differing library services and resources depending upon their academic needs. One finding across all groups was the users' general perceptions of the complexities associated with use of the Web site design.[45]

A survey of users from all academic libraries across Greece found that libraries are considered to be spaces that facilitate studying and reading as well as working with others.[46]

Ethnographic Methods

At the University of Rochester, library anthropologist Foster[47] and her colleagues used a number of ethnographic methods, including diaries, photos of the challenges faced by students when using the library, and asking students to provide feedback and design assistance, when the library was planning the renovation of library facilities. Although the goal of the Rochester research project was to improve the library's understanding of how students navigate the library environment and write research papers, the researchers did learn a fair amount about how students are using the existing space.

Previously, the MAYA Design Group used a variety of ethnographic methods to better understand the user experience at the main Carnegie Library of Pittsburgh. After gathering a plethora of data, the MAYA team, using information architecture principles, organized the data into three areas: space, people, and categorizations (e.g., Dewey).[48] The resulting presentations revealed a number of customer touchpoint failures, as shown in Figure 21.2. These "failure points" were the result of a patron not understanding library jargon, having difficulties in using a library-provided tool, encountering organization complexity (failing to find or understand signage), and so forth. After remodeling the physical library and the library's Web site, the central Pittsburgh library has become a destination—as evidenced by an increase in circulation, gate count, and attendance at programs.[49]

The Ethnographic Research in Illinois Academic Libraries (ERIAL) project, completed in 2009, provided some interesting results for the participating libraries, and also regarding the skills that were gained by the librarians who were involved in the project.[50]

The Georgia Tech library has found collaborating with various units on campus to be an effective way to engage both faculty and students so that the library can deliver a better overall library experience.[51]

Helpful UX Resources

Andy Priestner and Matt Borg (Eds.). *User Experience in Libraries: Applying Ethnography and Human-Centered Design*. London: Routledge, 2016. Contains 17 informative chapters that explore the topics of human-centered design and ethnography.

Designing Better Libraries blog with multiple contributors—http://dbl.lishost.org

Influx: Library User Experience provides a range of resources—http://weareinflux.com/ux-resources-inspiration/

Matthew Reidsma's blog provides a thoughtful and insightful perspective—https://matthew.reidsrow.com/

Aaron Schmidt's monthly "The User Experience" column in *Library Journal*

WeaveUX: The Journal of Library User Experience (peer-reviewed and open-source) is a great resource—weaveux.org

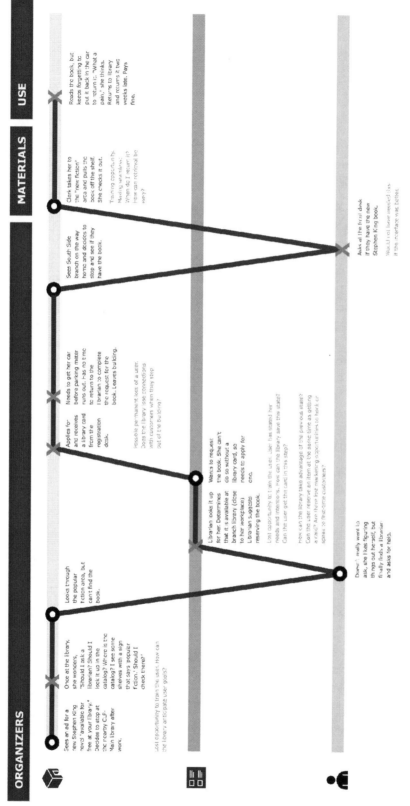

Figure 21.2. Customer Touchpoints in a Library Setting. Courtesy of MAYA Design.

SUMMARY

The whole notion of using the lens of the user experience (UX) is very simple—putting the user first. Sounds obvious, yet too often librarians make decisions without fully considering the impact of the decision on the user's experience. Because everything contributes to the overall user experience—whether it be a visit to the physical library or a visit to the library's Web site—everything can be evaluated using the UX perspective. Topics such as library policies, procedures, fines and fees, staff training, layout and signage of the library, how the collection is organized and presented, what portions of the collection are merchandized, and on and on all contribute to the total user experience. The really good news is that in most cases, a lot can be done to improve the user experience without spending a great deal of money.

NOTES

1. Andy Priestner. *User Experience in Libraries: Applying Ethnography and Human Centered Design.* London: Routledge, 2016.

2. Aaron Schmidt and Amanda Etches. *Useful, Usable, Desirable: Applying User Experience to Your Library.* Chicago: ALA Editions, 2014.

3. Courtney Greene McDonald. *Putting the User First: 30 Strategies for Transforming Library Service.* Chicago: Association of College and Research Libraries, 2014.

4. Kaya van Beynen, Patricia Pettijohn, and Marcy Carrel. Using Pedestrian Choice Research to Facilitate Resource Engagement in a Midsized Academic Library. *The Journal of Academic Librarianship*, 36 (5), 2010, 412–19.

5. Richard Krueger. *Focus Groups: A Practical Guide for Applied Research.* Thousand Oaks, CA: Sage Publications, 1994.

6. Olga Einasto. Investigating E-Service Quality Criteria for University Library: A Focus Group Study. *New Library World*, 115 (1/2), 2014, 4–14.

7. Candice Benjes-Small and Elizabeth Kocevar-Weidinger. Secrets to Successful Mystery Shopping. *College & Research Libraries News*, May 2011, 274–87.

8. M. Tygett, V. Lawson, and K. Weessies. Using Undergraduate Marketing Students in an Unobtrusive Reference Evaluation. *Reference Quarterly*, 36 (2), 1996, 270–76.

9. M. Stein, T. Edge, J. Kelley, D. Hewlett, and J. Trainer. Using Continuous Quality Improvement Methods to Evaluate Library Service Points. *Reference & User Services Quarterly*, 48 (1), 2008, 78–85.

10. Sarah Hammill and Eduardo Fojo. Using Secret Shopping to Assess Student Assistant Training. *Reference Services Review*, 41 (3), 2013, 514–31.

11. Crystal M. Boyce. Secret Shopping as User Experience Assessment Tool. *Public Services Quarterly*, 11 (4), 2015, 237–53.

12. Kathryn Crowe and Agnes Kathy Bradshaw. Taking a Page from Retail: Secret Shopping for Academic Libraries. *Evidence Based Library and Information Practice*, 11 (1), 2016. Available at https://journals.library.ualberta.ca/eblip/index.php/EBLIP/article/view/25311/20183

13. Phillip Calvert. It's a Mystery: Mystery Shopping in New Zealand's Public Libraries. *Library Review*, 54 (1), 2005, 24–35.

14. Kate Tesdell. Evaluating Public Library Service: The Mystery Shopper Approach. *Public Libraries*, 39 (3), May/June 2000, 145–53.

15. Marlu Burkamp and Diane Virbick. Through the Eyes of a Secret Shopper. *American Libraries*, 33 (10), November 2002, 56–57.

16. Steven Backs and Tim Kinder. Secret Shopping at the Monroe County Public Library. *Indiana Libraries*, 26 (4), 2007, 17–19.

17. Vanessa Czopek. Using Mystery Shoppers to Evaluate Customer Service in the Public Library. *Public Libraries*, 37 (6), 1998, 370.

18. Lynn Shostack. Designing Services that Deliver. *Harvard Business Review*, 62 (1), 1984, 133–39. See also Lynn Shostack. Understanding Services Through Blueprinting. *Advances in Services Marketing and Management*, 1, 1992, 6–23.

19. Bulu Maharana and Krushna Chandra Panda. Planning Business Process Reengineering (BPR) in Academic Libraries. *Malaysian Journal of Library & Information Science*, 6 (1), 2001, 105–11.

20. Judith Andrews and Eleanor Eade. Listening to Students: Customer Journey Mapping at Birmingham City University Library and Learning Resources. *New Review of Academic Librarianship*, 19 (2), 2014, 161–77.

21. Sue Sampson, Kim Granath, and Adrienne Alger. Journey Mapping the User Experience. *College & Research Libraries*, 78 (4), July 2017, 459–71.

22. Steven Bell. Blueprinting for Better Library Customer Service: From the Bell Tower. *Library Journal*, 2012. Available at http://lj.libraryjournal.com/2012/06/opinion/steven-bell/blueprinting-for-better-library-customer-service-from-the-bell-tower/#_

23. Steven Bell. Transforming the Library Starts with Mapping the Journey. Keynote speech presented at the American Library Association Virtual Conference, July 25, 2013).

24. Cassi Pretlow and Karen Sobel. Rethinking Library Service: Improving the User Experience with Service Blueprinting. *Public Services Quarterly*, 11 (1), 2015, 1–12.

25. Sue Samson, Kim Granath, and Adrienne Alger. Journey Mapping the User Experience. *College & Research Libraries*, July 2017. Available at http://crl.acrl.org/index.php/crl/article/view/16641

26. Joe Marquez, Annie Downey, and Ryan Clement. Walking a Mile in the User's Shoes: Customer Journey Mapping as a Method to Understanding the User Experience. *Internet Reference Services Quarterly*, 20, 2015, 135–50.

27. Mott Linn. Seating Sweeps: An Innovative Research Method to Learn about How Our Patrons Use the Library. Presentation at ACRL 2013 Conference, Association of College & Research Libraries, Indianapolis, IN: 2013, 511–17.

28. Lisa Given and Gloria Leckie. "Sweeping" the Library: Mapping the Social Activity Space of the Public Library. *Library & Information Science Research*, 25 (4), 2003, 365–85.

29. Gricel Dominguez. Beyond Gate Counts: Seating Studies and Observations to Assess Library Space Usage. *New Library World*, 117 (5/6), 2016, 321–28.

30. Envirosell. *San Jose Public Libraries and Hayward Public Libraries: Final Report.* New York: Envirosell, February 16, 2007. See also Envirosell. *Envirosell Final Report for the Metropolitan Library System.* New York: Envirosell, April 29, 2008. Available at https://www.webjunction.org/content/dam/WebJunction/Documents/webJunction/EnvirosellFinalReport.pdf

31. Julia Gross and Lutie Sheridan. Web Scale Discovery: The User Experience. *New Library World,* 112 (5/6), 236–47.

32. Junior Tidal. One Site to Rule Them All: Usability Testing of a Responsively Designed Library Website. ACRL 2015 Conference Proceedings, 2015. Available at http://www.ala.org/acrl/sites/ala.org.acrl/files/content/conferences/confsandpreconfs/2015/Tidal.pdf

33. Jakob Nielsen. Ten Usability Heuristics for User Interface Design. 2005. Available at https://www.nngroup.com/articles/ten-usability-heuristics/

34. Robin E. Miller, Bryan S. Vogh, and Eric J. Jennings. Library in an App: Testing the Usability of Boopsie as a Mobile Library Application. *Journal of Web Librarianship*, 7, 2013, 142–53.

35. Yan Quan Liu and Sarah Briggs. A Library in the Palm of Your Hand: Mobile Services in Top 100 University Libraries. *Information Technology and Libraries*, 34, June 2015, 133–48.

36. Jody Condit Fagan, Meris Mandernach, Carl Nelson, Jonathan Paulo, and Grover Saunders. Usability Test Results for a Discovery Tool in an Academic Library. *Information Technology and Libraries*, 31 (1), March 2012, 83–112.

37. Kelsey Brett, Ashley Lierman, and Cherie Turner. Lessons Learned: A Primo Usability Study. *Information Technology and Libraries*, 35, March 2016, 7–25.

38. Xianjin Zha, Jinchao Zhang, Yalan Yan, and Wento Wang. Comparing Flow Experience in Using Digital Libraries' Web and Mobile Context. *Library Hi Tech*, 33 (1), 2015, 41–53.

39. Nora Dethloff and Elizabeth M. German. Successes and Struggles with Building Web Teams: A Usability Committee Case Study. *New Library World*, 114 (5/6), 2013, 242–50.

40. Suzanne Chapman, Amy Fry, Amy Deschenes, and Courtney Greene McDonald. Strategies to Improve the User Experience. *Serials Review*, 42 (1), 2016, 47–58.

41. Jeffrey W. Gallant and Laura B. Wright. Planning for Iteration-Focused User Experience Testing in an Academic Library. *Internet Reference Services Quarterly*, 19 (1), 2014, 49–64.

42. Jakob Nielsen. Goal Composition: Extending Task Analysis to Predict Things People May Want to Do, January 1994. Available at https://www.nngroup.com/articles/goal-composition/

43. Merlen Prommann and Tao Zhang. Applying Hierarchical Task Analysis Method to Discovery Layer Evaluation. *Information Technology and Libraries*, March 2015, 77–105.

44. Katie Burn, Matthew Cunningham, Liz Waller, Emma Walton, and Graham Walton. Capturing the Student User Experience (UX) in York and Loughborough University Library Buildings. *Performance Measurement and Metrics*, 17 (2), 2016, 175–187.

45. Yong-Mi Kim. Users' Perceptions of University Library Websites: A Unifying View. *Library & Information Science Research*, 33, 2011, 63–72.

46. Angeliki Giannopoulou and Giannis Tsakonas. Affective Relationships Between Users and Libraries in Times of Economic Stress. *Library Management,* 36 (3), 2015, 248–57.

47. Nancy Foster and Susan Gibbons. (Eds.). *Studying Students: The Undergraduate Research Project at the University of Rochester.* Chicago: Association of College and Research Libraries, 2007.

48. Heather McQuaid, Aradhana Goel, and Mickey McManus. Designing for a Pervasive Information Architecture. *Proceedings of the Conference HCI 2003: Designing for Society.* Bath, UK, September 2003, 41–44.

49. Heather McQuaid, Aradhana Goel, and Mickey McManus. Designing for a Pervasive Information Environment: The Importance of Information Architecture. *Proceedings Volume 2 of the Conference HCI 2003: Designing for Society.* Bath, UK, September 2003, 41–44. See also Beth Dempsey. Library Buildings 2005: Power Users. *Library Journal*, December 15, 2005. Available at http://lj .libraryjournal.com/2005/12/managing-libraries/library-buildings-2005-power-users/

50. Lynda Duke and Andrew Asher. (Eds.). *College Libraries and Student Culture: What We Now Know.* Chicago, IL: American Library Association, 2012.

51. Robert Fox, Cathy Carpenter, and Ameet Doshi. Cool Collaborations: Designing a Better Library Experience. *College & Undergraduate Libraries*, 18 (2–3), 2011, 213–27.

Part V

Evaluation of Library Outcomes

22

Evaluating the Broader Perspective

Management is doing things right; leadership is doing the right things.

—Peter Drucker[1]

Libraries are often confronted with the need to demonstrate the value of the library and all of its services to interested stakeholders. Thus, rather than focusing on the evaluation of a specific library service, the library must attempt to assess the total impact of library services in the lives of its customers.

Attempting to answer the question, "How is the library doing?" is really trying to measure effectiveness or trying to answer the question, "Are we doing the *right* things?" An evaluation of the total library is an attempt to demonstrate how effective the library is in its community (city or county, academic campus, government agency, or company). Such an evaluation may also be attempting to demonstrate the value of the library in the lives of its customers and the broader community that it serves.

Funding any library is an expensive proposition: providing access to print and electronic collections, maintaining buildings and equipment, along with the ongoing costs of recruiting and retaining staff. Among the questions often raised by the funding stakeholders are:

- Are there demonstrable, tangible benefits that arise from library use?
- Does the library meet the needs of its community?
- Does the investment in libraries represent value for money?

The following chapters explore ways in which libraries have attempted to determine their effectiveness and define the value of the library. The primary means of describing the value of the library have occurred in the areas of accomplishments, economic benefits, and, for public libraries, social impacts of the library on the lives of customers.

Due to the elusive nature of organizational effectiveness (sometimes called "goodness"), Lawrence Mohr has called it the "Holy Grail of management research."[2] The pursuit of the Grail of Library Goodness has led to studies attempting to demonstrate the goodness of the library.[3]

337

One of the principal differences between a service organization such as a library and a for-profit business, according to Peter Drucker, is that a business receives resources (it must "earn" its revenues) by satisfying the customer, whereas the service organization receives a budget allocation from a funding source.[4] The problem is that there is no direct relationship between how effective a library is and the satisfaction experienced by the customer or user. Ultimately, it is not unusual for a budget-based institution such as a library to judge its effectiveness by the amount of next year's budget allocation. Often "performance" is the ability to maintain or increase the library's budget. Drucker suggests that service organizations like libraries should:

1. Answer the question, "What is our business and what should it be?"
2. Derive clear objectives and goals from their definition of function and mission.
3. Identify priorities of concentration that enable them to select targets, set deadlines, and make someone accountable for results.
4. Define measurements of performance.
5. Build feedback from results into their systems.
6. Perform an audit of objectives and results to identify those objectives that no longer serve a useful purpose.

Another challenge associated with assessing the goodness of the library is based on two different values. Librarians are primarily concerned about providing access to resources and information using professional and experienced staff members. As such, librarians have an *internal focus*, seeing themselves as "doing good," and are less concerned about assessing outputs and impacts. The library's funding decision makers have an *external view* and want to ensure that the library is operating efficiently and effectively—that is, meeting the needs of the community of users.

LIBRARY GOODNESS

Clearly, no single measure of library goodness is going to fulfill the expectations of the multiple groups that need to be satisfied. Without a clear understanding of and agreement on the mission and vision of the library, there may be conflicts over how well the goals of the library are actually being achieved. The reality is that the library is controlled to a large extent by the resources that are made available to it (and the library does not have direct control over the allocation of these resources).

In the past, little was required beyond adhering to budget allocations. In such an environment there was little encouragement and few rewards for being "good" beyond personal satisfaction. Although library stakeholders, including the funding decision makers, have historically accepted the conventional wisdom of the "community goodness" provided by the library, stakeholders are increasingly demanding tangible proof that the library is delivering quality library services that meet the needs of the customers using cost-efficient means. The bottom line is a demand for increased accountability.

This demand is not new. Back in 1973, Orr suggested that libraries needed to focus on providing answers to three "goodness" questions:[5]

- How good is the library? The focus is on quality and capabilities.
- What good does the library do? The focus is on beneficial use.
- How well is the library managed?

Nevertheless, librarians still have difficulty knowing how to approach this issue of reporting performance, for several reasons:

- **Lack of consensus.** The library profession has not spoken with one clear voice about what performance measures should be used to report a library's accomplishments.
- **Lack of definitions.** The library profession has failed to adopt a consistent set of definitions for the plethora of performance measures that already exist. The result is that two libraries can be reporting the same statistic but actually be measuring two different perspectives of a service, by collecting the data differently, and so forth.
- **Lack of understanding.** Library directors and managers often have a poor understanding of the potential value and utility of performance measures which, when consistently applied, can assist in improving the operation of the library.
- **Lack of structure.** There may be several reasons that prevent libraries from effectively using performance measures. Among these are the library's culture, a desire not to waste time and resources, the need for staff to embrace the value of performance measures, and the need for training.
- **Statistical overload.** Most libraries collect a great many performance measures. The state library and federal surveys often mandate the collection of a plethora of statistics, and often the local library continues to gather other measures that it has "always" collected. As a result, staff are more than likely to be overwhelmed by the prospect of collecting some "new" performance measures without considering the possibility of deciding to stop collecting others.
- **It is hard work.** As Orr noted, attempting to measure quality and beneficial use requires a great deal of thinking about the issues and how to measure the two concepts. Historically librarians have tended to fall back on measures that serve as surrogates—typically collection completeness and circulation.

As a result, the library profession has been unable to answer even such basic questions as:

- What is a good library?
- What is a bad library?
- How can we move from being "bad" to being "good"?

THE 90 PERCENT LIBRARY

An important strategic planning decision for library boards and stakeholders is: What percent of all service needs can be met by the resources contained within our library? Any library is going to be faced with a group of users with a wide variety of interests and information needs, yet no library can anticipate and plan for meeting all users' needs. Thus the question arises: What level of resources and services will meet "X" percent of the needs of our population? The library will handle the remainder of needs in some other way. The percent level selected by the library will determine, in large part, the budgetary needs of the library.

Charles Bourne asked: What does a library have to do to satisfy 90 percent of a library population's needs?[6] User requirements could be stated in the following terms:

90 percent of the information needs of a given user population is satisfied by:

Books that are less than _____ years old

A book collection size of _____ volumes

A media collection size of _____ items

> A print journal collection of _____ titles
> A print journal collection that is less than _____ years old
> An electronic journals collection of _____ titles
> Interlibrary loan journal articles delivered in _____ days
> Computer workstations to minimize wait times below _____ minutes

And so forth.

Note that all of these measures are internally focused and do not assess how well the library is moving toward being an important node in the networked world in which we are increasingly living.

MANAGEMENT FRAMEWORKS

Much confusion exists about the concept of organizational effectiveness, despite a fairly lengthy history of inquiry.[7] Conceptual questions, such as *what* to measure rather than *how* to measure effectiveness; *how* to define various components of effectiveness and *how* to link these factors in the assessment process to the organization's goals, objectives, and functions still persist. The three primary challenges that must be confronted are the definition, measurement, and determinants of effectiveness.

This chapter provides a brief overview of the challenges associated with organizational effectiveness and the role of performance measures as surrogates for demonstrating effectiveness.

Among the problems that must be confronted when attempting to assess organizational effectiveness is the need to address several issues: effectiveness is a reflection of individual values and preferences; different approaches to assess effectiveness are products of varying, arbitrary models of organizations; the construct of effectiveness has never been bounded; and not all relevant effectiveness criteria have been identified.[8]

One useful approach to the assessment of organizational effectiveness involves the four perspectives articulated by Kim Cameron:[9]

- The ***goal model*** (sometimes called the *goal attainment model* or the *rational system model*) views effectiveness in terms of achievement of specific goals and objectives. The focus is on productivity and outputs. If an organization does not have clearly defined goals, then it will be impossible to articulate criteria of effectiveness. The challenge in using this model is the complexity, ambiguity, diffuseness, and changeability that may typify organizational goals.

  Possible performance measures: goals and objectives, standards, outcomes

- The ***internal process model*** (sometimes called the *natural systems model*) sees an organization desiring to maintain itself as a social unit while at the same time seeking to achieve goals. Organizational health, internal processes, and the attainment of goals measure effectiveness in this case.

  Possible performance measures: input and process measures, benchmarks, peer comparisons

- The ***open systems model*** or *system resource model* focuses on the interdependence of the organization with its environment. The organization's survival and growth are dependent upon acquiring budgetary resources from external groups.

  Possible performance measures: total quality management, ISO 9000, quality awards

- The ***multiple constituencies model*** or *the participant satisfaction model* sees effectiveness as the degree to which the needs of the various constituencies or stakeholders are met. The challenge with this perspective is to reconcile the often-conflicting needs and wishes of different stakeholders, each of whom will have different criteria of effectiveness and may or may not control the purse strings.

Possible performance measures: holistic management frameworks

The significant challenges of assessing organizational effectiveness have been noted by March and Olson, who observed that organizations, especially those in higher education, are *"complex 'garbage cans'* into which a striking variety of problems, solutions, and participants may be dumped."[10]

Cameron's four models have been used to assess organizational effectiveness in a library setting.[11] Table 22.1 summarizes these models from a library's perspective by illustrating the possible performance measures that could be used to demonstrate organizational effectiveness. One of the real challenges facing libraries is a lack of consensus about the goals and objectives of the library.

Table 22.1. Models and Dimensions of Organizational Effectiveness

Goal Model	Process Model	System Resource Model	Multiple Constituencies Model
Outputs & Inputs	Internal Processes	Outputs & Inputs	Community Fit
Community Fit	Management Elements	Internal Processes	
Access to Materials		Physical Facilities	
Service Offerings		Management Elements	
Service to Special Groups			

Thomas Childers and Nancy Van House[12] argue that the principal reasons for the lack of consensus are:

- Revenues and outputs are separated
- A common metric (the "bottom line" in corporations) is lacking
- The decision-making process is not contained within the library
- The library has neither champions nor foes
- Library benefits are not widely self-evident

Role of Performance Measures

Performance measures can play a variety of roles in an organization. Although performance measures can stand alone, they can also be combined with other management techniques to create more useful organizational tools.

Performance measures are particularly effective when they are linked to organization's vision, goals and objectives—whether they are easy to collect or not. Almost all organizations will collect a plethora of performance measures, which are all characterized by the ease of their collection.

A library is provided with a set of *resources*. Those resources are transformed so that they have the *capability* to provide a set of services. These services are then *utilized*. And once used, the information and/or service that has been provided has the potential for a positive, beneficial *impact or effect,* first in the life of the individual user and ultimately on the community or organization. Richard Orr organized a set of performance measures reflecting these activities in a library setting using his Input-Process-Output-Outcomes model.[13]

Good performance measures are:[14]

- Balanced—include both financial and nonfinancial measures
- Aligned to the organization's strategies
- Flexible—can be changed as needed
- Timely and accurate
- Simple to understand
- Focused on improvement

Some suggest that performance measures should be SMART. The measure has a **S**pecific purpose, it is **M**easurable, the defined targets have to be **A**chievable, the measure has to be **R**elevant, and it must be **T**ime phased, which means the value or outcomes are shown for a predefined and relevant period.

Dashboards are a visual representation of a number of performance measures presented in the form of a control panel—somewhat similar to the dashboard of an automobile or airplane instrument panel. The plethora of measures displayed typically does not reflect a link between the measures and the organizational goals and objectives.

Key Performance Indicators

Key performance indicators (KPIs) help an organization define and evaluate how successful it is in terms of achieving its organizational goals. A university or college might consider the 5-year graduation rate as a key performance indicator, whereas an academic library might use a collection availability rate as a key performance indicator. The idea is to select a few key performance indicators that are reflective of organizational effectiveness.

Critical Success Factors

Critical success factor (CSF) is the term for an element that is necessary for an organization or project to achieve its vision. Success factors are those activities and capabilities that define the continuing success of an organization. The concept of "success factors" was refined by Jack Rockart[15] and has been applied in a number of settings: business process management, new service development, institutional repositories, a library digitization project,[16] and management of a special library.[17]

Critical success factors are concerned with what leads to organizational success. These factors might include such things as customer satisfaction, employee competencies and retention, service quality, innovation, information technology, and so forth.

Process Improvement Initiatives

W. Edwards Deming, Philip Crosby, and others who created the Total Quality Management (TQM) movement have brought greater focus to the importance of nonfinancial approaches and a management approach for implementing improvement activities. In particular, TQM focuses on using statistical process control methods to control and improve processes in organizations. Every process has variation, and tracking the quality of a process allows a determination of whether the variation exceeds defined limits.

Six Sigma. The term Six Sigma was developed by a Motorola engineer when it became clear that a method was needed to start measuring manufacturing defects per million opportunities, as opposed to per thousand opportunities. Six Sigma proponents believe that if the number of defects in a process is measured, these defects can be systematically eliminated. In order to achieve Six Sigma excellence, a process cannot produce more than 3.4 defects per million opportunities (an *opportunity* is defined as a chance for nonconformance).

Self-Assessment Award Models

The development of the quality award models has been driven by a desire to integrate both financial and nonfinancial approaches. The best-known models are the Malcolm Baldrige National Quality Awards (MBNQA) and the European Foundation for Quality Management (EFQM) Award—sometimes called the "Business Excellence Models."

The **Malcolm Baldrige National Quality Award (MBNQA)** is based on a set of seven criteria: leadership, the system, strategic planning, human resource development and management, process management, business results, and customer focus and satisfaction. These categories can also be defined by two key performance constructs of *results* and *drivers or enablers*—see Figure 22.1.

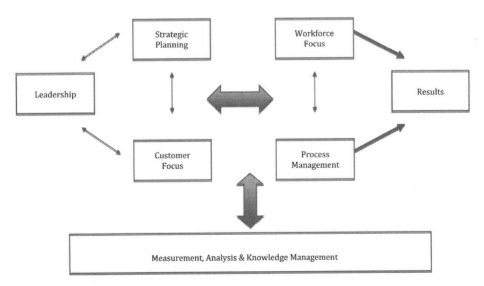

Figure 22.1. The Malcolm Baldrige Award Educational Framework. Adapted from Baldrige Performance Excellence Program. 2017. *2017–2018 Baldrige Excellence Framework: A Systems Approach to Improving Your Organization's Performance (Education).* Gaithersburg, MD: U.S. Department of Commerce, National Institute of Standards and Technology. https://www.nist.gov/baldrige.

Some organizations have lost sight of the objective of the award by focusing on winning the award rather than the end itself: high-quality products and services.[18]

EFQM Excellence Model—A performance self-assessment tool that provides a common language for communicating and sharing best practice among firms. Figure 22.2 presents the EFQM Excellence Model and its nine components. The five criteria that are controllable by managers are called "enablers" (or drivers) and the four criteria named "results" are what an organization strives to achieve.

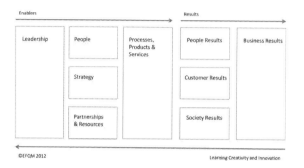

Figure 22.2. The EFQM Award Framework. EFQM Excellence Model available online at http://www.efqm.org/efqm-model/model-criteria. Reprinted with permission.

Essentially, the EFQM model suggests that leadership drives policy and strategy, people, partnerships, and resources and processes. The results of these efforts are measured in the model by people satisfaction (employee and customer) and impact on society. The ultimate outcome is excellence in key performance results.

It is generally accepted that the EFQM model is a self-assessment tool or static auditing tool. As such, the performance management framework is used for operational reporting instead of creating an adjustable model that interacts with business strategy.[19]

Performance Measurement Frameworks

Several frameworks provide a means for organizing a collection of related performance measures. Among these frameworks are:

- The Performance Pyramid
- The Performance Prism
- The Service Performance Framework

The Performance Pyramid—The Strategic Measurement Analysis and Reporting Technique (SMART) system, also known as the Performance Pyramid, was created as a management control system to define and sustain success, as shown in Figure 22.3. Large corporations usually embrace this framework. The top level focuses on the organization's mission, vision, and strategies. The second level defines the objectives for each operating unit, while the third level provides more specific measures of operating success. The fourth level provides measures that are applicable for a department.

The Performance Prism—The Performance Prism is designed to assist managers in the process of selecting the best performance measures for their organization.[20] The Performance Prism, which is illustrated in Figure 22.4, is comprised of five interrelated facets. Stakeholder

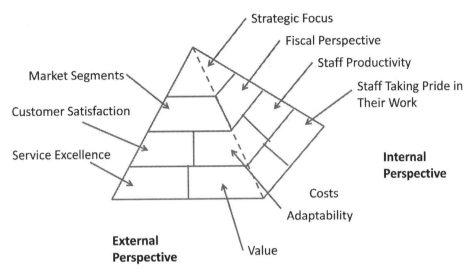

Figure 22.3. The Performance Pyramid. Adapted from Cross, K.F., and Lynch, R.L., The SMART way to define and sustain success, *National Productivity Review,* 1989; vol. 8, no. 1, pp. 23–33.

satisfaction, the first facet, is considered to be the most important aspect of performance measurement; it asks managers to identify who are the important stakeholders and then clarify their wants and needs. Strategies, the second facet, are focused on delivering value and ask the question: What strategies are required to ensure that the wants and needs of the stakeholders are satisfied?

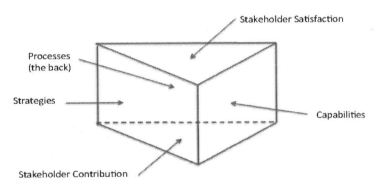

Figure 22.4. The Five Facets of the Performance Prism. Andy Neely, Chris Adams, and Paul Crowe. The Performance Prism in Practice. *Measuring Business Excellence,* 5 (2), 2001, p. 12.

The third facet, processes, identifies the processes that should be put in place in order to allow the firm's strategies to be achieved. Capabilities, the fourth facet of the prism, combine people, practices, infrastructure, and technology that enable the processes. Stakeholder contribution, the final facet, recognizes the importance of the firm's relationship with its stakeholders.

The strength of the Performance Prism is that it illustrates the interrelationships among the five components of the prism, thus assisting managers to understand the factors that drive performance.

The Service Performance Framework—includes six financial and nonfinancial criteria considered to be important to competitive success. Four factors *determine* competitive success (quality of service, flexibility, resource utilization, and innovation) and two factors reflect the *results* of success (competitiveness and financial performance).

Holistic Frameworks

The holistic approach focuses on providing both financial and nonfinancial performance measures using a framework that would encourage managers to gain a better understanding about what leads to organizational success. Among the holistic models or frameworks that have been developed are:

- The Results and Determinants Matrix
- The 3 Rs
- The Strategic Triangle
- Social Return on Investment
- The Big Picture
- The Balanced Scorecard
- Hierarchy of Community Needs

The Results and Determinants Matrix encourages managers to utilize both financial and nonfinancial measures in order to obtain richer feedback for better control of the business.[21] The matrix emphasizes "soft" measures such as competitive performance, quality of service, flexibility, resource utilization, and innovation, as well as the "hard" measures of financial performance. These dimensions are the basis of a generic performance framework for measuring performance. Similar to the other models, the matrix recognizes the two key dimensions of performance: the *determinants* (or *drivers)* and the *results*. The six generic performance dimensions are grouped into two categories of "results" and "determinants," as illustrated in Figure 22.5. The importance of the four determinants (flexibility, resource utilization, innovation, and quality of service) is contextually based.

The 3Rs provides a balanced approach to performance management by providing a strategic and comprehensive context for decision making.[22]

- *Resources* refers to the amount of time, money, and/or energy exerted as well as the type of resources used.
- *Reach* refers to the breadth and depth of influence over which available resources are spread. Physical (spatial) reach is one dimension, as well as the type of customers the library wishes to reach. As competition becomes an increasing concern, then market share becomes an important indicator of success.
- *Results* refers to the impact on the groups of customers reached by the resources used. Value has been added when the results are desirable from the customer's perspective. Customers may express themselves by indicating higher levels of satisfaction.

The Strategic Triangle illustrates that the point of all managerial activity is to create value, and in a public context to create public value.[23] Demonstrations of public value creation lie in evidence showing changes in social conditions. Moore has suggested that a strategic triangle, as shown in Figure 22.6, is an effective way to focus attention of managers on three complex

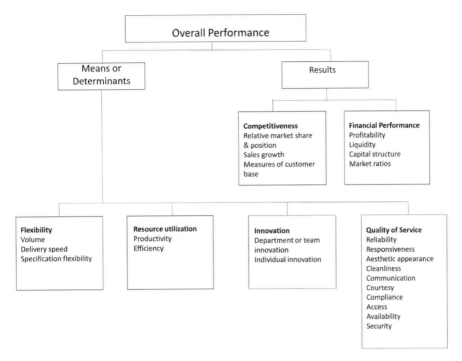

Figure 22.5. The Results and Determinants Matrix. Adapted from L. Fitzgerald, R. Johnston, S. Brignall, R. Silvestro, and C. Voss. *Performance Measurement in Service Businesses.* London: CIMA, 1991.

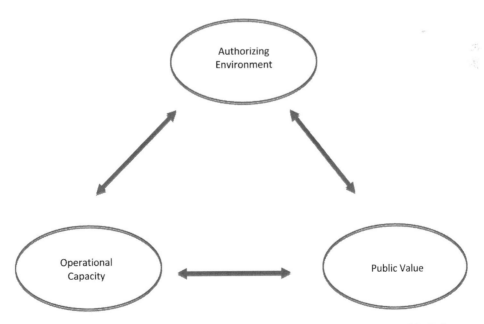

Figure 22.6. The Strategic Triangle. Adapted from Moore, Mark. *Creating Public Value: Strategic Management in Government.* Boston: Harvard University Press, 1997.

issues that must be considered before (or while) committing themselves and their organizations to a particular course of action:

- What is the important "public value" the organization is seeking to produce?
- What "sources of legitimacy and support" can be relied upon to authorize the organization to take action and provide the resources necessary to sustain the effort to create that value?
- What "operational capabilities" (including new investments and innovations) will the organization need to deliver the desired results?

The key to understanding *Public Values* are the outcomes that the organization is attempting to reach. The concept of pubic value underlines the importance of pursuing aims that will bring measurable benefit to the public sphere and address the expressed needs of a given population. The focus of *Legitimacy and Support* is to identify the ways in which the organization builds a team to support its programs. *Operational Capabilities* address how well an organization delivers services to achieve its declared objectives. The Strategic Triangle framework emphasizes three perspectives for managers:

- Upwards through institutional and political structures
- Downwards through management and operational lines
- Outwards toward customers and the public

Social Return on Investment (SROI) is an outcomes-based tool that helps organizations to understand and quantify three perspectives: the social effects, environmental impacts, and economic value they are creating. An SROI, sometimes called "the triple bottom line," provides a broader picture of the value of organizations to their communities; see Figure 22.7. An SROI analysis produces a narrative of how an organization creates and destroys value in the course of making change in the world, and calculates a ratio that states how much value (in dollars) is created for every dollar of investment.

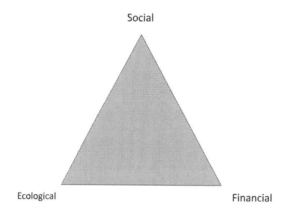

Figure 22.7. The Social Return on Investment

Preparing an SROI requires an understanding of the cause-and-effect relationships among inputs, outputs, and outcomes and requires a financial value to be assigned to each measure. The challenges for any library include developing the cause-and-effect relationships and then understanding and monetizing outcomes. Other initiatives that attempt to include the social perspective include the AA 1000 Assurance Standard; Cooperative, Environmental and Social

Performance Indicators (CESPI); the Global Reporting Initiative (GRI); the Social Impact Measurement for Local Economies; and the Practical Quality Assurance for Small Organizations (PQASO).

The Big Picture seeks to allow an organization to treat quality and impact issues in a holistic way.[24] The Big Picture is a two-by-two matrix. The four quadrants of The Big Picture include:

- *Direction* focuses on governance, purpose, strategy and policy, staffing, culture, and regulations.
- *Processes* concentrates on planning, managing people, managing money, managing other resources, managing activities, and monitoring and review.
- *Stakeholder Satisfaction* focuses on customers, paid staff, volunteers, funders, partners, and influencers.
- *Positive Impacts* spotlights strategic customers, financial health, evidence of standards, development, public profile, and impact on society.

The Balanced Scorecard is a comprehensive framework in which the mission and strategic directions of an organization can be understood using an array of performance measures.[25] The Balanced Scorecard framework contains a collection of financial and nonfinancial measures to assist an organization in implementing its specific success factors as identified in its vision, as shown in Figure 22.8.

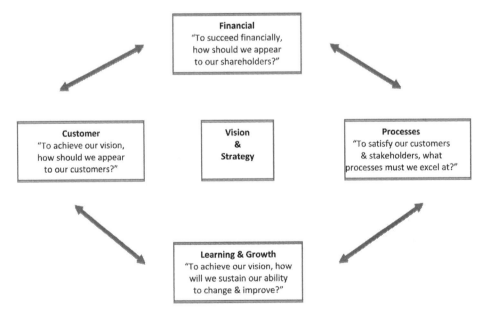

Figure 22.8. The Balanced Scorecard. Robert Kaplan and David Norton. Using the Balanced Scorecard as a Strategic Management System. *Harvard Business Review* 74, 1996, 75–85; Robert Kaplan and David Norton. Linking the Balanced Scorecard to Strategy. *California Management Review* 39, 1996, 53–79.

The Balanced Scorecard approach emphasizes the linkage of measurement to strategy and the cause-and-effect connections. The organization-specific scorecards contain a set of measures to improve performance according to the organization's needs and goals. The intent of this framework is that the measures should have a balance, not only of external measures and internal measures, but also between the result measures (outcomes) and the driver measures.

A commonly accepted strength of the Balanced Scorecard is the linkage of performance measures with organizational strategy.[26] Others stress that the scorecard's focus is on the implementation of strategy and not in determining strategy.[27] It is recommended that an organization develop a Strategy Map was a way to better understand the strategies being used.

The Balanced Scorecard is an organizing framework, rather than a "constraining straightjacket," which can be adjusted and built upon according to the needs of the organization to better understand cause-and-effect relationships.[28]

Library Balanced Scorecards have been developed and used by academic libraries, public libraries, and special libraries—particularly when the larger organization is also using a Balanced Scorecard. *Scorecards for Results: A Guide for Developing a Library Balanced Scorecard* suggests rearranging the perspectives as shown in Figure 22.9.[29]

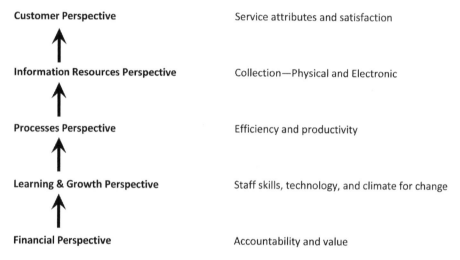

Figure 22.9. The Library Balanced Scorecard. Joseph R. Matthews. *Scorecard for Results: A Guide for Developing a Library Balanced Scorecard.* Westport, CN: Libraries Unlimited, 2008.

The **Hierarchy of Community Needs,** which is based on Maslow's Hierarchy of Needs, defines a path for a healthy, strong, and transformed community. The hierarchy provides the opportunity for a community to define a range of metrics that will enable the library and the community itself to track its progress in achieving its goals, as shown in Figure 22.10.[30]

Assessing the Frameworks

The use of a framework allows the library to begin to investigate and better understand the complexity of the relationships between drivers and results. These frameworks allow library managers to better understand how their strategies, capabilities, service offerings, and facilities affect student learning outcomes, teaching capabilities, and campus research activities.

Which Frameworks for What Purposes? Given all of these available frameworks, what would be best in your situation? The answer, not surprisingly, is that it depends. If the purpose is to provide a framework for a collection of performance measures for internal use by the library, then choose one of the Performance Measurement Frameworks. If the framework is to be shared with external decision makers, then one of the Integrated Management Frameworks would be a good selection.

Figure 22.10. Sample Strategy Map

What Criteria Should Be Used to Select a Framework? Among the most important criteria that can be used to select a framework are:

- **Fait accompli**—Has the larger organization already selected an management framework? If so, the library should use the same framework.
- **Focus**—Is the framework going to be used to track performance measures or organizational success?
- **Perspective**—Will library management use the framework as an internal tool, or is it to be used to communicate to stakeholders outside the library?
- **Resonation**—Does the framework resonate with funding decision makers? The framework *must resonate* with your stakeholders.

Should You Consider Using Multiple Frameworks? The short answer is no! Selecting, developing, using, and communicating a framework for the library is going to require considerable effort, and adding one or more other frameworks will only lead to confusion and complexity.

Note that none of the frameworks determine what outcome measures should be used. And it is outcomes that result from using the library and its services, be they student learning outcomes, better teaching skills, improved research productivity, and so forth that are becoming ever more important. This can be best accomplished if the library understands how it adds value for each type of use of the library and its services.

One of the real values of a framework is that it encourages the use of a few key measures. As Herb Simon has observed:

> "Information . . . consumes the attention of its recipients. Hence, a wealth of information creates a poverty of attention and a need to allocate that attention efficiently among the overabundance of information sources that might consume it.[31]

In conclusion, the use of a framework is but a tool in the library's efforts to accomplish two objectives: 1) better manage its resources by tacking its progress in reaching its goals, and 2) demonstrating the value of the library to its stakeholders! A management framework is simply a means, and not the end, in an effort to improve communication with campus (and off-campus) stakeholders about the value of the library.

If a framework does not resonate, then you might use an alternative approach suggested by Michael Buckland:[32]

> The financial crisis is looking even worse, but you will be pleased to know that the librarian reports that the library's performance went up a half a point on the library goodness scale last week.

NOTES

1. Peter Drucker. *The Daily Drucker: 366 Days of insight and Motivation for Getting the Right Things Done.* New York: HarperBusiness, 2004.

2. Lawrence B. Mohr. *Explaining Organizational Behavior: The Limits and Possibilities of Theory and Research.* San Francisco: Jossey-Bass, 1982.

3. Michael Buckland. *Library Services in Theory and Context.* New York: Pergamon, 1988, 241–44.

4. Peter F. Drucker. Managing the Service Institution. *The Interest,* 33, Fall 1973, 43–60.

5. Robert H. Orr. Measuring the Goodness of Library Services: A General Framework for Considering Quantitative Measures. *Journal of Documentation,* 29 (3), September 1973, 314–32.

6. Charles P. Bourne. Some User Requirements Stated Quantitatively in Terms of the 90 Percent Library, in Allen Kent and Orrin E. Taulbee (Eds.). *Electronic Information Handling.* Washington, DC: Spartan Books, 1965, 93–110.

7. Rosabeth Kanter. Organizational Performance: Recent Developments in Measurement. *Annual Review of Sociology,* 7, 1981, 321–49.

8. Kim Cameron and David Whetten. *Organizational Effectiveness: A Comparison of Multiple Models.* New York: Academic Press, 1983.

9. Kim Cameron. Domains of Organizational Effectiveness in Colleges and Universities. *Academy of Management Journal,* 24, 1981, 25–47; Kim Cameron. A Study of Organizational Effectiveness and Its Predictors. *Management Science,* 32, 1986, 87–112.

10. James G. March and Johan P. Olson. *Ambiguity and Choice in Organizations.* Oslo: Univesitetsforlaget, 1976, 49.

11. Thomas Childers and Nancy Van House. The Grail of Goodness: The Effective Library. *Library Journal,* 114, October 1, 1989, 44–49; Thomas Childers and Nancy Van House. Dimensions of Public Library Effectiveness. *Library & Information Science Research,* 11 (3), 1989, 273–301; Nancy Van House and Thomas Childers. Dimensions of Public Library Effectiveness II: Library Performance. *Library & Information Science Research,* 12 (2), 1990, 131–53.

12. Thomas Childers and Nancy Van House. *What's Good? Describing Your Public Library's Effectiveness.* Chicago: American Library Association, 1993.

13. Richard Orr. Measuring the Goodness of Library Services. *Journal of Documentation,* 29, 1973, 315–52.

14. Joseph R. Matthews. *Measuring for Results: The Dimensions of Public Library Effectiveness.* Westport, CN: Libraries Unlimited, 2004.

15. Jack F. Rockart. A Primer on Critical Success Factors, in Jack F. Rockart and Christine V. Bullen (Eds.). *The Rise of Managerial Computing: The Best of the Center for Information Systems Research.* Homewood, IL: Dow Jones-Irwin, 1986, 246–73.

16. Cory Lampert and Jason Vaughn. Success Factors and Strategic Planning: Rebuilding an Academic Library Digitization Program. *Information Technology and Libraries,* 28, September 2009, 116–36.

17. Jack Boberly. The Critical Success Factors Method: Its Application in a Special Library Environment. *Special Libraries,* 72, 1981, 201–8.

18. David A. Garvin. How the Baldrige Award Really Works. *Harvard Business Review,* 69, November-December 1991, 80–93.

19. Rodney McAdam and Michael Kelly. A Business Excellence Approach to Generic Benchmarking in SMEs. *Benchmarking: An International Journal,* 9, 2002, 7–27.

20. Andrew Neely, Chris Adams, and Mike Kennerley. *The Performance Prism: The Scorecard for Measuring and Managing Business Success.* London: Prentice Hall, 2002.

21. Adapted from L. Fitzgerald, R. Johnston, S. Brignall, R. Silvestro, and C. Voss. *Performance Measurement in Service Businesses.* London: CIMA, 1991.

22. Steve Montague. *The Three Rs of Performance: Core Concepts for Planning, Measurement, and Management.* Ottawa: Performance Management Network, 1997.

23. Mark Moore. *Creating Public Value: Strategic Management in Government.* Boston: Harvard University Press, 1997.

24. See http://www.thebigpicture.org.uk

25. Robert Kaplan and David Norton. Using the Balanced Scorecard as a Strategic Management System. *Harvard Business Review* 74, 1996, 75–85; Robert Kaplan and David Norton. Linking the Balanced Scorecard to Strategy. *California Management Review* 39, 1996, 53–79.

26. Henry Andersen, Gavin Lawrie, and Michael Shulver. *The Balanced Scorecard vs the EFQM Business Excellence Model—Which Is the Better Strategic Management Tool?* Maidenhead, England: 2GC Active Management, 2000.

27. Roselie McDevitt, Catherine Giapponi, and Norman Solomon. Strategy Revitalization in Academe: A Balanced Scorecard Approach. *International Journal of Educational Management* 22, 2008, 32–47.

28. John C. Anderson and Rungtusanatham Manus. A Theory of Quality Management Underlying the Deming Management Method." *Academy of Management Journal* 19 (1994): 472–509.

29. Joseph R. Matthews. *Scorecards for Results: A Guide for Developing a Library Balanced Scorecard.* Westport, CN: Libraries Unlimited, 2008.

30. John J. Huber and Steven V. Potter. *The Purpose-Based Library: Finding Your Path to Survival, Success, and Growth.* Chicago: Neal-Schuman, 2015.

31. Herbert A. Simon. Designing Organizations for an Information-Rich World, in Martin Greenberger (Ed.). *Computers, Communication, and the Public Interest.* Baltimore, MD: The Johns Hopkins Press, 1971, 71–92.

32. Michael K. Buckland. Concepts of Library Goodness. *Canadian Library Journal,* 39, April 1982, 64.

23

Outcomes and Value

Bad libraries build collections,
good libraries build services,
great libraries build communities.

—R. David Lankes[1]

When an individual uses a library, the immediate benefits will occur within hours, days, or weeks. The last category of Richard Orr's Input-Process-Output-Outcomes evaluation model (discussed in some detail in Chapter 2) is outcomes—how an individual translates the use of a library service into an accomplishment or benefit—which is the focus of this chapter.

Tefko Saracevic and Paul Kantor developed a useful framework or taxonomy for establishing the value that may arise from using library and information services.[2] They suggest that an individual has three potential reasons to use a library or information service: (1) to work on a task or project, (2) for personal reasons, or (3) to get an object or information, or to perform an activity.

They assert that when an individual interacts with a library service, there are three areas of interaction that should be considered:

Resources. From the individual's viewpoint, three perspectives might be considered in this area.

- *Accessibility.* This measure focuses on the ease with which the service can be accessed. Is a visit to the library required, for example? Is the resource available online?

- *Availability.* This traditional evaluation measure attempts to assess whether the library has the given resource, item, or service desired by the client.

- *Quality.* This measure assesses the degree to which a service or resource is accurate, current, timely, and complete.

Use of Resources, Services. In examining this area, the library could ask its customers to assess five potential measures:

- How much *effort* is required to move from one service to another?

- *Ease of use.* How difficult is it to use a resource or service?

- How *successful* is the client in using a library service or resource?
- The degree of *convenience* in using the resource or service.
- What *frustration*, if any, results from using the resource or service?

Operations and Environment. There are four categories in which an individual can be asked to rate the library and its services:

- Are the *facilities* adequate? Do the physical layout and organization of the library resources facilitate access to the resources and services?
- Is the *equipment* reliable and easy to use? Are user instructions or guides readily available? Is the library's Web site easy to use and kept current?
- Are library *staff members* helpful, efficient, and knowledgeable? Is there a clear understanding of the goals and objectives of the library?
- How reasonable and clear are the library's *policies and procedures*? Do they facilitate access or act as impediments?

Most importantly, Saracevic and Kantor focused on the results, outcomes, or impact that a library or information service has, first in the life of the user and ultimately on the organization. An *organization* can be defined as a community, an academic institution, or a profit or not-for-profit concern. The six outcome categories include:

1. **Cognitive results.** Use of the library may have an impact on the mind of the individual. The intention of this category is to ask, "What was learned?" Thus, the individual may have

   - Learned something new
   - Changed in viewpoint, outlook, or perspective
   - Refreshed memory of detail or facts
   - Substantiated or reinforced knowledge or belief
   - Gotten ideas with a slightly different or tangential perspective (serendipity)
   - Not learned anything

2. **Affective results.** Use of the library or its services may influence or have an emotional impact on the individual. The individual may experience

   - A sense of confidence, reliability, and trust
   - A sense of comfort, happiness, and good feelings
   - A sense of accomplishment, success, or satisfaction
   - A sense of frustration
   - A sense of failure

3. **Meeting expectations.** When using the library, the individual may

   - Be getting what was needed, sought, or expected
   - Have confidence in what was received
   - Be getting nothing
   - Receive more than expected
   - Seek substitute sources or action if expectations not met

4. **Accomplishments** in relation to tasks. As a result of using the library, the individual is

   - Able to make better-informed decisions
   - Achieve a higher-quality performance

- Able to point to a course of action
- Proceeding to the next step
- Discovering people and other sources of information
- Improving a policy, procedure, or plan

5. **Time aspects.** Some of the real value for the user of a library is the fact that the resources and/or services might lead to a savings in time
   - Save time
   - Waste time
   - Need to wait
   - Need time to understand how to use a service or resource
   - Experience a service that ranges from slow to fast

6. **Money aspects.** Using the library may result in saving money or generating new revenues. The individual may be able to
   - Estimate the dollar value of results obtained
   - Estimate the amount of money saved
   - Estimate the cost of using the service
   - Estimate what may be spent on a substitute service
   - Estimate value (in dollars) lost where the service was not available or use was not successful

It should be noted that the first three results (cognitive, affective, and expectations) would normally translate in some way to having an impact on the latter three outcomes (accomplishments, time, and money).

Saracevic and Kantor developed a taxonomy for establishing the value that arises from the use of the library, as shown in Figure 23.1. This taxonomy suggests that context helps establish value. Individuals have a reason for wanting to use the library, they have an interaction with the virtual or physical library, from which they derive value based on the result of their interactions.

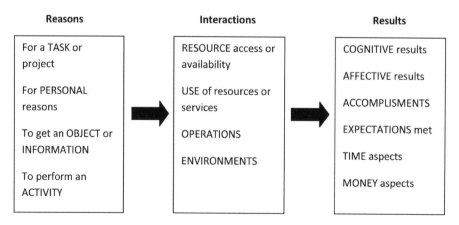

Figure 23.1. A Taxonomy of Value. Adapted from Figure 1 in Tefko Saracevic and Paul B. Kantor. Studying the Value of Library and Information Services. Part II. Methodology and Taxonomy. *Journal of the American Society of Information Science,* 48 (6), 1997, 543–63.

ISO 16439

This international standard specifies methods and defines terms for identifying the impact or output assessment of libraries on individuals, institutions, and society.[3] The standard discusses the various aspects of library outcomes:

- The outcome can be *limited* or *far-reaching* (changing the life of an individual)
- The outcome can be *immediate* or *long-term*
- *Actual* benefits may differ from *potential* benefits
- The outcomes can be *intended* or *unintended*

EVALUATION METHODS

A number of approaches can be used to assess the outcomes or impact of an academic library service in terms of student learning, teaching, and research, as shown in Table 23.1.

The small number of studies that have been done generally are limited by their small sample sizes, and most did not use a control group to better identify the actual impact of the library. For a more detailed discussion of the issues of assessment in the academic environment, consult *Library Assessment in Higher Education.*[4]

Table 23.1. Assessing the Outcomes of the Academic Library

	Student Learning	**Teaching**	**Research**
Access to the physical collection	Evaluation of term papers, projects. Do library users get better grades? Graduate sooner?	Teachers' assessment of materials presented during a course, assigned readings	Citation analysis of materials in research reports, articles and books published, conference presentations Value of the collection for research
Access to the electronic collection	Evaluation of term papers, projects. Do library users get better grades? Graduate sooner?	Teachers' assessment of materials presented during a course, assigned readings	Citation analysis of materials in research reports, articles and books published, conference presentations Value of the collection for research
Reference services	Value of the service to students	Value of the service to faculty	Value of the service to researchers
Instruction programs	Evaluation of term papers, projects. Do students who receive instruction get better grades? Graduate sooner?	Assessment of faculty of the value of the instruction: better papers, projects?	Assessment of researchers of the value of the instruction: better research, save time, assist in keeping current?

(continued)

Table 23.1. Assessing the Outcomes of the Academic Library (*continued*)

	Student Learning	Teaching	Research
Access to technology located in library	Indirect link to outcomes	Indirect link to outcomes	Indirect link to outcomes
Space for meetings in library	Indirect link to outcomes	Indirect link to outcomes	Indirect link to outcomes
Space for studying in library	Indirect link to outcomes	Indirect link to outcomes	Indirect link to outcomes

LIBRARY'S ROLE IN STUDENT LEARNING

One study examined student characteristics and undergraduate library use and found that five variables influenced library use: hours spent on campus, credit hour enrollment, gender (male), grade point average, and academic major.[5] However, a contrary point of view resulted from an analysis that found the quantity of time spent in the library was not associated with academic success, and a weak positive correlation was observed between academic achievement and the use of different library resources and services.[6] More recent studies have demonstrated a link between use of library collections and services and student learning.

The Hong Kong Baptist University Library. Thee library paired each student who used the library in some way with a nonuser counterpart with similar background, study major, and class level (undergraduate and graduate student). A total of 48 sample groups were analyzed and 31 of the 48 groups showed a positive statistical relationship between GPA and the borrowing of library materials.[7]

The Library Impact Data Project (England). Library transaction data that captured data for an individual (borrowing of materials, entering the library building, and downloading of e-resources) from eight UK-based universities (the data set involved several thousand records from each university) were analyzed and a statistically significant relationship between student GPA and two of the indicators—the downloading of e-resources and the borrowing of materials—was found.[8]

The Library Cube (Australia). The University of Wollongong Library created a data set called the Library Cube that combines library transaction data (borrowing of materials and the downloading of e-resources) with students' demographic and academic performance data. Interestingly, the library transaction data are updated every 15 minutes. The resulting data set can be used to explore possible relationships between use of the library and student learning. The analysis reveals that there is a positive relationship between the downloading of e-resources as well as the borrowing of library materials and student GPA.[9]

The University of Minnesota Library. The University of Minnesota-Twin Cities campus tracked the use of library services for entering freshmen students, controlling for the influence of demographic characteristics of each student ($N=5{,}368$). Freshmen students who used the library had a 0.23 higher GPA over those students who did not use the library.[10]

Stamford University Library. Using EZProxy log-in transaction data, an analysis revealed that students with a higher GPA logged in and downloaded more e-resources than their counterparts with lower GPAs.[11]

Midwest Public University Library (USA). An analysis of 3,757 freshmen and sophomore students over the course of a semester tracked the extent of what library services were used. A central database was created that captured use of the physical collections, e-resources, library computer lab, interlibrary loan, library instruction sessions, enrollment in credit-bearing information literacy courses, library-managed writing center, and the library-managed oral communication center. These library usage data were combined with student retention data; the results demonstrated that freshmen library use of any kind was nine times more likely to be retained than nonusers, and sophomore library users were four times more likely to be retained than nonusers.[12]

Examining the relatively consistent findings of the studies, it is possible to come to the following conclusions:

- There is no clear and consistent evidence that library use is linked to learning or academic success.
- A considerable proportion of all undergraduate students borrow no materials from the library.
- A small proportion of students (10 to 15 percent) are responsible for a majority of borrowed materials.
- Assigned readings and course-related readings (reserves) account for the majority of circulation in most undergraduate libraries.
- The amount of borrowing varies by discipline or field of study.
- Borrowing by undergraduates increases by class rank—lowest among freshmen and highest among seniors.
- A few courses on a campus will generate the majority of library use.
- The studies do not control for student abilities and typically rely on a single measure of use and success.
- The correlation between library use and academic achievement is weak at best.
- Few studies reported a link between bibliographic instruction and increased use of the library resources and services.

LIBRARY'S ROLE IN STUDENT RETENTION

The picture that emerges when examining the research about the role of the library in helping to retain students is mixed. There are two broad methods that can be used to study student retention and libraries: institutional-level data and individual-level data. When considering the former method, library usage data are combined with other institutional-level data, as Elizabeth Mezick did when she found no correlations between indicators of a culture of library assessment and student retention.[13]

Crawford created a "Total library service index per FTE" (sum of total circulations, interlibrary loans, gate counts, reference transactions, and instructional attendance—but not including number of downloaded e-resources) and found a positive and significant correlation between library use and six-year graduation rates. However, the correlation was weak and accounted for only a small proportion of the variation.[14]

Using individual-level data, Haddow and Joseph's study examined the number of items borrowed, number of online logins (regardless of location), and amount of computer usage located in the library. The authors found that students who withdrew from the university had little or no use of library resources, particularly at the start of the semester.[15] Retained students used library resources much more frequently than the students who dropped out.

The University of Minnesota focused its data collection efforts on the use of library services among entering freshmen students in their first semester.

LIBRARY'S ROLE IN TEACHING

Almost no research has been done to evaluate the library's role in helping professors provide instructional materials and course content. Professors spend a fair amount of time reading in an attempt to keep current in their field of specialization. Some of what these professors read obviously comes from the library.

A study at the University of California, Berkeley, found that professors include images and visual materials in course content in order to improve their students' learning, to integrate primary sources into their teaching, to provide students with a context for a topic, and to include materials that would otherwise not be available.[16]

A survey of faculty members found that use of the resources, services, and facilities provided by the library resulted in savings of time, money, and other resources. Faculty also noted that using the library improved their teaching and their development of course-related materials.[17]

For example, "bigness" seems to count at a basic level: Large universities produce a large number of publications, and their libraries spend large amounts of money on these and other materials and thus have large collections. One method to determine the actual productivity of an institution, especially when making comparisons to other universities, is to calculate the number of citations by faculty members or by full-time researchers. Examining the citations in the Institute for Scientific Information (ISI) and library measures derived from the Association of Research Libraries, John Budd found medium to high correlations between the number of publications and number of volumes, materials expenditures, total expenditures, and number of professional staff.[18] Similar results were noted by James Baughman and Martha Kieltyka.[19]

One interesting study combined ARL, IPEDS, and National Science Foundation grant funding data and found that high levels of research funding are associated with the performance measures most closely associated with research itself: staffing, space, and doctoral students (and that library characteristics such as collection size, staffing, and total expenditures *have no explanatory value* regarding research funding).[20]

Gerstberger and Allen found a direct relationship between perceived accessibility of information and several measures of utilization.[21] Researchers appeared to follow Zipf's Law of Least Effort: Individuals choose the option to obtain information that involves the least effort.[22]

Brinley Franklin and colleagues found that remote usage significantly exceeds in-library usage of electronic resources, sometimes by as much as four to one. Researchers depend more on electronic resources than on traditional print journals, and patterns of use vary by academic discipline.[23]

SCHOOL LIBRARIES

Keith Curry Lance and his colleagues have been involved in a series of studies that have sought to assess the impact of school library media centers on student academic achievement. Studies have been completed in a number of states, including Colorado, Alaska, Pennsylvania, Oregon, Iowa, and New Mexico.[24] These studies used a multivariate statistical analysis to control for competing predictors of achievement such as other school factors (teacher qualifications and experience, teacher-pupil ratio, per-pupil expenditures) and community conditions (adult educational attainment, racial and ethnic demographics, and poverty).[25]

The original Colorado study found that the size of the library in terms of staff and collection was a direct predictor of reading scores; the variation ranged from 5 to 15 percent. A majority of test score variation was explained by socioeconomic factors.

School principals have a strong impact on school library programs. They are willing to take risks, provide strong leadership, have problem-coping skills, and clearly communicate their expectations, which in turn lead to changed teacher behaviors.[26]

Examining these studies collectively, it is possible to identify three major sets of findings:

- **School library development:** Higher levels of professional and total staffing, larger collections of print and electronic resources, and more funding result in students doing better on standardized reading tests.
- **Leadership:** Meeting frequently with the principal, attending and participating in faculty meetings, serving on standards and curriculum committees, and meeting with library colleagues outside the local school resulted in students doing better academically.
- **Collaboration activities:** Identifying useful materials for teachers, planning instruction cooperatively with teachers, providing in-service training for teachers, and teaching students both with classroom teachers and independently were linked to higher reading scores.[27]

Ross Todd and other researchers at Rutgers University have conducted a number of large-scale state school library studies. Collectively, these studies have identified specific outcomes enabled through the school library, including:[28]

- **Mastery of resource-based competencies**—seeking, accessing, and evaluating resources
- **Mastery of research processes and learning management competencies**—prepare for, plan, and undertake research
- **Development of thinking-based competencies**—process of higher-order thinking and critical analysis
- **Development of affective, personal, and interpersonal competencies**—the social and cultural participation of inquiry
- **Outcomes related to reading to learn and reading for enjoyment**—reading for curriculum goals and for personal enjoyment

PUBLIC LIBRARIES

The Public Library Association received a grant from the Gates Foundation to develop standardized measures of effectiveness (outcomes) for the users of library services. During the course of the Project Outcome (www.projectoutcome.org), any public library can sign up and participate. Initially, a library asks participants in a library program (or a series of programs) to complete a brief survey. Surveys are available in seven areas: civic/community engagement, digital learning, early childhood literacy, economic development, education/lifelong learning, job skills, and summer reading. The survey asks four outcome-related questions with Likert-style response options:

- Learn something new?
- Gain confidence?
- Change their behavior?
- Gain awareness of library resources?

In addition, the survey respondents can indicate what worked well and what could be improved. As of the fall of 2016, the most heavily used surveys included the Early Childhood Literacy and the Education Lifelong Learning surveys (more than 3,600 respondents). The surveys are proving to be quite useful for identifying trends and identifying problems so that each participating library can take immediate corrective action, which results in the program getting incrementally better each time it is offered.

The Project Outcome team is developing additional tools to gather data in a variety of ways to ensure more reliable outcome-based data.

The value of a public library includes both use and nonuse, as shown in Figure 23.2. Use value can also be divided into two elements: direct and indirect benefits. The access to collections and services provides a range of benefits for users of the library that can be determined using several methods, as illustrated in Figure 23.2.

The direct and indirect value components for a typical public library are illustrated in Figure 23.3. Six areas in which the library may provide services are included: early childhood literacy and school readiness, local economic development, employment and career skills, encouraging small businesses, library as place, and recreational and personal learning.

				SERVICES & PROGRAMS	BENEFITS	MEASUREMENT METHODS
BENEFITS	USE	DIRECT	The direct benefits to library users	Collection—print Collection—non-print Collection—eResources Information technology Programs Flexible space in the facility	Financial savings Access to services Personal outcomes Social benefits Community outcomes	Consumer surplus Contingent valuation Survey of user willingness to pay
		INDIRECT	The follow-on benefits of using library services		Local amenity Environmental savings Contribution to literacy Complement educational institutions Facilitate career development	
	NON-USE	OPTION	The option for personal future use			Contingent valuation Survey of non-user willingness to pay
		EXISTENCE	Perceived value to the community			
		LEGACY	Value of preservation for future generations			

Figure 23.2. Ways to Determine Outcomes and Library Value

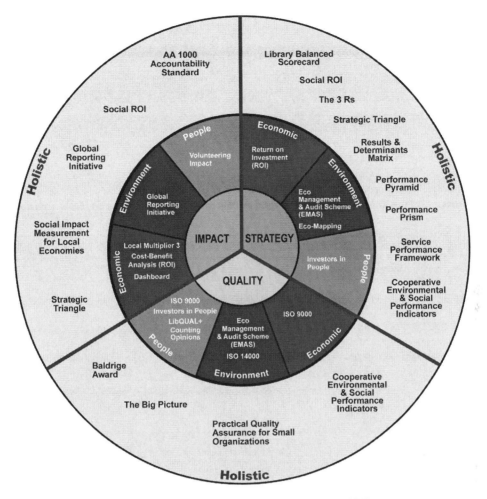

Figure 23.3. Tool Selector. © Joseph Matthews 2010.

A 2016 study found that although the public library is a valued community institution, there is no link between the perceived value and the level of funding among city mayors. Library advocacy efforts and a focus on library evaluation assist libraries in surviving; however, securing additional funding for a library is not about "library goodness."[29]

SUMMARY

Clearly, there are significant opportunities for the library community to begin to better understand the relationship of the library's resources and services to the outcomes and impacts in the lives of customers, students, faculty, and researchers. Research and assessment activities will require some creative approaches to better understand the contributions of the library. Seeking to assess impact will require any library to move from a traditional, library-centric view of the world to looking at the deeper issues associated with the library's actual contribution to learning, teaching, and research.

NOTES

1. R. David Lankes. Beyond the Bullet Points: Bad Libraries Build Collections, Good Libraries Build Services, Great Libraries Build Communities. R. David Lankes blog, 11 March 2012. Available at http://davidlankes.org/?p=1411

2. Tefko Saracevic and Paul B. Kantor. Studying the Value of Library and Information Services. Part I. Establishing a Theoretical Framework. *Journal of the American Society of Information Science*, 48 (6), 1997, 527–42; Tefko Saracevic and Paul B. Kantor. Studying the Value of Library and Information Services. Part II. Methodology and Taxonomy. *Journal of the American Society of Information Science*, 48 (6), 1997, 543–63.

3. ISO. *ISO 16439. Information and Documentation—Methods and Procedures for Assessing the Impact of Libraries.* Geneva: International Standards Organization, 2014.

4. Joseph R. Matthews. *Library Assessment in Higher Education.* Westport, CT: Libraries Unlimited, 2015.

5. Charles B. Harrell. *The Use of an Academic Library by University Undergraduates.* Doctoral dissertation, University of North Texas, 1988; Ethelene Whitmire. The Relationship Between Undergraduates' Background Characteristics and College Experiences and Their Academic Library Use. *College & Research Libraries*, 62 (6), November 2001, 528–40.

6. Jennifer Wells. The Influence of Library Usage on Undergraduate Academic Success. *Australian Academic & Research Libraries,* June 1995, 121–28.

7. Shun Han Wong and T. D. Webb. Uncovering Meaningful Correlation Between Student Academic Performance and Library Material Usage. *College & Research Libraries*, July 2011, 361–70.

8. Graham Stone. Library Impact Data Project: Looking for the Link Between Library Usage and Student Attainment. *College & Research Libraries*, November 2013, 546–59.

9. Brian Cox and Margie Jantti. Discovering the Impact of Library Use and Student Performance. *EDUCAUSE Review Online*, July 18, 2012. Available at http://er.educause.edu/articles/2012/7/discovering -the-impact-of-library-use-and-student-performance; see also Brian Cox and Margi Jantti. Capturing Business Intelligence Required for Targeted Marketing, Demonstrating Value, and Driving Process Improvement. *Library & Information Science Research*, 34 (4), 2012, 308–16; Margie Jantti and Jennifer Heath. What Role for Libraries in Learning Analytics? *Performance Measurement and Metrics*, 17 (2), 2016, 203–10.

10. Krista Soria, Jan Fransen, and Shane Nackerud. Library Use and Undergraduate Student Outcomes: New Evidence for Students Retention and Academic Success. *portal: Libraries and the Academy*, 13 (2), 2013, 147–64.

11. Karen Davidson, Stephanie Rollins, and Ed Cherry. Demonstrating Our Value: Tying Use of Electronic Resources to Academic Success. *Serials Librarian*, 65, 2013, 74–79.

12. Adam Murray, Ashley Ireland, and Jana Hackathorn. The Value of Academic Libraries: Library Services as a Predictor of Student Retention. *College & Research Libraries,* September 2016, 631–42.

13. Elizabeth Mezick. Relationship of Library Assessment to Student Retention. *Journal of Academic Librarianship*, 41 (1), 2014, 31–36.

14. Gregory Crawford. Pennsylvania Academic Libraries and Student Retention and Graduation: A Preliminary Investigation with Confusing Results. *Pennsylvania Libraries: Research & Practice*, 2 (2), 2014, 129–41.

15. Gaby Haddow and Jayanthi Joseph. Loans, Logins, and Lashing the Course: Academic Library Use and Student Retention. *Australian Academic & Research Libraries*, 41 (4), 2010, 233–44.

16. Diane Harley. Why Study Users? An Environmental Scan of Use and Users of Digital Resources in Humanities and Social Sciences Undergraduate Education. *First Monday*, 12 (1), January 2007. Available at https://firstmonday.org/ojs/index.php/fm/article/view/1423/1341

17. Rachel Fleming-May, Regina Mays, and Anne Pemberton. Academic Libraries' Support for Teaching: A LibValue Project. *Proceedings of the Library Assessment Conference*, 2014, 526–28. Available at http://libraryassessment.org/bm~doc/proceedings-lac-2014.pdf

18. John M. Budd. Faculty Publishing Productivity: An Institutional Analysis and Comparison with Library and Other Measures. *College & Research Libraries*, 56 (6), November 1995, 547–54; John M. Budd. Increases in Faculty Publishing Activity: An Analysis of ARL and ACRL Institutions. *College & Research Libraries*, 60, 1999, 308–15.

19. James C. Baughman and Martha E. Kieltyka. Farewell to Alexandria: Not Yet! *Library Journal*, 123 (5), 1999, 48–49.

20. Ryan P. Womack. ARL Libraries and Research: Correlates of Grant Funding. *The Journal of Academic Librarianship*, 42, 2016, 300–12.

21. Peter G. Gerstberger and Thomas J. Allen. Criteria Used by Research and Development Engineers in the Selection of an Information Source. *Journal of Applied Psychology*, 52 (4), August 1968, 272–79; see also Thomas J. Allen and Peter G. Gerstberger. *Criteria for Selection of an Information Source*. Cambridge, MA: MIT Press, 1967.

22. G. K. Zipf. *Human Behavior and the Principle of Least Effort*. Cambridge, MA: Addison-Wesley, 1949. See also Victor Resenberg. Factors Affecting the Preferences of Industrial Personnel for Information Gathering Methods. *Information Storage and Retrieval*, 3, 1967, 119–27.

23. Brinley Franklin and Terry Plum. Successful Web Survey Methodologies for Measuring the Impact of Networked Electronic Services (MINES for Libraries). *IFLA Journal,* 32 (1), 2006, 28–40; Brinley Franklin, Martha Kyrillidou, and Toni Olshen. The Story Behind the Numbers: Measuring the Impact of Networked Electronic Services (MINES) and the Assessment of the Ontario Council of University Libraries' Scholars Portal. Presented at the 6th Northumbria International Conference on Performance Measurement in Libraries and Information Services, Durham, England, August 22–24, 2005.

24. For a list of the many state projects that have focused on the value of school libraries, visit https://www.lrs.org/data-tools/school-libraries/impact-studies/

25. Keith Curry Lance and Becky Russell. Scientifically Based Research on School Libraries and Academic Achievement: What Is It? How Much of It Do We Have? How Can We Do It Better? *Knowledge Quest*, 32 (5), May/June 2004, 13–17.

26. Ken Haycock. Research in Teacher-Librarianship and the Institutionalization of Change, in A. Clyde (Ed.). *Sustaining the Vision: A Collection of Articles and Papers on Research in School Librarianship*. San Jose, CA: Hi Willow Research and Publishing, 1996, 13–22.

27. Keith Curry Lance. What Research Tells Us about the Importance of School Libraries. *Knowledge Quest,* 31 (1), September/October 2002, supplement, 17–22.

28. Ross Todd. *School Library Advocacy, Evidence and Actions in the USA: Principles for Planning and Implementing Advocacy Initiatives*. Presentation at the IFLA Conference in Lyon, France, 2014.

29. Edith Beckett. *Exploring the Relationship Between Constructs of Library Value and Local Government Public Library Funding: A Study of New Jersey Public Libraries*. Doctoral dissertation. New Brunswick, NJ: Rutgers, 2016.

24

Economic Impacts

*You may have heard the world is made up of atoms and molecules,
but it's really made up of stories.
When you sit with an individual that's been here,
you can give quantitative data a qualitative overlay.*

—William Turner[1]

Libraries must increasingly justify the money they receive and provide evidence about the impact of the library's use. It is possible to consider three categories of benefits:

Use Benefits

- Direct benefits
  - Cost savings from avoiding the purchase of materials (books, CDs, videos, magazines, newspapers, reference materials, and electronic resources)
  - Free or low-cost access to computers, photocopiers, audio and video equipment, meeting rooms, and programs
  - Access to trained professionals
  - Economic impact of library spending on jobs, supplies, and so forth in the local community
  - Economic spending by library users in nearby business establishments
- Indirect benefits
  - Improving skills—reading literacy, job skills, computer skills—for children and adults of all ages
  - Educational programs
  - Library as a community amenity
  - Community interactions
  - Support for a democratic society
  - Social welfare

Nonuse Benefits

- Option for an individual to use the library at some time in the future. The library is appreciated and valued as an institution that improves the quality of life in the community.
- Option for others to use now and in the future—sometimes called altruistic motivation. Indicates the willingness of individuals to support the library so that others may benefit. Nonuse benefits are difficult to quantify and if measured are open to considerable discussion and debate. Thus, nonuse benefits are typically ignored in order to produce a more conservative estimate of benefits.

The total value of a library can be determined by adding use and nonuse values.

It is also critical to think about value from the perspective of the library customer. Value should be considered as the worth of a product or service in terms of organizational, operational, social, and financial benefit to the customer. All library product offerings and services have both a value and a cost in the mind of the customer. The cost of the offering may be monetary, but it more than likely also includes such factors as time, effort, or equipment needed to make use of a library service. And the customer will be comparing the value and the costs associated with using the library with the value and costs of using an alternative.

METHODOLOGIES

The method most frequently used for evaluation of the economic benefits of a library is the use of a survey, or multiple surveys to different groups of individuals. Any evaluation must address several important issues: who receives the value, when the value accrues, whether an immediate benefit also translates into a long-term value, and how to identify and quantify the tangible and intangible benefits derived from library use. The end result is the preparation of a cost-benefit analysis, which attempts to compare the total costs and the value of the total benefits to make an evaluation of the utility of the library.

Several methods have been used in an attempt to determine the economic value of a library, including:

Direct survey

Client value model

Contingent valuation

Consumer surplus

Formula approach

Return on capital investment

Impact analysis

Economic impact analysis

Data envelopment analysis

A meta-analysis of a variety of research studies resulted in the well-known report, *Worth Their Weight*, which concluded that

> [p]ublic library valuation researchers have sought out and adopted valuation methods from the field of economists that allow the library to put a dollar value on its programs and services and show efficient use of tax dollars in cost/benefit terminology. The studies we reviewed clearly demonstrate the field's growing

sophistication, showing advancement from simple questionnaires to complex surveys, and from simple economic cost/benefit assessments to complex economic algorithms and forecasts.[2]

A subsequent meta-analysis by Svanhild Aabø of 38 library return-on-investment (ROI) studies concluded that

> ROI increases considerably, as expected, when both direct and indirect benefits are included . . . and that cost/benefit analysis (CBA) combined with market analogy methods or measurement of secondary economic impacts gives a higher ROI figure than CBA combined with contingent valuation.[3]

DIRECT SURVEY

The outcomes or impacts the library and its information services have on the larger organization can be summarized by using three major outcome categories: *accomplishments, time,* and *money.*

Accomplishments can be viewed as the category of outcome or impact that is not related to time or money impacts. Further, accomplishments can be viewed both from a positive perspective and from the perspective of avoiding negative consequences, as articulated most clearly by Joanne Marshall in some of her studies. For example, Marshall suggests that information services can assist the organization by avoiding[4]

- poor business decisions,
- conflict within the institution, and
- conflict with another institution.

A case in point illustrates the consequences of a poor decision-making process when incomplete information about a particular topic becomes one of the components of a decision. A medical researcher at Johns Hopkins University conducted an online search about the potential side effects of a particular chemical compound, which was being considered for testing on humans.[5] The researcher did not conduct a thorough search of the published paper-based literature, found in the library, which preceded the start of an online database. Based on the online search results, the trial for human testing commenced and one of the volunteers subsequently died. For a period of time, all medical trials at Johns Hopkins University were stopped. Now researchers must collaborate with a librarian and a pharmacist to ensure that a search of medical literature is comprehensive and thorough.

Time. One of the principal values of a library and its information services is that it significantly improves the productivity of the clients of the library, and thus the efficiency of the larger organization is improved. The principal reason this is so is that the librarian is more knowledgeable and skilled in the area of information retrieval and, at the same time, are paid less than other professionals (for example, doctors, engineers, lawyers, and senior managers).

Helen Manning surveyed library users and asked them to identify the impact of library services on their job, the number of hours saved as a result of using library services, and the number of hours saved by the librarian. Manning calculated that the total savings attributable to use of the library resulted in a benefit/cost ratio of 5.15:1.[6]

In a wide range of studies, José-Marie Griffiths and Don King have focused on the apparent value of information services. That is, they focused on the time and effort that would be required for an individual to identify, locate, order, receive, and use the needed information compared to the time (and thus, cost) if these tasks were performed by a library. If the library were eliminated and other sources of information were used to provide the equivalent information, the organization would spend considerably more than it does for a library—a 3:1 return on investment.[7]

The net result of the Griffiths and King studies is that libraries provide better information, faster and less expensively, than is possible considering other alternatives. By providing timely, quality information services that meet the needs of the professionals within an organization, the library helps to increase the quality, timeliness, and productivity of these individuals and ultimately enhances the performance of the larger organization.

Griffiths and King also report that professionals spend a considerable amount of time reading journal articles, books, internal reports, and other documents (professionals average 198 readings per year). These professionals spend a considerable amount of time acquiring and reading documents (an average of 288 hours per year). This reading, in turn, leads these professionals to avoid having to do certain work, modify their existing work, or stop an unproductive line of work.

Professional employees spend an average of 9.5 hours a week obtaining, reviewing, and analyzing information that represents a significant expenditure of their time at the workplace. These same professionals have also estimated the value of receiving information from the library as opposed to their acquiring the documents themselves. On average, the return on investment ranged from 7.8:1 to 14.2:1.[8]

Gwen Harris and Joanne Marshall prepared a cost-benefit analysis that examined a library's current awareness bulletin and found a benefit-to-cost ratio of 9:1.[9] Readers of the current awareness bulletin felt that they not only saved time, but also were introduced to new ways of doing things, avoided duplication of effort, and increased their individual productivity.

There is a flip side to the positive impact of improving a person's productivity, as noted by Marshall.[10] Without the appropriate information, a person can experience loss (waste) of his or her own time or loss of another person's time. This expenditure of time or attention is the currency of exchange for information. This scarcity of attention relative to the abundant amount of available information creates an *attention economy*, according to Warren Thorngate.[11]

The constantly increasing volume of information means that any criteria developed to separate the informational wheat from the chaff are going to be problematic. As we seek information, we are likely to make two kinds of errors: of commission (reading something that has little or no value) and of omission (overlooking something we shouldn't). Sampling an ever-decreasing proportion of worthwhile articles, reports, and so forth means that we are ever more likely to overlook that which would provide insight, solve a problem, suggest a new direction for research, and so forth.

Money. Two approaches to identifying the cost aspects of the library and its information services can be used: ascertaining (1) the relative value and (2) the consequential value of an information service.

The *relative value* approach seeks to identify the cost to use alternative sources of information compared to the nominal cost of providing the library service. According to Griffiths and King, on average, an organization without a library will spend more than three times per year as much per professional to obtain information services as an organization with a library. This estimated value approach is based on the assumption that each service transaction results in true "savings" for an organization, but clearly this is not always the case. Yet this approach can be an effective starting point for the library director when discussing the value of the library with the management team of the organization.

The second approach is to identify the *consequential value* of using the library and its information services. The approach here is to ask the library client (user) what is the financial impact of each information service transaction (or of a sample of transactions). The decision of whether to use a sample would be based on the volume of activity within the library (a sample size of several hundred would be desirable, assuming that the total transactions exceed several thousand).

Some libraries wait about a week and then contact by telephone or e-mail the individual who responded to the survey. The survey questions are repeated. In some cases, the individual is able to think of some additional benefits that will accrue through use of the information service that he or she overlooked initially.

Once the data about the financial impact have been gathered, a cost-benefit analysis can be prepared. On the one hand, the benefits from using the library have been identified by the clients (quantifying the benefits). On the other hand, the costs for providing library services are fairly well known (using the library's budget and preparing an activity-based costing analysis to identify the indirect and overhead costs to the organization).[12] The cost-benefit analysis allows the library to prepare an estimate of the library's return on investment, or ROI.

Frank Portugal suggests that two variations can be followed when the cost-benefit analysis is prepared.[13] The first approach tallies all the financial benefits in the form of savings and reports the result. The second approach tallies all the financial benefits in the form of savings and also includes estimates of losses that may have occurred as the result of using the information service.

Depending on which option is chosen, the cost-benefit ratio for special libraries, according to Portugal, will range from 28:1 to 18.8:1. Clearly, either option demonstrates that the library is providing real dividends as the result of its services, and thus the library should not be considered an overhead expense.

Other studies report similar results. Leigh Estabrook, in her analysis of document delivery studies, found that there was a range of benefits that varied from $2 to $48 saved for every dollar spent.[14] In an earlier review of cost-benefit studies, Manning reported a ratio of savings to cost of about 5 to 1.[15] And Michael Koenig, in an article that reviewed the cost-benefit methodologies, identified a number of studies that resulted in a range of benefits to cost of 2.5:1 to 26:1.[16]

Freeing up a professional's time to identify and obtain relevant information can have a considerable beneficial impact on an organization. One survey of nine corporations found that the professionals were able to quantify the value of information received—the value of which ranged from $2,500 to $15,000 per document used.[17]

In addition to saving money, the information provided by the library may spur additional revenues (revenues from existing products and services to existing customers and/or attracting and retaining new customers), lead to the development of new products and services, shorten the product/service development life cycle, and so forth.[18]

The U.S. Department of Transportation produced a study which demonstrated that good information reduces costs, saves time, improves decision making, and improves customer satisfaction.[19] More recently, a toolkit for transportation librarians, *Proving Your Library's Value*, was developed to

> [a]ddress the perception that libraries are less relevant than they once were. Perhaps on-site usage is not what it used to be. With changes in technology, however,

the . . . services which libraries provide have remained the same (or increased), staff has found ways to do more with less, and improved services continue to be offered. It is the responsibility of librarians to prove this.[20]

Duplication, Replication, and Complementarity

A majority of research is conducted to discover new things. However, in some cases, research may be conducted for other reasons.

- *Replication* is the deliberate and conscious repetition of research intended to confirm or extend previous (and in some cases uncertain) research.
- *Complementarity* involves using several independent methods to overturn, confirm, or extend specific research findings.
- Duplication represents inadvertent, unconscious, or deliberate repetition of research efforts. Duplication often occurs due to a lack of knowledge about prior research findings.

Failing to conduct a thorough search for relevant information can lead to significant expenditures of funds that would not have been spent if the information had been known. A survey in England estimated that between 10 and 20 percent of research was unintentionally duplicated, costing British companies from £6 to £12 million in 1962.[21] The belated discovery of information, if previously known, would have led to significant changes, as shown in Figure 24.1.

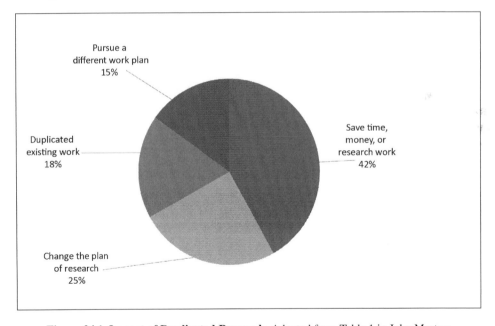

Figure 24.1. Impact of Duplicated Research. Adapted from Table 1 in John Martyn. Unintentional Duplication of Research. *New Scientist,* 377, 1968, 338.

A more recent study conducted by the UK Patent Office found that few companies investigated previous research and development results. Further, the Patent Office found that about one-third of the applications had already been patented and thus the efforts had been duplicated. This duplication of effort was estimated to cost the European Union £20 billion a year in 1998.[22] Also, many companies pay other companies millions each year for infringing intellectual patent property rights.

CLIENT VALUE MODEL

Guillaume Van Moorsel has suggested creating a client value model, which establishes a common "value vocabulary" for libraries and their customers, thereby establishing a basis for making planning decisions about library product and service offerings. A relative value index is created for alternative products or service offerings that can be used to assess each alternative.[23]

CONTINGENT VALUATION

The *contingent valuation* (CV) method, developed by Nobel laureate economists Kenneth Arrow and Robert Solow, uses surveys to value nonmarket or public goods and services. The strength of the contingent valuation method is its directness. Contingent valuation has been applied to more than 50 cultural studies, including assessing the value of cultural and national heritage, museums, theaters, art and paintings, and libraries.[24] Another study examined more than 2,000 papers and studies from more than 40 countries that applied the technique in different contexts.[25]

The respondent is presented with a description of the service, its present quantity and quality, and an anticipated or planned change. In order to be valid, contingent valuation must not violate the assumption of rationality. The respondent is then asked to state the value of the proposed change in terms of his or her maximum willingness to pay or asked how much the respondent would accept to give up something he or she already has.

Ideally the two contingent valuation methods—willingness to pay and willingness to accept—would provide similar estimates of benefits. However, the willingness to accept method will typically provide the highest benefits estimates, as respondents normally include not only direct benefits but also societal or collective benefits. The willingness-to-pay approach provides a more conservative estimate, because some respondents assume that someone else in society will fund the service even if they choose not to support it—the "free rider" problem.

The role of altruism must be addressed when a contingent valuation study is conducted so that the study strength can be addressed before any conclusions can be drawn. Altruism can be divided into several categories: local versus global, and nonpaternalistic versus paternalistic altruism. Aabø and Strand found that 40 percent of a library's total value is motivated by nonuse value, and from 15 to 30 percent of total value is motivated by global altruism.[26]

Although contingent valuation has been used in a variety of settings, it is not without its detractors. Potential bias can stem from at least three perspectives: strategic, information, or hypothetical bias. These biases may appear depending on the manner in which questions are structured, combined with the respondent having sufficient information (or familiarity due to experience) with the goods or services being valued in order to formulate an appropriate response.[27]

St. Louis Public Library. Two contingent valuation methods were used at the St. Louis Public Library to determine a cost-benefit ratio. The first approach asked a random sample of library card holders (sample size was 332) what they would be willing to pay in taxes to enjoy the library services as they then existed. The respondents indicated that they would be willing to pay at the same rate as the library's budget—a 1:1 ratio.[28]

A second approach, the willingness-to-accept method, asked what the respondents would accept in terms of a reduced tax bill if the library system were to close. The respondents indicated that the average amount that they would accept would be a $7 reduction. However, 88 percent of the respondents refused to answer the question, indicating that the library was too valuable or too important to consider closing; that the community and their children needed the public library. The end result using the willingness-to-accept method was a 7:1 benefit-to-cost ratio; however, use of this ratio should be carefully considered given the low response rate of values provided by respondents.

Respondents' expectations, reasons for using a public library, and prior experiences in using the library will in large part determine their assessment of the value of library services.

Phoenix Public Library. In the Phoenix Public Library study, telephone interviews were conducted with a random sample of library cardholders, who were asked how much they would be willing to pay (in taxes) to enjoy the library privileges they already had. Respondents were also asked how much of a tax cut they would accept in exchange for closing all public libraries (80 percent of the households interviewed refused to answer the willingness-to-accept question).[29]

In addition, a sample of teachers was asked how much their school budgets would have to increase to provide the same quality of resources and services if the Phoenix Public Library did not exist. Similarly, businesses were asked how much their firms would have to be compensated to be made "whole" again if services of the library were no longer available. The benefit-to-cost ratio using the willingness-to-pay method was 10.1:1; the willingness-to-accept method produces a much higher ratio of 51.2:1.

The study also used the consumer surplus method as well as calculating the return to capital assets; these methods are discussed later in this chapter. Overall, the study found that for each dollar of the library's budget, its patrons received benefits of more than $10.

The British Library. The British Library commissioned a study to determine the library's contribution to the national economy. The study used the contingent valuation method to determine the direct and indirect benefits arising from use of the library. More than 2,000 people were interviewed, and the study concluded that for every £1 pound of public finding the British Library receives annually, £4.40 was generated for the UK economy. If the British Library did not exist, the UK would lose £280 million of economic value per annum.[30]

Norway. A contingent valuation study was conducted throughout all of Norway using a telephone survey of 999 individuals. The sample reflected the characteristics of the total population of Norway. This study was unique in that it asked the respondents to assign a value to the motivations for using a public library—direct, indirect, and nonuser values.

The results revealed that direct use had the highest value among the respondents—40 percent. The value of having the option to use the public library should the need arise, sometimes called the potential use value, was the second highest value—20 percent. The altruistic motivation value for others in the community, not the respondents or their family, and their use of the public library, was the third highest value—17 percent. Adding all the other options to the altruistic value provides a total of 40 percent for nonuse values.[31] The importance of nonuse values shows that a majority of the respondents appreciate and value social benefits of public libraries and will support libraries from a broader perspective than direct self-interest only. Interestingly, households with higher education and fewer children are more likely to give greater weight to altruistic or nonuse values. Further, some 94 percent of the Norwegian population perceive that they have property rights to their local library. Also, using a willingness-to-accept method, a cost-benefit ratio was reported as 4:1.[32]

CONSUMER SURPLUS

Consumer surplus is used by economists to determine the value consumers place on the consumption of a good or service in excess of what they must pay to get it. Although library services are free, customers do pay in the form of time and direct transportation costs to use the public library. This effort to use the library represents an implicit price or transaction cost to the customer. Because many alternatives to almost all library services are available in the market-place, it is possible to determine the price of the market alternative plus its transaction cost.

In conducting a consumer surplus survey, respondents are asked, for example, about the number of books that they borrow from the library, the number of books that they buy, and the number of additional books that they would buy if they could not borrow from the library. Comparing the number of borrowed books with the number of purchased books, it is possible to calculate the value that the library user places on borrowing privileges. Such estimates can also be made for each library service used by each user surveyed. All of these estimates are then totaled to provide an estimate of the total direct annual benefits for all library users measured in dollars.

A survey of general users, teachers, and businesspeople using the consumer surplus method, conducted on behalf of the Phoenix Public Library, found a benefit-to-cost ratio of 16:1.

State of Florida. In a study of public libraries in Florida, survey participants were asked to indicate, in dollar terms, the value to them of individual library programs and services. The study team calculated overall user benefits by deriving an average retail price for each service. The value for each service was then totaled to derive the total benefits received by library users. A return on investment of $6.27 was calculated for each tax dollar invested.[33]

Another study of the economic contribution and return on taxpayer investment in Florida's public libraries employed both the contingent valuation method and an economic impact analysis, using data gathered from a statewide telephone survey of adults, in-library user surveys of adults, a follow-up survey of libraries, and surveys of organizations (schools, businesses, and so forth).

The study found that in addition to borrowing materials for recreational or entertainment reasons, adults used the public library for three reasons:

- **Personal or family needs:** job seeking, health issues, consumer purchasing, and so forth.
- **Educational needs:** as students, teachers, home schooling, and lifelong learning.
- **Work-related purposes:** contributions to businesses, schools, universities, nonprofit organizations, government agencies, and hospitals.

The study found an overall return on investment of 6.54 to 1.[34]

An earlier survey of 1,991 Florida public library customers, reported by Bruce Fraser et al., found that a significant number of respondents felt that the library had contributed to the patrons' financial well-being, provided benefits to local businesses, and contributed to the prosperity of the local/state community.[35]

State of South Carolina. A study found that the total direct economic impact for South Carolina's public libraries (only the value of circulation and reference services were calculated) resulted in a benefit-to-cost ratio of 2.86:1.

Survey respondents also agreed that the public library improves the quality of life (92 percent), enhances personal fulfillment (73 percent), nurtures a love of reading (73 percent), and is a source of personal enjoyment (64 percent); 78 percent of business users felt that the public library helped improve the success of their business.

The indirect economic impact of public library expenditures—wages, supplies, new materials, construction, and so forth—was almost $126 million. The indirect benefits provide a benefit-to-cost ratio of 1.62 to 1. Thus, the total direct and indirect return on investment is $4.48 for every dollar spent by South Carolina public libraries—a benefit-to-cost ratio of 4.48:1.[36] Note, though, that the use of an indirect economic impact analysis is a weak argument from the perspective of a funding stakeholder, given that other departments could spend the same amount of money and achieve the same results.

British Public Libraries. Analyzing the available statistical data, a study team concluded that British public libraries produce £98 million more value than they cost to provide—a return on investment of 13.6 percent. The borrowing of books and the dominant use of the public library allows the user to obtain the benefit at a fraction of what it would cost to purchase the book or to read books that would be too expensive to buy. Thus, different types of people, according to their education, wealth, age, and personal interest, generate a mixture of educational, informative, cultural, and recreational benefits.[37]

A SHORTCUT METHOD

Conducting a telephone or paper survey using the consumer surplus method is obviously costly and time-consuming. A shortcut method is available that will produce very similar results without incurring the costs of the survey. For each library service, a substitute price is determined by checking various sources in the local community or online. The results of such an analysis are shown in Table 24.1. The prices are then multiplied by the total activity levels for each category—annual circulation, attendance at programs, number of reference queries answered, and so forth.

As shown in Figure 24.2, the San Diego Public Library concluded that the benefits exceed costs by a factor of 6:1. Similar results were noted by the Miami-Dade Public Library System, which also found a benefit-to-cost ratio of 6:1 (see Table 24.2). Using this shortcut method, a library can calculate its own cost-benefit ratio. Determining and communicating the cost-benefit ratio for your library is important for both interested funding stakeholders and the citizens of a community.

One of the problems associated with the use of the cost-benefit ratio as calculated in Table 24.2 is that each use of a particular item is treated as if it were a new purchase by the library on behalf of the user. In addition, the material in the library's collection will be there for several years and will be used with less frequency over time. Clearly, material in a library's collection is going to have a value each time it is used, but from an economic viewpoint the value will be less than the original purchase price. A number of studies have attempted to calculate a more realistic value of an item being circulated (used by a library customer) as a percent of the purchase price of the item.

Table 24.1. Pricing of Substitute Market Services

Service	Substitute	Price ($)	Source
Children's books (paperback)	Bookstore	8.00	*Bowker Annual*
Books for adults (paperback)	Bookstore	14.00	*Bowker Annual*
Video/DVD films	Rental	4.00	Netflix
Audio/music	Purchase	13.00	Wal-Mart
Magazines	Newsstand	3.00	Local newsstand
Newspapers	Newsstand	1.00	Local newsstand
Toys	Educational store	15.00	Local educational store
Reference and research services	Information broker	50.00/hour	Information broker
Special events	Cultural center	9.00	Local cultural center
Craft and activity programs	YMCA	1.00/hour	YMCA
Social skills/ etiquette training	YMCA	1.00/hour	YMCA
WiFi	Local coffee shop	Free	Local coffee shop
Adult education	Public schools	40.00 per class	Public schools
Family or parenting programs	Public schools	40.00 per class	Public schools
Storytelling programs	Local bookstore	Free	Local bookstore
Meeting space	Local public school	25.00 per hour	Local public school
Encyclopedia	Purchase a CD	75.00	World Book
Dictionaries and almanacs	Local bookstore	10.00	Local bookstore

The business of the public library is to gather books, information, and related material to make them available, **Free** to the residents of the City of San Diego, CA. If our patrons had had to buy these materials and services in Fiscal Year 2001 they would have paid at least . . . .
$160,207,881!

For example:

- 6,587,872 items (including books, audiovisual materials, etc.) were borrowed. At an average retail price of $20, these would have cost **$131,757,540**.
- 1,617,633 books, periodicals and newspapers were used in libraries but not checked out. Had the library user had to purchase these materials at an average retail price of $10 these would have cost **$16,176,330**.
- 1,835,706 questions were answered in person and by telephone by library staff. Had the library user had to pay $2 for each inquiry, the cost would have been **$3,671,412**.
- 308,362 persons used the electronic magazines and newspapers on the library's IAC database. If the user had to purchase these materials or pay for access at $5 each, these activities would be worth **$1,541,810**.
- 536,974 persons signed up and used the Internet on a Library workstation. If the user had to pay for access at $10 each, these activities would be worth **$5,369,740**.
- 154,017 persons attended 4,370 library programs (excluding the film and Chamber Music series). At a $2.50 admission these activities would be worth **$385,034**.
- 22,400 children and teens registered for the Summer Reading Program. If each had paid a $5 registration fee, this would have cost **$110,200**.
- 618 literacy and ESL tutors provided 43,554 hours of tutoring to 839 learners. At $25/hour, this service would have cost **$1,088,850**.
- 227 students spent 6,170 hours using computer resources at the Library's Literacy Computer Lab. At $10/hour, this would have cost **$61,700**.
- 4,853 persons attended Monday evening and Sunday afternoon film series. At a $5 admission, these activities would be worth **$24,285**.
- 2,100 persons attended the Chamber Music series at the Central Library. At $10 admission, these activities would be worth **$21,000**.

These are just some of the services the public library provided in FY 2001. The value was much more to many more users than the estimate of $160,207,881. However, all of the library's services in FY 2001 cost the taxpayer of the City of San Diego only $27,675,365.

Figure 24.2. How Much Is Library Service Really Worth? Based on information from the San Diego Public Library.

Table 24.2. Miami-Dade Public Libraries Estimated Return on Investment, 1998–1999

Materials and Services	Estimated Benefits ($)
4,751,514 books and materials borrowed at an average retail price of $20 each.	95,030,280
4,614,903 books, periodicals, and newspapers were used in libraries; if purchased, the average retail price of each would be $10.	46,149,030
5,435,095 reference questions answered in person by library staff, if each charge were $2 per inquiry.	10,870,190
625,292 Internet sessions at a $2 per session access fee.	1,250,584
420,581 persons attended 8,546 programs and exhibitions, if there were a $2 admission fee.	841,162
19,000 children and teens participated in the Mayor's Summer Reading Program, if there were a $5 registration fee.	95,000
279 literacy tutors provided 10,015 hours of one-on-one tutoring to 239 Project LEAD participants, if each charge were $25/hour.	250,375
Total Benefits	154,486,621
Less Taxpayers' Investment (Annual Library Budget)	–24,645,113
Total Return on Investment	**129,841,508**
Benefit-to-Cost Ratio	**6.3:1**

Based on information from the Miami-Dade Public Library System.

Joseph Newhouse and A. J. Alexander constructed an economic model based on data collected at the Beverly Hills (California) Public Library which suggested that the value of an item being loaned was 10 percent of the purchase price of a book. They concluded that the maximum benefit was derived from books that were issued frequently over a long period of time.[38]

VALUE-ADDED LIBRARY METHODOLOGY

A "Value-Added Library Methodology" (V+LM) was developed in New Zealand that was based on the assumption of a hypothetical commercial market with willing buyers and sellers that would price the outputs of the service. The results of the New Zealand approach were derived using an average book loan value of 25 percent of the average book purchase price.[39] The V+LM approach was intended to identify and quantify what the library does that adds value, what activities add the greatest value, whether the budget allocation is appropriate, and any inconsistencies between principles and actions.[40] A library's service is valued with the V+LM methodology using three main measures:

- **Market price proxy,** which estimates the market price in an imagined situation where there is a willing seller and a willing buyer.
- **Replacement cost,** which estimates what it would cost to replace the service.
- **Opportunity cost,** which estimates the value from using a service assuming that less time is spent on searching for information.

Public, academic, and special libraries have used the V+LM methodology. For example, the Manakau Public Libraries, located in New Zealand, calculated a 66 percent return on the library's annual budget.

Two studies were conducted to identify the benefits from cataloging records provided by national libraries. A study performed for the National Library of Canada (NLC), using NLC records as the basis for copy cataloging rather than doing original cataloging of items, found that a total of $1,725,000 was saved by Canadian university libraries and large urban public libraries.[41] A similar study performed on behalf of the National Library of New Zealand found a total economic benefit of NZD $160.6 million.[42]

FORMULA APPROACH

A project in England to determine the value of public library benefits estimated the value of the loaning of materials and found that the value of benefits slightly exceeded the costs of providing the service. The project developed a simplified equation to estimate benefits:

$$V = 0.15 \; IP$$

where V=value, I=circulation of books, and P=the average price of acquiring the book.[43] This formula has the following attributes:

- Books acquired but not loaned will depress the value.
- The higher the circulation, the higher the value.
- More expensive books have a greater impact on value (the user receives more benefit).
- The value of paperback books is accurately reflected.
- Hardback books have a longer lending life than paperbacks.
- The formula is simple to use.

The disadvantage of this method is that only circulation of materials is being valued, to the exclusion of all other services. Adding additional components to the formula for other library services would probably make the formula too complicated.

Library ROI to Grants Income

An international study was conducted to determine the return on investment (ROI) in electronic resources in terms of grant dollars generated. A survey was distributed to faculty members with the intent to demonstrate that the library and its resources can be viewed as an asset, as faculty generate income through grants and use the library and its collections in developing their grant proposals and conducting their research. The intent was to demonstrate that the availability of electronic resources (from the desktop) increased faculty efficiency, enabling them to write more successful grant proposals more quickly with the result of increased revenue to the university. The outcome was a formula that in simplistic terms identified the amount of grant funding received with the library's help divided by the library's budget.[44] The actual formula used is shown in Figure 24.3.

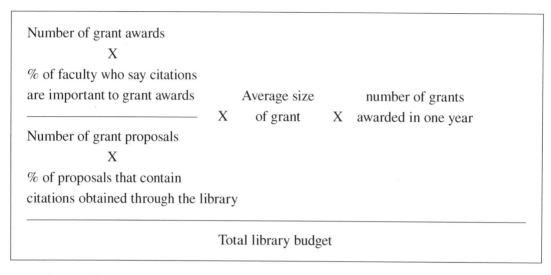

Figure 24.3. Library ROI in Grants Formula. Judy Luther. University Investment in the Library: What's the Return? A Case Study at the University of Illinois at Urbana-Champaign (White Paper). *Elsevier Library Connect,* 6 (1), 2008. Available at https://libraryconnect.elsevier.com/articles/university -investment-library-what-s-return-case-study-university-illinois-urbana-champaign

There are significant problems in attempting to calculate a library ROI using grant income as a surrogate measure of value. Grants are awarded and tracked each year and yet the university may receive the revenue over a several-year period. The formula tracks revenues and costs for a single year, yet a more conservative and accurate approach would be to track grant awards over a multi-year period. Ray Lyons provides a much more detailed discussion of the challenges of the library grant ROI formula shown here in his blog (Lib)rary Performance.[45]

The University of Colorado librarians decided to measure the institutional value of library resources used by faculty in their research using a variation of this approach. A total of three quantitative methods were used to gather data: cost-benefit analysis (CBA), a citation analysis of journal articles published by faculty, and return on investment (ROI); in addition, the researchers employed qualitative in-person interviews with faculty. The librarians assigned a monetary value to the journal articles used in research, identified relevant costs, and constructed a formula for determining faculty benefits.[46] In general, ROI is usually expressed as a percentage and represents the "rate of return" or the value of the benefits compared to the initial "investment" or total costs. The formula used in this study was:

$$((\text{Benefits} - \text{Costs}) \div \text{Costs}) \times 100 = \text{ROI}$$

The specific steps used to develop this model are shown in Figure 24.4. The table identifies the source of data so that other libraries can more easily apply this model in their own setting.

The results of this analysis suggested that for every dollar invested in journal subscriptions, the ROI model produced a positive return of 66 percent and 144 percent for the Denver

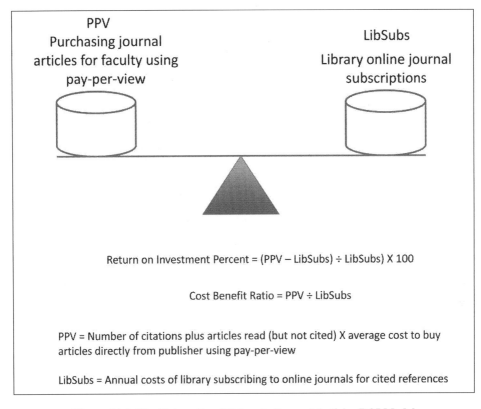

Figure 24.4. The University of Colorado Journal Articles ROI Model

and Boulder campuses respectively (and a negative return of -19 percent for the Anschutz Medical Center Campus).[47] Although a variety of factors will influence the ROI calculations, the reality is that ROI and CBA metrics are only meaningful when used as a suite of measures so that the entire library operations can be understood in context. The authors' unexpected bonus for conducting the study was that it helped to build relationships with academic departments, increased awareness of the library's resource needs, and provided evidence to explore alternative acquisition models.

RETURN ON CAPITAL INVESTMENT

Comparing annual benefits of the library with the annual tax-supported budget provides an estimate of the annual percent return on taxes paid. Tax support is the base that makes the existence of the library possible and hence makes its provision of services feasible. Determining the rate of return on the public library capital investment requires valuation of the physical assets of the library. These assets include land and buildings, furniture and equipment, and collections. Land is typically valued at estimated market value. Other assets are valued at their current replacement costs. The return on capital investment for several libraries is shown in Figure 24.5.[48]

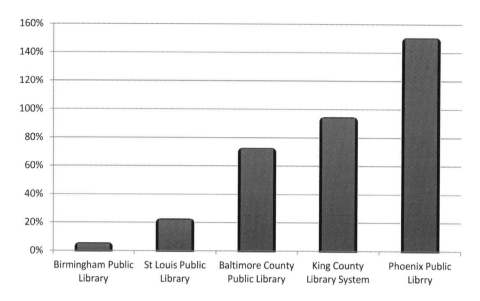

Figure 24.5. Return on Capital Investment for Selected Public Libraries. Glen E. Holt, Donald S. Elliott, Leslie E. Holt, and Anne Watts. *Public Library Benefits Valuation Study: Final Report to the Institute of Museum and Library Services for National Leadership Grant.* St. Louis, MO: St. Louis Public Library, 2001; Donald S. Elliott, Glen E. Holt, Sterling W. Hayden, and Leslie Edmonds Holt. *Measuring Your Library's Value: How to Do a Cost-Benefit Analysis for Your Public Library.* Chicago: ALA Editions, 2006.

ECONOMIC IMPACT ANALYSIS

A study conducted on behalf of the Free Library of Philadelphia estimated the economic impact of the library in helping Philadelphians learn to read and acquire working skills, locate job opportunities and develop career skills, develop or enhance their own businesses, and determine the increased value of neighborhood homes located near a branch public library. This study did not determine the ROI for the library, but did discover:[49]

Literacy. The economic value of the library services that help Philadelphians learn to read and acquire working skills totaled $21.8 million for FY10, comprised of
- $18.4 million in literacy-related reading and lending
- $2.6 million in literacy-related programming
- $818,000 in literacy-related online activities

Business Development. The economic value of the library services that help Philadelphians develop or enhance their own businesses totaled $3.8 million for FY10, comprised of
- $2.9 million in business development online and database activities
- $819,285 in business development book-reading and lending
- $55,385 in business development programming

Value to Homes and Neighborhoods. Homes within one-quarter mile of a library are worth, on average, $9,630 more than homes more than one-quarter mile from a library. For homes between one-quarter and one-half mile of a library, the additional value is $650.

A 2012 study by the Pew Charitable Trusts found that while Philadelphians see neighborhood branch facilities as multipurpose community centers, they use their libraries less when compared to a set of peer libraries, and also have fewer public access computers per capita. In addition, the Philadelphia Public Library has been slow to provide teen centers, adjust hours to encourage maximum patronage, and revamp facilities to make them more flexible and more welcoming.[50]

ECONOMIC IMPACT STUDIES

Economic impact studies compare local or regional economic conditions with an activity present versus the activity's absence. The economic benefit calculation estimates the change in economic indictors due to the activity.[51] An economic impact analysis uses a basic input-output model of economic activity to identify the specific stimulus, such as an investment in a new library building or the annual expenditures for the library's operations. The model identifies how transactions affect the production and consumption of goods and services in an economy. As the result of direct spending by the library for salaries and supplies, the model estimates the recycling of funds in the local or regional economy. This magnification of spending is known as the *multiplier effect.*

The library provides data on the location of vendors and suppliers for all library expenditures. A survey of library customers is then conducted to determine the value of their expenditures as a result of their visit to the library. Library customers might spend money on transportation, parking, food, shopping, movie, museum, motels, and so forth.

Seattle Public Library. The opening of a new downtown main library in Seattle, Washington, resulted in a 250 percent increase in the number of visitors to the Central Library. Approximately 30 percent of the 2.5 million individuals who visited the library were projected to be out-of-town visitors (based on a survey of people entering the library). An economic impact analysis demonstrated that these out-of-town visitors would spend $16 million annually in net new spending in downtown Seattle (hotels, restaurants, car rentals, ferries, and so forth).[52]

Carnegie Library of Pittsburgh. An economic impact analysis was prepared for the Carnegie Library of Pittsburgh, and the analysis concluded that the library provides an economic benefit of $3 for every dollar it spends. The Carnegie Library of Pittsburgh is *the most visited* regional asset. These visitors to the library spend a total of $9.8 to $15.6 million annually at nearby businesses. The library supported more than 900 jobs and $80 million in economic output in Allegheny County through its operations and renovations. The library provides more than $75 worth of benefits for every resident of Allegheny County.[53]

State of Florida. As part of a study conducted on behalf of the state of Florida, an econometric input-output model was used to estimate the economic effects of public libraries on the gross regional product (GRP), employment, and real disposable income (wages) from the public funding, investment, and earnings for 2004. The statewide GRP was estimated to have increased by $4.0 billion as a result of publicly funded public library expenditures in the state. A total of 68,700 jobs were created from the spending increases, and personal income increased by $5.6 million.[54]

On a larger or more macro scale, Liu examined the potential contributions of a nation's public libraries to the national economy using a statistical method known as path analysis. Liu found a causal relationship between public library expenditures, literacy rates, and economic productivity, with libraries having a direct effect on literacy rates and an indirect effect of national gross domestic product (GDP).[55]

DATA ENVELOPMENT ANALYSIS

Data envelopment analysis (DEA), developed by Charnes, Cooper, and Rhodes, is a statistical technique used to evaluate a number of producers, or (in the jargon of the DEA literature) a "decision making unit." A library can be a decision-making unit for the purposes of analysis. The production process for each decision-making unit is to convert a set of inputs and produce a set of outputs.[56]

A DEA analysis compares each producer with only the "best" producers. A data envelopment analysis might be prepared for a group of separate libraries or all branch libraries in a system. The inputs used in the analysis might be size of the facility, total number of materials in the collection, number of staff members, hours open per week, and so forth. The output measures might include circulation, reference queries answered, attendance at programs, gate count, and so forth.

The data envelopment analysis provides three types of evaluation information:

- A single summative score is assigned to each library. This series of efficiency scores can then be used to relate one decision-making unit to all others.
- Any perceived slack (or waste) in the input used and the output produced is identified.
- A set of weights is attached to each decision-making unit relative to all other units.

Obviously, the choice of what inputs and outputs to include in the analysis is very important. In most cases, a statistical technique called *correlation* is used to test for a statistical relationship between the input variables and the output variables. After all, preparing a data envelopment analysis using variables that are not related to one another will not produce any helpful information. The strengths of a DEA include the following:

- Multiple input and output models can be handled.
- It does not require an assumption of a functional form relating inputs to outputs.
- A producer is compared to a peer or a combination of peers.
- Inputs and outputs can have different units—dollars, counts, and so forth.
- Insights are gained into ways to increase outputs /or conserve inputs to make a library more efficient.
- The analysis can be run several times, changing the mix of input and output measures, in order to better understand the operations of the libraries.

One DEA study compared different size university libraries. The study team developed a "service index" for 24 university libraries in Taiwan. The input variables included data concerning collections, personnel, expenditures, buildings, and services provided.[57]

A DEA analysis of the Association of Research Libraries showed that about 49 percent of the public institutions appear inefficient, while only 17 percent of the private institutions do so.[58]

Another study compared 118 university libraries from German-speaking countries and English-speaking countries. Ten libraries were rated fully efficient; however, there were no significant differences between libraries from English-speaking and German-speaking countries or between small and large university libraries.[59] Chen prepared a study that evaluated the 23 university libraries in Taipei—using four input and five output variables—and found that 11 libraries were relatively efficient.[60]

An application of the data envelopment analysis examined the 47 branch public libraries in Hawaii. Four input measures (collection size, number of library staff, days open, and non-personnel expenditures) and three output measures (circulation, patron visits, and reference transactions) were used in the analysis. Among a number of additional library characteristics that were analyzed, only floor space and the size of the collection had positive effects on library performance—that is, larger libraries did better.[61]

OTHER METHODS

Other measures that might be used to determine the economic value of the library that have not been discussed in this chapter are:

- Subsidies the public library provides to other organizations in the community, such as schools, nonprofit organizations, and other government agencies.
- Cost avoidance resulting from the fact that the library provides a service and thus other government or nonprofit organizations need not expend monetary resources.[62]
- Conjoint analysis using statistical techniques to compare one attribute of a service with all other attributes to ascertain people's preferences.
- Path analysis using a series of regressions with a different number of variables entered at different stages to examine the causal relationships. Lewis Liu used path analysis to examine the relationships among public libraries, literacy levels, and economic productivity measured by gross domestic product per capita. Liu concluded that public libraries contribute to long-term economic productivity primarily through literacy programs.[63]

A report by the Urban Libraries Council summarizes the public library's contributions to local economic development. This readable report discusses the impact of library services in the areas of early literacy and school readiness, strategies for building workforce participation, small business support, and the power of place.[64]

SUMMARY

This chapter has presented a number of methods that can be used to determine the economic value of a library. As shown in Table 24.3, the various methods produce a range of benefits compared to cost. The good news is that regardless of the method selected, the results generally fall into the same range. That is, the typical benefit-to-cost ratio ranges from 4:1 to 6:1.

In a review of library valuation studies, Kim suggested it is possible to divide the studies into two frameworks: a *marketing framework* that aims to improve communication between libraries and their stakeholders (advocacy), and an *evaluation framework* that tries to describe the current state of affair in a library.[65] Each framework has contrasting purposes, objectives, and methodologies that must be acknowledged.

Several meta-analyses of library valuation studies have been completed. Aabø summarized 38 studies and found that ROI increased when both direct and indirect benefits were included in the calculations.[66] Another meta-analysis used regression analysis to examine a total of 42 library valuation studies and found that per capita GDP explained ROI scores.[67]

Table 24.3. Summary of Return on Investment (ROI) Studies

Study	Year	ROI
Single Library Studies—USA		
Baltimore Public Library[i]	2001	$4.50
Birmingham Public Library[ii]	2001	$2.00
Cortez Public Library (CO)[iii]	2009	$31.07
Kanawha County Public Library (Charleston, SC)[iv]	2009	$3.64
King County Public Library	2001	$7.50[v]
Mastic-Moriches-Shirley Community Library (Suffolk County, NY)	2006	$2.97
Middle Country Public Library (Suffolk County, NY)[vi]	2006	$4.59
Northport-East Northport Public Library (Suffolk County, NY)[vii]	2006	$3.30
Phoenix Public Library[viii]	2001	$10.00
Port Jefferson Free Library (Suffolk County, NY)	2006	$4.14
St. Louis Public Library[ix]	2001	$3.75
Mean ROI $9.21 Median ROI $4.14		
Studies of Libraries with Branches—USA		
Buffalo & Erie County Public Library[x]	2007	$6.70
Carnegie Library of Pittsburgh (PA)[xi]	2006	$3.00
Charlotte Mecklenburg County Library (NC)[xii]	2010	$4.61 to $6.03
Denver Public Library (CO)[xiii]	2006	$4.96
Douglas County Libraries (CO)[xiv]	2006	$5.02
Eagle Valley Library District (CO)[xv]	2006	$4.28
Fort Morgan Public Library (CO)[xvi]	2006	$8.80
Johnson County Library (KS)[xvii]	2015	$4.13
Mesa County Public Library District (CO)[xviii]	2006	$4.57
Montrose Library District (CO)[xix]	2006	$5.33
Nashville Public Library (TN)[xx]	2016	$3.06
New York City Public Libraries (NY)[xxi]	2012	—

(continued)

Table 24.3. Summary of Return on Investment (ROI) Studies (*continued*)

Study	Year	ROI
Studies of Libraries with Branches—USA		
Philadelphia, Free Library of (PA)[xxii]	2010	—
Phoenix Public Library (AZ)	2001	$10.00
Rangeview Library District (CO)[xxiii]	2006	$4.81
Salt Lake County Library (UT)[xxiv]	2013	$5.47 to $6.07
San Francisco Public Library (CA)[xxv]	2007	$3.34
San Francisco Public Library (CA), Branch Library Improvement Project[xxvi]	2015	$5.19 to $9.11
Santa Clara County Library District (CA)[xxvii]	2013	$2.50 to $5.17
St. Louis Public Library (MO)	1999	$4.00
Seattle Public Library (WA)[xxviii]	2005	—
Toledo-Lucas County Public Library (OH)[xxix]	2011	$2.86
Mean ROI $ 4.82 Median ROI $4.81		
Studies of a Group of Libraries—USA		
Montgomery County public libraries (OH), 25 locations[xxx]	2006	3.69
Nine southwestern Ohio public libraries[xxxi]	2006	$3.81
Nine public libraries from Illinois, Texas, and Washington	2003	$1.02 to $1.24
Suffolk Cooperative Library System (42 public libraries in New York)[xxxii]	2005	$3.87
State Studies—USA		
Florida[xxxiii]	2004	$6.54
Florida[xxxiv]	2010	$8.32
Hawaii[xxxv]	2003	$4.10
Illinois[xxxvi]	2000	$3.58
Indiana[xxxvii]	2007	$2.38
Minnesota[xxxviii]	2011	$4.62
Ohio[xxxix]	2016	$3.89

(*continued*)

Table 24.3. Summary of Return on Investment (ROI) Studies (*continued*)

Study	Year	ROI
State Studies—USA		
Pennsylvania[xl]	2006	$5.53
South Carolina[xli]	2005	$2.86
Texas[xlii]	2012	$4.42
Texas[xliii]	2017	$4.64
Utah[xliv]	2008	$7.35
Vermont[xlv]	2008	$7.26
Wisconsin[xlvi]	2008	$4.06
Mean ROI 4.99 Median ROI 4.42		
Canadian Studies		
Halifax Public Library[xlvii]	2009	—
Halton Hills Public Library[xlviii]	2014	$4.04
Kawartha Lakes Public Library, Ontario[xlix]	2014	$7.05
London Public Library, Ontario[l]	2015	$6.65
Markham Public Library, Ontario[li]	2013	$2.75 to $9.77
Milton Public Library, Ontario[lii]	2014	$5.67
Ottawa Public Library[liii]	2016	$5.17
Pickering Public Library, Ontario[liv]	2014	$5.85
Sault Ste. Marie Public Library, Ontario[lv]	2015	$1.54
Stratford Public Library, Ontario[lvi]	2015	$7.48
Toronto Public Library, Ontario[lvii]	2013	$5.63
Vancouver Island Regional Library[lviii]	2016	$5.36
Mean ROI $5.49 Median ROI $5.63		
International Studies		
Barcelona, Spain[lix]	2013	€2.25
Bolton, England[lx]	2005	£1.2 to £1.7

(*continued*)

Table 24.3. Summary of Return on Investment (ROI) Studies (*continued*)

Study	Year	ROI
International Studies		
British Library[lxi]	2004	£4.44
Christchurch City Libraries[lxii]	2012	$5.10
Hutt City, New Zealand[lxiii]	2013	$1.27 to $1.44
Latvia[lxiv]	2012	€1.37
New South Wales, Australia[lxv]	2008	AU$4.24
National Library of Australia[lxvi]	1995	AU$2.00
National Library of New Zealand[a]	2002	NZ$3.50
Norway[lxvii]	2005	4.00 kr
Prague[lxviii]	2015	2.55 Kč
South Korea (22 public libraries)[lxix]	2012	₩3.66
Spain (all public, university, and research libraries)[lxx]	2010	€2.80 to €3.83
Sunshine Coast Regional Library, Australia[lxxi]	2008	AU$5.45
State of New South Wales, Australia[lxxii]	2008	$4.24
State of Victoria, Australia[lxxiii]	2011	$3.56
State of Queensland, Australia[lxxiv]	2012	$2.30 to $4.10
United Kingdom[lxxv]	2001	£1.13
Wagga Wagga, Australia[lxxvi]	2008	AU$1.33
Mean ROI 3.31 Median ROI 3.50		

i. Donald Elliott, Glen Holt, Sterling Hayden, and Leslie Edmonds Holt. *Measuring Your Library's Value: How to Do a Cost-Benefit Analysis for Your Public Library*. Chicago: American Library Association, 2009.
ii. Elliott et al., 2009.
iii. Library Research Service. *Public Libraries—A Wise Investment: Cortez Public Library*. Denver, CO: Library Research Service, Colorado State Library, 2009. Available at http://www.lrs.org/documents/roi/cortez.pdf
iv. Charleston: A Great Community Deserves a Great Library. 2009. Available at http://old.kanawhalibrary.org/pdfs/positionpaper.pdf
v. Elliott et al., 2009.
vi. Pearl Kamer. *The Economic Value of the Middle Country Public Library in Suffolk County, New York* (A Research Report by the Long Island Association). 2006. Available at http://www.mcpl.lib.ny.us/pdf/economicvalueofMCPL.pdf
vii. Pearl Kamer. *Placing an Economic Value on the Services of the Northport-East Northport Public Library in Suffolk County, New York* (A Research Report by the Long Island Association). 2006. Available at http://www.nenpl.org/main/aboutus/economicstudy.php

(*continued*)

Table 24.3. Summary of Return on Investment (ROI) Studies (*continued*)

viii. Elliott et al., 2009.

ix. Elliott et al., 2009.

x. Available at http://www.buffalolib.org/.

xi. Center for Economic Development. *Carnegie Library of Pittsburgh: Community Impact and Benefits.* Pittsburgh, PA: Carnegie Mellon University, April 2006.

xii. UNC Charlotte Urban Institute. *Expanding Minds, Empowering Individuals, and Enriching Our Community: A Return on Investment Study of the Charlotte Mecklenburg Library 2010.* Charlotte: UNC Charlotte Urban Institute, 2010.

xiii. Library Research Service. *Public Libraries—A Wise Investment: Denver Public Library.* Denver, CO: Library Research Service, Colorado State Library, 2009. Available at http://www.lrs.org/documents/roi/denver.pdf

xiv. Library Research Service. *Public Libraries—A Wise Investment: Douglas County Public Library.* Denver, CO: Library Research Service, Colorado State Library, 2009. Available at http://www.lrs.org/documents/roi/douglas.pdf

xv. Library Research Service. *Public Libraries—A Wise Investment: Eagle Valley Library District.* Denver, CO: Library Research Service, Colorado State Library, 2009. Available at http://www.lrs.org/documents/roi/eagle.pdf

xvi. Library Research Service. *Public Libraries—A Wise Investment: Fort Morgan Public Library.* Denver, CO: Library Research Service, Colorado State Library, 2009. Available at http://www.lrs.org/documents/roi/ftmorgan.pdf

xvii. Marilu Goodyear et al. Analyzing the Return on investment in Johnson County Library. Edwards, KS: School of Public Affairs, University of Kansas, November 2015. Available at https://www.jocolibrary.org/sites/default/files/FINAL_JohnsonCountyLibrary_ROI_Report_2015-11-19.pdf

xviii. Library Research Service. *Public Libraries—A Wise Investment: Mesa County Public Library.* Denver, CO: Library Research Service, Colorado State Library, 2009. Available at http://www.lrs.org/documents/roi/ftmorgan.pdf

xix. Library Research Service. *Public Libraries—A Wise Investment: Montrose Library District.* Denver, CO: Library Research Service, Colorado State Library, 2009. Available at http://www.lrs.org/documents/roi/montrose.pdf

xx. The Research Center. *Economic Impact and Contribution Analysis: Nashville Public Library.* Nashville, TN: Nashville Area Chamber of Commerce, The Research Center, April 2016.

xxi. R. Newman. *Economic Impact of Libraries in New York City.* New York: New York City Council, Committee on Cultural Affairs, Libraries and International Intergroup Relations, 2012.

xxii. Fels Research & Consulting. *The Economic Value of The Free Library in Philadelphia.* University of Pennsylvania, 2010.

xxiii. Library Research Service. *Public Libraries—A Wise Investment: Rangeview Library District.* Denver, CO: Library Research Service, Colorado State Library, 2009. Available at http://www.lrs.org/documents/roi/rangeview.pdf

xxiv. Javaid Lai. A Return on Investment Study of Salt Lake County Library Services. Salt Lake City: The University of Utah, July 2013.

xxv. BERK. *Providing for Knowledge, Growth and Prosperity: A Benefit Study of the San Francisco Public Library.* Seattle: BERK, 2007.

xxvi. BERK. *Reinvesting and Renewing for the 21st Century: A Community and Economic Benefits Study of San Francisco's Branch Library Improvement Program.* Seattle: BERK, September 2015.

xxvii. BERK. *Santa Clara County Library District 2013 Return on Investment Report.* Seattle: BERK, 2013.

xxviii. BERK. *The Seattle Public Library Central Library: Economic Benefits Assessment.* Seattle: BERK, 2005.

xxix. Oleg Smirnov. *Toledo-Lucas County Public Library: Economic Value and Return on Investment.* Toledo, OH: University of Toledo, 2011.

xxx. Dayton Metro Library. Return on Investment: Valuing Montgomery County's Public Libraries. Dayton, OH: Dayton Metro Library, 2007.

xxxi. Devin, Driscoll & Fleeter. *Value for Money: Southwestern Ohio's Return from Investment in Public Libraries.* Columbus, OH: Devin, Driscoll & Fleeter, June 2006.

xxxii. Pearl Kamer. *Placing an Economic Value on the Services of Public Libraries in Suffolk County, New York* (A Research Report by the Long Island Association). Melville, NY: Long Island Association, 2005.

xxxiii. José-Marie Griffiths, Donald W. King, Christinger Tomer, Thomas Lynch, and Julie Harrington. *Taxpayer Return on Investment in Florida Public Libraries* (Summary Report). Chapel Hill, NC: University of North Carolina iSchool, 2004.

(*continued*)

Table 24.3. Summary of Return on Investment (ROI) Studies (*continued*)

xxxiv. Phyllis Pooley et al. *Taxpayer Return on Investment in Florida Public Libraries*. Pensacola: The University of West Florida, Haas Center for Business Research and Economic Development, May 2010.

xxxv. Joe Ryan and Charles McClure. *Economic Impact of the Hawaii State Public Library System (HSPLS) on the Business and Tourism Industries Study: Final Report*. Honolulu: HSPLS, 2003.

xxxvi. Norman Walzer, Karen Stott, and Lori Sutton. *Managing Illinois Libraries: Providing Services Customers Value*. Macomb, IL: IIRA, 2000. ED 445686.

xxxvii. Indiana Business Research Center. *The Economic Impact of Libraries in Indiana*. Indiana University, Indiana Business Research Center, November 2007.

xxxviii. Bureau of Business and Economic Research. *Minnesota Public Libraries' Return on Investment*. Duluth: University of Minnesota Duluth, Bureau of Business and Economic Research, December 2011.

xxxix. Howard Fleeter & Associates. *The Return on Investment of Ohio's Public Libraries & a Comparison with Other States*. April 2016.

xl. José-Marie Griffiths, Donald King, and Sarah Aerni. *Taxpayer Return-on-Investment (ROI) in Pennsylvania Public Libraries*. Chapel Hill: University of North Carolina, School of Information and Library Science, January 2007. Available at https://c.ymcdn.com/sites/www.palibraries.org/resource/resmgr/roi_docs/roi_fullreport.pdf

xli. School of Library and Information Science. *The Economic Impact of Public Libraries on South Carolina*. January 2005. Available at http://www.libsci.sc.edu/SCEIS/final%20report%2026%20january.pdf

xlii. Bureau of Business Research. *Texas Public Libraries: Economic Benefits and Return on Investment*. Austin: University of Texas, Bureau of Business Research, December 2012.

xliii. Bureau of Business Research IC² Institute. *Texas Public Libraries: Economic Benefits and Return on Investment*. Austin, TX: Bureau of Business Research IC² Institute, January 2017. Available at https://www.tsl.texas.gov/roi

xliv. Steven Decker. *Economic Impact of Utah Libraries: Pilot Study*. Cedar City, UT: Cedar City Public Library, 2006.

xlv. Retrieved from http://libraries.vermont.gov/sites/libraries/files/misc/plvalue06-07.pdf

xlvi. North Star Economics. *The Economic Contribution of Wisconsin Public Libraries to the Economy of Wisconsin*. Madison, WI: North Star Economics, May 2008.

xlvii. Canmac Economics Limited. *Halifax Central Library: An Economic Impact Assessment* [of the Construction of the Central Library]. Halifax, Canada: Canmac Economics Limited, July 2009.

xlviii. *Economic Impact of Halton Hills Public Library*. Halton Hills, Ontario, Canada, June 2014.

xlix. Mary Riley. City Council Given an Overview of Library Operations and Value to the Community. *Kawartha Lakes This Week,* September 29, 2014.

l. *The Economic Impact of London Public Library on the City of London*. London, Ontario, Canada: The London Public Library, 2015.

li. Shaun McDonough. Markham Public Library: Economic Impact Assessment Executive Summary. Markham, Ontario, Canada: Markham Public Library, 2013 (updated 2016).

lii. *The Economic Impact of Milton Public Library on the City of Milton*. Milton, Ontario, Canada: The Milton Public Library, 2014.

liii. Ottawa Public Library. *Check Out the Benefit: The Economic Benefits of the Ottawa Public Library*. November 2016.

liv. *The Economic Impact of the Pickering Public Library on the City of Pickering*. Pickering, Canada: The Pickering Public Library, 2014.

lv. NORDIK Institute. *Building Strong and Vibrant Communities: The Value of Sault Ste. Marie's Public Library*. Sault Ste. Marie, Ontario, Canada: NORDIK Institute, March 2015.

lvi. Mike Beitz. Economic Impact of Stratford Public Library Estimated at Nearly $15 Million. *Stratford Beacon Herald*, January 27, 2015.

lvii. Martin Prosperity Institute. *So Much More: The Economic Impact of the Toronto Public Library on the City of Toronto*. Toronto: Martin Prosperity Institute, 2013.

lviii. Vancouver Island Regional Library Administration. Assessing the Economic Impact of Vancouver Island Regional Library on Our Member Communities. July 2016. Available at http://virl.bc.ca/sites/default/files/documents/Reports/ROI%20Report%20-%20PRINT.pdf

lix. Maria Luria I Roig and Joel Pintor Gonzalez. *Return on Investment of Municipal Libraries Network of the Barcelona Province (2007-2011)*. Barcelona, Spain: Library Services Management Office, 2013.

(*continued*)

Table 24.3. Summary of Return on Investment (ROI) Studies (*continued*)

lx. Jura Consultants. *Bolton's Museum, Library and Archive Services: An Economic Valuation.* Bolton, England: Bolton Metropolitan Borough Council and MLA North West, 2005.

lxi. Caroline Pung, Ann Clarke, and Laurie Pattern. Measuring the Economic Impact of the British Library. *New Review of Academic Librarianship,* 10 (1), 2004, 79–102.

lxii. Janet Mansell, Alice Chuickshank, Jane Rodgers, and Dan Daly. *Mapping, Measuring and Valuing the Social & Economic Benefit of Christchurch City Libraries—Post Earthquake.* LIANZA Conference 2012, 23–26 September, Palmerston North, Ipukarea—Celebrate, Sustain, Transform.

lxiii. Hutt City Libraries. *Social Return on Investment Analysis.* Hutt City, New Zealand: Hutt City Libraries, 2013.

lxiv. Leva Strode, Alfreds Vanags, Renate Strazdina, Janis Dirveiks, Helena Dombrovska, Daina Pakalna, and Kristine Paberza. *Economic Value and Impact of Public Libraries in Latvia: Study Report.* 2012. Available at http://www.kis.gov.lv/download/Economic%20value%20and%20impact%20of%20public%20libraries%20in%20Latvia.pdf

lxv. J.L. Management Services. *Enriching Communities: The Value of Public Libraries in New South Wales Summary Report.* Sydney, Australia: Library Council of New South Wales, March 2008.

lxvi. Brian Haratsis. Justifying the Economic Value of Public Libraries in a Turbulent Local Government Environment. *APLIS,* 8 (4), 1995, 164–72.

lxvii. Svanhild Aabø. *The Value of Public Libraries: A Methodological Discussion and Empirical Study Applying the Contingent Valuation Method.* Oslo, Norway: University of Oslo, 2005.

lxviii. Jan Stejskal and Petr Hajek. Evaluating the Economic Value of a Public Service: The Case of the Municipal Library of Prague. *Public Money & Management,* 35 (2), 2015, 145–52.

lxix. Young Man Ko, Wonsik Shim, Soon-Hee Pyo, Ji Sang Chang, and Hye Kyung Chung. An Economic Valuation Study of Public Libraries in Korea. *Library & Information Science Research,* 34, 2012, 117–24.

lxx. José Antonio Gómez Yáñez. *The Economic and Social Value of Information Services: Libraries.* Barcelona, Spain: FESABID (Spain's Federation of Archive, Library, Documentation and Museum Science Associations), 2014.

lxxi. Ross Duncan. Best Bang for the Buck: The Economic Impact of Sunshine Coast Libraries Queensland. *APLIS,* 21 (4), December 2008, 140–53.

lxxii. J.L. Management Services. *Enriching Communities: The Value of Public Libraries in New South Wales* (Summary Report). Sydney, Australia: Library Council of New South Wales, 2008.

lxxiii. SGS Economics and Planning. *Dollars, Sense and Public Libraries: The Landmark Study of the Socio-Economic Value of Victorian Public Libraries.* Melbourne, Victoria, Australia: State Library of Victoria, 2011.

lxxiv. SGS Economics and Planning. *The Library Dividend: A Guide to Socio-Economic Value of Queensland's Public Libraries.* Brisbane, Australia: State Library of Queensland, 2012.

lxxv. Anne Morris, Margaret Hawkins, and John Sumsion. *The Economic Value of Public Libraries.* London: Resource: The Council for Museums, Archives and Libraries, 2001.

lxxvi. Philip Hider. Using the Contingent Valuation Method for Dollar Valuations of Library Services. *Library Quarterly,* 78 (4), 2008, 437–58.

a. Valuation of the national bibliographic database and the national union catalog.

Other observations about determining the economic value of a library include the following:

- No single evaluation method is going to provide a solution for multiple libraries.
- The actual benefits or outcomes received by people as they use a library's services or collections will likely be invisible and difficult to measure.
- Demonstration of a causal relationship, though the ultimate goal, must overcome many methodological issues.
- A direct survey of library customers can be used to determine the positive impact of the library in reducing costs, saving time, accomplishments, and so forth. The direct survey is

most often used in the special library environment, but has also been used in academic and public libraries.

- A contingent valuation study is time-consuming and expensive because it typically involves a telephone survey to gather the needed data. Hence, this method is beyond the means of most libraries.
- The consumer surplus method can be readily adapted and has been used successfully by a number of libraries.
- The shortcut method can be easily used by a library to demonstrate its value to its community.
- The return on capital investment can be easily determined for most libraries, and the findings may resonate with local stakeholders.
- The economic impact method can be used to show both the direct and indirect economic benefits of a local library or a group of libraries.
- If two or more methods are used to estimate the economic benefits, there will likely be increased confidence in the results.
- Some studies have only reported the direct benefits, in order to communicate a more conservative estimate of the economic benefits.
- Economic studies in advocacy may ultimately be self-defeating, in that the vast majority of studies have only mediocre "economic" impacts.
- Regardless of the method selected, the results should be clearly and consistently communicated to the library's funding decision makers and its customers.

As I previously noted,

> Unfortunately the evidence to date about the positive impacts of library ROI studies is underwhelming. Feedback from library directors indicates that ROI may have a place in justifying public library funding, but the ROI number may not be compelling enough to prevent budget reductions or lead to budget increases.[68]

NOTES

1. William Turner. *History of Philosophy.* New York: Forgotten Books, 2016, 82. (Originally published by Ginn & Company, 1903.)

2. Susan Imholz and Jennifer Weil Arns. *Worth Their Weight: An Assessment of the Evolving Field of Library Valuation.* Washington, DC: Americans for Libraries Council, 2007, 5.

3. Svanhild Aabø. Libraries and Return-on-Investment (ROI): A Meta-Analysis. *New Library World*, 110 (7/8), 2009, 311–24.

4. Joanne Gard Marshall. *The Impact of the Special Library on Corporate Decision-Making.* Washington, DC: Special Libraries Association, 1993.

5. Collaboration with Librarian Required in Hopkins' Report. *Corporate Library Update*, 10 (13), September 15, 2001, 1.

6. Helen Manning. The Corporate Librarian: Great Return on Investment, in James M. Matarazzo et al. (Eds.). *President's Task Force on the Value of the Information Professional* (Final Report. Preliminary Study). Washington, DC: Special Libraries Association, 1987, 23–34.

7. José-Marie Griffiths and Donald W. King. *Special Libraries: Increasing the Information Edge.* Washington, DC: Special Libraries Association, 1993.

8. Mary Corcoran and Anthea Stratigos. *Knowledge Management: It's All About Behavior. Information About Information Briefing.* Burlingame, CA: Outsell, January 2001.

9. Gwen Harris and Joanne G. Marshall. Building a Model Business Case: Current Awareness Service in a Special Library. *Special Libraries*, 87 (2), Summer 1996, 181–94.

10. Joanne Gard Marshall. *The Impact of the Special Library on Corporate Decision-Making.* Washington, DC: Special Libraries Association, 1993.

11. Warren Thorngate. On Paying Attention, in William J. Baker, Leendert P. Mos, Hans V. Rappard, and Henderikus J. Stam (Eds.). *Recent Trends in Theoretical Psychology.* New York: Springer-Verlag, 1987, 247–63.

12. Alison M. Keyes. The Value of the Special Library: Review and Analysis. *Special Libraries*, 86 (3), Summer 1995, 172–87.

13. Frank H. Portugal. *Valuating Information Intangibles: Measuring the Bottom-Line Contribution of Librarians and Information Professionals.* Washington, DC: Special Libraries Association, 2000.

14. Leigh Estabrook. Valuing a Document Delivery System. *RQ*, 27 (1), Fall 1986, 59–62.

15. Helen Manning. The Corporate Librarian: Great Return on Investment, in *President's Task Force on the Value of the Information Professional.* Washington, DC: Special Libraries Association, 1987, 49–67.

16. Michael Koenig. The Importance of Information Services for Productivity "Under-Recognized" and Under-Invested. *Special Libraries*, 83 (3), Fall 1992, 199–210.

17. Margareta Nelke. Swedish Corporations Value Information. *Information Outlook*, 3 (2), February 1999, 10.

18. For a more detailed discussion of the economic value of special libraries, see Joseph R. Matthews. *The Bottom Line: Determining and Communicating the Value of Special Libraries.* Westport, CT: Libraries Unlimited, 2002.

19. Susan C. Dresley and Annalynn Lacombe. *Value of Information and Information Services.* Cambridge, MA: U.S. Department of Transportation, Volpe National Transportation Systems Center, October 1998.

20. A. J. Million, Sheila M. Hatchell, and Roberto A. Sarmiento. *Proving Your Library's Value: A Toolkit for Transportation Librarians* (CMR 13-007). Jefferson City, MO: Missouri Department of Transportation, 2012, 6.

21. John Martyn. Unintentional Duplication of Research. *New Scientist*, 377, 1968, 338.

22. Patent Omission Costs £20b. *Professional Engineering*, 11 (11), June 10, 1998, 12.

23. Guillaume Van Moorsel. Client Value Models Providing a Framework for Rational Library Planning (or, Phrasing the Answer in the Form of a Question). *Medical Reference Services Quarterly*, 24 (2), Summer 2005, 25–40.

24. D. Noonan. *Contingent Valuation Studies in the Arts and Culture: An Annotated Bibliography.* Chicago: The Cultural Policy Center at the University of Chicago, 2002.

25. Richard T. Carson, Jennifer L. Wright, N. J. Carson, A. Alberini, and Nicholas E. Flores. *A Bibliography of Contingent Value Papers and Studies.* La Jolla, CA: Natural Resource Damage Assessment, 1995.

26. Svanhild Aabø and Jon Strand. Public Library Valuation, Nonuse Values, and Altruistic Motivations. *Library & Information Science Research*, 26, 2004, 351–72.

27. Richard T. Carson. Contingent Valuation: A User's Guide. *Environmental Science and Technology*, 34 (8), 2000, 1413–18. See also Richard T. Carson, Nicholas E. Flores, and Norman F. Meade. Contingent Valuation: Controversies and Evidence. *Environmental and Resource Economics*, 19, 2001, 173–210.

28. Glen E. Holt and Donald Elliott. Proving Your Library's Worth: A Test Case. *Library Journal*, 123 (18), November 1998, 42–44; Glen E. Holt, Donald Elliott, and Christopher Dussold. A Framework for Evaluating Public Investment in Urban Libraries. *The Bottom Line*, 9 (4), Summer 1996, 4–13; Glen Holt, Donald Elliott, and Amonia Moore. Placing a Value on Public Library Services: A St. Louis Case Study. *Public Libraries*, 38 (2), March–April 1999, 98+.

29. Donald Elliott. *Cost-Benefit Analysis of Phoenix Public Library*. Phoenix: Phoenix Public Library, April 2001.

30. Spectrum Strategy Consultants and Independent. *Measuring Our Value*. London: The British Library, 2004. Available at http://www.bl.uk/pdf/measuring.pdf; Caroline Pung, Ann Clarke, and Laurie Patten. Measuring the Economic Impact of the British Library. *New Review of Academic Librarianship*, 10 (1), 2004, 79–102; Gary Warnaby and Jill Fenney. Creating Customer Value in the Not-for-Profit Sector: A Case Study of the British Library. *International Journal of Nonprofit Voluntary Sector Marketing*, 10, 2005, 183–95.

31. Svanhild Aabø and Jon Strand. Public Library Valuation, Nonuse Values, and Altruistic Motivations. *Library & Information Science Research*, 26, 2004, 351–72. See also Svanhild Aabø and Ragnar Audunson. Rational Choice and Valuation of Public Libraries: Can Economic Models for Evaluating Non-Market Goods Be Applied to Public Libraries? *Journal of Librarianship and Information Science*, 34 (1), March 2002, 5–15; Svanhild Aabø. Valuation of Public Libraries, in Carl Gustav Johannsen and Leif Kajberg (Eds.). *New Frontiers in Public library Research*. Lanham, MD: Scarecrow Press, 2005, 127–141.

32. Svanhild Aabø. Are Public Libraries Worth Their Price? *New Library World*, 106 (11/12), 2005, 487–95.

33. Charles McClure, Bruce Fraser, Timothy W. Nelson, and Jane B. Robbins. *Economic Benefits and Impacts from Public Libraries in the State of Florida*. Tallahassee: Florida State University, Information Use Management and Policy Institute, January 2001.

34. José-Marie Griffiths, Donald W. King, and Christinger Tomer. *Taxpayers Return-on-Investment (ROI) in Florida Public Libraries. Part I: The Use, Impact and Value of Florida's Public Libraries—Detailed Study Methods and Summary Results*. Tallahassee: Center for Economic Forecasting and Analysis, Florida State University, August 2004; Tim Lynch and Julie Harrington. *Taxpayers Return-on-Investment (ROI) in Florida Public Libraries. Part II: The Economic Impact and Value of Public Libraries in Florida—The REMI Analysis*. Tallahassee: Center for Economic Forecasting and Analysis, Florida State University, August 2004.

35. Bruce T. Fraser, Timothy W. Nelson, and Charles R. McClure. Describing the Economic Impacts and Benefits of Florida Public Libraries: Findings and Methodological Applications for Future Work. *Library & Information Science Research*, 24, 2002, 211–33.

36. David D. Barron, Robert V. Williams, Stephen Bajjaly, Jennifer Arns, and Steven Wilson. *The Economic Impact of Public Libraries on South Carolina*. Columbia: University of South Carolina, School of Library and Information Science, January 2005.

37. Anne Morris, Margaret Hawkins, and John Sumsion. *The Economic Value of Public Libraries*. London: Resource: The Council for Museums, Archives and Libraries, 2001. See also Anne Morris, John Sumsion, and Margaret Hawkins. The Economic Value of Public Libraries. *Libri*, 52, 2002, 78–87.

38. Joseph P. Newhouse and A. J. Alexander. *An Economic Analysis of Public Library Services*. Santa Monica, CA: Rand Corporation, 1972.

39. Library & Information Association of New Zealand. *Manukau Libraries: Trial of the V+LM Value Added Library Methodology* (Trial Report). New Zealand: LIANZA, October 12, 2000.

40. Ruth MacEachern. Measuring the Added Value of Library and Information Services: The New Zealand Approach. *IFLA Journal* 27, (4), 2001, 232–37.

41. Jamshid Beheshti. *The Use of NLC MARC Records in Canadian Libraries, Phase 1: University and Large Urban Public Libraries, Final Report, 31 March 2002*. Montreal: McGill University, Graduate School of Library and Information Studies, 2002.

42. McDermott Miller, Ltd. *National Bibliographic Database and National Union Catalogue: Economic Evaluation for the National Library of New Zealand*. Wellington, New Zealand: McDermott Miller, Ltd., 2002.

43. John Sumsion, Margaret Hawkins, and Anne Morris. Estimating the Economic Value of Library Benefits. *Performance Measurement and Metrics*, 4 (1), 2003, 13–27.

44. Judy Luther. University Investment in the Library: What's the Return? A Case Study at the University of Illinois at Urbana-Champaign (White Paper). *Elsevier Library Connect*, 6 (1), 2008.

Available at https://libraryconnect.elsevier.com/articles/university-investment-library-what-s-return-case-study-university-illinois-urbana-champaign

45. Ray Lyons. Quantitative Thinking Improves Mental Alertness. November 9, 2014. Lib(rary) Performance blog. See also Ray Lyons. Do No Quantitative Harm. January 20, 2015. Lib(rary) Performance blog. Available at https://libperformance.com/

46. Denise Pan, Gabrielle Wiersma, Leslie Williams, and Yem Fong. More Than a Number: Unexpected Benefits of Return on Investment Analysis. *The Journal of Academic Librarianship*, 39 (6), November 2013, 566–72.

47. Denise Pan, Gabrielle Wiersma, and Yem Fong. Towards Demonstrating Value: Measuring the Contributions of Library Collections to University Research and Teaching Goals. Presentation at the ACRL Conference, March 30-April 2, 2011, in Philadelphia, Pennsylvania. Available at http://www.ala.org/acrl/sites/ala.org.acrl/files/content/conferences/confsandpreconfs/national/2011/papers/towards_demonstratin.pdf

48. Glen E. Holt, Donald S. Elliott, Leslie E. Holt, and Anne Watts. *Public Library Benefits Valuation Study: Final Report to the Institute of Museum and Library Services for National Leadership Grant*. St. Louis, MO: St. Louis Public Library, 2001. See also Donald S. Elliott, Glen E. Holt, Sterling W. Hayden, and Leslie Edmonds Holt. *Measuring Your Library's Value: How to Do a Cost-Benefit Analysis for Your Public Library*. Chicago: ALA Editions, 2006.

49. Fels Institute of Government. *The Economic Value of the Free Library of Philadelphia*. Philadelphia: The University of Pennsylvania, Fels Institute of Government, October 2010.

50. Pew Charitable Trusts. *The Library in the City: Changing Demands and a Challenging Future*. New York: Pew Charitable Trusts, 2012.

51. Glen E. Holt, Donald S. Elliott, and Christopher Dussold. A Framework for Evaluating Public Investment in Urban Libraries. *The Bottom Line*, 9 (4), 1996, 4–13.

52. Berk & Associates. *The Seattle Public Library Central Library: Economic Benefits Assessment. The Transformative Power of a Library to Redefine Learning, Community, and Economic Development*. Seattle: Berk & Associates, 2005.

53. Carnegie Mellon University. *Carnegie Library of Pittsburgh: Community Impact and Benefits*. Pittsburgh: Carnegie Mellon University, Center for Economic Development, April 2006.

54. José-Marie Griffiths, Donald W. King, and Christinger Tomer. *Taxpayers Return-on-Investment (ROI) in Florida Public Libraries. Part I: The Use, Impact and Value of Florida's Public Libraries—Detailed Study Methods and Summary Results*. Tallahassee: Center for Economic Forecasting and Analysis, Florida State University, August 2004; Tim Lynch and Julie Harrington. *Taxpayers Return-on-Investment (ROI) in Florida Public Libraries. Part II: The Economic Impact and Value of Public Libraries in Florida—The REMI Analysis*. Tallahassee: Center for Economic Forecasting and Analysis, Florida State University, August 2004.

55. Lewis G. Liu. The Contribution of Public Libraries to Countries' Economic Productivity: A Path Analysis. *Library Review*, 53 (9), 2004, 435–41.

56. Abraham Charnes, William W. Cooper, and E. Rhodes. Measuring the Efficiency of Decision Making Units. *European Journal of Operations Research*, 2, 1978, 429–44. See also Abraham Charnes, William W. Cooper, Arie Y. Lewin, and Lawrence M. Seiford (Eds.). *Data Envelopment Analysis: Theory, Methodology and Applications*. Norwell, MA: Kluwer Academic Publishers, 1994.

57. Chiang Kao and Ya-Chi Lin. Comparing University Libraries of Different University Size. *Libri*, 49, 1999, 150–58.

58. Wonsik Shim and Paul B. Kantor. A Novel Economic Approach to the Evaluation of Academic Research Libraries. *Proceedings of the American Society for Information Science*, 35, 1998, 400–10.

59. Gerhard Reichmann. Measuring University Library Efficiency Using Data Envelopment Analysis. *Libri*, 54, 2004, 136–46.

60. Tser-yieth Chen. An Evaluation of the Relative Performance of University Libraries in Taipei. *Library Review*, 46 (3), 1997, 190–201.

61. Khem R. Sharma, PingSun Leung, and Lynn Zane. Performance Measurement of Hawaii State Public Libraries: An Application of Data Envelopment Analysis (DEA). *Agricultural and Resource Economics Review*, 28 (2), October 1999, 190–98.

62. Jennifer Abend and Charles R. McClure. Recent Views on Identifying Impacts from Public Libraries. *Public Library Quarterly*, 17 (3), 1999, 3–29.

63. Lewis G. Liu. The Contribution of Public Libraries to Countries' Economic Productivity: A Path Analysis. *Library Review*, 53 (9), 2004, 435–41.

64. The Urban Libraries Council. *Making Cities Stronger: Public Library Contributions to Local Economic Development*. Evanston, IL: The Urban Libraries Council, 2007.

65. Giyeong Kim. A Critical Review of Valuation Studies to Identify Frameworks in Library Services. *Library & Information Science Research*, 33, 2011, 112–19.

66. Svanhild Aabø. Libraries and Return on Investment (ROI): A Meta-Analysis. *New Library World*, 110 (7/8), 2009, 311–24.

67. Hye-Kyung Chung, Young-Man Ko, Won-Sik Shim, and Soon-Hee Pyo. An Exploratory Meta Analysis of Library Economic Valuation Studies. *Journal of the Korean Society for Library and Information Science*, 43 (4), 2009, 117–37.

68. Joseph R. Matthews. What's the Return on ROI: The Benefits and Challenges of Calculating Your Library's Return on Investment. *Library Leadership & Management*, 25 (1), February 2011, 10.

25

Evaluation of Social Impacts

Public libraries do have impact on the community in which they oper-
ate. They sustain local community and identity, support people whose
main activities are out of the labour market, foster cultural enrichment
and diversity, promote a sense of social cohesion, develop confidence in
individuals and communities, stimulate imagination and creativity, health
and well-being.

—Svanhild Aabø[1]

The evaluation of the social impacts of a library will focus exclusively on public libraries. Most special libraries are designed to serve only a very narrowly defined clientele and not the public. School and academic libraries have the potential for impacting the larger community they serve, but most of the use and therefore the benefits are going to accrue to those who use the academic library—students and faulty members and not the general public.

The majority of the literature pertaining to the social benefits of public libraries involves the author asserting what the benefits are rather than reporting on a research project. One of the most visible examples of this is a Canadian project that produced a report called "Dividends: The Value of Public Libraries in Canada."[2] This report drew upon a number of sources and suggested that the benefits of the public library can easily be divided into two categories: economic and social (see Figure 25.1).

The notion that public libraries have a social impact is an old one. Historically, the purpose of public libraries was to safeguard democracy and divert behavior from socially destructive activities by exposing the population of a community to literature and acceptable recreation.[3] The terms "social impact," "social benefit," social cohesion," and "social inclusion" are often used interchangeably. However, these terms are all descriptors of the broader concept of "social capital."

Social capital accumulates as a byproduct of interactions, which result in a sense that a service or institution enhances functioning within the wider society. In general, *social capital* refers to the networks and links within a community. It encompasses the level of cooperation, trust, mutual support, and participation of residents in community activities that strengthen their

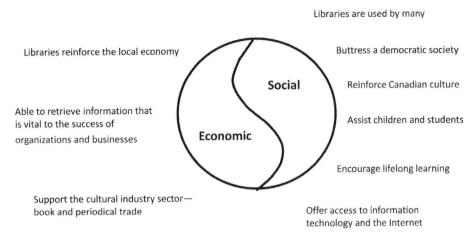

Figure 25.1. The Benefits of Public Libraries. Leslie Fitch and Jody Warner. Dividends: The Value of Public Libraries in Canada. *The Bottom Line,* 11 (4), 1998, 158–79, n. 2.

sense of social belonging and community well-being. Social capital consists of relationships among individuals, organizations, businesses, and government. Social network theory offers a robust conceptual and methodological framework for better understanding the relational value of library services.[4]

Social capital can be thought to exist in three ways:

- **Bonding social capital** refers to the ties between people and organizations.
- **Bridging social capital** refers to ties across groups that are not alike.
- **Linking social capital** promotes involvement and inclusion across social strata.[5] Almost all of the research to identify the social benefits of a public library has involved qualitative methods. Surveys have been used occasionally, primarily to determine the level of support for public libraries in a community, in a state, or across the nation.

Stephen Town, former York University Library director in England, has developed the phrase "relationship capital" as a broader, encompassing term that can be characterized by the following:[6]

- It is personal and individual
- It applies externally as well as internally (to the library)
- It results in problem solving and knowledge sharing
- It supports connections that build brand and enhance reputation
- The reality that relationships depend on character and behavior
- The fact that relationships can build or destroy value

Town has expanded on the concept of relationship capital and has developed a Library Value Scorecard as shown in Figure 25.2.

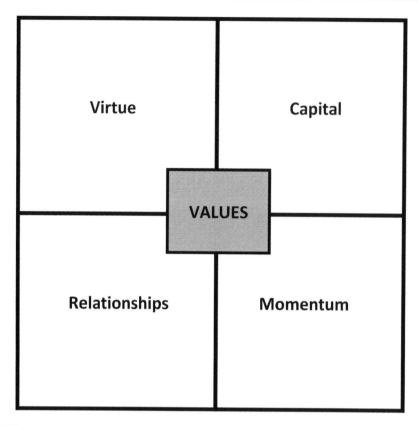

Figure 25.2. Town's Library Value Scorecard. J. S. Town and M. Kyrillidou. Developing a Values Scorecard. *Performance Measurement and Metrics,* 14(1), 2013, 7–16.

QUALITATIVE METHODS

Most of the studies exploring the social impacts or benefits of the public library in a community have relied on qualitative measures. Among these are focus groups, observations, interviews, asking users to keep diaries, and so forth.

Barbara Debono, in a review of the social impact of public libraries, suggests that two approaches can be taken in investigating the effects, experiences, or differences: an emphasis on a neutral outcome and an emphasis on positive impacts or benefits.[7]

An analysis in England suggested that libraries needed to move beyond the lending of materials and traditional library services to embrace new services and partnerships and work as a tool for active development with life-enhancing consequences for the community.[8] Fran Matarasso suggests that there is a broader value of library services in alleviating social problems and laying the foundations of sustainable communities.[9]

One study investigated the impact of providing in-library access to information technology resources and found a positive impact on both the communities and the individuals in that the library supported a range of activities—from study to job seeking to building and maintaining social networks using the Internet.[10]

An examination of the economic and social benefits of the public library in an Australian community found that the library contributed to key social values in the community, especially equity and social justice; contributed to the quality of life; and was a symbol and institution of the community.[11]

A study of 10 public libraries in the Sydney, Australia, area found that the library was accessed not only for its resources but also for the opportunity to socialize. Parents generally regarded libraries as safe places and were happy to allow their children to frequently spend time at the library. The desire to socialize with staff was also noted for older, more frequent users of the library.[12]

Another Australian study involving all 43 public library systems in the state of Victoria analyzed more than 10,000 surveys designed to gather views about the contribution to and impact of their libraries on their local communities. This *Libraries/Building/Communities* project reported the contributions of public libraries to their communities under four main themes:[13]

- Developing social capital
    - Providing a welcoming environment
    - Creating pride of place
    - Attracting users from all walks of life
    - Reaching out to the community
    - Appreciating cultural differences
    - Building bridges to the government
    - Encouraging collaboration across the community
- Overcoming the digital divide
    - Making technology accessible
    - Exploiting technology to benefit the community
- Creating informed communities
    - Community information
    - Government information
    - Gateway to the world of information
- Convenient and comfortable places of learning
    - Developing information skills
    - Stimulating ideas and discussion
    - Supporting vulnerable learners
    - Supporting students

Public libraries create social capital in several ways, through[14]

- Encouraging trust through social cohesion and inclusion by providing resources and a meeting place accessible to everyone—creating communities;
- Facilitating local dialogue and dissemination of local information—building bonding social capital;
- Encouraging civic engagement by delivering programs that bring citizens together—breaking down barriers;

- Upholding democratic ideals by making information freely available to all citizens—creating an informed citizenry;
- Providing a public space where citizens can work together on personal and community problems—fostering community participation; and
- Engaging in partnerships with other community organizations—building bridging social capital.

A 2016 report prepared for the State Library of Queensland, Australia, suggested that public libraries have been expanding their access to a variety of digital technologies and community exchange, teaching creativity, as well as stimulating people to connect with each other and the world.[15]

The Social Audit

In England, the British Library financed several research projects to examine the utility of a social audit as a potential tool in assessing the social and economic impacts of public libraries.[16] A social audit assesses the social impact of an organization in relation to its aim and those of its stakeholders. The social audit team interviews actual and potential library users and focuses especially on the needs of library nonusers.

Rebecca Linley and Bob Usherwood used a "social process audit," which collects information through the use of interviews and focus groups with stakeholders.[17] When conducting a social audit, the main criterion for evaluation is the impact of policy on social need, which raises the obvious question of what constitutes social need and what the public library's responsibility is in meeting some portion of a social need.[18]

The results of the social audit suggested that the public library's established roles (culture, education, reading and literacy, and information) have enduring relevance:

- The library remains important as a source of *free* reading material, especially for people with limited economic means.
- The library supports the development of children's reading skills.
- Library services support both adults' and children's educational needs.

The library provides equitable access to information and other resources. The public library also has a social and caring role:

- The library is a center of cultural life.
- The library is a suitable "nonstigmatized" place for adult literacy classes.
- Individuals gain new skills and confidence from using the library.
- The library is a place where people meet and share interests, sometimes described as "the cement in the social fabric."
- The library promotes greater understanding among different cultural groups.
- The library sustains local identity by developing and maintaining community self-esteem.
- The library has a beneficial effect on psychological health and well-being, especially for the isolated and vulnerable.

The findings of a social audit are derived from qualitative, often anecdotal, evidence and suggest that public libraries enrich the lives of many people. Proponents of the social audit process argue that use of this technique is what makes the enriching process visible. Opponents of the technique point to the lack of any objective or quantitative performance measures to support the conclusions made as a result of the audit.

QUANTITATIVE METHODS

The Pew Research Center conducts a number of periodic surveys related to libraries. All survey reports are available from the Pew Research Center. Among these surveys are:

Libraries and Learning. A majority of Americans think public libraries serve the educational needs of their communities and families fairly well, and library users often outperform others in learning activities. However, notable shares of Americans do not know that libraries offer learning-related programs and materials.[19]

Libraries at the Crossroads. The public is interested in new and innovative services and thinks libraries are important to their communities. Two-thirds say that closing their local public library would have a major impact on their community and they would like their local library to:[20]

- Support local education
- Serve special constituents such as veterans, active-duty military personnel, and immigrants
- Help local businesses, job seekers, and those upgrading their work skills
- Embrace new technologies such as 3-D printers and provide services to help patrons learn about high-tech gadgetry

Younger Americans and Public Libraries. Although the lives of younger generations are full of technology, they will most likely have read a book, visited the library, and used a library Web site in the past year.[21]

From Distant Admirers to Library Lovers. Public library users and proponents are not a niche group: 30 percent are highly engaged with libraries and another 39 percent fall into the medium engaged category. A connection (or lack of a connection) with the local library is part of a broader information and social landscape. Life stage and special circumstances influence use of the library. Engagement categories include:[22]

High Engagement

- Library Lovers
- Information Omnivores

Medium Engagement

- Solid Center
- Print Traditionalists

Low Engagement

- Not for Me
- Young and Restless
- Rooted and Roadblocked

Nonengagement

- Distant Admirers
- Off the Grid

7 Surprises About Libraries in Our Surveys. Several surveys suggest that:[23]

1. Older Americans are least likely to use libraries.
2. Ten percent of Americans have never used a library, but they still think libraries are good for their communities.
3. Although e-reading is on the rise, print remains most popular.
4. The choice of reading print or e-books depends on the circumstances.
5. Library users want recommendations based on their prior book-reading habits.
6. Libraries should consider different ways of arranging their collections.
7. Those who use libraries are more likely than others to be book buyers.

How Americans Value Public Libraries in Their Communities. The survey showed that:[24]

1. Libraries are appreciated
   - 91 percent indicated that libraries are important to their communities
   - 76 percent say libraries are important to them and their families
2. Libraries compare well with other organizations (military, police, church, medical system, and so forth)
3. People like librarians
   - 81 percent of visitors say librarians are "very helpful"
4. Libraries have rebranded themselves as tech hubs
   - 77 percent say free access to computers and the Internet is a very important service
   - 80 percent say borrowing books is a very important service

The Marist College Institute for Public Opinion 2003 telephone poll suggests that people are willing to pay for improved library services even when they may not be active library users.[25] Specifically, the survey found that:

- 67 percent of the respondents felt it was *very valuable* to have access to a public library in their community, and another 27 percent felt it was valuable
- Almost two-thirds of the respondents would support an increase in taxes to support public library services
- The respondents would, on average, be willing to pay an additional $49 per year for public libraries
- The priorities for library services included programs for children, open hours in evenings and on weekends, computers for public use, and homework help centers, among many more

A New York State Zogby poll[26] revealed that:

- Almost all respondents felt the public library was important to them (95 percent) and almost three-fourths indicated that the library was "very important"
- More than 75 percent of the respondents would be willing to increase their taxes to improve support for the library
- A sizable majority (89 percent) felt it was important for state government to do more for local public libraries

The *Counting on Results* project analyzed survey responses from more than 5,500 respondents from 45 libraries in 20 states. The purpose of the project was to learn more about the outcomes of public library use. The results indicated the following:[27]

- **General information outcomes:** Reading for pleasure was the most popular response (74 percent), followed by learning more about a skill, hobby, or other personal interest (56 percent) and finding information for school, work, or a community group.

- **Local history and genealogy outcomes:** Respondents made progress researching family history (53 percent), identified a new source to search (50 percent), and obtained a document or record.

- **Library as place (Commons) outcomes:** Respondents learned about new books, videos, or music (67 percent); found a quiet place to think, read, write, or study (59 percent); and met a friend or coworker (30 percent).

- **Information literacy outcomes:** Respondents found what they were looking for by asking a librarian for help (51 percent), using the library catalog, and searching the Web.

- **Business and career information outcomes:** Respondents explored or started or developed a business (36 percent), developed job-related skills, and explored job/careers.

- **Basic literacy outcomes:** Respondents became a citizen (42 percent), read to a child or assisted a child to choose a book, and managed personal finances better.

US Impact Study. Funded by the Bill and Melinda Gates Foundation, the US Impact Study evaluated the effect of library Internet computers on users over the course of several years. Data from almost 50,000 online surveys suggested that the availability of the computers has an impact in seven areas: social connection (maintain personal connections); education (e.g., using library computers to do schoolwork and taking online classes); employment (e.g., search for a job opportunities; submit an application online or work on a resume); health and wellness (learning about medical conditions, finding health care providers, and assessing health insurance options); e-government (e.g., learn about laws and regulations, find out about a government program or service); community and civic engagement (e.g., learn about politics, news, and the community; keep up with current events); and personal finance (e.g., manage personal finances, do online banking, and make purchases online).

Public Libraries in Africa. A survey in six African countries showed that all groups surveyed (national and local stakeholders as well as library users and nonusers) agree that libraries are essential to individuals as well as communities in general and that they have the potential to contribute to community development in important areas such as health, employment, and agriculture.[28]

Libraries Building Communities (Australia). Data were gathered in a variety of ways (surveys, focus groups, interviews) from almost 10,000 individuals. The results of this study suggest that libraries and librarians make a fundamental contribution to the communities they serve in four ways: overcoming the digital divide; creating informed communities; being convenient and comfortable places of learning; and building social capital. On the community level, libraries are perceived to add value in the fields of social interaction; promoting social inclusion, bridging the generation gap, and providing a focal point for the community.[29]

Enriching Communities (Australia). This project surveyed library service managers in all public libraries in the State of New South Wales, developed 10 case studies, and interviewed representatives from other organizations to learn how public libraries benefit other institutions. The project demonstrated how public libraries sustain the community and contribute positively to several fields reflecting four types of well-being in society: *cultural* (participating in literary events; celebrating cultural diversity; working with local theaters to promote their events; hosting local artists and travelling exhibitions; cooperating with other cultural institutions); *social* (safe, harmonious, welcoming, and inclusive environment; promote acceptance and understanding of others; ensure free and equitable access to collections; contribute to developing, maintaining, and improving literacy levels; and preserving the past through extensive local and family history collections); *economic* (enable users to avoid or reduce expenditures, enlarge job opportunities; support of local businesses; assists small to medium-sized enterprises (SMEs) to maintain high professional standards and compete with larger organizations; contributes to tourism); and *environmental*.[30]

Public Libraries—Arenas for Citizenship (PLACE). In Norway, two surveys were carried out in 2006 and again in 2011 in three communities to measure the role of the library as a meeting place based on actual use.[31] The different types of meetings that can take place were grouped into six categories:

1. A resource for information about other meetings in the community.
2. A public space for accidental meetings and conversations.
3. A space where cultural and political ideas are presented and discussed.
4. An arena to acquire information and knowledge so the individual can be an informed and participating citizen.
5. A space to meet with colleagues and friends.
6. A virtual meeting space for meetings on the Web.

OUTCOME MEASURES

All types of libraries have long used output measures to demonstrate "capacity utilization" of library services. Outputs are counts of activities or services provided by a library to its customers. Demonstrating the actual impact on or benefit in the lives of a library's customers relies on *outcome measures* that:

- Reflect changes or improvements brought about in people's lives
- Typically are reported according to amount of change in knowledge, skills, attitude, behavior, or condition (social status/life condition)
- Help answer the question, "Why do libraries matter?"

In an extensive literature review, Rooney-Browne identified 11 possible impacts and outcomes that contribute to social value: improved self-esteem, enhanced life chances, employability, empowerment, social networks, promoting civic values, sense of place, community engagement, social cohesion, informed citizens, and social, human, and intellectual capital.[32]

To date there has been little sustained effort to develop outcome measures that demonstrate the benefits received by individuals who use library collections and services. There are, however, a few projects that have started work in this area.

How Libraries and Librarians Help. Joan Durrance and Karen Fisher used a variety of qualitative data collection methods to capture outcomes in a variety of setting in their "How Libraries and Librarians Help" project.[33] Durrance and Fisher suggest a four step process to identify outcomes:

Step One—Prepare to conduct an outcomes study by determining what outcomes are important.

Step Two—Choose the approaches and tools that can be used to collect data.

Step Three—Analyze outcomes data.

Step Four—Maximize the results of the outcomes study.

Outcomes in Everyday Life (Finland). A sample of 1,000 individuals responded to a survey which asked them to identify the ways in which they benefited from their use of the public library. The 22 possible types of benefits were grouped into three categories following a factor analysis: everyday activities, cultural interests, and career benefits. A majority of the respondents used the public library for recreational, cultural, or educational purposes in their leisure time.[34]

Scandinavian Comparison. A survey in Finland, Norway, and the Netherlands found that Finns perceive more benefits (38 percent) than their peers in Norway (14 percent) and the Netherlands (12 percent). Benefits were perceived most commonly in education, cultural activities, and everyday activities, followed by work. Interestingly, Dutch users receive very few benefits in work and business from services provided by the public library.[35]

University of Colorado. Denise Pan and her colleagues used an embedded, mixed-methods, longitudinal approach to gather data and assess student learning outcomes that measure and describe the value of library services. Interestingly, the authors used a cost-benefit analysis to demonstrate the impact of services using the approach they followed.[36]

Public Library Association's Project Outcome

The Public Library Association's Project Outcome is developing a set of tools that will assist libraries to transition to an outcome-oriented approach to determine the library's benefits in the lives of its customers. Project Outcome recommends a four-step outcome measurement process, as shown in Figure 25.3: 1) set goals, 2) measure outcomes, 3) review results, and 4) take action.

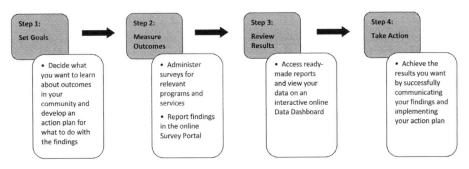

Figure 25.3. Project Outcome Measurement Process. Used with permission of Project Outcome.

More than several hundred public libraries are currently collecting data from their patrons using an online survey (visit ProjectOutcome.Org to learn more about the available tools). The online surveys will gather outcome data in seven areas: civic/community engagement, digital learning, economic development, education/lifelong learning, early childhood literacy, job skills, and summer reading. Patrons may complete a survey shortly after the conclusion of a program or a series of programs (called Immediate Surveys) or several weeks (or months) later (called Follow-Up Surveys). The surveys are designed to capture outcome data in four key areas (see Table 25.1).

Table 25.1. Project Outcome—Four Outcome-Related Survey Questions

	Captures if a patron. . . .	**Why use this metric**
Knowledge	learned something	Most programs & services have a learning component or objective; this metric measures if that objective was achieved
Confidence	feels confident using what they learned	A patron is more likely to try to apply what they learned after leaving the library if they have confidence doing so; this metric, when combined with the immediate survey's intent to change outcome, point to a great likelihood that action will be taken at a later date
Application	intends to or has changed	This gets to the "action" metric communities, boards or funders want to know: did they actually do something with that they learned
Awareness	has increased their awareness of library resources	This metric measures how well the library is integrating their other, supporting resources, into the program or service they are offering; it points to a more comprehensive usage picture of the library

Used with permission of Project Outcome.

Once the data have been gathered, the project portal allows a library to download a set of standard reports. The libraries that have been using the surveys have found that they are easy to set up, patron participation is high, and the results are quite valuable.

SUMMARY

The social benefits impacts of the public library on the local community have been documented by studies conducted in the United States, England, and Australia, among others. These benefits may affect an individual in a number of different ways.

Joseph Matthews has suggested that a public library can begin to identify both the direct and indirect (social) benefits arising from the use of the library, as shown in Figure 25.4.

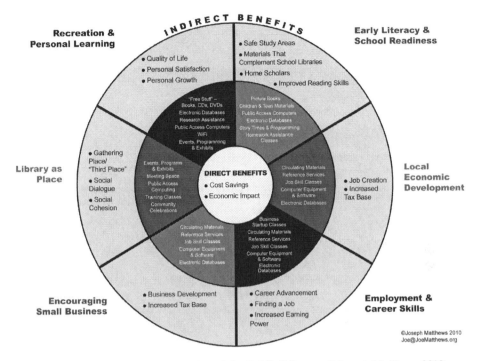

Figure 25.4. Determining the Value of the Public Library. © Joseph Matthews 2010.

Margaret Weaver has used the concept of the student journey through higher education as a framework for how libraries can support students as they work to attain their objectives as well as show how libraries contribute to the university's bottom line.[37]

Nevertheless, a number of difficulties arise when attempting to assess the social impact of public libraries, including the following:

- Library initiatives are often not sustained, and "best practices" are not shared.
- Increased funding for a broader definition of the role of the library seldom appears.
- The same activity in different libraries will differ in terms of the number of people served or impacted.
- Tools to demonstrate value are difficult to find and use—although this is changing with the Public Library Association's *Project Outcome.*
- Most people find it difficult to estimate the impact of the library on their lives.
- It is difficult to draw a causal relationship between the availability of a service and a social impact.
- It is difficult to extrapolate the results from several local studies into a broader picture.
- It is difficult to arrive at an operational definition of a social impact and an appropriate method for gathering useful data so that the method could be replicated across several studies.
- Qualitative data can be difficult and expensive to gather, and the results are often viewed with suspicion.

NOTES

1. Svanhild Aabø. The Value of Public Libraries: A Socio-Economic Analysis. In M. Belotti (Ed.). *Verso un'economia della biblioteca: Finanziamenti, programmazione e valorizzazione in tempo di crisi.* Milan, Italy: Editrice Bibliografica, 2011, 169–76.

2. Leslie Fitch and Jody Warner. Dividends: The Value of Public Libraries in Canada. *The Bottom Line,* 11 (4), 1998, 158–79.

3. Barbara Debono. Assessing the Social Impact of Public Libraries: What the Literature Is Saying. *Australasian Public Libraries and Information Services*, 15 (2), June 2002, 80–95.

4. Paul Bracke. Social Networks and Relational Capital in Library Service Assessment. *Performance Measurement and Metrics*, 17 (2), 2016, 134–41.

5. J. Cavaye. *Social Capital: A Commentary on Issues, Understanding and Measurement.* Sydney, Australia: PASCAL Observatory, 2002.

6. J. Stephen Town. Measures of Relationship Capital for the Value Scorecard. *Library Management*, 36 (3), 2015, 235-47; J. Stephen Town. Implementing the Value Scorecard. *Performance Measurement and Metrics,* 16 (3), 2015, 234–51; J. Stephen Town. The Value of People: A Review and Framework for Human Capital Assessment in Academic and Research Libraries. *Performance Measurement and Metrics,* 15 (1/2), 2014, 67–80; J. Stephen Town and Martha Kyrillidou. Developing a Values Scorecard. *Performance Measurement and Metrics,* 14 (1), 2013, 7–16.

7. Barbara Debono, Assessing the Social Impact of Public Libraries: What the Literature Is Saying. *Australasian Public Libraries and Information Services*, 15 (2), June 2002, 80–95.

8. Ronald B. McCabe. *Civic Librarianship: Renewing the Social Mission of the Public Library.* London: Scarecrow Press, 2003.

9. Fran Matarasso. *Learning Development: An Introduction to the Social Impact of Public Libraries.* London: British Library Research and Innovation Centre, 1998.

10. J. Eve and Peter Brophy. *The Value and Impact of End User IT Services in Public Libraries.* Manchester, England: Centre for Research in Library & Information Management, 2001.

11. S. Briggs, H. Guldberg, and S. Sivaciyan. *Lane Cove Library—A Life: The Social Role and Economic Benefit of Public Libraries.* Sydney, Australia: Library Council of NSW, 1996.

12. Eva Cox, Kathleen Swinbourne, Chris Pip, and Suzanne Laing. *A Safe Place to Go: Libraries and Social Capital.* Sydney, Australia: State Library of New South Wales, June 2000.

13. Carol Oxley. *Libraries/Building/Communities. The Vital Contribution of Victoria's Public Libraries—A Research Report for the Library Board of Victoria and the Victorian Public Library Network. Executive Summary; Report One: Setting the Scene; Report Two: Logging the Benefits; Report Three: Bridging the Gaps; Report Four: Showcasing the Best.* Sydney, Australia: State Library of Sydney, 2005.

14. Candy Hillenbrand. Public Libraries as Developers of Social Capital. *APLIS*, 18 (1), March 2005, 4–12.

15. Queensland University of Technology. *Advancing Queensland's Public Libraries: A Research Report for State Library of Queensland.* Brisbane, Australia: PwC Chair in Digital Economy, Queensland University of Technology, June 2016.

16. Evelyn Kerslake and Margaret Kinnel. *The Social Impact of Public Libraries: A Literature Review* (British Library Research and Innovation Centre). London: Community Development Foundation, 1997.

17. Rebecca Linley and Bob Usherwood. *New Measures for the New Library: A Social Audit of Public Libraries* (British Library Research & Innovation Centre Report 89). London: British Library Board, 1998.

18. D. H. Blake, W. C. Frederick, and M. S. Myers. *Social Auditing: Evaluating the Impact of Corporate Programmes.* New York: Praeger, 1976.

19. Lee Rainie. *Libraries and Learning.* New York: Pew Research Center, April 2016.

20. John Horrigan. *Libraries at the Crossroads.* New York: Pew Research Center, September 2015.

21. *Younger Americans and Public Libraries.* New York: Pew Research Center, September 2014.

22. Lee Rainie. *From Distant Admirers to Library Lovers—and Beyond: A Typology of Public Library Engagement in America.* New York: Pew Research Center, March 13, 2014.

23. Lee Rainie, *7 Surprises About Libraries in Our Surveys.* New York: Pew Research Center, June 30, 2014.

24. Lee Rainie. *The Next Library and the People Who Will Use It.* Presentation to the Arizona Library Association/Mountain Plains Libraries on November 13, 2014.

25. Lee Miringoff. *The Public Library: A National Survey.* Poughkeepsie, NY: The Marist College Institute for Public Opinion, 2003.

26. Survey results available at http://readme.readmedia.com/New-Poll-Shows-Continued-Public -Support-For-Increase-in-State-Aid-for-Libraries/42311

27. Keith Curry Lance, Marcia J. Rodney, Nicolle O. Steffen, Suzanne Kaller, Rochelle Logan, Christie M. Koontz, and Dean K. Jue. *Counting on Results: New Tools for Outcome-Based Evaluation of Public Libraries.* Aurora, CO: Bibliographic Center for Research, 2002. See also Nicolle O. Steffen, Keith Curry Lance, and Rochelle Logan. Time to Tell the Whole Story: Outcome-Based Evaluation and the Counting on Results Project. *Public Libraries,* 41 (4), July/August 2002, 222–28; Nicolle O. Steffen and Keith Curry Lance. Who's Doing What: Outcome-Based Evaluation and Demographics in the Counting on Results Project. *Public Libraries,* 41 (5), September/October 2002, 271–76, 278–79.

28. Monika Elbert, David Fuegi, and Ugne Lipeikaite. Perceptions of Public Libraries in Africa. *Ariadne. Web Magazine for Information Professionals,* 2012. Available at http://www.ariadne.ac.uk /issue68/elbert-et-al

29. State Library of Victoria. *Libraries Building Communities.* Melbourne, Australia: State Library of Victoria, 2005. This consists of four reports: Report One: *Setting the Scene;* Report Two: *Logging the Benefits;* Report Three: *Bridging the Gaps;* and Report Four: *Showcasing the Best.*

30. Library Council of New South Wales. *Enriching Communities: The Value of Libraries in New South Wales.* Sydney, Australia: Library Council of New South Wales, 2008.

31. Svanhild Aabø, Ragnar Audunson, and Andreas Vårheim. How Do Public Libraries Function as Meeting Places? *Library & Information Science Research,* 32 (1), 2010, 16–26.

32. Christine Rooney-Browne. Methods for Demonstrating the Value of Public Libraries in the UK: A Literature Review. *Library and Information Research,* 35 (109), 2011, 3–39.

33. Joan Durrance and Karen Fisher. *How Libraries and Librarians Help: A Guide to Identifying User-Centered Outcomes.* Chicago: American Library Association, 2005.

34. Pertti Vakkari and S. Serola. Perceived Outcomes of Public Libraries. Paper presented at the Nordic Conference on Public Library Research, Oslo, September 12, 2010.

35. Pertti Vakkari, Svanhild Aabø, Ragnar Audunson, Frank Huysmans, and Marjolein Oomes. Perceived Outcomes of Public Libraries in Finland, Norway and the Netherlands. *Journal of Documentation,* 70 (5), 2014, 927–44.

36. Denise Pan, Ignacio J. Ferrer-Vinent, and Margret Bruehl. Library Value in the Classroom: Assessing Student Learning Outcomes from Instruction and Collections. *The Journal of Academic Librarianship,* 40, 2014, 332–38.

37. Margaret Weaver. Student Journey Work: A Review of Academic Library Contributions to Student Transition and Success. *New Review of Academic Librarianship,* 19, 2013, 101–24.

26

Communicating the Library's Story

If creating value in libraries lies in adopting stakeholder priorities as library priorities and understanding and authentically measuring what matters most to stakeholders, then communicating that value involves sharing the results of assessment with stakeholder groups in a way that is most appealing and meaningful to them.

—Amanda Albert[1]

Libraries, by and large, have done little to create a proactive communication plan that enlightens various stakeholders about the impact and value of the library. Historically, library managers have relied on a range of performance metrics, usually consisting of input and output metrics, as a surrogate measure for value. However, what has significance and relevance to the typical stakeholder is not the typical performance measures shared by libraries.[2] The communication plan should focus on what stakeholders value and how they want the information presented.

Libraries have a variety of reasons for communicating with their stakeholders, such as to demonstrate accountability, to present a point of view, to inform and persuade them, and to reduce any communication barriers. Effectively communicating the benefits that arise from the use of the library and its facilities, staff, collections, services, programs, and technology must start with a clear understanding of the library's mission and goals. The goal is the alignment of the library's mission, goals, and objectives with those of the larger organization or community being served.

A communications plan is a means of ensuring that the appropriate messages are delivered and evaluating the impact of those messages. The plan, which should parallel the strategic plan, typically addresses:

- The organizational and institutional mission
- Library goals and objectives
- The strategy, which identifies the ways in which the objectives can be accomplished
- The multiple audiences that need to be informed

412

- The tools that will be used to deliver the messages
- The message to deliver (each message should have a unique audience)
- Timing (the time frame for the communications)
- Evaluation of the effectiveness of the messages
- Use of the evaluation results to adjust and improve the communication tools and messages

Many stakeholders become lost in the minutia of fact and figures if they are not given some context in which to better understand the statistics being presented. Glen Holt has suggested that developing a multipronged approach to communicating the value of the library has several advantages:[3]

- Alerting library customers as to the availability of additional services
- Reaching out to nonusers about the availability and value of library services
- Informing the community about the value of the library
- Informing the library's stakeholders about the value of the library

UNDERSTAND THE AUDIENCE

Good communication is built on a clear understanding of the intended audience. Funding decision makers, for instance, are confronted with a plethora of budget requests, so the experiences and perspectives of these individuals must first be understood and acknowledged before the best way to communicate with them can be formulated. Increasingly, stakeholders want to ensure that the library is operating in an efficient and transparent manner, as well as to understand the library's value proposition.

One nationwide survey of public officials and library directors found a wide perceptions gap when comparing library services to other community services: police, fire, streets, sewage, parks and recreation, and so forth.[4] Three-fourths of the responding library directors believed they initiated interactions with the stakeholders, whereas half of the public officials considered the library to be proactive. There was, however, general agreement among all respondents about the goals, importance, and overall quality of the public library in their community.

Robert Cialdini, a noted social psychologist, has demonstrated that there are six tendencies of human behavior that will positively impact compliance with a request (which is at the heart of advocacy): liking, reciprocity, social proof, authority, consistency, and scarcity.[5] Ken Haycock and Joseph Matthews have explored these six tendencies in a library context in an effort to encourage librarians to adopt and use these tendencies as the librarians advocate for libraries. At the end of the day, relationships that are built over time are what matter as far as key stakeholders are concerned.[6]

People learn in a variety of ways (some are visual, others are auditory, and still others prefer to absorb information by reading). Thus, it is important for library managers to visit the library's stakeholders, whether in their offices, at community social gatherings, and by having lunch or dinner with them. Learn as much as you can about the stakeholder before the first face-to-face meeting, so that the time spent together is spent in relationship building and in delivering information that will be of value to the stakeholder.

Once ongoing relationships with the library's stakeholders have been developed, carefully select the performance metrics that will reflect the value of the library from the stakeholder's perspective, and deliver the information in the manner in which the stakeholder prefers. Clearly, library managers must eliminate library jargon and terminology and in their place use the language used by these stakeholders. Managers should practice their presentations on nonlibrarians, and eliminate words or phrases that they do not understand.

Any library manager must choose the appropriate method for conveying information about the library based on the manager's knowledge of the preferences of the audience.[7] It is important to package the information for each audience in a way that is distinctive (consistent use of logos and colors is helpful). The information to be conveyed might best be presented in a written report, summarized using an infographic, provided as a PowerPoint presentation, or communicated orally during a meeting.

EMPHASIZE BENEFITS

When communicating the message about the impact and value of the library, managers should focus on the benefits and impacts that result from the use of the library (and not report use or efficiency metrics). For stakeholders, the value proposition centers on:

- Saving time. Individuals save a significant amount of time when accessing the library's high-quality collections and downloading e-resources.
- Saving money. Customers do not need to purchase materials or access to materials if they use the library (as the library has purchased or licensed access to content). In addition, customers can visit the library and use the latest technology for a wide variety of purposes.
- Contributing to productivity. Gaining access to library resources, especially desktop access, significantly increases productivity.
- Growing economic development programs. Many libraries offer programs, collections, and other services to encourage entrepreneurs in starting up new businesses, as well as to assist people in improving their employment skills, applying for jobs, and doing job training.

OFFER CONTEXT

Providing context or comparison about a particular statistic or performance measure will improve the communication process. Comparing the monthly attendance (gate count) at the library to attendance at local theaters and museums may make a more meaningful impression about how frequently the library is being used. Developing some memorable one-liners about the value and impact of the library will ensure that brief opportunities for conversation (the memorable elevator speech) are not missed. Combining a quantitative measure with a story about the impact of the library in the life of one individual can make a lasting and fruitful impression.

BE CREDIBLE

The goal of engaging stakeholders is to gain stakeholder trust by listening to and learning about the stakeholder's perspective, which "can be a significant competitive advantage for organizations. By understanding what influences and drives stakeholder trust, firms can identify risks, focus their strategies for maximum benefit, and develop initiatives to help them weather erosions of trust."[8] Library managers gain credibility based on their knowledge of the literature, experience, understanding of assorted issues, and trustworthiness. By regularly engaging with campus or community stakeholders, managers build trust and are better received when making presentations about the library and its value.

When managers present information, it is important for them to:

- Ensure that the results are accurately portrayed and that any limitations (every study or evaluation has limitations) are clearly articulated and acknowledged.
- Compare the results with those from other comparable libraries (acknowledging that selecting a set of peer libraries can take many paths).
- Clearly document the process used to gather the data and what statistical tools were used to analyze the resulting data.
- Contrast the results with those found in the literature, especially if the results differ.

UPGRADE COMMUNICATION SKILLS

Before developing a presentation, one must determine what message(s) are to be conveyed. Consider the most effective manner in which to deliver the message. A wide variety of channels exists, and it is important to select a combination of them.

The dependence on *PowerPoint* (and its various offshoots) means that many presentations turn out to be dull or boring—especially if the presenter is simply reading the bullet points. Suggestions for improving a graphical presentation include:

- Ensure that the graphic (chart, table, or figure) can stand on its own.
- Ensure that the graphic is large enough to be seen by most people in the room.
- Reduce the number of words per line to five or six.
- Use a combination of stories plus statistics for maximum effect.
- Be informative, not boring.
- Test each slide for library jargon.
- Edit appropriately: Should each graphic be used? Are all of the slides really necessary?

STAGE THE RELEASE OF INFORMATION

Any communications plan must acknowledge that the process of communicating the value of the library is more effective if the message is delivered in an ongoing manner. A combination of written and oral messages should be used to convey the impact and value of the library to the stakeholders. The library might consider:[9]

- Preparing an executive summary of the library's annual report that has real visual appeal, using colorful charts and graphs.
- Creating an infographic of the library's accomplishments and its contributions in the lives of its customers. Tools such as Inkscape, Piktochart, Venngage, and Canva provide templates and tips, making the creation of an infographic something that anyone can do.
- Maintaining an effective social media presence on Twitter, Facebook, Flickr, Pinterest, WhatsApp, Snapchat, and so forth. Post snippets of a report on social media.
- Capturing human-interest stories about the effectiveness of the library and its services.
- Using the library's newsletter to focus on the progress being made to achieve the goals set by the library.

One effective way to put information into context and some life into dull and staid statistics is through the use of a story. Stories assist people in making sense of things. Stories allow a library to put a face on its services and demonstrate how the customer values the library. A memorable story will often be retained by and sometimes shared by a stakeholder with other stakeholders. When the opportunity presents itself, begin your conversation by saying, "Let me tell you a story . . .".

In addition to formal prepared presentations, it is important that all library managers prepare, rehearse, and be ready to deliver short and informative speeches that provide a quick summary of the value of the library.

ASK FOR FEEDBACK

One characteristic of successful managers is that they continuously seek to improve their presentation skills. As part of this process, they should ask their peers to objectively critique their presentation skills. Joining Toastmasters is one way to refine one's presentation skills. Most importantly, they should ask for feedback from library stakeholders about the library's communication strategy and the effectiveness of the library's message. Is the message about how the library is affecting the institution or larger organization's mission and goals resonating? Acknowledging that people have different ways of learning and absorbing information, managers can tailor the library's message in ways that the stakeholders prefer.

Regardless of the specific metrics (output, return on investment, or outcomes) selected to demonstrate impact and value, it is important to show trends over time (trend data over the past five years will usually be more than sufficient) and to make comparisons to capture audience attention. Here is one example:

> The value of Santa Clara County Library District's services was between $83 and $171.8 million. This means for every dollar spent by SCCLD, the community receives at least $2.50 to $5.17 in direct benefits.[10]

The library's senior management team and the library board members will often find opportunities to share the value of the library with interested stakeholders and community members. Whether making a presentation, communicating in writing, or simply having a conversation, it is best if the senior management team all understand the value of the library and can communicate that message in an effective manner.

Some Thoughts about Performance Measures

The use of performance measures is not an end in itself, but rather a means to improve operations and services and for reporting to various stakeholders how much the library is used and how efficiently the library is operating. It is important for the library director and the management team to assist in the process of helping the library's stakeholders define success for the institution. It is also important to recognize that the library cannot be all things to all people, and so must focus on what services are provided to meet the needs of specific segments of potential users of the library. Defining success is

WHY MEASURE PERFORMANCE?
If you don't measure results, you can't tell success from failure.
If you can't see success, you can't reward it.
If you can't reward success, you're probably rewarding failure.
If you can't see success, you can't learn from it.
If you can't recognize failure, you can't correct it.
If you can demonstrate results, you can win public support.
—David Osborne and Ted Gaebler[11]

not a destination but a journey, and the definition of success will change over time as the library meets and exceeds its goals.

It is possible to consider the variety of potential measures as forming a hierarchy (see Figure 26.1). The library can utilize a variety of input, process, output, and outcome or impact performance measures.[12]

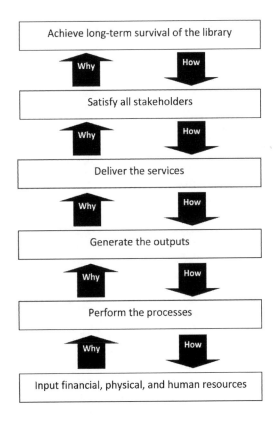

Figure 26.1. Hierarchy of Performance Measures. Jennifer Cram. Performance Management, Measurement and Reporting in a Time of Information-Centred Change. *Australian Library Journal,* 45 (3), August 1996, 225–38.

The key to communicating how effective the library is to its customers is to actively involve the various stakeholders, especially the funding decision makers, in determining what information they would like to know about the library. In particular, asking these individuals what questions about the library they would like answered is very important to gain a better understanding of what issues and perspectives are important to them individually and collectively. With this understanding in hand, it is possible to identify a set of performance measures that will have maximum impact in communicating value.

Neil McLean and Clare Wilde have revised and expanded upon the evaluation model originally developed by Orr (see Figure 26.2).[13] This revised model clearly demonstrates the wide variety of measures that can be selected by a library and differentiates the activities in the library that are performed by staff to prepare materials for use (technical processes) from the activities performed by staff who interact with the users of the library (public processes). Remember that a performance measure is simply a quantitative description of a specific process or activity; some context and analysis are required in order to understand the underlying meaning of a measure.

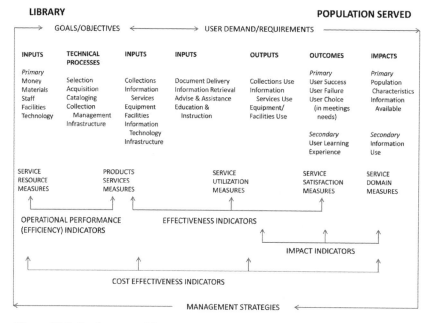

Figure 26.2. Performance Measurement Framework. Adapted from Neil McLean and Clare Wilde. Evaluating Library Performance: The Search for Relevance. *Australian Academic & Research Libraries,* 22 (3), September 1991, 201.

Ultimately, the success of a library director and of the library's budget is a political judgment on the part of the various stakeholders, particularly the funding decision makers and of the citizens themselves (especially if they are called upon to vote for an increased tax levy), about the utility and value of the library to its customers and the larger organizational context.

This judgment can be positively swayed by first identifying the strategies that the library will be using to deliver the services it has selected as most responsive to the needs of its customers. Then the library has to identify that set of input, process, output, and outcome measures that will reflect the contribution of the library to individuals and to the larger organizational context. Once these have been selected, it is important to ensure that the collection and use of the measures are clearly understood by all library staff members.

To achieve the library's vision of the future, goals are set for each measure (usually interim goals are also established). Finally, the performance measures are collected and distributed to all staff members and stakeholders on a quarterly basis. The measures are then discussed in regular library management and staff meetings so that the importance of the measures is clear. Any corrective actions, if any, can then be discussed and planned.

It is also important to select performance measures of activities and services over which the library has complete control. An effective performance measurement system has the following attributes:

- **Clarity of purpose.** The audience for which the measures are being collected and analyzed is clearly stated. Those in the target audience should readily understand the indicators.
- **Focus.** The measures chosen should reflect the service objectives of the library.
- **Alignment.** The performance measures should be synchronized with the goals and objectives of the library. Too many libraries routinely collect too many statistics and performance measures that are then casually ignored.
- **Balance.** The measures should present a balanced view of the library and its overall performance. Some of the measures should include outcomes and the user perspective. Measures describe different characteristics of performance:
  - *Absolute/relative.* An absolute measure is one that can stand on its own. A relative performance measure is compared to the same measure in other "similar" libraries.
  - *Process/function oriented.* A process measure looks at the various tasks and activities that constitute a functional activity, such as cataloging. A functional measure takes a broader view.
  - *Performance or diagnostic.* Some performance measures are designed to measure the achievements of a particular service, whereas others are gathered to assist in analyzing a process or activity with the goal of improving it.
  - *Objective/subjective.* Objective measures reflect a specific activity, (e.g., circulation), whereas subjective measures reflect an opinion or observation by a trained professional (e.g., adequacy and depth of a collection) or by customers (e.g., satisfaction surveys). Sometimes objective data are referred to as hard measures, and subjective data have been called soft measures.
  - *Direct/indirect.* A direct indicator measures a specific activity (e.g., circulation). An indirect indicator provides an estimate for an activity (the number of online catalog searches is used as a surrogate in order to estimate the number of people who used the online catalog; e.g., 2.5 searches = 1 person).

- *Leading/lagging.* A leading performance measure provides some advance warning that another activity will increase or decrease. A lagging measure reflects actual performance (e.g., circulation).
- *Social/economic.* Combinations of social and economic outcome measures can be used.

- **Regular refinement.** The performance indicators should be periodically reviewed to ensure that their continued use provides the library with real value. In some cases, a new measure should be introduced and another dropped.

- **Vigorous performance indicators.** Each performance measure should be clearly defined and relevant. The data collected should be unambiguous and not open to manipulation. Readily available statistics, such as the number of Web site hits, are often more dangerous than useful.

The selection, collection, and sharing of performance measures are designed to provide improved services, as well as increased accountability, by informing all of the library's stakeholders how well the library is actually doing. In the measures that are reported to stakeholders, there should be a balance among input, process (efficiency), output, and outcome measures. The library might want to consider grouping the measures into categories.

> *Few libraries exist in a vacuum, accountable only to themselves. There is always a larger context for assessing library quality, that is, what and how well does the library contribute to achieving the overall goals of the parent constituencies?"*
>
> —Sarah Pritchard[14]

For example, Don Mills, the former long-time director of the Mississauga Public Library in Ontario, Canada, has developed eight categories—the 8 Bs—that are used for planning purposes as well as communicating the library's results to its stakeholders:[15]

- Books—physical and electronic resources
- Bricks—facilities issues
- Bytes—information technology plan
- Bucks—revenue generation (Friends, partnerships, ads)
- Bodies—staff-related topics
- Bridges—partnerships
- Boasts—marketing and promotion, celebration of accomplishments
- Board

SUMMARY

As a library puts together its communications plan, it is important to tailor the library's message to fit the preferences of the stakeholders. The library's message will be strengthened if managers remember to:

- Nurture personal relationships with each stakeholder so that they see the library director (and others on the management team) more than once a year at the budget presentation
- Communicate the message that the library provides real value to customers in unique and compelling ways
- Ask library stakeholders to visit the library to see the high quality and diversity of services being delivered
- Provide context for the statistics that are presented, to make the message more understandable and meaningful
- Use the jargon and vocabulary of the stakeholders
- Avoid *overselling* the library's services—*over-deliver* and look for ways to add more value in customers' lives

The management team should make sure they have devoted the time and energy needed to be prepared so that when opportunity arises, they are ready to take center stage. Remember, the goal is to keep your stakeholders focused on the library's message rather than getting lost in a sea of numbers.[16]

NOTES

1. Amanda Albert. Communicating Library Value—The Missing Piece of the Assessment Puzzle. *The Journal of Academic Librarianship*, 40, 2014, 634–37.

2. See Peter Hernon, Robert E. Dugan, and Joseph R. Matthews. *Getting Started with Evaluation.* Chicago: American Library Association, 2014, ch. 10.

3. Glen Holt. Balancing Buildings, Books, Bytes, and Bucks: Steps to Secure the Public Library Future in the Internet Age. *Library Trends* 46, (1), Summer 1997, 92–116.

4. The Library Research Center. A Survey of Public Libraries and Local Government. *Illinois State Library Special Report Series* 4 (1), 1997, 1–62.

5. Robert Cialdini. *Influence: Science and Practice.* 4th ed. New York: Allyn & Bacon, 2001.

6. Ken Haycock and Joseph R. Matthews. Persuasive Advocacy. *Public Library Quarterly*, 35 (2), 2016, 1–10.

7. Christine Olsen. What's in It for Them? Communicating the Value of Information Services. *Information Outlook*, November 2002, 19–23.

8. The Conference Board of Canada. *Stakeholder Trust: A Competitive Strategy* (report by Michael Bassett). Ottawa: Conference Board of Canada, 2008. Available at http://www.conferenceboard.ca/e -library/abstract.aspx?did=2798

9. Peter Hernon and Joseph R. Matthews. *Listening to the Customer.* Santa Barbara, CA: Libraries Unlimited, 2011.

10. SCCLD. *Santa Clara County Library District 2013 Return on Investment Report.* Seattle: BERK, 2014, 2.

11. David Osborne and Ted Gaebler. *Reinventing Government: How the Entrepreneurial Spirit Is Transforming the Public Sector.* New York: Addison-Wesley, 1992.

12. Jennifer Cram. Performance Management, Measurement and Reporting in a Time of Information-Centred Change. *Australian Library Journal*, 45 (3), August 1996, 225–38.

13. Neil McLean and Clare Wilde. Evaluating Library Performance: The Search for Relevance. *Australian Academic & Research Libraries*, 22 (3), September 1991, 201.

14. Sarah Pritchard. Determining Quality in Academic Libraries. *Library Trends*, 44 (3), Winter 1996, 572–94.

15. E-mail communication from Don Mills, February 5, 2007.

16. Joseph R. Matthews. *Adding Value to Libraries, Archives, and Museums: Harnessing the Force That Drives Your Organization's Future*. Santa Barbara, CA: Libraries Unlimited, 2016.

Author/Title Index

Page numbers followed by *t* indicate tables and *f* indicate figures

Subject Index

Page numbers followed by *t* indicate tables and *f* indicate figures

431

About the Author

JOSEPH R. MATTHEWS is president of JRM Consulting and has provided consulting assistance to numerous academic, public, and special libraries and local governments. He was an instructor at the School of Library Information Science (SLIS) at San Jose State University, where he was honored as a SLIS Outstanding Scholar. Matthews has taught evaluation of library services, library information systems, strategic planning, management, and research methods. He is author of numerous articles as well as more than 30 books, including *Adding Value to Libraries, Museums, and Archives: Harnessing the Force That Drives Your Organization's Future*; *Managing with Data and Metrics: Using ACRLMetrics and PLAmetrics*; *Getting Started with Evaluation*; *Reflecting on the Future of Academic and Public Libraries*; *Listening to the Customer*; *Library Assessment in Higher Education*; *The Customer-Focused Library: Re-Inventing the Public Library from the Outside-In*; *The Evaluation and Measurement of Library Services*; and *Strategic Planning and Management for Library Managers*. Matthews is an invited conference speaker and is active in the American Library Association and the Association of College & Research Libraries. He is editor of *Public Library Quarterly* and is on the editorial boards of *Performance Measurement and Metrics* and *Library Hi Tech*.

Made in the USA
Monee, IL
03 May 2022

95807500R00262